D1348222

COMPACT EDITION

SPANISH-ENGLISH
ENGLISH-SPANISH
DICTIONARY

LUCEM LIBRIS
DISSEMINAMUS

GEDDES&
GROSSET

Abbreviations / Abreviaturas

abrev	abbreviation	abreviatura
adj	adjective	adjectivo
adv	adverb	adverbio
art	article	artículo
auto	automobile	automóvil
aux	auxiliary	auxiliar
bot	botany	botánica
chem	chemistry	química
col	colloquial term	lengua familiar
com	commerce	comercio
compd	in compounds	usada en palabras compuestas
comput	computers	informática
conj	conjunction	conjunción
dep	sport	deporte
excl	exclamation	exclamación
f	feminine noun	sustanrivo femenino
fam	colloquial term	lengua familiar
ferro	railway	ferrocarrilero
fig	figurative use	uso figurado
gr	grammar	gramática
imp	impersonal	impersonal
inform	computers	informática
interj	interjection	interjección
invar	invariable	invariable
irr	irregular	irregular
jur	law term	jurisprudencia
law	law term	jurisprudencia
ling	linguistics	lingüística
m	masculine noun	sustantivo masculino
mar	marine term	vocablo marítimo
mat, math	mathematics	matemáticas
med	medicine	medicina
mil	military term	lo militar
mus	music	música
n	noun	sustantivo
pej	pejorative	peyorativo
pl	plural	plural
pn	pronoun	pronombre
poet	poetical term	vocablo poético

prep	preposition	preposición
quím	chemistry	química
rad	radio	radio
rail	railway	ferrocarilero
sl	slang	argot
teat	theatre	teatro
tec	technology	técnica, tecnologia
TV	television	televisión
vb	verb	verbo
vi	intransitive verb	verbo intransitivo
vr	reflexive verb	verbo reflexivo
vt	transitive verb	verbo transitivo

Spanish–English
Dictionary

a *prep* (a) el, according to, for, on, by, for, of.

abacería *f* grocery.

abacero *m* grocer.

ábaco *m* abacus.

abad *m* abbot.

abadejo *m* cod.

abadesa *f* abbess.

abadía *f* abbey.

abajo *adv* below, underneath, down; ~ **de** *prep* under, below.

abalanzarse *vr* to rush forward, to dash.

abanderado *m* standard-bearer, colour bearer.

abandonado/da *adj* derelict, abandoned, neglected.

abandonar *vt* to abandon, to leave; ~ **se** *vr* ~ **a** to give oneself up to.

abandono *m* desertion, neglect; retirement.

abanicar *vt* to fan.

abanico *m* fan.

abaratar *vt* to lower the price of.

abarca *f* sandal.

abarcar *vt* to include.

abarrancarse *vr* to get into difficulties.

abarrotado/da *adj* packed.

abarrotar *vt* to tie down.

abastecedor/ra *m/f* supplier, purveyor.

abastecer *vt* to supply, provide.

abastecimiento *m* supplying, provisions.

abasto *m* supply of provisions.

abate *m* abbé, French abbot.

abatido/da *adj* dejected, low-spirited.

abatimiento *m* low spirits *pl*; depression.

A

a *prep* to; in; at; according to; on; by; for; of.

abaceria *f* grocery.

abacero *m* grocer.

ábaco *m* abacus.

abad *m* abbot.

abadejo *m* cod.

abadesa *f* abbess.

abadía *f* abbey.

abajo *adv* under; underneath; below; ~ **de** *prep* under, below.

abalanzarse *vr* to rush forward.

abalorio *m* glass bead.

abanderado *m* (*mil*) ensign; standard bearer.

abandonado/da *adj* derelict; abandoned; neglected.

abandonar *vt* to abandon; to leave; ~**se** *vr* ~ **a** to give oneself up to.

abandono *m* desertion; neglect; retirement.

abanicar *vt* to fan.

abanico *m* fan.

abaratar *vt* to lower the price of.

abarca *f* sandal.

abarcar *vt* to include.

abarrancarse *vr* to get into difficulties.

abarrotado/da *adj* packed.

abarrotar *vt* to tie down.

abastecedor/ra *m/f* supplier, purveyor.

abastecer *vt* to supply, provide.

abastecimiento *m* supplying; provisions.

abasto *m* supply of provisions.

abate *m* abbé, French abbot.

abatido/da *adj* dejected, low-spirited.

abatimiento *m* low spirits *pl*; depression.

abatir *vt* to knock down; to humble.

abdicación *f* abdication.

abdicar *vt* to abdicate.

abdomen *m* abdomen.

abdominal *adj* abdominal.

abecé *m* alphabet.

abecedario *m* alphabet; spelling book, primer.

abedul *m* birch tree.

abeja *f* bee; ~ **reina** queen bee.

abejar *m* beehive.

abejarrón *m* bumblebee.

abejón *m* drone; hornet.

abejorro *m* bumblebee.

aberración *f* aberration.

abertura *f* aperture, chink, opening.

abeto *m* fir tree.

abetunado/da *adj* dark-skinned.

abierto/ta *adj* open; sincere; frank.

abigarrado/da *adj* multicoloured.

ab intestato *adj* intestate.

abismal *adj* abysmal.

abismo *m* abyss; gulf; hell.

abjuración *f* abjuration.

abjurar *vt* to abjure, to recant; *vi*: ~ **de** to abjure, to recant.

ablandamiento *m* softening.

ablandar *vt, vi* to soften.

ablativo *m* (*gr*) ablative.

ablución *f* ablution.

abnegación *f* self-denial.

abnegado/da *adj* selfless.

abnegar *vt* to renounce.

abobado/da *adj* silly.

abobamiento *m* stupefaction.

abobar *vt* to stupefy.

abocado/da *adj* light (wine).

abocar *vt* to seize with the mouth; ~**se** *vr* to meet by agreement.

11

abochornar *vt* to swelter; **~se** *vr* to shame.

abofetear *vt* to slap.

abogacía *f* legal profession.

abogado/a *m/f* lawyer; barrister.

abogar *vi* to intercede; **~ por** to advocate.

abolengo *m* ancestry; inheritance from ancestors.

abolición *f* abolition, abrogation.

abolir *vt* to abolish.

abolladura *f* dent.

abollar *vt* to dent.

abominable *adj* abominable, cursed.

abominación *f* abomination.

abominar *vt* to detest.

abonado/da *adj* ready; prepared; * *m/f* subscriber; season ticket holder.

abonar *vt* to settle; to fertilize; to endorse; **~se** *vr* to subscribe; * *vi* to clear up.

abono *m* payment; subscription; dung, manure.

abordaje *m* boarding.

abordar *vt* (*mar*) to board; to broach.

aborigen *m* aborigine.

aborrecer *vt* to hate, to abhor.

aborrecible *adj* hateful, detestable.

aborrecimiento *m* abhorrence, hatred.

abortar *vi* to miscarry; to have an abortion.

abortivo/va *adj* abortive.

aborto *m* abortion; monster.

abortón *m* abortion.

abotagado/da *adj* swollen.

abotinado/da *adj* tied up.

abotonar *vt* to button.

abovedado/da *adj* vaulted.

abrasar *vt* to burn; to parch; **~se** *vr* to burn oneself.

abrazadera *f* bracket; clasp.

abrazar *vt* to embrace; to surround.

abrazo *m* embrace.

abrebotellas *m invar* bottle opener.

abrecartas *m invar* letter opener.

abrelatas *m invar* can opener.

abrevadero *m* watering place.

abrevar *vt* to water (cattle).

abreviación *f* abbreviation, abridgement; shortening.

abreviar *vt* to abridge, to cut short.

abreviatura *f* abbreviation.

abridor *m* opener.

abrigar *vt* to shelter; to protect; **~se** *vr* to take shelter.

abrigo *m* coat; shelter; protection; aid.

abril *m* April.

abrillantar *vt* to polish.

abrir *vt* to open; to unlock; **~se** *vr* to open up; to clear the way; to be open.

abrochador *m* buttonhook.

abrochar *vt* to button; to do up.

abrogar *vt* to abrogate.

abrumador/ra *adj* overwhelming; annoying.

abrumar *vt* to overwhelm.

abrupto/ta *adj* abrupt; steep.

absceso *m* abscess.

absentismo *m* absenteeism.

absolución *f* forgiveness, absolution.

absoluto/ta *adj* absolute.

absolutorio/a *adj* absolutory.

absolver *vt* to absolve.

absorbente *adj* absorbent.

absorber *vt* to absorb.

absorción *f* absorption; takeover.

absorto *adj* engrossed.

abstemio *adj* teetotal.

abstención *f* abstention.

abstenerse *vr* to abstain.

abstinencia *f* abstinence.

abstinente *adj* abstinent, abstemious.

abstracción *f* abstraction.

abstracto/ta *adj* abstract.

abstraer *vt* to abstract; **~se** *vr* to be absorbed.

abstraído *adj* absent-minded.

absuelto/ta *adj* absolved.

absurdidad *f*, **absurdo** *m* absurdity.

absurdo *adj* absurd.

abuela *f* grandmother.

abuelo *m* grandfather.

abulia *f* lethargy.

abultado/da *adj* bulky, large, massive.

abultar *vt* to increase, to enlarge; * *vi* to be bulky.

abundancia *f* abundance.

abundante *adj* abundant, copious.

abundar *vi* to abound.

aburrido/da *adj* boring, dull.

aburrimiento *m* boredom.

aburrir *vt* to bore.

abusar *vt* to abuse.

abusivo/va *adj* abusive.

abuso *m* abuse.

abyección *f* abjectness.

abyecto/ta *adj* abject, wretched.

acá *adv* here.

acabado/da *adj* perfect, accomplished.

acabar *vt* to finish, to complete; to achieve; **~se** *vr* to finish; to be over; to run out; * *vi* to finish; to die, to expire.

acabose *m*: **el ~** the last straw.

acacia *f* acacia.

academia *f* academy.

académico/ca *m/f* academician; * *adj* academic.

acaecer *vi* to happen.

acallar *vt* to quiet, to hush; to soften, to appease.

acalorado/da *adj* heated.

acalorarse *vr* to become heated.

acampar *vt* to camp.

acanalado/da *adj* grooved; fluted.

acanalar *vt* to corrugate.

acanto *m* acanthus.

acantonamiento *m* cantonment.

acantonar *vt* to billet.

acaparar *vt* to monopolize; to hoard.

acariciar *vt* to fondle, to caress.

acarrear *vt* to transport; to occasion.

acarreo *m* carriage, transportation.

acaso *m* chance; * *adv* perhaps.

acatarrarse *vr* to catch (a) cold.

acaudalado/da *adj* rich, wealthy.

acaudalar *vt* to hoard.

acaudillar *vt* to command.

acceder *vi* to agree; **~ a** to have access to.

accesible *adj* attainable; accessible.

acceso *m* access; fit.

accesorio/ria *adj*, *m* accessory.

accidentado/da *adj* uneven; hilly; eventful.

accidental *adj* accidental; casual.

accidentarse *vr* to have an accident.

accidente *m* accident.

acción *f* action, operation; share.

accionar *vt* to work.

accionista *m* shareholder.

acebo *m* holly tree.

acebuche *m* wild olive tree.

acechador/ra *m/f* spy, observer.

acechar *vt* to lie in wait for; to spy on, observe.

acecho *m* spying, watching; ambush.

aceitar *vt* to oil.

aceite *m* oil.

aceitera *f* oilcan.

aceitoso/sa *adj* oily.

aceituna *f* olive.

aceitunado/da *adj* olive-green.

aceitunero *m* olive seller.

aceituno *m* olive tree.

aceleración f acceleration.

aceleradamente adv swiftly, hastily.

acelerador m accelerator.

acelerar vt to accelerate; to hurry.

acelga f (bot) chard (a variety of beet).

acento m accent.

acentuación f accentuation.

acentuar vt to accentuate.

aceña f water mill.

acepción f acceptation.

aceptable adj acceptable.

aceptación f acceptance; approval.

aceptar vt to accept, to admit.

acequia f canal, channel; drain.

acera f pavement.

acerado/da adj steel compd, made of steel; sharp; steely.

acerbo/ba adj rigorous, harsh; cruel.

acerca prep about, relating to.

acercar vt to move nearer; ~se vr ~ a to approach.

acerico m pincushion.

acero m steel.

acérrimo/ma adj staunch; bitter.

acertado/da adj correct, proper; prudent.

acertar vt to hit; to guess right; * vi to get it right; to turn out true.

acertijo m riddle.

acervo m heap, pile.

acetato m (quim) acetate.

achacar vt to impute.

achacoso/sa adj sickly, unhealthy.

achantar vt (fam) to scare; ~se vr to back down.

achaparrado/da adj stunted; stocky.

achaque m ailment; excuse; subject, matter.

achicar vt to diminish; to humiliate; to bale (out).

achicharrar vt to scorch; to overheat.

achicoria f (bot) chicory.

achisparse vr to get tipsy.

aciago/ga adj unlucky; ominous.

acíbar m aloes; (fig) bitterness; displeasure.

acicalar vt to polish; ~se vr to dress in style.

acicate m spur.

acidez f acidity.

ácido m acid; * ~/da adj acid, sour.

acierto m success; solution; dexterity.

aclamación f acclamation.

aclamar vt to applaud, to acclaim.

aclaración f clarification.

aclarar vt to clear; to brighten; to explain; to clarify; ~se vr to understand; * vi to clear up.

aclimatar vt to acclimatize; ~se vr to become acclimatized.

acne m acne.

acobardar vt to intimidate.

acodarse vr to lean.

acogedor/ra adj welcoming.

acoger vt to receive; to welcome; to harbour; ~se vr to take refuge.

acogida f reception; asylum.

acolchar vt to quilt; to cushion.

acólito m acolyte; assistant.

acometer vt to attack; to undertake.

acometida f attack, assault.

acomodadizo adj accommodating.

acomodado/da adj suitable, convenient, fit; wealthy.

acomodador/ra m/f usher, usherette.

acomodar vt to accommodate, to arrange; ~se vr to comply.

acomodaticio/cia adj accomodating; pliable.

acompañamiento m (mus) accompaniment.

acompañar vt to accompany; to join; (mus) to accompany.

acompasado/da *adj* measured; well proportioned.

acondicionado/da *adj* conditioned.

acondicionar *vt* to arrange; to condition.

acongojar *vt* to distress.

aconsejable *adj* advisable.

aconsejar *vt* to advise; ~**se** *vr* to take advice.

acontecer *vi* to happen.

acontecimiento *m* event, incident.

acopio *m* gathering, storing.

acopiar *vt* to gather, to store up.

acoplamiento *m* coupling.

acoplar *vt* to couple; to fit; to connect.

acorazado/da *adj* armoured; * *m* battleship.

acordado/da *adj* agreed.

acordar *vt* to agree; to remind; ~**se** *vr* to agree; to remember.

acorde *adj* harmonious; * *m* chord.

acordeón *m* accordion.

acordonado/da *adj* cordoned-off.

acordonar *vt* to tie up; to cordon off.

acorralar *vt* to round up, corral; corner.

acortar *vt* to abridge, to shorten; ~**se** *vr* to become shorter.

acosar *vt* to pursue closely; to pester.

acostado/da *adj* in bed; lying down.

acostar *vt* to put to bed; to lay down; ~**se** *vr* to go to bed; to lie down.

acostumbrado/da *adj* usual.

acostumbrar *vi* to be used to; ~**se** *vr* ~ **a** to get used to; * *vt* to accustom.

acotación *f* boundary mark; quotation in the margin; stage direction.

acotar *vt* to set bounds to; to annotate.

ácrata *m/f* anarchist.

acre *adj* acid; sharp; * *m* acre.

acrecentamiento *m* increase.

acrecentar *vt* to increase, to augment.

acreditar *vt* to guarantee; to assure, to affirm; to authorize; to credit; ~**se** *vr* to become famous.

acreedor *m* creditor.

acribillar *vt* to riddle with bullets; to molest, to torment.

acriminar *vt* to incriminate; to accuse.

acrimonia *f* acrimony.

acrisolar *vt* to refine, to purify.

acritud *f* acrimony.

acróbata *m/f* acrobat.

acta *f* act; ~**s** *fpl* records *pl*.

actitud *f* attitude; posture.

activar *vt* to activate; to speed up.

actividad *f* activity; liveliness.

activo/va *adj* active; diligent.

acto *m* act, action; act of a play; ceremony.

actor *m* actor; plaintiff.

actriz *f* actress.

actuación *f* action; behaviour; proceedings *pl*.

actual *adj* actual, present.

actualidad *f* present time; ~**es** *fpl* current events *pl*.

actualizar *vt* to update.

actualmente *adv* at present.

actuar *vt* to work; to operate; * *vi* to work; to act.

acuarela *f* watercolour.

acuario *m* tank.

Acuario *m* Aquarius (sign of the zodiac).

acuartelamiento *m* quartering of troops.

acuartelar *vt* (*mil*) to quarter (troops).

acuático/ca *adj* aquatic.

acuchillar *vt* to cut; to plane.

acuciar *vt* to urge on.

acuclillarse *vr* to crouch.

acudir *vi* to go to; to attend; to assist.

acueducto *m* aqueduct.

acuerdo *m* agreement; **de ~** *fam* OK, all right.

acumular *vt* to accumulate, to collect.

acuñación *f* coining.

acuñar *vt* to coin, to mint; to wedge in.

acuoso/sa *adj* watery.

acupuntura *f* acupuncture.

acurrucarse *vr* to squat; to huddle up.

acusación *f* accusation.

acusador/ra *m/f* accuser; * *adj* accusing.

acusar *vt* to accuse; to reveal; to denounce; **~se** *vr* to confess.

acusativo *m* (*gr*) accusative.

acuse *m*: **~ de recibo** acknowledgement of receipt.

acústica *f* acoustics *pl.*

acústico/ca *adj* acoustic.

adagio *m* adage, proverb; (*mus*) adagio.

adalid *m* chief, commander.

adamascado/da *adj* damask.

adaptable *adj* adaptable.

adaptación *f* adaptation.

adaptador *m* adapter.

adaptar *vt* to adapt.

adecuado/da *adj* adequate, fit; appropriate.

adecuar *vt* to fit/to accommodate/to proportion.

adefesio *m* folly/nonsense.

adelantado/da *adj* advanced; fast.

adelantamiento *m* progress/ improvement/advancement; overtaking.

adelantar *vt*, *vi* to advance, to accelerate; to pass; to ameliorate, to improve; **~se** *vr* to advance; to outdo.

adelante *adv* forward(s); **de hoy en ~** from now on; **más ~** later on; further on; * *excl* come in!

adelanto *m* advance; progress; improvement.

adelfa *f* (*bot*) rosebay.

adelgazar *vt* to make thin *or* slender; * *vi* to lose weight.

ademán *m* gesture; attitude.

además *adv* moreover, besides; **~ de** besides.

adentrarse *vr* to get inside; to penetrate.

adentro *adv* in; inside.

adepto/ta *m/f* supporter.

aderezar *vt* to dress, to adorn; to prepare; to season.

aderezo *m* adorning; seasoning; arrangement.

adeudado/da *adj* in debt.

adeudar *vt* to owe; **~se** *vr* to run into debt.

adherencia *f* adhesion, cohesion; alliance.

adherente *adj* adhering to, cohesive.

adherir *vi*: **~ a** to adhere to; to espouse.

adhesión *f* adhesion; cohesion.

adición *f* addition.

adicionar *vt* to add.

adicto/ta *adj*: **~ a** addicted to; devoted to; * *m* supporter; addict.

adiestrar *vt* to guide; to teach, to instruct; **~se** *vr* to practise.

adinerado/da *adj* wealthy, rich.

adiós *excl* goodbye; hello.

aditivo *m* additive.

adivinanza *f* enigma; riddle.

adivinar *vt* to foretell; to guess.

adivino/na *m/f* fortune-teller.

adjetivo *m* adjective.

adjudicación f adjudication.
adjudicar vt to adjudge; ~**se** vr to appropriate.
adjuntar vt to endorse.
adjunto/ta adj united, joined, annexed; * m/f assistant.
administración f administration.
administrador/a m/f administrator.
administrar vt to administer.
administrativo/va adj administrative.
admirable adj admirable, marvellous.
admiración f admiration; wonder; (gr) exclamation mark.
admirar vt to admire; to surprise; ~**se** vr to be surprised.
admisible adj admissible.
admisión f admission, acceptance.
admitir vt to admit; to let in; to concede; to permit.
admonición f warning.
adobado m pickled pork.
adobar vt to dress; to season.
adobe m adobe, sun-dried brick.
adobo m dressing; pickle sauce.
adoctrinar vt to indoctrinate; to teach.
adolecer vi to suffer from.
adolescencia f adolescence.
adolescente adj, m/f adolescent.
adonde adv (to) where.
adónde adv where.
adopción f adoption.
adoptar vt to adopt.
adoptivo/va adj adoptive; adopted.
adoquín m paving stone.
adoración f adoration, worship.
adorar vt to adore; to love.
adormecer vt to put to sleep; ~**se** vr to fall asleep.
adormidera f (bot) poppy.
adornar vt to embellish, to adorn.

adorno m adornment; ornament, decoration.
adosado/da adj semidetached.
adquirir vt to acquire.
adquisición f acquisition.
adrede adv on purpose.
adscribir vt to appoint.
aduana f customs pl.
aduanero m customs officer; ~/**ra** adj customs compd.
aducir vt to adduce.
adueñarse vr: ~ **de** to take possession of.
adulación f adulation.
adulador/ra m/f flatterer.
adular vt to flatter.
adulterar vt to adulterate; * vi to commit adultery.
adulterio m adultery.
adúltero/ra m/f adulterer, adulteress.
adulto/ta adj, m/f adult, grown-up.
adusto/ta adj gloomy; stern.
advenedizo m upstart.
advenimiento m arrival; accession.
adverbio m adverb.
adversario m adversary; antagonist.
adversidad f adversity; setback.
adverso/sa adj adverse.
advertencia f warning, foreword.
advertido/da adj sharp.
advertir vt to notice; to warn.
Adviento m Advent.
adyacente adj adjacent.
aéreo/rea adj aerial.
aerobic m aerobics pl.
aerodeslizador m hovercraft.
aerodeslizante m hovercraft.
aerogenerador m wind turbine.
aeromozo/za m/f air steward/ess.
aeronauta m aeronaut.
aeronáutica f aeronautics.
aeronave f spaceship.

aeroplano *m* aeroplane.

aeropuerto *m* airport.

aerosol *m* aerosol.

aerostática *f* aerostatics.

afabilidad *f* affability.

afable *adj* affable.

afán *m* hard work; desire.

afanar *vt* to harass; (*col*) to pinch; ~**se** *vr* to strive.

afanoso/sa *adj* hard, industrious.

afear *vt* to deform, to misshape.

afección *f* affection; fondness; attachment; disease.

afectación *f* affectation.

afectadamente *adv* affectedly.

afectado/da *adj* affected.

afectar *vt* to affect, to feign.

afectísimo/ma *adj* affectionate; ~ **suyo** yours truly.

afectivo/va *adj* fond, tender.

afecto *m* affection; passion; ~/**ta** *adj* affectionate; disposed; reserved.

afectuoso/sa *adj* affectionate; moving; tender.

afeitar *vt*, ~**se** *vr* to shave.

afeite *m* make-up, rouge.

afeminado/da *adj* effeminate.

afeminar *vt* to make effeminate.

aferrado/da *adj* stubborn.

aferrar *vt* to grapple, to grasp, to seize.

afianzamiento *m* strengthening.

afianzar *vt* to strengthen; to prop up; ~**se** *vr* to become established.

afiche *m* poster.

afición *f* affection; hobby; fans *pl*.

aficionado/da *adj* keen; * *m/f* lover, fan; amateur.

aficionar *vt* to inspire affection; ~**se** *vr* ~ **a** to grow fond of.

afiladera *f* grindstone.

afilado *adj* sharp.

afilar *vt* to sharpen, to grind.

afín *m* related; similar.

afinar *vt* to tune; to refine.

afincarse *vr* to settle.

afinidad *f* affinity; analogy; relationship.

afirmación *f* affirmation.

afirmado *m* road surface.

afirmar *vt* to secure, to fasten; to affirm, to assure.

afirmativo/va *adj* affirmative.

aflicción *f* affliction, grief.

aflictivo/va *adj* distressing.

afligir *vt* to afflict, to torment.

aflojar *vt* to loosen, to slacken, to relax; * *vi* to grow weak; to abate; to relent; ~**se** *vr* to relax.

aflorar *vi* to emerge.

afluente *adj* flowing; * *m* tributary.

afluir *vi* to flow.

afónico/ca *adj* hoarse; voiceless.

aforismo *m* aphorism.

afortunado/da *adj* fortunate, lucky.

afrancesado/da *adj* Frenchified.

afrenta *f* outrage; insult.

afrentar *vt* to affront; to insult.

afrontar *vt* to confront; to bring face to face.

afuera *adv* out, outside.

afueras *fpl* outskirts *pl*.

agacharse *vr* to stoop, to squat.

agalla *f* gill; ~**s** *pl* pluck, guts; tonsils *pl*; tonsillitis.

agarradero *m* handle.

agarrado/da *adj* miserly, stingy.

agarrar *vt* to grasp, to seize; ~**se** *vr* to hold on tightly.

agarrotar *vt* to tie down; to squeeze tightly; to garrotte.

agasajar *vt* to receive and treat kindly; to regale.

agasajo *m* graceful reception; kindness.

ágata *f* agate.

agazaparse *vr* to crouch.

agencia *f* agency.

agenciarse *vr* to obtain.

agenda *f* diary.

agente *m* agent; policeman.

ágil *adj* agile.

agilidad *f* agility, nimbleness.

agitación *f* shaking; stirring; agitation.

agitanado/da *adj* Gypsy-like.

agitar *vt* to wave; to move; ~**se** *vr* to become excited; to become worried.

aglomeración *f* crowd; ~ **de tráfico** traffic jam.

aglomerar *vt*, ~**se** *vr* to crowd together.

agnóstico/ca *adj*, *m/f* agnostic.

agobiar *vt* to weigh down; to oppress; to burden.

agolparse *vr* to assemble in crowds.

agonía *f* death throes *pl*.

agonizante *adj* dying.

agonizar *vi* to be dying.

agorar *vt* to predict.

agostar *vt* to parch.

agosto *m* August.

agotado/da *adj* exhausted; finished; sold out.

agotador/ra *adj* exhausting.

agotamiento *m* exhaustion.

agotar *vt* to exhaust; to drain; to misspend.

agraciado/da *adj* attractive; lucky.

agraciar *vt* to pardon; to reward.

agradable *adj* pleasant; lovely.

agradar *vt* to please, to gratify.

agradecer *vt* to be grateful for; to thank.

agradecido/da *adj* thankful.

agradecimiento *m* gratitude, gratefulness, thanks *pl*.

agrado *m* agreeableness, courteousness; will, pleasure; liking.

agrandar *vt* to enlarge; to exaggerate; to aggrandize; ~**se** *vr* to get bigger.

agrario/ria *adj* agrarian; agricultural.

agravante *f* further difficulty.

agravar *vt* to oppress; to aggrieve; to aggravate; to exaggerate; ~**se** *vr* to get worse.

agraviar *vt* to wrong; to offend; ~**se** *vr* to be aggrieved; to be piqued.

agravio *m* offence; grievance.

agredir *vt* to attack.

agregado *m* aggregate; attaché.

agregar *vt* to aggregate, to heap together; to collate; to appoint.

agresión *f* aggression, attack.

agresivo/va *adj* aggressive.

agresor *m* aggressor, assaulter.

agreste *adj* rustic, rural.

agriar *vt* to sour; to exasperate.

agrícola *adj* farming *compd*.

agricultor/ra *m/f* farmer.

agricultura *f* agriculture; ~ **biológica** organic farming.

agridulce *adj* sweet and sour.

agrietarse *vr* to crack.

agrimensor *m* surveyor.

agrimensura *f* surveying.

agrio *adj* sour, acrid; rough, sharp, rude, unpleasant.

agronomía *f* agronomy.

agropecuario/ria *adj* farming *compd*.

agrupación *f* group(ing).

agrupar *vt* to group, to cluster; to crowd.

agua *f* water; slope of a roof; ~ **fuerte** etching; ~ **bendita** holy water; ~**s** *pl* waters *pl*.

aguacate *m* avocado pear.

aguacero *m* short, heavy shower of rain.

aguachirle *f* slops *pl*.

aguado/da *adj* watery.

aguador *m* water carrier.

aguafuerte *m* etching.

aguamarina *f* aquamarine (precious stone).

aguanieve *f* sleet.

aguantar *vt* to bear, to suffer; to hold up.

aguante *m* firmness; patience.

aguar *vt* to water down.

aguardar *vt* to wait for.

aguardiente *m* brandy.

aguarrás *f* turpentine.

agudeza *f* keenness, sharpness; acuteness; acidity; smartness.

agudizar *vt* to make worse; **~se** *vr* to get worse.

agudo/da *adj* sharp; keen-edged; smart; fine; acute; witty; brisk.

aguero *m*: **buen/mal ~** good/bad omen.

aguijar *vt* to prick, to spur, to goad; to stimulate.

aguijón *m* sting of a bee, wasp etc; stimulation.

aguijonear *vt* to prick; to spur; to stimulate.

águila *f* eagle; genius.

aguileño/ña *adj* aquiline; sharp-featured.

aguilucho *m* eaglet.

aguinaldo *m* Christmas box.

aguja *f* needle; spire; hand; magnetic needle; (*ferro*) points *pl*.

agujerear *vt* to pierce, to bore.

agujero *m* hole.

agujetas *fpl* stitch; stiffness; pains *pl* from fatigue.

agustino *m* monk of the order of St Augustine.

aguzar *vt* to whet, to sharpen; to stimulate.

ahí *adv* there.

ahijada *f* goddaughter.

ahijado *m* godson.

ahijar *vt* to adopt (as one's own child).

ahínco *m* earnestness; eagerness.

ahogar *vt* to smother; to drown; to suffocate; to oppress; to quench; **~se** *vr* to drown; to suffocate.

ahogo *m* breathlessness; financial difficulty.

ahondar *vt* to deepen; to study deeply; * *vi*: **~ en** to penetrate into.

ahora *adv* now, at present; just now.

ahorcar *vt* to hang; **~se** *vr* to hang oneself.

ahorrar *vt* to save; to avoid.

ahorrativo/va *adj* thrifty, careful with money.

ahorro *m* saving; thrift.

ahuecar *vt* to hollow, to scoop out; **~se** *vr* to get pig-headed.

ahumar *vt* to smoke, to cure (in smoke); **~se** *vr* to fill with smoke.

ahuyentar *vt* to drive off; to dispel.

airado/da *adj* angry.

airarse *vr* to get angry.

airbag *m* airbag.

aire *m* air; wind; aspect; musical composition.

airearse *vr* to take the air.

airoso/sa *adj* airy; windy; graceful; successful.

aislado/da *adj* insulated; isolated.

aislar *vt* to insulate; to isolate.

ajar *vt* to spoil; to abuse.

ajardinado/da *adj* landscaped.

ajedrez *m* chess.

ajedrezado/da *adj* chequered.

ajenjo *m* wormwood, absinth.

ajeno/na *adj* someone else's; foreign; ignorant; improper.

ajetrearse *vr* to exert oneself; to bustle; to toil; to fidget.

ajetreo *m* activity; bustling.

ají *m* red pepper.

ajo *m* garlic.

ajorca *f* bracelet.

ajuar *m* household furniture; trousseau.

ajustado/da *adj* tight; right; close.

ajustar *vt* to regulate, to adjust; to settle (a balance); to fit; to agree on; * *vi* to fit.

ajuste *m* agreement; accommodation; settlement; fitting.

ajusticiar *vt* to execute.

al = a el.

ala *f* wing; aisle; row, file; brim; winger.

alabanza *f* praise; applause.

alabar *vt* to praise; to applaud.

alabastro *m* alabaster.

alacena *f* cupboard, closet.

alacrán *m* scorpion.

alado/da *adj* winged.

alambique *m* still.

alambrada *f* wire fence; wire netting.

alambrado *m* wire fence; wire netting.

alambre *m* wire.

alambrista *m/f* tightrope walker.

alameda *f* avenue; poplar grove.

álamo *m* poplar.

alano *m* mastiff.

alarde *m* show.

alargador *m* extension lead.

alargar *vt* to lengthen; to extend; to hasten; to stretch out; to spin out; ~**se** *vr* to get longer; to drag on.

alarido *m* outcry, shout; **dar** ~**s** to howl.

alarma *f* alarm.

alarmante *adj* alarming.

alarmar *vt* to alarm.

alarmista *m* alarmist.

alazán *m* sorrel.

alba *f* dawn.

albacea *m* executor.

albahaca *f* (*bot*) basil.

albañil *m* bricklayer.

albañilería *f* bricklaying.

albarán *m* invoice.

albarda *f* saddle.

albaricoque *m* apricot.

albedrío *m* free will.

alberca *f* reservoir; swimming pool.

albergar *vt* to lodge, to harbour; ~**se** to shelter.

albergue *m* shelter; ~ **de juventud** youth hostel.

albóndiga *f* meatball.

albor *m* dawn; whiteness.

alborada *f* dawn; reveille.

alborear *vi* to dawn.

albornoz *m* bath robe.

alborotado/da *adj* restless, turbulent.

alborotar *vi* to make a row; * *vt* to stir up; ~**se** to get excited; to get rough.

alboroto *m* noise; disturbance, riot.

alborozar *vt* to exhilarate; ~**se** *vr* to rejoice.

alborozo *m* joy.

albricias *fpl* good news *pl*.

albufera *f* lagoon.

álbum *m* album.

albumen *m* egg white.

alcachofa *f* artichoke.

alcahuete/ta *m/f* pimp, bawd.

alcalde *m* mayor.

alcaldesa *f* mayoress.

alcaldía *f* office and jurisdiction of a mayor; mayor's office.

alcalino/na *adj* alkaline.

alcance *m* reach; bad balance.

alcancía *f* money box.

alcanfor *m* camphor.

alcantarilla *m* sewer; gutter.

alcanzar vt to reach; to get, to obtain; to hit; * vi to suffice; to reach.

alcaparra f caper.

alcatraz m gannet.

alcayata f hook.

alcázar m castle, fortress.

alcoba f bedroom.

alcohol m alcohol.

alcohólico/ca adj, m/f alcoholic.

alcoholismo m alcoholism.

alcornoque m cork tree.

aldaba f knocker.

aldea f village.

aldeano/na m/f villager; * adj rustic.

ale excl come on!

aleación f alloy.

aleatorio/ria adj random.

aleccionar vt to instruct; to train.

alegación f allegation.

alegar vt to allege; to quote.

alegato m allegation; argument.

alegoria f állegory.

alegórico/ca adj allegorical.

alegrar vt to cheer; to poke; to liven up; **~se** vr to get merry.

alegre adj happy; merry, joyful; content.

alegría f happiness; merriment.

alegrón m sudden joy; flicker.

alejamiento m remoteness; removal.

alejar vt to remove; to estrange; **~se** vr to go away.

aleluya f hallelujah.

alemán/ana adj, m/f German; * m German language.

alentador/ra adj encouraging.

alentar vt to encourage.

alergia f allergy.

alero m gable-end; eaves pl.

alerta adj, f alert.

alertar vt to alert.

aleta f fin; wing; flipper; fender.

aletargarse vr to get drowsy.

aletazo m flap.

aletear vi to flutter.

aleteo m fluttering.

alevosía f treachery.

alevoso/sa adj treacherous.

alfabéticamente adv alphabetically.

alfabético/ca adj alphabetical.

alfabeto m alphabet.

alfalfa f (bot) lucerne.

alfarería f pottery.

alfarero m potter.

alféizar m window sill.

alférez m second lieutenant; (US navy) ensign.

alfil m bishop (at chess).

alfiler m pin; clip; clothes peg.

alfiletero m pincushion.

alfombra f carpet; rug.

alfombrar vt to carpet.

alfombrilla f mouse mat.

alforja f saddlebag; knapsack.

alga f (bot) seaweed.

algarabia f gabble, gibberish.

algarroba f (bot) carob.

algarrobo m (bot) carob tree.

algazara f din.

álgebra f algebra.

álgido/da adj chilly; crucial.

algo pn something; anything; * adv somewhat.

algodón m cotton; cotton plant; cotton wool.

algodón azucarado m candyfloss.

algodonero m cotton plant; dealer in cotton.

alguacil m bailiff; mounted official.

alguien pn someone, somebody; anyone, anybody.

alguno/na adj some; any; no; * pn someone, somebody.

alhaja f jewel.

alhelí m wallflower.

aliado/da adj allied.

alianza f alliance, league; wedding ring.

aliar vt to ally; ~**se** vr to form an alliance.

alias adv alias.

alicaído/da adj weak; downcast.

alicates mpl pincers pl, nippers pl.

aliciente m attraction; incitement.

alienación f alienation.

aliento m breath; respiration.

aligerar vt to lighten; to alleviate; to hasten; to ease.

alijo m lightening of a ship; alleviation; cache.

alimaña f pest.

alimentación f nourishment; food; grocery.

alimentar vt to feed, to nourish; ~**se** vr to feed.

alimenticio/cia adj food compd; nutritious.

alimento m food; ~**s** mpl alimony.

alineación m alignment; line-up.

alinear vt to arrange in line; ~**se** vr to line up.

aliñar vt to adorn; to season.

aliño m dressing; ornament, decoration.

alisar vt to plane; to polish; to smooth.

alistarse vr to enlist, to enrol.

aliviar vt to lighten; to ease; to relieve, to mollify.

alivio m alleviation; mitigation; relief; comfort.

aljibe m cistern.

allá adv there; over there; then.

allanamiento m: ~ **de morada** burglary.

allanar vt to level, to flatten; to overcome difficulties; to pacify; to subdue; to burgle; ~**se** vr to submit; to tumble down.

allegado/da adj near; * m/f follower.

allí adv there, in that place.

alma f soul; human being.

almacén m warehouse, store; magazine.

almacenaje m storage.

almacenar vt to store (up).

almanaque m almanac.

almeja f clam.

almena f battlement.

almendra f almond.

almendrado/da adj almond-shaped; * m macaroon.

almendro m almond tree.

almiar m haystack.

almíbar m syrup.

almidón m starch.

almidonado/da adj starched; affected; spruce.

almidonar vt to starch.

almirantazgo m admiralty.

almirante m admiral.

almirez m mortar.

almizcle m musk.

almohada f pillow; cushion.

almohadilla f small pillow; pad; pincushion.

almohadón m large cushion.

almorranas fpl haemorrhoids pl.

almorzar vt to have for lunch; * vi to have lunch.

almuerzo m lunch.

alocado/da adj crazy; foolish; inconsiderate.

alocución f allocution.

áloe m (bot) aloes.

alojamiento m lodging; housing.

alojar vt to lodge; ~**se** vr to stay.

alondra f lark.

alpargata f rope-soled shoe.

alpinismo m mountaineering.

alpinista m/f mountaineer.

alpiste m canary seed.

alquería f farmhouse.
alquilar vt to let, to rent; to hire.
alquiler m renting, letting; hiring; rent; hire.
alquimia f alchemy.
alquimista m alchemist.
alquitrán m tar, liquid pitch.
alquitranado/da adj tarred.
alrededor adv around.
alrededores mpl surroundings pl.
alta f discharge from hospital.
altanería f haughtiness.
altanero/ra adj haughty, arrogant, vain, proud.
altar m altar; ~ **mayor** high altar.
altavoz m loudspeaker.
alterable adj changeable.
alteración f alteration; disturbance, tumult.
alterar vt to alter, to change; to disturb; ~**se** vr to get upset.
altercado m altercation, controversy; quarrel.
alternar vt, vi to alternate.
alternativa f alternative.
alternativo/va adj alternate.
alterno/na adj alternate; alternating.
Alteza f Highness (title).
altibajos mpl ups and downs pl.
altillo m hillock.
altiplanicie f high plateau.
altísimo/ma adj extremely high, most high; * m **el A~** the Most High, God.
altisonante, altísono/na adj high-sounding, pompous.
altitud f height; altitude.
altivez f haughtiness.
altivo/va adj haughty, proud, high-flown.
alto/ta adj high; elevated; tall; sharp; arduous, difficult; eminent; enormous; * m height; story; highland;

(mil) halt; (mus) alto; **i~!, i~ ahí!** interj stop!
altramuz m (bot) lupin.
altura f height; depth; mountain summit; altitude; ~**s** pl: **las ~s** the heavens.
alubia f bean.
alucinación f hallucination.
alucinar vt to blind, to deceive; * vi to hallucinate; ~**se** vr to deceive oneself, to labour under a delusion.
aludir vi to allude.
alumbrado m lighting; illumination.
alumbramiento m lighting; illumination; childbirth.
alumbrar vt to light; * vi to give birth.
aluminio m aluminium.
alumno/na m/f student, pupil.
alunizar vi to land on the moon.
alusión f allusion; hint.
alusivo/va adj allusive.
aluvión f alluvium; flood.
alvéolo m socket; cell of a honeycomb.
alza f rise; sight.
alzacuello m dog collar.
alzada f height; appeal.
alzamiento m rise; elevation; higher bid; uprising.
alzar vt to raise, to lift up; to construct, to build; to gather (in); ~**se** vr to get up; to rise in rebellion; ~**se con algo** vr to make off with something.
ama f mistress, owner; housewife; foster mother; ~ **de llaves** housekeeper; ~ **de leche** nurse.
amabilidad f kindness, niceness.
amable adj kind, nice.
amaestrado/da adj performing.
amaestrar vt to teach; to instruct; train.

amagar vt to threaten; to shake one's fist at; * vi to feint.

amago m threat; indication; symptom.

amalgama f amalgam.

amalgamar vt to amalgamate.

amamantar vt to suckle.

amanecer vi to dawn; **al ~** at daybreak.

amanerado/da adj affected.

amansar vt to tame; to soften; to subdue; **~se** vr to calm down.

amante m/f lover.

amanuense m amanuensis, clerk, copyist.

amapola f (bot) poppy.

amar vt to love.

amargar vt to make bitter; to exasperate; **~se** vr to be bitter.

amargo/ga adj bitter, acrid; painful; * m bitterness.

amargor m bitterness; sorrow, distress.

amargura f bitterness; sorrow.

amarillear vi to turn yellow.

amarillento/ta adj yellowish.

amarillo/lla adj yellow; * m yellow.

amarra f mooring rope.

amarrar vt to moor; to tie, to fasten.

amartelar vt to court, to woo; **~se** vr to fall in love with.

amartillar vt to hammer; to cock (a gun or pistol).

amasar vt to knead; (fig) to arrange, to settle; to prepare.

amasijo m dough; mixed mortar; medley.

amateur m/f amateur.

amatista f amethyst.

amatorio/ria adj relating to love.

amazona f amazon; masculine woman.

ambages mpl: **sin ~** in plain language.

ámbar m amber.

ambición f ambition.

ambicionar vt to crave, to covet.

ambicioso/sa adj ambitious.

ambidextro/tra adj ambidextrous.

ambientación f setting; sound effects pl.

ambiente m atmosphere; environment.

ambigüedad f ambiguity.

ambiguo/gua adj ambiguous; doubtful, equivocal.

ámbito m circuit, circumference; field; scope.

ambos/bas adj, pn both.

ambrosía f ambrosia.

ambulancia f ambulance.

ambulante adj travelling.

ambulatorio m state-run clinic.

ameba f amoeba.

amedrentar vt to frighten, to terrify; to intimidate.

amén f amen; so be it; **~ de** besides; except.

amenaza f threat.

amenazar vt to threaten.

amenizar vt to make pleasant.

ameno/na adj pleasant; delicious; flowery (of language).

América f America; **~ del Norte/del Sur** North/South America.

americano/na adj, m/f (Latin) American.

ametralladora m machine gun.

amianto m asbestos.

amiga f (female) friend.

amigable adj amicable, friendly; suitable.

amigo m friend; comrade; lover; **~/ga** adj friendly.

amilanar vt to frighten, to terrify; **~se** vr to get scared.

aminorar vt to diminish; to reduce.

amistad f friendship.
amistoso/sa adj friendly, cordial.
amnesia f amnesia.
amnistía f amnesty.
amo m owner; boss.
amodorrarse vr to grow sleepy.
amohinar vt to annoy; **~se** vr to sulk.
amoldar vt to mould; to adapt; **~se** vr to adapt oneself.
amonestación f advice; admonition; **~ones** fpl publication of marriage banns.
amonestar vt to advise; to admonish; to publish banns of marriage of.
amoníaco m ammoniac.
amor m love; fancy; lover; **~ mío** my love; **por ~ de Dios** for God's sake; **~ propio** self-love.
amoratado adj livid.
amordazar vt to muzzle; to gag.
amorfo/fa adj shapeless.
amorío m love affair.
amoroso/sa adj affectionate, loving; lovely.
amortajar vt to shroud.
amortiguador m shock absorber.
amortiguadores mpl suspension.
amortiguar vt to mortify; to deaden; to temper; to muffle.
amortización f repayment; redemption.
amortizar vt to entail (an estate), to render inalienable; to pay, to liquidate, to discharge (a debt).
amotinamiento m mutiny.
amotinar vt to incite rebellion; **~se** vr to mutiny.
amparar vt to shelter, to protect; to favour; **~se** vr to claim protection.
amparo m protection, support; help; refuge, asylum.
amperio m amp.

ampliación f amplification, enlargement.
ampliar vt to amplify, to enlarge; to extend; to expand.
amplificación f enlargement.
amplificador m amplifier.
amplificar vt to amplify.
amplio/lia adj ample, extensive.
amplitud f amplitude, extension, largeness.
ampolla f blister; ampoule.
ampuloso/sa adj pompous.
amputación f amputation.
amputar vt to amputate.
amueblar vt to furnish.
amuleto m amulet.
amurallar vt to surround with walls.
anacoreta m anchorite, hermit.
anacronismo m anachronism.
ánade m/f duck.
anadear vi to waddle.
anagrama f anagram.
anales mpl annals pl.
analfabetismo m illiteracy.
analfabeto/ta adj illiterate.
analgésico m painkiller.
análisis m analysis.
analista m/f analyst.
analítico/ca adj analytical.
analizar vt to analyze.
analogía f analogy.
analógico/ca, análogo/ga adj analogous.
ananá m pineapple.
anaquel m shelf (in a bookcase).
anaranjado/da adj orange-coloured.
anarquía f anarchy.
anárquico/ca adj anarchic, chaotic.
anarquismo m anarchism.
anarquista m/f anarchist.
anatema f anathema.
anatomía f anatomy.
anatómico/ca adj anatomical.

anca f rump.
ancho/cha adj broad, wide, large; * m breadth, width.
anchoa f anchovy.
anchura f width, breadth.
anciano/na adj old; * m/f old man/woman.
ancla f anchor.
ancladero m anchorage.
anclaje m anchorage.
anclar vi to anchor.
andaderas fpl baby walker.
andadura f walk; pace; amble.
andamio m scaffold.
andamiaje m scaffolding.
andanada f (mar) broadside.
andar vi to go, to walk; to fare; to act, to proceed, to work; to behave; to elapse; to move; * vt to go, to travel; * m walk, pace.
andariego/ga adj wandering.
andarín m fast walker.
andas fpl stretcher.
andén m pavement, sidewalk; (ferro) platform; quayside.
andrajo m rag.
andrajoso/sa adj ragged.
andurriales mpl byways pl.
anécdota f anecdote.
anegar vt to inundate, to submerge; ~se vr to drown; to sink.
anejo/ja adj attached.
anemia f anaemia.
anestésico m anaesthetic.
anexar vt to annex; to join.
anexión f annexation.
anexionamiento m annexation.
anexo/xa adj annexed.
anfibio/bia adj amphibious.
anfiteatro m amphitheatre.
anfitrión/ona m/f host/ess.
ángel m angel.
angelical adj angelic, heaven-born.

angélico/ca adj angelic.
angina f angina.
anglicano/na adj, m/f Anglican.
anglicismo m anglicism.
angosto/ta adj narrow, close.
anguila f eel.
angula f elver.
angular adj angular; **piedra ~** f cornerstone.
ángulo m angle, corner.
anguloso/sa adj angled, cornered.
angustia f anguish; heartache.
angustiar vt to cause anguish.
anhelante adj eager; longing.
anhelar vi to gasp; * vt to long for.
anhelo m desire, longing.
anidar vi to nestle, to make a nest; to dwell, to inhabit.
anillo m ring.
ánima f soul.
animación f liveliness; activity.
animado/da adj lively.
animador/ora m/f host(ess).
animadversión f ill-will.
animal adj, m animal.
animar vt to animate, to liven up; to comfort; to revive; ~se vr to cheer up.
ánimo m soul; courage; mind; intention, meaning; will; thought; * excl come on!
animosidad f valour, courage; boldness.
animoso/sa adj courageous, spirited.
aniñarse vr to act in a childish manner.
aniquilar vt to annihilate, to destroy; ~se vr to decline, to decay.
anís m aniseed; anisette.
aniversario/ria adj annual; * m anniversary.
ano m anus.
anoche adv last night.

anochecer vi to grow dark; * m nightfall.

anodino/na adj (med) anodyne.

anomalía f anomaly.

anómalo/la adj anomalous.

anonadar vt to annihilate; to lessen; ~se vr to humble oneself.

anonimato m anonymity.

anónimo/ma adj anonymous.

anormal adj abnormal.

anotación f annotation, note.

anotar vt to comment, to note.

anquilosamiento m paralysis.

ánsar m goose.

ansia f anxiety, eagerness, hankering.

ansiar vt to desire.

ansiedad f anxiety.

ansioso/sa adj anxious, eager.

antagónico/ca adj antagonistic; opposed.

antagonista m antagonist.

antaño adv formerly.

antártico/ca adj antarctic; * m: **el A~** the Antarctic.

ante m suede; * prep before; in the presence of; faced with.

anteanoche adv the night before last.

anteayer adv the day before yesterday.

antebrazo m forearm.

antecámara f antechamber.

antecedente adj, m antecedent.

anteceder vt to precede.

antecesor/ra m/f predecessor; * m forefather.

antedicho/cha adj aforesaid.

antelación f; **con ~** in advance.

antemano adv: **de ~** beforehand.

antena f feeler, antenna; aerial; **~ parabólica** satellite dish.

anteojo m eyeglass; **~ de larga vista** telescope; **~s** mpl glasses pl.

antepasado/da adj passed, elapsed; **~s** mpl ancestors pl.

antepecho m (mil) parapet; ledge.

anteponer vt to place in front; to prefer.

anteproyecto m sketch; blueprint.

anterior adj preceding; former.

anterioridad f priority; preference.

antes prep, adv before; * conj before.

antesala f antechamber.

antiaéreo/rea adj anti-aircraft.

antibalas adj bullet-proof.

antibiótico m antibiotic.

anticiclón m anticyclone.

anticipación f anticipation.

anticipado/da adj advance.

anticipar vt to anticipate; to forestall; to advance.

anticipo m advance.

anticonceptivo m contraceptive.

anticongelante m antifreeze.

anticuado/da adj antiquated.

anticuario m antiquary, antiquarian.

anticuerpo m antibody.

antídoto m antidote.

antífona f antiphony; anthem.

antiestético/ca adj unsightly.

antifaz m mask.

antigualla f monument of antiquity; antique.

antiguamente adv in ancient times, of old.

antigüedad f antiquity, oldness.

antiguo/gua adj antique, old, ancient; * m senior; **~s** mpl: **los ~s** the ancients.

antílope m antelope.

antinatural adj unnatural.

antimonio m antimony.

antipatía f antipathy.

antipático/ca adj unpleasant.

antípodas mpl antipodes.

antirrobo *adj* anti-theft.

antisemita *adj* anti-Semitic.

antiséptico/ca *adj* antiseptic.

antítesis *f* (*gr*) antithesis.

antojadizo/za *adj* capricious, fanciful.

antojarse *vr* to long, to desire; to itch.

antojo *m* whim, fancy; longing.

antología *f* anthology.

antorcha *f* torch; taper.

antro *m* (*poet*) cavern, den, grotto.

antropófago *m* cannibal.

antropología *f* anthropology.

antropólogo/ga *m/f* anthropologist.

anual *adj* annual.

anualidad *f* annuity.

anublar *vt* to cloud, to obscure; **~se** *vr* to become clouded.

anudar *vt* to knot; to join; **~se** *vr* to get into knots.

anulación *f* annulment; cancellation.

anular *vt* to annul; to revoke; to cancel; * *adj* annular.

anunciación *f* announcement.

anunciante *m/f* advertiser.

anunciar *vt* to announce; to advertise.

anuncio *m* advertisement.

anverso *m* obverse.

anzuelo *m* hook; allurement.

añadidura *f* addition.

añadir *vt* to add.

añejo/ja *adj* old; stale, musty.

añicos *mpl* bits *pl*, small pieces *pl*; **hacer ~** to shatter.

añil *m* indigo plant; indigo.

año *m* year.

añojo *m* yearling calf.

añoranza *f* longing.

aorta *f* aorta.

aovar *vi* to lay eggs.

apabullar *vt* to squash.

apacentar *vt* to graze.

apacible *adj* affable; gentle; placid, quiet.

apaciguar *vt* to appease; to pacify, to calm.

apadrinar *vt* to support, to favour; to be godfather to.

apagado/da *adj* dull; quiet; muted; listless.

apagar *vt* to put out; to turn off; to quench, to extinguish; to damp; to destroy; to soften.

apagón *m* power cut, outage.

apalabrar *vt* to agree to; to engage.

apalancar *vt* to lever.

apalear *vt* to cane, to drub; to winnow.

apañado/da *adj* skilful; suitable.

apañar *vt* to grasp; to pick up; to patch; **~se** *vr* to manage.

aparador *m* sideboard; store window.

aparato *m* apparatus; machine; ostentation, show.

aparatoso/sa *adj* showy; spectacular.

aparcamiento *m* car park.

aparcar *vt, vi* to park.

aparcería *f* partnership in a farm (*or* other business).

aparcero/ra *m/f* partner; associate.

aparecer *vi* to appear; **~se** *vr* to appear.

aparecido/da *m/f* ghost.

aparejar *vt* to prepare; to harness (horses); to rig (a ship).

aparejo *m* preparation; harness, gear; (*mar*) tackle, rigging; **~s** *mpl* tools *pl*, implements *pl*.

aparentar *vt* to look; to pretend; to deceive.

aparente *adj* apparent; convenient.

aparición *f* apparition; appearance.

apariencia f outward appearance.

apartadero m (ferro) siding.

apartado m paragraph; ~ **de correos** o **postal** PO Box.

apartamento m flat, apartment.

apartamiento m isolation; separation; flat, apartment.

apartar vt to separate, to divide; to remove; to sort; ~**se** vr to go away; to be divorced; to desist.

aparte m aside; new paragraph; * adv apart, separately; besides; aside.

apasionado/da adj passionate; devoted; fond; biased.

apasionar vt to excite; ~**se** vr to get excited.

apatía f apathy.

apático/ca adj apathetic, indifferent.

apeadero m halt, stopping place; station.

apearse vr to dismount; to get down/out/off.

apechugar vt to face up to.

apedrear vt to stone; * vi to hail.

apegarse vr: ~ **a** to become fond of.

apego m attachment, fondness.

apelación f (jur) appeal.

apelar vi (jur) to appeal; ~ **a** to have recourse to.

apelativo adj (gr): **nombre** ~ m generic name.

apellidar vt to call by name; to proclaim; ~**se** vr to be called.

apellido m surname; family name; epithet.

apelmazar vt to compress.

apenar vt to grieve; to embarrass; ~**se** vr to grieve; to be embarrassed.

apenas adv scarcely, hardly; * conj as soon as.

apéndice m appendix, supplement.

apendicitis f appendicitis.

apercibido/da adj provided; ready.

apercibirse vr to notice.

aperitivo m aperitif; appetizer.

apero m agricultural implement.

apertura f aperture, opening, chink; cleft.

apesadumbrar vt to sadden.

apestar vt to infect; * vi: ~ **a** to stink of.

apetecer vt to fancy.

apetecible adj desirable; appetizing.

apetito m appetite.

apetitoso/sa adj pleasing to the taste, appetizing; tempting.

apiadarse vr to take pity.

ápice m summit, point; smallest part of a thing.

apilar vt to pile up; ~**se** vr to pile up.

apiñado/da adj crowded; pyramidal; pine-shaped.

apiñarse vr to clog, to crowd.

apio m (bot) celery.

apisonadora f steamroller.

apisonar vt to ram down.

aplacar vt to appease, to pacify; ~**se** vr to calm down.

aplanar vt to level, to flatten.

aplastar vt to flatten, to crush.

aplatanarse vr to get weary.

aplaudir vt to applaud; to extol.

aplauso m applause; approbation, praise.

aplazamiento m postponement.

aplazar vt to postpone.

aplicable adj applicable.

aplicación f application; effort.

aplicado/da adj studious; industrious.

aplicar vt to apply; to clasp; to attribute; ~**se** vr: ~ **a** to devote oneself to.

aplique *m* wall light.

aplomo *m* self-assurance.

apocado/da *adj* timid.

Apocalipsis *m* Apocalypse.

apocamiento *m* timidity; depression.

apocar *vt* to lessen, to diminish; to contract; ~**se** *vr* to feel humiliated.

apócrifo/fa *adj* apocryphal; fabulous.

apodar *vt* to nickname.

apoderado/da *m/f* proxy, attorney; agent.

apoderar *vt* to authorize; to give the power of attorney to; ~**se** *vr*: ~ **de** to take possession of.

apodo *m* nickname, sobriquet.

apogeo *m* peak.

apolillar *vt* to gnaw or eat (clothes); ~**se** *vr* to be moth-eaten.

apología *f* eulogy; defence.

apoltronarse *vr* to grow lazy; to loiter.

apoplejía *f* apoplexy.

apoplético/ca *adj* apoplectic.

apoquinar *vt* (*fam*) to fork out.

aporrear *vt* to beat up.

aportar *vi* to arrive at a port; to arrive; * *vt* to contribute.

aposentar *vt* to harbour; to put up.

aposento *m* room.

aposición *f* (*gr*) apposition.

apósito *m* (*med*) external dressing.

aposta *adv* on purpose.

apostar *vt* to bet, to wager; to post soldiers; * *vi* to bet.

apostasia *f* apostasy.

apóstata *m* apostate.

apostatar *vi* to apostatize.

apostilla *f* marginal note; postscript.

apóstol *m* apostle.

apostolado *m* apostleship.

apostólico/ca *adj* apostolical.

apostrofar *vt* to apostrophize.

apóstrofe *m* apostrophe.

apóstrofo *m* (*gr*) apostrophe.

apostura *f* neatness.

apoteosis *f* apotheosis.

apoyar *vt* to rest; to favour, to patronize, to support; ~**se** *vr* to lean.

apoyo *m* support; protection.

apreciable *adj* appreciable; valuable; respectable.

apreciar *vt* to appreciate; to estimate, to value.

aprecio *m* appreciation; esteem.

aprehender *vt* to apprehend, to seize.

aprehensión *f* apprehension, seizure.

apremiante *adj* urgent.

apremiar *vt* to press; to compel.

apremio *m* pressure, constriction; judicial compulsion.

aprender *vt* to learn; ~ **de memoria** to learn by heart.

aprendiz/za *m/f* apprentice.

aprendizaje *m* apprenticeship.

aprensión *f* apprehension.

aprensivo/va *adj* apprehensive.

apresar *vt* to seize, to grasp.

apresurado/da *adj* hasty.

apresuramiento *m* hurry.

apresurar *vt* to accelerate, to hasten, to expedite; ~**se** *vr* to hurry.

apretado/da *adj* tight; cramped;, difficult.

apretar *vt* to compress, to tighten; to constrain; to distress; to urge earnestly; * *vi* to be too tight.

apretón *m* squeeze.

apretura *f* squeeze.

aprieto *m* conflict; tight spot.

aprisa *adv* quickly, swiftly; promptly.

aprisco *m* sheepfold.

aprisionar *vt* to imprison.

aprobación *f* approbation, approval.

aprobar *vt* to approve; to pass; * *vi* to pass.

apropiación *f* appropriation, assumption.

apropiado/da *adj* appropriate.

apropiarse *vr* to appropriate.

aprovechable *adj* profitable.

aprovechado/da *adj* industrious; thrifty; selfish.

aprovechamiento *m* use; exploitation.

aprovechar *vt* to use; to exploit; to profit from; to take advantage of; * *vi* to be useful; to progress; **~se** *vr*: ~ **de** to use; to take advantage of.

aproximación *f* approximation; closeness.

aproximado/da *adj* approximate.

aproximar *vt* to approach; **~se** *vr* to approach.

aptitud *f* aptitude, fitness, ability.

apto/ta *adj* apt; fit, able; clever.

apuesta *f* bet, wager.

apuesto/ta *adj* neat.

apuntado/da *adj* pointed.

apuntador *m* prompter.

apuntalar *vt* to prop up.

apuntar *vt* to aim; to level, to point at; to mark; * *vi* to begin to appear or show itself; to prompt (theatre); **~se** *vr* to score; to enrol.

apunte *m* annotation; prompting (theatre).

apuñalar *vt* to stab.

apurado/da *adj* poor, destitute of means; exhausted; hurried.

apurar *vt* to purify; to clear up, to verify; to exhaust; to tease and perplex; **~se** *vr* to worry; to hurry.

apuro *m* want; pain, affliction; haste; jam.

aquejado/da *adj* afflicted.

aquel/~la *adj* that; **~los/~las** *pl* those.

aquél/~la *pn* that (one); **~los/~las** *pl* those (ones).

aquello *pn* that.

aquí *adv* here; now.

aquietar *vt* to quiet, to appease.

aquilino *adj* aquiline.

aquilón *m* north wind.

ara *f* altar.

árabe *adj*, *m/f*, *m* (*ling*) Arabic.

arabesco *m* arabesque.

arado *m* plough.

arancel *m* tariff.

arándano *m* bilberry; blueberry.

arandela *f* washer.

araña *f* spider; chandelier.

arañar *vt* to scratch; to scrape; to corrode.

arar *vt* to plough.

arbitraje *m* arbitration.

arbitrar *vt*, *vi* to arbitrate; to referee.

arbitrariedad *f* arbitrariness.

arbitrario/ria *adj* arbitrary.

arbitrativo/va *adj* arbitrary.

arbitrio *m* free will; arbitration.

árbitro *m* arbitrator; referee; umpire.

árbol *m* tree; (*mar*) mast; shaft.

arbolado/da *adj* forested; wooded; * *m* woodland.

arboladura *f* rigging; masts *pl*.

arbolar *vt* to hoist, to set upright.

arboleda *f* grove.

arbusto *m* shrub.

arca *f* chest, wooden box.

arcada *f* arch; arcade; **~s** *fpl* retching.

arcaico/ca *adj* archaic.

arcaísmo *m* archaism.

arcángel *m* archangel.

arce *m* maple tree.

archipiélago *m* archipelago.

archivador *m* filing cabinet.

archivar *vt* to file.

archivero, archivista *m* keeper of records, archivist.

archivo *m* file(s) (*pl*); archives *pl*.

arcilla *f* clay.

arcilloso/sa *adj* clayey.

arcipreste *m* archpriest.

arco *m* arc; arch; fiddle bow; hoop; ~ **iris** rainbow.

arder *vi* to burn, to blaze.

ardid *m* stratagem, artifice; cunning.

ardiente *adj* burning; ardent, passionate; active; fiery.

ardilla *f* squirrel.

ardor *m* heat; valour; vivacity; fieriness, fervour.

ardoroso/sa *adj* fiery; restless.

arduo/dua *adj* arduous, difficult; high.

área *f* area.

arena *f* sand; grit; arena.

arenal *m* sandy ground.

arenga *f* harangue; speech.

arengar *vi* to harangue.

arenisca *f* sandstone; grit.

arenoso/sa *adj* sandy.

arenque *m* herring; ~ **ahumado** smoked herring, kipper.

argamasa *f* mortar.

argamasar *vi* to mix mortar.

argolla *f* large ring.

argot *m* slang.

argucia *f* subtlety.

argüir *vi* to argue, to dispute; * *vt* to deduce; to argue; to imply.

argumentación *f* argumentation.

argumentar *vt, vi* to argue, to dispute; to conclude.

argumento *m* argument.

aria *f* (*mus*) aria; tune, air.

aridez *f* drought, want of rain.

árido/da *adj* dry; barren.

Aries *m* Aries (sign of the zodiac).

ariete *m* battering ram.

ario/a *adj* Aryan.

arisco/ca *adj* fierce; rude; intractable.

aristocracia *f* aristocracy.

aristócrata *m* aristocrat.

aristocrático/ca *adj* aristocratic.

aritmética *f* arithmetic.

arlequín *m* harlequin, buffoon.

arma *f* weapon, arm.

armada *f* fleet, armada.

armadillo *m* armadillo.

armado/da *adj* armed; reinforced.

armador *m* ship owner; privateer; jacket, jerkin.

armadura *f* armour; framework; skeleton; armature.

armamento *m* armament.

armar *vt* to man; to arm; to fit; ~**la** to kick up a fuss.

armario *m* wardrobe; cupboard.

armatoste *m* hulk; contraption.

armazón *f* chassis; skeleton; frame.

armería *f* arsenal; heraldry; gunsmith's.

armero *m* gunsmith.

armiño *m* ermine.

armisticio *m* armistice.

armonía *f* harmony.

armonioso/sa *adj* harmonious.

armonizar *vt* to harmonize; to reconcile.

arnés *m* harness; ~**eses** *mpl* gear, trappings *pl*.

aro *m* ring; earring.

aroma *m* aroma, fragrance.

aromaterapia *f* aromatherapy.

aromático/ca *adj* aromatic.

arpa *f* harp.

arpegio *m* (*mus*) arpeggio.

arpía *f* (*poet*) shrew.

arpillera *f* sackcloth.

arpón *m* harpoon.

arqueado/da *adj* arched, vaulted.

arquear *vt* to arch; to bend.

arqueo *m* arching; gauging (of a ship).

arqueología *f* archaeology.

arqueólogo/ga *m/f* archaeologist.

arquero *m* archer.

arqueta *f* small trunk.

arquetipo *m* archetype.

arquitecto *m* architect.

arquitectónico/ca *adj* architectural.

arquitectura *f* architecture.

arrabal *m* suburb; slum.

arrabalero *m* suburbanite.

arraigado *adj* deep-rooted; established.

arraigar *vi* to root; to establish; * *vt* to establish; ~**se** *vr* to take root; to settle.

arrancar *vt* to pull up by the roots; to pull out; to wrest; to extract; * *vi* to start; to move.

arranque *m* sudden start; start; outburst.

arras *fpl* security.

arrasar *vt* to demolish, to destroy.

arrastrado/da *adj* miserable; painstaking; servile.

arrastrar *vt* to drag; * *vi* to creep, to crawl; to lead a trump at cards; ~**se** *vr* to crawl; to grovel.

arrastre *m* dragging.

¡arre! *excl* gee!, go on!

arrear *vt* to drive on; * *vi* to hurry along.

arrebañar *vt* to scrape together; to pick up.

arrebatado/da *adj* rapid; violent, impetuous; rash, inconsiderate.

arrebatar *vt* to carry off, to snatch; to enrapture.

arrebato *m* fury; rapture.

arrebol *m* rouge.

arrebujar *vt* to crumple; to wrap up.

arrecife *m* reef.

arrecirse *vr* to grow stiff with cold.

arreglado *adj* neat; regular, moderate.

arreglar *vt* to regulate; to tidy; to adjust; ~**se** *vr* to come to an understanding.

arreglo *m* rule, order; agreement; arrangement.

arrellanarse *vr* to sit at ease; to make oneself comfortable.

arremangar *vt* to roll up; ~**se** *vr* to roll up one's sleeves.

arremeter *vi* to attack; to seize suddenly.

arremetida *f* attack, assault.

arrendador *m* landlord.

arrendamiento *m* leasing; hire; lease.

arrendar *vt* to rent, to let out, to lease.

arrendatario/ria *m/f* tenant.

arreo *m* dress, ornament; ~**s** *mpl* harness.

arrepentido/da *adj* repentant.

arrepentimiento *m* repentance, penitence.

arrepentirse *vr* to repent.

arrestar *vt* to arrest; to imprison.

arresto *m* boldness; prison; arrest.

arriada *f* flood, overflowing.

arriar *vt* (*mar*) to lower, to strike; to pay out.

arriate *m* bed; causeway.

arriba *adv* above, over, up; high, on high, overhead; aloft.

arribada *f* (*mar*) arrival (of a vessel) in port.

arribar *vi* (*mar*) to put into harbour.

arribista *m/f* upstart.

arriendo *m* lease; farm rent.

arriero *m* muleteer.

arriesgado/da *adj* risky; daring.

arriesgar *vt* to risk, to hazard; to expose to danger; **~se** *vr* to take a chance.

arrimar *vt* to approach, to draw near; (*mar*) to stow (cargo); **~se** *vr* to side up; to lean.

arrinconar *vt* to put in a corner; to lay aside.

arrobado/da *adj* enchanted.

arrobamiento *m* rapture; amazement.

arrobarse *vr* to be totally amazed; to be out of one's senses.

arrocero/ra *adj* rice-producing.

arrodillarse *vr* to kneel down.

arrogancia *f* arrogance, haughtiness.

arrogante *adj* arrogant; haughty, proud; stout.

arrojadizo/za *adj* easily thrown.

arrojar *vt* to throw, to fling; to dash; to emit; to shoot, to sprout; **~se** *vr* to hurl oneself.

arrojo *m* boldness, fearlessness.

arrollador/ra *adj* overwhelming.

arrollar *vt* to run over; to defeat heavily.

arropar *vt* to clothe, to dress; **~se** *vr* to wrap up.

arrostrar *vt* to face (up to).

arroyo *m* stream; gutter.

arroz *m* rice.

arrozal *m* rice field.

arruga *f* wrinkle; rumple.

arrugar *vt* to wrinkle; to rumple; to fold; **~ la frente** to frown; **~se** *vr* to shrivel.

arruinar *vt* to demolish; to ruin; **~se** *vr* to go bankrupt.

arrullador/ra *adj* flattering, cajoling.

arrullar *vt* to lull; * *vi* to coo.

arrullo *m* cooing (of pigeons); lullaby.

arrumaco *m* caress.

arsenal *m* arsenal; dockyard.

arsénico *m* arsenic.

arte *m/f* art; skill; artfulness.

artefacto *m* appliance.

arteria *f* artery.

artero/ra *adj* dexterous, cunning, artful.

artesa *f* kneading trough.

artesanía *f* craftsmanship.

artesano *m* artisan, workman.

ártico/ca *adj* arctic; * *m*: **el A~** the Arctic.

articulación *f* articulation; joint.

articulado/da *adj* articulated; jointed.

articular *vt* to articulate; to joint.

artículo *m* article; clause; point; (*gr*) article; condition.

artífice *m* artisan; artist.

artificial *adj* artificial.

artificio *m* workmanship, craft; artifice, cunning trick.

artificioso/sa *adj* skilful, ingenious; artful, cunning.

artillería *f* gunnery; artillery.

artillero *m* artillery man.

artimaña *f* trap; cunning.

artista *m* artist; craftsman.

artístico/ca *adj* artistic.

artritis *f* arthritis.

arzobispado *m* archbishopric.

arzobispo *m* archbishop.

as *m* ace.

asa *f* handle; lever.

asado *m* roast meat; barbecue.

asador *m* spit.

asadura *f* offal.

asalariado/da *adj* salaried.

asaltador/a *m/f* assailant.

asaltante *m/f* assailant.

asaltar *vt* to assault; to storm (a position); to assail.

asalto *m* assault, attack.

asamblea *f* assembly, meeting.

asar *vt* to roast.

asbesto *m* asbestos.

ascendencia *f* ascendancy; ancestry.

ascendente *adj* ascending; (*ferro*) **tren** ~ *m* up train.

ascender *vi* to be promoted; to rise; * *vt* to promote.

ascendiente *m* forefather; influence.

Ascensión *f* feast of the Ascension.

ascenso *m* promotion; ascent.

ascensor *m* elevator.

asceta *m* ascetic.

ascético/ca *adj* ascetic.

asco *m* nausea; loathing.

ascua *f* red-hot coal.

aseado/da *adj* clean; elegant; neat.

asear *vt* to clean; to tidy.

asediar *vt* to besiege; to chase.

asedio *m* siege.

asegurado/da *adj* insured.

asegurador *m* insurer.

asegurar *vt* to secure; to insure; to affirm; to bail; ~**se** *vr* to make sure.

asemejarse *vr* to be like, to resemble.

asentado/da *adj* established.

asentar *vt* to sit down; to affirm, to assure; to note; * *vi* to suit.

asentir *vi* to acquiesce, to concede.

aseo *m* cleanliness; neatness; ~**s** *mpl* toilets *pl*.

aséptico/ca *adj* germ-free.

asequible *adj* attainable; obtainable.

aserción *f* assertion, affirmation.

aserradero *m* sawmill.

aserrar *vt* to saw.

aserrín *m* sawdust.

asertivo/va *adj* affirmative.

asesinar *vt* to assassinate; to murder.

asesinato *m* assassination; murder.

asesino *m* assassin; murderer.

asesor *m* counsellor, adviser, consultant.

asesorar *vt* to advise; to act as consultant to; ~**se** *vr* to consult.

asestar *vt* to aim, to point; to strike.

aseverar *vt* to affirm.

asfalto *m* asphalt.

asfixia *f* suffocation.

asfixiar *vt* to suffocate; ~**se** *vr* to suffocate.

así *adv* so, thus, in this manner; like this; therefore; so that; also; ~ **que** so that; therefore; **así, así** so-so; middling.

asidero *m* handle.

asiduidad *f* assiduousness.

asiduo/dua *adj* assiduous.

asiento *m* chair; bench, stool; seat; contract; entry; residence.

asignación *f* assignation; destination.

asignar *vt* to assign, to attribute.

asignatura *f* subject; course.

asilado/da *m/f* inmate; refugee.

asilo *m* asylum, refuge; ~ **político** political asylum.

asimilación *f* assimilation.

asimilar *vt* to assimilate.

asimismo *adv* similarly, in the same manner.

asir *vt* to grasp, to seize; to hold, to grip; * *vi* to take root.

asistencia *f* audience; presence; assistance, help.

asistente *m* assistant, helper.

asistir *vi* to be present; to assist; * *vt* to help.

asma *f* asthma.

asmático/ca *adj* asthmatic.

asno *m* ass.

asociación *f* association; partnership.

asociado *m* associate.

asociar vt to associate; **~se** vr to associate.

asolar vt to destroy; to devastate.

asolear vt to expose to the sun; **~se** vr to sunbathe.

asomar vi to appear; **~se** vr to appear, to show up.

asombrar vt to amaze; to astonish; **~se** vr to be amazed; to get a fright.

asombro m dread, terror; astonishment.

asombroso/sa adj astonishing, marvellous.

asomo m mark, token, indication; conjecture.

asonancia f assonance; harmony.

aspa f cross; sail.

aspaviento m astonishment; fuss.

aspecto m appearance; aspect.

aspereza f roughness; surliness.

áspero/ra adj rough, rugged; craggy, knotty; horrid; harsh, hard; severe, austere; gruff.

asperón m grindstone.

aspersión f sprinkling; aspersion.

áspid m asp.

aspiración f breath; pause.

aspirante m aspirant, aspirer.

aspirar vt to breathe; to aspire; (gr) to aspirate.

aspirina f aspirin.

asquear vt to sicken; * vi to be sickening; **~se** vr to feel disgusted.

asqueroso/sa adj disgusting.

asta f lance; horn; handle.

astado/da adj horned.

asterisco m asterisk.

astilla f chip (of wood), splinter.

astillero m dockyard.

astral adj astral.

astringente adj astringent.

astro m star.

astrología m astrology.

astrológico/ca adj astrological.

astrólogo/ga m/f astrologer.

astronauta m/f astronaut.

astronave f spaceship.

astronomía f astronomy.

astronómico/ca adj astronomical.

astrónomo/ma m/f astronomer.

astucia f cunning, slyness.

astuto/ta adj cunning, sly; astute.

asueto m time off; holiday, vacation.

asumir vt to assume.

Asunción f Assumption.

asunto m subject, matter; affair, business.

asustar vt to frighten; **~se** vr to be frightened.

atacar vt to attack.

atajo m short cut.

atalaya f watchtower.

atañer vi: **~ a** to concern.

ataque m attack.

atar vt to tie; to fasten.

atardecer vi to get dark; * m dusk; evening.

atareado/da adj busy.

atascar vt to jam; to hinder; **~se** vr to become bogged down.

atasco m traffic jam.

ataúd m coffin.

ataviar vt to dress up, to trim, to adorn.

atavío m dress; ornament; **~s** mpl finery.

ateísmo m atheism.

atemorizar vt to frighten; **~se** vr to get scared.

atenazar vt to grip; to torment.

atención f attention, heedfulness; civility; observance, consideration.

atender vi to be attentive; * vt to attend to; to heed, to expect, to wait for; to look at.

atenerse vr: ~ **a** to adhere to.

atentado m terrorist attack; transgression, offence.

atentamente adv observantly; **le saluda** ~ yours faithfully.

atentar vt to attempt; to commit.

atento/ta adj attentive; heedful; observing; mindful; polite, courteous, mannerly.

atenuante adj extenuating.

atenuar vt to diminish; to lessen.

ateo/a adj, m/f atheist.

aterciopelado/da adj velvety.

aterido/da adj frozen stiff.

aterirse vr to grow stiff with cold.

aterrador/a adj frightening.

aterrar vt to terrify; ~**se** vr to be terrified.

aterrizaje m landing.

aterrizar vi to land.

aterrorizar vt to frighten, to terrify.

atesorar vt to treasure or hoard up (riches).

atestación f testimony, evidence.

atestado/da adj packed; * m affidavit.

atestar vt to cram, to stuff; to attest, to witness.

atestiguar vt to witness, to attest.

atiborrar vt to stuff; ~**se** vr to stuff oneself.

ático m attic.

atildar vt to punctuate with a tilde; to censure.

atinado/da adj wise; correct.

atisbar vt to pry into; to examine closely.

atizar vt to stir (the fire) with a poker; to stir up.

atlántico/ca adj atlantic; * m: **el A~** the Atlantic.

atlas m atlas.

atleta m/f athlete.

atlético/ca adj athletic.

atletismo m athletics.

atmósfera f atmosphere.

atmosférico/ca adj atmospheric.

atolladero m bog; obstacle; impediment.

atollar vi to stick; ~**se** vr to get stuck.

atolondramiento m stupefaction, consternation.

atolondrar vt to stun, to stupefy; ~**se** vr to be stupefied.

atómico/ca adj atomic.

atomizador m spray.

átomo m atom.

atónito/ta adj astonished, amazed.

atontado/da adj stunned; silly.

atontar vt to stun, to stupefy; ~**se** to grow stupid.

atormentar vt to torture; to harass; to torment.

atornillar vt to screw on; to screw down.

atosigar vt to poison; to harass; to oppress.

atracadero m landing-place.

atracador/a m/f robber.

atracar vt to moor; to rob; ~**se** vr: ~ **(de)** to stuff oneself (with).

atracción f attraction.

atractivo/va adj attractive; magnetic; * m charm.

atraer vt to attract, to allure.

atragantarse vr to stick in the throat, to choke.

atrancar vt to bar (a door).

atrapar vt to trap; to nab; to deceive.

atrás adv backward(s); behind; previously, **hacia** ~ backward(s).

atrasado/da adj slow; backward; in arrears.

atrasar vi to be slow; * vt to postpone; ~ **el reloj** to put back a watch; ~**se** vr to stay behind; to be late.

atraso *m* backwardness; slowness; delay.

atravesado/da *adj* oblique; cross; perverse; mongrel; degenerate.

atravesar *vt* to cross; to pass over; to pierce; to go through; **~se** *vr* to get in the way; to meddle.

atrayente *adj* attractive.

atreverse *vr* to dare, to venture.

atrevido/da *adj* bold, audacious, daring.

atrevimiento *m* boldness, audacity.

atribución *f* attribution, imputation.

atribuir *vt* to attribute, to ascribe; to impute.

atribular *vt* to vex, to afflict.

atributivo/va *adj* attributive.

atributo *m* attribute.

atrición *f* attrition.

atril *m* lectern; music stand.

atrio *m* porch; portico.

atrocidad *f* atrocity.

atrochar *vi* to take a short cut.

atropellado/da *adj* hasty, precipitate.

atropellar *vt* to trample; to run down; to hurry; to insult; **~se** *vr* to hurry.

atropello *m* accident; push; outrage.

atuendo *m* attire.

atroz *adj* atrocious, heinous; cruel.

atufar *vt* to vex, to plague; **~se** *vr* turn sour; to get mad.

atún *m* tuna (fish).

aturdido/da *adj* hare-brained.

aturdimiento *m* stupefaction; astonishment; dullness.

aturdir *vt* to stun, to confuse; to stupefy.

atusar *vt* to smooth.

audacia *f* audacity, boldness.

audaz *adj* audacious, bold.

audible *adj* audible.

audiencia *f* audience.

auditivo/va *adj* auditory.

auditor *m* auditor.

auditoría *f* audit.

auditorio *m* audience; auditorium.

auge *m* boom; climax.

augurar *vt* to predict.

augurio *m* omen.

aula *f* lecture room.

aullar *vi* to howl.

aullido/aullo *m* howling.

aumentar *vt* to augment, to increase; to magnify; to put up; * *vi* to increase; to grow larger.

aumento *m* increase; promotion, advancement.

aún *adv* even; **~ así** even so.

aun *adv* still; yet.

aunar *vt* to unite, to assemble.

aunque *adv* though, although.

¡aúpa! *excl* come on!

áureo/rea *adj* golden, gilt *compd*.

aureola *f* glory; nimbus.

auricular *m* receiver; **~es** *mpl* headphones *pl*.

aurora *f* dawn.

auscultar *vt* to sound.

ausencia *f* absence.

ausentarse *vr* to go out.

ausente *adj* absent.

auspicio *m* auspice; prediction; protection.

austeridad *f* austerity.

austero/ra *adj* austere, severe.

austral *adj* southern.

autenticar *vt* to authenticate.

autenticidad *f* authenticity.

auténtico/ca *adj* authentic.

autillo *m* brown owl.

auto *m* judicial sentence; car; edict, ordinance; **~ de fe** auto-da-fe.

autoadhesivo/va *adj* self-adhesive.

autobiografía *f* autobiography.

autobús *m* bus.

autocar *m* bus.

autocracia *f* autocracy.

autócrata *m* autocrat.

autóctono/na *adj* native.

autodefensa *f* self defence.

autodeterminación *f* self-determination.

autoedición *f* desktop publishing.

autoescuela *f* driving school.

autoestop, autostop *f* hitchhiking; **hacer ~** to hitchhike.

autoestopista, autostopista *m/f* hitchhiker.

autógrafo *m* autograph.

autómata *m* automaton.

automático/ca *adj* automatic.

automatización *f* automation.

automedicación *f* self-medication.

automotor *m* diesel train.

automóvil *m* automobile.

automovilismo *m* motoring; motor racing.

automovilista *m/f* motorist, driver.

automovilístico/ca *adj* car *compd*.

autonomía *f* autonomy.

autónomo/ma *adj* autonomous.

autonómico/ca *adj* autonomous.

autopista *f* motorway; **~ de la información** information superhighway.

autopsía *f* post mortem, autopsy.

autor/ra *m/f* author; maker; writer.

autoridad *f* authority.

autorización *f* authorization.

autorizar *vt* to authorize.

autorradio *m* car radio.

autorretrato *m* self-portrait.

autoservicio *m* self-service store; restaurant.

autosuficiencia *f* self-sufficiency.

autovía *f* state highway.

auxiliar *vt* to aid, to help, to assist; to attend; * *adj* auxiliary.

auxilio *m* aid, help, assistance.

aval *m* guarantee; guarantor.

avalancha *f* avalanche.

avance *m* advance; attack; trailer (for a film).

avanzada *f* (*mil*) vanguard.

avanzar *vt, vi* to advance.

avaricia *f* avarice.

avaricioso/sa *adj* avaricious, covetous.

avaro/ra *adj* miserly; * *m/f* miser.

avasallar *vt* to subdue; to enslave.

ave *f* bird; fowl.

avecinarse *vr* to be on the way.

avellana *f* hazelnut.

avellano *m* hazelnut tree.

ave maría *f* Hail Mary.

avena *f* oats *pl*.

avenencia *f* agreement, bargain; union.

avenida *f* avenue.

avenido/da *adj* agreed.

avenir *vt* to reconcile; **~se** *vr* to reach a compromise.

aventajado/da *adj* advantageous, profitable; beautiful; excellent.

aventajar *vt* to surpass, to excel.

aventar *vt* to fan; to expel.

aventura *f* adventure; event, incident.

aventurado/da *adj* risky.

aventurar *vt* to venture, to risk.

aventurero/ra *adj* adventurous.

avergonzar *vt* to shame, to abash; **~se** *vr* to be ashamed.

avería *f* breakdown.

averiado/da *adj* broken down; out of order.

averiarse *vr* to break down.

averiguación *f* discovery; investigation.

averiguar *vt* to inquire into; to investigate, to explore.

aversión f aversion, dislike; abhorrence.

avestruz m ostrich.

aviación f aviation; air force.

aviador/a m/f aviator.

avicultura f poultry farming.

avidez f covetousness.

ávido/da adj (poet) greedy, covetous.

avieso/sa adj irregular, out of the way; mischievous, perverse.

avinagrado/da adj sour.

avinagrarse vr to go sour.

avío m preparation, provision.

avión m aeroplane.

avioneta f light aircraft.

avisado/da adj prudent, cautious; **mal ~** ill-advised.

avisar vt to inform; to warn; to advise.

aviso m notice; warning; hint.

avispa f wasp.

avispado/da adj lively, brisk; vivacious.

avisparse vr to worry.

avispero m wasp's nest.

avispón m hornet.

avistar vt to sight.

avituallar vt (mil) to supply (with food).

avivar vt to quicken, to enliven; to encourage.

avutarda f bustard.

axioma m axiom, maxim.

¡ay! excl ouch!; ow! **¡~ de mí!** alas! poor me!

aya f governess, instructress.

ayer adv yesterday.

ayuda f help, aid; support; * m deputy, assistant.

ayudante m (mil) adjutant; assistant.

ayudar vt to help, to assist; to further.

ayunar vi to fast, to abstain from food.

ayuno m fasting, abstinence from food.

ayuntamiento m town/city hall.

azabache m jet.

azada f spade; hoe.

azafata f air hostess.

azafrán m saffron.

azahar m orange or lemon blossom.

azar m unforeseen disaster; unexpected accident; fate; **por ~** by chance; **al ~** at random.

azaroso/sa adj unlucky, ominous; risky.

azogue m mercury.

azor m goshawk.

azorar vt to frighten, to terrify.

azotaina f drubbing, sound flogging.

azotar vt to whip, to lash.

azote m whip.

azotea f flat roof of a house.

azteca m/f Aztec.

azúcar m/f sugar.

azucarado/da adj sugared; sugary.

azucarar vt to sugar, to sweeten.

azucarero m sugar bowl.

azucena f white lily.

azufre m sulphur, brimstone.

azul adj blue; **~ celeste** sky blue.

azulado/da adj azure, bluish.

azulejo m tile.

azuzar vt to irritate, to stir up.

B

baba f dribble, spittle.
babear vi to dribble, to drool.
babel m bedlam.
babero m bib.
babia f: **estar en ~** to be absent-minded or dreaming.
baboso/sa adj dribbling, drooling.
babucha f slipper.
baca f (auto) roof rack.
bacalao m cod.
bache m pothole.
bachillerato m baccalaureate.
báculo m stick.
bagaje m baggage.
bagatela f trifle.
bahía f bay.
bailador/ra m/f dancer.
bailar vi to dance.
bailarín/ina m/f dancer.
baile m dance, ball; **~ de disfraces** fancy-dress ball.
baja f fall; casualty.
bajada f descent; inclination; slope; ebb.
bajamar f low tide, low water.
bajar vt to lower, to let down; to lessen; to humble; to go/come down; to bend downward(s); * vi to descend; to go/come down; to grow less; **~se** vr to crouch; to lessen.
bajeza f meanness; lowliness.
bajío m shoal, sandbank; lowlands pl.
bajo/ja adj low; abject, despicable; common; dull (of colours); deep; humble; * prep under, underneath, below; * adv softly; quietly; * m (mus) bass; low place.
bajón m fall.
bakalao m (fam) rave music.

bala f bullet.
baladronada f boast, brag; bravado.
balance m hesitation; balance sheet; balance; rolling (of a ship).
balancear vt, vi to balance; to roll; to waver; **~se** vr to swing.
balancín m balance beam; rocker arm; seesaw; balancing pole.
balanza f scale; balance.
balar vi to bleat.
balaustrada f balustrade, banister.
balazo m shot.
balbucear vt, vi to stutter.
balbuciente adj stammering, stuttering.
balcón m balcony.
baldar vt to cripple.
balde m bucket; **de ~** adv gratis, for nothing; **en ~** in vain.
baldío/día adj waste; uncultivated.
baldosa f floor; tile; flagstone.
balido m bleating, bleat.
balín m buckshot.
balística f ballistics pl.
ballena f whale; whalebone.
ballenato m calf of a whale.
ballenero m (mar) whaler.
ballesta f crossbow; **a tiro de ~** at a great distance.
ballestero m archer; crossbow-maker.
ballet m ballet.
balneario m spa.
balón m ball.
baloncesto m basketball.
balonmano m handball.
balonvolea m volleyball.
balsa[1] f balsa wood; raft, float.
balsa[2] f pool, pond.
bálsamo m balsam, balm.
baluarte m bastion; bulwark.

bamba *f* fat; (*bot*) swelling; flabbiness.
bambolear *vi* to reel; **~se** *vr* to sway.
bamboleo *m* reeling, staggering.
bambú *m* bamboo.
banana *f* banana; plantain.
banano *m* banana tree.
banasta *f* large basket.
banca *f* bench; banking; **~ electrónica** electronic banking.
bancario/ria *adj* bank(ing) *compd*.
bancarrota *f* bankruptcy.
banco *m* bench; work bench; bank.
banda *f* band; sash; ribbon; troop; party; gang; touchline.
bandada *f* flock; shoal.
bandearse *vr* to move to and fro.
bandeja *f* tray, salver.
bandera *f* banner, standard; flag.
banderilla *f* small decorated dart used at a bullfight.
banderillear *vt* to plant banderillas in a bull's neck or shoulder.
banderillero *m* thrower of banderillas.
banderín *m* small flag, pennant.
bandido *m* bandit, outlaw.
bando *m* faction, party; edict.
bandolera *f* bandoleer.
bandolero *m* bandit.
bandurria *f* bandore (musical instrument resembling a lute).
banquero/ra *m/f* banker.
banqueta *f* three-legged stool; pavement, sidewalk.
banquete *m* banquet; formal dinner.
banquillo *m* dock; bench.
bañador *m* swimsuit.
bañar *vt* to bathe; to dip; to coat (with varnish); **~se** *vr* to bathe; to swim.
bañera *f* bath (tub).
bañero *m* lifeguard.
bañista *m/f* bather.
baño *m* bath; dip; bathtub; varnish; coating.

baptista *m/f* Baptist.
bar *m* bar.
baraja *f* pack of cards.
barajar *vt* to shuffle (cards); to jumble up.
baranda *f* rail.
barandilla *f* small balustrade, small railing.
baratijas *fpl* trifles *pl*, toys *pl*; trash, junk.
baratillo *m* secondhand goods *pl*; junkshop; bargain sale.
barato/ta *adj* cheap; **de ~** gratis; * *m* cheapness; bargain sale; money extracted from winning gamblers.
baraúnda *f* noise, hurly-burly.
barba *f* chin; beard; **~ a ~** face to face; * *m* actor who impersonates old men.
barbacoa *f* barbecue.
barbaridad *f* barbarity, barbarism; outrage.
barbarie *f* barbarism; savagery.
barbarismo *m* barbarism (form of speech).
bárbaro/ra *adj* barbarous; cruel; rude; rough.
barbecho *m* first ploughing, fallow land.
barbería *f* barber's shop.
barbero *m* barber.
barbilampiño/ña *adj* clean-shaven; (*fig*) inexperienced.
barbilla *f* (tip of the) chin.
barbo *m* barbel.
barbudo/da *adj* bearded.
barca *f* boat.
barco *m* boat; ship.
barítono *m* (*mus*) baritone.
barman *m* barman.
barniz *m* varnish; glaze.
barnizar *vt* to varnish.
barómetro *m* barometer.

barón *m* baron.
baronesa *f* baroness.
barquero *m* boatman.
barquilla *f* (*mar*) log; basket (of an air balloon).
barquillo *m* wafer; cornet, cone.
barra *m* bar; rod; lever; French loaf; sandbank; **de ~ a ~** from place to place.
barrabasada *f* trick, plot.
barraca *f* hut.
barranco *m* gully, ravine; (*fig*) great difficulty.
barranquismo *m* canyoning.
barrena *f* drill, bit, auger.
barrenar *vt* to drill, to bore; (*fig*) to frustrate.
barrendero *m* sweeper.
barreno *m* large drill; borehole.
barreño *m* tub.
barrer *vt* to sweep; to overwhelm.
barrera *f* barrier; turnpike, claypit.
barriada *f* suburb, area of a city.
barricada *f* barricade.
barrido *m* sweep.
barriga *f* abdomen; belly.
barrigudo/da *adj* pot-bellied.
barril *m* barrel; cask.
barrio *m* area, district.
barrizal *m* claypit.
barro *m* clay, mud.
barroco/ca *adj* baroque.
barrote *m* ironwork (of doors, windows, tables); crosspiece.
barruntar *vt* to guess; to foresee; to conjecture.
barrunto *m* conjecture.
bártulos *mpl* gear, belongings *pl*.
barullo *m* uproar.
basamento *m* base.
basalto *m* basalt.
basar *vt* to base; **~se** *vr* **~ en** to be based on.

basca *f* squeamishness, nausea.
báscula *f* scales *pl*.
base *f* base, basis.
básico/ca *adj* basic.
basílica *f* basilica.
basilisco *m* basilisk.
bastante *adj* sufficient, enough; * *adv* quite.
bastar *vi* to be sufficient, to be enough.
bastardo/da *adj*, *m/f* bastard.
bastidor *m* embroidery frame; **~es** *mpl* scenery (on stage).
basto/ta *adj* coarse, rude, unpolished.
bastón *m* cane, stick; truncheon; (*fig*) command.
bastonazo *m* beating.
bastos *mpl* clubs *pl* (one of the four suits at cards).
basura *f* rubbish, trash, refuse; dung.
basurero *m* refuse collector, dustman; dunghill.
bata *f* dressing gown; overall; laboratory coat.
batacazo *m* noise of a fall.
batalla *f* battle, combat; fight.
batallador/a *adj* battling.
batallar *vi* to battle, to fight; to fence with foils; to waver.
batallón *m* (*mil*) battalion.
batata *f* sweet potato.
bate *m* bat.
batería *m* battery; percussion.
batida *f* beating (of woodland/ moorland); search; chase.
batido/da *adj* shot (of silk); well-trodden (of roads); * *m* batter; **~ de leche** milk shake.
batidora *f* food mixer; whisk.
batir *vt* to beat; to whisk; to dash; to demolish; to defeat.

batista *f* fine cotton cloth, cambric.
batuta *f* baton.
baúl *m* trunk; (*fam*) belly.
bautismal *adj* baptismal.
bautismo *m* baptism.
bautizar *vt* to baptize, to christen.
bautizo *m* baptism.
baya *f* berry.
bayeta *f* cloth.
bayo/ya *adj* bay (colour of a horse).
bayoneta *f* bayonet.
bayonetazo *m* thrust with a bayonet.
baza *f* card trick.
bazar *m* bazaar.
bazo *m* spleen.
bazofia *f* refuse; hogwash.
be *m* baa (cry of sheep).
beatificación *f* beatification.
beatificar *vt* to beatify; to hallow, to sanctify, to make blessed.
beato/ta *adj* happy; blessed; devout; * *m* lay brother; *m/f* pious person; beatified person.
bebé *m/f* baby.
bebedero *m* drinking trough.
bebedizo *m* (love) potion.
bebedor/ra *m/f* (hard) drinker.
beber *vt, vi* to drink.
bebida *f* drink, beverage.
beca *f* fellowship; grant, bursary, scholarship; sash; hood.
becada *f* woodcock.
becerro *m* yearling calf.
bedel *m* janitor; uniformed employee.
befa *f* jeer, taunt.
befarse *vr*: ~ **de** to mock, to ridicule.
beldad *f* beauty.
belén *m* nativity scene.
bélico/ca *adj* warlike, martial.
belicoso/sa *adj* warlike; aggressive.
beligerante *adj* belligerent.
bellaco/ca *adj* artful; cunning.

belladona *f* (*bot*) deadly nightshade.
belleza *f* beauty.
bello/lla *adj* beautiful; handsome; lovely; fine.
bellota *f* acorn; (*med*) Adam's apple; pomander.
bemol *m* (*mus*) flat.
bencina *f* benzine.
bendecir *vt* to bless; to consecrate; to praise.
bendición *f* blessing, benediction.
bendito/ta *adj* saintly; blessed; simple; happy.
benedictino/na/benito/ta *adj, m/f* Benedictine.
beneficiado *m* incumbent; beneficiary.
beneficiar *vt* to benefit; to be of benefit to.
beneficiario/ria *m/f* beneficiary.
beneficio *m* benefit, advantage; profit; benefit night.
beneficioso/sa *adj* beneficial.
benéfico/ca *adj* beneficent, kind.
benemérito/ta *adj* worthy, meritorious.
beneplácito *m* consent, approbation.
benevolencia *f* benevolence.
benévolo/la *adj* benevolent, kindhearted.
benigno/na *adj* benign; kind; mild.
beodo/da *adj* drunk, drunken.
berberecho *m* cockle.
berenjena *f* eggplant.
bergantín *m* (*mar*) brig.
bermejo/ja *adj* red.
berrear *vi* to low, to bellow.
berrido *m* bellowing (of a calf).
berrinche *m* anger, rage, tantrum (applied to children).
berro *m* watercress.
berza *f* cabbage.

besamanos *m invar* levee; royal audience.

besamel *f* white sauce.

besar *vt* to kiss; to graze; **~se** *vr* to kiss.

beso *m* kiss; collision of persons or things.

bestia *f* beast, animal; idiot.

bestial *adj* bestial; (*fam*) marvellous, great.

bestialidad *f* bestiality.

besugo *m* sea bream.

besuquear *vt* to cover with kisses.

besuqueo *m* repeated kisses *pl*.

betún *m* shoe polish.

bezo *m* thick lip; swollen tissue in a wound.

biberón *m* feeding bottle.

Biblia *f* Bible.

bíblico/ca *adj* biblical.

bibliófilo/la *m/f* book-lover, bookworm.

bibliografía *f* bibliography.

bibliográfico/ca *adj* bibliographical.

bibliógrafo/fa *m/f* bibliographer.

biblioteca *f* library.

bibliotecario/ra *m/f* librarian.

bicarbonato *m* bicarbonate.

bicho *m* small animal; bug; **mal ~** villain.

bici *f* (*fam*) bike.

bicicleta *f* bicycle; **~ de montaña** mountain bike.

bidé *m* bidet.

bielda *f* pitchfork.

bien *m* good, benefit; profit; **~es** *mpl* goods *pl*, property; wealth; * *adv* well, right; very; willingly; easily; **~ que** *conj* although; **está ~** he is well.

bienal *adj* biennial.

bienaventuranza *f* blessedness; bliss; happiness; prosperity; **~s** *fpl* the Beatitudes.

bienestar *m* well-being.

bienhablado/da *adj* well-spoken.

bienhecho/cha *adj* well-shaped.

bienhechor/ra *m/f* benefactor.

bienio *m* space of two years.

bienvenida *f* welcome.

bifurcación *f* fork.

bigamia *f* bigamy.

bígamo/ma *m/f* bigamist.

bigote *m* moustache; whiskers *pl*.

bigotudo/da *adj* with a big moustache.

bikini *m* bikini.

bilingüe *adj* bilingual.

bilioso/sa *adj* bilious.

bilis *f* bile.

billar *m* billiards *pl*.

billete *m* note, banknote; ticket; (*ferro*) ticket; **~ sencillo** single ticket; **~ de ida y vuelta** return ticket.

billetero *m* wallet.

billón *m* trillion.

bimensual *adj* twice monthly.

bimotor *m* twin-engined plane.

binario *m* binary.

binoculares *mpl* binoculars *pl*; opera glasses *pl*.

biodegradable *adj* biodegradable.

biodiversity *f* biodiversity.

biografía *f* biography.

biógrafo/fa *m/f* biographer.

biología *f* biology.

biológico/ca *adj* biological.

biólogo/ga *m/f* biologist.

biombo *m* screen.

biopsia *f* biopsy.

bípedo *m* biped.

birlar *vt* to knock down at one blow; to pinch (*fam*).

birreta *f* biretta.

bis *excl* encore.

bisabuela *f* great-grandmother.

bisabuelo *m* great-grandfather.

bisagra *f* hinge.

bisexual *adj* bisexual.

bisexualidad *f* bisexuality.

bisiesto *adj*: **año ~** leap year.

bisnieto/ta *m/f* great-grandson/daughter.

bisoño/na *adj* raw, inexperienced; novice.

bisonte *m* bison.

bistec *m* steak.

bisturí *m* scalpel.

bisutería *f* costume jewellery.

bizarro/rra *adj* brave, gallant; generous.

bizco/ca *adj* cross-eyed.

bizcocho *m* sponge cake; biscuit; ship's biscuit.

bizquear *vi* to squint.

blanco/ca *adj* white; blank; * *m* whiteness; white person; blank, blank space; target (to shoot at).

blancura *f* whiteness.

blandir *vt* to brandish a sword; **~se** *vr* to swing.

blando/da *adj* soft, smooth; mild, gentle; (*fam*) cowardly.

blanducho/cha *adj* flabby.

blandura *f* softness; gentleness, mildness.

blanquear *vt* to bleach; to whitewash; to launder (money); * *vi* to show white.

blanquecino/na *adj* whitish.

blanqueo *m* laundering (of money).

blasfemador/ra *m/f* blasphemer.

blasfemar *vi* to blaspheme.

blasfemia *f* blasphemy; verbal insult.

blasfemo/ma *adj* blasphemous; * *m* blasphemer.

blasón *m* heraldry, honour, glory.

blasonar *vt* to emblazon; to praise highly.

bledo *m*: **me importa un ~** I don't give a damn (*sl*).

blindado/da *adj* armour-plated; bullet-proof.

bloc *m* writing pad.

bloque *m* block.

bloquear *vt* to block; to blockade.

bloqueo *m* blockade.

blusa *f* blouse.

boato *m* ostentation, pompous show.

bobada *f* folly, foolishness.

bobear *vt* to act or talk in a stupid manner.

bobería *f* silliness, foolishness.

bobina *f* bobbin.

bobo/ba *m/f* idiot, fool; clown, funny man; * *adj* stupid, silly.

boca *f* mouth; entrance, opening; mouth of a river; **~ en ~** *adv* by word of mouth; **a pedir de ~** to one's heart's content.

bocacalle *f* entrance to a street.

bocadillo *m* sandwich, roll.

bocado *m* mouthful.

bocal *m* pitcher; mouthpiece of a trumpet.

bocamanga *f* cuff.

bocanada *f* mouthful (of liquor); gust.

bocazas *m/f invar* loudmouth.

boceto *m* sketch.

bochorno *m* sultry weather, scorching heat; blush.

bochornoso/sa *adj* sultry; shameful.

bocina *f* trumpet; megaphone; horn (of a car).

boda *f* wedding.

bodega *f* wine cellar; warehouse; bar.

bodegón *m* cheap restaurant; still life (in art).

bodoque *m* pellet; lump; (*fam*) idiot.

bodorrio *m* quiet wedding.

bofes *mpl* lungs; lights.

bofetada *f* slap (in the face).

bofetón *m* hard slap.

boga *f* fashion; (*ferro*) bogey; rower; rowing; **estar en ~** to be fashionable.

bogar *vi* to row, to paddle.

bohemio *m/f* Bohemian.

boicot *m* boycott.

boicotear *vt* to boycott.

boina *f* beret.

boj *m* box, box tree.

bola *f* ball; marble; globe; slam (in cards); shoe polish; (*fam*) lie, fib.

bolazo *m* blow with a ball.

bolchevique *adj* Bolshevik.

bolear *vi* to knock balls about (billiards); * *vt* to throw (a ball).

bolera *f* bowling alley.

bolero *m* bolero jacket; bolero dance.

boleta *f* entrance ticket; pass, permit.

boletín *m* bulletin; journal, review.

boleto *m* ticket.

boli *m* (*fam*) (ballpoint) pen.

boliche *m* jack (at bowls); bowls, bowling alley; dragnet.

bolígrafo *m* (ballpoint) pen.

bolillo *m* bobbin.

bollo *m* bread roll; lump.

bolo *m* ninepin; (large) pill.

bolsa *f* handbag; bag; pocket; sac; stock exchange.

bolsillo *m* pocket; purse.

bolsista *m/f* stockbroker.

bolso *m* purse.

bomba *f* pump; bomb; surprise; **dar a la ~** to pump; **~ de gasolina** petrol pump.

bombardear *vt* to bombard.

bombardeo *m* bombardment.

bombardero *m* bomber.

bombazo *m* explosion; bombshell.

bombero *m* fireman.

bombilla *f* light bulb.

bombín *m* bowler hat.

bombo *m* large drum.

bombón *m* sweet; chocolate.

bonachón/ona *adj* good-natured.

bonanza *f* fair weather (at sea); prosperity; bonanza.

bondad *f* goodness, kindness; courtesy.

bondadoso/sa *adj* good, kind.

bonete *m* clerical hat; college cap.

bonito *adj* pretty, nice-looking; pretty good, passable; * *m* tuna (fish).

bono *m* (financial) bond.

boñiga *f* cow pat.

bonsái *m* bonsai.

boqueada *f* act of opening the mouth; **la última ~** the last gasp.

boquear *vi* to gape;, to gasp; to breathe one's last; * *vt* to pronounce, to utter (a word).

boquerón *m* anchovy; large hole.

boquete *m* gap, narrow entrance.

boquiabierto/ta *adj* open-mouthed; gaping.

boquilla *f* mouthpiece of a musical instrument; nozzle.

borbollón/borbotón *m* bubbling; **salir a borbollones** to gush forth.

borda *f* (*mar*) gunwale; hut.

bordado *m* embroidery.

bordadora *f* embroiderer.

bordar *vt* to embroider; to do anything very well.

borde *m* border; margin; (*mar*) board.

bordear *vi* (*mar*) to tack; * *vt* to go along the edge of; to flank.

bordillo *m* kerb.

bordo *m* (*mar*) board of a ship.

boreal *adj* boreal, northern.

borgoña *m* burgundy wine.

borla *f* tassel; tuft.

borona *f* millet; corn; corn bread.

borrachera *f* drunkenness; hard drinking; spree.

borracho/cha *adj* drunk, intoxicated; blind with passion; * *m/f* drunk, drunkard.

borrador *m* first draft; scribbling pad; eraser.

borraja *f* (*bot*) borage.

borrar *vt* to erase, to rub out; to blur; to obscure.

borrasca *f* storm; violent squall of wind; hazard; danger.

borrascoso/sa *adj* stormy.

borrego/ga *m/f* yearling lamb; simpleton, blockhead.

borrico/ca *m/f* donkey, ass; blockhead.

borrón *m* blot, blur; rough draft of a writing; first sketch of a painting; stain, blemish.

borronear *vt* to sketch.

boscaje *m* grove, small wood; landscape (in painting).

bosque *m* forest; wood.

bosquejar *vt* to make a sketch of (a painting); to make a rough model of (a figure).

bosquejo *m* sketch (of a painting); unfinished work.

bostezar *vi* to yawn; to gape.

bostezo *m* yawn; yawning.

bota *f* leather wine-bag; boot.

botánica *f* botany.

botánico/ca *adj* botanic; * *m/f* botanist.

botanista *m/f* botanist.

botar *vt* to cast, to fling; to launch.

bote *m* bounce; thrust; tin, can; boat.

botella *f* bottle.

botica *f* pharmacy.

boticario/ria *m/f* pharmacist.

botijo *m* earthenware jug.

botín *m* high boot, half-boot; gaiter; booty.

botiquín *m* medicine chest.

botón *m* button; knob (of a radio etc); (*bot*) bud.

botonadura *f* set of buttons.

botones *m invar* bellboy.

bóveda *f* arch; vault, crypt.

boxeador *m* boxer.

boxeo *m* boxing.

boya *f* (*mar*) buoy.

boyante *adj* buoyant, floating; (*fig*) fortunate, successful.

bozal *m* muzzle.

bozo *m* down (on the upper lip or chin); head collar (of a horse).

braceada *f* violent movement of the arms.

bracear *vi* to swing the arms.

bracero *m* day-labourer; farm-hand.

braga *f* sling, rope; nappy; **~s** *fpl* panties *pl*.

bragazas *m invar* henpecked husband.

braguero *m* truss.

bragueta *f* fly, flies *pl* (of trousers).

braille *m* braille.

bramante *m* twine, string.

bramar *vi* to roar, to bellow; to storm, to bluster.

bramido *m* roar, bellow, howl.

brasa *f* live coal; **estar hecho una ~** to be very flushed.

brasero *m* brazier.

bravamente *adv* bravely, gallantly; fiercely; roughly; extremely well.

bravío/vía *adj* ferocious, savage, wild; coarse; * *m* fierceness, savageness.

bravo/va *adj* brave, valiant; bullying; savage, fierce; rough; sumptuous; excellent, fine; * *excl* well done!

bravura *f* ferocity; courage.

braza *f* fathom.

brazada *f* extension of the arms; armful.

brazado *m* armful.

brazal *m* armband; irrigation channel.

brazalete *m* bracelet.

brazo *m* arm; branch (of a tree); enterprise; courage; **luchar a ~ partido** to fight hand to hand.

brea *f* pitch; tar.

brear *vt* to pitch; to tar; to abuse, to ill-treat; to play a joke on.

brebaje *m* potion.

brecha *f* (*mil*) breach; gap, opening; **batir en ~** (*mil*) to make a breach.

bregar *vi* to struggle; to quarrel; to slog away.

breva *f* early fig; early large acorn.

breve *m* papal brief; * *f* (*mus*) breve; * *adj* brief, short; **en ~** shortly.

brevedad *f* brevity, shortness, conciseness.

breviario *m* breviary; (*fig*) daily reading.

brezo *m* (*bot*) heather.

bribón/ona *adj* dishonest, rascally.

bribonear *vi* to be idle; to play dirty tricks.

bricolaje *m* do-it-yourself.

brida *f* bridle; clamp, flange.

bridge *m* bridge (cards).

brigada *f* brigade; squad, gang.

brigadier *m* brigadier.

brillante *adj* brilliant; bright, shining; * *m* diamond.

brillar *vi* to shine; to sparkle, to glisten; to shine, to be outstanding.

brillo *m* brilliance, brightness.

brincar *vi* to skip; to leap, to jump; to gambol; to fly into a passion.

brinco *m* leap, jump; bounce.

brindar *vi* : **~ a la salud de/~ por** to drink the health of, to toast; * *vt* to offer, to present.

brindis *m invar* toast.

brío *m* spirit, dash.

briosamente *adv* spiritedly, dashingly.

brioso/sa *adj* dashing, full of spirit; lively.

brisa *f* breeze.

brisca *f* card game.

broca *f* reel; drill; shoemaker's tack.

brocado *m* gold or silver brocade; **~/da** *adj* embroidered; like brocade.

brocal *m* rim, mouth; curb.

brocha *f* large brush; **~ de afeitar** shaving brush.

brochada *f* brushstroke.

broche *m* clasp; brooch; cufflink.

broma *f* joke.

bromear *vi* to joke.

bromista *m/f* joker.

bronca *f* row.

bronce *m* bronze.

bronceado/da *adj* tanned; * *m* bronzing, suntan.

broncearse *vr* to get a suntan.

bronco/ca *adj* rough, coarse; rude; harsh.

bronquitis *f* bronchitis.

broquel *m* shield.

brotar *vi* (*bot*) to bud, to germinate; to gush, to rush out; (*med*) to break out.

brote *m* (*bot*) shoot; (*med*) outbreak.

bruces *adv*: **de ~** face downward(s).

bruja *f* witch.

brujería *f* witchcraft.

brujo *m* sorcerer, magician, wizard.

brújula *f* compass.

bruma *f* mist; (*mar*) sea mist.

brumoso/sa *adj* misty.

bruñido *m* polish.

bruñir *vt* to polish; to put rouge on.

brusco/ca *adj* rude; sudden; brusque.

brutal *adj* brutal, brutish.

brutalidad *f* brutality; brutal action.

bruto *m* brute, beast; **~/ta** *adj* stupid; gross; brutish.

buba *f* tumour.

bucal *adj* oral.

bucear *vi* to dive.

buceo *m* diving.

bucle *m* curl.

bucólica *f* pastoral poetry; (*fam*) food.

buche *m* craw, maw; (*fam*) guts *pl*; mouthful; crease in clothes.

budismo *m* Buddhism.

buen *adj* (*before m nouns*) good.

buenamente *adv* easily; willingly.

buenaventura *f* fortune, good luck.

bueno/na *adj* good, perfect; fair; fit, proper; good-looking; **¡buenos días!** good morning!; **¡buenas tardes!** good afternoon!; **¡buenas noches!** good night!; **¡~!** right!

buey *m* ox, bullock.

bufa *f* joke, mock.

búfalo *m* buffalo.

bufanda *f* scarf.

bufar *vi* to choke with anger; to snort.

bufete *m* desk, writing-table; lawyer's office.

bufido *m* snorting (of an animal).

bufo/fa *adj* comic; **ópera ~a** *f* comic opera.

bufón *m* buffoon; jester; **~/ona** *adj* funny, comical.

bufonada *f* buffoonery; joke.

buhardilla *f* attic.

búho *m* owl; unsocial person.

buhonero *m* pedlar, hawker.

buitre *m* vulture.

bujía *f* candle; spark plug.

bula *f* papal bull.

bulbo *m* (*bot*) bulb.

bulboso/sa *adj* bulbous.

bulevar *m* boulevard.

bulla *f* confused noise, clatter; crowd; **meter ~** to make a noise.

bullicio *m* bustle; uproar.

bullicioso/sa *adj* lively, restless, noisy, busy; turbulent; boisterous.

bulto *m* bulk; tumour, swelling; bust; baggage.

buñuelo *m* doughnut; fritter.

buque *m* vessel, ship, tonnage, capacity(of a ship); hull (of a ship).

burbuja *f* bubble.

burbujear *vi* to bubble.

burdel *m* brothel.

burdo/da *adj* coarse, rough.

burgués/esa *adj* bourgeois.

burguesía *f* bourgeoisie.

buril *m* engraver's chisel.

burla *f* trick; gibe; joke; **de ~s** in fun.

burlar *vt* to hoax; to defeat; to play tricks on, to deceive; to frustrate; **~se** *vr* to joke, to laugh at.

burlesco/ca *adj* burlesque; comical, funny.

burlón/ona *m/f* joker.

burocracia *f* bureaucracy.

burócrata *m/f* bureaucrat.

burrada *f* drove of asses; stupid action.

burro *m* ass, donkey; idiot; sawhorse.

bursátil *adj* stock exchange *compd*.

bus *m* bus.

busca *f* search, hunt; bleeper.

buscapiés *m invar* jumping jack (fireworks).

buscar vt to seek, to search for; to look for; to hunt after; * vi to look, to search, to seek.

buscavidas m prying person, busybody.

buscón m petty thief, small-time crook.

búsqueda f search.

busto m bust.

butaca f armchair; seat.

butano m butane.

butifarra f Catalan sausage.

buzo m diver.

buzón m letter box, postbox; conduit, canal; cover of a jar.

C

cabal adj just, exact; right; complete; accomplished.

cábalas fpl intrigue.

cabalgada f cavalcade; (mil) cavalry raid.

cabalgadura f mount horse, beast of burden.

cabalgar vi to ride, to go riding.

cabalgata f procession.

cabalístico/ca adj cabalistic.

caballa f mackerel.

caballar adj equine.

caballería f mount, steed; cavalry; cavalry horse; chivalry; knighthood.

caballeriza f stable; stud; stable hands pl.

caballerizo m groom.

caballero m knight; gentleman; rider, horseman; horse soldier; ~ andante knight errant.

caballerosidad f chivalry.

caballeroso/sa adj noble; gentlemanlike.

caballete m ridge of a roof; painter's easel; trestle; bridge (of the nose).

caballo m horse; ~ de carreras racehorse; (at chess) knight; queen (in cards); a ~ on horseback.

cabaña f hut, cabin; hovel; livestock; balk (in billiards).

cabaré m cabaret.

cabecear vi to nod (with sleep); to shake one's head; (mar) to pitch.

cabeceo m nod; shaking (of the head).

cabecera f headboard; head; far end; pillow; headline; vignette.

cabecilla m ringleader.

cabellera f head of hair; wig; tail of a comet.

cabello m hair.

cabelludo/da adj hairy, shaggy.

caber vi to fit.

cabestrillo m sling.

cabestro m halter; bell-ox.

cabeza f head; chief, leader; main town, chief centre.

cabezada f butt; nod/shake of the head.

cabezal m pillow; compress.

cabezón m collar (of a shirt); opening in a garment for the head.

cabezudo/da adj big-headed; pigheaded.

cabida f room, capacity; tener ~ con una persona to have influence with someone.

cabildo m chapter (of a church); meeting of a chapter; corporation of a town.

cabina f cabin; telephone booth.

cabizbajo/ja, cabizcaído/da *adj* crestfallen; pensive, thoughtful.

cable *m* cable, lead, wire.

cabo *m* end, extremity; cape, headland; (*mar*) cable, rope.

cabra *f* goat.

cabrero *m* goatherd.

cabrío/a *adj* goatish.

cabriola *f* caper; gambol.

cabritilla *f* kidskin.

cabrito *m* kid.

cabrón *m* cuckold; ¡~! (*fam*) bastard! (*sl*).

cacahuete *m* peanut.

cacao *m* (*bot*) cacao tree; cocoa.

cacarear *vi* to crow; to brag, to boast.

cacareo *m* crowing of a cock, cackling of a hen; boast, brag.

cacería *f* hunting-party.

cacerola *f* pan, saucepan; casserole.

cachalote *m* sperm whale.

cacharro *m* pot; piece of junk.

cachear *vt* to frisk.

cachemir *m* cashmere.

cacheo *m* frisking.

cachete *m* cheek; slap in the face.

cachiporra *f* truncheon.

cachivache *m* pot; piece of junk.

cacho *m* slice, piece (of lemons, oranges, etc); horn.

cachondeo *m* (*fam*) farce.

cachondo/da *adj* randy; funny.

cachorro/ra *m/f* puppy; cub (of any animal).

cacique *m* chief; local party boss.

caco *m* pickpocket; coward.

cacofonía *f* cacophony.

cacto/cactus *m* cactus.

cada *adj invar* each; every.

cadalso *m* scaffold.

cadáver *m* corpse, cadaver.

cadavérico/ca *adj* cadaverous.

cadena *f* chain; series, link; radio or TV network.

cadencia *f* cadence.

cadente *adj* harmonious.

cadera *f* hip.

cadete *m* (*mil*) cadet.

caducar *vi* to become senile; to expire, to lapse; to deteriorate.

caducidad *f* expiry.

caduco/ca *adj* worn out; decrepit; perishable; expired, lapsed.

caer *vi* to fall; to tumble down; to lapse; to happen; to die; ~se *vr* to fall down.

café *m* coffee; cafe, coffee house.

cafetera *f* coffee pot.

cafetería *f* cafe.

cafetero/ra *m/f* coffee merchant; cafe owner.

cafre *adj* savage, inhuman; rude.

cagar *vi* (*fam*) to have a shit (*sl*).

caída *f* fall, falling; slope, descent.

caimán *m* caiman, alligator.

caja *f* box, case; casket; cashbox; cash desk; check-out, till; ~ **de ahorros** savings bank; ~ **de cambios** gearbox; ~ **negra** black box.

cajero/ra *m/f* cashier, teller; ~ **automático** cash machine.

cajetilla *f* packet.

cajón *m* chest of drawers; locker.

cal *f* lime; ~ **viva** quick lime.

cala *f* creek, small bay; small piece of melon, etc; (*mar*) hold; dipstick.

calabacín *m* small marrow, courgette.

calabaza *f* pumpkin, squash.

calabozo *m* prison; cell.

calada *f* soaking; lowering of nets; puff, drag; swoop.

calado *m* openwork in metal, wood or linen.

calafatear *vt* (*mar*) to calk.

calamar *m* squid.
calambre *m* cramp.
calamidad *f* calamity, disaster.
calamitoso/sa *adj* calamitous.
calaña *f* model; pattern.
calandria *f* calendra lark.
calar *vt* to soak, to drench; to penetrate, to pierce; to see through; to lower; ~**se** *vr* to stall (of a car).
calavera *f* skull; madcap.
calaverada *f* ridiculous or foolish action.
calcañar *m* heel.
calcar *vt* to trace, to copy.
calcáreo/rea *adj* calcareous.
calceta *f* (knee-length) stocking.
calcetín *m* sock.
calcinar *vt* to calcine.
calcio *m* calcium.
calco *m* tracing.
calcomanía *f* transfer.
calculable *adj* calculable.
calculadora *f* calculator.
calcular *vt* to calculate, to reckon; to compute.
cálculo *m* calculation, estimate; calculus; (*med*) gallstone.
caldear *vt* to weld; to warm, to heat up.
caldera *f* kettle, boiler; **las ~s de Pero Botero** (*fam*) hell.
calderada *f* stew.
calderilla *f* holy water fount; small change.
caldero *m* small boiler.
caldo *m* stock; broth.
caldoso/sa *adj* having too much broth or gravy.
calefacción *f* heating.
calendario *m* calendar.
calentador *m* heater.
calentamiento *m* ~ **global** global warming.

calentar *vt* to warm up, to heat up; ~**se** *vr* to grow hot; to dispute.
calentura *f* fever.
calenturiento/ta *adj* feverish.
calesa *f* calash, cab.
calibre *m* calibre; (*fig*) calibre.
calidad *f* grade, quality, condition; kind.
cálido/da *adj* hot; (*fig*) warm.
caliente *adj* hot; fiery; **en ~** in the heat of the moment.
califa *m* caliph.
califato *m* caliphate.
calificación *f* qualification; grade.
calificar *vt* to qualify; to assess, to mark; ~**se** *vr* to register as a voter.
caligrafía *f* calligraphy.
calistenia *f* callisthenics.
cáliz *m* chalice.
calizo/za *adj* calcareous.
callado/da *adj* silent, quiet.
callandico *adv* softly, silently.
callar *vi*, ~**se** *vr* to be silent, to keep quiet.
calle *f* street; road.
calleja *f* lane, narrow passage.
callejear *vi* to loiter about the streets.
callejero/ra *adj* loitering.
callejón *m* alley.
callejuela *f* lane, narrow passage; subterfuge.
callista *m/f* chiropodist.
callo *m* corn; callus; ~**s** *mpl* tripe.
callosidad *f* callosity.
calloso/sa *adj* callous; horny.
calma *f* calm, calmness.
calmante *m* (*med*) sedative.
calmar *vt* to calm, to quiet, to pacify. * *vi* to become calm.
calmoso/sa *adj* calm; tranquil.
calor *m* heat, warmth; ardour, passion.

caloría f calorie.

calumnia f calumny, slander.

calumniar vt to slander.

calumnioso/sa adj slanderous.

caluroso/sa adj warm; hot; lively.

calva f bald patch.

calvario m Calvary; (fig) debts pl.

calvicie f baldness.

calvinismo m Calvinism.

calvinista m/f Calvinist.

calvo/va adj bald; bare, barren.

calza f wedge.

calzado m footwear.

calzador m shoehorn.

calzar vt to put on (shoes); to wear (shoes); to stop (a wheel); ~**se** vr to put on one's shoes.

calzón m shorts pl; pants pl; panties pl.

calzonazos m invar stupid guy; **es un** ~ he is a weak-willed guy.

calzoncillos mpl underpants pl, shorts pl.

cama f bed; **hacer la** ~ to make the bed.

camada f litter (of animals); ~ **de ladrones** gang of thieves.

camafeo m cameo.

camaleón m chameleon.

camandulero/ra adj prudish; hypocritical; sly, tricky.

cámara f hall; chamber; room; camera; cine camera.

camarada m/f comrade, companion.

camarera f waitress; maid.

camarero m waiter.

camarilla f clique; lobby.

camarín m dressing room; lift car.

camarón m shrimp, prawn.

camarote m berth, cabin.

cambalache m exchange, swap.

cambalachear vt to exchange, to swap.

cambiable adj changeable, variable; interchangeable.

cambiar vt to exchange; to change. * vi to change, to alter; ~**se** vr to move house.

cambio m change, exchange; rate of exchange; bureau de change.

cambista m/f exchange broker.

camelar vt to flirt with.

camello m camel.

camilla f couch; cot; stretcher.

caminante m/f traveller, walker.

caminar vi to travel; to walk, to go.

caminata f long walk; hike.

camino m road; way.

camión m truck.

camioneta f van.

camisa f shirt; chemise.

camiseta f T-shirt; vest.

camisón m nightgown.

camorra f quarrel, dispute.

camorrista m/f quarrelsome person.

campamento m (mil) encampment, camp.

campana f bell.

campaña f countryside; level country, plain; (mil) campaign.

campanada f peal of a bell; (fig) scandal.

campanario m belfry.

campaneo m bellringing, chime.

campanero m bell founder; bellringer.

campanilla f handbell; (med) uvula.

campante adj excelling, outstanding; smug.

campánula f bellflower.

campear vi to go out to pasture; to work in the fields.

campechano/na adj open.

campeón/ona m/f champion.

campeonato m championship.

campesino/na, campestre adj rural.

campiña f flat tract of cultivated farmland.

camping m camping, campsite.

campista m/f camper.

campo m country; field; camp; ground; pitch; ~ **de refugiados** refugee camp.

campus m invar campus.

camuflaje m camouflage.

caña f cane, reed; stalk; shinbone; glass of beer; ~ **dulce** sugar cane.

canal m channel, canal.

canalizar vt to canalize.

canalla f mob, rabble.

canalón m large gutter.

cáñamo m hemp.

cañamón m hemp seed.

canana f cartridge belt.

canapé m couch, sofa.

canario m canary.

canas fpl grey hair; **peinar** ~ to grow old.

canasta f basket, hamper.

canastilla f small basket.

canasto m large basket.

cañaveral m reedbed.

cancel m storm door.

cancelación f cancellation.

cancelar vt to cancel; to write off.

Cáncer m Cancer (sign of the zodiac).

cáncer m cancer.

cancerígeno/na adj carcinogenic.

canceroso/sa adj cancerous.

cancha f (tennis) court.

canciller m chancellor; foreign minister.

canción f song.

cancionero m songbook.

candado m padlock.

candela f candle.

candelabro m candlestick.

candente adj red-hot.

candidato/ta m/f candidate.

cándido/da adj simple, naive; white, snowy.

candil m oil lamp.

candilejas fpl footlights pl.

candor m candour; innocence.

canela f cinnamon.

canelón m icicle.

cañería f conduit of water, water pipe.

cangrejo m crab; crayfish.

canguro m kangaroo; * f baby-sitter.

caníbal m/f cannibal, man-eater.

canica f marble.

canícula f dog days pl.

canijo/ja adj weak, sickly.

canilla f shinbone; arm-bone; tap of a cask; spool.

canino/na adj canine; **hambre** ~**a** f ravenous hunger.

canje m exchange.

canjear vt to exchange.

caño m tube, pipe; sewer.

cano/na adj grey-haired; white-haired.

canoa f canoe.

canon m canon; tax; royalty; rent.

cañón m tube, pipe; barrel; gun; canyon.

cañonazo m gunshot; (fig) bombshell.

cañonear vt to shell, to bombard.

cañoneo m shelling, gunfire.

cañonera f gunboat.

canónico/ca adj canonical.

canónigo m canon, prebendary.

canonización f canonization.

canonizar vt to canonize.

canoso/sa adj grey-haired; white-haired.

cansado/da adj weary, tired; tedious, tiresome.

cansancio m tiredness, fatigue.

cansar *vt* to tire, to tire out; to bore; ~**se** *vr* to get tired, to grow weary.

cantable *adj* suitable for singing.

cantante *m/f* singer.

cantar *m* song. * *vt* to sing; to chant. * *vi* to sing; to chirp.

cántara *f* pitcher.

cantarín/ina *m/f* someone who sings a lot.

cántaro *m* pitcher; jug; **llover a ~s** to rain heavily, to pour.

cantera *f* quarry.

cantero *m* quarryman.

cántico *m* canticle.

cantidad *f* quantity, amount; number.

cantimplora *f* water bottle; hip flask.

cantina *f* buffet, refreshment room; canteen; cellar; snack bar; bar.

cantinela *f* ballad, song.

canto *m* stone; singing; song; edge.

cantón *m* corner; canton.

cantonear *vi* to loaf around.

cantor/ra *m/f* singer.

canuto *m* (*fam*) joint (*sl*), marijuana cigarette.

caoba *f* mahogany.

caos *m* chaos; confusion.

capa *f* cloak; cape; layer, stratum; cover; pretext; ~ **de ozono** ozone layer.

capacho *m* hamper; big basket.

capacidad *f* capacity; extent; talent.

capar *vt* to geld; to castrate; (*fig*) to curtail.

caparazón *m* caparison.

capataz *m* foreman, overseer.

capaz *adj* capable; capacious, spacious, roomy.

capazo *m* large basket; carrycot.

capcionar *vt* to seize, to arrest.

capcioso/sa *adj* wily, deceitful.

capear *vt* to flourish (one's cloak in front of a bull); * *vi* (*mar*) to ride out or weather (a storm).

capellán *m* chaplain.

capeo *m* challenging of a bull with a cloak.

caperuza *f* hood.

capilar *adj* capillary.

capilla *f* hood, cowl; chapel.

capirote *m* hood.

capital *m* capital; capital sum; * *f* capital, capital city; * *adj* capital; principal.

capitalismo *m* capitalism.

capitalista *m/f* capitalist.

capitalizar *vt* to capitalize.

capitán *m* captain.

capitana *f* flagship; (woman) captain (in sport).

capitanear *vt* to captain; to command.

capitanía *f* captaincy.

capitel *m* capital (of a column).

capitolio *m* capitol.

capitulación *f* capitulation; agreement; ~**ones** *fpl* marriage contract.

capitular *vi* to come to terms, to make an agreement.

capítulo *m* chapter of a cathedral; chapter (of a book).

capó *m* (*auto*) bonnet.

capón *m* capon.

caporal *m* chief, ringleader.

capota *f* hat, bonnet.

capote *m* greatcoat; bullfighter's cloak.

capricho *m* caprice, whim, fancy.

caprichoso/sa *adj* capricious, whimsical; obstinate.

Capricornio *m* Capricorn (sign of the zodiac).

cápsula *f* capsule.

captar *vt* to captivate; to understand; (*rad*) to tune in to, to receive.

captura *f* capture, arrest.

capturar *vt* to capture.

capucha *f* circumflex (accent); cap, cowl, hood of a cloak.

capuchino *m* Capuchin monk; **(café)** ~ cappuccino (coffee).

capullo *m* cocoon of a silkworm; rosebud; coarse cloth made of spun silk.

caqui *m, adj* khaki.

cara *f* face; appearance; ~ **a** ~ face to face.

carabina *f* carbine, rifle.

carabinero *m* carabineer.

caracol *m* snail; seashell; spiral.

caracola *f* shell.

caracolear *vi* to prance about (of a horse).

carácter *m* character; quality; condition; handwriting.

característico/ca *adj* characteristic.

caracterizar *vt* to characterize.

caradura *m/f*: **es un** ~ he's got a nerve.

caramba *excl* well!

carámbano *m* icicle.

carambola *f* cannon (at billiards); trick.

caramelo *m* candy.

caramente *adv* dearly.

caramillo *m* small flute; piece of gossip.

carantoña *f* hideous mask; dressed-up old woman; ~**s** *fpl* caresses *pl*.

carátula *f* pasteboard mask; **la** ~ the stage.

caravana *f* caravan; tailback (of traffic).

caray *excl* well!

carbón *m* coal; charcoal; carbon; carbon paper.

carbonada *f* grill; kind of pancake.

carboncillo *m* charcoal.

carbonera *f* coal tip; coal mine.

carbonería *f* coalyard.

carbonero *m* coal merchant; *(mar)* collier.

carbónico/ca *adj* carbonic.

carbonilla *f* coaldust.

carbonizar *vt* to carbonize.

carbono *m* *(quim)* carbon.

carbunclo/carbunco *m* carbuncle.

carburador *m* carburettor.

carcaj *m* quiver.

carcajada *f* (loud) laugh.

carcamal *m* nickname for an old person.

cárcel *f* prison; jail.

carcelero *m* warder, jailer.

carcoma *f* deathwatch beetle; woodworm; anxious concern.

carcomer *vt* to gnaw, to corrode; ~**se** *vr* to grow worm-eaten.

carcomido/da *adj* worm-eaten.

cardar *vt* to card (wool).

cardenal *m* cardinal; cardinal bird; *(med)* bruise, weal.

cardenalicio/cia *adj* belonging to a cardinal.

cárdeno/na *adj* purple; livid.

cardíaco/ca, cardiaco/ca *adj* cardiac; * heart *compd*.

cardinal *adj* cardinal, principal.

cardo *m* thistle.

carear *vt* to bring face to face; to compare; ~**se** *vr* to come face to face.

carecer *vi*: ~ **de** to want, to lack.

carencia *f* lack.

careo *m* confrontation.

carero/ra *adj* pricey.

carestía *f* scarcity, want; famine.

careta *f* pasteboard mask.

carga *f* load; freight; cargo; *(mil)* charge; duty, obligation; tax.

cargadero *m* loading place.

cargado/da *adj* loaded; (*elec*) live.

cargador *m* loader; carrier; longshoreman.

cargamento *m* cargo.

cargar *vt* to load, to burden; to charge; * *vi* to charge; to load (up); to lean.

cargo *m* burden, loading; employment, post; office; charge, care; obligation; accusation.

carguero *m* freighter.

cariarse *vr* to decay.

caricatura *f* caricature.

caricia *f* caress.

caridad *f* charity.

caries *f* (*med*) tooth decay, caries.

carilargo/ga *adj* long-faced.

carilla *f* side (of paper); beekeeper's mask.

cariño *m* fondness, tenderness; love.

cariñoso/sa *adj* affectionate; loving.

caritativo/va *adj* charitable.

cariz *m* look.

carmelita *adj*, *m/f* Carmelite.

carmesí *adj*, *m* crimson.

carmín *m* carmine; rouge; lipstick.

carnada *f* bait, lure.

carnal *adj* carnal, of the flesh; **primo ~** first cousin.

carnaval *m* carnival.

carn *f* flesh; meat; pulp (of fruit).

carné, carnet *m* driving licence; **~ de identidad** identity card.

carnero *m* sheep; mutton.

carnicería *f* butcher's shop; carnage, slaughter.

carnicero/ra *m/f* butcher. * *adj* carnivorous.

carnívoro/ra *adj* carnivorous.

carnoso/sa, carnudo *adj* beefy, fat; fleshy.

caro/ra *adj* dear; affectionate; dear, expensive; * *adv* dearly.

carótida *f* carotid artery.

carpa *f* carp (fish); tent.

carpeta *f* table cover; folder, file, portfolio.

carpintería *f* carpentry; carpenter's shop.

carpintero *m* carpenter.

carraca *f* carrack (ship); rattle.

carrasca *f*, **carrasco** *m* evergreen oak.

carraspera *f* hoarseness.

carrera *f* career; course; race; run, running; route; journey; **a ~ abierta** at full speed.

carreta *f* long narrow cart.

carrete *m* reel, spool, bobbin.

carretera *f* road.

carretero *m* carter, cartwright.

carretilla *f* carter; truck; trolley; gocart; squib, cracker; wheel barrow.

carretón *m* small cart.

carril *m* lane (of highway); furrow; **~ bus** bus lane.

carrillo *m* cheek; pulley.

carro *m* cart; car.

carrocería *f* bodywork, coachwork.

carromato *m* covered wagon, (Gypsy) caravan.

carroña *f* carrion.

carroza *f* state coach; (*mar*) awning.

carruaje *m* carriage; vehicle.

carrusel *m* merry-go-round.

carta *f* letter; map; document; playing card; menu; **~ blanca** carte blanche; **~ bomba** letter-bomb; **~ credencial** *o* **de creencia** credentials *pl*; **~ certificada** registered letter.

cartabón *m* square (tool).

cartapacio *m* notebook; folder.

cártel *m* cartel.

cartel *m* placard; poster; wall chart; cartel.

cartera f satchel; handbag; briefcase; postwoman.

carterista m/f pickpocket.

cartero m postman.

cartilaginoso/sa adj cartilaginous.

cartílago m cartilage.

cartilla f first reading book, primer.

cartón m cardboard, pasteboard; cartoon.

cartuchera f (mil) cartridge belt.

cartucho m (mil) cartridge.

cartuja f Carthusian order.

cartujo m Carthusian monk.

cartulina f card, pass; thin cardboard.

casa f house; home; firm, company; ~ **de campo** country house; ~ **de moneda** mint; ~ **de huéspedes** boarding house.

casaca f coat.

casación f abrogation.

casadero/ra adj marriageable.

casado/da adj married.

casamentero/ra m/f marriage-maker, matchmaker.

casamiento m marriage, wedding.

casar vt to marry; to couple; to abrogate; to annul; ~**se** vr to marry, to get married.

cascabel m small bell; rattlesnake.

cascada f cascade, waterfall.

cascanueces m invar nutcracker.

cascar vt to crack, to break into pieces; (fam) to beat; ~**se** vr to be broken open.

cáscara f rind, peel; husk, shell; bark.

cascarón m eggshell.

casco m skull; helmet; fragment; shard; hulk (of a ship); crown (of a hat); hoof; empty bottle, returnable bottle; ~**s azules** blue berets.

cascote m rubble, fragment of material used in building.

casera f landlady.

caserío m country house; hamlet.

casero m landlord; janitor; * ~**/ra**, adj domestic; household compd; home-made.

caset(t)e m cassette; * f cassette-player.

casi adv almost, nearly; ~ **nada** next to nothing; ~ **nunca** hardly ever, almost never.

casilla f hut, cabin; box office; square (on a chess board); pigeon-hole, compartment.

casillero m (set of) pigeonholes pl; luggage locker.

casino m club, social club.

caso m case; occurrence, event; hap, casuality; occasion; (gr) case; **en ese** ~ in that case; **en todo** ~ in any case; ~ **que** in case.

casorio m unwise marriage.

caspa f dandruff; scurf.

casquete m helmet.

casquillo m bottle top; tip, cap; point.

casta f caste; race; lineage; breed; kind, quality.

castaña f chestnut; demijohn.

castañar m chestnut grove.

castañetear vi to play the castanets.

castaño m chestnut tree; ~**/ña** adj chestnut(-coloured), brown.

castañuela f castanet.

castellano m Castilian, Spanish.

castidad f chastity.

castigar vt to castigate, to punish; to afflict.

castigo m punishment; correction; penalty.

castillo m castle.

castizo/za adj pure, thoroughbred.

casto/ta adj pure, chaste.

castor m beaver.

castrar *vt* to geld, to castrate; to prune; to cut the honeycombs out of (beehives).

casual *adj* casual, accidental.

casualidad *f* chance, accident.

casucha *f* hovel; slum.

casulla *f* chasuble.

cata *f* tasting.

catacumbas *fpl* catacombs *pl*.

catador/ra *m/f* wine tester.

catadura *f* looks *pl*, face.

catalejo *m* telescope.

catalizador *m* catalyst; catalytic converter.

catálogo *m* catalogue.

catamarán *m* catamaran.

cataplasma *f* poultice.

catapulta *f* catapult.

catar *vt* to taste; to inspect, to examine; to look at; to esteem.

catarata *f* (*med*) cataract; waterfall.

catarro *m* catarrh.

catarroso/sa *adj* catarrhal.

catástrofe *f* catastrophe.

catavino *m* small cup for tasting wine; **~s** *m/f invar* wine-taster; tippler.

catecismo *m* catechism.

cátedra *f* professor's chair.

catedral *f* cathedral.

catedrático/ca *m/f* professor (of a university).

categoría *f* category; rank.

categórico/ca *adj* categorical, decisive.

catequismo *m* catechism.

caterva *f* mob.

catolicismo *m* catholicism.

católico/ca *adj*, *m/f* catholic.

catorce *adj*, *m* fourteen.

catre *m* cot.

cauce *m* riverbed; (*fig*) channel.

caucho *m* rubber; tyre.

caución *f* caution; (*jur*) security, bail.

caucionar *vt* to prevent, to guard against; (*jur*) to bail.

caudal *m* volume, flow; property, wealth; plenty.

caudaloso/sa *adj* carrying much water (of rivers); wealthy, rich.

caudillo *m* leader.

causa *f* cause; motive, reason; lawsuit; **a ~ de** considering, because of.

causal *adj* causal.

causante *m/f* originator; * *adj* causing, originating.

causar *vt* to cause; to produce; to occasion.

cáustico *m* caustic; **~/ca** *adj* caustic.

cautela *f* caution, cautiousness.

cauteloso/sa *adj* cautious, wary.

cauterizar *vt* (*med*) to cauterize; to apply a drastic remedy to.

cautivar *vt* to take prisoner in war; to captivate, to charm.

cautiverio *m* captivity.

cautividad *f* captivity.

cautivo/va *adj*, *m/f* captive.

cauto/ta *adj* cautious, wary.

cava *f* digging and earthing of vines; wine cellar; sparkling wine.

cavar *vt* to dig up, to excavate; * *vi* to dig, to delve; to think profoundly.

caverna *f* cavern, cave.

cavernoso/sa *adj* cavernous.

cavidad *f* cavity, hollow.

cavilación *f* deep thought.

cavilar *vt* to ponder, to consider carefully.

caviloso/sa *adj* obsessed; suspicious.

cayada *f*, **cayado** *m* shepherd's crook.

caza *f* hunting; shooting; chase; game; * *m* fighter-plane.

cazador/ra *m/f* hunter; *m* huntsman; ~ **furtivo** poacher.

cazamoscas *m invar* flycatcher (bird).

cazar *vt* to chase, to hunt; to catch.

cazo *m* saucepan; ladle.

cazuela *f* casserole; pan.

cazurro/rra *adj* silent, taciturn.

cebada *f* barley.

cebar *vt* to feed (animals), to fatten.

cebo *m* feed, food; bait, lure; priming.

cebolla *f* onion; bulb.

cebolleta *f* spring onion, scallion.

cebollino *m* onion seed; chive.

cebón *m* fattened pig.

cebra *f* zebra.

cecear *vt* to pronounce s the same as c; to lisp.

cecina *f* dried meat; salt beef.

cedazo *m* sieve, strainer.

ceder *vt* to hand over; to transfer, to make over; to yield, to give up; * *vi* to submit, to comply, to give in; to diminish, to grow less.

cederrón *m* CD-ROM.

cedro *m* cedar.

cédula *f* certificate; document; slip of paper; bill; ~ **de cambio** bill of exchange.

cegar *vi* to grow blind; * *vt* to blind; to block up.

cegato/ta *adj* short-sighted.

ceguera *f* blindness.

ceja *f* eyebrow; edging of clothes; (*mus*) bridge of a stringed instrument; brow of a hill.

cejar *vi* to go backward(s); to slacken, to give in.

celada *f* helmet; ambush; trick.

celador *m* watchman.

celda *f* cell.

celdilla *f* cell; cavity.

celebración *f* celebration; praise.

celebrar *vt* to celebrate; to praise; ~ **misa** to say mass.

célebre *adj* famous, renowned; witty, funny.

celebridad *f* celebrity, fame.

celeridad *f* speed, velocity.

celeste *adj* heavenly; sky-blue.

celestial *adj* heavenly; delightful.

celibato *m* celibacy.

célibe *m/f* bachelor, spinster.

celo *m* zeal; rut (in animals); Sellotape™; ~**s** *mpl* jealousy.

celofán *m* cellophane.

celosía *f* lattice (of a window).

celoso/sa *adj* zealous; jealous.

célula *f* cell.

celular *adj* cellular.

celulitis *f* cellulitis.

celuloide *m* celluloid.

cementerio *m* graveyard.

cemento *m* cement.

cena *f* dinner, supper.

cenador *m* arbour.

cenagoso/sa *adj* miry, marshy.

cenagal *m* quagmire.

cenar *vt* to have for dinner; * *vi* to have supper, to have dinner.

cencerro *m* jangle, clatter.

cenicero *m* ashtray.

ceniciento/ta *adj* ash-coloured.

ceñido/da *adj* tight-fitting; sparing, frugal.

ceñir *vt* to surround, to circle; to abbreviate, to abridge; to fit tightly.

cenit *m* zenith.

ceniza *f* ashes *pl*; **miércoles de** ~ Ash Wednesday.

ceño *m* frown.

censo *m* census; tax; ground rent; ~ **electoral** electoral roll.

censor/ra *m/f* censor; reviewer, critic.

censura f censorship; review; censure, blame.

censurar vt to review, to criticize; to censure, to blame.

centella f lightning; spark.

centellear vi to sparkle.

centena f hundred.

centenadas adv: **a ~** by hundreds.

centenar m hundred.

centenario/ia adj centenary; * m centenary.

centeno m rye.

centésimo/ma adj hundredth; * m hundredth.

centígrado m centigrade.

centímetro m centimetre.

céntimo m cent.

centinela f sentry, guard; lookout.

central adj central; * f head office, headquarters; (telephone) exchange; **~ nuclear** nuclear power station.

centralización m centralization.

centralizar vt to centralize.

céntrico adj central.

centrífugo/ga adj centrifugal.

centrista adj centrist.

centro m centre; **~ comercial** shopping centre.

centuplicar vt to increase a hundredfold.

céntuplo/pla adj centuple, hundredfold.

ceñudo/da adj frowning, grim.

cepa f stock (of a vine); origin (of a family).

cepillar vt to brush.

cepillo m brush; plane (tool).

cepo m branch, bough; trap; snare; poor box.

cera f wax; **~s** fpl honeycomb.

cerámica f pottery.

cerca f enclosure; fence; **~s** mpl objects pl in the foreground of a painting; * adv near, at hand, close by; **~ de** close, near.

cercanías fpl outskirts.

cercano/na adj near, close by; neighbouring, adjoining.

cercar vt to enclose, to circle; to fence in.

cerciorar vt to assure, to ascertain, to affirm; **~se** vr to find out.

cerco m enclosure; fence; (mil) siege.

cerdo m pig.

cereal m cereal.

cerebelo m cerebellum.

cerebro m brain.

ceremonia f ceremony.

ceremonial adj, m ceremonial.

ceremonioso/sa adj ceremonious.

cereza f cherry.

cerezo m cherry tree.

cerilla f wax taper; ear wax; match, safety match.

cerner vt to sift; * vi to bud, to blossom; to drizzle; **~se** vr to hover; to swagger.

cernido m sifting.

cero m nothing, zero.

cerquita adv close by.

cerrado/da adj closed, shut; locked; overcast, cloudy; broad (of accent).

cerradura f locking-up; lock.

cerrajería f trade of a locksmith; locksmith's shop.

cerrajero m locksmith.

cerrar vt to close, to shut; to block up; to lock; **~ una cuenta** to close an account; **~se** vr to close; to heal; to cloud over; vi to close, to shut; to lock.

cerril adj mountainous; rough, wild, untamed.

cerro *m* hill; neck (of an animal); backbone; combed flax or hemp; **en ~** bareback.

cerrojo *m* bolt (of a door).

certamen *m* competition, contest.

certero *adj* accurate; well-aimed.

certeza, certidumbre *f* certainty.

certificación *f* certificate.

certificado *m* certificate; **~/da** *adj* registered (of a letter).

certificar *vt* to certify, to affirm.

cervato *m* fawn.

cervecería *f* bar; brewery.

cervecero *m* brewer.

cerveza *m* beer.

cerviz *f* nape of the neck; cervix.

cesación *f* cessation, stoppage.

cesar *vt* to cease, to stop; to fire (*sl*); to remove from office; * *vi* to cease, to stop; to retire.

cese *m* suspension; dismissal.

cesión *f* cession; transfer.

césped *m* grass; lawn.

cesta *f* basket, pannier.

cestería *f* basket shop; basketwork.

cesto *m* (large) basket.

cetrino/na *adj* greenish-yellow; sallow; jaundiced, melancholic.

cetro *m* sceptre.

chabacano/na *adj* coarse, vulgar; shoddy.

chabola *f* shack.

cháchara *f* chitchat, chatter, idle talk.

chacolí *m* light white wine with a sharp taste.

chafar *vt* to crush; to ruin.

chal *m* shawl.

chalado/da *adj* crazy.

chale(t) *m* detached house.

chaleco *m* waistcoat.

chalupa *f* (*mar*) boat, launch.

chamarra *f* sheepskin jacket.

champán *m* champagne.

champiñón *m* mushroom.

champú *m* shampoo.

chamuscar *vt* to singe, to scorch.

chamusquina *f* scorching; (*fig*) row, quarrel.

chanchullo *m* (*fam*) fix, fiddle (*sl*).

chanciller *m* chancellor.

chancleta *f* slipper.

chanclo *m* clog; galosh.

chándal *m* tracksuit.

chanfaina *f* cheap stew.

chantaje *m* blackmail.

chanza *f* joke, jest; **~s** *fpl* fun.

chapa *f* metal plate; panel; (*auto*) numberplate.

chaparrón *m* heavy shower (of rain).

chapotear *vt* to wet with a sponge; * *vi* to paddle (in water).

chapucear *vt* to botch, to bungle.

chapucero *m* bungler; **~/ra** *adj* clumsy, crude.

chapurrar *vt* to speak (a language) badly; to mix (drinks).

chapuza *f* badly done job.

chapuzarse *vr* to duck; to dive.

chaqueta *f* jacket.

charca *f* pool.

charco *m* pool, puddle.

charcutería *f* shop selling pork meat products.

charla *f* chat, talk.

charlar *vi* to chat.

charlatán/ana *m/f* chatterbox.

charlatanería *f* talkativeness.

charol *m* varnish; patent leather.

charrada *f* coarse thing; bad breeding; bad taste.

charretera *f* shoulder pad.

charro *m* coarse individual; **~/rra** *adj* coarse; gaudy.

charter *m* charter flight.

chasco *m* disappointment; joke, jest.

chasis *m invar* (*auto*) chassis.

chasquear *vt* to crack (a whip); to disappoint.

chasquido *m* crack; click.

chatarra *f* scrap.

chato/ta *adj* flat, flattish; snub-nosed.

chaval/la *m/f* lad/lass.

cheque *m* cheque.

chequeo *m* check-up; service.

chequera *f* chequebook.

chicano/na *adj* Chicano.

chicha *f* corn liquor; meat.

chicharra *f* harvest fly.

chicharrón *m* (pork) crackling.

chichón *m* lump, bump.

chichonera *f* helmet.

chicle *m* chewing gum.

chico/ca *adj* little, small; * *m/f* boy/girl.

chifla *f* whistle; hiss.

chiflado/da *adj* crazy.

chiflar *vt* to boo.

chile *m* chilli pepper.

chillar *vi* to scream, to shriek; to howl; to creak.

chillido *m* squeak; shriek, howl.

chillón/ona *adj* loud, noisy; gaudy; * *m/f* whiner, moaner.

chimenea *f* chimney; fireplace.

china *f* pebble; porcelain, chinaware; China silk.

chinche *f* bug; drawing pin, thumbtack; * *m* nuisance.

chincheta *f* drawing pin.

chinela *f* slipper.

chino/na *adj*, *m/f* Chinese; * *m* Chinese language.

chiquero *m* pig sty.

chiripa *f* fluke.

chirla *f* mussel.

chirriar *vi* to hiss; to creak; to chirp.

chirrido *m* chirping (of birds); squeaking.

chis *excl* sh!

chisgarabís *m* (*fam*) meddler.

chisme *m* tale; thingummyjig.

chismear *vi* to tell tales.

chismoso/sa *adj* gossiping; * *m/f* gossip.

chispa *f* spark; sparkle; wit; drop (of rain); drunkenness.

chispazo *m* spark.

chispeante *adj* sparkling.

chispear *vi* to sparkle; to drizzle.

chisporrotear *vi* to crackle; to sparkle; to hiss (of liquids).

chistar *vi* to speak.

chiste *m* funny story, joke.

chistoso/sa *adj* witty; amusing, funny.

chivato *m* kid; child.

chivo/va *m/f* billy/nanny goat.

chocante *adj* startling; odd.

chocar *vi* to strike, to knock; to crash; * *vt* to shock.

chochear *vi* to dodder, to be senile; to dote.

chocho *adj* doddering; doting.

chocolate *m* chocolate.

chocolatera *f* chocolate pot.

chófer *m* driver.

chollo *m* bargain.

chopo *m* (*bot*) black poplar.

choque *m* shock; crash, collision; clash, conflict.

chorizo *m* pork sausage.

chorlito *m* plover.

chorrear *vi* to spout, to gush; to drip.

chorrera *f* channel; frill.

chorro *m* gush; jet; stream; **a ~s** abundantly.

choto *m* kid; calf.

choza *f* hut, shack.

chubasco *m* squall.

chuchería *f* trinket.

chucho *m* mongrel.

chufleta f joke; taunt, jeer.

chulada f funny speech or action.

chulear vi to brag.

chuleta f chop.

chulo m rascal; pimp.

chunga f fun, joke; **estar de ~** to be in good humour.

chunguearse vr to be in good humour.

chupado/da adj skinny; easy.

chupar vt to suck; to absorb.

chupete m dummy.

chupetear vi to suck gently.

chupón/ona m/f swindler, sponger (sl).

churro m fritter.

churruscarse vr to scorch.

churrusco m burnt toast.

chusco/ca adj pleasant; funny.

chusma f rabble, mob.

chuzo m little spear or spike; **llover a ~s** to pour heavily.

cianuro m cyanide.

ciática f sciatica.

ciático/ca adj sciatic.

cibercafé m Internet café.

ciberespacio m cyberspace.

cicatear vi to be mean.

cicatriz f scar.

cicatrizar vt to heal.

ciclismo m cycling.

ciclista m/f cyclist.

ciclo m cycle.

ciclón m cyclone.

cicloturismo m bicycle touriism.

cicuta f (bot) hemlock.

ciegamente adv blindly.

ciego/ga adj blind.

cielo m sky; heaven; atmosphere; climate.

cien adj, m a hundred.

ciénaga f swamp.

ciencia f science.

cieno m mud; mire.

cienpiés m invar centipede.

científico/ca adj scientific.

ciento adj, m a hundred.

cierne m: **en ~** in blossom; **estar en ~** to be in its infancy.

cierto/ta adj certain, sure; right, correct; **por ~** certainly.

cierva f hind.

ciervo m deer, hart, stag; **~ volante** stag beetle.

cierzo m cold northerly wind.

cifra f number, numeral; quantity; cipher; abbreviation.

cifrar vt to write in code; to abridge.

cigala f langoustine.

cigarra f cicada.

cigarrera m cigar case.

cigarrillo m cigarette.

cigarro m cigar; cigarette.

cigüeña f stork; crank (of a bell).

cilicio m hair shirt; spiked belt.

cilíndrico/ca adj cylindrical.

cilindro m cylinder.

cima f summit; peak; top.

címbalo m cymbal.

cimbor(r)io m cupola, dome.

cimbr(e)ar vt to shake, to swish, to swing; **~ a uno** to give one a clout (with a stick); **~se** vr to sway.

cimentado m refinement of gold.

cimentar vt to lay the foundation of (a building); to found; to refine (metals); to strengthen, to cement.

cimiento m foundation, groundwork; basis, origin.

cinc m zinc.

cincel m chisel.

cincelar vt to chisel, to engrave.

cincha f girth.

cinchar vt to girth.

cinco adj, m five.

cincuenta adj, m fifty.

cine *m* cinema.

cineasta *m/f* film maker.

cinematográfico/ca *adj* cinematographic.

cínico/ca *adj* cynical.

cinismo *m* cynicism.

cinta *f* band, ribbon; reel.

cinto *m* belt.

cintura *f* waist.

cinturón *m* belt, girdle; (*fig*) zone; ~ **de seguridad** seatbelt.

ciprés *m* cypress tree.

circo *m* circus.

circuito *m* circuit; circumference.

circulación *f* circulation; traffic.

circular *adj* circular; circulatory; * *vt* to circulate; * *vi* (*auto*) to drive.

círculo *m* circle; (*fig*) scope, compass.

circuncidar *vt* to circumcize.

circuncisión *f* circumcision.

circundar *vt* to surround, to encircle.

circunferencia *f* circumference.

circunflejo/ja *adj*: **acento ~** *m* circumflex.

circunscribir *vt* to circumscribe.

circunscripción *f* division; electoral district.

circunspección *f* circumspection.

circunspecto/ta *adj* circumspect, cautious.

circunstancia *f* circumstance.

circunstante *m/f* bystander.

circunvalación *f*: **carretera de ~** bypass.

cirio *m* wax candle.

ciruela *f* plum; ~ **pasa** prune.

ciruelo *m* plum tree.

cirugía *f* surgery.

cirujano *m* surgeon.

cisco *m* coaldust.

cisma *m* schism; discord.

cismático/ca *adj* schismatic.

cisne *m* swan.

cisterna *f* cistern.

cisura *f* incision.

cita *f* quotation; appointment, meeting.

citación *f* quotation; (*jur*) summons.

citar *vt* to make an appointment with; to quote; (*jur*) to summon.

cítrico/ca *adj* citric; ~**s** *mpl* citric fruits *pl*.

ciudad *f* city; town.

ciudadanía *f* citizenship.

ciudadano/na *m/f* citizen; * *adj* civic.

ciudadela *f* citadel.

cívico/ca *adj* civic.

civil *adj* civil; polite, courteous; * *m* Civil Guard; civilian.

civilización *f* civilization.

civilizar *vt* to civilize.

civismo *m* public spirit; patriotism.

cizaña *f* discord.

clamar *vt* to clamour for.

clamor *m* clamour, outcry; peal of bells.

clamoroso/sa *adj* noisy, loud.

clandestino/na *adj* clandestine, secret, concealed.

clara *f* egg-white.

claraboya *f* skylight.

clarear *vi* to dawn; ~**se** *vr* to be transparent.

clarete *adj*, *m* claret.

claridad *f* brightness, clearness.

clarificar *vt* to brighten; to clarify.

clarín *m* bugle; bugler.

clarinete *m* clarinet; * *m/f* clarinetist.

claro/ra *adj* clear, bright; evident, manifest; * *m* opening; clearing (in a wood); skylight.

claroscuro *m* chiaroscuro (in painting).

clase *f* class; rank; order.

clásico/ca *adj* classical.

clasificación *f* classification.

clasificar *vt* to classify.

claudicar *vi* to limp; to act deceitfully; to back down.

claustro *m* cloister; faculty (of a university); womb, uterus.

cláusula *f* clause.

clausura *f* closure, closing.

clavado/da *adj* tight-fitting; nailed.

clavar *vt* to nail; to fasten in, to force in; to drive in; (*fam*) to cheat, to deceive; ~**se** *vr* to penetrate.

clave *f* key; (*mus*) clef; * *m* harpsichord.

clavel *m* (*bot*) carnation.

clavetear *vt* to decorate with studs.

clavicordio *m* clavichord.

clavícula *f* clavicle, collar bone.

clavija *f* pin, peg.

clavo *m* nail; corn (on the feet); clove.

claxon *m* horn.

clemencia *f* clemency.

clemente *adj* clement, merciful.

cleptómano/na *m/f* kleptomaniac.

clerecía *f* clergy.

clerical *adj* clerical.

clérigo *m* priest; clergyman.

clero *m* clergy.

clic, click *m* click.

cliché *m* cliché; negative (of a photo).

cliente *m/f* client.

clientela *f* clientele.

clima *m* climate.

climatizado/da *adj* air-conditioned.

clínica *f* clinic; private hospital.

clínico/ca *adj* clinical.

clip *m* paper clip.

cloaca *f* sewer.

cloquear *vi* to cluck.

clon *m* clone.

clonación *f* cloning.

clonar *vt* to clone.

clónico/ca *adj* cloned.

club *m* club.

clueca *f* broody hen.

coacción *f* coercion, compulsion.

coactivo/va *adj* coercive.

coadjutor/ra *m/f* coadjutor, assistant.

coagular *vt*, ~**se** *vr* to coagulate; to curdle.

coágulo *m*: ~ **sanguíneo** blood clot.

coalición *f* coalition.

coartada *f* (*jur*) alibi.

coartar *vt* to limit, to restrict, to restrain.

cobalto *m* cobalt.

cobarde *adj* cowardly, timid.

cobardía *f* cowardice.

cobaya *f* guinea pig.

cobertizo *m* small shed; shelter.

cobertura *f* cover; coverage; bedspread.

cobijar *vt* to cover; to shelter.

cobra *f* cobra.

cobrador/ra *m/f* conductor/conductress; collector.

cobrar *vt* to recover; ~**se** *vr* (*med*) to come to.

cobre *m* copper; kitchen utensils *pl*; (*mus*) brass.

cobrizo/za *adj* coppery.

cobro *m* encashment; payment; recovery.

cocaína *f* cocaine.

cocción *f* cooking.

cocear *vt* to kick; (*fig*) to resist.

cocer *vt* to boil; to bake (bricks); * *vi* to boil; to ferment; ~**se** *vr* to suffer intense pain.

cochambre *m* dirty, stinking object.

cochambroso/sa *adj* nasty; filthy; stinking.

coche *m* car; coach, carriage; pram, baby carriage; ~ **bomba** car bomb; (*ferro*) ~ **cama** sleeping car; ~ **restaurante** restaurant car.

cochera *f* garage, lockup, carport, depot.

cochero *m* coachman.

cochinilla *f* woodlouse; cochineal.

cochino/na *adj* dirty, filthy; nasty; * *m* pig.

cochiquera *f* pigsty.

cocido/da *adj* boiled; (*fig*) skilled, experienced; * *m* stew.

cocina *f* kitchen; cooker; cookery.

cocinero/ra *m/f* cook.

coco *m* coconut; bogeyman.

cocodrilo *m* crocodile.

codazo *m* blow given with the elbow.

codear *vt, vi* to elbow; ~**se** *vr*: ~**se con** to rub shoulders with.

códice *m* codex, old manuscript.

codicia *m* covetousness, greediness.

codiciable *adj* covetable.

codiciar *vt* to covet, to desire.

codicilo *m* (*jur*) codicil.

codicioso/sa *adj* greedy, covetous.

código *m* law; set of rules; code; ~ **postal** post code.

codillo *m* knee of a four-legged animal; angle; (*tec*) elbow (joint).

codo *m* elbow.

codorniz *f* quail.

coerción *f* coercion; restraint.

coercitivo/va *adj* coercive.

coetáneo/nea *adj* contemporary.

coexistencia *f* coexistence.

coexistente *adj* coexistent.

coexistir *vi* to coexist.

cofia *f* (nurse's) cap.

cofrade *m* member (of a brotherhood).

cofradía *f* brotherhood, fraternity.

cofre *m* trunk.

cogedor *m* shovel; dustpan.

coger *vt* to catch, to take hold of; to occupy, to take up; ~**se** *vr* to catch.

cognitivo/va *adj* cognitive.

cogollo *m* heart of a lettuce or cabbage; shoot of a plant.

cogote *m* back of the neck.

cohabitar *vi* to cohabit, to live together.

cohechar *vt* to bribe, to suborn.

cohecho *m* bribery.

coherencia *f* coherence.

coherente *adj* coherent.

cohete *m* rocket.

cohibido/da *adj* shy.

cohibir *vt* to prohibit; to restrain.

cohorte *m* cohort.

coincidencia *f* coincidence.

coincidente *adj* coincidental.

coincidir *vi* to coincide.

coito *m* intercourse, coitus.

cojear *vi* to limp, to hobble; (*fig*) to go astray.

cojera *f* lameness; limp.

cojín *m* cushion.

cojo/ja *adj* lame, crippled.

col *f* cabbage.

cola[1] *f* tail; queue; last place.

cola[2] *f* glue.

colaborador/ra *m/f* collaborator; contributor.

colaborar *vi* to collaborate.

colación *f* collation, comparison; light meal.

colada *f* wash, washing; (*quím*) bleach; sheep run.

coladero *m* colander, strainer.

colador *m* sieve.

colapso *m* collapse.

colar *vt* to strain, to filter; * *vi* to ooze; ~**se en** to get into without paying.

colateral *adj* collateral.

colcha f bedspread, counterpane.

colchón m mattress.

colchoneta f mattress.

coleada f wagging (of an animal's tail).

colear vi to wag the tail.

colección f collection.

coleccionar vt to collect.

coleccionista m/f collector.

colecta f collection (for charity).

colectar vt to collect (taxes).

colectivo/va adj collective.

colector m collector; sewer.

colega m/f colleague.

colegial m schoolboy.

colegiala f schoolgirl.

colegiata f collegiate church.

colegio m college; school.

colegir vt to collect; to deduce, to infer.

cólera f bile; anger; fury, rage.

coléricamente adv in a rage.

colérico/ca adj angry; furious; bad-tempered.

colesterol m cholesterol.

coleta f pigtail.

colgadero m hook, hanger, peg.

colgadura f tapestry; hangings pl, drapery.

colgajo m tatter, rag.

colgante adj hanging; * m pendant.

colgar vt to hang; to suspend; to decorate with tapestry; * vi to be suspended.

colibrí m hummingbird.

cólico m colic.

coliflor m cauliflower.

colilla f end or butt of a cigarette.

colina f hill.

colindante adj neighbouring.

colindar vi to adjoin.

coliseo m coliseum; opera house; theatre.

colisión f collision; friction.

collar m necklace; (dog) collar.

colmar vt to heap up; * vi to fulfill, to realize.

colmena f hive, beehive.

colmenar m beehive stand; bee-house.

colmillo m eyetooth; tusk.

colmo m height; summit; extreme; **a ~** plentifully.

colocación f employment; placing; situation.

colocar vt to arrange; to place; to provide with a job; **~se** vr to get a job.

colon m (med) colon.

colonia f colony; silk ribbon.

colonial adj colonial.

colonización f colonization.

colonizador/a m/f settler; * adj colonizing.

colonizar vt to colonize.

colono m colonist; farmer.

coloquio m conversation; conference.

color m colour, hue; dye; rouge; suit (of cards).

coloración f colouring, coloration.

colorado/da adj ruddy; red.

colorar vt to colour; to dye.

colorear vt to colour; to excuse.

colorete m rouge.

colorido m colouring.

colosal adj colossal.

columna f column.

columnata f colonnade.

columpiar vt, **~se** vr to swing to and fro.

columpio m swing, seesaw.

colusión f collusion.

colza f (bot) rape; rape seed.

coma f (gr) comma; * m (med) coma.

comadre f midwife; godmother; neighbour.

comadreja f weasel.

comadrón/ona m/f midwife.

comandancia f command.

comandante m commander.

comandar vt to command.

comarca f territory, district.

comba f curve; warp (of timber); skipping rope.

combar vt to bend; ~**se** vr to warp.

combate m combat, conflict; fighting.

combatiente m combatant.

combatir vt to combat, to fight; to attack; * vi to fight.

combinación f combination; (quím) compound; (cocktail; scheme.

combinar vi to combine.

combustible adj combustible; * m fuel.

combustión f combustion.

comedero m dining room; trough.

comedia f comedy; play, drama.

comediante m/f player, actor/ actress.

comedido/da adj moderate, restrained.

comedirse vr to restrain oneself.

comedor/ra m/f glutton; * m dining room.

comendatorio/ria adj introductory (of letters).

comensal m/f fellow diner.

comentar vt to comment on, to expound.

comentario m comment, remark; commentary.

comentarista m/f commentator.

comenzar vi to commence, to begin.

comer vt to eat; to take (a piece at chess); * vi to have lunch.

comercial adj commercial.

comerciante m/f trader, merchant, dealer.

comerciar vi to trade, to do business.

comercio m trade, commerce; business; ~ **electrónico** e-commerce; ~ **justo** fair trade.

comestible adj eatable; * mpl ~**s** food, foodstuffs pl.

cometa m comet; * f kite.

cometer vt to commit, to charge; to entrust.

cometido m task.

comezón f itch; itching.

comicios mpl elections pl.

cómico/ca adj comic, comical.

comida f food; eating; meal; lunch; ~ **basura** junk food.

comienzo m beginning.

comillas fpl quotation marks pl.

comilón/ona m/f great eater, glutton; * f blow-out.

comino m cumin (plant or seed).

comisaría f police station; commissariat.

comisario/-a m/f commissioner.

comisión f commission; committee.

comisionado/da m/f; commissioner; committee member.

comisionar vt to commission.

comité m committee.

comitiva f suite, retinue, followers pl.

como adv as; like; such as.

cómo adv how?; why? * excl what?

cómoda f chest of drawers.

comodidad f comfort; convenience; ~**es** fpl wealth, comforts pl.

comodín m joker.

cómodo/da adj convenient; comfortable.

compact disc m compact disc.

compacto/ta adj compact; close, dense.

compadecer *vt* to pity; **~se** *vr* to agree with each other.

compadre *m* godfather; friend.

compaginar *vt* to arrange, to put in order; **~se** *vr* to tally.

compañero/ra *m/f* companion, friend; comrade; partner.

compañia *f* company.

comparación *f* comparison.

comparar *vt* to compare.

comparativo/va *adj* comparative.

comparecer *vi* to appear in court.

comparsa *m/f* extra (in the theatre).

compartimento *m* compartment.

compartir *vt* to divide into equal parts.

compás *m* compass; pair of compasses; (*mus*) measure, beat.

compasión *f* compassion, commiseration.

compasivo/va *adj* compassionate.

compatibilidad *f* compatibility.

compatible *adj*: **~ con** compatible with, consistent with.

compatriota *m/f* countryman; countrywoman; fellow citizen.

compeler *vt* to compel, to constrain.

compendiar *vt* to abridge.

compendio *m* abridgment; summary.

compensación *f* compensation; recompense.

compensar *vt* to compensate; to recompense.

competencia *f* competition, rivalry; competence.

competente *adj* competent; adequate.

competer *vi* to be one's responsibility.

competición *f* competition.

competidor/ra *m/f* competitor, contestant; rival.

competir *vi* to vie; **~ con** to compete with, to rival.

compilación *f* compilation.

compilador *m* compiler.

compilar *vt* to compile.

compinche *m* pal, mate (*sl*).

complacencia *f* pleasure; indulgence.

complacer *vt* to please; **~se** *vr* to be pleased with.

complaciente *adj* pleasing.

complejo *m* complex; **~/ja** *adj* complex.

complementario/ria *adj* complementary.

complemento *m* complement.

completar *vt* to complete.

completo/ta *adj* complete; perfect.

complexión *f* constitution, temperament; build.

complicado/da *adj* complicated.

complicar *vt* to complicate.

cómplice *m/f* accomplice.

complicidad *f* complicity.

complot *m* plot.

componer *vt* to compose; to constitute; to mend, to repair; strengthen, to restore; to adorn; to adjust; to reconcile; to compose, to calm; **~se** *vr*: **~se de** to consist of.

comportamiento *m* behaviour.

comportarse *vr* to behave.

composición *f* composition; composure, agreement; settlement.

compositor/ra *m/f* composer; compositor.

compostura *f* composition, composure; mending, repairing; discretion; modesty, demureness.

compota *f* stewed fruit.

compra *f* purchase; **~ a plazos** hire purchase.

comprador/ra *m/f* buyer; customer, shopper.

comprar *vt* to buy, to purchase.

comprender *vt* to include, to contain; to comprehend, to understand.

comprensible *adj* comprehensible.

comprensión *f* comprehension, understanding.

comprensivo/va *adj* comprehensive.

compresa *f* sanitary towel.

compresión *f* compression.

comprimido *m* pill.

comprimir *vt* to compress; to repress, to restrain.

comprobante *vt* receipt; voucher.

comprobar *vt* to verify, to confirm; to prove.

comprometer *vt* to compromise; to embarrass; to implicate; to put in danger; **~se** *vr* to compromise oneself.

compromiso *m* compromise.

compuerta *f* hatch; sluice.

compuesto *m* compound; **~/ta** *adj* composed; made up of.

compulsar *vt* to collate, to compare; to make an authentic copy.

compulsivo/va *adj* compulsive.

compunción *f* compunction, regret.

compungirse *vr* to feel remorseful.

computador *m*, **computadora** *f* computer.

computar *vt* to calculate; to compute.

cómputo *m* computation; calculation.

comulgar *vt* to administer communion to; * *vi* to receive communion.

común *adj* common, usual, general; * *m* community; public; **en ~** in common.

comunal *adj* communal.

comunicación *f* communication; report.

comunicado *m* announcement.

comunicar *vt* to communicate; **~se** *vr* to communicate (with each other).

comunicativo/va *adj* communicative.

comunidad *f* community; **Comunidad Europea** European Community.

comunión *f* communion.

comunismo *m* communism.

comunista *adj*, *m/f* communist.

comunitario/ria *adj* of the European Union.

con *prep* with; by; **~ que** so then, providing that.

coñac *m* brandy, cognac.

conato *m* endeavour; effort; attempt.

concavidad *f* concavity.

cóncavo/va *adj* concave.

concebir *vt* to conceive; * *vi* to become pregnant.

conceder *vt* to give; to grant; to concede, to allow.

concejal/la *m/f* member of a council.

concejo *m* council.

concentración *f* concentration.

concentrar *vt*, **~se** *vr* to concentrate.

concéntrico/ca *adj* concentric.

concepción *f* conception; idea.

concepto *m* conceit, thought; judgement, opinion.

concerniente *adj*: **~ a** concerning, relating to.

concernir *v imp* to regard, to concern.

concertar *vt* to coordinate; to settle; to adjust; to agree; to arrange, to fix up; * *vi* (*mus*) to harmonize, to be in tune.

concesión *f* concession.

concesionario *m* agent.

concha f shell; tortoise-shell.
conchabar vt to mix, to blend; **~se**
  vr to plot, to conspire.
conciencia f conscience.
concienciar vt to make aware; **~se**
  vr to become aware.
concierto m concert; agreement;
  concerto; **de ~** in agreement, in
  concert.
conciliación f conciliation, reconciliation.
conciliar vt to reconcile; * adj council.
conciliatorio/ra adj conciliatory.
concilio m council.
concisión f conciseness.
conciso/sa adj concise, brief.
conciudadanía f joint-citizenship.
conciudadano/na m/f fellow citizen.
cónclave m conclave.
concluir vt to conclude, to end, to
  complete; to infer, to deduce; **~se**
  vr to conclude.
conclusión f conclusion.
concluyente adj conclusive.
concordancia f concordance, concord; harmony.
concordar vt to reconcile, to make
  agree; * vi to agree, to correspond.
concordato m concordat.
concordia f conformity, agreement.
concretar vt to make concrete; to
  specify.
concreto/ta adj concrete.
concubina f concubine.
concubinato m concubinage.
concupiscencia f lust.
concurrencia f concurrence; coincidence;   competition;   crowd,
  gathering.
concurrido/da adj busy.
concurrir vi to meet; to contribute;
  to coincide; to compete.
concursante m/f competitor.

concurso m crowd; competition;
  help, cooperation.
concusión f concussion.
condado m county.
conde m earl, count.
condecoración f medal.
condecorar vt to adorn; (mil) to decorate.
condena f condemnation.
condenable adj culpable.
condenar vt to condemn; to find
  guilty; **~se** vr to blame oneself; to
  confess (one's guilt).
condenatorio/ria adj condemnatory.
condensación f condensation.
condensar vt to condense.
condesa f countess.
condescendencia   f   helpfulness,
  willingness; acquiescence; compliance.
condescender vi to acquiesce, to
  comply.
condición f condition, state; quality;
  status; rank; stipulation.
condicionado/da adj conditioned.
condicional adj conditional.
condimentar vt to flavour, to season.
condimento m condiment, seasoning.
condiscípulo/la m/f fellow pupil; fellow student.
condolerse vr to sympathize.
condón m condom.
condonar vt to condone; to forgive.
conducción f conveyance; management; (auto) driving.
conducente adj: **~ a** leading to.
conducir vt to convey, to conduct; to
  drive; to manage; * vi to drive; **~**
  (a) to lead (to); **~se** vr to conduct
  oneself.
conducta f conduct, behaviour;
  management.

conducto *m* conduit, pipe; drain; (*fig*) channel.

conductor/ra *m/f* conductor, guide; (*ferro*) guard; driver.

conectado/da *adj* on-line.

conectar *vt* to connect.

conejera *f* warren, burrow.

conejo *m* rabbit.

conexión *f* connection; plug; relationship.

conexo/xa *adj* connected, related.

confabularse *vr* to conspire.

confección *f* preparation; clothing industry.

confeccionar *vt* to make up.

confederación *f* confederacy.

confederado/da *adj* confederate.

confederarse *vr* to confederate.

conferencia *f* conference; telephone call.

conferenciar *vi* to confer; to be in conference.

conferir *vt* to award; to compare.

confesar *vt* to confess; to admit.

confesión *f* confession.

confesionario *m* confessional.

confeso/sa *adj* (*jur*) self-confessed.

confesonario *m* confessional.

confesor *m* confessor.

confeti *m* confetti.

confiado/da *adj* trusting; confident; arrogant.

confianza *f* trust; confidence; conceit; familiarity; **en ~** confidential.

confiar *vt* to confide, to entrust; * *vi* to trust.

confidencia *f* confidence.

confidencial *adj* confidential.

confidente *m/f* confidante; informer.

configurar *vt* to shape, to form.

confín *m* limit, boundary.

confinar *vt* to confine; * *vi*: **~ con** to border upon.

confirmación *f* confirmation.

confirmar *vt* to confirm; to corroborate.

confiscación *f* confiscation.

confiscar *vt* to confiscate.

confite *m* candy.

confitería *f* sweet shop.

confitero/ra *m/f* confectioner.

confitura *f* preserve; jam.

conflagración *f* conflagration.

conflictivo/va *adj* controversial.

conflicto *m* conflict.

confluencia *f* confluence.

confluir *vi* to join (applied to rivers); to gather (applied to people).

conformar *vt* to shape; to adjust, to adapt; * *vi* to agree; **~se** *vr* to conform; to resign oneself.

conforme *adj* alike, similar; agreed; * *prep* according to.

conformidad *f* similarity; agreement; resignation.

conformista *m/f* conformist.

confortable *adj* comfortable.

confortar *vt* to comfort; to strengthen; to console.

confortativo/va *adj* comforting.

confraternidad *f* fraternity.

confrontación *f* confrontation.

confrontar *vt* to confront.

confundir *vt* to confound, to jumble; to confuse; **~se** *vr* to make a mistake.

confusamente *adv* confusedly.

confusión *f* confusion.

confuso/sa *adj* confused.

congelación *f* freezing.

congelado/da *adj* frozen; * *mpl*: **~s** frozen food.

congelador *m* freezer.

congelar *vt* to freeze; **~se** *vr* to congeal.

congeniar *vi* to get on well.

congestión f congestion.

congestionar vt to congest.

congoja f anguish, distress, grief.

congraciarse vr to ingratiate oneself.

congratulación f congratulation.

congratular vt to congratulate.

congregación f congregation, assembly.

congregar(se) vt (vr) to assemble, to meet, to collect.

congresista m/f delegate.

congreso m congress.

cónico/ca adj conical.

conjetura f conjecture, guess.

conjeturar vt to conjecture, to guess.

conjugación f (gr) conjugation.

conjugar vt (gr) to conjugate; to combine.

conjunción f conjunction.

conjuntamente adv together.

conjunto/ta adj united, joint; * m whole; (mus) ensemble, band; team.

conjuración f conspiracy, plot.

conjurado/da m/f conspirator.

conjurar vt to exorcise; * vi to conspire, to plot.

conjuro m incantation, exorcism.

conmemoración f commemoration.

conmemorar vt to commemorate.

conmigo pn with me.

conminación f threat.

conminar vt to threaten.

conminatorio/ria adj threatening.

conmiseración f commiseration, pity, sympathy.

conmoción f shock; upheaval; commotion; (med) concussion.

conmovedor/ra adj touching.

conmover vt to move; to disturb.

conmutación f commutation, exchange.

conmutador m switch.

conmutar vt (jur) to commute; to exchange.

connotar vt to imply.

coño excl (fam) hell!, damn! (sl).

cono m cone.

conocedor/ra m/f connoisseur.

conocer vt to know, to understand; ~se vr to know one another.

conocido/da m/f acquaintance.

conocimiento m knowledge, understanding; (med) consciousness; acquaintance; (mar) bill of lading.

conque m condition.

conquista f conquest.

conquistador m conqueror; * adj ~/ra conquering.

conquistar vt to conquer.

consabido/da adj well known; above mentioned.

consagración f consecration.

consagrar vt to consecrate.

consanguíneo/nea adj related by blood.

consanguinidad f blood relationship.

consecución f acquisition; attainment.

consecuencia f consequence; conclusion; consistency; **por** ~ therefore.

consecuente adj consistent.

consecutivo/va adj consecutive.

conseguir vt to attain; to get, to obtain.

consejero/ra m/f adviser; councillor.

consejo m advice; council.

consenso m consensus.

consentido/da adj spoiled (of children).

consentimiento m consent.

consentir vt to consent to; to allow; to admit; to spoil (a child).

conserje *m/f* doorman, porter; caretaker; janitor.

conservación *f* conservation.

conservante *m* preservative.

conservar *vt* to conserve; to keep; to preserve (fruit).

conservas *fpl* canned food.

conservatorio *m* (*mus*) conservatoire.

considerable *adj* considerable.

consideración *f* consideration; respect.

consideradamente *adv* considerately.

considerado/da *adj* respected; considerate.

considerar *vt* to consider.

consigna *f* (*mil*) watchword; order, instruction; (*ferro*) left-luggage office.

consignación *f* consignment.

consignar *vt* to consign, to dispatch; to assign; to record, to register.

consignatario/ria *m/f* consignee.

consigo *pn* (*m*) with him; (*f*) with her; (*vd*) with you; (*reflexivo*) with oneself.

consiguiente *adj* consequent.

consistencia *f* consistence, consistency.

consistente *adj* consistent; firm, solid.

consistir *vi*: ~ **en** to consist of; to be due to.

consistorio *m* town council; town hall.

consocio/cia *m/f* fellow member; partner.

consola *f* control panel; console.

consolación *f* consolation.

consolador/ra *adj* consoling, comforting.

consolar *vt* to console, to comfort, to cheer.

consolidar *vt* to consolidate.

consomé *m* consommé.

consonancia *f* consonance.

consonante *m* rhyme; * *f* (*gr*) consonant; * *adj* consonant, harmonious.

consorcio *m* partnership.

consorte *m/f* consort, companion, partner; accomplice.

conspiración *f* conspiracy, plot.

conspirador/ra *m/f* conspirator, plotter.

conspirar *vi* to conspire, to plot.

constancia *f* constancy; steadiness.

constante *adj* constant; firm.

constar *vi* to be evident, to be certain; to be composed of, to consist of.

constatar *vt* to note; to check.

constelación *f* constellation.

consternación *f* consternation.

consternar *vt* to dismay; to shock.

constipado/da *adj*: estar ~ to have a cold.

constiparse *vr* to catch a cold.

constitución *f* constitution.

constitucional *adj* constitutional.

constituir *vt* to constitute; to establish; to appoint.

constitutivo/va *adj* constitutive; essential.

constituyente *adj* constituent.

constreñimiento *m* constraint.

constreñir *vt* to restrict; to force; (*med*) to constipate; to constrict.

constricción *f* constriction, contraction.

construcción *f* construction.

constructor/ra *m/f* builder.

construir *vt* to form; to build, to construct; to construe.

consuegro/gra *m/f* father-in-law/ mother-in-law of one's son or daughter.

consuelo *m* consolation, comfort.

cónsul *m* consul.

consulado *m* consulate.

consulta *f* consultation.

consultar *vt* to consult, to ask for advice.

consultivo/va *adj* consultative.

consultor/ra *m/f* adviser, consultant.

consultorio *m* (*med*) surgery.

consumación *f* consummation, finishing.

consumado/da *adj* consummate; complete; accomplished; perfect.

consumar *vt* to consummate, to finish; to carry out.

consumición *f* consumption; drink.

consumidor/ra *m/f* consumer.

consumir *vt* to consume; to burn, to use; to waste, to exhaust; ~**se** *vr* to waste away, to be consumed.

consumismo *m* consumerism.

consumo *m* consumption.

contabilidad *f* accounting; bookkeeping.

contable *m/f* accountant.

contacto *m* contact; (*auto*) ignition.

contado/da *adj*: ~**s** scarce, few; * *m*: **pagar al** ~ to pay (in) cash.

contador *m* meter; counter in a cafe; ~/~**a** *m/f* accountant.

contaduría *f* accountancy; accountant's office.

contagiar *vt* to infect; ~**se** *vr* to get infected.

contagio *m* contagion.

contagioso/sa *adj* contagious.

contaminación *f* contamination; pollution.

contaminar *vt* to contaminate; to pollute; to corrupt.

contante *m* cash.

contar *vt* to count, to reckon; to tell; * *vi* to count; ~ **con** to rely upon.

contemplación *f* contemplation.

contemplar *vt* to look at; to contemplate, to consider; to meditate.

contemplativo/va *adj* contemplative.

contemporáneo/nea *adj* contemporary.

contemporizar *vi* to temporize.

contencioso/sa *adj* contentious; quarrelsome.

contender *vi* to contend, to compete.

contendiente *m/f* competitor.

contenedor *m* container.

contener *vt* to contain, to hold; to hold back; to repress; ~**se** *vr* to control oneself.

contenido/da *adj* moderate, restrained; * *m* contents *pl*.

contentar *vt* to content, to satisfy; to please; ~**se** *vr* to be pleased or satisfied.

contento/ta *adj* glad; pleased; content; * *m* contentment; (*jur*) release.

contestación *f* answer, reply.

contestador *m*: ~ **automático** answering machine.

contestar *vt* to answer, to reply; to prove, to corroborate.

contexto *m* context.

contienda *f* contest, dispute.

contigo *pn* with you.

contigüidad *f* contiguity.

contiguo/gua *adj* contiguous, close.

continencia *f* continence, abstinence, moderation.

continental *adj* continental.

continente *m* continent, mainland; * *adj* continent.

contingencia *f* risk; contingency.

contingente *adj* contingent, accidental; * *m* contingent.

continuación *f* continuation; sequel.

continuar *vt, vi* to continue.

continuidad f continuity.

continuo/nua adj continuous.

contonearse vr to walk affectedly.

contoneo m affected manner of walking.

contorno m environs pl; contour, outline; **en ~** round about.

contorsión f contortion.

contra prep against; contrary to; opposite.

contraataque m counter-attack.

contrabajo m (mus) double bass; bass guitar; low bass.

contrabandista m/f smuggler.

contrabando m contraband; smuggling.

contracción f contraction.

contrachapado m plywood.

contradecir vt to contradict.

contradicción f contradiction.

contradictorio/ria adj contradictory.

contraer vt to contract, to shrink; to make (a bargain); **~se** vr to shrink, to contract.

contrafuerte m buttress; foothill; heel-pad.

contragolpe m backlash.

contrahecho/cha adj deformed; hunchbacked; counterfeit, fake, false.

contralto m (mus) contralto.

contramaestre m (mar) boatswain; foreman.

contrapartida f (com) balancing entry.

contrapaso m back step.

contrapelo adv: **a ~** against the grain.

contrapesar vi to counterbalance.

contrapeso m counterpoise; counterweight.

contraponer vt to compare, to oppose.

contraposición f comparison; contrast.

contraproducente adj counterproductive.

contraprogramación f competitive scheduling.

contrapunto m (mus) counterpoint.

contrariar vt to contradict, to oppose; to vex.

contrariedad f opposition; setback; annoyance.

contrario/ria m/f opponent; * adj contrary, opposite; **por el ~** on the contrary.

contrarreloj f time trial.

contrarrestar vt to return a ball; (fig) to counteract.

contrarrevolución f counter-revolution.

contraseña f countersign; (mil) watchword.

contrasentido m contradiction.

contrastar vt to resist; to contradict; to assay (metals); to verify (measures and weights); * vi to contrast.

contraste m contrast.

contrata f contract.

contratación f signing-up, hiring.

contratar vt to contract; to hire, to engage.

contratiempo m setback; accident.

contratista m contractor.

contrato m contract, agreement.

contravención f contravention.

contraveneno m antidote.

contravenir vi to contravene, to transgress; to violate.

contraventana f shutter.

contribución f contribution; tax.

contribuir vt, vi to contribute.

contribuyente m/f contributor; taxpayer.

contrincante m competitor.

contrito/ta *adj* contrite, penitent.
controlador/ra *m/f* controller.
controlar *vt* to control; to check.
controversia *f* controversy, dispute.
contumacia *f* obstinacy, stubbornness; (*jur*) contempt of court.
contumaz *adj* obstinate, stubborn; (*jur*) guilty of contempt of court.
contundente *adj* overwhelming; blunt.
contusión *f* bruise.
convalecencia *f* convalescence.
convalecer *vi* to recover from sickness, to convalesce.
convaleciente *m/f, adj* convalescent.
convalidar *vt* to recognize.
convencer *vt* to convince.
convencimiento *m* conviction.
convención *f* convention, pact.
convencional *adj* conventional.
conveniencia *f* suitability; usefulness; agreement; ~s *fpl* property.
conveniente *adj* useful; suitable.
convenio *m* convention, agreement, treaty.
convenir *vi* to agree, to suit.
convento *m* convent, nunnery; monastery.
conventual *adj* monastic.
convergencia *f* convergence.
converger *vi* to converge.
conversación *f* conversation, talk; communication.
conversar *vi* to talk, to converse.
conversión *f* conversion, change.
converso/sa *m/f* convert.
convertir *vt*, ~se *vr* to convert.
convexo/xa *adj* convex.
convicción *f* conviction.
convicto/ta *adj* convicted (found guilty).
convidado/da *m/f* guest.
convidar *vt* to invite.

convincente *adj* convincing.
convite *m* invitation; banquet.
convivencia *f* living together.
convocar *vt* to convoke, to assemble.
convocatoria *f* summons; notice of a meeting.
convoy *m* convoy.
convulsión *f* convulsion.
convulsivo/va *adj* convulsive.
conyugal *adj* conjugal, married.
cónyuge *m/f* spouse.
cooperar *vi* to cooperate.
cooperativa *f* cooperative.
cooperativo/va *adj* cooperative.
coordinadora *f* coordinating committee.
coordinar *vt* to arrange, to coordinate.
copa *f* cup; glass; top of a tree; crown of a hat; ~s *fpl* hearts *pl* (at cards).
copete *m* quiff; pride.
copia *f* plenty, abundance; copy, duplicate.
copiador/ra *m/f* copyist; copier; **libro** ~ letter book.
copiar *vt* to copy; to imitate.
copioso/sa *adj* copious, abundant, plentiful.
copla *f* verse; (*mus*) popular song, folk song.
copo *m* small bundle; flake of snow.
copropietario/ria *m/f* joint owner.
cópula *f* copulation; conjunction; (*gr*) copula.
copulativo/va *adj* copulative.
coqueta *f* coquette, flirt.
coquetear *vi* to flirt.
coquetería *f* coquetry, flirtation.
coraje *m* courage; anger, passion.
coral *m* coral; choir; * *adj* choral.
coraza *f* cuirass; armour-plating.

corazón *m* heart; core; **de ~** willingly.

corazonada *f* feeling; inspiration; quick decision; presentiment.

corbata *f* tie.

corbeta *f* corvette.

corcel *m* steed, charger.

corchea *f* (*mus*) quaver.

corchete *m* clasp; hook and eye.

corcho *m* cork; float (for fishing); cork bark.

cordel *m* cord, rope; (*mar*) line.

cordero *m* lamb; lambskin; meek, gentle person.

cordial *adj* cordial, affectionate; * *m* cordial.

cordialidad *f* cordiality.

cordillera *f* range of mountains.

cordón *m* cord, string; lace; cordon.

cordura *f* prudence, good sense, wisdom.

corista *m/f* chorister.

cornada *f* thrust with a bull's horn.

cornadura *f* horns *pl*.

cornamenta *f* horns of an animal *pl*.

córnea *f* cornea.

cornear *vt* to gore.

córneo/ea *adj* horny, corneous.

corneta *f* bugle.

cornisa *f* cornice.

cornudo/da *adj* horned.

coro *m* choir; chorus.

corona *f* crown; coronet; top of the head; crown (of a tooth); tonsure; halo.

coronación *f* coronation.

coronar *vt* to crown; to complete, to perfect.

coronario/ria *adj* coronary.

coronel *m* (*mil*) colonel.

coronilla *f* crown of the head.

corpiño *m* bodice.

corporación *f* corporation.

corporal *adj* corporal.

corpóreo/rea *adj* corporeal.

corpulencia *f* corpulence.

corpulento/ta *adj* corpulent, bulky.

Corpus *m* Corpus Christi.

corral *m* yard; farmyard; corral; playpen.

correa *f* leather strap, thong; flexibility.

correaje *m* leather straps *pl*.

corrección *f* correction; reprehension; amendment.

correccional *m* reformatory.

correctivo/va *adj* corrective.

correcto/ta *adj* exact, correct.

corrector/ra *m/f* proof-reader.

corredizo/za *adj* sliding; easy to be untied.

corredor/ra *adj* running; * *m/f* broker, runner; *m* corridor.

corregir *vt* to correct, to amend; to reprehend; **~se** *vr* to reform.

correlación *f* correlation.

correo *m* post, mail; courier; postman; **~ electrónico** e-mail; **a vuelta de ~** by return of post; **~s** *mpl* post office.

correoso/sa *adj* flexible, leathery.

correr *vt* to run; to flow; to travel over; to pull (a drape); * *vi* to run, to rush; to flow; to blow (applied to the wind); **~se** *vr* to be ashamed; to slide, to move; to run (of colours).

correría *f* incursion.

correspondencia *f* correspondence; communication; agreement.

corresponder *vi* to correspond; to answer; to be suitable; to belong; to concern; **~se** *vr* to love one another.

correspondiente *adj* corresponding, suitable.

corresponsal *m/f* correspondent.

corretear *vi* to rush around; to hang about the streets.

corrida *f* run, dash; bullfight.

corrido/da *adj* expert; knowing; ashamed.

corriente *f* current; course, progression; (electric) current; * *adj* current; common, ordinary, general; fluent; flowing, running.

corrillo *m* circle of persons; clique.

corro *m* circle of people.

corroborar *vt* to corroborate.

corroer *vt* to corrode, to erode.

corromper *vt* to corrupt; to rot; to turn bad; to seduce; to bribe; ~**se** *vr* to rot; to become corrupted; * *vi* to stink.

corrosión *f* corrosion.

corrosivo/va *adj* corrosive.

corrupción *f* corruption; rot, decay.

corruptible *adj* corruptible.

corrupto/ta *adj* corrupted, corrupt.

corruptor/ra *m/f* corruptor, perverter.

corrusco *m* broken bread.

corsé *f* corset.

cortacésped *m* lawn mower.

cortado *m* coffee with a little milk; ~**/da** *adj* cut; sour; embarrassed.

cortadura *f* cut; cutting; incision; fissure; ~**s** *fpl* shreds *pl*, cuttings *pl*, parings *pl*.

cortafuegos *m invar* fire lane, firebreak.

cortaplumas *m invar* penknife.

cortar *vt* to cut; to cut off, to curtail; to intersect; to carve; to chop; to cut (at cards); to interrupt; ~**se** *vr* to be ashamed or embarrassed; to curdle.

cortauñas *m invar* nail clippers *pl*.

corte *m* cutting; cut; section; length (of cloth); style; * *f* (royal) court; capital (city); **C~s** *fpl* Spanish Parliament.

cortedad *f* shortness, smallness; stupidity; bashfulness.

cortejar *vt* to court.

cortejo *m* entourage; courtship; procession; lover.

cortés/esa *adj* courteous, polite.

cortesana *f* courtesan.

cortesía *f* courtesy, good manners *pl*.

corteza *f* bark; peel; crust; (*fig*) outward appearance.

cortina *f* curtain.

cortinaje *m* set of curtains.

corto/ta *adj* short; scanty, small; stupid; bashful; **a la ~a o a la larga** sooner or later.

corvo/va *adj* bent, crooked.

corzo/za *m/f* roe deer, fallow deer.

cosa *f* thing; matter, affair; **¡no hay tal ~!** nothing of the sort!.

cosaco *m* cossack.

cosecha *f* harvest; harvest time; **de su ~** of one's own invention.

cosechar *vt* to harvest, to reap.

coser *vt* to sew; to join.

cosido *m* stitching, sewing.

cosmético/a *adj*, *m* cosmetic.

cosmopolita *adj*, *m* cosmopolitan.

cosquillas *fpl* tickling; (*fig*) agitation.

costa *f* cost, price; charge, expense; coast, shore; **a toda ~** at all events.

costado *m* side; (*mil*) flank; side of a ship.

costal *m* sack, large bag.

costalada *f* heavy fall.

costar *vt* to cost; to need.

coste *m* cost, expense.

costear *vt* to pay for.

costera *f* side; slope; coast.

costero/ra *adj* coastal; (*mar*) coasting.

costilla *f* rib; (*fig*) wife; cutlet; ~**s** *fpl* back, shoulders *pl*.

costillar *m* human ribs *pl*.

costo *m* cost, price; expense.

costoso/sa *adj* costly, dear, expensive.

costra *f* crust; (*med*) scab.

costumbre *f* custom, habit.

costura *f* sewing; seam; needlework.

costurera *f* seamstress.

costurero *m* sewing box.

cotejar *vt* to compare.

cotejo *m* comparison, collation.

cotidiano/na *adj* daily.

cotilla *m/f* gossip.

cotización *f* quotation.

cotizar *vt* to quote; ~**se** *vr*: ~ **a** to sell at; to be quoted at.

coto *m* enclosure; reserve; boundary stone.

cotorra *f* magpie; small parrot; (*col*) chatterbox.

covacha *f* small cave, grotto.

coyote *m* coyote.

coyuntura *f* joint, articulation; juncture.

coz *f* kick; recoil (of a gun); ebbing (of a flood); (*fig*) insult.

cráneo *m* skull.

cráter *m* crater.

creación *f* creation.

creador/ra *adj* creative; * *m/f* creator.

crear *vt* to create, to make; to establish.

crecer *vi* to grow, to increase; to rise.

creces *fpl* increase.

crecida *f* swell (of rivers).

crecido/da *adj* full-grown (of a person); large; (*fig*) vain.

creciente *f* crescent (moon); (*mar*) flood tide; * *adj* growing; crescent.

crecimiento *m* increase; growth.

credenciales *fpl* credentials *pl*.

credibilidad *f* credibility.

crédito *m* credit; belief, faith; reputation.

credo *m* creed.

credulidad *f* credulity.

crédulo/la *adj* credulous.

creencia *f* credence, belief.

creer *vt*, *vi* to believe; to think; to consider.

crema *f* cream; custard.

cremallera *f* zipper.

crepúsculo *m* twilight.

crespo/pa *adj* curled; angry, displeased.

crespón *m* crepe.

cresta *f* crest (of birds).

creyente *m/f* believer.

cría *f* breeding; young.

criada *f* servant, maid.

criadero *m* (*bot*) nursery; breeding place.

criadilla *f* testicle; small loaf; truffle.

criado/da *m/f* servant; *adj* reared, brought up, bred.

criador *f* creator; breeder.

crianza *f* breeding, rearing.

criar *vt* to create, to produce; to breed; to nurse; to breast-feed; to bring up, to raise.

criatura *f* creature; child.

criba *f* sieve.

cribar *vt* to sift.

crimen *m* crime.

criminal *adj*, *m/f* criminal.

criminalista *m/f* criminologist; criminal lawyer.

crin *f* mane; horsehair.

crío/a *m/f* (*fam*) kid.

criollo/lla *adj*, *m/f* Creole.

cripta *f* crypt.
crisis *f invar* crisis.
crisma *f* chrism.
crisol *m* crucible; melting pot.
crispar *vt* to set on edge; to tense up.
cristal *m* crystal; glass; pane; lens.
cristalino/na *adj* crystalline.
cristalización *f* crystallization.
cristalizar *vt* to crystallize.
cristiandad *f* Christianity.
cristianismo *m* Christianity.
cristiano/na *adj, m/f* Christian.
Cristo *m* Christ.
criterio *m* criterion.
crítica *m/f* criticism.
criticar *vt* to criticize.
crítico/ca *m/f* critic; * *adj* critical.
croar *vi* to croak.
cromo *m* chrome.
crónica *f* chronicle; news report; feature.
crónico/ca *adj* chronic.
cronista *m/f* chronicler; reporter, columnist.
cronología *f* chronology.
cronológico/ca *adj* chronological.
cronómetro *m* stopwatch.
cruce *m* crossing; crossroads.
crucero *m* cruiser; cruise; transept; crossing; Southern Cross (constellation).
crucificar *vt* to crucify; to torment.
crucifijo *m* crucifix.
crucigrama *m* crossword.
crudeza *f* unripeness; crudeness; undigested food (in the stomach).
crudo/da *adj* raw; green, unripe; crude; cruel; hard to digest.
cruel *adj* cruel.
crueldad *f* cruelty.
cruento/ta *adj* bloody; cruel.
crujido *m* crack; creak; clash; crackling.

crujiente *adj* crunchy.
crujir *vi* to crackle; to rustle.
crustáceo *m* crustacean.
cruz *f* cross; tails (of a coin).
cruzada *f* crusade.
cruzado *m* crusader; ~/da *adj* crossed.
cruzar *vt* to cross; (*mar*) to cruise ~se *vr* to cross; to pass each other.
cuaderna *f* fourth part; timber; rib.
cuaderno *m* notebook; exercise book; logbook.
cuadra *f* block; stable.
cuadrado/da *adj, m* square.
cuadragenario/ria *adj* forty-year-old.
cuadragésimo/ma *adj, m* fortieth.
cuadrangular *adj* quadrangular, four-cornered.
cuadrángulo *m* quadrangle.
cuadrante *m* quadrant; dial.
cuadrar *vt, vi* to square; to fit, to suit, to correspond.
cuadricular *adj* squared.
cuadrilátero/ra *adj, m* quadrilateral.
cuadrilla *f* party, group; gang, crew.
cuadro *m* square; picture, painting; window frame; scene; chart; (*dep*) team; executive.
cuadrúpedo/da *adj* quadruped.
cuádruple *adj* quadruple.
cuádruplo/pla *adj* quadruple, fourfold.
cuajada *f* curd.
cuajar *vt* to coagulate; to thicken; to adorn; to set; ~se *vr* to coagulate, to curdle; to set; to fill up.
cuál *pn* which (one).
cual *pn* which; who; whom; * *adv* as; like; * *adj* such as.
cualidad *f* quality.
cualquier *adj* any.
cualquiera *adj* anyone, anybody;

someone, somebody; whoever; whichever.

cuándo *adv* when; **¿de ~ acá?** since when?

cuando *adv* when; if; even; * *conj* since; **de ~ en ~** from time to time; **~ más, ~ mucho** at most, at best; **~ menos** at least.

cuantía *f* quantity, amount; importance.

cuantioso/sa *adj* numerous; substantial.

cuantitativo/va *adj* quantitive.

cuánto *adj* what a lot of; how much?; **¿~s?** how many?; * *pn, adv* how; how much; how many.

cuanto/ta *adj* as many as; as much as; all; whatever; * *adv* **en ~ as** soon as; **en ~ a** as regards; **~ más** moreover, the more as.

cuarenta *adj, m* forty.

cuarentena *f* space of forty days; Lent; quarantine.

cuaresma *f* Lent.

cuarta *f* fourth; span; (*mar*) point (of the compass).

cuartear *vt* to quarter, to divide up; **~se** *vr* to split into pieces.

cuartel *m* quarter, district; barracks *pl*.

cuarteta *f* (*poet*) quatrain.

cuartilla *f* fourth part; sheet of paper.

cuarto *m* fourth part; quarter; room, apartment; span; **~s** *mpl* cash, money; **~/ta** *adj* fourth.

cuarzo *m* quartz.

cuatrero *m* horse thief.

cuatro *adj, m* four.

cuatrocientos/tas *adj* four hundred.

cuba *f* cask; tub; (*fig*) drunkard.

cubeta *f* small cask.

cúbico/ca *adj* cubic.

cubierta *f* cover; deck of a ship; (*auto*) bonnet; tyre; pretext.

cubierto *m* cover; shelter; place at table; meal at a fixed charge; **~s** *mpl* cutlery.

cubil *m* lair.

cubilete *m* tumbler; dice box.

cubo *m* cube; bucket.

cubo de la basura *m* dustbin.

cubrecama *m* bedspread.

cubrir *vt* to cover; to disguise; to protect; to roof a building; **~se** *vr* to become overcast.

cucaña *f* (*fam*) soft job (*sl*); bargain; cinch (*sl*).

cucaracha *f* cockroach.

cuchara *f* spoon.

cucharada *f* spoonful; ladleful.

cucharadita *f* teaspoonful.

cucharita *f* teaspoon.

cucharón *m* ladle; large spoon.

cuchichear *vi* to whisper.

cuchicheo *m* whispering.

cuchilla *f* large kitchen knife; chopping knife; blade.

cuchillada *f* cut; gash; **~s** *fpl* wrangles, quarrels.

cuchillo *m* knife.

cuchitril *m* pigsty.

cuclillas *adv*: **en ~** squatting.

cuclillo *m* cuckoo; (*fig*) cuckold.

cuco *m* cuckoo; **~/ca** *adj* sharp.

cucurucho *m* paper cornet.

cuello *m* neck; collar.

cuenca *m* bowl, deep valley; hollow; socket of the eye.

cuenco *m* earthenware bowl.

cuenta *f* calculation; account; bill (in a restaurant); count, counting; bead; importance.

cuentakilómetros *m invar* mileometer.

cuentarrevoluciones *m invar* rev counter.

cuentista *m/f* storyteller.

cuento *m* tale, story, narrative.

cuerda *f* rope; string; spring.

cuerdo/da *adj* sane; prudent, judicious, canny.

cuerno *m* horn.

cuero *m* hide, skin, leather.

cuerpo *m* body; cadaver, corpse.

cuervo *m* raven.

cuesta *f* slope, hill; incline; **ir ~ abajo** to go downhill; **~ arriba** uphill.

cuestión *f* question, matter; dispute; quarrel; problem.

cuestionable *adj* questionable, problematic.

cuestionar *vt* to question, to dispute.

cueva *f* cave; cellar.

cuidado *m* care, worry, concern; charge.

cuidadosamente *adv* observantly.

cuidadoso/sa *adj* careful; anxious.

cuidar *vt* to care for; to mind, to look after.

culata *f* butt; breech (of a gun); hindquarters *pl* (of an animal); rear of a horse.

culebra *f* snake.

culinario/ria *adj* culinary.

culminación *f* culmination.

culo *m* backside; bum (*sl*); bottom.

culpa *f* fault, blame; guilt.

culpabilidad *f* guilt.

culpable *adj* culpable; guilty; * *m/f* culprit.

culpar *vt* to accuse, to blame.

cultivación *f* cultivation, culture.

cultivar *vt* to cultivate.

cultivo *m* cultivation; crop.

culto/ta *adj* cultured; refined, civilized; * *m* culture; worship.

cultura *f* culture.

cumbre *f* top, summit.

cumpleaños *m invar* birthday.

cumplido/da *adj* large, plentiful; complete, perfect, courteous; * *m* compliment.

cumplidor/ora *adj* reliable.

cumplimentar *vt* to compliment.

cumplimiento *m* fulfilment; accomplishment; completion.

cumplir *vt* to carry out, to fulfil; to serve (a prison sentence); to carry out (death penalty); to attain, to reach (a certain age); **~se** *vr* to be fulfilled; to expire, to be up.

cúmulo *m* heap, pile.

comunicado *m* communiqué.

cuna *f* cradle.

cuña *f* wedge.

cuñado/da *m/f* brother/sister-in-law.

cundir *vi* to spread; to grow, to increase.

cuneta *f* ditch.

cuota *f* quota; fee.

cupé *m* (*auto*) coupé.

cupo *m* share.

cupón *m* coupon.

cúpula *f* cupola, dome.

cura *m* priest; * *f* cure; treatment.

curable *adj* curable.

curación *f* cure; curing.

curandero *m* quack (doctor).

curar *vt* to cure; to treat, to dress (a wound); to salt; to dress; to tan.

curativo/va *adj* curative, healing.

curia *f* ecclesiastical court.

curiosear *vt* to glance at; * *vi* to look round.

curiosidad *f* curiosity.

curioso/sa *adj* curious; * *m/f* bystander.

currante *m/f* (*fam*) worker.

currar *vi* (*fam*) to work.

currículum *m* curriculum vitae.

cursado/da *adj* skilled; versed.

cursar *vt* to frequent a place; to send, to dispatch); to study.

cursillo *m* short course of lectures (in a university).

cursivo/va *adj* italic (type).

curso *m* course, direction; year (at university); subject.

cursor *m* cursor.

curtidor *m* tanner.

curtidos *mpl* tanned leather.

curtir *vt* to tan leather; **~se** *vr* to become sunburned; to become inured.

curva *f* curve, bend.

curvatura *f* curvature.

curvilíneo/nea *adj* curvilinear.

curvo/va *adj* curved, bent.

cuscurro *m* little crust of bread.

cúspide *f* summit, peak; apex.

custodia *f* custody, safekeeping, care; monstrance.

custodio *m* guard, keeper; watchman.

cutáneo/nea *adj* cutaneous.

cutícula *f* cuticle.

cutis *m* skin.

cutre *adj* (*fam*) mean, grotty (*sl*).

cuyo/ya *pn* whose, of which, of whom.

D

dactilógrafo/fa *m/f* typist.

dádiva *f* gift, present; donation.

dadivoso/sa *adj* generous, openhanded.

dado *m* die; **~s** dice.

daga *f* dagger.

dale *excl* come on!

daltónico/ca *adj* colour-blind.

dama *f* lady, gentlewoman; mistress; queen; actress who performs principal parts.

damasco *m* damask (fabric); damson (plum).

damasquino/na *adj* damask.

damero *m* checkers board.

damnificar *vt* to hurt, to injure, to damage.

danza *f* dance.

danzar *vi* to dance; to meddle.

danzarín *m* fine dancer; meddler.

dañar *vt* to hurt, to injure; to damage.

dañino/na *adj* harmful; noxious; mischievous.

daño *m* harm, damage; prejudice; loss.

dar *vt* to give; to supply, to administer, to afford; to deliver; to bestow; to strike, to beat, to knock; to communicate; **~se** *vr* to conform (to the will of another); to give oneself up; **~se prisa** to hurry.

dardo *m* dart.

datar *vt* to date.

dátil *m* (*bot*) date.

dativo *m* (*gr*) dative.

dato *m* fact.

de *prep* of; from; for; by; on; to; with.

deambular *vi* to stroll.

deán *m* dean.

debajo *adv* under, underneath, below.

debate *m* debate, discussion; contest; altercation.

debatir *vt* to debate, to argue, to discuss.

debe *m* (*com*) debit; **~ y haber** debit and credit.

deber *m* obligation, duty; debt; * *vt* to owe; to be obliged to; * *vi*: **debe (de)** it must, it should.

debidamente *adv* justly, duly; exactly, perfectly.

débil *adj* feeble, weak; sickly; frail.
debilidad *f* dimness; weakness.
debilitar *vt* to debilitate, to weaken.
débito *m* debt; duty.
debutar *vi* to make one's debut.
década *f* decade.
decadencia *f* decay, decline.
decaer *vi* to decay, to moulder; to decline, to fade.
decaimiento *m* decay, decline.
decálogo *m* decalogue.
decano *m* senior; dean.
decantar *vt* to decant.
decapitación *f* decapitation, beheading.
decapitar *vt* to behead.
decena *f* ten.
decencia *f* decency.
decente *adj* decent; honest.
decepción *f* disappointment.
decidir *vt* to decide, to determine.
decimal *adj* decimal.
décimo/ma *adj, m* tenth.
decir *vt* to say; to tell; to speak; to name.
decisión *f* decision; determination, resolution; sentence.
decisivo/va *adj* decisive; final.
declamación *f* declamation, discourse, oration.
declamar *vi* to declaim; to harangue.
declaración *f* declaration; explanation, interpretation; (*jur*) deposition.
declarar *vt* to declare; to manifest; to expound; to explain; (*jur*) to decide; **~se** *vr* to declare one's opinion; * *vi* to testify.
declinación *f* declination, descent; decline.
declinar *vi* to decline; to decay, to degenerate; * *vt* (*gr*) to decline.
declive *m* slope; decline.

decolorarse *vr* to become discoloured.
decomiso *m* confiscation.
decoración *f* decoration.
decorado *m* scenery.
decorar *vt* to decorate, to adorn; to illustrate.
decorativo/va *adj* decorative.
decoro *m* honour, respect; circumspection; honesty; decency.
decoroso/sa *adj* decorous, decent.
decrecer *vi* to decrease.
decrépito/ta *adj* decrepit, worn out with age.
decrepitud *f* decrepitude.
decretar *vt* to decree, to determine.
decreto *m* decree; decision; judicial decree.
dechado *m*: **~ de virtudes** model of virtue and perfection.
dedal *m* thimble; very small drinking glass.
dedicación *f* dedication; consecration.
dedicar *vt* to dedicate, to devote; to consecrate; **~se** *vr* to apply oneself to.
dedicatoria *f* dedication.
dedo *m* finger; toe; small bit; **~ meñique** little finger; **~ pulgar** thumb; **~ índice** index finger; **~ corazón** middle finger; **~ anular** ring finger.
deducción *f* deduction, inference; derivation.
deducir *vt* to deduce, to infer; to allege in pleading; to subtract.
defección *f* defection; apostasy.
defectivo/va *adj* defective.
defecto *m* defect; defectiveness.
defectuoso/sa *adj* defective, imperfect, faulty.
defender *vt* to defend, to protect; to

justify, to assert, to maintain; to prohibit, to forbid; to resist, to oppose.

defensa f defence, justification, apology; guard, shelter, protection, fence.

defensiva f defensive.

defensivo m defence, safeguard; ~/**va** adj defensive.

defensor/ra m/f defender, protector; lawyer, defence counsel.

deferente adj pliant, docile, yielding.

deferir vi to defer; to yield (to another's opinion); * vt to communicate.

deficiencia f deficiency.

deficiente adj defective.

déficit m deficit.

definición f definition; decision.

definir vt to define, to describe, to explain; to decide.

definitivo/va adj definitive; positive.

deformar vt to deform; ~**se** vr to become deformed.

deforme adj deformed; ugly.

deformidad f deformity; ugliness; gross error.

defraudación f fraud; usurpation.

defraudar vt to defraud, to cheat; to usurp; to disturb.

defunción f death; funeral.

degeneración f degeneration; degeneracy.

degenerar vi to degenerate.

degollación f beheading.

degollar vt to behead; to destroy, to ruin.

degradación f degradation.

degradar vt to degrade; ~**se** vr to degrade or demean oneself.

degustar vt to taste.

dehesa f pasture.

deidad f deity, divinity; goddess.

dejadez f slovenliness, neglect.

dejado/da adj slovenly, idle, indolent; dejected.

dejar vt to leave, to quit; to omit; to let; to permit, to allow; to leave, to forsake; to bequeath; to pardon; ~ **de** to stop; to fail to; ~**se** vr to abandon oneself.

dejo m accent; aftertaste, tang.

del adj of the (contraction of de and el).

delantal m apron.

delante adv in front; opposite; ahead; ~ **de** in front of; before.

delantera f front, forepart (of something); advantage; forward line.

delantero/ra adj front; * m/f forward.

delatar vt to accuse; to denounce.

delator m accuser; informer, denouncer.

delegación f delegation; substitution.

delegado/da m/f delegate; deputy.

delegar vt to delegate; to substitute.

deleitar vt to delight.

deletrear vt to spell; to examine; to conjecture.

delfín m dolphin; dauphin.

delgadez f thinness.

delgado/da adj thin; delicate, fine; light; slender, lean; acute; ingenious; little, scanty.

deliberación f deliberation; resolution.

deliberadamente adv deliberately.

deliberar vi to consider, to deliberate; * vt to debate; to consult.

delicadeza f tenderness, softness; delicacy, daintiness; subtlety.

delicado/da adj delicate, tender; faint; exquisite; delicious, dainty; slender, subtle.

delicia f delight, pleasure.
delicioso/sa adj delicious; delightful.
delincuencia f delinquency.
delincuente m delinquent.
delineante m/f draftsman/woman.
delinear vt to delineate, to sketch; to describe.
delinquir vi to offend.
delirante adj delirious.
delirar vi to rave; to talk nonsense.
delirio m delirium; dotage; nonsense.
delito m offence; crime.
demacrado/da adj pale and drawn.
demagogia f demagogy.
demagogo m demagogue.
demanda f demand, claim; pretension, complaint; challenge; request.
demandado/da m/f defendant.
demandante m/f claimant.
demandar vt to demand; to ask; to claim; to sue.
demarcación f demarcation; boundary line.
demarcar vt to mark out (limits).
demás adj other; remaining; * pn **los/las ~** the others, the rest; **estar ~** to be over and above; to be useless or superfluous; **por ~** in vain, to no purpose.
demasía f excess; arduous enterprise; rudeness; want of respect; abundance, plenty; **en ~** excessively.
demasiado/da adj too; excessive; * adv too, too much.
demencia f madness.
demente adj mad, insane.
democracia f democracy.
demócrata m/f democrat.
democrático/ca adj democratic.

demoler vt to demolish; to destroy.
demolición f demolition.
demonio m demon.
demora f delay; demurrage.
demorar vt to delay; **~se** vr to be delayed; * vi to linger.
demostrable adj demonstrable.
demostración f demonstration; manifestation.
demostrar vt to prove, to demonstrate; to manifest.
demostrativo/va adj demonstrative.
denegación f denial; refusal.
denegar vt to deny; to refuse.
dengue m prudery.
denigración f defamation; stigma, disgrace.
denigrar vt to blacken; to insult.
denominación f denomination.
denominar vt to name; to designate.
denotar vt to denote; to express.
densidad f density; obscurity.
denso/sa adj dense, thick; compact.
dentado/da adj jagged, toothed; perforated (of stamps).
dentadura f set of teeth.
dentellada f gnashing of the teeth; nip; pinch with the teeth; **a ~s** snappishly, peevishly.
dentera f (fig) the shivers pl.
dentición f dentition, teething.
dentífrico m toothpaste.
dentista m/f dentist.
dentro adv within; * pn: **~ de** in, inside.
denuncia f denunciation; accusation; report.
denunciar vt to advise; to denounce; to report.
deparar vt to offer, to present.
departamento m department; (ferro) compartment; apartment.
dependencia f dependency; relation,

affinity; dependence; office; business, affair.

depender *vi*: ~ **de** to depend on, to be dependent on.

dependienta *f* saleswoman.

dependiente *m* shop assistant; * *adj* dependent.

depilar *vt* to depilate, remove hair from.

depilatorio *m* hair remover.

deplorable *adj* deplorable, lamentable.

deplorar *vt* to deplore.

deponer *vt* to depose; to declare; to displace; to deposit.

deportación *f* deportation.

deportar *vt* to deport.

deporte *m* sport.

deportista *m/f* sportsman/woman.

deportivo/va *adj* sports *compd*.

deposición *f* deposition; assertion, affirmation; (*jur*) deposition upon oath.

depositar *vt* to deposit; to confide; to put away for safekeeping.

depósito *m* deposit; warehouse; tank.

depravación *f* depravity.

depravar *vt* to deprave, to corrupt.

depreciar *vt* to depreciate.

depredador/ra *adj* predatory; * *m* predator.

depresión *f* depression.

deprimido/da *adj* depressed.

deprimir *vt* to depress; ~**se** *vr* to become depressed.

deprisa *adv* quickly.

depuración *f* purification.

depuradora *f* purifier.

depurar *vt* to cleanse; to purify; to filter.

de quitapón *adj* detachable, removable.

derecha *f* right hand, right side; right.

derecho/cha *adj* right; straight; just; perfect; certain; * *m* right, justice; law; tax, duty; fee; * *adv* straight.

derivación *f* derivation; source; origin.

derivado/da *adj* derivative; * *m* derivative; by-product.

derivar *vt, vi* to derive; (*mar*) to drift.

dermatología *f* dermatology.

dermatólogo/ga *m/f* dermatologist.

derogar *vt* to derogate, to abolish; to reform.

derogatorio/ria *adj* derogatory.

derramamiento *m* effusion; waste; dispersion; ~ **de sangre** bloodshed.

derramar *vt* to drain off (water); to spread; to spill, to scatter; to waste, to shed; ~**se** *vr* to pour out.

derrame *m* spelling; overflow; discharge; leakage.

derredor *m* circumference, circuit; **al** ~, **en** ~ around, about.

derrengado/da *adj* bent, crooked.

derrengar *vt* to sprain.

derretir *vt* to melt; to consume; to thaw; ~**se** *vr* to melt.

derribar *vt* to demolish; to flatten.

derribo *m* demolition; ruins of a demolished building *pl*.

derrocar *vt* to pull down, to demolish.

derrochador *m* spendthrift.

derrochar *vt* to dissipate; to squander.

derroche *m* waste.

derrota *f* ship's course; road, path; defeat.

derrotar *vt* to destroy; to defeat.

derrotero *m* collection of sea charts; ship's course; (*fig*) course, way.

derruir *vt* to demolish.

derrumbar *vt* to throw down; **~se** *vr* to collapse.

desabastecer *vt* to cut off supplies from.

desabillé *m* deshabille.

desabollar *vt* to take bulges out of.

desabotonar *vt* to unbutton; **~se** *vr* to come undone.

desabrido/da *adj* tasteless, insipid; rude; unpleasant.

desabrigado/da *adj* uncovered; unsheltered.

desabrigar *vt* to uncover; to deprive of clothes or shelter.

desabrochar *vt* to undo; **~se** *vr* to come undone.

desacatar *vt* to treat in a disrespectful manner.

desacato *m* disrespect, incivility.

desacertado/da *adj* mistaken; unwise; inconsiderate.

desacierto *m* error, gross mistake, blunder.

desaconsejado/da *adj* inconsiderate; ill-advised.

desaconsejar *vt* to advise against.

desacorde *adj* discordant.

desacostumbrado/da *adj* unusual.

desacreditar *vt* to discredit.

desacuerdo *m* blunder; disagreement; forgetfulness.

desafiar *vt* to challenge; to defy.

desafilado/da *adj* blunt.

desafinado/da *adj* out of tune.

desafinar *vi* to be out of tune.

desafío *m* challenge; struggle; contest, combat.

desaforado/da *adj* huge; disorderly, lawless; impudent.

desafortunadamente *adv* unfortunately.

desafortunado/da *adj* unfortunate, unlucky.

desafuero *m* outrage; excess.

desagradable *adj* disagreeable, unpleasant.

desagradar *vt* to displease; to pester.

desagradecido/da *adj* ungrateful.

desagradecimiento *m* ingratitude.

desagrado *m* harshness; displeasure.

desagraviar *vt* to make amends for.

desagravio *m* amends *pl*; satisfaction.

desaguar *vt* to drain; * *vi* to drain off.

desagüe *m* channel, drain; drainpipe; drainage.

desaguisado *m* outrage.

desahogado/da *adj* comfortable; roomy.

desahogar *vt* to ease; to vent; **~se** *vr* to recover; to relax; to let off steam.

desahogo *m* ease, relief; freedom.

desahuciar *vt* to cause to despair; to give up; to evict.

desahucio *m* eviction.

desairado/da *adj* disregarded; slighted.

desairar *vt* to disregard, to take no notice of.

desaire *m* disdain, disrespect; unattractiveness.

desajustar *vt* to make uneven; to unbalance; **~se** *vr* to get out of order.

desajuste *m* disorder; imbalance.

desalentador/ra *adj* disheartening.

desalentar *vt* to put out of breath; to discourage.

desaliento *m* dismay.

desaliño *m* slovenliness; carelessness.

desalinizadora *f* desalination plant.

desalinizar *vt* to desalinate.

desalmado/da *adj* cruel, inhuman.

desalojar *vt* to eject; to move out; * *vi* to move out.

desamarrar *vt* to cast off (a ship); to untie; to remove.

desamor *m* indifference.

desamparado/da *adj* helpless.

desamparar *vt* to forsake, to abandon; to relinquish.

desamparo *m* abandonment; helplessness; dereliction.

desamueblar *vt* to remove the furniture from.

desandar *vt* to retrace; to go back the same road.

desangrar *vt* to bleed; to drain (a pond); (*fig*) to exhaust (one's means); ~**se** *vr* to lose a lot of blood.

desanimado/da *adj* downhearted.

desanimar *vt* to discourage; ~**se** *vr* to lose heart.

desapacible *adj* disagreeable; unpleasant, harsh.

desaparecer *vi* to disappear.

desaparecido/da *adj* missing; * *mpl* ~**s** missing people.

desaparejar *vt* to unharness, unhitch (beasts); (*mar*) to unrig (a ship).

desaparición *f* disappearance.

desapego *m* coolness; lack of interest.

desapercibido/da *adj* unnoticed.

desaplicado/da *adj* lazy; careless, neglectful.

desapolillar *vt* to free from moths; ~**se** *vr* (*fig*) to get rid of the cobwebs.

desaprensivo/va *adj* unscrupulous.

desaprobación *f* disapproval.

desaprobar *vt* to disapprove; to condemn; to reject.

desaprovechado/da *adj* useless; unprofitable; backward; slack.

desaprovechar *vt* to waste, to turn to a bad use.

desarmar *vt* to disarm; to disband (troops); to dismantle; (*fig*) to pacify.

desarme *m* disarmament.

desarraigar *vt* to uproot; to root out; to extirpate.

desarraigo *m* eradication.

desarrapado/da *adj* ragged.

desarreglado/da *adj* untidy.

desarreglar *vt* to disorder, to upset.

desarreglo *m* disorder; untidiness.

desarrollar *vt* to develop; to unroll; to unfold; ~**se** *vr* to develop; to be unfolded; to open.

desarrollo *m* development.

desarropar *vt* to undress.

desarticular *vt* to take apart.

desasir *vt* to loosen, to disentangle; ~**se** *vr* to extricate oneself.

desasosegar *vt* to disquiet, to disturb.

desasosiego *m* restlessness; anxiety.

desastrado/da *adj* wretched, miserable; ragged.

desastre *m* disaster; misfortune.

desastroso/sa *adj* disastrous.

desatado/da *adj* untied; wild.

desatar *vt* to untie, to loose; to separate; to solve; ~**se** *vr* to come undone; to break.

desatascar *vt* to unblock; to clear.

desatender *vt* to pay no attention to; to disregard.

desatinado/da *adj* foolish; extravagant; * *m* fool, madman.

desatinar *vi* to talk nonsense; to reel, to stagger.

desatino *m* blunder; nonsense.

desatornillar *vt* to unscrew.

desatrancar *vt* to unbar; to unblock.

desautorizado/da *adj* unauthorized.

desautorizar *vt* to deprive of authority; to deny.

desavenencia *f* discord, disagreement.

desavenido/da *adj* contrary, disagreeing.

desaventajado/da *adj* disadvantageous, unprofitable.

desayunar *vt* to have for breakfast; ~**se** *vr* to breakfast; * *vi* to have breakfast;

desayuno *m* breakfast.

desazón *f* disgust; uneasiness; annoyance.

desazonado/da *adj* ill-adapted; ill-humoured.

desazonar *vt* to annoy; ~**se** *vr* to be annoyed; to be anxious.

desbancar *vt* to break (the bank in gambling); (*fig*) to supplant.

desbandarse *vr* to disband; to go off in all directions.

desbarajuste *m* confusion.

desbaratar *vt* to destroy.

desbarrar *vi* to talk rubbish.

desbastar *vt* to smooth; to polish; to waste.

desbloquear *vt* to unblock.

desbocado/da *adj* open-mouthed; wild (applied to a horse); foul-mouthed; indecent.

desbocarse *vr* to bolt.

desbordar *vt* to exceed; ~**se** *vr* to overflow.

descabalgar *vi* to dismount.

descabellado/da *adj* dishevelled; disorderly; wild, unrestrained; disproportional; violent.

descabellar *vt* to ruffle.

descafeinado/da *adj* decaffeinated.

descalabrado/da *adj* wounded on the head; imprudent.

descalabrar *vt* to wound on the head; to smash.

descalabro *m* blow; misfortune; considerable loss.

descalificar *vt* to disqualify; to discredit.

descalzar *vt*, ~**se** *vr* to take off one's shoes.

descalzo/za *adj* barefooted; (*fig*) destitute.

descambiar *vt* to exchange.

descaminado/da *adj* (*fig*) misguided.

descaminar *vt* to misguide, to lead astray.

descamisado/da *adj* shirtless.

descampado/da *adj* disengaged; free; open; * *m* open space.

descansado/da *adj* rested, refreshed; quiet.

descansar *vt* to rest; * *vi* to rest; to lie down.

descansillo *m* landing.

descanso *m* rest, repose; break; interval.

descapotable *m* convertible.

descarado/da *adj* cheeky, barefaced.

descararse *vr* to behave insolently.

descarga *f* unloading; volley, discharge.

descargar *vt* to unload, to discharge; ~**se** *vr* to unburden oneself.

descargo *m* discharge; evidence; receipt.

descarnado/da *adj* scrawny.

descarnar *vt* to strip the flesh from; to clean away the flesh from; to corrode; ~**se** *vr* to grow thin.

descarado/da *adj* cheeky.

descaro *m* nerve.

descarriar *vt* to lead astray; to misdirect; **~se** *vr* to lose one's way; to stray; to err.

descarrilamiento *m* (*ferro*) derailment.

descarrilar *vi* (*ferro*) to leave or run off the rails.

descarrío *m* losing of one's way.

descartar *vt* to discard; to dismiss; to rule out; **~se** *vr* to excuse oneself.

descascarillado/da *adj* peeling.

descastado *adj* degenerate; ungrateful.

descendencia *f* descent, offspring.

descendente *adj* descending; **tren ~** *m* (*ferro*) down train.

descender *vt* to take down; * *vi* to descend, to walk down; to flow; to fall; **~ de** to be derived from.

descendiente *adj* descending; * *m/f* descendant.

descenso *m* descent; drop; relegation.

descerrajar *vt* to force the lock (of a door etc); to discharge firearms.

descifrar *vt* to decipher; to unravel.

desclavar *vt* to draw out nails (from).

descocado/da *adj* bold, impudent.

descodificador *m* decoder (for TV).

descolgar *vt* to take down; to pick up; **~se** *vr* to let oneself down.

descollar *vi* to excel.

descolorido/da *adj* pale, colourless.

descomedido/da *adj* impudent, insolent; huge.

descompaginar *vt* to disarrange.

descomponer *vt* to discompose, to set at odds; to disconcert; (*quim*) to decompose.

descomposición *f* disagreement; discomposure; decomposition.

descompuesto/ta *adj* decomposed; broken.

descomunal *adj* uncommon; huge.

desconcertado/da *adj* disconcerted; bewildered.

desconcertar *vt* to disturb; to confound; to disconcert; **~se** *vr* to be bewildered; to be upset.

desconchado/da *adj* peeling.

desconchar *vt* to peel off.

desconcierto *m* disorder, confusion; uncertainty.

desconectar *vt* to disconnect.

desconfiado/da *adj* mistrustful, distrustful.

desconfianza *f* distrust; jealousy.

desconfiar *vi*: **~ de** to mistrust, to suspect.

descongelar *vt* to defrost.

descongestionar *vt* to clear.

desconocer *vt* to disown, to disavow; to be totally ignorant of (a thing); not to know (a person); not to acknowledge (a favour received).

desconocido/da *adj* unknown; disguised; * *m/f* stranger.

desconocimiento *m* ignorance.

desconsiderado/da *adj* inconsiderate; imprudent.

desconsolado/da *adj* disconsolate; painful; sad.

desconsolar *vt* to distress.

desconsuelo *m* distress; trouble; despair.

descontado *adj*: **por ~** of course; **dar por ~** to take for granted.

descontar *vt* to discount; to deduct.

descontento *m* dissatisfaction; disgust.

descorazonar *vt* to dishearten, to discourage.

descorchar *vt* to uncork.

descorrer *vt* to draw.

descortés/esa *adj* impolite, rude.

descortesía *f* rudeness.

descoser *vt* to undo, take apart; to separate; ~**se** *vr* to come apart at the seams.

descosido/da *adj* unstitched; disjointed.

descoyuntar *vt* to dislocate; to vex, to annoy.

descrédito *m* discredit.

descreído/da *adj* incredulous.

descremado/da *adj* skimmed.

describir *vt* to describe; to draw, to delineate.

descripción *f* description; delineation; inventory.

descriptivo/va *adj* descriptive.

descuartizar *vt* to quarter; to carve.

descubierto *m* deficit; overdraft; ~/**ta** *adj* uncovered.

descubrimiento *m* discovery; revelation.

descubrir *vt* to discover, to disclose; to uncover; to reveal; to show; ~**se** *vr* to reveal oneself; to take off one's hat; to confess.

descuento *m* discount; decrease.

descuida *excl* don't worry!

descuidado/da *adj* careless, negligent.

descuidar *vt* to neglect; * *vi*, ~**se** *vr* to be careless.

descuido *m* carelessness, negligence; forgetfulness; incivility; improper action.

desde *prep* since; after; from; ~ **luego** of course; ~ **entonces** since then.

desdecirse *vr* to retract one's words.

desdén *m* disdain, scorn.

desdentado/da *adj* toothless.

desdentar *vt* to draw out (teeth).

desdeñable *adj* contemptible, despicable.

desdeñar *vt* to disdain, to scorn; ~**se** *vr* to be disdainful.

desdeñoso/sa *adj* disdainful; contemptuous.

desdicha *f* misfortune, calamity; great poverty.

desdichado/da *adj* unfortunate; wretched, miserable.

desdoblar *vt* to unfold, to spread open.

desear *vt* to desire, to wish; to require, to demand.

desecación *f* desiccation.

desecar *vt* to dry up.

desechar *vt* to depreciate; to reject; to refuse; to throw away.

desecho *m* residue; ~**s** *mpl* rubbish.

desembalar *vt* to unpack.

desembarazado/da *adj* free.

desembarazar *vt* to free; to clear; ~**se** *vr*: ~ **de** to get rid of.

desembarcadero *m* landing stage.

desembarcar *vt* to unload, to disembark; * *vi* to disembark, to land.

desembarco *m* landing.

desembargo *m* (*jur*) raising an embargo.

desembarque *m* landing.

desembocadura *f* mouth.

desembocar *vi*: ~ **en** to flow into.

desembolsar *vt* to pay out.

desembolso *m* expenditure.

desembragar *vi* to declutch.

desembuchar *vt* to disgorge; to tell all.

desempaquetar *vt* to unpack.

desempatar *vi* to hold a play-off.

desempate *m* play-off.

desempeñar *vt* to redeem; to extricate from debt; to fulfil (any duty or promise); to acquit; ~**se** *vr* to get out of debt.

desempeño *m* redeeming a pledge; occupation.

desempleado/da *adj* unemployed; * *m/f* unemployed person.

desempleo *m* unemployment.

desempolvorar *vt* to dust.

desencadenar *vt* to unchain; ~**se** *vr* to break loose; to burst.

desencajar *vt* to disjoint; to dislocate; to disconnect.

desencallar *vt* to refloat.

desencanto *m* disenchantment.

desenchufar *vt* to unplug.

desenfadado/da *adj* free; unembarrassed.

desenfado *m* ease; facility; calmness, relaxation.

desenfocado/da *adj* out of focus.

desenfrenado/da *adj* outrageous; ungovernable.

desenfreno *m* wildness; lack of self-control.

desenganchar *vt* to unhook; to uncouple.

desengañado/da *adj* disillusioned.

desengañar *vt* to disillusion; ~**se** *vr* to become disillusioned.

desengaño *m* disillusionment; disappointment.

desengrasar *vt* to take the grease off.

desenhebrar *vt* to unthread; to unravel.

desenlace *m* climax; outcome.

desenmarañar *vt* to disentangle; to unravel.

desenmascarar *vt* to unmask.

desenredar *vt* to disentangle.

desenrollar *vt* to unroll.

desenroscar *vt* to untwist; to unroll.

desentenderse *vr* to feign not to understand; to pass by without noticing.

desenterrar *vt* to exhume; to dig up.

desentonar *vi* to be out of tune; to clash.

desentrañar *vt* to unravel.

desentumecer *vt* to stretch; to loosen up.

desenvainar *vt* to unsheath; to show.

desenvoltura *f* sprightliness; cheerfulness; impudence, boldness.

desenvolver *vt* to unfold; to unroll; to decipher, to unravel; to develop; ~**se** *vr* to develop; to cope.

desenvuelto/ta *adj* forward; natural.

deseo *m* desire, wish.

deseoso/sa *adj* anxious.

desequilibrado/da *adj* unbalanced.

deserción *f* desertion; defection.

desertar *vt* to desert; (*jur*) to abandon (a cause).

desertificación *f* desertification.

desertor *m* deserter; fugitive.

desesperación *f* despair, desperation; anger, fury.

desesperado/da *adj* desperate, hopeless.

desesperar *vi*, ~**se** *vr* to despair; * *vt* to make desperate.

desestabilizar *vt* to destabilize.

desestimar *vt* to disregard, to reject.

desfachatez *f* impudence.

desfalcar *vt* to embezzle.

desfalco *m* embezzlement.

desfallecer *vi* to get weak; to faint.

desfallecimiento *m* fainting.

desfasado/da *adj* old-fashioned.

desfase *m* gap.

desfavorable *adj* unfavorable.

desfigurar *vt* to disfigure, to deform; to disguise.

desfiladero *m* gorge.

desfilar *vi* (*mil*) to parade.

desfogarse *vr* to give vent to one's passion or anger.

desforestación *f* desforestation.

desgajar vt to tear off; to break in pieces; **~se** vr to be separated; to be torn to pieces.

desgana f disgust; loss of appetite; aversion, reluctance.

desganado/da adj not hungry; half-hearted; **estar ~** to lose all pleasure in doing a thing; to lose one's appetite.

desgañitarse vr to scream, to bawl.

desgarrador/a adj heartrending.

desgarrar vt to tear; to shatter.

desgarro m tear; grief; impudence.

desgarrón m large tear.

desgastar vt to waste; to corrode; **~se** vr to get worn out.

desgaste m wear (and tear).

desglosar vt to break down.

desgracia f misfortune; disgrace; accident; setback.

desgraciado/da adj unfortunate; unhappy, miserable; out of favour; disagreeable.

desgreñado/da adj dishevelled.

desgreñar vt to dishevel (the hair); to disorder.

desguarnecer vt to strip down; to dismantle.

deshabitado/da adj deserted, uninhabited; desolate.

deshacer vt to undo, to destroy; to cancel, to efface; to rout (an army); to solve; to melt; to break up, to divide; to dissolve in a liquid; to violate (a treaty); to diminish; to disband (troops); **~se** vr to melt; to come apart.

desharrapado/da adj shabby; ragged, in tatters.

deshecho/cha adj undone, destroyed; wasted; melted; in pieces.

deshelar vt to thaw; **~se** vr to thaw, to melt.

desheredar vt to disinherit.

deshidratado/da adj dehydrated.

deshidratar vt to dehydrate.

deshielo m thaw.

deshilachar vt to unravel.

deshilar vt to fray.

deshinchar vt to deflate; **~se** vr to go flat, to go down.

deshojar vt to strip the leaves off.

deshollinador m chimney sweep.

deshonesto/ta adj indecent.

deshonra f dishonour; shame.

deshonrar vt to affront, to insult, to defame; to dishonour.

deshonroso/sa adj dishonourable, indecent.

deshora f unseasonable time.

deshuesar vt to rid of bones; to stone.

desidia f idleness, indolence.

desierto/ta adj deserted; solitary; * m desert; wilderness.

designación f designation.

designar vt to design; to intend; to appoint; to express, to name.

designio m design, purpose; road, course.

desigual adj unequal, unlike; uneven, craggy.

desigualdad f inequality, dissimilitude; inconstancy; roughness, unevenness.

desilusión f disappointment.

desilusionar vt to disappoint; **~se** vr to become disillusioned.

desinfección f disinfection.

desinfectar vt to disinfect.

desinflar vt to deflate.

desintegración f disintegration.

desinterés m unselfishness; disinterestedness.

desinteresado/da adj disinterested; unselfish.

desistir vi to desist, to cease.

desleal adj disloyal; unfair.

deslealtad f disloyalty, breach of faith.

desleír vt to dilute; to dissolve.

deslenguado/da adj foul-mouthed.

desligar vt to separate; to loosen, to unbind; ~**se** vr to extricate oneself.

desliz m slip, sliding; lapse, weakness.

deslizadizo/za adj slippery, slippy; glib.

deslizar vt to slip, to slide; to let slip (a comment); ~**se** vr to slip; to skid; to flow softly; to creep in.

deslucido/da adj tarnished; dull; shabby.

deslucir vt to tarnish; to damage; to discredit.

deslumbramiento m glare; confusion.

deslumbrar vt to dazzle; to puzzle.

desmán m outrage; disaster; misconduct.

desmandarse vr to behave badly.

desmantelar vt to dismantle; to abandon, to forsake.

desmaquillador m make-up remover.

desmarañar vt to disentangle.

desmayado/da adj unconscious; dismayed; appalled; weak.

desmayar vi to be dispirited or faint-hearted; ~**se** vr to faint.

desmayo m unconsciousness; faint, swoon; dismay.

desmedido/da adj disproportionate.

desmejorar vt to impair; to weaken.

desmembrar vt to dismember; to separate.

desmemoriado/da adj forgetful.

desmentir vt to give the lie to; ~**se** vr to contradict oneself.

desmenuzar vt to crumble; to chip at; to fritter away; to examine minutely.

desmerecer vt to be unworthy of; * vi to deteriorate.

desmesurado/da adj excessive; huge; immeasurable.

desmontar vt to level; to remove (a heap of rubbish); to dismantle; * vi to dismount.

desmoralización f demoralization.

desmoralizar vt to demoralize.

desmoronar vt to destroy little by little; ~**se** vr to fall into disrepair.

desnatado/da adj skimmed.

desnatar vt to skim (milk); to take the choicest part of.

desnaturalizar vt to divest of naturalization rights; ~**se** vr to forsake one's country.

desnivel m unevenness of the ground.

desnucar vt to break (one's neck).

desnudar vt to undress; to strip; to discover, to reveal; ~**se** vr to undress.

desnudez f nakedness.

desnudo/da adj naked; bare, uncovered; ill-clothed; (fig) plain, evident.

desnutrición f malnutrition.

desnutrido/da adj undernourished.

desobedecer vt, vi to disobey.

desobediencia f disobedience; insubordination.

desobediente adj disobedient.

desocupado/da adj empty; at leisure.

desocupar vt to vacate; to empty; ~**se** vr to retire from a business; to withdraw from an arrangement.

desodorante m deodorant.

desolación f destruction; affliction.

desolado/da *adj* desolate, disconsolate.

desolar *vt* to lay waste; to harass.

desollar *vt* to flay, to skin; (*fig*) to extort.

desorden *m* disorder, confusion.

desordenado/da *adj* disorderly; untidy.

desordenar *vt* to disorder; to untidy; ~**se** *vr* to get out of order.

desorganización *f* disorganization.

desorganizar *vt* to disorganize.

desorientar *vt* to mislead; to confuse; ~**se** *vr* to lose one's way.

desovar *vi* to spawn.

despabilado/da *adj* watchful, vigilant; wide-awake.

despabilar *vt* to snuff (a candle); (*fig*) to dispatch quickly; to sharpen; ~**se** *vr* to wake up.

despacio *adv* slowly, leisurely; little by little; ¡~! softly!, gently!

despachar *vt* to dispatch; to expedite; to sell; to send.

despacho *m* dispatch, expedition; cabinet; office; commission; warrant, patent; expedient; smart answer.

despachurrar *vt* to squash, to crush; to mangle.

desparejar *vt* to make unequal or uneven.

desparpajo *m* ease; savoir-faire.

desparramar *vt* to disseminate, to spread; to spill; to squander, to lavish; ~**se** *vr* to be dissipated.

despavorido *adj* frightened.

despectivo/va *adj* pejorative, derogatory.

despecho *m* indignation; displeasure; spite; dismay; despair; deceit; derision, scorn; **a** ~ **de** in spite of.

despedazar *vt* to tear into pieces; to mangle.

despedida *f* farewell; sacking.

despedir *vt* to discharge; to dismiss (from office); to see off; ~**se** *vr*: ~ **de** to say goodbye to.

despegado/da *adj* cold; detached.

despegar *vt* to unglue; to take off; ~**se** *vr* to come loose.

despego *m* detachment; coolness.

despegue *m* take-off.

despeinado/da *adj* dishevelled.

despeinar *vt* to ruffle.

despejado/da *adj* sprightly, quick; clear.

despejar *vt* to clear away; ~**se** *vr* to cheer up; to clear; * *vi* to clear.

despellejar *vt* to skin.

despensa *f* pantry, larder; provisions *pl*.

despeñadero *m* precipice.

despeñar *vt* to precipitate; ~**se** *vr* to throw oneself headlong.

despepitarse *vr* to bawl.

desperdiciar *vt* to squander.

desperdicio *m* waste; ~**s** *mpl* rubbish; waste.

desperdigar *vt* to separate; to scatter.

desperezarse *vr* to stretch oneself.

desperfecto *m* slight damage; flaw.

despertador *m* alarm clock.

despertar *vt* to wake up, to rouse from sleep; to excite; * *vi* to wake up; to grow lively or sprightly; ~**se** *vr* to wake up.

despiadado/da *adj* heartless; merciless.

despido *m* dismissal.

despierto/ta *adj* awake; vigilant; fierce; brisk, sprightly.

despilfarrar *vt* to waste.

despilfarro *m* slovenliness; waste; mismanagement.

despintar *vt* to deface (a painting); to obscure (things); to mislead; **~se** to lose its colour.

despistar *vt* to mislead; to throw off the track; **~se** *vr* to take the wrong way; to become confused.

desplante *m* bold statement; wrong stance; insolence.

desplazamiento *m* displacement.

desplazar *vt* to move; to scroll; **~se** *vr* to travel.

desplegar *vt* to unfold, to display; to explain, to elucidate; (*mar*) to unfurl; **~se** *vr* to open out; to travel.

despliegue *m* display.

desplomarse *vr* to fall to the ground; to collapse.

desplumar *vt* to fleece; to pluck.

despoblado *m* desert.

despoblar *vt* to depopulate; to desolate; **~se** *vr* to become depopulated.

despojar *vt*: **~ (de)** to strip (of); to deprive (of); **~se** *vr* to undress.

despojo *m* plunder; loot; **~s** *mpl* giblets *pl*; remains *pl*; offal.

desposado/da *adj* newlywed.

desposar *vt* to marry, to betroth; **~se** *vr* to be betrothed or married.

desposeer *vt* to dispossess.

desposeimiento *m* dispossession.

déspota *m* despot.

despótico/ca *adj* despotic.

despotismo *m* despotism.

despreciable *adj* contemptible, despicable.

despreciar *vt* to offend; to despise.

desprecio *m* scorn, contempt.

desprender *vt* to unfasten, to loosen; to separate; **~se** *vr* to give way; to fall down; to extricate oneself.

desprendimiento *m* alienation, disinterestedness.

despreocupado/da *adj* careless; unworried.

despreocuparse *vr* to be carefree.

desprestigiar *vt* to run down.

desprevenido/da *adj* unawares, unprepared.

desproporción *f* disproportion.

desproporcionado/da *adj* disproportionate.

desproporcionar *vt* to disproportion.

despropósito *m* absurdity.

desprovisto/ta *adj* unprovided.

después *adv* after, afterwards; next.

despuntar *vt* to blunt; * *vi* to sprout; to dawn; **al ~ del día** at break of day.

desquiciar *vt* to upset; to discompose; to disorder.

desquitar *vt* to retrieve (a loss); **~se** *vr* to win one's money back again; to return by giving like for like; to take revenge.

desquite *m* recovery of a loss; revenge, retaliation.

desrizar *vt* to uncurl.

destacamento *m* (*mil*) detachment.

destacar *vt* to emphasize; (*mil*) to detach (a body of troops); **~se** *vr* to stand out.

destajo *m* piecework; **trabajar a ~** to do piecework.

destapar *vt* to uncover; to open; **~se** *vr* to be uncovered.

destartalado/da *adj* untidy.

destello *m* signal light; sparkle.

destemplado/da *adj* out of tune; incongruous (applied to paintings); intemperate.

desteñir *vt* to discolour; **~se** *vr* to fade.

desternillarse *vr*: **~ de risa** to roar with laughter.

desterrar vt to banish; to expel, to drive away.

destetar vt to wean.

destete m weaning.

destierro m exile, banishment.

destilación f distillation.

destilar vt, vi to distil.

destinar vt to destine for, to intend for.

destinatario/a m/f addressee.

destino m destiny; fate, doom; destination; office.

destitución f destitution, abandonment.

destituir vt to dismiss.

destornillador m screwdriver.

destornillar vt to unscrew.

destreza f dexterity, cleverness, cunning, expertness, skill.

destripar vt to disembowel; to trample.

destronar vt to dethrone.

destrozar vt to destroy, to break into pieces; (mil) to defeat.

destrozo m destruction; (mil) defeat, massacre.

destrucción f destruction, ruin.

destructivo/va adj destructive.

destruir vt to destroy.

desunir vt to separate, to disunite; to cause discord between.

desuso m disuse.

desvaído/da adj tall and graceless.

desvalido/da adj helpless; destitute.

desvalijar vt to rob; to burgle.

desván m garret.

desvanecer vt to dispel; ~se vr to grow vapid, to become insipid; to vanish; to be affected with giddiness.

desvanecimiento m pride, haughtiness; giddiness; swoon.

desvariar vi to be delirious.

desvarío m delirium; giddiness; inconstancy, caprice; extravagance.

desvelar vt to keep awake; ~se vr to stay awake.

desvelo m want of sleep; watchfulness.

desvencijado/da adj rickety.

desvencijar vt to disunite, to divide; to weaken; ~se vr to be ruptured; to come apart.

desventaja f disadvantage; damage.

desventura f misfortune; calamity.

desventurado/da adj unfortunate; calamitous.

desvergonzado/da adj impudent, shameless.

desvergonzarse vr to behave in an impudent manner.

desvergüenza f impudence; shamelessness.

desvestir vt, ~se vr to undress.

desviar vt to divert; to dissuade; to parry (at fencing); ~se vr to go off course.

desvío m turning away, going astray; aversion; disdain; indifference.

desvivirse vr: ~ por to long for.

detallar vt to detail, to relate minutely.

detalle m detail.

detallista m retailer.

detención f detention; delay.

detener vt to stop, to detain; to arrest; to keep back; to reserve; to withhold; ~se vr to stop; to stay.

detenidamente adv carefully.

detenido/da adj detailed; sparing niggardly; slow, inactive.

detergente m detergent.

deterioración f deterioration; damage.

deteriorar vt to damage.

deterioro m deterioration.

determinación *f* determination, resolution; boldness.

determinado/da *adj* determined; resolute.

determinar *vt* to determine; **~se** *vr* to decide.

detestable *adj* detestable.

detestar *vt* to detest, to abhor.

detonación *f* detonation.

detonar *vi* to detonate.

detractar *vt* to denigrate, to defame, to slander.

detrás *adv* behind; at the back, in the back.

detrimento *m* detriment; damage; loss.

deuda *f* debt; fault; offence.

deudor/ra *m/f* debtor.

devaluación *f* devaluation.

devanar *vt* to reel; to wrap up.

devastación *f* devastation, desolation.

devastador/ra *adj* devastating.

devastar *vt* to devastate.

devengar *vt* to accrue.

devoción *f* devotion, piety; strong affection; ardent love.

devolución *f* return; (*jur*) devolution.

devolutivo/va *adj* (*jur*) transferable.

devolver *vt* to return; to send back; to refund; to throw up; * *vi* to be sick.

devorar *vt* to devour, to swallow up.

devoto/ta *adj* devout, pious; devotional; strongly attached.

día *m* day.

diablo *m* devil.

diablura *f* prank.

diabólico/ca *adj* diabolical; devilish.

diácono *m* deacon.

diadema *m/f* diadem; halo.

diafragma *m* diaphragm; midriff.

diagnosis *f invar* diagnosis.

diagnóstico *m* diagnosis.

diagonal *adj* diagonal.

diagrama *m* diagram.

dialecto *m* dialect.

diálisis *f invar* dialysis.

diálogo *m* dialogue.

diamante *m* diamond.

diámetro *m* diameter.

diana *f* (*mil*) reveille; bull's-eye.

diapasón *m* (*mus*) diapason, octave.

diapositiva *f* transparency, slide.

diario *m* journal, diary; daily newspaper; daily expenses *pl*; **~/ria** *adj* daily.

diarrea *f* diarrhoea.

dibujar *vt* to draw, to design.

dibujo *m* drawing; sketch, draft; description.

dicción *f* diction; style; expression.

diccionario *m* dictionary.

diciembre *m* December.

dictado *m* dictation.

dictador *m* dictator.

dictadura *f* dictatorship.

dictamen *m* opinion, notion; suggestion, insinuation; judgement.

dictar *vt* to dictate.

dicha *f* happiness, good fortune; **por ~** by chance.

dicho *m* saying; sentence; declaration; promise of marriage; **~/cha** *adj* said.

dichoso/sa *adj* happy, prosperous.

diecinueve *adj*, *m* nineteen.

dieciocho *adj*, *m* eighteen.

dieciséis *adj*, *m* sixteen.

diecisiete *adj*, *m* seventeen.

diente *m* tooth; fang; tusk.

diestro/tra *adj* right; dexterous, skilful, clever; sagacious, prudent; sly, cunning; * *m* skilful fencer; halter; bridle.

diesel, diésel adj diesel compd.
dieta f diet, regimen; diet, assembly; daily salary of judges.
diez adj, m ten.
diezmar vt to decimate.
diezmo m tithe.
difamación f defamation.
difamar vt to defame, to libel.
difamatorio/ria adj defamatory, calumnious.
diferencia f difference.
diferencial adj differential.
diferenciar vt to differentiate, to distinguish; ~se vr to differ, to distinguish oneself.
diferente adj different, unlike.
diferido/da adj recorded.
diferir vt to defer, to put off; to differ.
difícil adj difficult.
dificultad f difficulty.
dificultar vt to put difficulties in the way of; to render difficult.
dificultoso/sa adj difficult; painful.
difundir vt to diffuse, to spread; to divulge; ~se vr to spread (out).
difunto/ta adj dead, deceased; late.
difusión f diffusion.
difuso/sa adj diffusive, copious; large; prolix, circumstantial.
digerir vt to digest; to bear with patience; to adjust, to arrange; (chem) to digest.
digestión f digestion; concoction.
digestivo/va adj digestive.
digital adj digital.
digitalizar vt to digitize.
dignarse vr to condescend, to deign.
dignidad f dignity, rank.
digno/na adj worthy; suitable.
dije m relic; trinket.
dilapidar vt to squander, to waste.
dilatación f dilation, extension; greatness of mind; calmness.

dilatado/da adj large; numerous; prolix; spacious, extensive.
dilatar vt to dilate, to expand; to spread out; to defer, to protract.
dilatorio/ria adj dilatory.
dilema m dilemma.
diligencia f diligence; affair, business; call of nature; stage coach.
diligente adj diligent, assiduous; prompt, swift.
dilucidar vt to elucidate, to explain.
diluir vt to dilute.
diluviar vi to rain in torrents.
diluvio m flood, deluge, inundation; abundance.
dimensión f dimension; extent; capacity, bulk.
diminutivo/va adj diminutive.
diminuto/ta adj defective, faulty; minute, small.
dimisión f resignation.
dimitir vt to give up, to abdicate; * vi to resign.
dinámica f dynamics.
dinámico/ca adj dynamic.
dinamita f dynamite.
dínamo, dinamo f dynamo.
dinastía f dynasty.
dineral m large sum of money.
dinero m money.
diocesano/na adj diocesan.
diócesis f diocese.
Dios m God.
diosa f goddess.
diploma m diploma, patent.
diplomacia, diplomática f diplomacy.
diplomado/da adj qualified.
diplomático/ca adj diplomatic; * m/f diplomat.
diptongo m diphthong.
diputación f deputation.
diputado m deputy.

diputar *vt* to depute.

dique *m* dike, dam.

dirección *f* direction, guidance; administration; steering.

directivo/va *adj* governing.

directo/ta *adj* direct, straight; apparent, evident; live.

director/ra *m/f* director; conductor; president; manager; headmaster.

dirigir *vt* to direct; to conduct; to regulate, to govern; **~se** *vr* to go toward(s); to address oneself to.

discernimiento *m* discernment.

discernir *vt* to discern, to distinguish.

disciplina *f* discipline.

discípulo *m* disciple; scholar.

disco *m* disc; record; discus; light; face (of the sun or moon); lens (of a telescope) ; **~ compacto** compact disc.

díscolo/la *adj* ungovernable; peevish.

disconforme *adj* differing.

discordancia *f* disagreement, discord.

discordante *adj* dissonant, discordant.

discordar *vi* to clash, to disagree.

discorde *adj* discordant; (*mus*) dissonant.

discordia *f* discord, disagreement.

discoteca *m* discotheque, disco.

discreción *f* discretion; acuteness of mind.

discrecional *adj* discretionary.

discrepancia *f* discrepancy.

discrepar *vi* to differ.

discreto/ta *adj* discreet; ingenious; witty, eloquent.

discriminación *f* discrimination.

disculpa *f* apology; excuse.

disculpar *vt* to exculpate, to excuse; to acquit, to absolve; **~se** *vr* to apologize; to excuse oneself.

discurrir *vi* to ramble about; to run to and fro; to discourse (upon a subject); * *vt* to invent, to contrive; to meditate.

discurso *m* speech; conversation; dissertation; space of time.

discusión *f* discussion.

discutir *vt, vi* to discuss.

disecar *vt* to dissect; to stuff.

disección *f* dissection.

diseminar *vt* to scatter; to disseminate, to propagate.

disentería *f* dysentery.

disentir *vi* to dissent, to disagree.

diseñador/ra *m/f* designer.

diseñar *vt* to draw; to design.

diseño *m* design; draft; description; picture.

disfraz *m* disguise; mask.

disfrazar *vt* to disguise, to conceal; to cloak, to dissemble; **~se** *vr* to disguise oneself as.

disfrutar *vt* to enjoy; **~se** *vr* to enjoy oneself.

disgustar *vt* to disgust; to offend; **~se** *vr* to be displeased; to fall out.

disgusto *m* disgust, aversion; quarrel; annoyance; grief, sorrow.

disidente *adj* dissident; * *m/f* dissident, dissenter.

disimular *vt* to hide; to tolerate.

disimulo *m* dissimulation; tolerance.

disipado/da *adj* prodigal, lavish.

disipar *vt* to dissipate, to disperse, to scatter; to lavish.

dislocación *f* dislocation.

dislocarse *vr* to be dislocated or out of joint.

disminución *f* diminution.

disminuir *vt* to diminish; to decrease.

disolución f dissolution; liquidation.

disolver vt to loosen, to untie; to dissolve; to disunite; to melt, to liquefy; to interrupt.

disonancia f dissonance; disagreement, discord.

disparar vt to shoot, to discharge, to fire; to let off; to throw with violence; * vi to shoot, to fire.

disparatado/da adj inconsistent; absurd, extravagant.

disparate m nonsense, absurdity, extravagance.

disparo m shot; discharge; explosion.

dispensar vt to dispense; to excuse; to dispense with; to distribute.

displicencia f displeasure; dislike.

disponer vt to arrange, to prepare; to dispose.

disponible adj available; disposable.

disposición f disposition, order; resolution; command; power, authority.

dispositivo m device.

dispuesto/ta adj disposed; fit, ready.

disputa f dispute, controversy.

disputar vt to dispute, to controvert, to question; * vi to debate, to argue.

disquete m floppy disk.

distancia f distance; interval; difference.

distanciarse vr to become estranged.

distante adj distant, far off.

distinción f distinction; difference; prerogative.

distinguido/da adj distinguished, conspicuous.

distinguir vt to distinguish; to discern; ~**se** vr to distinguish oneself.

distintivo m distinctive mark; particular attribute.

distinto/ta adj distinct, different; clear.

distracción f distraction, want of attention.

distraer vt to distract; ~**se** vr to be absent-minded, to be inattentive.

distraído/da adj absent-minded, inattentive.

distribución f distribution; division, separation; arrangement.

distribuidor m distributor.

distribuir vt to distribute.

distrito m district; territory.

disturbar vt to disturb, to interrupt.

disturbio m riot; disturbance, interruption.

disuadir vt to dissuade.

disuasión f dissuasion.

diurno/na adj daily.

diva f prima donna.

divagar vt to digress.

diván m divan.

divergencia f divergence.

divergente adj divergent.

diversidad f diversity; variety of things.

diversificar vt to diversify; to vary.

diversión f diversion; sport; amusement; (mil) diversion.

diverso/sa adj diverse, different; several, sundry.

divertido/da adj amused; amusing.

divertir vt to divert (the attention); to amuse, to entertain; (mil) to draw off; ~**se** vr to amuse oneself.

dividir vt to divide; to disunite; to separate; to share out.

divieso m (med) boil.

divinidad f divinity.

divino/na adj divine, heavenly; excellent.

divisa f emblem.

divisar vt to perceive.

divisible *adj* divisible.

división *f* division; partition; separation; difference.

divorciar *vt* to divorce; to separate; ~**se** *vr* to get divorced.

divorcio *m* divorce; separation, disunion.

divulgación *f* publication; dissemination.

divulgar *vt* to publish, to divulge.

dobladillo *m* hem; turn-up.

dobladura *f* fold.

doblar *vt* to double; to fold; to bend; * *vi* to turn; to toll; ~**se** *vr* to bend, to bow, to submit.

doble *adj* double; dual; deceitful; **al** ~ doubly; * *m* double.

doblegar *vt* to bend; ~**se** *vr* to yield.

doblez *m* crease; fold; turn-up; * *f* duplicity.

doce *adj*, *m* twelve.

docena *f* dozen.

docente *adj* teaching.

dócil *adj* docile, tractable.

docilidad *f* docility, gentleness; compliance.

doctor/ra *m/f* doctor.

doctorado *m* doctorate.

doctrina *f* doctrine, instruction; science.

doctrinal *m* catechism; * *adj* doctrinal.

documentación *f* documentation.

documento *m* document; record.

dogma *m* dogma.

dólar *m* dollar.

dolencia *f* disease; affliction.

doler *vi* to feel pain; to ache; ~**se** *vr* to feel for the sufferings of others; to complain.

dolor *m* pain; aching, ache; affliction.

doloroso/sa *adj* painful.

domador/ra *m/f* tamer.

domar *vt* to tame; to subdue, to master.

domesticar *vt* to domesticate.

domiciliarse *vr* to establish oneself in a residence.

domicilio *m* domicile; home, abode.

dominación *f* domination; dominion; authority, power.

dominante *adj* dominant; domineering.

dominar *vt* to dominate; to be fluent in; ~**se** *vr* to moderate one's passions.

domingo *m* Sunday; (Christian) Sabbath.

dominguero/ra *adj* done or worn on Sunday; * *m/f* Sunday driver.

dominical *adj* Sunday.

dominio *m* dominion; domination; power, authority; domain.

donación *f* donation; gift.

donar *vt* to donate; to bestow.

donativo *m* contribution.

doncella *f* virgin, maiden; lady's maid.

donde *adv* where.

dónde *adv* where; **¿de dónde?** from where?; **¿por dónde?** where?

dondequiera *adv* anywhere.

dorado/da *adj* gilt *compd*; golden; * *m* gilding.

dorar *vt* to gild; (*fig*) to palliate.

dormilón/ona *m/f* dull, sleepy person.

dormir *vi* to sleep; ~**se** *vr* to fall asleep.

dormitorio *m* dormitory.

dorsal *adj* dorsal.

dos *adj*, *m* two.

doscientos/tas *adj pl* two hundred.

dosis *f invar* dose.

dotado/da *adj* gifted.

dotar *vt* to endow.

dote *f* dowry; **~s** *fpl* gifts *pl* of nature; endowments *pl*.

dragón *m* dragon; (*mil*) dragoon.

drama *m* drama.

dramático/ca *adj* dramatic.

dramatizar *vt* to dramatize.

dramaturgo/ga *m/f* dramatist.

droga *f* drug; stratagem; artifice, deceit.

drogadicción *f* drug addiction.

drogadicto/ta *m/f* drug addict.

droguería *f* hardware store.

dromedario *m* dromedary.

dubitativo/va *adj* doubtful, dubious; uncertain.

ducado *m* duchy; ducat.

ducha *f* shower; (*med*) douche.

ducharse *vr* to have a shower.

ducho/cha *adj* skilled, experienced.

duda *f* doubt; suspense; hesitation.

dudar *vt* to doubt.

dudoso/sa *adj* doubtful, dubious.

duelo *m* grief, affliction; mourning.

duende *m* elf, hobgoblin.

dueño/ña *m/f* owner; landlord/lady; employer.

dulce *adj* sweet; mild, gentle, meek; soft; * *m* sweet, candy.

dulcificar *vt* to sweeten.

dulzura *f* sweetness; gentleness; softness.

dúo *m* (*mus*) duo, duet.

duodécimo/ma *adj* twelfth.

duplicación *f* duplication.

duplicado *m* duplicate.

duplicar *vt* to duplicate, to double; to repeat.

duplicidad *f* duplicity; falseness.

duplo *m* double.

duque *m* duke.

duquesa *f* duchess.

duración *f* duration.

duradero/ra *adj* lasting, durable.

durante *adv* during.

durar *vi* to last, to continue.

durazno *m* peach; peach tree.

duraznero *m* peach tree.

dureza *f* hardness; harshness; **~ de oído** hardness of hearing.

durmiente *adj* sleeping; * *m* (*ferro*) sleeper.

duro/ra *adj* hard; cruel; harsh, rough; * *m* five peseta coin; * *adv* hard.

duunviro *m* magistrate in ancient Rome.

E

e *conj* and (before words starting with i and hi).

ea *interj* hey!, come on!; **¡~ pues!** well then!, let's see!

ebanista *m* cabinet-maker, carpenter.

ébano *m* ebony.

ebrio/ia *adj* drunk.

ebullición *f* boiling.

eccema *m* eczema.

echar *vt* to throw; to add; to fire; to pour out; to mail; to give off; to bud; **~se** *vr* to lie down; to rest; to stretch out.

eclesiástico/ca *adj* ecclesiastical.

eclipsar *vt* to eclipse; to outshine.

eclipse *m* eclipse.

eco *m* echo.

ecografía *f* ultrasound scan.

ecología *f* ecology.

ecologismo m green movement.

ecologista m/f ecologist, environmentalist.

economato m cut-price store.

economía f economy.

económico/ca adj economic; cheap; thrifty; financial; avaricious.

economista m/f economist.

ecosistema m ecosystem.

ecotasa f ecotax.

ecoturismo m ecotourism.

ecuación f equation.

ecuador m equator.

ecuánime adj level-headed.

ecuestre adj equestrian.

ecuménico/ca adj ecumenical; universal.

edad f age.

edecán m (mil) aide-de-camp.

edición f edition; publication.

edicto m edict.

edificación f construction.

edificante adj edifying, instructive.

edificar vt to build, to construct; to edify.

edificio m building; structure.

editar vt to edit; to publish.

editor/ra m/f editor; publisher.

educación f education; upbringing; (good) manners pl.

educador/ra m/f teacher, educator.

educando/da m/f pupil.

educar vt to educate, to instruct; to bring up.

efectivamente adv exactly; really; in fact.

efectivo/va adj effective; true; certain.

efecto m effect; consequence; purpose; ~ **invernadero** greenhouse effect ~**s** mpl effects pl, goods pl; **en** ~ in fact, really.

efectuar vt to effect, to carry out.

efeméride f event (remembered on its anniversary).

efervescencia f effervescence, fizziness.

eficacia f effectiveness, efficacy.

eficaz adj efficient; effective.

eficiente adj efficient.

efigie f effigy, image.

efímero/ra adj ephemeral.

efluvio m outflow.

efusión f effusion.

efusivo/va adj effusive.

égloga f (poet) eclogue.

egoísmo m selfishness.

egoísta m/f self-seeker; * adj selfish.

egregio/gia adj eminent, remarkable.

eje m axle; axis.

ejecución f execution.

ejecutar vt to execute, to carry out, to perform; to put to death; (jur) to attach, to seize.

ejecutivo/va adj executive; * m/f executive.

ejecutor/ra m/f executor; (jur) distrainer.

ejecutoria f (jur) writ of execution.

ejecutorio/ria adj (jur) executory.

ejemplar m specimen; copy; example; * adj exemplary.

ejemplificar vt to exemplify.

ejemplo m example; **por** ~ for example, for instance.

ejercer vt to exercise.

ejercicio m exercise.

ejercitación f exercise, practice.

ejercitar vt to exercise; ~**se** vr to train.

ejército m army.

ejote m green bean.

el art, m the.

él pn he, it.

elaboración f elaboration.

elaborado/da *adj* elaborate.

elaborar *vt* to elaborate.

elasticidad *f* elasticity.

elástico/ca *adj* elastic.

elección *f* election; choice.

elector/ra *m/f* elector.

electorado *m* electorate.

electoral *adj* electoral.

electricidad *f* electricity.

electricista *m/f* electrician.

eléctrico/ca *adj* electric, electrical.

electrización *f* electrification.

electrizar *vt* to electrify.

electrocardiograma *m* electrocardiogram.

electrocutar *vt* to electrocute.

electrodoméstico *m* (electrical) domestic appliance.

electrónico/ca *adj* electronic.

electrotecnia *f* electrical engineering.

elefante *m* elephant.

elegancia *f* elegance.

elegante *adj* elegant, fine.

elegía *f* elegy.

elegir *vt* to choose, to elect.

elemental *adj* elemental; elementary.

elemento *m* element; ~s *mpl* elements *pl*, rudiments *pl*, first principles *pl*.

elevación *f* elevation; highness; rise; haughtiness, pride; height; altitude.

elevar *vt* to raise; to elevate; ~se *vr* to rise; to be enraptured; to be conceited.

eliminar *vt* to eliminate, to remove.

eliminatoria *f* preliminary (round).

elipse *f* (*geom*) ellipse.

elipsis *f* (*gr*) ellipsis.

elite, élite *f* elite.

elixir *m* elixir.

ella *pn* she; it.

ello *pn* it.

elocución *f* elocution.

elocuencia *f* eloquence.

elocuente *adj* eloquent.

elogiar *vt* to praise, to eulogize.

elogio *m* eulogy, praise.

elote *m* corn on the cob.

elucidación *f* elucidation, explanation.

eludir *vt* to elude, to escape.

emanación *f* emanation.

emanar *vi* to emanate.

emancipación *f* emancipation.

emancipar *vt* to emancipate, to set free.

embadurnar *vt* to smear, to bedaub.

embajada *f* embassy.

embajador/ra *m/f* ambassador.

embalaje *m* packing, package.

embalar *vt* to bale, to pack in bales.

embaldosar *vt* to pave with tiles.

embalsamador *m* embalmer.

embalsamar *vt* to embalm.

embalse *m* reservoir.

embarazada *f* pregnant woman; * *adj* pregnant.

embarazar *vt* to embarrass; to make pregnant; ~se *vr* to become intricate.

embarazo *m* pregnancy; embarrassment; obstacle.

embarazoso/sa *adj* difficult; intricate, entangled.

embarcación *f* embarkation; any vessel or ship.

embarcadero *m* quay, wharf; port; harbour.

embarcar *vt* to embark; ~se *vr* to go on board; (*fig*) to get involved (in a matter).

embargar *vt* to lay on an embargo; to impede, to restrain.

embargo *m* embargo; **sin ~** still, however.

embarque *m* embarkation.

embastar *vt* to stitch, to tack.

embate *m* breakers *pl*, surf, surge; sudden attack.

embaucador/ra *m/f* swindler; impostor.

embaucar *vt* to deceive; to trick.

embebecer *vt* to fascinate; **~se** *vr* to be fascinated.

embebecimiento *m* amazement, astonishment; fascination.

embeber *vt* to soak; to saturate; * *vi* to shrink; **~se** *vr* to be enraptured; to be absorbed.

embelesamiento *m* rapture.

embelesar *vt* to amaze, to astonish.

embeleso *m* amazement, enchantment.

embellecer *vt* to embellish, to beautify.

emberrincharse *vr* to have a tantrum.

embestida *f* assault, violent attack.

embestir *vt* to assault, to attack.

emblanquecer *vt* to whiten; **~se** *vr* to grow white; to bleach.

emblema *m* emblem.

embobado/da *adj* amazed; fascinated.

embobamiento *m* astonishment; fascination.

embobar *vt* to amaze; to fascinate; **~se** *vr* to be amazed; to stand gaping.

embobecer *vt* to make silly; **~se** *vr* to get silly.

embobecimiento *m* silliness.

émbolo *m* plunger; piston.

embolsar *vt* to put money into (a purse); to pocket.

emborrachar *vt* to intoxicate, to inebriate; **~se** *vr* to get drunk.

emboscada *f* (*mil*) ambush.

emboscarse *vr* (*mil*) to lie in ambush.

embotar *vt* to blunt; **~se** *vr* to go numb.

embotellamiento *m* traffic jam.

embotellar *vt* to bottle (wine).

embozado/da *adj* covered; covert.

embozar *vt* to muffle (the face); (*fig*) to cloak, to conceal.

embozo *m* part of a cloak, veil or anything with which the face is muffled; covering of one's face.

embrague *m* clutch.

embrear *vt* to cover with tar or pitch.

embriagar *vt* to intoxicate, to inebriate; to transport, to enrapture.

embriaguez *f* intoxication, drunkenness; rapture, delight.

embrión *m* embryo.

embrollador/ra *m/f* troublemaker.

embrollar *vt* to muddle; to entangle, to embroil.

embrollo *m* muddle.

embromar *vt* to tease; to cajole, to wheedle.

embrujar *vt* to bewitch.

embrutecer *vt* to brutalize; **~se** *vr* to become depraved.

embudo *m* funnel.

embuste *m* fraud; lie, fib (*sl*).

embustero/ra *m/f* impostor, cheat; liar; * *adj* deceitful.

embutido *m* sausage; inlay.

embutir *vt* to insert; to stuff; to inlay; to cram, to scoff.

emergencia *f* emergency.

emerger *vi* to emerge, to appear.

emético/ca *adj* emetic.

emigración *f* emigration; migration.

emigrado/da *adj* emigrated; * *m/f* emigrant.

emigrante *m/f* emigrant.

emigrar *vi* to emigrate.
eminencia *f* eminence.
eminente *adj* eminent, high; excellent, conspicuous.
emisario *m* emissary.
emisión *f* emission; broadcasting; programme; issue.
emisora *f* broadcasting station.
emitir *vt* to emit, to send forth; to issue; to broadcast.
emoción *f* emotion; feeling; excitement.
emocionante *adj* exciting.
emocionar *vt* to excite; to move, to touch.
emoliente *adj* emollient, softening.
emolumento *m* emolument.
emotivo/va *adj* emotional.
empacar *vt* to pack; to crate.
empachar *vt* to give indigestion; ~se *vr* to have indigestion.
empacho *m* (*med*) indigestion.
empachoso/sa *adj* indigestible.
empadronamiento *m* register; census.
empadronarse *vr* to register.
empalagar *vt* to sicken; to disgust.
empalago *m* disgust; boredom.
empalagoso/sa *adj* cloying; tiresome.
empalizada *f* (*mil*) palisade.
empalmadura *f* join; weld; splice.
empalmar *vt* to join.
empalme *m* (*ferro*) junction; connection.
empanada *f* (meat) pie.
empanar *vt* to cover with breadcrumbs.
empantanarse *vr* to get swamped; to get bogged down.
empañar *vt* to put a nappy on; to mist; to steam up; ~se *vr* to steam up; to tarnish one's reputation.

empapar *vt* to soak; to soak up; ~se *vr* to soak.
empapelar *vt* to paper.
empaquetar *vt* to pack, to parcel up.
emparedado *m* sandwich.
emparejar *vt* to level; to match, to fit; to equalize.
emparentar *vi* to be related by marriage.
emparrado *m* vine arbor.
empastar *vt* to paste; (*med*) to fill (a tooth).
empaste *m* (*med*) filling.
empatar *vi* to draw.
empate *m* draw.
empedernido/da *adj* inveterate; heartless.
empedernir *vt* to harden; ~se to be inflexible.
empedrado *m* paving.
empedrador *m* paver.
empedrar *vt* to pave.
empeine *m* instep.
empellón *m* push; heavy blow.
empeñado/da *adj* determined; pawned.
empeñar *vt* to pawn, to pledge; ~se *vr* to pledge oneself to pay debts; to get into debt; ~se en algo to insist on something.
empeño *m* obligation; determination; perseverance.
empeorar *vt* to make worse; * *vi*, ~se *vr* to grow worse.
empequeñecer *vt* to dwarf; (*fig*) to belittle.
emperador *m* emperor.
emperatriz *f* empress.
emperifollarse *vt* to dress oneself up.
empero *conj* yet, however.
emperrarse *vr* to get stubborn; to be obstinate.

empezar *vt* to begin, to start.

empinado/da *adj* high; proud.

empinar *vt* to raise; to exalt; * *vi* to drink heavily; ~**se** *vr* to stand on tiptoe; to soar.

empírico/ca *adj* empirical.

empirismo *m* empiricism.

empizarrado *m* slate roofing.

empizarrar *vt* to slate, to roof with slate.

emplasto *m* plaster.

emplazamiento *m* summons; location.

emplazar *vt* to summon; to locate.

empleado/da *m/f* official; employee.

emplear *vt* to employ; to occupy; to commission.

empleo *m* employ, employment, occupation.

empobrecer *vt* to reduce to poverty; * *vi* to become poor.

empobrecimiento *m* impoverishment.

empollar *vt* to incubate; to hatch; (*fam*) to swot (up).

empolvar *vt* to powder; to sprinkle powder upon.

emponzoñador/ra *m/f* poisoner.

emponzoñamiento *m* poisoning.

emponzoñar *vt* to poison; to taint, to corrupt.

emporio *m* emporium.

empotrado/da *adj* built-in.

empotrar *vt* to embed; to build in.

emprendedor/ra *m/f* entrepreneur.

emprender *vt* to embark on; to tackle; to undertake.

empresa *f* (*com*) company; enterprise, undertaking.

empresario/ria *m/f* manager.

empréstito *m* loan.

empujar *vt* to push; to press forward.

empuje *m* thrust; pressure; (*fig*) drive.

empujón *m* push; impulse; **a ~ones** in fits and starts.

empuñadura *f* hilt (of a sword).

empuñar *vt* to clench, to grip with the fist; to clutch.

emulación *f* emulation.

emular *vt* to emulate, to rival.

emulsión *f* emulsion.

en *prep* in; for; on, upon.

enaguas *fpl* petticoat.

enajenación *f* alienation; absent-mindedness.

enajenamiento *m* alienation; absent-mindedness.

enajenar *vt* to alienate; ~**se** *vr* to fall out.

enamoradamente *adv* lovingly.

enamoradizo/za *adj* inclined to fall in love.

enamorado/da *adj* in love, lovesick.

enamoramiento *m* falling in love.

enamorar *vt* to inspire love in; ~**se** *vr* to fall in love.

enano/na *adj* dwarfish; * *m* dwarf.

enarbolar *vt* to hoist, to raise high.

enardecer *vt* to fire with passion, to inflame.

enarenar *vt* to fill with sand.

encabezamiento *m* heading; foreword.

encabezar *vt* to head; to put a heading to; to lead.

encabritarse *vr* to rear (of horses).

encadenamiento *m* linking together, chaining.

encadenar *vt* to chain, to link together; to connect, to unite.

encajadura *f* insertion; socket; groove.

encajar *vt* to insert; to drive in; to encase; to intrude; ~**se** *vr* to squeeze; to gatecrash; * *vi* to fit (well).

encaje *m* encasing; joining; socket; groove; inlaid work.

encajera *f* lacemaker.

encajonamiento *m* packing into boxes, etc.

encajonar *vt* to pack up in a box.

encalabrinar *vt* to make confused; ~se *vr* to become obstinate.

encaladura *f* whitening, whitewash.

encalar *vt* to whitewash.

encallar *vi* (*mar*) to run aground.

encallecer *vi* to get corns.

encamarse *vr* to take to one's bed.

encaminar *vt* to guide, to show the way; ~se *vr*: ~ a to take the road to.

encandilar *vt* to dazzle.

encanecer *vi* to grow grey; to grow old.

encantado/da *adj* bewitched; delighted; pleased.

encantador/ra *adj* charming; *m/f* magician.

encantamiento *m* enchantment.

encantar *vt* to enchant, to charm; (*fig*) to delight.

encanto *m* enchantment; spell, charm.

encañonar *vt* to hold up; to point a gun at; * *vi* to grow feathers.

encapotar *vt* to cover with a cloak; ~se *vr* to be cloudy.

encapricharse *vr* to become stubborn.

encapuchar *vt* to cover with a hood.

encaramar *vt* to raise; to extol.

encararse *vr*: ~ a to come face to face with.

encarcelación *f* incarceration.

encarcelar *vt* to imprison.

encarecer *vt* to raise the price of; ~se *vr* to get dearer.

encarecimiento *m* price increase; con ~ insistently.

encargado/da *adj* in charge; * *m/f* representative; person in charge.

encargar *vt* to charge; to commission.

encargo *m* charge; commission; job; order.

encariñarse *vr*: ~ con to grow fond of.

encarnación *f* incarnation, embodiment.

encarnado/da *adj* incarnate; flesh-coloured; * *m* flesh colour.

encarnar *vt* to embody, to personify.

encarnizado/da *adj* bloodshot, inflamed; bloody, fierce.

encarrilar *vt* to put back on the rails; to put on the right track.

encasillar *vt* to pigeonhole; to typecast.

encasquetar *vt* to pull on (a hat).

encastillarse *vr* to refuse to yield.

encauzar *vt* to channel.

encebollado *m* casserole of beef or lamb and onions, seasoned with spice.

encenagado/da *adj* muddy, mud-stained.

encenagamiento *m* wallowing in mud.

encenagarse *vr* to wallow in mud.

encendedor *m* lighter.

encender *vt* to kindle, to light, to set on fire; to inflame, to incite; to switch on, to turn on; ~se *vr* to catch fire; to flare up.

encendido/da *adj* inflamed; high-coloured; * *m* ignition (of car).

encerado *m* blackboard.

encerar *vt* to wax; to polish.

encerrar *vt* to shut up, to confine; to contain; ~se *vr* to withdraw from the world.

encespedar *vt* to turf.

enchapar *vt* to veneer.

encharcarse *vr* to be flooded.

enchufar *vt* to plug in; to connect.

enchufe *m* plug; socket; connection; (*fam*) contact, connection.

encía *f* gum (of the teeth).

encíclica *f* encyclical.

enciclopedia *f* encyclopedia.

enciclopédico/ca *adj* encyclopedic.

encierro *m* confinement; enclosure; prison; bull-pen; penning (of bulls).

encima *adv* above; over; at the top; besides; ~ **de** *prep* above; over; at the top of; besides.

encina *f* holm oak, evergreen oak.

encinar *m* oakwood; oak grove.

encinta *adj* pregnant.

enclaustrado/da *adj* cloistered; hidden away.

enclenque *adj* weak, sickly; * *m* weakling.

encoger *vt* to contract, to shorten; to shrink; to discourage; ~**se** *vr* to shrink; (*fig*) to cringe.

encogidamente *adv* shyly, timidly, bashfully.

encogido/da *adj* shy, timid, bashful.

encogimiento *m* contraction; shrinkage; shyness; timidness; bashfulness.

encoladura *f* gluing.

encolar *vt* to glue.

encolerizar *vt* to provoke, to irritate; ~**se** *vr* to get angry.

encomendar *vt* to recommend; to entrust; ~**se** *vr*: ~ **a** to entrust oneself to; to put one's trust in.

encomiar *vt* to praise.

encomienda *m* commission, charge; message; (*mil*) command; patronage, protection; parcel post.

encomio *m* eulogy, praise; commendation.

enconar *vt* to inflame; to irritate.

encono *m* ill-feeling, rancour.

enconoso/sa *adj* hurtful, prejudicial; malevolent.

encontrado/da *adj* conflicting; hostile.

encontrar *vt* to meet, to encounter; *vr*: ~**se con** to run into; * *vi* to assemble, to come together.

encopetado/da *adj* presumptuous, boastful.

encorvadura *f* curvature; crookedness.

encorvar *vt* to bend, to curve.

encrespar *vt* to curl, to frizzle (hair); (*fig*) to anger; ~**se** *vr* to get rough (of the sea); (*fig*) to get cross.

encrucijada *f* crossroads; junction.

encuadernación *f* binding.

encuadernador/ra *m/f* bookbinder.

encuadernar *vt* to bind (books).

encubiertamente *adv* secretly; deceitfully.

encubierto/ta *adj* hidden, concealed.

encubridor/ra *m/f* concealer, harbourer; receiver of stolen goods.

encubrimiento *m* concealment, hiding; receiving of stolen goods.

encubrir *vt* to hide, to conceal.

encuentro *m* meeting; collision, crash; match, game.

encuesta *f* inquiry; opinion poll.

encumbrado/da *adj* high; elevated.

encumbramiento *m* elevation; height.

encumbrar *vt* to raise, to elevate; ~**se** *vr* to be raised; (*fig*) to become conceited.

encurtir *vt* to pickle.

endeble *adj* feeble, weak.

endecasílabo/ba *adj* consisting of eleven syllables.

endecha *f* dirge, lament.

endemoniado/da *adj* possessed with the devil; devilish.

enderezamiento *m* guidance, direction.

enderezar *vt* to straighten out; to set right; ~**se** *vr* to stand upright.

endeudarse *vr* to get into debt.

endiablado/da *adj* devilish, diabolical; ugly.

endiosar *vt* to deify; ~**se** *vr* to be high and mighty.

endosar *vt* to endorse.

endoso *m* endorsement.

endrina *f* sloe.

endrino *m* blackthorn, sloe.

endulzar *vt* to sweeten; to soften.

endurecer *vt* to harden, to toughen; ~**se** *vr* to become cruel; to grow hard.

endurecidamente *adv* cruelly.

endurecimiento *m* hardness; obstinacy; hard-heartedness.

enebro *m* (*bot*) juniper.

enemigo/ga *adj* hostile; * *m* enemy.

enemistad *f* enmity.

enemistar *vt* to make an enemy; ~**se** *vr* to become enemies; to fall out.

energía *f* energy, power, drive; strength of will; ~ **nuclear** nuclear power; ~ **solar** solar energy; ~ **renovables** renewable forms of energy.

enérgico/ca *adj* energetic; forceful.

energúmeno/na *m/f* (*fam*) madman/woman.

enero *m* January.

enervar *vt* to enervate.

enfadadizo/za *adj* irritable, crotchety.

enfadar *vt* to anger, to irritate; to trouble; ~**se** *vr* to become angry.

enfado *m* trouble; anger.

enfadoso/sa *adj* annoying, troublesome.

énfasis *m* emphasis.

enfático/ca *adj* emphatic.

enfermar *vi* to fall ill; * *vt* to make sick; to weaken.

enfermedad *f* illness.

enfermería *f* infirmary; sick bay.

enfermero/ra *m/f* nurse.

enfermizo/za *adj* infirm, sickly.

enfermo/ma *adj* sick, ill; * *m/f* invalid, sick person; patient.

enfervorizar *vt* to arouse; to inflame, to incite.

enflaquecer *vt* to weaken; to make thin.

enflaquecimiento *m* loss of weight; (*fig*) weakening.

enfocar *vt* to focus; to consider (a problem).

enfoque *m* focus.

enfrascarse *vr* to be deeply embroiled.

enfrentar *vt* to confront; to put face to face; ~**se** *vr* to face each other; to meet (two teams).

enfrente *adv* over against, opposite; in front.

enfriamiento *m* refrigeration; (*med*) cold.

enfriar *vt* to cool; to refrigerate; ~**se** *vr* to cool down; (*med*) to catch a cold.

enfurecer *vt* to madden, to enrage; ~**se** *vr* to get rough (of the wind and sea); to become furious or enraged.

enfurruñarse *vr* to get sulky; to frown.

engalanar *vt* to adorn, to deck.

engallarse *vr* to be arrogant.

engañabobos *m invar* trickster; trick, trap.

engañadizo/za *adj* gullible, easily deceived.

engañador/ra *adj* cheating; deceptive; * *m/f* cheat, impostor, deceiver.

engañar *vt* to deceive, to cheat; ~se *vr* to be deceived; to make a mistake.

enganchar *vt* to hook, to hang up; to hitch up; to couple, to connect; to recruit into military service; ~se *vr* (*mil*) to enlist.

engañifa *f* deceit, trick.

engaño *m* mistake; misunderstanding; deceit, fraud.

engañoso/sa *adj* deceitful, artful, false.

engarzar *vt* to thread; to link; to curl.

engastar *vt* to set, to mount.

engaste *m* setting, mount.

engatusamiento *m* deception, coaxing.

engatusar *vt* to coax.

engendrar *vt* to beget, to engender; to produce.

engendro *m* foetus, embryo; (*fig*) monstrosity; brainchild.

englobar *vt* to include.

engolfarse *vr* (*mar*) to sail out to sea; ~ **en** to be deeply involved in.

engolosinar *vt* to entice; ~se *vr* to find delight in.

engomadura *f* gluing.

engomar *vt* to glue.

engordar *vt* to fatten; * *vi* to grow fat; to put on weight.

engorro *m* nuisance, bother.

engorroso/sa *adj* troublesome, cumbersome.

engranaje *m* gear; gearing.

engrandecer *vt* to augment; to magnify; to speak highly of; to exaggerate.

engrandecimiento *m* increase; aggrandizement; exaggeration.

engrasar *vt* to grease, to lubricate.

engreído/da *adj* conceited, vain.

engreimiento *m* presumption, vanity.

engreír *vt* to make proud; ~se *vr* to grow proud.

engrosar *vt* to enlarge; to increase.

engrudo *m* paste.

engullidor/ra *m/f* devourer; guzzler.

engullir *vt* to swallow; to gobble, to devour.

enharinar *vt* to cover or sprinkle with flour.

enhebrar *vt* to thread.

enhilar *vt* to thread.

enhorabuena *f* congratulations *pl*; * *interj* congratulations.

enhoramala *interj* good riddance.

enigma *m* enigma, riddle.

enigmático/ca *adj* enigmatic; dark, obscure.

enjabonar *vt* to soap; (*fam*) to tick off.

enjaezar *vt* to harness (a horse).

enjalbegar *vt* to whitewash.

enjambre *m* swarm (of bees); crowd, multitude.

enjaular *vt* to shut up in a cage; to imprison.

enjoyar *vt* to adorn with jewels.

enjuagar *vt* to rinse out; to wash out.

enjuague *m* (*med*) mouthwash; rinsing, rinse.

enjugar *vt* to dry (the tears); to wipe off.

enjuiciar *vt* to prosecute, to try; to pass judgement on, to judge.

enjuto/ta *adj* dried up; (*fig*) lean.

enlace *m* connection, link; relationship.

enladrillado *m* brick paving.

enladrillador *m* bricklayer.

enladrillar *vt* to pave with bricks.

enlazable *adj* able to be fastened together.

enlazar *vt* to join, to unite; to tie.

enlodar *vt* to cover in mud; (*fig*) to stain.

enloquecer *vt* to madden, to drive crazy; * *vi* to go mad.

enloquecimiento *m* madness.

enlosar *vt* to lay with flags.

enlutar *vt* to put into mourning; ~**se** *vr* to go into mourning.

enmaderar *vt* to roof with timber.

enmarañar *vt* to entangle; to complicate; to confuse; ~**se** *vr* to become entangled; to get confused.

enmascarar *vt* to mask; ~**se** *vr* to go in disguise, to masquerade.

enmendar *vt* to correct; to reform; to repair, to compensate for; to amend; ~**se** *vr* to mend one's ways.

enmienda *f* correction, amendment.

enmohecer *vt* to make mouldy; to rust; ~**se** *vr* to grow mouldy or musty; to rust.

enmohecido/da *adj* mouldy. **enmudecer(se)** *vt* to silence; ~**se** *vr* to grow dumb; to be silent.

ennegrecer *vt* to blacken; to darken; to obscure.

ennoblecer *vt* to ennoble.

ennoblecimiento *m* ennoblement.

enojadizo/za *adj* peevish; short-tempered, irritable.

enojar *vt* to irritate, to make angry; to annoy; to upset; to offend; ~**se** *vr* to get angry.

enojo *m* anger, annoyance.

enojoso/sa *adj* offensive, annoying.

enorgullecerse *vr*: ~ **(de)** to be proud (of).

enorme *adj* enormous, vast, huge; horrible.

enormidad *f* enormity; monstrousness.

enramar *vt* to cover with the branches of trees.

enranciarse *vr* to grow rancid.

enrarecer *vt* to thin, to rarefy.

enredadera *f* climbing plant; bindweed.

enredador/ra *m/f* gossip; troublemaker; busybody.

enredar *vt* to entangle, to ensnare, to confound, to perplex; to puzzle; to sow discord among; ~**se** *vr* to get entangled; to get complicated; to get embroiled.

enredo *m* entanglement; mischievous lie; plot of a play.

enredoso/sa *adj* complicated.

enrejado *m* trelliswork.

enrejar *vt* to fix a grating to (a window); to grate, to lattice.

enrevesado/da *adj* complicated.

enriquecer *vt* to enrich; to adorn; ~**se** *vr* to grow rich.

enristrar *vt* to string (garlic); to straighten out; to go straight to.

enrobustecer *vt* to strengthen.

enrojecer *vt* to redden; * *vi* to blush.

enrolar *vt* to recruit; ~**se** *vr* (*mil*) to join up.

enrollar *vt* to roll (up).

enronquecer *vt* to make hoarse; * *vi* to grow hoarse.

enroscadura *f* twist.

enroscar *vt* to twist; ~**se** *vr* to curl or roll up.

ensalada *f* salad.

ensaladera *f* salad bowl.

ensaladilla (rusa) *f* Russian salad.

ensalmar *vt* to set (dislocated bones); to heal by spells.

ensalmo *m* enchantment, spell.

ensalzar *vt* to exalt, to aggrandize; to exaggerate.

ensamblador/ra *m/f* joiner.

ensamblar *vt* to assemble.

ensanchar *vt* to widen; to extend; to enlarge; ~**se** *vr* to expand; to assume an air of importance.

ensanche *m* dilation, augmentation; widening; expansion.

ensangrentar *vt* to stain with blood.

ensañar *vt* to irritate, to enrage; ~**se con** *vr* to treat brutally.

ensartar *vt* to string (beads, etc).

ensayar *vt* to test; to rehearse.

ensayo *m* test, trial; rehearsal of a play; essay.

ensenada *f* creek.

enseña *f* colours *pl*, standard.

enseñanza *f* teaching, instruction; education.

enseñar *vt* to teach, to instruct; to show.

enseres *mpl* belongings *pl*.

ensillar *vt* to saddle.

ensimismarse *vr* to be or become lost in thought.

ensoberbecer *vt* to make proud; ~**se** *vr* to become proud; (*mar*) to get rough.

ensordecer *vt* to deafen; * *vi* to grow deaf.

ensordecimiento *m* deafness.

ensortijamiento *m* curling the hair.

ensortijar *vt* to fix a ring in; to curl.

ensuciar *vt* to stain, to soil; to defile; ~**se** *vr* to wet oneself; to dirty oneself.

ensueño *m* fantasy; daydream; illusion.

entablar *vt* to board (up); to strike up (conversation).

entablillar *vt* (*med*) to put in a splint.

entallar *vt* to tailor (a suit); * *vi* to fit.

ente *m* organization; entity, being; (*fam*) odd character.

entendederas *fpl* understanding; brains *pl*.

entender *vt*, *vi* to understand, to comprehend; to remark, to take notice (of); to reason, to think; **a mi ~** in my opinion; ~**se** *vr* to understand each other.

entendido/da *adj* understood; wise; learned, knowing.

entendimiento *m* understanding; knowledge; judgement.

enteramente *adv* entirely, completely.

enterar *vt* to inform; to instruct; ~**se** *vr* to find out.

entereza *f* entireness, integrity; firmness of mind.

enternecer *vt* to soften; to move (to pity); ~**se** *vr* to be moved.

enternecimiento *m* compassion, pity.

entero/ra *adj* entire, complete; perfect; honest; resolute; **por ~** entirely, completely.

enterrador *m* gravedigger.

enterrar *vt* to inter, to bury.

entibiar *vt* to cool.

entidad *f* entity; company; body; society.

entierro *m* burial; funeral.

entoldar *vt* to cover with an awning.

entomología *f* entomology.

entonación *f* intonation; modulation; (*fig*) presumption, pride.

entonar *vt* to tune, to intone; to tone; * *vi* to be in tune; ~**se** *vr* to give oneself airs.

entonces *adv* then, at that time.

entontecer *vt* to fool; * *vi*, ~**se** *vr* to get silly.

entontecimiento *m* silliness.

entornar *vt* to half close.

entorpecer *vt* to dull; to make lethargic; to hinder; to delay.

entorpecimiento *m* numbness; lethargy.

entrada *f* entrance, entry; (*com*) receipts *pl*; entree; ticket (for cinema, theatre, etc).

entrambos/bas *pn, pl* both.

entrampar *vt* to trap, to snare; to mess up; to burden with debts; ~**se** *vr* get into debt.

entrañable *adj* intimate; affectionate.

entrañas *fpl* entrails *pl*, intestines *pl*.

entrante *adj* coming, next.

entrar *vi* to enter, to go in; to commence.

entre *prep* between; among(st); in; ~ **manos** in hand.

entreabrir *vt* to half open (a door), to leave ajar.

entrecano/na *adj* grey-black, greyish.

entrecejo *m* space between the eyebrows; frown.

entrecortado/da *adj* faltering; difficult.

entredicho *m* (*jur*) injunction; **estar en** ~ to be banned; **poner en** ~ to cast doubt on.

entrega *f* delivery; instalment.

entregar *vt* to deliver; to hand over; ~**se** *vr* to surrender; to devote oneself.

entrelazar *vt* to interlace.

entremedias *adv* in the meantime.

entremeses *mpl* hors d'oeuvres.

entremeter *vt* to put (one thing) between (others); ~**se** *vr* to interfere, to meddle.

entremetido/da *m/f* meddler; * *adj* meddling.

entremetimiento *m* insertion; meddling.

entrenador/ra *m/f* trainer, coach.

entrenar *vt* to train; ~**se** *vr* to train.

entreoír *vt* to half hear.

entrepaño *m* panel.

entrepierna *f* crotch.

entresaca *f* thinning out (of trees).

entresacar *vt* to thin out; to sift, to separate.

entresuelo *m* entresol; mezzanine.

entretanto *adv* meanwhile.

entretejer *vt* to interweave.

entretela *f* interfacing, stiffening, interlining.

entretener *vt* to amuse; to entertain, to divert; to hold up; to maintain; ~**se** *vr* to amuse oneself; to linger.

entretenido/da *adj* pleasant; amusing; entertaining.

entretenimiento *m* amusement, entertainment.

entrever *vt* to have a glimpse of.

entreverado/da *adj* patchy; streaky.

entrevista *f* interview.

entrevistar *vt* to interview; ~**se** *vr* to have an interview.

entristecer *vt* to sadden.

entrometer *vt* to put (one thing) between (others); ~**se** *vr* to interfere, to meddle.

entrometido/da *m/f* meddler; * *adj* meddling.

entroncar *vi* to be related or connected.

entronización *f* enthronement.

entronizar *vt* to enthrone.

entumecer *vt* to swell; to numb; ~**se** *vr* to become numb.

entumecido/da *adj* numb, stiff.

entumecimiento *m* numbness.

enturbiar *vt* to make cloudy; to obscure, to confound; ~**se** *vr* to become cloudy; (*fig*) to get confused.

entusiasmar *vt* to excite, to fill with enthusiasm; to delight.

entusiasmo *m* enthusiasm.

entusiasta *m/f* enthusiast.

enumeración *f* enumeration.

enumerar *vt* to enumerate.

enunciación *f*, **enunciado** *m* enunciation, declaration.

enunciar *vt* to enunciate, to declare.

envainar *vt* to sheathe, to sheath.

envalentonar *vt* to give courage to; ~**se** *vr* to boast.

envanecer *vt* to make vain; to swell with pride; ~**se** *vr* to become proud.

envaramiento *m* stiffness; numbness.

envarar *vt* to numb.

envasar *vt* to pack; to bottle; to can.

envase *m* packing; bottling; canning; container; package; bottle; can.

envejecer *vt* to make old; * *vi*, ~**se** *vr* to grow old.

envenenador/ra *m/f* poisoner.

envenenar *vt* to poison; to embitter.

envenenamiento *m* poisoning.

envergadura *f* (*fig*) scope.

envés *m* wrong side (of material).

enviado/da *m/f* envoy, messenger.

enviar *vt* to send, to transmit, to convey, to dispatch.

enviciar *vt* to vitiate, to corrupt; ~**se** *vr* to get corrupted.

envidia *f* envy; jealousy.

envidiable *adj* enviable.

envidiar *vt* to envy; to grudge; to be jealous of.

envidioso/sa *adj* envious; jealous.

envilecer *vt* to vilify, to debase; ~**se** *vr* to degrade oneself.

envío *m* (*com*) dispatch, remittance of goods; consignment.

enviudar *vi* to become a widower or widow.

envoltorio *m* bundle of clothes.

envoltura *f* cover; wrapping.

envolver *vt* to involve; to wrap up.

enyesar *vt* to plaster; (*med*) to put in a plaster cast.

enzarzarse *vr* to get involved in a dispute; to get oneself into trouble.

épico/ca *adj* epic.

epicúreo/rea *adj* epicurean.

epidemia *f* epidemic.

epidémico/ca *adj* epidemic.

epidermis *f* epidermis; cuticle.

Epifanía *f* Epiphany.

epígrafe *f* epigraph, inscription; motto; headline.

epigrama *m* epigram.

epilepsia *f* epilepsy.

epílogo *m* epilogue.

episcopado *m* episcopacy; bishopric.

episcopal *adj* episcopal.

episódico/ca *adj* episodic.

episodio *m* episode, instalment.

epístola *f* epistle, letter.

epistolar *adj* epistolary.

epistolario *m* collected letters *pl*.

epitafio *m* epitaph.

epíteto *m* epithet.

epítome *m* epitome; compendium.

época *f* epoch; period, time.

epopeya *f* epic.

equidad *f* equity, honesty; impartiality, justice.

equidistar *vi* to be equidistant.

equilátero/ra *adj* equilateral.

equilibrar *vt* to balance; to poise.

equilibrio *m* balance, equilibrium.

equinoccial *adj* equinoctial.

equinoccio *m* equinox.

equipaje *m* luggage; equipment.

equipar *vt* to fit out, to equip, to furnish.

equipararse *vr*: ~ **con** to be on a level with.

equipo *m* equipment; team; shift.

equitación *f* horsemanship; riding.

equitativo/va *adj* equitable; just.

equivalencia *f* equivalence.

equivalente *adj* equivalent.

equivaler *vi* to be of equal value.

equivocación *f* mistake, error; misunderstanding.

equivocado/da *adj* mistaken, wrong.

equivocar *vt* to mistake; ~**se** *vr* to make a mistake, to be wrong.

equívoco/ca *adj* equivocal, ambiguous; * *m* equivocation; quibble.

era *f* era, age; threshing floor.

erario *m* treasury, public funds *pl*.

erección *f* foundation, establishment; erection, elevation.

erguir *vt* to erect, to raise up straight; ~**se** *vr* to straighten up.

erial *m* fallow land.

erigir *vt* to erect, to raise, to build; to establish.

erizamiento *m* standing on end (of hair, etc).

erizarse *vr* to bristle; to stand on end.

erizo *m* hedgehog; ~ **de mar** sea urchin.

ermita *f* hermitage.

ermitaño *m* hermit.

erosionar *vt* to erode.

erótico/ca *adj* erotic.

erotismo *m* eroticism.

errante *adj* errant; stray; roving.

errar *vi* to be mistaken; to wander.

errata *f* misprint.

erre: ~ **que** ~ *adv* obstinately.

erróneo/nea *adj* erroneous.

error *m* error, mistake, fault.

eructar *vi* to belch, to burp.

eructo *m* belch, burp.

erudición *f* erudition, learning.

erudito/ta *adj* learned, erudite.

erupción *f* eruption, outbreak.

esa : *f* of **ese**.

ésa : *f* of **ése**.

esbelto/ta *adj* slim, slender.

esbirro *m* bailiff; henchman; killer.

esbozo *m* outline.

escabechar *vt* to marinate; to pickle.

escabeche *m* pickle; pickled fish.

escabel *m* footstool.

escabrosidad *f* unevenness, roughness; harshness.

escabroso/sa *adj* rough, uneven; craggy; rude, risqué, blue.

escabullirse *vr* to escape, to evade; to slip through one's fingers.

escafandra *f* diving suit; space suit.

escala *f* ladder; (*mus*) scale; stopover.

escalador/ra *m/f* climber.

escalar *vt* to climb.

escaldado/da *adj* cautious, suspicious, wary.

escaldar *vt* to scald.

escalera *f* staircase; ladder.

escalfar *vt* to poach (eggs).

escalofríos *mpl* shivers *pl*.

escalofriante *adj* chilling.

escalón *m* step of a stair; rung.

escama *f* (fish) scale.

escamado/da *adj* wary, cautious.

escamar *vt* to scale, to take off the scales; ~**se** *vr* to flake off; to become suspicious.

escamoso/sa *adj* scaly.

escamotear *vt* to swipe; to make disappear.

escampar *vi* to stop raining.

escanciador *m* wine waiter; cupbearer.

escanciar *vt* to pour (wine).

escandalizar *vt* to scandalize; ~**se** *vr* to be shocked.

escándalo *m* scandal; uproar.

escandaloso/sa *adj* scandalous; shocking.

escanear *vt* to scan.

escáner *m* scanner.

escaño *m* bench with a back; seat (parliament).

escapada *f* escape, flight.

escapar *vi* to escape; **~se** *vr* to get away; to leak (water, etc).

escaparate *m* shop window; wardrobe.

escapatoria *f* escape, flight; excuse.

escape *m* escape, flight; leak; exhaust (of motor); **a todo ~** at full speed.

escapulario *m* scapulary.

escarabajo *m* beetle.

escaramuza *f* skirmish; dispute, quarrel.

escaramuzar *vt* to skirmish.

escarbadura *f* act and effect of scratching.

escarbar *vt* to scratch (the earth as hens do); to inquire into.

escarcha *f* white frost.

escarchar *vi* to be frosty.

escardador *m* weeding hoe.

escardillo *m* small weeding hoe.

escarlata *adj* scarlet.

escarlatina *f* scarlet fever.

escarmentar *vi* to learn one's lesson; * *vt* to punish severely.

escarmiento *m* warning, caution; punishment.

escarnecer *vt* to mock, to ridicule.

escarnio *m* gibe, ridicule.

escarola *f* (*bot*) endive.

escarpa *f* slope; escarpment.

escarpado/da *adj* sloped; craggy.

escarpín *m* sock; pump (shoe).

escasear *vi* to be scarce.

escasez *f* shortage; poverty.

escaso/sa *adj* small, short, little; sparing; scarce; scanty.

escatimar *vt* to curtail, to lessen; to be scanty with.

escena *f* stage; scene.

escenario *m* stage; set.

escepticismo *m* scepticism.

escéptico/ca *adj* sceptic, sceptical.

esclarecer *vt* to lighten; to illuminate; to illustrate; to shed light on (problem, etc).

esclarecido/da *adj* illustrious, noble.

esclarecimiento *m* clarification; enlightenment.

esclavina *f* short cloak or cape.

esclavitud *f* slavery, servitude.

esclavizar *vt* to enslave.

esclavo/va *m/f* slave; captive.

esclusa *f* sluice, floodgate.

escoba *f* broom, brush.

escobazo *m* blow given with a broom.

escobilla *f* brush, small broom; blade.

escocer *vt* to sting; to burn; **~se** *vr* to chafe.

escoger *vt* to choose, to select.

escolar *m/f* schoolboy/girl; * *adj* scholastic.

escolástico/ca *adj* scholastic; * *m* scholar.

escollo *m* reef, rock.

escolta *f* escort.

escoltar *vt* to escort.

escombros *mpl* rubbish; debris.

esconder *vt* to hide, to conceal; **~se** *vr* to be hidden.

escondidas: a ~ *adv* in a secret manner.

escondite *m* hiding place; **juego del ~** hide-and-seek.

escondrijo *m* hiding place.

escopeta f shotgun; **a tiro de ~** within gunshot.

escopetazo m gunshot; gunshot wound.

escopetero m gunsmith.

escoplo m chisel.

escorbuto m scurvy.

escoria f dross; scum; dregs pl.

Escorpio m Scorpio (sign of the zodiac).

escorpión m scorpion.

escotado/da adj low-cut.

escotadura f low neck(line).

escotar vt to cut low in front.

escote m low neck (of a dress).

escotilla f (mar) hatchway.

escozor m smart; burning pain; sting(ing).

escriba m scribe (of the Hebrews).

escribanía f clerk's office; writing desk.

escribano m court clerk; notary.

escribiente m copyist.

escribir vt to write; to spell; * vi to write.

escrito m document; manuscript; text.

escritor/ra m/f writer, author.

escritorio m writing desk; office, study.

escritura f writing; deed.

escrúpulo m doubt, scruple, scrupulousness.

escrupulosidad f scrupulousness.

escrupuloso/sa adj scrupulous; exact.

escrutar vt to examine; to count (ballot papers).

escrutinio m scrutiny, inquiry.

escrutiñador m scrutinizer, inquirer.

escuadra f square; squadron; squad.

escuadrar vt to square.

escuadrón m squadron.

escuálido/da adj skinny; squalid.

escucha f listening(-in); * m scout.

escuchar vt to listen to, to heed.

escudar vt to shield; to guard from danger; **~se** vr to protect oneself.

escudero m squire; page.

escudilla f bowl.

escudo m shield.

escudriñamiento m investigation, scrutiny.

escudriñar vt to search, to examine; to pry into.

escuela f school; **~ primaria** primary school; **~ secundaria** secondary school.

escueto/ta adj plain; simple.

esculpir vt to sculpt.

escultor/ra m/f sculptor.

escultura f sculpture.

escupidera f cuspidor.

escupidura f spit.

escupir vt to spit.

escurreplatos m invar plate rack.

escurridizo/za adj slippery.

escurrir vt to drain; to drip; **~se** vr to slip away; to slip, to slide; * vi to wring out.

ese/esa adj that; **esos/as** pl those.

ése/ésa pn that (one); **ésos/as** pl those (ones).

esencia f essence.

esencial adj essential; principal.

esfera f sphere; globe.

esférico/ca adj spherical.

esferoide f spheroid.

esfinge m sphinx.

esforzado/da adj strong, vigorous; valiant.

esforzarse vr to exert oneself, to make an effort.

esfuerzo m effort.

esfumarse vr to fade away.

esgrima f fencing.

esgrimidor *m* fencer.

esgrimir *vi* to fence.

esguince *m* (*med*) sprain.

eslabón *m* link of a chain; steel; shackle.

eslabonar *vt* to link; to unite.

esmaltador *m* enameller.

esmaltar *vt* to enamel.

esmalte *m* enamel.

esmerado/da *adj* careful, neat.

esmeralda *m* emerald.

esmerar *vt* to polish; ~**se** *vr* to take great care; to work hard.

esmeril *m* emery.

esmerillar *vt* to polish with emery.

esmero *m* careful attention, great care.

esnob *adj* snobbish; posh; * *m/f* snob.

eso *pn* that.

esófago *m* oesophagus; throat.

esos, ésos *pl* of **ese, ése**.

espabilar *vt* to wake up; ~**se** *vr* to wake up; (*fig*) to get a move on.

espacial *adj* space *compd*.

espaciar *vt* to spread out; to space (out).

espacio *m* space; (radio or TV) programme.

espaciosidad *f* spaciousness, capacity.

espacioso/sa *adj* spacious, roomy.

espada *f* sword; ace of spades.

espadachín *m* bully.

espadaña *f* (*bot*) bulrush.

espadín *m* small short sword.

espaguetis *mpl* spaghetti.

espalda *f* back, back-part; ~**s** *fpl* shoulders *pl*.

espaldilla *f* shoulder blade.

espantadizo/za *adj* timid, easily frightened.

espantajo *m* scarecrow; bogeyman.

espantapájaros *m invar* scarecrow.

espantar *vt* to frighten; to chase or drive away.

espanto *m* fright; menace, threat; astonishment.

espantoso/sa *adj* frightful, dreadful; amazing.

español/la *adj* Spanish; * *m/f* Spaniard; * *m* Spanish (language).

esparadrapo *m* sticking plaster.

esparcir *vt* to scatter; to divulge; ~**se** *vr* to amuse oneself.

espárrago *m* asparagus.

esparto *m* (*bot*) esparto.

espasmo *m* spasm.

espátula *f* spatula.

especia *f* spice.

especial *adj* special; particular; **en** ~ especially.

especialidad *f* speciality.

especie *f* species; kind, sort; matter.

especificación *f* specification.

especificar *vt* to specify.

específico/ca *adj* specific.

espectáculo *m* spectacle; show.

espectador/ra *m/f* spectator.

espectro *m* spectre, phantom, ghost, apparition.

especulación *f* speculation; contemplation; venture.

especulador/ra *m/f* speculator.

especular *vt* to speculate.

especulativo/va *adj* speculative; thoughtful.

espejismo *m* mirage.

espejo *m* mirror.

espeluznante *adj* horrifying.

espera *f* stay, waiting; (*jur*) respite, adjournment, delay.

esperanza *f* hope.

esperanzar *vt* to give hope to.

esperar *vt* to hope; to expect, to wait for.

esperma f sperm.
espesar vt to thicken; to condense; ~**se** vr to grow thick; to solidify.
espeso/sa adj thick, dense.
espesor m thickness.
espesura f thickness; density, solidity.
espía m/f spy.
espiar vt to spy.
espiga f ear (of corn).
espigón m ear of corn; sting; (mar) breakwater.
espina f thorn; fishbone.
espinaca f (bot) spinach.
espinazo m spine, backbone.
espinilla f shinbone.
espino m hawthorn.
espinoso/sa adj thorny; dangerous.
espionaje m spying, espionage.
espiral adj, f spiral.
espirar vt to exhale.
espíritu m spirit, soul; mind; intelligence; **el E~ Santo** the Holy Ghost; ~**s** pl demons pl, hobgoblins pl.
espiritual adj spiritual; ghostly.
espiritualidad f spirituality.
espiritualizar vt to spiritualize.
esplendidez f splendour.
espléndido/da adj splendid.
esplendor m splendour.
espliego m (bot) lavender.
espolear vt to spur, to instigate, to incite.
espolón m spur (of a cock); spur (of a mountain range); sea wall; jetty; (mar) buttress.
espolvorear vt to sprinkle.
espondeo m (poet) spondee.
esponja f sponge.
esponjar vt to sponge; ~**se** vr to be puffed up with pride.
esponjoso/sa adj spongy.

esponsales mpl betrothal.
espontaneidad f spontaneity.
espontáneo/nea adj spontaneous.
esposa f wife.
esposar vt to handcuff.
esposas fpl handcuffs pl.
esposo m husband.
espuela f spur; stimulus; (bot) larkspur.
espuerta f pannier, basket.
espulgar vt to delouse; to examine closely.
espuma f froth, foam.
espumadera f skimmer.
espumajear vi to foam at the mouth.
espumar vt to skim, to take the scum off.
espumarajo m foam, froth (from the mouth).
espumoso/sa adj frothy, foamy; sparkling (wine).
espurio/ria adj spurious; adulterated; illegitimate.
esputo m spit, saliva.
esqueje m cutting (of plant).
esquela f note, slip of paper.
esqueleto m skeleton.
esquema m scheme; diagram; plan.
esquí m ski; skiing.
esquiar vi to ski.
esquife m skiff, small boat.
esquilador m sheep-shearer.
esquilar vt to shear sheep.
esquina f corner, angle.
esquinado/da adj cornered, angled.
esquinar vt to form a corner with.
esquirol m blackleg.
esquivar vt to shun, to avoid, to evade.
esquivez f disdain; shyness.
esquivo/va adj scornful; shy, reserved.
esta: f of **este**.

ésta: *f* of **éste**.
estabilidad *f* stability.
estable *adj* stable.
establecer *vt* to establish.
establecimiento *m* establishment.
establo *m* stable.
estaca *f* stake; stick; post.
estacada *f* fence; fencing; stockade.
estacazo *m* blow with a stick.
estación *f* season (of the year); station; railroad station, terminus; ~ **de autobuses** bus station; ~ **de servicio** filling station.
estacional *adj* seasonal.
estacionamiento *m* parking; car park; (*mil*) stationing.
estacionar *vt* to park; (*mil*) to station.
estacionario/ria *adj* stationary.
estadio *m* phase; stadium.
estadista *m* statesman; statistician.
estadística *f* statistics *pl*.
estadístico/ca *adj* statistical.
estado *m* state, condition.
Estados Unidos *mpl* United States (of America).
estafa *f* trick, fraud.
estafador/ra *m/f* swindler, racketeer.
estafar *vt* to deceive, to defraud.
estafeta *f* post office.
estallar *vi* to crack; to burst; to break out.
estallido *m* explosion; (*fig*) outbreak.
estambre *m* stamen.
estamento *m* estate; body; layer; class.
estameña *f* serge.
estampa *f* print; engraving; appearance.
estampado/da *adj* printed; * *m* printing; print; stamping.
estampar *vt* to print.

estampida *f* stampede.
estampido *m* report (of a gun); crack.
estampilla *f* seal, stamp.
estancar *vt* to check (a current); to monopolize; to prohibit, to suspend; ~**se** *vr* to stagnate.
estancia *f* stay; bedroom; ranch; (*poet*) stanza.
estanco *m* tobacconist's (shop); ~/**ca** *adj* watertight.
estándar *adj*, *m* standard.
estandarizar *vt* to standardize.
estandarte *m* banner, standard.
estanque *m* pond, pool; reservoir.
estanquero/ra *m/f* tobacconist.
estante *m* shelf (for books).
estantería *f* shelves *pl*, shelving.
estaño *m* tin.
estar *vi* to be; to be (in a place).
estatal *adj* state *compd*.
estática *f* statics *pl*.
estático/ca *adj* static.
estatua *f* statue.
estatura *f* stature.
estatuto *m* statute, law.
este *m* east.
este/ta *adj* this; **estos/tas** *pl* these.
éste *pn m* this (one); **éstos/tas** *pl* these (ones).
estera *f* mat.
estercolar *vt* to manure.
estercolero *m* dunghill.
estéreo *adj invar*, *m* stereo.
estereotipar *vt* to stereotype.
estereotipo *m* stereotype.
estéril *adj* sterile, infertile.
esterilidad *f* sterility, infertility.
esterilla *f* mat.
esterlina *adj*: **libra** ~ pound sterling.
estético/ca *adj* aesthetic; * *f* aesthetics.

estiércol *m* dung; manure.

estilar(se) *vi* (*vr*) to be in fashion; to be used.

estilo *m* style; fashion; stroke (in swimming).

estima *f* esteem.

estimable *adj* estimable, worthy of esteem.

estimación *f* estimation, valuation.

estimar *vt* to estimate, to value; to esteem; to judge; to think.

estimulante *adj* stimulating; * *m* stimulant.

estimular *vt* to stimulate, to excite; to goad.

estímulo *m* stimulus.

estío *m* summer.

estipendiario *m* stipendiary.

estipulación *f* stipulation.

estipular *vt* to stipulate.

estirado/da *adj* stretched tight; (*fig*) pompous.

estirar *vt* to stretch out.

estirón *m* pulling; tugging; **dar un ~** to grow rapidly.

estirpe *f* race, origin, stock.

estival *adj* summer *compd*.

esto *pn* this.

estocada *f* stab.

estofa *f*: **de baja ~** poor quality.

estofado *m* stew.

estola *f* stole.

estolidez *f* stupidity.

estólido/da *adj* stupid.

estomacal *adj* stomach *compd*.

estómago *m* stomach.

estopa *f* tow.

estoque *m* rapier, sword.

estorbar *vt* to hinder; (*fig*) to bother; * *vi* to be in the way.

estorbo *m* obstacle, hindrance, impediment.

estornudar *vi* to sneeze.

estornudo *m* sneeze.

estos, éstos *pl* of **este, éste**.

estrada *f* highway.

estrado *m* drawing room; stage, platform.

estrafalario/ria *adj* slovenly; eccentric.

estrago *m* ruin, destruction; havoc.

estrambótico/ca *adj* eccentric, odd.

estrangulador/ra *m/f* strangler.

estrangulamiento *m* bottleneck.

estrangular *vt* to strangle; (*med*) to strangulate.

estraperlo *m* black market.

estratagema *f* stratagem, trick.

estrategia *f* strategy.

estratégico/ca *adj* strategic.

estrato *m* stratum, layer.

estraza *f* rag; **papel de ~** brown paper.

estrechar *vt* to tighten; to contract, to constrain; to compress; **~se** *vr* to grow narrow; to embrace; **~ la mano** to shake hands.

estrechez *f* strictness, narrowness; shortage of money.

estrecho *m* straits *pl*; **~/cha** *adj* narrow, close; tight; intimate; rigid, austere; short (of money).

estrella *f* star.

estrellado/da *adj* starry; **huevos ~s** fried eggs.

estrellar *vt* to dash to pieces; **~se** *vr* to smash; to crash; to fail.

estremecer *vt* to shake, to make tremble; **~se** *vr* to shake, to tremble.

estremecimiento *m* trembling, shaking.

estrenar *vt* to wear for the first time; to move into (a house); to show (a film) for the first time; **~se** *vr* to make one's debut.

estreñido/da *adj* constipated.

estreñimiento *m* constipation.

estrépito *m* noise, racket; fuss.

estrepitoso/sa *adj* noisy.

estribar *vi*: ~ **en** to be supported by; to be based on.

estribillo *m* chorus.

estribo *m* buttress; stirrup; running board; **perder los ~s** to fly off the handle (*fam*).

estribor *m* (*mar*) starboard.

estricto/ta *adj* strict; severe.

estrofa *f* (*poet*) verse, strophe.

estropajo *m* scourer.

estropajoso/sa *adj* tough, leathery; despicable; mean; stammering.

estropear *vt* to spoil; to damage; ~**se** *vr* to get damaged.

estructura *f* structure.

estruendo *m* clamour, noise; confusion, uproar; pomp, ostentation.

estrujar *vt* to press, to squeeze.

estrujón *m* pressing, squeezing.

estuario *m* estuary.

estuche *m* case (for scissors, etc); sheath.

estudiante *m/f* student.

estudiantil *adj* student *compd*.

estudiar *vt* to study.

estudio *m* study; studio; ~**s** *mpl* studies *pl*; learning.

estudioso/sa *adj* studious.

estufa *f* heater, fire.

estufilla *f* muff; small stove.

estupefacción *f* stupefaction.

estupefaciente *m* narcotic.

estupefacto *adj* speechless; thunderstruck.

estupendo/da *adj* terrific, marvellous.

estupidez *f* stupidity.

estúpido/da *adj* stupid.

estupor *m* stupor; astonishment.

estupro *m* rape.

etapa *f* stage; stopping place; (*fig*) phase.

etcétera *adv* etcetera, and so on.

éter *m* ether.

etéreo/rea *adj* ethereal.

eternidad *f* eternity.

eternizar *vt* to eternalize, to perpetuate.

eterno/na *adj* eternal.

ética *f* ethics.

ético/ca *adj* ethical, moral.

etimología *f* etymology.

etimológico/ca *adj* etymological.

etiqueta *f* etiquette; label.

Eucaristía *f* Eucharist.

eufemismo *m* euphemism.

euforia *f* euphoria.

euro *m* euro.

eurocámara *f* European Parliament.

euroconector *m* Euroconnector.

eurodiputado/da *m/f* Euro-MP.

euroescéptico/ca *m/f* Eurosceptic.

Europa *f* Europe.

eurotúnel *m* Eurotunnel, Channel tunnel.

evacuación *f* evacuation.

evacuar *vt* to evacuate, to empty.

evadir *vt* to evade, to escape.

evaluar *vt* to evaluate.

evangélico/ca *adj* evangelical.

evangelio *m* gospel.

evangelista *m* evangelist.

evangelizar *vt* to evangelize.

evaporar *vt* to evaporate; ~**se** *vr* to vanish.

evasión *f* evasion, escape.

evasivo/va *adj* evasive; * *f* excuse.

eventual *adj* possible; temporary, casual (worker).

evidencia *f* evidence, proof.

evidente *adj* evident, clear.

evitable *adj* avoidable.

evitar *vt* to avoid.

evocación *f* evocation; invocation.

evocar *vt* to call out; to invoke.

evolución *f* evolution, development; change; (*mil*) manoeuvre.

evolucionar *vi* to evolve.

ex *adj* ex.

exacción *f* exaction; extortion.

exacerbar *vt* to exacerbate; to irritate.

exactamente *adv* exactly.

exactitud *f* exactness.

exacto/ta *adj* exact; punctual; accurate.

exageración *f* exaggeration.

exagerar *vt* to exaggerate.

exaltación *f* exaltation, elation.

exaltar *vt* to exalt, to elevate; to praise, to extol; ~**se** *vr* to get excited.

examen *m* exam, examination, test, inquiry.

examinador *m* examiner.

examinar *vt* to examine.

exánime *adj* lifeless, weak.

exasperación *f* exasperation.

exasperar *vt* to exasperate, to irritate.

excavación *f* excavation.

excavadora *f* excavator; digger.

excavar *vt* to excavate, to dig out.

excedente *adj* excessive.

exceder *vt* to exceed, to surpass, to excel, to outdo.

excelencia *f* excellence.

Excelencia *f* Excellency (title).

excelente *adj* excellent.

excelso/sa *adj* elevated, sublime, lofty.

excentricidad *f* eccentricity.

excéntrico/ca *adj* eccentric.

excepción *f* exception.

excepto *adv* excepting, except (for).

exceptuar *vt* to except, to exempt.

excesivo/va *adj* excessive.

exceso *m* excess.

excitación *f* excitement; excitation.

excitar *vt* to excite; ~**se** *vr* to get excited.

exclamación *f* exclamation.

exclamar *vt* to exclaim, to cry out.

excluir *vt* to exclude.

exclusión *f* exclusion.

exclusiva *f* exclusive; (*com*) sole right.

exclusivamente, exclusive *adv* exclusively.

exclusivo/va *adj* exclusive.

excomulgar *vt* to excommunicate.

excomunión *f* excommunication.

excremento *m* excrement.

excursión *f* excursion, trip.

excusa *f* excuse, apology.

excusable *adj* excusable.

excusado *m* toilet.

excusar *vt* to excuse; to avoid; ~ **de** to exempt from; ~**se** *vr* to apologize.

execrable *adj* execrable, abhorrent.

execrar *vt* to execrate, to curse.

exención *f* exemption; immunity, privilege.

exento/ta *adj* exempt, free.

exequias *fpl* funeral rites *pl*, obsequies *pl*.

exhalación *f* exhalation; fumes *pl*, vapour.

exhalar *vt* to exhale; to give off; to heave (a sigh).

exhausto/ta *adj* exhausted.

exhibición *f* exhibition, display.

exhibir *vt* to exhibit.

exhortación *f* exhortation.

exhortar *vt* to exhort.

exhumación *f* exhumation.

exhumar *vt* to disinter, to exhume.

exigencia *f* demand, requirement.

exigir *vt* to demand, to require.

exiguo/gua *adj* meagre, small.

exiliado/da *adj* exiled; * *m/f* exile.

exilio *m* exile.

eximir *vt* to exempt, to free; to excuse.

existencia *f* existence, being.

existente *adj* existing, in existence.

existir *vi* to exist, to be.

éxito *m* outcome; success; (*mus, etc*) hit; **tener ~** to be successful.

exoneración *f* exoneration.

exonerar *vt* to exonerate.

exorbitante *adj* exhorbitant, excessive.

exorcismo *m* exorcism.

exorcista *m* exorcist.

exorcizar *vt* to exorcize.

exótico/ca *adj* exotic.

expandir *vt* to expand.

expansión *f* expansion; extension.

expansivo/va *adj* expansive.

expatriarse *vr* to emigrate; to go into exile.

expectativa *f* expectation; prospect.

expectoración *f* expectoration.

expectorar *vt* to expectorate.

expedición *f* expedition.

expedicionario/ria *adj* expeditionary.

expediente *m* expedient; means; (*jur*) proceedings *pl*; dossier, file.

expedir *vt* to send, to forward, to dispatch.

expeditivo/va *adj* expeditious.

expedito/ta *adj* speedy; clear, free.

expeler *vt* to expel.

expensas *fpl:* **a ~ de** at the expense of.

experiencia *f* experience; trial.

experimentado/da *adj* experienced; expert.

experimental *adj* experimental.

experimentar *vt* to experience; * *vi:* **~ con** to experiment with.

experimento *m* experiment, trial.

experto/ta *adj* expert; experienced.

expiación *f* expiation; purification.

expiar *vt* to atone for; to purify.

expiatorio/ria *adj* expiatory.

expirar *vi* to expire.

explanada *f* esplanade.

explayarse *vr* to speak at length.

explicación *f* explanation.

explicar *vt* to explain, to expound; **~se** *vr* to explain oneself.

explícito/ta *adj* explicit.

exploración *f* exploration.

explorador/ra *m/f* explorer.

explorar *vt* to explore.

explosión *f* explosion.

explotación *f* exploitation; running.

explotar *vt* to exploit; to run; * *vi* to explode.

exponente *m* (*mat*) exponent.

exponer *vt* to expose; to explain.

exportación *f* export; exports *pl*.

exportar *vt* to export.

exposición *f* exposure; exhibition; explanation; account.

expresar *vt* to express.

expresión *f* expression.

expresivo/va *adj* expressive; energetic.

expreso/sa *adj* express, clear, specific; fast (train).

express *m* (*ferro*) express train.

exprimidor *m* squeezer.

exprimir *vt* to squeeze out.

ex profeso *adv* on purpose.

expropiar *vt* to expropriate.

expuesto/ta *adj* exposed; on display.

expulsar *vt* to expel, to drive out.

expulsión *f* expulsion.

exquisito/ta *adj* exquisite; excellent.

éxtasis *m* ecstasy, enthusiasm.
extático/ca *adj* ecstatic.
extender *vt* to extend, to stretch out;
~**se** *vr* to extend; to spread.
extensión *f* extension; extent.
extensivo/va *adj* extensive.
extenso/sa *adj* extensive.
extenuación *f* emaciation; debility,
exhaustion.
extenuar *vt* to exhaust, to debilitate.
exterior *adj* exterior, external; * *m*
exterior, outward appearance.
exteriormente *adv* externally.
exterminador *m* exterminator.
exterminar *vt* to exterminate.
exterminio *m* extermination.
externo/na *adj* external, outer; * *m/f*
day pupil.
extinción *f* extinction.
extinguir *vt* to wipe out; to
extinguish.
extintor *m* (fire) extinguisher.
extirpación *f* extirpation,
extermination.
extirpar *vt* to extirpate, to root out.
extorsión *f* extortion.
extra *adj invar* extra; good quality;
* *m/f* extra; * *m* bonus.
extracción *f* extraction.
extracto *m* extract.

extradición *f* extradition.
extraditar *vt* to extradite.
extraer *vt* to extract.
extranjero/ra *m/f* stranger; foreigner; * *adj* foreign, alien.
extrañar *vt* to find strange; to miss; ~**se**
vr to be surprised; to grow apart.
extrañeza *f* strangeness; surprise.
extraño/ña *adj* foreign; rare;
singular, strange, odd.
extraordinario/ria *adj* extraordinary,
uncommon, odd.
extravagancia *f* extravagance.
extravagante *adj* extravagant.
extraviado/da *adj* lost, missing.
extraviar *vt* to mislead; ~**se** *vr* to
lose one's way.
extravío *m* deviation; loss.
extremado/da *adj* extreme;
accomplished.
extremaunción *f* extreme unction.
extremidad *f* extremity; brim; tip;
~**es** *fpl* extremities *pl*.
extremo/ma *adj* extreme, last; * *m*
extreme, highest degree; **en**
~extremely.
extrínseco/ca *adj* extrinsic,
external.
extrovertido/da *adj*, *m/f* extrovert.
exuberancia *f* exuberance; luxuriance.

F

fábrica *f* factory.
fabricación *f* manufacture,
production.
fabricante *m/f* producer,
manufacturer.
fabricar *vt* to build, to construct; to
manufacture; (*fig*) to fabricate.
fabril *adj* manufacturing *compd*,
industrial.

fábula *f* fable; fiction; rumour,
common talk.
fabulista *m/f* writer of fables.
fabuloso/sa *adj* fabulous, fictitious.
facción *f* (political) faction; feature.
faccioso/sa *adj* factious, turbulent.
facha *f* appearance, look; face.
fachada *f* facade, face, front.
fácil *adj* facile, easy.

facilidad *f* facility, easiness; **con ~** *adv* cosily, easily.

facilitar *vt* to facilitate.

fácilmente *adv* easily.

facineroso *adj* wicked, criminal.

facsímil *m* facsimile, fax.

factible *adj* feasible, practicable.

factor *m* (*mat*) factor; (*com*) factor, agent.

factoría *f* agency; factory.

factura *f* invoice.

facultad *f* faculty.

facultativo/va *adj* optional; * *m/f* doctor, practitioner.

faena *f* task, job; hard work.

faisán *m* pheasant.

faja *f* band, sash; strip (of land); corset.

fajo *m* bundle; wad.

falacia *f* fallacy; fraud.

falange *f* phalanx.

falaz *adj* deceitful, fraudulent; fallacious.

falda *f* skirt; lap; flap; train; slope, hillside.

faldero/ra *adj*: **hombre ~** ladies' man; **perrito ~** lap-dog.

faldón *m* coat-tails *pl*; skirt.

falible *adj* fallible.

fallar *vt* (*jur*) to pronounce sentence on, to judge; * *vi* to fail.

fallecer *vi* to die.

fallecimiento *m* decease, death.

fallido/da *adj* unsuccessful, frustrated.

fallo *m* judgement, sentence; failure.

falsamente *adv* falsely.

falsario/ria *adj* falsifying, forging.

falsear *vt* to falsify, to counterfeit.

falsedad *f* falsehood; untruth, fib (*sl*); hypocrisy.

falsete *m* (*tec*) plug; bung; (*mus*) falsetto.

falsificación *f* falsification.

falsificador/ora *m/f* forger, counterfeiter.

falsificar *vt* to falsify, to forge, to counterfeit.

falso/sa *adj* false, untrue; deceitful; fake.

falta *f* fault, defect; want; flaw, mistake; (*dep*) foul.

faltar *vi* to be wanting; to fail; not to fulfil one's promise; to need; to be missing.

falto/ta *adj* wanting, deficient, lacking; miserable, wretched.

faltriquera *f* pocket.

fama *f* fame; reputation, name.

famélico/ca *adj* starving.

familia *f* family.

familiar *adj* familiar; homely, domestic; * *m/f* relative, relation.

familiaridad *f* familiarity.

familiarizarse *vr*: **~ con** to familiarize oneself with.

famoso/sa *adj* famous.

fan *m/f* fan.

fanático/ca *adj* fanatical; enthusiastic; * *m/f* fanatic; fan.

fandango *m* fandango.

fanfarrón/ona *m/f* bully, braggart.

fanfarronada *f* boast, brag.

fanfarronear *vi* to bully, to brag.

fanfarronería *f* boast, brag.

fango *m* mire, mud.

fangoso/sa *adj* muddy, miry.

fantasía *f* fancy; fantasy; caprice; presumption.

fantasma *f* phantom, ghost.

fantástico/ca *adj* fantastic, whimsical; presumptuous.

fardo *m* bale, parcel.

farfullar *vi* to talk with a stammer.

farisaico/ca *adj* pharisaical; hypocritical.

fariseo *m* Pharisee; hypocrite.

farmacéutico/ca *adj* pharmaceutical; * *m/f* pharmacist.

farmacia *f* pharmacy.

faro *m* (*mar*) lighthouse; (*auto*) headlamp; floodlight.

farol *m* lantern.

farola *f* street light.

farsa *f* farce.

farsante *m/f* fraud, fake.

fascículo *m* part, instalment.

fascinación *f* fascination.

fascinar *vt* to fascinate; to enchant.

fascismo *m* fascism.

fascista *adj, m/f* fascist.

fase *f* phase.

fastidiar *vt* to annoy; to offend; to spoil.

fastidio *m* annoyance; boredom; disgust.

fastidioso/sa *adj* annoying; tedious.

fatal *adj* fatal; mortal; awful.

fatalidad *f* fatality; mischance, ill-luck.

fatalismo *m* fatalism.

fatalista *m/f* fatalist.

fatiga *f* weariness, fatigue.

fatigar *vt* to fatigue, to tire; to harass.

fatigoso/sa *adj* tiresome, troublesome.

fatuidad *f* fatuity, foolishness, silliness.

fatuo/tua *adj* fatuous, stupid, foolish; conceited.

fauces *fpl* jaws *pl*, gullet.

fausto/ta *adj* happy, fortunate; * *m* splendour, pomp.

favor *m* favour; protection; good turn.

favorable *adj* favourable.

favorecer *vt* to favour, to protect.

favorito/ta *adj* favourite.

fax *m* fax.

faz *f* face.

fe *f* faith, belief.

fealdad *f* ugliness.

febrero *m* February.

febril *adj* feverish.

fecha *f* date (of a letter etc).

fechar *vt* to date.

fechoría *f* misdeed; exploit.

fecundar *vt* to fertilize.

fecundidad *f* fecundity, fertility.

fecundo/da *adj* fruitful, fertile.

federación *f* federation.

felicidad *f* happiness.

felicitar *vt* to congratulate.

feligrés/esa *m/f* parishioner.

feliz *adj* happy, fortunate.

felpa *f* plush; towelling.

felpudo *m* doormat.

femenil *adj* feminine, womanly.

femenino/na *adj* feminine; female.

feminismo *m* feminism.

feminista *adj, m/f* feminist.

fenómeno *m* phenomenon; (*fig*) freak, accident; * *adj* (*fam*) great (*sl*), marvellous.

feo/ea *adj* ugly; bad, nasty.

feracidad *f* productivity, fertility.

feraz *adj* fertile, fruitful.

féretro *m* bier, casket.

feria *f* fair, rest day; village market.

fermentación *f* fermentation.

fermentar *vi* to ferment.

fermento *m* ferment; leaven.

ferocidad *f* ferocity, wildness; cruelty.

feroz *adj* ferocious, savage; cruel.

ferretería *f* ironmonger's, hardware store.

ferrocarril *m* railway.

ferroviario/ria *adj* rail *compd*.

ferry *m* ferry.

fértil *adj* fertile, fruitful.

fertilidad *f* fertility, fruitfulness.

fertilización f fertilization.

fertilizar vt to fertilize.

férula f ferule; (med) splint.

ferviente adj fervent; ardent.

fervor m fervour, zeal; ardour.

fervoroso/sa adj fervent, ardent, passionate.

festejar vt to feast; to court, to woo.

festejo m courtship; feast.

festín m feast.

festividad f festivity.

festivo/va adj festive, merry; witty; día ~ holiday.

festón m garland; festoon.

festonear vt to ornament with garlands.

fétido/da adj foetid, stinking.

feto m foetus.

feudal adj feudal.

fiable adj trustworthy; reliable.

fiador/ra m/f guarantor; (com) backer.

fiambre m cold meat.

fiambrera f dinner pail.

fianza f (jur) surety.

fiar vt to entrust, to confide; to bail; to sell on credit; to buy on credit; * vi to trust.

fibra f fibre.

fibroso/sa adj fibrous.

ficción f fiction.

ficha f token, counter (at games); (index) card.

ficticio/cia adj fictitious.

fidedigno/na adj reliable, trustworthy.

fideicomisario/ria m/f trustee.

fideicomiso f trust.

fidelidad f fidelity; loyalty.

fideos mpl vermicelli pl.

fiebre f fever.

fiel adj faithful, loyal; * mpl los ~es the faithful pl.

fieltro m felt.

fiera f wild beast.

fiereza f fierceness, ferocity; cruelty.

fiero/ra adj fierce, ferocious; cruel; rough, harsh.

fiesta f party; festivity; ~s fpl holidays pl, vacations pl.

figura f figure, shape.

figurado/da adj figurative.

figurar vt to figure; ~se vr to fancy, to imagine.

figurilla f ridiculous little figure.

fijador m fixative; gel (for the hair).

fijar vt to fix, to fasten; ~se vr to become fixed; to establish oneself; ~se en to notice.

fijo/ja adj fixed, firm; settled, permanent.

fila f row, line; (mil) rank; en ~ in a line, in a row.

filamento m filament.

filantropía f philanthropy.

filántropo/pa m/f philanthropist.

filete m fillet; fillet steak.

filiación f lineage; personal description, particulars pl.

filial adj filial; * f (com) subsidiary.

filibustero m pirate.

filigrana f filigree.

filmar vt to film.

filo m edge, blade.

filología f philology.

filológico/ca adj philological.

filólogo/ga m/f philologist.

filosofar vt to philosophize.

filosofía f philosophy.

filosófico/ca adj philosophical.

filósofo/fa m/f philosopher.

filtración f filtration.

filtrar vt to filter, to strain.

filtro m filter.

fin m end; termination, conclusion; aim, purpose; al ~ at last; en ~ (fig) well then; por ~ finally, lastly.

final *adj* final; * *m* end; termination, conclusion; * *f* (*dep*) final.

finalizar *vt* to finish, to conclude; * *vi* to be finished.

finalmente *adv* finally, at last.

financiar *vt* to finance.

finca *f* land, property, real estate; country house; farm.

fineza *f* fineness, perfection; elegance; courtesy; small gift.

fingido/da *adj* feigned, fake, sham.

fingimiento *m* simulation, pretence.

fingir *vt* to feign, to fake; to invent; to imitate; ~**se** *vr* to pretend to be; * *vi* to pretend.

finito/ta *adj* finite.

fino/na *adj* fine, pure; slender; polite; acute; dry (of sherry).

finura *f* fineness.

firma *f* signature; (*com*) company.

firmamento *m* firmament, sky, heaven.

firmar *vt* to sign.

firme *adj* firm, stable, strong, secure; constant; resolute; * *m* road surface.

firmeza *f* firmness, stability, constancy.

fiscal *adj* fiscal.

fiscalía *f* office and business of the district attorney.

fiscalizar *vt* to inspect; to criticize.

fisco *m* treasury, exchequer.

fisgar *vt* to pry into.

fisgón/ona *m/f* prying person, snooper (*sl*).

física *f* physics.

físico/ca *adj* physical; * *m/f* physicist; * *m* physique.

fisonomía *f* physiognomy.

fisonomista *m/f*: **ser buen ~** to have a good memory for faces.

flaco/ca *adj* lean, skinny; feeble.

flagelación *f* flagellation.

flagrante *adj* flagrant.

flamante *adj* flaming, bright; brand-new.

flan *m* crème caramel.

flanco *m* flank.

flanquear *vt* (*mil*) to flank.

flaquear *vi* to flag; to weaken.

flaqueza *f* thinness, leanness; feebleness, weakness.

flash *m* flash.

flato *m* (*med*) flatulence; depression.

flatulento/ta *adj* flatulent.

flauta *f* (*mus*) flute.

flautista *m/f* flute player, flautist.

flecha *f* arrow.

fleco *m* fringe.

flema *f* phlegm.

flemático/ca *adj* phlegmatic.

flemón *m* ulcer in the gums.

flequillo *m* fringe (of hair), bangs *pl*.

fletar *vt* to freight (a ship).

flete *m* (*mar*) freight; charter.

flexibilidad *f* flexibility.

flexible *adj* flexible; compliant; docile.

flojedad *f* feebleness; laxity, laziness; negligence.

flojera *f*: **me da ~** I can't be bothered.

flojo/ja *adj* loose; flexible; lax, slack; lazy.

flor *f* flower.

florecer *vi* to blossom.

florero *m* vase.

floresta *f* wood, grove; beauty spot.

florete *m* fencing foil.

florido/da *adj* full of flowers; in bloom; choice.

florista *m/f* florist.

flota *f* fleet.

flotador *m* float; rubber ring.

flotante *adj* floating.

flotar *vi* to float.

flote m: **a ~** afloat.

flotilla f small fleet, flotilla.

fluctuación f fluctuation; uncertainty.

fluctuar vi to fluctuate; to waver.

fluidez f fluidity; fluency.

fluido/da adj fluid; (fig) fluent; * m fluid.

fluir vi to flow.

flujo m flux; flow; **~ de sangre** (med) loss of blood.

fluvial adj fluvial, river compd.

foca f seal.

foco m focus; centre; source; floodlight; (light)bulb.

fofo/fa adj spongy; soft; bland.

fogata f blaze; bonfire.

fogón m stove; hearth.

fogonazo m flash; explosion.

fogosidad f dash, verve; fieriness.

fogoso/sa adj fiery; ardent, fervent; impetuous, boisterous.

folk m folk (music).

follaje m foliage.

folletista m/f pamphleteer.

folleto m pamphlet; folder, brochure.

follón m (fam) mess; fuss.

fomentar vt to encourage; to promote.

fomento m promotion.

fonda f hotel; inn; boarding house.

fondeadero m anchorage.

fondear vi to drop anchor.

fondista m/f innkeeper.

fondo m bottom; back; background; space; **~s** mpl stock, funds pl, capital; **a ~** perfectly, completely.

fontanería f plumbing.

fontanero/ra m/f plumber.

footing m jogging.

forajido m outlaw.

foral adj belonging to the statute law of a country.

forastero/ra adj strange, exotic; * m/f stranger.

forcejear vi to struggle.

forense adj forensic; * m/f forensic scientist.

forjador/ra m/f framer; forger.

forjadura f forging.

forjar vt to forge; to frame; to invent.

forma f form, shape; pattern; (med) fitness; (dep) form; means, method; **de ~ que** in such a manner that.

formación f formation; form, figure; education; training.

formal adj formal; proper, genuine; serious, grave.

formalidad f formality; gravity.

formalizar vt (jur) to formalize; to regularize; **~se** vr to be regularized.

formar vt to form, to shape.

formidable adj formidable, dreadful; terrific (sl).

fórmula f formula.

formulario m formulary.

fornicación f fornication.

fornicador m fornicator.

fornicar vi to commit fornication.

fornido/da adj well-built.

foro m court of justice; forum.

forraje m forage.

forrajear vt to forage.

forrar vt to line; to face; to cover.

forro m lining; book jacket.

fortalecer vt to fortify, to strengthen.

fortaleza f courage; strength, vigour; (mil) fortress, stronghold.

fortificación f fortification.

fortificar vt to strengthen; to fortify (a place).

fortín m (mil) small fort.

fortuito/ta adj fortuitous.

fortuna f fortune; wealth.

forzar *vt* to force.
forzoso/sa *adj* indispensable, necessary.
forzudo/da *adj* strong, vigorous.
fosa *f* grave; pit.
fósforo *m* phosphorus; **~s** *mpl* matches *pl*.
fósil *adj*, *m* fossil.
foso *vt* pit; moat, ditch, fosse.
foto *f* photo.
fotocopia *f* photocopy.
fotografía *f* photography; photograph.
fotógrafo/fa *m/f* photographer.
frac *m* evening coat, dress coat.
fracasar *vi* to fail.
fracaso *m* failure.
fracción *f* fraction.
fractura *f* fracture.
fracturar *vt* to break (a bone).
fragancia *f* fragrance, sweetness of smell.
fragante *adj* fragrant, scented.
fragata *f* (*mar*) frigate.
frágil *adj* fragile, frail.
fragilidad *f* fragility, brittleness; frailty.
fragmento *m* fragment.
fragosidad *f* roughness; denseness.
fragoso/sa *adj* craggy, rough, uneven.
fragua *f* forge.
fraguar *vt* to forge; to contrive; * *vi* to solidify, to harden.
fraile *m* friar, monk.
frambuesa *f* raspberry.
francés/sa *adj* French; * *m* French (language); * *m/f* Frenchman/woman.
franco/ca *adj* frank; candid; free, gratis.
franela *f* flannel; vest.
franja *f* fringe.

franquear *vt* to clear; to overcome; to stamp (letters); **~se** to unbosom oneself.
franqueo *m* postage.
franqueza *f* frankness.
franquicia *f* immunity from taxes.
frasco *m* flask.
frase *f* phrase.
fraternal *adj* fraternal, brotherly.
fraternidad *f* fraternity, brotherhood.
fratricida *m/f* fratricide (person).
fratricidio *m* fratricide (murder).
fraude *m* fraud, deceit; cheat.
fraudulento/ta *adj* fraudulent, deceitful.
frazada *f* blanket.
frecuencia *f* frequency.
frecuentar *vt* to frequent.
frecuente *adj* frequent.
fregadero *m* (kitchen) sink.
fregado *m* scouring, scrubbing; (*fig*) intrigue; underhand work.
fregar *vt* to scrub; to wash up.
fregona *f* kitchen maid; (*perj*) skivvy.
freír *vt* to fry.
frenar *vt* to brake; (*fig*) to check.
frenesí *m* frenzy.
frenético/ca *adj* frantic; frenzied, wild.
frenillo *m* speech impediment.
freno *m* bit; brake; (*fig*) check.
frente *f* front; face; **~ a ~** face to face; **en ~** opposite; (*mil*) front; * *m* forehead.
fresa *f* strawberry.
fresal *m* strawberry plant; ground bearing strawberry plants.
fresco/ca *adj* fresh; cool; new; ruddy; * *m* fresh air; * *m/f* (*fam*) shameless or impudent person.
frescura *f* freshness; frankness; cheek, nerve.

fresno *m* ash tree.

frialdad *f* coldness; indifference.

fricción *f* friction.

friega *f* rubbing; nuisance.

frígido/da *adj* frigid.

frigorífico *m* fridge.

frijol *m* bean.

frío/fría *adj* cold; indifferent; * *m* cold; indifference.

friolento/ta *adj* chilly.

friolera *f* trifle

friso *m* frieze; wainscot.

fritada *f* dish of fried meat or fish.

frito/ta *adj* fried.

frivolidad *f* frivolity.

frívolo/la *adj* frivolous.

frondosidad *f* foliage.

frondoso/sa *adj* leafy.

frontera *f* frontier.

fronterizo/za *adj* frontier *compd*; bordering.

frontón *m* (*dep*) pelota court; pelota.

frotación, frotadura *f* friction, rubbing.

frotar *vt* to rub.

fructífero/ra *adj* fruit-bearing, fruitful.

fructificar *vi* to bear fruit; to come to fruition.

fructuoso/sa *adj* fruitful.

frugal *adj* frugal, sparing.

frugalidad *f* frugality, parsimony.

fruncir *vt* to pleat; to knit; to contract; ~ **las cejas** to knit the eyebrows.

frustrar *vt* to frustrate.

fruta *f* fruit; ~ **del tiempo** seasonal fruit.

frutal *m* fruit tree.

frutera *f* fruit dish.

frutería *f* fruit shop, greengrocer's shop.

frutero/ra *m/f* fruiterer, fruit seller, greengrocer; * *m* fruit basket.

frutilla *f* strawberry.

fruto *m* fruit; benefit, profit.

fuego *m* fire.

fuelle *m* bellows *pl*.

fuente *f* fountain; spring; source; large dish.

fuera *adv* out(side); away; ~ **de** *prep* outside; ¡~! out of the way!

fueraborda *m* outboard motor.

fuero *m* statute law of a country; jurisdiction.

fuerte *m* (*mil*) fortification, fort; forte; * *adj* vigorous, tough; strong; loud; heavy; * *adv* strongly; hard.

fuerza *f* force, strength; (*elec*) power; violence; **a** ~ **de** by dint of; ~**s** *mpl* troops *pl*.

fuga *f* flight, escape; leak (of gas).

fugarse *vr* to escape, to flee.

fugaz *adj* fleeting.

fugitivo/va *adj, m/f* fugitive.

fulano/na *m/f* so-and-so, what's-his-name/what's-her-name.

fulgurar *vi* to flash.

fullería *f* cheating.

fullero *m* cardsharp, cheat.

fulminar *vt* to fulminate; * *vi* to explode.

fumador/ra *m/f* smoker.

fumar *vt, vi* to smoke.

fumigación *f* fumigation.

funambulista *m/f* tightrope walker.

función *f* function; duties *pl*; show, performance.

funcionar *vi* to function; to work (of a machine).

funcionario/ria *m/f* official; civil servant.

funda *f* case, sheath; ~ **de almohada** pillowcase.

fundación *f* foundation.

fundador/ra *m/f* founder.

fundamental *adj* fundamental.
fundamentalismo *m* fundamentalism.
fundamentalista *adj, m/f* fundamentalist.
fundamento *m* foundation; groundwork; reason, cause.
fundar *vt* to found; to establish; to ground.
fundición *f* fusion; foundry.
fundir *vt* to fuse; to melt; to smelt; (*com*) to merge; to bankrupt; (*elec*) to fuse, to blow.
fúnebre *adj* mournful, sad; funereal.
funeral *m* funeral; **~es** *mpl* funeral, obsequies *pl*.
funerario/ria *adj* funeral *compd*, funereal.
funesto/ta *adj* ill-fated, unfortunate; fatal.

furgón *m* wagon.
furgoneta *f* pick-up (truck).
furia *f* fury, rage.
furibundo/da *adj* furious; frenzied.
furioso/sa *adj* furious.
furor *m* fury, rage.
furtivamente *adv* furtively.
furtivo/va *adj* furtive.
furúnculo *m* (*med*) boil.
fusible *m* fuse.
fusil *m* rifle.
fusilar *vt* to shoot.
fusilero *m* rifleman.
fusión *f* fusion; (*com*) merger.
fusta *f* riding crop.
fútbol *m* football.
futbolista *m/f* footballer.
fútil *adj* futile; trifling.
futilidad *f* futility.
futuro/ra *adj, m* future.

G

gabán *m* overcoat.
gabardina *f* gabardine; raincoat.
gabarra *f* (*mar*) lighter (boat).
gabinete *m* (*pol*) cabinet, study; office (of solicitors, etc).
gaceta *f* gazette.
gachas *fpl* porridge, pap.
gacho/cha *adj* curved, bent downward.
gafas *fpl* glasses *pl*, spectacles *pl*.
gafe *m* jinx.
gaita *f* bagpipe; flageolet.
gaitero/ra *m/f* bagpiper, bagpipe player.
gaje *m*: **~s del oficio** occupational hazards *pl*.
gajo *m* segment (of orange).
gala *f* full dress; (*fig*) cream, flower; **~s** *fpl* finery; **hacer ~ de** to display, to show off.

galán *m* lover; handsome young man; (*teat*) male lead.
galante *adj* gallant.
galanteador *m* lover, suitor.
galantear *vt* to court, to woo.
galanteo *m* gallantry, courtship.
galantería *f* gallantry; politeness; compliment.
galápago *m* tortoise.
galardón *m* reward, prize.
galardonar *vt* to reward, to recompense.
galaxia *f* galaxy.
galbana *f* laziness, idleness.
galeón *m* (*mar*) galleon.
galera *f* (*mar*) galley; wagon; (type-)galley.
galería *f* gallery.
galgo *m* greyhound.

gallardete m (*mar*) pennant, streamer.

gallardía f fineness, elegance, gracefulness; dash.

gallardo/da adj graceful, elegant; brave, daring.

galleta f biscuit.

gallina f hen; * m/f (*fig*) coward; ~ **ciega** blindman's buff.

gallinero m henhouse, coop; poulterer; (*teat*) top gallery; hubbub.

gallineta f woodcock (bird).

gallo m cock.

galón m (*mil*) stripe; braid; gallon.

galopar vi to gallop.

galope m gallop.

galvánico/ca adj galvanic.

galvanismo m galvanism.

gama[1] f (*mus*) scale; (*fig*) range, gamut.

gama[2] f doe (of the fallow deer).

gamba f shrimp; prawn.

gamberro/rra m/f hooligan.

gamo m buck of the fallow deer.

gamuza f chamois.

gana f desire, wish; appetite; will, longing; **de buena** ~ with pleasure, voluntarily; **de mala** ~ unwillingly, with reluctance.

ganadería f cattle raising; cattle; livestock.

ganadero m rancher; cattle dealer.

ganado m livestock, cattle pl; ~ **mayor** horses and mules pl; ~ **menor** sheep, goats and pigs pl.

ganancia f gain, profit; increase.

ganancial adj lucrative.

ganar vt to gain; to win; to earn; * vi to win.

gancho m hook; crook.

gandul adj, m/f layabout.

ganga f bargain.

gangoso/sa adj nasal.

gangrena f gangrene.

gangrenarse vr to become gangrenous.

gangrenoso/sa adj gangrenous.

ganso/sa m/f gander; goose; (*fam*) idiot.

garabatear vi, vt to scrawl, to scribble.

garabatos mpl scrawling letters or characters pl.

garaje m garage.

garante m/f guarantor; * adj responsible.

garantía f warranty, guarantee.

garañón m jackass, male donkey.

garapatear vi, vt to scrawl, to scribble.

garapiñar vt to freeze; to ice.

garbanzo m chickpea.

garbo m gracefulness, elegance; stylishness; generosity.

garboso/sa adj graceful; elegant, stylish; generous.

garduña f marten.

gargajo m phlegm, spit.

garganta f throat, gullet; instep; neck (of a bottle); narrow pass between mountains or rivers.

gargantilla f necklace.

gárgara f noise made by gargling.

gargarismo m gargling, gargle.

gargarizar vi to gargle.

garita f (*mil*) sentry box; (*ferro*) signal box.

garra f claw; talon; paw.

garrafa f carafe; (gas) cylinder.

garrafal adj great, vast, huge.

garrapata f tick (insect).

garrotazo m blow with a stick or club.

garrote m stick, club, cudgel; (*jur*) garrotte.

garrotillo m (*med*) croup.

garrucha f pulley.

garza f heron.

garzo/za adj blue-eyed.

gas m gas.

gasa f gauze.

gaseoso/sa adj fizzy; * f lemonade.

gasfitero/ra m/f plumber.

gasoil m diesel (oil).

gasolina f petrol.

gasolinera f filling station, petrol station.

gasómetro m gasometer.

gastador/ra m/f spendthrift.

gastar vt to spend; to expend; to waste; to wear away; to use up; ~**se** vr to wear out; to waste.

gasto m expense, expenditure; use.

gastronomía f gastronomy.

gata f she-cat; **a ~s** on all fours.

gatear vi to go on all fours.

gatera f cat hole.

gatillazo m click of the trigger in firing.

gatillo m trigger of a gun; (med) dental forceps.

gato m cat; jack.

gatuno/na adj catlike, feline.

gaveta f drawer of a desk, locker.

gavilán m sparrow hawk.

gavilla f sheaf of corn.

gaviota f seagull.

gay (fam) adj invar, m gay (sl), homosexual.

gazapo m young rabbit; lie.

gazmoñada, gazmoñería f prudery; hypocrisy.

gazmoñero/ra, gazmoño/ña adj hypocritical.

gaznate m throttle, wind pipe.

gazpacho m Spanish cold tomato soup.

gazuza f ravenous hunger.

gelatina f jelly; gelatine.

gemelo/la m/f twin.

gemido m groan, moan, howl.

Géminis m Gemini (sign of the zodiac).

gemir vi to groan, to moan.

genciana f (bot) gentian.

gendarme m policeman.

gendarmería f police.

genealogía f genealogy.

genealógico/ca adj genealogical.

generación f generation; progeny, race.

general m general; * adj general; **en ~** generally, in general.

generalidad f generality.

generalizar vt to generalize.

generalmente adv generally.

genérico/ca adj generic.

género m genus; kind, type; gender; cloth, material; ~**s** mpl goods pl, commodities pl.

generosidad f generosity.

generoso/sa adj noble, generous.

Génesis f Genesis.

genial adj inspired, brilliant; genial.

genio m nature, character; genius.

genital adj genital; * mpl ~**es** genitals pl.

genitivo m (gr) genitive case.

gente f people; nation; family.

gentil m/f pagan, heathen; * adj elegant; graceful; charming.

gentileza f grace; charm; politeness.

gentilhombre m gentleman.

gentío m crowd, throng.

genuflexión f genuflection.

genuino/na adj genuine; pure.

geografía f geography.

geográfico/ca adj geographical.

geógrafo/fa m/f geographer.

geología f geology.

geólogo/ga m/f geologist.

geometría f geometry.

geométrico/ca adj geometrical, geometric.

geranio m (bot) geranium.
gerente m/f manager; director.
geriatría f (med) geriatrics.
germen m germ, bud; source, origin.
germinar vi to germinate, to bud.
gerundio m (gr) gerund.
gesticular vi to gesticulate.
gestión f management; negotiation.
gesto m face; grimace; gesture.
giganta f giantess.
gigante m giant; * adj gigantic.
gigantesco/ca adj gigantic, giant.
gilipollas adj invar (fam) stupid; * m/f invar wimp (sl).
gimnasia f gymnastics.
gimnasio m gymnasium.
gimnasta m/f gymnast.
gimnástico/ca adj gymnastic.
ginebra f gin.
ginecólogo/ga m/f gynaecologist.
gira f trip, tour.
girar vt to turn around; to swivel; (com) to draw, to issue; * vi to go round, to revolve; (com) to do business; to draw.
giratorio/ria adj revolving.
girasol m sunflower.
giro m turning round; tendency; change; (com) draft.
gitano/na m/f Gypsy.
glacial adj icy.
glaciar m glacier.
glándula f gland.
glandular adj glandular.
globalización f globalization.
globo m globe; sphere; orb; balloon; ~ aerostático air balloon.
glóbulo m globule; corpuscle.
gloria f glory.
gloriarse vr: ~ en to glory in, to take pride in; to take delight in.
glorieta f bower, arbour; roundabout.
glorificación f glorification; praise.

glorificar vt to glorify.
glorioso/sa adj glorious.
glosa f gloss; comment.
glosar vt to gloss; to comment on.
glotón/ona m/f glutton.
glotonería f gluttony.
gobernación f government.
gobernador/ra m/f governor.
gobernar vt to govern; to regulate; to direct.
gobierno m government.
goce m enjoyment.
gol m goal.
goleta f schooner.
golf m golf.
golfa f (fam) slut.
golfo[1] m gulf, bay.
golfo[2] m (fam) urchin; lout.
golondrina f swallow.
golosina f dainty, titbit; sweet.
goloso/sa adj sweet-toothed.
golpe m blow, stroke, hit; knock; clash; coup; de ~ suddenly.
golpear vt to beat, to knock; to punch.
goma f gum; rubber; elastic.
gomosidad f stickiness, viscosity.
gomoso/sa adj gummy, viscous.
góndola f gondola; (ferro) freight truck.
gondolero m gondolier.
gordinflón/ona m/f very fat person.
gordo/da adj fat, plump, big-bellied; first, main; (fam) enormous.
gordura f grease; fatness, corpulence, obesity.
gorgojo m grub, weevil.
gorgorito m trill, warble.
gorila m gorilla.
gorjear vi to twitter, to chirp.
gorjeo m chirping.
gorra f cap; bonnet; (mil) bearskin.
gorrión m sparrow.
gorro m cap; bonnet.

gorrón/ona *m/f* scrounger.
gota *f* drop; (*med*) gout.
gotear *vt* to drip; to drizzle.
gotera *f* leak.
gótico/ca *adj* Gothic.
gotoso/sa *adj* gouty.
gozar *vt* to enjoy, to have, to possess;
~**se** *vr* to enjoy oneself, to rejoice.
gozne *m* hinge.
gozo *m* joy, pleasure.
gozoso/sa *adj* joyful, cheerful; content, glad, pleased.
grabación *f* recording.
grabado *m* engraving.
grabador *m* engraver.
grabadora *f* tape recorder.
grabar *vt* to engrave; to record.
gracejo *m* wit;, charm; gracefulness.
gracia *f* grace, gracefulness; wit;
¡(muchas) ~**s!** thanks (very much); **tener ~** to be funny.
gracioso/sa *adj* graceful; beautiful;
funny; pleasing; * *m* comic character.
grada *f* step of a staircase; tier, row;
~**s** *fpl* seats *pl* of a stadium or theatre.
gradería *f* (flight of) steps *pl*; row of seats.
grado *m* step; degree; **de buen ~** willingly.
graduación *f* graduation; (*mil*) rank.
gradual *adj* gradual.
graduar *vt* to graduate.
gráfico/ca *adj* graphic; * *m* diagram;
* *f* graph.
graja *f* rook.
grajo *m* rook.
grama *f* grass.
gramática *f* grammar.
gramatical *adj* grammatical.
gramático/ca *m/f* grammarian.
gramo *m* gram(me).

gran *adj* = **grande**.
grana *f* grain; scarlet.
granada *f* (*mil*) grenade; pomegranate.
granadero *m* (*mil*) grenadier.
granadilla *f* passionflower; passion fruit.
granado *m* pomegranate tree.
granate *m* garnet (precious stone).
grande *adj* great; big; tall; grand;
* *m/f* adult.
grandeza *f* greatness; grandeur; size.
grandiosidad *f* greatness; grandeur, magnificence.
grandioso/sa *adj* grand, magnificent.
granel *adv*: **a ~** in bulk.
granero *m* granary.
granito *m* granite.
granizada *f* hail; hailstorm; shower, volley.
granizado *m* iced drink.
granizar *vi* to hail.
granizo *m* hail.
granja *f* farm.
granjero/ra *m/f* farmer.
grano *m* grain.
granuja *m/f* rogue; urchin.
grapa *f* staple; clamp.
grasa *f* suet; fat; grease.
grasiento/ta *adj* greasy; rusty; filthy.
gratificación *f* gratification; recompense.
gratificar *vt* to gratify; to reward, to recompense.
gratis *adj* free; *adv* freely.
gratitud *f* gratitude, gratefulness.
grato/ta *adj* pleasant, agreeable.
gratuito/ta *adj* gratuitous; free.
gravamen *m* charge, obligation; nuisance; tax.
gravar *vt* to burden; (*com*) to tax.

grave *adj* weighty, heavy; grave, important; serious.

gravedad *f* gravity; graveness.

gravemente *adv* gravely, seriously.

gravilla *f* gravel.

gravitación *f* gravitation.

gravitar *vt* to gravitate; to weigh down on.

gravoso/sa *adj* onerous, burdensome; costly.

graznar *vi* to croak; to cackle; to quack.

graznido *m* croak; cackle; quack.

greda *f* clay.

gremio *m* union, guild; society; company, corporation.

greña *f* tangle; shock of hair.

greñudo/da *adj* dishevelled.

gresca *f* clatter; outcry; confusion; wrangle, quarrel.

grieta *f* crevice, crack, chink.

grifo *m* tap; petrol station.

grilletes *mpl* shackles *pl*; fetters *pl*.

grillo *m* cricket; bud, shoot; ~s *mpl* fetters *pl*, irons *pl*.

grima *f* disgust; annoyance.

gripe *f* flu, influenza.

gris *adj* grey.

gritar *vi* to cry out, to shout, to yell.

gritería *f* shouting, clamour, uproar.

grito *m* shout, cry, scream.

grosella *f* redcurrant; ~ **negra** blackcurrant.

grosellero *m* currant bush.

grosería *f* coarseness, rudeness; vulgar comment.

grosero/ra *adj* coarse; rude, bad-mannered.

grosor *m* thickness.

grotesco/ca *adj* grotesque.

grúa *f* crane (machine); derrick.

grueso/sa *adj* thick; bulky; large; coarse; * *m* bulk.

grulla *f* crane (bird).

grumo *m* clot; curd.

grumoso/sa *adj* clotted.

gruñido *m* grunt; growl.

gruñidor/ra *m/f* grunter, mumbler; (*fig*) grumbler.

gruñir *vi* to grunt; to grumble; to creak (of hinges etc).

grupa *f* rump.

grupo *m* group.

gruta *f* grotto.

guadaña *f* scythe.

guagua *f* baby; bus.

gualdrapa *f* trappings *pl* (of a horse); tatter, rag.

guantada *f* slap.

guante *m* glove.

guapo/pa *adj* good-looking; handsome; smart.

guarda *m/f* guard, keeper; * *f* custody, keeping.

guardaagujas *m invar* (*ferro*) switchman.

guardabosque *m* gamekeeper; ranger.

guardacostas *m invar* coastguard vessel.

guardaespaldas *m/f invar* bodyguard.

guardafuegos *m invar* fireguard, fender.

guardameta *m/f* goalkeeper.

guardapolvo *m* dust cover; overall.

guardar *vt* to keep, to preserve; to save (money); to guard; ~se *vr* to be on one's guard; ~se de to avoid, to abstain from.

guardarropa *f* wardrobe; cloakroom.

guardia *f* guard; (*mar*) watch; care, custody; * *m/f* guard; policeman/woman; * *m* (*mil*) guardsman.

guardián/ana *m/f* keeper; guardian.

guardilla *f* garret, attic.
guarecer *vt* to protect; to shelter; **~se** *vr* to take refuge.
guarida *f* den, lair; shelter; hiding place.
guarismo *m* figure, numeral.
guarnecer *vt* to provide, to equip; to reinforce; to garnish, to set (in gold, etc); to adorn.
guarnición *f* trimming; gold setting; sword guard; garnish; (*mil*) garrison.
guasa *f* joke.
guasón/ona *m/f* joker, jester.
gubernativo/va *adj* governmental.
guedeja *f* lock of hair.
guerra *f* war; hostility.
guerrear *vi* to fight, to wage war.
guerrero/ra *m/f* warrior; * *adj* martial, warlike.
guerrilla *f* guerrilla warfare; guerrilla group.
gueto *m* ghetto.
guía *m/f* guide; * *f* guidebook.
guiar *vt* to guide; (*auto*) to steer.
guijarral *m* stony place.
guijarro *m* pebble.
guillotina *f* guillotine.
guillotinar *vt* to guillotine.

guinda *f* cherry.
guindal *m* cherry tree.
guindilla *f* chilli pepper.
guiñapo *m* tatter, rag; rogue.
guiñar *vt* to wink.
guión *m* hyphen (in writing); script (of film).
guirigay *m* gibberish, confused language.
guirnalda *f* garland, wreath.
guisado *m* stew.
guisante *m* (*bot*) pea.
guisar *vt* to cook.
guiso *m* cooked dish; stew; seasoning.
guisote *m* hash, poor quality stew.
guitarra *f* guitar.
guitarrista *m/f* guitar player.
gula *f* gluttony.
gusano *m* maggot, worm.
gustar *vt* to taste; to sample; * *vi* to please, to be pleasing; **me gusta . . .** I like . . . .
gusto *m* taste; pleasure; delight; liking.
gustosamente *adv* gladly, with pleasure.
gustoso/sa *adj* pleasant; tasty.
gutural *adj* guttural.

H

haba *f* (*bot*) broad bean.
haber *vt* to get, to lay hands on; to occur; * *v imp*: **hay** there is, there are; * *v aux* to have; **~se** *vr*: **habérselas con uno** to have it out with somebody; * *m* income, salary; assets *pl*; (*com*) credit.
habichuela *f* bean.
hábil *adj* able, clever, skilful, dexterous, apt.

habilidad *f* ability, ableness, dexterity, aptitude.
habilitación *f* entitlement, qualification.
habilitar *vt* to qualify, to enable; to finance.
habitable *adj* inhabitable.
habitación *f* habitation, abode, lodging, dwelling, residence; room.
habitante *m/f* inhabitant, occupant.

habitar *vt* to inhabit, to live in.

hábito *m* dress; habit, custom.

habitual *adj* habitual, customary.

habituar *vt* to accustom; **~se** *vr* to become accustomed to.

habla *f* speech; language; dialect.

hablador/ra *m/f* talkative person.

habladuría *f* rumour; **~s** *fpl* gossip.

hablante *adj* speaking; * *m/f* speaker.

hablar *vt, vi* to speak; to talk.

hacedor/ra *m/f* maker; author.

hacendado *m* landowner; rancher.

hacendoso/sa *adj* industrious.

hacer *vt* to make; to do; to put into practice; to perform; to effect; to prepare; to imagine; to force; (*mat*) to amount to, to make; * *vi* to act, to behave; **~se** *vr* to become.

hacha *f* torch; axe, hatchet.

hachazo *m* blow with an axe.

hacia *adv* toward(s); about; **~ arriba/ abajo** up(wards)/down-(wards).

hacienda *f* property; large farm; ranch; **H~** Treasury.

hacinar *vt* to stack or pile up; to hoard.

hada *f* fairy.

hado *m* fate, destiny.

halagar *vt* to cajole, to flatter.

halago *m* cajolery; pleasure.

halagüeño *adj* attractive, flattering.

halcón *m* falcon.

halconero *m* falconer.

hálito *m* breath; gentle breeze.

hall *m* hall; foyer.

hallar *vt* to find; to meet with; to discover; **~se** *vr* to find oneself; to be.

hallazgo *m* finding, discovery.

hamaca *f* hammock.

hambre *f* hunger; famine; longing.

hambriento/ta *adj* hungry; starved.

hamburguesa *f* hamburger.

haragán/ana *m/f* idler, good-for-nothing.

haraganear *vi* to idle, to loiter.

haraganería *f* idleness, laziness.

harapo *m* rag, tatter.

haraposo *adj* ragged.

hardware *m* hardware.

harina *f* flour; **~ de maíz** cornflour.

harinoso/sa *adj* floury.

hartar *vt* to satiate; to glut; to tire, to sicken; **~se** *vr* to gorge oneself (with food); to get fed up.

harto/ta *adj* full; fed up; * *adv* enough.

hartura *f* surfeit; plenty, abundance.

hasta *prep* up to; down to; until, as far as; * *adv* even.

hastío *m* loathing; disgust; boredom.

hatajo *m* lot, collection.

hato *m* clothes *pl*; herd of cattle, flock of sheep; provisions *pl*; crowd, gang, collection.

haya *f* beech tree.

haz *m* bunch, bundle; beam (of light).

hazaña *f* exploit, achievement.

hazmerreír *m* *invar* ridiculous person, laughing stock.

hebilla *f* buckle.

hebra *f* thread; vein of minerals or metals; grain of wood.

hebraico/ca *adj* belonging to the Hebrews.

hebreo/ea *m/f* Hebrew; Israeli; * *m* Hebrew language; * *adj* Hebrew; Israeli.

hechicería *f* witchcraft; charm.

hechicero/ra *adj* charming, bewitching; * *m/f* sorcerer/ sorceress.

hechizar *vt* to bewitch, to enchant; to charm.

hechizo *m* bewitchment, enchantment.

hecho/cha *adj* made; done; mature; ready-to-wear; cooked; * *m* action; act; fact; matter; event.

hechura *f* form, shape; fashion; making; workmanship; creature.

hectárea *f* hectare.

heder *vi* to stink, to smell bad.

hediondez *f* strong stench.

hediondo/da *adj* foetid, stinking.

hedor *m* stench, stink.

helada *f* frost; freeze-up.

helado/da *adj* frozen; glacial, icy; astonished; astounded; * *m* ice cream.

helar *vt* to freeze; to congeal; to astonish, to amaze; ~**se** *vr* to be frozen; to turn into ice; to congeal; * *vi* to freeze; to congeal.

helecho *m* fern.

hélice *f* helix; propeller.

helicóptero *m* helicopter.

hembra *f* female.

hemisferio *m* hemisphere.

hemorragia *f* haemorrhage.

hemorroides *fpl* haemorrhoids *pl*, piles *pl*.

henchir *vt* to fill up; ~**se** *vr* to fill or stuff oneself.

hendedura *f* fissure, chink, crevice.

hender *vt* to crack, to split; to go through; to open a passage.

hendidura *f* = **hendedura**.

heno *m* hay.

heraldo *m* herald.

herborizar *vi* to pick herbs; to collect plants.

heredad *f* patrimony, inherited property; farm.

heredar *vt* to inherit.

heredera *f* heiress.

heredero *m* heir.

hereditario/ria *adj* hereditary.

hereje *m/f* heretic.

herejía *f* heresy.

herencia *f* inheritance, heritage, heredity.

herida *f* wound, injury.

herido/da *adj* wounded, hurt.

herir *vt* to wound, to hurt; to beat, to strike; to affect, to touch, to move; to offend.

hermafrodita *m* hermaphrodite.

hermana *f* sister.

hermanar *vt* to match, to suit, to harmonize.

hermanastra *f* step-sister, half-sister.

hermanastro *m* step-brother, half-brother.

hermandad *f* fraternity; brotherhood.

hermano *m* brother; ~/**na** *adj* matched; resembling.

hermético/ca *adj* hermetic, watertight.

hermoso/sa *adj* beautiful, handsome, lovely; large, robust.

hermosura *f* beauty.

hernia *f* hernia, rupture.

héroe *m* hero.

heroicidad *f* heroism; heroic deed.

heroico/ca *adj* heroic.

heroína[1] *f* heroine.

heroína[2] *f* heroin (drug).

heroísmo *m* heroism.

herpes *m* herpes; * *fpl* (*med*) shingles.

herrador *m* farrier, blacksmith.

herradura *f* horseshoe.

herramienta *f* tool.

herrar *vt* to shoe (horses).

herrería *f* ironworks; forge.

herrero *m* smith.

hervidero *m* boiling; unrest; swarm.

hervir *vt* to boil; to cook; * *vi* to boil; to bubble; to seethe.

hervor *m* boiling; fervour, passion.

heterogeneidad *f* heterogeneous-ness.

heterogéneo/nea *adj* heterogeneous.
heterosexual *adj*, *m/f* heterosexual.
heterosexualidad *f* heterosexuality.
hexámetro *m* hexameter.
hez *f* lees *pl*, dregs *pl*.
hidalgo *m* nobleman.
hidalguía *f* nobility.
hidra *f* hydra.
hidráulica *f* hydraulics.
hidráulico/ca *adj* hydraulic.
hidroavión *m* seaplane.
hidrofobia *f* hydrophobia.
hidrógeno *m* (*quím*) hydrogen.
hidromasaje *m* whirlpool bath.
hiedra *f* ivy.
hiel *f* gall, bile.
hielo *m* frost; ice.
hiena *f* hyena.
hierba *f* grass; herb.
hierro *m* iron.
hígado *m* liver; (*fig*) courage, pluck.
higiene *f* hygiene.
higiénico/ca *adj* hygienic.
higo *m* fig.
higuera *f* fig tree.
hijastro/tra *m/f* stepson/daughter.
hijo/ja *m/f* son/daughter; child; offspring.
hilandero/ra *m/f* spinner.
hilar *vt* to spin.
hilera *f* row, line, file.
hilo *m* thread; wire.
hilván *m* tacking.
hilvanar *vt* to tack; to perform in a hurry.
himno *m* hymn.
hincapié *m*: **hacer ~ en** to emphasize.
hincar *vt* to thrust in, to drive in.
hincha *m/f* (*fam*) fan.
hinchado/da *adj* swollen; vain, arrogant.
hinchar *vt* to swell; to inflate; (*fig*) to

exaggerate; **~se** *vr* to swell; to become vain.
hinchazón *f* swelling, lump.
hinojo *m* (*bot*) fennel.
hipar *vi* to hiccup.
hipérbola *f* hyperbola, section of a cone.
hipérbole *f* hyperbole, exaggeration.
hiperbólico/ca *adj* hyperbolic, hyperbolical.
hipermercado, híper *m* hypermarket, superstore.
hípica *f* horseracing; showjumping.
hipnotismo *m* hypnotism.
hipo *m* hiccups *pl*.
hipocondria *f* hypochondria.
hipocondríaco/ca *adj* hypochondriac.
hipocresía *f* hypocrisy.
hipócrita *adj* hypocritical; * *m/f* hypocrite.
hipódromo *m* racetrack.
hipopótamo *m* hippopotamus.
hipoteca *f* mortgage.
hipotecar *vt* to mortgage.
hipotecario/ria *adj* belonging to a mortgage.
hipótesis *f* hypothesis.
hipotético/ca *adj* hypothetical.
hisopo *m* (*bot*) hyssop; water sprinkler; paintbrush.
hispano/na *adj* Hispanic.
Hispanoamérica *f* Spanish America.
hispanoamericano/na *adj*, *n* Spanish American.
histeria *f* hysteria.
histérico/ca *adj* hysterical.
historia *f* history; tale, story.
historiador/ra *m/f* historian.
histórico/ca *adj* historical; historic.
historieta *f* short story; short novel; comic strip.
hito *m* landmark; boundary post; target.

hocico *m* snout; **meter el ~ en todo** to meddle in everything.

hogar *m* hearth, fireplace; (*fig*) house, home; family life.

hogaza *f* large loaf of bread.

hoguera *f* bonfire; blaze.

hoja *f* leaf; petal; sheet of paper; blade.

hojalata *f* tin (plate).

hojaldre *f* puff pastry.

hojarasca *f* dead leaves *pl*; rubbish.

hojear *vt* to turn the pages of.

hola *excl* hello!

holgado/da *adj* loose, wide, baggy; at leisure; idle, unoccupied; well-to-do; well-off.

holgar *vi* to rest; to be out of work; to be superfluous.

holgazán/ana *m/f* idler, slacker.

holgazanear *vt* to idle, to loaf around, to lounge around.

holgazanería *f* idleness, laziness.

holgura *f* looseness, bagginess; leisure; comfort; enjoyment.

hollín *m* soot.

holocausto *m* holocaust.

hombre *m* man; human being.

hombrera *f* shoulder pad.

hombro *m* shoulder.

hombruno/na *adj* manlike; virile, manly.

homenaje *m* homage.

homicida *m/f* murderer; * *adj* murderous, homicidal.

homicidio *m* murder.

homilía *f* homily.

homogeneidad *f* homogeneity.

homogéneo/nea *adj* homogeneous.

homólogo/ga *adj* homologous; synonymous.

homosexual *adj*, *m/f* homosexual.

honda *f* sling, catapult.

hondazo *m* throw with a sling.

hondo/da *adj* deep; profound; intense.

hondonada *f* dale, hollow; ravine.

hondura *f* depth, profundity.

honestidad *f* honesty; modesty; decency.

honesto/ta *adj* honest; modest.

hongo *m* mushroom; fungus; bowler hat.

honor *m* honour.

honorable *adj* honourable.

honorario/ria *adj* honorary; **~s** *mpl* fees *pl*.

honorífico/ca *adj* creditable, honourable.

honra *f* honour, reverence; self-esteem; reputation; integrity; **~s funebres** *pl* funeral honours *pl*.

honradez *f* honesty, integrity.

honrado/da *adj* honest; honourable; reputable.

honrar *vt* to honour.

honroso/sa *adj* honourable; respectable; honest.

hora *f* hour; time.

horadar *vt* to drill, to bore.

horario/ria *adj* hourly, hour *compd*; * *m* timetable.

horca *f* gallows; pitchfork.

horcajadas *adv*: **a ~** astride.

horchata *f* tiger-nut milk.

horizontal *adj* horizontal.

horizonte *m* horizon.

horma *f* mould, form.

hormiga *f* ant.

hormigón *m* concrete.

hormiguear *vi* to itch; to swarm, to team.

hormiguero *m* anthill; place swarming with people.

hormona *f* hormone.

hornada *f* batch.

horno *m* oven; furnace.

horóscopo *m* horoscope.

horquilla *f* pitchfork; hairpin.

horrendo/da *adj* horrible; frightful.

hórreo *m* granary.

horrible *adj* horrid, horrible.

horripilante *adj* hair-raising.

horror *m* horror, fright; atrocity.

horrorizar *vt* to horrify; **~se** *vr* to be terrified.

horroroso/sa *adj* horrid, hideous, frightful.

hortaliza *f* vegetable.

hortelano/na *m/f* gardener; market gardener.

hortera *m* shop assistant; (*fig*) coarse person.

hosco/ca *adj* sullen, gloomy.

hospedaje *m* board and lodging.

hospedar *vt* to put up, to lodge; to entertain.

hospedería *f* inn; guest room; hospice.

hospedero/ra *m/f* landlord/lady; host/hostess.

hospicio *m* orphanage; hospice.

hospital *m* hospital.

hospitalario/ria *adj* hospitable.

hospitalidad *f* hospitality.

hostal *m* small hotel.

hostelería *f* hotel business or trade.

hostería *f* inn, tavern, hostelry.

hostia *f* host; wafer; (*fam*) whack (*sl*), punch.

hostigar *vt* to lash, to whip; to trouble, to pester, to bore.

hostil *adj* hostile; adverse.

hostilidad *f* hostility.

hostilizar *vt* (*mil*) to harry, to harass.

hotel *m* hotel.

hoy *adv* today; now, nowadays; **de ~ en adelante** as from today.

hoya *f* hole, pit.

hoyo *m* hole, pit; excavation.

hoz *f* sickle; gorge.

hozar *vi* to grub (of pigs).

hucha *f* money-box.

hueco/ca *adj* hollow, concave; empty; vain, ostentatious; * *m* interval; gap, hole; vacancy.

huelga *f* strike.

huella *f* track, footstep.

huérfano/na *adj*, *m/f* orphan.

huero/ra *adj* empty; addled.

huerta *f* market garden; irrigated region.

huerto *m* orchard; kitchen garden; **~ de hortalizas** market garden.

hueso *m* bone; stone, core.

huésped/da *m/f* guest, lodger; innkeeper.

hueste *f* army; crowd.

huesudo/da *adj* bony.

huevera *f* eggcup.

huevo *m* egg.

huida *f* flight, escape.

huir *vi* to flee, to escape.

hule *m* oilcloth.

humanidad *f* humanity; corpulence; **~es** *fpl* humanities *pl*.

humano/na *adj* human; humane, kind.

humareda *f* cloud of smoke.

humeante *adj* smoking; steaming.

humear *vi* to smoke.

humedad *f* humidity, moisture; wetness.

humedecer *vt* to moisten; to wet; to soak.

húmedo/da *adj* humid; wet; moist; damp.

humildad *f* humility, humbleness; submission.

humilde *adj* humble.

humillación *f* humiliation, submission.

humillar *vt* to humble; to subdue; **~se** *vr* to humble oneself.

humo *m* smoke; fumes *pl*.

humor *m* mood, temper; humour.

hundir *vt* to submerge; to sink; to ruin; **~se** *vr* to sink, to go to the bottom; to collapse; to be ruined.

huracán *m* hurricane.

huraño/ña *adj* shy; unsociable.

hurgar *vt* to stir; to poke.

hurón *m* ferret; (*fig*) shy person; busybody.

huronear *vt* to ferret out.

hurtadillas *adv*: **a ~** by stealth.

hurtar *vt* to steal, to rob.

hurto *m* theft, robbery.

húsar *m* hussar.

husmear *vt* to scent; to pry into.

huso *m* spindle.

I

ictericia *f* jaundice.

ida *f* departure, going; **(viaje de) ~** outward journey; **~ y vuelta** round trip; **~s y venidas** comings and goings *pl*.

idea *f* idea; scheme.

ideal *adj* ideal.

idealmente *adv* ideally.

idear *vt* to conceive; to think, to contrive.

ídem *pn* ditto.

idéntico/ca *adj* identical.

identidad *f* identity.

identificar *vt* to identify.

ideología *f* ideology.

idilio *m* idyll.

idioma *m* language.

idiosincrasia *f* idiosyncrasy.

idiota *m/f* idiot.

idiotez *f* idiocy.

idólatra *m/f* idolater.

idolatrar *vt* to idolize; to worship.

idolatría *f* idolatry.

ídolo *m* idol.

idoneidad *f* aptitude, fitness.

idóneo/nea *adj* suitable, fit.

iglesia *f* church.

ignominia *f* ignominy; infamy.

ignominioso/sa *adj* ignominious.

ignorancia *f* ignorance.

ignorante *adj* ignorant, uninformed.

ignorar *vt* to be ignorant of, not to know.

igual *adj* equal; similar; the same; **al ~** equally.

igualar *vt* to equalize, to equal; to match; to level off; **~se** *vr* to be equal; to agree.

igualdad *f* equality.

igualmente *adv* equally.

ijar *m* flank.

ilegal *adj* illegal, unlawful.

ilegalidad *f* illegality.

ilegitimidad *f* illegitimacy.

ilegítimo/ma *adj* illegal; illegitimate.

ileso/sa *adj* unhurt.

ilícito/ta *adj* illicit, unlawful.

ilimitado/da *adj* unlimited.

illustrar *vt* to illustrate; to instruct.

iluminación *f* illumination.

iluminar *vt* to illumine, to illuminate, to enlighten.

ilusión *f* illusion; hope; **hacerse ~ones** to build up one's hopes.

ilusionista *m/f* conjurer.

iluso/sa *adj* easily deceived.

ilusorio/ria *adj* illusory.

ilustración *f* illustration; enlightenment.

ilustre *adj* illustrious, famous.

imagen *f* image.
imaginable *adj* imaginable.
imaginación *f* imagination; fancy.
imaginar *vt* to imagine; to think up; *vi*, ~**se** *vr* to imagine.
imán *m* magnet.
imbécil *m/f* imbecile, idiot.
imbecilidad *f* imbecility.
imbuir *vt* to imbue; to infuse.
imitable *adj* imitable.
imitación *f* imitation; **a** ~ **de** in imitation of.
imitador/ra *m/f* imitator.
imitar *vt* to imitate, to copy; to counterfeit.
impaciencia *f* impatience.
impacientar *vt* to make impatient; to irritate.
impaciente *adj* impatient.
impacto *m* impact.
impar *adj* odd.
imparcial *adj* impartial.
imparcialidad *f* impartiality.
impasibilidad *f* impassivity.
impasible *adj* impassive.
impavidez *f* intrepidity; cheek(iness).
impávido/da *adj* dauntless, intrepid; cheeky.
impecable *adj* impeccable.
impedimento *f* impediment, obstacle.
impedir *vt* to impede, to hinder; to prevent.
impeler *vt* to drive, to propel; to impel; to incite, to stimulate.
impenetrable *adj* impenetrable, impervious; incomprehensible.
impenitente *adj* impenitent.
impensado/da *adj* impenitent.
imperativo/va *adj*, *m* imperative.
imperceptible *adj* imperceptible.
imperdible *m* safety pin.
imperdonable *adj* unforgivable.

imperfección *f* imperfection.
imperfecto/ta *adj* imperfect.
imperial *adj* imperial.
impericia *f* lack of experience.
imperio *m* empire.
imperioso/sa *adj* imperious; arrogant, haughty; urgent.
impermeable *adj* waterproof; * *m* raincoat.
impermutable *adj* immutable.
impersonal *adj* impersonal.
impertérrito/ta *adj* intrepid, fearless.
impertinencia *f* impertinence; irrelevance.
impertinente *adj* not pertinent; touchy; impertinent.
imperturbable *adj* imperturbable; unruffled.
ímpetu *m* impetus; impetuosity.
impetuoso/sa *adj* impetuous.
implacable *adj* implacable, inexorable.
implicación *f* implication.
implicar *vt* to implicate, to involve.
implícito/ta *adj* implicit.
implorar *vt* to beg, to implore.
imponderable *adj* imponderable; (*fig*) priceless.
imponer *vt* to impose; to command; ~**se** *vr* to assert oneself; to prevail.
impopular *adj* unpopular.
importación *f* importing; imports *pl*.
importancia *f* importance; significance, weight; size.
importante *adj* important, considerable.
importar *vi* to be important, to matter; * *vt* to import; to be worth.
importe *m* amount, cost.
importunar *vt* to bother, to pester.
importunidad *f* pestering; annoyance.
importuno/na *adj* annoying; unreasonable.

imposibilidad f impossibility.

imposibilitar vt to make impossible.

imposible adj impossible; extremely difficult; slovenly.

imposición f imposition; tax; deposit.

impostor/ra m/f impostor, fraud.

impostura f imposture, deceit, cheat.

impotencia f impotence.

impotente adj impotent.

impracticable adj impracticable, unworkable.

imprecación f curse.

imprecar vt to curse.

imprecatorio/ria adj containing curses, full of evil wishes.

impreciso/sa adj imprecise, vague.

impregnarse vr to be impregnated.

imprenta f printing; press; printing office.

imprescindible adj essential.

impresión f impression; stamp; print; edition.

impresionante adj impressive; marvellous; tremendous.

impresionar vt to move; to impress; ~se vr to be impressed; to be moved.

impreso m printed paper; printed book.

impresor m printer.

impresora f printer; ~ láser laser printer.

imprevisto/ta adj unforeseen, unexpected.

imprimir vt to print; to imprint; to stamp.

improbable adj improbable, unlikely.

improperio m insult, taunt.

impropio/pia adj improper; unfit; unbecoming.

improvisar vt to extemporize; to improvize.

improviso/sa adj: de ~ unexpectedly.

imprudencia f imprudence; indiscretion; carelessness.

imprudente adj imprudent; indiscreet; unwise.

impudencia f shamelessness.

impudente adj shameless.

impúdico/ca adj shameless; lecherous.

impuesto/ta adj imposed; * m tax, duty.

impugnación f opposition, contradiction.

impugnar vt to oppose; challenge; impugn.

impulsivo/va adj impulsive.

impulso m impulse; thrust; (fig) impulse.

impune adj unpunished.

impunidad f impunity.

impureza f impurity.

impuro/ra adj impure;, foul.

imputable adj attributable, chargeable.

imputar vt to impute, to attribute.

inaccesible adj inaccessible.

inacción f inaction, inactivity.

inadmisible adj inadmissible.

inadvertencia f carelessness, inadvertence.

inadvertido/da adj unnoticed.

inagotable adj inexhaustible.

inaguantable adj unbearable, intolerable.

inalterable adj unalterable.

inapelable adj without appeal.

inapreciable adj imperceptible; invaluable.

inaudito/ta adj unheard-of.

inauguración f inauguration, opening.

inaugurar *vt* to inaugurate.
incalculable *adj* incalculable.
incandescente *adj* incandescent.
incansable *adj* untiring, tireless.
incapacidad *f* incapacity, inability.
incapaz *adj* incapable, unable.
incauto/ta *adj* incautious, unwary.
incendiar *vt* to kindle, to set on fire.
incendiario/ria *adj* incendiary; * *m/f* arsonist.
incendio *m* fire.
incentivo *m* incentive.
incertidumbre *f* doubt, uncertainty.
incesante *adj* incessant, continual.
incesto *m* incest.
incestuoso/sa *adj* incestuous.
incidencia *f* incidence; incident.
incidente *m* incident.
incidir *vi*: ~ **en** to fall upon; to influence, to affect.
incienso *m* incense.
incierto/ta *adj* uncertain, doubtful.
incineración *f* incineration; cremation.
incipiente *adj* incipient.
incisión *f* incision, cut.
incisivo/va *adj* incisive.
inciso *m* (*gr*) comma.
incitación *f* incitement.
incitar *vt* to incite, to excite.
incivil *adj* uncivil, rude.
inclemencia *f* inclemency, severity; inclemency (of the weather).
inclinación *f* inclination.
inclinar *vt* to incline; to nod, to bow (the head); ~**se** *vr* to bow; to stoop.
incluir *vt* to include, to comprise; to incorporate; to enclose.
inclusión *f* inclusion.
inclusive *adv* inclusive.
incluso/sa *adj* included; * *adv* inclusively; even.

incógnito/ta *adj* unknown; **de** ~ incognito.
incoherencia *f* incoherence.
incoherente *adj* incoherent.
incombustible *adj* incombustible, fireproof.
incomodar *vt* to inconvenience; to bother, to annoy.
incomodidad *f* inconvenience; annoyance; discomfort.
incómodo/da *adj* uncomfortable; annoying; inconvenient.
incomparable *adj* incomparable, matchless.
incompatibilidad *f* incompatibility.
incompatible *adj* incompatible.
incompetencia *f* incompetence.
incompetente *adj* incompetent.
incompleto/ta *adj* incomplete.
incomprehensible *adj* incomprehensible.
incomunicación *f* isolation; lack of communication.
incomunicado/da *adj* isolated, cut off; in solitary confinement.
inconcebible *adj* inconceivable.
incondicional *adj* unconditional; wholehearted; staunch.
inconexo/xa *adj* unconnected, disconnected.
inconfundible *adj* unmistakable.
incongruencia *adj* incongruity, incongruence.
incongruo/grua *adj* incongruous.
inconmensurable *adj* immeasurable.
inconsciencia *f* unconsciousness; thoughtlessness.
inconsciente *adj* unconscious; thoughtless.
inconsecuencia *f* inconsequence.
inconsiderado/da *adj* inconsiderate, thoughtless.

inconsolable *adj* inconsolable.

inconstancia *f* inconstancy, unsteadiness.

inconstante *adj* inconstant, variable, fickle.

incontestable *adj* indisputable, incontrovertible, undeniable.

incontinencia *f* incontinence.

incontinente *adj* incontinent.

inconveniencia *f* inconvenience; impoliteness; unsuitability.

inconveniente *adj* inconvenient, unsuitable; impolite.

incorporación *f* incorporation, involvement.

incorporar *vt* to incorporate; ~**se** *vr* to sit up; to join (an organization), to become incorporated.

incorrecto/ta *adj* incorrect.

incorregible *adj* incorrigible.

incorruptible *adj* incorruptible.

incredulidad *f* incredulity.

incrédulo/la *la adj* incredulous.

increíble *adj* incredible.

incremento *m* increment, increase; growth; rise.

increpar *vt* to reprehend, to reprimand.

incruento/ta *adj* bloodless.

inculcar *vt* to inculcate.

inculpar *vt* to accuse, to blame.

inculto/ta *adj* uncultivated; uneducated; uncouth.

incumbencia *f* obligation; duty.

incumbir *vi*: ~ **a uno** to be incumbent upon one.

incurable *adj* incurable; irremediable.

incurrir *vt*: ~ **en** to incur; to commit (a crime).

incursión *f* incursion, raid.

indagación *f* search, inquiry.

indagar *vt* to inquire into.

indebido/da *adj* undue; illegal, unlawful.

indecencia *f* indecency.

indecente *adj* indecent.

indecible *adj* unspeakable, unutterable.

indecisión *f* hesitation; indecision.

indeciso/sa *adj* hesitant; undecided.

indecoroso/sa *adj* unseemly, unbecoming.

indefectible *adj* infallible.

indefenso/sa *adj* defenceless.

indefinible *adj* indefinable.

indefinido/da *adj* indefinite.

indeleble *adj* indelible.

indemnización *f* indemnification, compensation.

indemnizar *vt* to indemnify, to compensate.

independencia *f* independence.

independiente *adj* independent.

indestructible *adj* indestructible.

indeterminado/da *adj* indeterminate; indefinite.

indicación *f* indication.

indicador *m* indicator; gauge.

indicar *vt* to indicate.

indicativo/va *adj, m* indicative.

índice *m* ratio, rate; hand (of a watch or clock); index, table of contents; catalogue; forefinger, index finger.

indicio *m* indication, mark; sign, token; clue.

indiferencia *f* indifference, apathy.

indiferente *adj* indifferent.

indígena *adj* indigenous, native; * *m/f* native.

indigencia *f* indigence, poverty, need.

indigente *adj* indigent, poor, destitute.

indigestión *f* indigestion.

indigesto/ta *adj* undigested; indigestible.

indignación *f* indignation, anger.

indignar *vt* to irritate; to provoke, to tease; **~se** *vr*: **~ por** to get indignant about.

indigno/na *adj* unworthy, contemptible, low.

indirecta *f* innuendo, hint.

indirecto/ta *adj* indirect.

indisciplinado/da *adj* undisciplined.

indiscreción *f* indiscretion, tactlessness; gaffe.

indiscreto/ta *adj* indiscreet, tactless.

indisoluble *adj* indissoluble.

indispensable *adj* indispensable.

indisponer *vt* to spoil, to upset; to make ill; **~se** *vr* to fall ill.

indisposición *f* indisposition, slight illness.

indispuesto/ta *adj* indisposed.

indisputable *adj* indisputable, incontrovertible.

indistinto/ta *adj* indistinct.

individual *adj* individual; single (of a room); * *m* (*dep*) singles.

individualidad *f* individuality.

individualizar *vt* to specify individually.

individuo *m* individual.

indivisible *adj* indivisible.

indocilidad *f* disobedience.

índole *f* disposition, nature, character; soft, kind.

indolencia *f* indolence, laziness.

indolente *adj* indolent, lazy.

indómito/ta *adj* untamed, ungoverned.

inducción *f* induction, persuasion.

inducir *vt* to induce, to persuade.

inductivo/va *adj* inductive.

indudable *adj* undoubted; unquestionable.

indulgencia *f* indulgence.

indulgente *adj* indulgent.

indultar *vt* to pardon; to exempt.

indulto *m* pardon; exemption.

industria *f* industry; skill.

industrial *adj* industrial.

industrialización *f* industrialization.

inédito/ta *adj* unpublished; (*fig*) new.

inefable *adj* ineffable, unspeakable, indescribable.

ineficacia *f* inefficacy.

ineficaz *adj* ineffective; inefficient.

ineptitud *f* inability; unfitness, ineptitude.

inepto/ta *adj* inept, unfit, useless.

inercia *f* inertia, inactivity.

inerme *adj* unarmed; defenceless.

inerte *adj* inert; dull; sluggish, motionless.

inescrutable *adj* inscrutable.

inesperado/da *adj* unexpected, unforeseen.

inestable *adj* unstable.

inestimable *adj* inestimable.

inevitable *adj* unavoidable.

inexactitud *f* inaccuracy.

inexacto/ta *adj* inaccurate, untrue.

inexorable *adj* inexorable.

inexperto/ta *adj* inexperienced.

infalibilidad *f* infallibility.

infalible *adj* infallible.

infame *adj* infamous.

infancia *f* infancy, childhood.

infanta *f* infanta, princess.

infante *m* infante, prince; (*mil*) infantryman.

infantería *f* infantry.

infanticida *m/f* infanticide (person).

infanticidio *m* infanticide (murder).

infantil *adj* infantile; childlike; children's.

infarto *m* heart attack; **~ de miocardio** heart attack.

infatigable *adj* tireless, untiring.
infección *f* infection.
infectar *vt* to infect.
infeliz *adj* unhappy, unfortunate.
inferior *adj* inferior.
inferioridad *f* inferiority.
inferir *vt* to infer.
infernal *adj* infernal, hellish.
infestar *vt* to harass; to infest.
infidelidad *f* infidelity, unfaithfulness.
infiel *adj* unfaithful; disloyal; inaccurate.
infierno *m* hell.
infiltración *f* infiltration.
infiltrarse *vr* to infiltrate.
ínfimo/ma *adj* lowest; of very poor quality.
infinidad *f* infinity; immensity.
infinitivo *m* (*gr*) infinitive.
infinito/ta *adj* infinite; immense.
inflación *f* inflation.
inflamable *adj* flammable.
inflamación *f* ignition; inflammation.
inflamar *vt* to inflame; to excite, to arouse; **~se** *vr* to catch fire.
inflamatorio/ria *adj* inflammatory.
inflar *vt* to inflate, to blow up; (*fig*) to exaggerate.
inflexibilidad *f* inflexibility.
inflexible *adj* inflexible.
influencia *f* influence.
influir *vt* to influence.
influjo *m* influence.
infografía *f* computer graphics.
información *f* information; news; (*mil*) intelligence; investigation, judicial inquiry.
informal *adj* irregular, incorrect; untrustworthy; informal.
informalidad *f* irregularity; untrustworthiness; informality.

informar *vt* to inform; to reveal, to make known; **~se** *vr* to find out; * *vi* to report; (*jur*) to plead; to inform.
informática *f* computer science, information technology.
informe *m* report, statement; piece of information, account; * *adj* shapeless, formless.
infortunio *m* misfortune, ill luck.
infracción *f* infraction; breach, infringement.
infractor/ra *m/f* offender.
infructuoso/sa *adj* fruitless, unproductive, unprofitable.
infundado/da *adj* groundless.
infundir *vt* to infuse, to instil.
infusión *f* infusion.
infuso/sa *adj* infused; introduced.
ingeniar *vt* to devise; **~se** *vr*: **~ para** to manage to.
ingeniería *f* engineering; **~ genética** genetic engineering.
ingeniero/ra *m/f* engineer.
ingenio *m* talent; wit; ingenuity; engine; **~ de azúcar** sugar mill.
ingenioso/sa *adj* ingenious, clever; witty.
ingenuidad *f* ingenuousness; candour, frankness.
ingenuo/nua *adj* ingenuous.
ingerir *vt* to ingest; to swallow; to consume.
ingle *f* groin.
inglés/esa *adj* English; * *m* English (language); * *m/f* Englishman/woman.
ingratitud *f* ingratitude, unthankfulness.
ingrato/ta *adj* ungrateful, thankless; disagreeable.
ingrediente *m* ingredient.
ingresar *vt* to deposit; * *vi* to come in.

ingreso *m* entry; admission; **~s** *mpl* income; takings *pl*.

inhabilitar *vt* to disqualify, to disable.

inhabitable *adj* uninhabitable.

inherente *adj* inherent.

inhibición *f* inhibition.

inhibir *vt* to inhibit; to restrain.

inhumano/na *adj* inhuman.

inicial *adj*, *f* initial.

iniciar *vt* to initiate; to begin.

iniciativa *f* initiative.

inimaginable *adj* unimaginable, inconceivable.

inimitable *adj* inimitable.

ininteligible *adj* unintelligible.

iniquidad *f* iniquity, injustice.

injertar *vt* to graft.

injerto *m* graft.

injuria *f* offence; insult.

injuriar *vt* to insult, to wrong.

injurioso/sa *adj* insulting; offensive.

injusticia *f* injustice.

injusto/ta *adj* unjust.

inmaculado/da *adj* immaculate.

inmadurez *f* immaturity.

inmediaciones *fpl* neighbourhood; surrounding area.

inmediatamente *adv* immediately, at once.

inmediato/ta *adj* immediate.

inmemorial *adj* immemorial.

inmensidad *f* immensity.

inmenso/sa *adj* immense.

inmensurable *adj* immeasurable.

inmigración *f* immigration.

inmigrante *m/f* immigrant.

inmigrar *vi* to immigrate.

inminente *adj* imminent.

inmobiliario/ria *adj* real-estate *compd*; * *f* estate agency.

inmoral *adj* immoral.

inmortal *adj* immortal.

inmortalidad *f* immortality.

inmortalizar *vt* to immortalize.

inmóvil *adj* immovable.

inmovilidad *f* immobility.

inmueble *m* property; * *adj*: **bienes ~s** real estate.

inmundicia *f* nastiness, filth.

inmundo/da *adj* filthy, dirty; nasty.

inmune *adj* (*med*) immune; free, exempt.

inmunidad *f* immunity; exemption.

inmutabilidad *f* immutability.

inmutable *adj* immutable.

inmutarse *vr* to turn pale.

innato/ta *adj* inborn, innate.

innecesario/ria *adj* unnecessary.

innegable *adj* undeniable.

innovación *f* innovation.

innovador/ra *m/f* innovator.

innovar *vt* to innovate.

innumerable *adj* innumerable, countless.

inocencia *f* innocence.

inocentada *f* practical joke.

inocente *adj* innocent.

inoculación *f* inoculation.

inocular *vt* to inoculate.

inodoro *m* toilet.

inofensivo/va *adj* harmless.

inolvidable *adj* unforgettable.

inopinado/da *adj* unexpected.

inoxidable *adj*: **acero ~** stainless steel.

inquietar *vt* to worry, to disturb; **~se** *vr* to worry, to get worried.

inquieto/ta *adj* anxious, worried.

inquietud *f* uneasiness, anxiety.

inquilino/na *m/f* tenant; lodger.

inquirir *vt* to inquire into, to investigate.

insaciable *adj* insatiable.

insalubre *adj* unhealthy.

insalubridad *f* unhealthiness.

insano/na adj insane, mad.

inscribir vt to inscribe; to list, to register.

inscripción f inscription; enrolment, registration.

insecticida m insecticide.

insecto m insect.

inseguridad f insecurity.

inseminación f insemination; ~ **artificial** artificial insemination.

insensatez f stupidity, folly.

insensato/ta adj senseless, stupid; mad.

insensibilidad f insensitivity; callousness.

insensible adj insensitive; imperceptible; numb.

insensiblemente adv insensitively; imperceptibly.

inseparable adj inseparable.

inserción f insertion.

insertar vt to insert.

inservible adj useless.

insidioso/sa adj insidious.

insigne adj notable.

insignificante adj insignificant.

insignia f badge; ~s fpl insignia pl.

insinuación f insinuation.

insinuar vt to insinuate; ~**se** vr: to make advances; ~ **en** to worm one's way into.

insipidez f insipidness.

insípido/da adj insipid.

insistencia f persistence; insistence.

insistir vi to insist.

insolación f (med) sunstroke.

insolencia f insolence, rudeness, effrontery.

insolente adj insolent, rude.

insólito/ta adj unusual.

insolvencia f insolvency.

insolvente adj insolvent.

insomnio m insomnia.

insondable adj unfathomable; inscrutable.

insoportable adj unbearable.

inspección f inspection, survey; check.

inspeccionar vt to inspect; to supervise.

inspector/ra m/f inspector; superintendent.

inspiración f inspiration.

inspirar vt to inspire; (med) to inhale.

instalación f installation.

instalar vt to install.

instancia f instance.

instantáneo/nea adj instantaneous; * f snap(shot); **café** ~ instant coffee.

instante m instant; **al** ~ immediately, instantly.

instar vt to press, to urge.

instigación f instigation.

instigar vt to instigate.

instinto m instinct.

institución f institution.

instituir vt to institute.

instituto m institute.

institutriz f governess.

instrucción f instruction.

instructivo/va adj instructive; educational.

instructor/ra m/f instructor, teacher.

instruir vt to instruct, to teach.

instrumento m instrument; tool, implement.

insuficiencia f lack, inadequacy.

insuficiente adj insufficient, inadequate.

insufrible adj insufferable, insupportable.

insulina f insulin.

insulso/sa adj insipid; dull.

insultar vt to insult.

insulto *m* insult.

insuperable *adj* insuperable, insurmountable.

insurgente *m/f* insurgent.

insurrección *f* insurrection.

intacto/ta *adj* untouched; entire; intact.

integral *adj* integral, whole; **pan ~** wholewheat bread.

integrar *vt* to make up; to integrate.

integridad *f* integrity; completeness.

íntegro/gra *adj* integral, entire.

intelectual *adj*, *m/f* intellectual.

inteligencia *f* intelligence; understanding.

inteligente *adj* intelligent.

inteligible *adj* intelligible.

intemperie *f*: **a la ~** out in the open.

intempestivo/va *adj* untimely.

intención *f* intention, purpose; plan.

intencionado/da *adj* meaningful; deliberate.

intendencia *f* administration, management.

intendente *m* manager.

intensidad *f* intensity; strength.

intenso/sa *adj* intense, strong; deep.

intentar *vt* to try, to attempt.

intento *m* intent, purpose; attempt.

intercalación *f* insertion.

intercalar *vt* to insert.

intercambio *m* exchange, swap.

interceder *vi* to intercede.

interceptar *vt* to intercept.

intercesión *f* intercession, mediation.

intercesor/ra *m/f* intercessor, mediator.

interés *m* interest; share, part; concern, advantage; profit.

interesado/da *adj* interested; prejudiced; mercenary.

interesante *adj* interesting; useful, convenient.

interesar *vt* to be of interest to, to interest; **~se** *vr*: **~ en**, **por** to take an interest in; * *vi* to be of interest.

interfaz, interface *f* interface.

interferir *vt* to interfere with; to jam (a telephone); * *vi* to interfere.

interfono *m* intercom.

interinidad *f* temporary holding of office.

interino/na *adj* provisional, temporary; * *m/f* temporary holder of a post; stand-in.

interior *adj* interior, internal; * *m* interior, inside.

interioridad *f* inwardness.

interiorismo *m* interior design.

interiorista *m/f* interior designer.

interjección *f* (*gr*) interjection.

interlocutor/ra *m/f* speaker.

intermediar *vt* to interpose.

intermedio/dia *adj* intermediate; * *m* interval.

interminable *adj* interminable, endless.

intermitente *adj* intermittent; *m* (*auto*) indicator.

internacional *adj* international.

internado *m* boarding school.

internar *vt* to intern; to commit; **~se** *vr* to penetrate.

interno/na *adj* interior, internal; * *m/f* boarder.

interpelación *f* interpellation, appeal, plea.

interpelar *vt* to appeal to.

interpolar *vt* to interpolate; to interrupt.

interponer *vt* to interpose, to put in.

interposición *f* insertion; interjection.

interpretación *f* interpretation.

interpretar *vt* to interpret, to explain; (*teat*) to perform; to translate.

intérprete *m/f* interpreter; translator; (*teat*) performer.
interracial *adj* interracial.
interrogación *f* interrogation; question mark.
interrogante *adj* questioning.
interrogar *vt* to interrogate.
interrogatorio *m* questioning; (*jur*) examination; questionnaire.
interrumpir *vt* to interrupt.
interrupción *f* interruption.
interruptor *m* switch.
intervalo *m* interval.
intervención *f* supervision, control; (*com*) auditing; (*med*) operation; intervention.
intervenir *vt* to control, to supervise; (*com*) to audit; (*med*) to operate on; * *vi* to participate; to intervene.
interventor/ra *m/f* inspector; (*com*) auditor.
interviú *f* interview.
intestino/na *adj* internal, interior; * *m* intestine.
intimar *vt* to intimate; * *vi* to become friendly.
intimidad *f* intimacy; private life.
intimidar *vt* intimidate.
íntimo/ma *adj* internal, innermost; intimate, private.
intolerable *adj* intolerable, insufferable.
intolerancia *f* intolerance.
intolerante *adj* intolerant.
intranquilizarse *vr* to get anxious or worried.
intranquilo/la *adj* worried.
intransigente *adj* intransigent.
intransitable *adj* impassable.
intransitivo/va *adj* (*gr*) intransitive.
intratable *adj* intractable, difficult.
intrepidez *f* intrepidity; fearlessness.
intrépido/da *adj* intrepid, daring.

intriga *f* intrigue.
intrigante *m/f* intriguer.
intrigar *vt*, *vi* to intrigue.
intrínseco/ca *adj* intrinsic.
introducción *f* introduction.
introducir *vt* to introduce; to insert.
introductor *m* introducer.
introvertido/da *adj*, *m/f* introvert.
intrusión *f* intrusion.
intruso/sa *adj* intrusive; * *m/f* intruder.
intuición *f* intuition.
intuitivo/va *adj* intuitive.
inundación *f* inundation, flood(ing).
inundar *vt* to inundate, to overflow; to flood.
inusitado/da *adj* unusual.
inútil *adj* useless.
inutilidad *f* uselessness.
inutilizar *vt* to render useless.
invadir *vt* (*mil*) to invade; to overrun.
invalidar *vt* to invalidate, to render null and void.
inválido/da *adj* invalid, null and void; * *m/f* invalid.
invariable *adj* invariable.
invasión *f* invasion.
invasor/ra *adj* invading; * *m/f* invader.
invencible *adj* invincible.
invención *f* invention.
inventar *vt* to invent.
inventario *m* inventory.
invento *m* invention.
inventor/ra *m/f* inventor.
invernadero *m* greenhouse.
invernar *vi* to pass the winter.
inverosímil *adj* unlikely, improbable.
inverosimilitud *f* unlikeliness, improbability.
inversión *f* (*com*) investment; inversion.

inverso/sa *adj* inverse; inverted; contrary.
invertir *vt* (*com*) to invest; to invert.
investidura *f* investiture.
investigación *f* investigation, research.
investigar *vt* to investigate; to do research into.
investir *vt* to confer.
invicto/ta *adj* unconquerable.
invierno *m* winter.
inviolabilidad *f* inviolability.
inviolable *adj* inviolable.
invisible *adj* invisible.
invitado/da *m/f* guest.
invitar *vt* to invite; to entice; to pay for.
invocación *f* invocation.
invocar *vt* to invoke.
involuntario/ria *adj* involuntary.
invulnerable *adj* invulnerable.
inyección *f* injection.
ir *vi* to go; to walk; to travel; ~**se** *vr* to go away, to depart.
ira *f* anger, wrath.
iracundo/da *adj* irate; irascible.
iris *m* iris (eye); **arco** ~ rainbow.
ironía *f* irony.
irónico/ca *adj* ironic(al).
irracional *adj* irrational.
irradiación *f* irradiation.
irrazonable *adj* unreasonable.
irreal *adj* unreal.
irreconciliable *adj* irreconcilable.

irreflexión *f* rashness, thoughtlessness.
irregular *adj* irregular; abnormal.
irregularidad *f* irregularity; abnormality.
irremediable *adj* irremediable; incurable.
irremisible *adj* irretrievable; unpardonable.
irreparable *adj* irreparable.
irresistible *adj* irresistible.
irresoluto/ta *adj* irresolute; hesitant.
irreverencia *f* irreverence; disrespect.
irreverente *adj* irreverent; disrespectful.
irrevocable *adj* irrevocable.
irrisorio/ria *adj* derisory, ridiculous.
irritación *f* irritation.
irritar *vt* to irritate, to exasperate; to stir up; to inflame.
irrupción *f* irruption; invasion.
isla *f* island, isle.
Islam *m* Islam.
islámico/ca *adj* Islamic.
islote *m* small island.
istmo *m* isthmus.
italiano/na *adj* Italian; * *m* Italian (language); * *m/f* Italian man/woman.
ítem *m* item.
itinerario *m* itinerary.
izar *vt* (*mar*) to hoist.
izquierdo/da *adj* left; left-handed; * *f* left; left(-wing).

J

jabalí *m* wild boar.
jabalina *f* wild sow; (*dep*) javelin.
jabón *m* soap.
jabonar *vt* to soap.
jaca *f* pony.

jacinto *m* hyacinth.
jacuzzi *m* jacuzzi.
jactancia *f* boasting.
jactancioso/sa *adj* boastful.
jactarse *vr* to boast.

jadear *vi* to pant.
jaguar *m* jaguar.
jalea *f* jelly.
jaleo *m* racket, uproar.
jalón *m* pull, tug.
jamás *adv* never; **para siempre ~** for ever.
jamón *m* ham; **~ de York** (cooked) ham; **~ serrano** cured ham.
jaque *m* check (at game of chess); **~ mate** checkmate.
jaqueca *f* migraine.
jarabe *m* syrup.
jarcia *f* (*mar*) ropes *pl*, rigging.
jardín *m* garden.
jardinería *f* gardening.
jardinero/ra *m/f* gardener.
jarra *f* jug, jar, pitcher; **en ~s, de ~s** with arms akimbo; with hands to the sides.
jarro *m* jug.
jarrón *m* vase.
jaspe *m* jasper.
jaspear *vt* to marble; to speckle.
jaula *f* cage; cell for mad people.
jauría *f* pack of hounds.
jazmín *m* jasmin.
jazz *m* jazz.
jefatura *f*: **~ de policía** police headquarters.
jefe *m* chief, head, leader; (*ferro*) **~ de tren** guard, conductor.
jengibre *m* ginger.
jerarquía *f* hierarchy.
jerárquico/ca *adj* hierarchical.
jerga *f* coarse cloth; jargon.
jergón *m* coarse mattress.
jerigonza *f* jargon, gibberish.
jeringa *f* syringe.
jeroglífico/ca *adj* hieroglyphic; * *m* hieroglyph, hieroglyphic.
jersey *m* sweater, pullover.
Jesucristo *m* Jesus Christ.

jesuita *m* Jesuit.
jesuítico/ca *adj* jesuitical.
jibia *f* cuttlefish.
jícara *f* small cup (for chocolate).
jilguero *m* goldfinch.
jinete/ta *m/f* horseman/woman, rider.
jipijapa *m* straw hat.
jirafa *f* giraffe.
jirón *m* rag, shred.
jocosidad *f* humour, jocularity.
jocoso/sa *adj* good-humoured.
jornada *f* journey; day's journey; working day.
jornal *m* day's wage.
jornalero *m* (day) labourer.
joroba *f* hump; * *m/f* hunchback.
jorobado/da *adj* hunchbacked.
jorobar *vt* to pester, to annoy.
jota *f* jot, iota; Spanish dance.
joven *adj* young; * *m/f* youth; young woman.
jovial *adj* jovial, cheerful.
jovialidad *f* joviality, cheerfulness.
joya *f* jewel; **~s** *fpl* jewellery.
joyería *f* jewellery; jeweller's shop.
joyero/ra *m/f* jeweller.
juanete *m* (*med*) bunion.
jubilación *f* retirement.
jubilado/da *adj* retired; * *m/f* senior citizen.
jubilar *vt* to pension off; to superannuate; to discard; **~se** *vr* to retire.
jubileo *m* jubilee.
júbilo *m* joy, rejoicing.
judaico/ca *adj* Judaic, Jewish.
judaísmo *m* Judaism.
judía *f* bean; **~ verde** green bean, French bean.
judicatura *f* judicature; office of a judge.
judicial *adj* judicial.
judío/día *adj* Jewish; * *m/f* Jewish man/woman.

juego *m* play; amusement; sport; game; gambling; **~s Olímpicos** Olympic Games.

juerga *f* binge; party.

jueves *m invar* Thursday.

juez *m/f* judge.

jugada *f* playing of a card; stroke, shot.

jugador/ra *m/f* player; gambler.

jugar *vt, vi* to play, to sport, to gamble.

jugarreta *f* bad play, unskilful play.

jugo *m* sap, juice.

jugoso/sa *adj* juicy, succulent.

juguete *m* toy, plaything.

juguetear *vi* to play.

juguetón/ona *adj* playful.

juicio *m* judgement, reason; sanity; opinion.

juicioso/sa *adj* judicious, prudent.

julio *m* July.

junco *m* (*bot*) rush; junk (small Chinese ship).

jungla *f* jungle.

junio *m* June.

junta *f* meeting; assembly; congress; council.

juntamente *adv* jointly; at the same time.

juntar *vt* to join; to unite; **~se** *vr* to meet, to assemble; to draw closer.

junto/ta *adj* joined; united; near; adjacent; **~s** together; * *adv*: **todo ~** all at once.

juntura *f* junction; joint.

Júpiter *m* Jupiter (planet).

jurado *m* jury; juror; member of a panel.

juramento *m* oath; curse.

jurar *vt, vi* to swear.

jurídico/ca *adj* lawful, legal; juridical.

jurisdicción *f* jurisdiction; district.

jurisprudencia *f* jurisprudence.

jurista *m/f* jurist.

justa *f* joust, tournament.

justamente *adv* justly; just.

justicia *f* justice; equity.

justificación *f* justification.

justificante *m* voucher; receipt.

justificar *vt* to justify.

justo/ta *adj* just; fair, right; exact, correct; tight; * *adv* exactly, precisely; just in time.

juvenil *adj* youthful.

juventud *f* youthfulness, youth; young people *pl*.

juzgado *m* tribunal; court.

juzgar *vt, vi* to judge.

K

karaoke *m* karaoke.

ketchup *m* ketchup.

kilogramo *m* kilogram.

kilometraje *m* distance in kilometres.

kilómetro *m* kilometre.

kilovatio *m* kilowatt.

kiosco *m* kiosk.

L

la *art f* the; * *pn* her; you; it.
laberinto *m* labyrinth.
labia *f* fluency; (*fam*) the gift of the gab (*sl*).
labio *m* lip; edge.
labor *f* labour, task; needlework; farmwork; ploughing.
laboratorio *m* laboratory.
laboriosidad *f* laboriousness.
laborioso/sa *adj* laborious; hard-working.
labrado/da *adj* worked; carved; wrought; * *m* cultivated land.
labrador/ra *m/f* farmer; peasant.
labranza *f* farming; cultivation; farmland.
labrar *vt* to work; to carve; to farm; (*fig*) to bring about.
labriego/ga *m/f* peasant.
laca *f* lacquer; hairspray.
lacayo *m* lackey, footman.
lacerar *vt* to tear to pieces, to lacerate.
lacio/cia *adj* faded, withered; languid; lank (hair).
lacónico/ca *adj* laconic.
laconismo *m* laconic style, terseness.
lacra *f* scar; blot, blemish.
lacrar *vt* to seal (with sealing wax).
lacre *m* sealing wax.
lactancia *f* lactation; breast-feeding.
lácteo/tea *adj*: **productos ~s** dairy products.
ladear *vt* to move to one side; to incline; **~se** *vr* to lean; to tilt.
ladera *f* slope.
ladino/na *adj* cunning, crafty.
lado *m* side; faction, party; favour,

protection; (*mil*) flank; **al ~ de** beside; **poner a un ~** to put aside; **por todos ~s** on all sides.
ladrar *vt* to bark.
ladrido *m* bark, barking.
ladrillo *m* brick.
ladrón/ona *m/f* thief, robber, burglar.
lagar *m* wine press.
lagartija *f* (small) lizard.
lagarto *m* lizard.
lago *m* lake.
lágrima *f* tear.
lagrimal *m* corner of the eye.
lagrimoso/sa *adj* weeping, shedding tears.
laguna *f* lake; lagoon; gap.
laico/ca *adj* lay.
lamedura *f* licking.
lamentable *adj* lamentable, deplorable; pitiable.
lamentación *f* lamentation.
lamentar *vt* to be sorry about; to lament, to regret; * *vi*, **~se** *vr* to lament, to complain; to mourn.
lamento *m* lament.
lamer *vt* to lick, to lap.
lámina *f* plate, sheet of metal; engraving.
lámpara *f* lamp.
lamparilla *f* nightlight.
lamparón *m* grease spot.
lampiño/ña *adj* beardless.
lamprea *f* lamprey (fish).
lana *f* wool.
lance *m* cast, throw; move, play (in a game); event, incident.
lancero *m* (*mil*) lancer.
lancha *f* barge, lighter; launch.

langosta *f* locust; lobster.

langostino *m* king prawn.

languidez *f* langour.

lánguido/da *adj* languid, faint, weak.

lanudo/da *adj* woolly, fleecy.

lanza *f* lance, spear.

lanzada *f* stroke with a lance.

lanzadera *f* shuttle.

lanzamiento *m* throwing; (*mar*, *com*) launch, launching.

lanzar *vt* to throw; (*dep*) to bowl, to pitch; to launch, to fling; (*jur*) to evict.

lapicero *m* pencil, ballpoint pen.

lápida *f* flat stone, tablet.

lapidario *m*; ~/ria *adj* lapidary.

lápiz *m* pencil; mechanical pencil.

lapso *m* interval; error.

lapsus *m* error, mistake.

largamente *adv* for a long time.

largar *vt* to loosen, to slacken; to let go; to launch; to throw out; ~se *vr* (*fam*) to beat it (*sl*).

largo/ga *adj* long; lengthy, generous; copious; **a la ~a** in the end, eventually.

largueza *f* liberality, generosity.

largura *f* length.

laringe *f* larynx.

laringitis *f* laryngitis.

las *art fpl* the; * *pn* them; you.

lascivia *f* lasciviousness; lewdness.

lascivo/va *adj* lascivious; lewd.

láser *m* laser.

lasitud *f* lassitude, weariness.

lástima *f* compassion, pity; shame.

lastimar *vt* to hurt; to wound; to feel pity for; ~se *vr* to hurt oneself.

lastimero/ra *adj* pitiful, pathetic.

lastimoso/sa *adj* pathetic, mournful.

lastrar *vt* to ballast (a ship).

lastre *m* ballast; good sense.

lata *f* tin; can; (*fam*) nuisance.

lateral *adj* lateral.

latido *m* (heart)beat.

latifundio *m* large estate.

latigazo *m* lash, crack (of a whip).

látigo *m* whip.

latín *m* Latin.

latinizar *vt* to Latinize.

latino/na *adj* Latin.

Latinoamérica *f* Latin America.

latinoamericano/na *adj, m/f* Latin American.

latir *vi* to beat, to palpitate.

latitud *f* latitude.

latón *m* brass.

latoso/sa *adj* annoying; boring.

latrocinio *m* theft, robbery.

laúd *f* lute (musical instrument).

laudable *adj* laudable, praiseworthy.

láudano *m* laudanum.

laureado/da *adj* honoured; * *m* laureate.

laurel *m* (*bot*) laurel; reward.

lava *f* lava.

lavabo *m* washbasin; washroom.

lavadero *m* washing place; laundry.

lavado *m* washing; laundry.

lavadora *f* washing machine.

lavanda *f* lavender.

lavandera *f* laundress.

lavandería *f* laundry; ~ **automática** Launderette™.

lavaparabrisas *m invar* windscreen washer.

lavaplatos *m invar* dishwasher.

lavar *vt* to wash; to wipe away; ~se *vr* to wash oneself.

lavativa *f* (*med*) enema; (*fig*) nuisance.

laxante *m* (*med*) laxative.

laxitud *f* laxity, slackness, laxness.

laxo/xa *adj* lax, slack.

lazada *f* bow, knot.

lazarillo m: **perro ~** guide dog.

lazo m knot; bow; snare, trap; tie; bond.

le pn him; you; (dativo) to him; to her; to it; to you.

leal adj loyal; faithful.

lealtad f loyalty.

lebrel m greyhound.

lebrillo m glazed earthenware pan.

lección f reading; lesson; lecture; class.

leche f milk.

lechera f milkmaid, dairymaid; milk churn.

lechería f dairy.

lecho m bed; layer.

lechón m sucking pig.

lechuga f lettuce.

lechuza f owl.

lector/ra m/f reader.

lectura f reading.

leer vt, vi to read.

legado m bequest, legacy; legate.

legajo m file.

legal adj legal; trustworthy.

legalidad f legality.

legalización f legalization.

legalizar vt to legalize.

legaña f sleep (in eyes).

legar vt to leave, to bequeath.

legible adj legible.

legión f legion.

legionario/ria m&f legionary.

legislación f legislation.

legislador/ra m/f legislator, lawmaker.

legislar vt to legislate.

legislativo/va adj legislative.

legislatura f legislature.

legitimar vt to legitimize.

legitimidad f legitimacy.

legítimo/ma adj legitimate, lawful; authentic.

legua f league.

legumbres fpl pulses pl.

leído/da adj well-read.

lejano/na adj distant, remote; far.

lejía f bleach.

lejos adv at a great distance, far off.

lelo/la adj stupid, ignorant; * m/f idiot.

lema m motto; slogan.

lencería f linen, drapery.

lengua f tongue; language.

lenguado m sole.

lenguaje m language.

lente m/f lens; **~ de contacto** contact lense.

lenteja f lentil.

lentilla f contact lens.

lentitud f slowness.

lento/ta adj slow.

leña f wood, timber.

leñador m woodsman, woodcutter.

leño m block, log; trunk of a tree.

leñoso/sa adj woody.

Leo m Leo (sign of the zodiac).

león m lion.

leona f lioness.

leonado/da adj lion-coloured, tawny.

leopardo m leopard.

leotardos mpl tights.

lepra f leprosy.

leproso/sa adj leprous; * m/f leper.

lerdo/da adj slow, heavy; dull; slow-witted.

les pn them; you; (dativo) to them; to you.

lesbiana adj, f lesbian.

lesión f wound; injury; damage.

letal adj mortal, deadly.

letanía f litany.

letárgico/ca adj lethargic.

letargo m lethargy.

letra f letter; handwriting; printing type; draft of a song; bill, draft; **~s** fpl letters pl, learning.

letrado/da *adj* learned, lettered; * *m/f* lawyer; counsel.

letrero *m* sign; label.

letrina *f* latrine.

leucemia *f* leukaemia.

leva *m* (*mar*) weighing anchor; (*mil*) levy.

levadizo/za *adj* that can be lifted or raised; **puente ~** drawbridge.

levadura *f* yeast; brewer's yeast.

levantamiento *m* raising; insurrection.

levantar *vt* to raise, to lift up; to build; to elevate; to hearten, to cheer up; **~se** *vr* to get up; to stand up.

levante *m* Levant; east; east wind.

leve *adj* light; trivial.

levita *f* greatcoat, frock coat.

léxico *m* vocabulary.

ley *f* law; standard (for metal).

leyenda *f* legend.

liar *vt* to tie, to bind; to confuse.

libelo *m* petition; satire, lampoon.

libélula *f* dragonfly.

liberación *f* liberation; release.

liberal *adj* liberal, generous; * *m/f* liberal.

liberalidad *f* liberality, generosity.

libertad *f* liberty, freedom.

libertador/ra *m/f* liberator.

libertar *vt* to free, to set at liberty; to exempt, to clear from an obligation or debt.

libertinaje *m* licentiousness.

libertino/na *m/f* permissive person.

libra *f* pound; **~ esterlina** pound sterling.

Libra *f* Libra (sign of the zodiac).

librar *vt* to free, to deliver; (*com*) to draw; to make out (a cheque); (*jur*) to exempt; to fight (a battle); **~se** *vr* to escape.

libre *adj* free; exempt; vacant.

libremente *adv* freely.

librería *f* bookshop.

librero/ra *m/f* bookseller.

libreta *f* notebook; **~ de ahorros** savings book.

libro *m* book.

licencia *f* licence; licentiousness.

licenciado/da *adj* licensed; * *m/f* graduate.

licenciar *vt* to permit, to allow; to license; to discharge; to confer a degree upon; **~se** *vr* to graduate.

licencioso/sa *adj* licentious, dissolute.

liceo *m* lyceum; secondary school.

lícitamente *adv* lawfully.

lícito/ta *adj* lawful, fair; permissible.

licor *m* liquor.

licuadora *f* blender.

lid *m* contest, fight; dispute.

líder *m/f* leader.

liderazgo *m* leadership.

liebre *f* hare.

lienzo *f* linen; canvas; face or front of a building.

liga *f* suspender; birdlime; league; coalition; alloy.

ligadura *f* (*med*, *mus*) ligature; binding; bond, tie.

ligamento *m* ligament; tie; bond.

ligar *vt* to tie, to bind, to fasten; **~se** *vr* to commit oneself; * *vi* to mix, blend; (*fam*) to pick up.

ligazón *f* union, connection.

ligereza *f* lightness; swiftness; agility; superficiality.

ligero/ra *adj* light, swift; agile; superficial.

liguero *m* suspender belt.

lija *f* dogfish; sandpaper.

lijar *vt* to smooth, to sandpaper.

lila *f* lilac.

lima f file.

limadura f filing.

limar vt to file; to polish.

limitación f limitation, restriction.

limitado/da adj limited.

limitar vt to limit; to restrict; to cut down.

límite m limit, boundary.

limítrofe adj neighbouring, bordering.

limón m lemon.

limonada f lemonade.

limonar m plantation of lemon trees.

limosna f alms pl, charity.

limpiabotas m/f invar shoeshine boy/ girl.

limpiaparabrisas m invar windscreen wiper.

limpiar vt to clean; to cleanse; to purify; to polish; (fig) to clean up.

limpieza f cleanliness; cleaning; cleansing; polishing; purity.

limpio/pia adj clean; neat; pure.

linaje m lineage, family, descent.

linaza f linseed.

lince m lynx.

linchar vt to lynch.

lindar vi to be adjacent.

linde m boundary.

lindero m edge; boundary.

lindo/da adj pretty; lovely.

línea f line; cable; outline.

lineal adj linear.

lingote m ingot.

lingüista m/f linguist.

lino m flax.

linterna f lantern, lamp; torch, flashlight.

lío m bundle, parcel; (fam) muddle, mess.

liposucción f liposuction.

liquidación f liquidation.

liquidar vt to liquidate; to settle (accounts).

líquido/da adj liquid.

lira f (mus) lyre.

lirio m (bot) iris.

lirón m dormouse; (fig) sleepy- head.

lisiado/da adj injured; * m/f cripple.

lisiar vt to injure; to hurt.

liso/sa adj plain, even, flat, smooth.

lisonja f adulation, flattery.

lisonjear vt to flatter.

lisonjero/ra m/f flatterer; * adj flattering; pleasing.

lista f list; school register; catalogue; menu.

lista de correos f poste restante.

listo/ta adj ready; smart, clever.

listón m ribbon; strip (of wood or metal).

litera f berth; bunk, bunk bed.

literal adj literal.

literario/ria adj literary.

literato/ta adj literary; * m/f writer, literary person; ~s mpl literati pl.

literatura f literature.

litigar vt to fight; * vi (jur) to go to law; (fig) to dispute.

litigio m lawsuit.

litografía f lithography.

litográfico/ca adj lithographic.

litoral adj coastal; * m coast.

litro m litre (measure).

liturgia f liturgy.

litúrgico/ca adj liturgical.

liviandad f fickleness; triviality; lightness.

liviano/na adj light; fickle; trivial.

lívido/da adj livid.

llaga f wound; sore.

llama f flame; llama (animal).

llamada f call.

llamador m door-knocker.

llamamiento m call.

llamar vt to call; to name; to summon; to ring up, to telephone; * vi to knock at the door; to ring up, to telephone; ~se vr to be named.

llamarada f blaze; outburst.

llamativo/va adj showy; loud (colour).

llano/na adj plain; even, level, smooth; clear, evident; * m plain.

llanta f (wheel) rim; tyre; inner (tube).

llanto m flood of tears, crying.

llanura f evenness, flatness; plain, prairie.

llave f tap; key; ~ maestra master key.

llavero m key ring.

llegada f arrival, coming.

llegar vi to arrive; ~ a to reach; ~se vr to come near, to approach.

llenar vt to fill; to cover; to fill out (a form); to satisfy, to fulfil; ~se vr to gorge oneself.

lleno/na adj full, full up; complete.

llevadero/ra adj tolerable.

llevar vt to take; to wear; to carry; to convey, to transport; to drive; to lead; to bear; ~se vr to carry off, to take away.

llorar vt, vi to weep, to cry.

lloriquear vt to whine.

lloro m weeping, crying.

llorón/ona m/f tearful person; crybaby.

lloroso/sa adj mournful, full of tears.

llover vi to rain.

lloviznar vi to drizzle.

lluvia f rain; ~ ácida acid rain.

lluvioso/sa adj rainy.

lo pn it; him; you; * art the.

loable adj laudable.

loar vt to praise.

lobato m young wolf.

lobo m wolf.

lóbrego/ga adj murky, dark, gloomy.

lóbulo m lobe.

local adj local; * m place, site.

localidad f locality; location.

localizar vt to localize.

loción f lotion.

loco/ca adj mad; * m/f mad person.

locomotora f locomotive.

locuacidad f loquacity.

locuaz adj loquacious, talkative.

locución f expression.

locura f madness, folly.

locutor/ra m/f (rad) announcer; (TV) newsreader.

locutorio m telephone booth.

lodazal m muddy place.

lodo m mud, mire.

logaritmo m logarithm.

lógica f logic.

lógico/ca adj logical.

lograr vt to achieve; to gain, to obtain.

logro m achievement; success.

loma f hillock.

lombarda f red cabbage.

lombriz f worm.

lomo m loin; back (of an animal); spine (of a book); **llevar**, **traer a ~** to carry on the back.

lona f canvas.

loncha f slice; rasher.

longaniza f pork sausage.

longitud f length; longitude.

lonja[1] f slice; rasher.

lonja[2] f market, exchange; ~ de pescado fish market.

loro m parrot.

los art mpl the; * pn them; you.

losa f flagstone.

lote m lot; portion.

lotería f lottery.

loza f crockery.

lozanía f luxuriance, lushness; vigour; self-assurance.

lozano/na *adj* luxuriant, lush; sprightly.

lubricante *m* lubricant.

lucero *m* morning star, bright star.

lucha *f* struggle, fight.

luchador/ra *m/f* fighter; * *m* wrestler.

luchar *vi* to struggle; to wrestle.

lúcido/da *adj* lucid.

luciérnaga *f* glowworm.

lucimiento *m* splendour, lustre; brightness.

lucir *vt* to light (up); to show off; * *vi* to shine; ~**se** *vr* to make a fool of oneself.

lucrativo/va *adj* lucrative.

lucro *m* gain, profit.

luego *adv* next; afterward(s); **desde** ~ of course.

lugar *m* place, spot; village; reason; **en** ~ **de** instead of, in lieu of.

lugareño/ña *adj* belonging to a village; * *m/f* inhabitant of a village.

lugarteniente *m* deputy.

lúgubre *adj* lugubrious; sad, gloomy.

lujo *m* luxury; abundance.

lujoso/sa *adj* luxurious; showy; profuse, lavish.

lujuria *f* lust.

lujurioso/sa *adj* lustful, lewd.

lumbre *f* fire; light.

lumbrera *f* luminary; skylight.

luminaria *f* illumination.

luminoso/sa *adj* luminous, shining.

luna *f* moon; glass plate for mirrors; lens.

lunar *m* mole, spot; * *adj* lunar.

lunático/ca *adj*, *m/f* lunatic.

lunes *m invar* Monday.

lupa *f* magnifying glass.

lupanar *m* brothel.

lustre *m* gloss, lustre; splendour.

lustro *m* lustrum (space of five years).

lustroso/sa *adj* bright, brilliant.

luteranismo *m* Lutheranism.

luterano/na *adj*, *m/f* Lutheran.

luto *m* mourning (dress); grief.

luz *f* light.

M

macarrones *mpl* macaroni.

macedonia *f*: ~ **de frutas** fruit salad.

macerar *vt* to macerate, to soften.

maceta *f* flowerpot.

machacar *vt* to pound, to crush; * *vi* to insist, to go on.

machacón/ona *adj* wearisome, tedious.

machete *m* machete, cutlass.

machista *adj*, *m* sexist.

macho *adj* male; (*fig*) virile; * *m* male; (*fig*) he-man.

machucar *vt* to pound, to bruise.

macilento/ta *adj* lean; haggard, withered.

macizo/za *adj* massive; solid; * *m* mass, chunk.

madeja *f* skein of thread; mop of hair.

madera *f* timber, wood.

madero *m* beam of timber.

madrastra *f* stepmother.

madraza *f* loving mother.

madre *f* mother; womb.

madreperla *f* mother-of-pearl.

madreselva *f* honeysuckle.

madrigal *m* madrigal.

madriguera *f* burrow; den.

madrina *f* godmother.

madroño *m* strawberry plant.

madrugada f dawn; **de ~** at day break.

madrugador/ra m/f early riser.

madrugar vi to get up early; to get ahead.

madurar vt to ripen; * vi to ripen, to grow ripe; to mature.

madurez f maturity; ripeness; wisdom.

maduro/ra adj ripe, mature.

maestra f mistress; schoolmistress; teacher.

maestría f mastery, skill.

maestro m master; teacher; **~/tra** adj masterly, skilled; principal.

magia f magic.

mágico/ca adj magical.

magisterio m teaching; teaching profession; teachers pl.

magistrado/da m/f magistrate.

magistral adj magisterial; masterly.

magistratura f magistracy.

magnanimidad f magnanimity.

magnánimo/ma adj magnanimous.

magnate m magnate.

magnético/ca adj magnetic.

magnetismo m magnetism.

magnetizar vt to magnetize.

magnetofón, magnetófono m tape recorder.

magnetofónico/ca adj: **cinta magnetofónica** recording tape.

magnificencia f magnificence, splendour.

magnífico/ca adj magnificent, splendid.

magnitud f magnitude.

mago/ga m/f magician.

magro/gra adj thin, lean; meagre.

magulladura f bruise.

magullar vt to bruise; to damage; to bash (sl).

mahometano/na m/f, adj Muslim.

mahometanismo m Islam.

mahonesa f mayonnaise.

maíz m maize, Indian corn.

maizal m maize field.

majada f sheepfold.

majadería f absurdity; silliness.

majadero/ra adj dull; silly, stupid; * m idiot.

majestad f majesty.

majestuoso/sa adj majestic.

majo/ja adj nice; attractive; smart.

majuelo m vine newly planted; hawthorn.

mal m evil; hurt; harm, damage; misfortune; illness; * adj (before masculine nouns) bad.

malamente adv badly.

malaria f malaria.

malcriado/da adj rude, ill-behaved; naughty; spoiled.

maldad f wickedness.

maldecir vt to curse.

maldición f curse.

maldito/ta adj wicked; damned, cursed.

malear vt to damage; to corrupt.

malecón m pier.

maledicencia f slander; scandal.

maleducado/da adj bad-mannered, rude.

maleficio m curse; spell; witchcraft.

maléfico/ca adj harmful, damaging, evil.

malestar m discomfort; (fig) uneasiness; unrest.

maleta f suitcase; (auto) boot.

maletero f (auto) boot.

malevolencia f malevolence.

malévolo/la adj malevolent.

maleza f weeds pl; thicket.

malgastar vt to waste; to ruin.

malhablado/da adj foul-mouthed.

malhechor/ra m/f malefactor; criminal.

malhumorado/da *adj* cross, bad-tempered.

malicia *f* malice, wickedness; suspicion; cunning.

malicioso/sa *adj* malicious, wicked, evil; sly, crafty; spiteful.

malignidad *f* (*med*) malignancy; evil nature; malice.

maligno/na *adj* malignant; malicious.

malla *f* mesh, network; **~s** *fpl* leotard.

malo/la *adj* bad; ill; wicked; * *m/f* villain.

malograr *vt* to spoil; to upset (a plan); to waste; **~se** *vr* to fail; to die early.

malparado/da *adj*: **salir ~** to come off badly.

malparida *f* woman who has had a miscarriage.

malparir *vi* to miscarry, to have a miscarriage.

malsano/na *adj* unhealthy.

malteada *f* milk shake.

maltratamiento *m* ill-treatment.

maltratar *vt* to ill-treat, to abuse, to mistreat.

malva *f* (*bot*) mallow.

malvado/da *adj* wicked, villainous.

malversación *f* embezzlement.

malversador/ra *m/f* embezzler.

malversar *vt* to embezzle.

mama *f* teat; breast.

mamá *f* (*fam*) mum, mummy.

mamar *vt, vi* to suck.

mamarrachada *f* ridiculous sight.

mamarracho *m* mess, botch-up.

mamífero *m* mammal.

mamón/ona *m/f* small baby; scrounger.

mampara *f* partition; screen.

mampostería *f* masonry; stone-masonry.

maná *m* manna.

manada *f* flock, herd; pack; crowd.

manantial *m* source, spring; origin.

manar *vt* to run with, to flow; * *vi* to spring from; to flow; to abound.

mancha *f* stain, spot.

manchado/da *adj* spotted.

manchar *vt* to stain, to soil.

mancilla *f* spot, blemish.

manco/ca *adj* one-armed; one-handed; maimed; faulty.

mancomunar *vt* to associate, to unite; to make jointly responsible.

mancomunidad *f* union, fellowship; community; (*jur*) joint responsibility.

mandado *m* command; errand, message.

mandamiento *m* order, command; commandment.

mandar *vt* to command, to order; to bequeath; to send.

mandarín *m* mandarin.

mandarina *f* tangerine, mandarin orange.

mandatario/ria *m/f* agent; leader.

mandato *m* mandate, order; term of office.

mandíbula *f* jaw.

mandil *m* apron.

mando *m* command, authority, power; term of office; **~ a distancia** remote control.

mandón/ona *adj* bossy, domineering.

manecilla *f* small hand (of a watch or meter); book-clasp.

manejable *adj* manageable.

manejar *vt* to manage; to operate; to handle; (*auto*) to drive; **~se** *vr* to manage; to behave.

manejo *m* management; handling; driving; confidence.

manera *f* manner, way; fashion; kind.

manga *f* sleeve; hose.

mango[1] *m* handle.

mango[2] *m* mango.

mangonear *vi* to interfere; * *vt* to boss about.

manguera *f* hose; pipe.

manguito *m* muff.

maní *m* peanut.

manía *f* mania; craze; dislike; spite.

maniatar *vt* to tie the hands of; to handcuff.

maniático/ca *adj* maniac, mad, frantic; * *m/f* maniac.

manicomio *m* lunatic asylum.

manicura *f* manicure.

manifestación *f* manifestation; show; demonstration; mass meeting.

manifestar *vt* to manifest, to declare.

manifiesto/ta *adj* manifest, open, clear; * *m* manifesto.

manija *f* handle.

maniobra *f* manoeuvring; handling; (*mil*) manoeuvre.

maniobrar *vt* to manoeuvre; to handle.

manipulación *f* manipulation.

manipular *vt* to manipulate.

maniquí *m* dummy; * *m/f* model.

manirroto/ta *adj* lavish, extravagant.

manivela *f* crank.

manjar *m* (tasty) dish.

mano *f* hand; hand (of a clock or watch); foot, paw (of an animal); coat (of paint); lot, series; hand (at game); **a ~** by hand; **a ~s llenas** liberally, generously.

manojo *m* handful, bunch.

manopla *f* glove; face cloth.

manosear *vt* to handle; to mess up.

manoseo *m* handling.

manotazo *m* slap, smack.

manoteo *m* gesticulation.

mansalva *f*: **a ~** *adv* indiscriminately.

mansedumbre *f* meekness, gentleness.

mansión *f* mansion.

manso/sa *adj* tame; gentle, soft.

manta *f* blanket.

manteca *f* fat; **~ de cerdo** lard.

mantecado *m* cake eaten at Christmas; ice cream.

mantecoso/sa *adj* greasy.

mantel *m* tablecloth.

mantelería *f* table linen.

mantener *vt* to maintain, to support; to nourish; to keep; **~se** *vr* to hold one's ground; to support oneself.

mantenimiento *m* maintenance; subsistence.

mantequilla *f* butter.

mantilla *f* mantilla (head covering for women); **~s** *fpl* baby clothes *pl*.

manto *m* mantle; cloak, robe.

mantón *m* shawl.

manual *adj* manual; * *m* manual, handbook.

manufactura *f* manufacture.

manufacturar *vt* to manufacture.

manuscrito *m* manuscript; * *adj* hand-written.

manutención *f* support, maintenance.

manzana *f* apple.

manzanilla *f* camomile; camomile tea; manzanilla sherry.

manzano *m* apple tree.

maña *f* handiness, dexterity, cleverness, cunning; habit, custom; trick.

mañana *f* morning; * *adv* tomorrow.

mañoso/sa *adj* skilful, handy; cunning.

mapa *m* map.

mapamundi *f* map of the world.

maquillaje *m* make-up; making up.

maquillar *vt* to make up; **~se** *vr* to put on make-up.

máquina *f* machine; (*ferro*) engine; camera; (*fig*) machinery; plan, project.
maquinación *f* machination.
maquinador/ra *m/f* schemer, plotter.
maquinalmente *adv* mechanically.
maquinar *vt, vi* to machinate; to conspire.
maquinaria *f* machinery; mechanism.
maquinilla *f*: ~ **de afeitar** razor.
maquinista *m* (*ferro*) train driver; operator; (*mar*) engineer.
mar *m/f* sea.
maraña *f* shrub, thicket; tangle.
maravilla *f* wonder.
maravillar *vt* to astonish, to amaze; ~**se** *vr* to be amazed, to be astonished.
maravilloso/sa *adj* wonderful, marvellous.
marca *f* mark; stamp; (*com*) make, brand.
marcado/da *adj* strong, marked.
marcador *m* scoreboard; scorer.
marcar *vt* to mark; to dial; to score; to record; to set (hair); * *vi* to score; to dial.
marcha *f* march; running; gear; speed; (*fig*) progress.
marchar *vi* to go; to work; ~**se** *vr* to go away.
marchitar *vt* to wither; to fade.
marchito/ta *adj* faded; withered.
marcial *adj* martial, warlike.
marciano/na *adj* martian.
marco *m* frame; framework; (*dep*) goalposts *pl*.
marea *f* tide; ~ **negra** oil slick.
marear *vt* (*mar*) to sail, to navigate; to annoy, to upset; ~**se** *vr* to feel sick; to feel faint; to feel dizzy.
marejada *f* swell, heavy sea, surge.

mareo *m* sick feeling; dizziness; nuisance.
marfil *m* ivory.
margarina *f* margarine.
margarita *f* daisy.
margen *m* margin; border; * *f* bank (of river).
marginal *adj* marginal.
marginar *vt* to exclude; to leave margins on (a page); to make notes in the margin of.
marica *m* (*fam*) sissy.
maricón *m* (*fam*) queer (*sl*).
marido *m* husband.
mariguana, marihuana *f* cannabis.
marimacho *f* (*fam*) mannish woman.
marina *f* navy.
marinero/ra *adj* sea *compd*; seaworthy; * *m* sailor.
marino/na *adj* marine; * *m* sailor, seaman.
marioneta *f* puppet.
mariposa *f* butterfly.
mariquita *f* ladybug.
mariscal *m* marshal.
marisco *m* shellfish.
marital *adj* marital.
marítimo/ma *adj* maritime, marine.
marmita *f* pot.
mármol *m* marble.
marmóreo/rea *adj* marbled, marble *compd*.
marmota *f* marmot.
maroma *f* rope.
marqués *m* marquis.
marquesa *f* marchioness.
marrano *m* pig, boar.
marrón *adj* brown.
marrullería *f* plausibility; plausible excuse; ~**s** *fpl* cajolery.
marrullero/ra *adj* crafty, cunning.
marta *f* marten, sable.
Marte *m* Mars (planet).

martes *m invar* Tuesday.
martillar *vt* to hammer.
martillo *m* hammer.
mártir *m/f* martyr.
martirio *m* martyrdom.
martirizar *vt* to martyr.
marxismo *m* Marxism.
marxista *adj, m/f* Marxist.
marzo *m* March.
mas *adv* but, yet.
más *adv* more; most; besides, moreover; **a ~ tardar** at latest; **sin ~ ni ~** without more ado.
masa *f* dough, paste; mortar; mass.
masacre *m* massacre.
masaje *m* massage.
mascar *vt* to chew.
máscara *m/f* masked person; * *f* mask.
mascarada *f* masquerade.
mascarilla *f* (*med*) mask.
masculino/na *adj* masculine, male.
mascullar *vt* to mumble, to mutter.
masivo/va *adj* massive, en masse.
masoquista *m/f* masochist.
masticación *f* mastication.
masticar *vt* to masticate, to chew.
mástil *m* (*mar*) mast.
mastín *m* mastiff.
masturbación *f* masturbation.
masturbarse *vr* to masturbate.
mata *f* shrub; sprig, blade; grove, group of trees; mop of hair.
matadero *m* slaughterhouse.
matador/ra *adj* killing; * *m/f* killer; * *m* bullfighter.
matanza *f* slaughtering; massacre.
matar *vt* to kill; to execute; to murder; **~se** *vr* to kill oneself, to commit suicide.
matasanos *m invar* quack (doctor).
matasellos *m invar* postmark.
mate[1] *m* checkmate.
mate[2] *adj* matt.

matemáticas *fpl* mathematics.
matemático/ca *adj* mathematical; * *m/f* mathematician.
materia *m* matter, materials *pl*; subject.
material *adj* material, physical; * *m* equipment, materials *pl*.
materialidad *f* outward appearance.
materialismo *m* materialism.
materialista *m/f* materialist.
maternal *adj* maternal, motherly.
maternidad *f* motherhood.
materno/na *adj* maternal.
matinal *adj* morning *compd*.
matiz *m* shade of colour; shading.
matizar *vt* to mix colours; to tinge, to tint.
matón *m* bully.
matorral *m* shrub, thicket.
matraca *f* rattle.
matricida *m/f* matricide (person).
matricidio *m* matricide (murder).
matrícula *f* register, list; (*auto*) registration number; numberplate.
matricular *vt* to register, to enrol.
matrimonial *adj* matrimonial.
matrimonio *m* marriage, matrimony.
matriz *f* matrix; womb; mould, form.
matrona *f* matron.
matutino/na *adj* morning.
maullar *vi* to mew.
maullido *m* mew (of a cat).
mausoleo *m* mausoleum.
máxima *f* maxim.
máxime *adv* principally.
máximo/ma *adj* maximum; top; highest.
mayo *m* May.
mayonesa *f* mayonnaise.
mayor *adj* main, chief; (*mus*) major; biggest; eldest; greater, larger; elderly; * *m* chief, boss; adult; **al por ~** wholesale; **~es** *mpl* forefathers.

mayoral *m* foreman.

mayordomo *m* steward.

mayoría *f* majority, greater part; ~ de edad coming of age.

mayorista *m/f* wholesaler.

mayormente *adv* principally, chiefly.

mayúsculo/la *adj* (*fig*) tremendous; * *f* capital letter.

maza *f* club; mace.

mazada *f* blow with a club.

mazapán *m* marzipan.

mazmorra *f* dungeon.

mazo *m* bunch; club, mallet; bat.

mazorca *f* ear of corn.

me *pn* me; to me.

mear *vi* (*fam*) to pee, to piss (*sl*).

mecánica *f* mechanics.

mecánico/ca *adj* mechanical; * *m/f* mechanic.

mecanismo *m* mechanism.

mecanografía *f* typing.

mecanógrafo/fa *m/f* typist.

mecate *m* rope.

mecedora *f* rocking chair.

mecer *vt* to rock; to dandle (a child).

mecha *f* wick; fuse.

mechar *vt* to lard; to stuff.

mechero *m* (cigarette) lighter.

mechón *m* lock of hair; large bundle of threads or fibres.

medalla *f* medal.

medallón *m* medallion.

media *f* stocking; sock; average.

mediación *f* mediation, intervention.

mediado/da *adj* half full; half complete; **a ~s de** in the middle of.

mediador/ra *m/f* mediator; go-between.

mediana *f* central reserve.

medianero/ra *adj* dividing; adjacent.

mediano/na *adj* medium; middling; mediocre.

medianoche *f* midnight.

mediante *prep* by means of.

mediar *vi* to intervene; to mediate.

medias *fpl* tights *pl*.

medicación *f* medication.

medicamento *m* medicine.

medicina *f* medicine.

medicinal *adj* medicinal.

médico/ca *adj* medical; * *m/f* doctor.

medida *f* measure.

medio/dia *adj* half; **a medias** partly; * *m* middle; average; way, means; medium.

mediocre *adj* middling; moderate; mediocre.

mediocridad *f* mediocrity.

mediodía *m* noon, midday.

medir *vt* to measure; ~se *vr* to be moderate.

meditación *f* meditation.

meditar *vt* to meditate.

mediterráneo/nea *adj* Mediterranean; * *m*: **el M~** the Mediterranean.

medrar *vi* to grow, to thrive, to prosper; to improve.

medroso/sa *adj* fearful, timid.

médula *f* marrow; essence, substance; pith.

medusa *f* jellyfish.

megáfono *m* megaphone.

mejilla *f* cheek.

mejillón *m* mussel.

mejor *adj*, *adv* better; best.

mejora *f* improvement.

mejorar *vt* to improve, to ameliorate; to enhance; * *vi* to improve; (*med*) to recover, to get better; ~se *vr* to improve, to get better.

mejoría *f* improvement; recovery.

melancolía *f* melancholy.

melancólico/ca *adj* melancholy, sad, gloomy.

melena *f* long hair, loose hair, mane.
melenudo/da *adj* long-haired.
melindroso/sa *adj* prudish, finicky.
mella *f* notch in edged tools; gap.
mellado/da *adj* jagged; gap-toothed.
mellar *vt* to notch.
mellizo/za *adj, m/f* twin.
melocotón *m* peach.
melodía *f* melody.
melodioso/sa *adj* melodious.
melodrama *f* melodrama.
melón *m* melon.
melosidad *f* sweetness.
meloso/sa *adj* honeyed; mellow.
membrana *f* membrane.
membranoso/sa *adj* membranous.
membrete *m* letter head.
membrillo *m* quince; quince tree.
membrudo/da *adj* strong, robust; burly.
memorable *adj* memorable.
memorándum *m* notebook; memorandum.
memoria *f* memory; report; record; ~s *fpl* memoirs *pl.*
memorial *m* memorial; petition.
mención *f* mention.
mencionar *vt* to mention.
mendigar *vt* to beg.
mendigo/ga *m/f* beggar.
mendrugo *m* crust.
menear *vt* to move from place to place; (*fig*) to handle; ~se *vr* to move; to shake; to sway.
meneo *m* movement; shake; swaying.
menester *m* necessity; need; want; ~es *mpl* duties *pl.*
menesteroso/sa *adj* needy.
menestra *f* vegetable soup or stew.
menguante *f* decreasing.
menguar *vi* to diminish; to discredit.
menopausia *f* menopause.

menor *m/f* young person, juvenile; * *adj* less; smaller; minor; **al por ~** retail.
menoría *f*: **a ~** retail.
menos *adv* less; least; **a lo ~** *o* **por lo ~** at least; * *prep* except; minus.
menoscabar *vt* to damage; to harm; to lessen; to discredit.
menoscabo *m* damage; harm; loss.
menospreciar *vt* to undervalue; to despise, to scorn.
menosprecio *m* contempt, scorn; undervaluation.
mensaje *m* message.
mensajero/ra *m/f* messenger; courier.
menstruación *f* menstruation.
mensual *adj* monthly.
menta *f* mint.
mental *adj* mental; intellectual.
mentar *vt* to mention.
mente *f* mind; understanding.
mentecato/ta *adj* silly, stupid; * *m/f* idiot.
mentir *vt* to feign; to pretend; * *vi* to lie.
mentira *f* lie, falsehood.
mentiroso/sa *adj* lying; * *m/f* liar.
menú *m* menu; set meal.
menudencia *f* trifle, small thing; minuteness; ~s *fpl* odds and ends *pl.*
menudillos *mpl* giblets *pl.*
menudo/da *adj* small; minute; petty, insignificant; **a ~** frequently, often.
meñique *m* little finger.
meollo *m* marrow; (*fig*) core.
mequetrefe *m* good-for-nothing; busybody.
meramente *adv* merely, solely.
mercader *m* dealer, trader.
mercadería *f* commodity; trade; ~s *fpl* merchandise.

mercado *m* market; marketplace.

mercancía *f* commodity; **~s** *fpl* goods *pl*, merchandise.

mercantil *adj* commercial, mercanile.

mercenario/ria *adj* mercenary; * *m* mercenary; labourer.

mercería *f* haberdashery, draper's shop.

mercurio *m* mercury.

Mercurio *m* Mercury (planet).

merecedor/ra *adj* deserving.

merecer *vt* to deserve, to merit.

merecido/da *adj* deserved.

merendar *vi* to have tea; to have a picnic.

merengue *m* meringue.

meridiano *m* meridian.

meridional *adj* southern.

merienda *f* (light) tea; afternoon snack; picnic.

mérito *m* merit; worth, value.

meritorio/ria *adj* meritorious.

merluza *f* hake.

merma *f* waste, leakage.

mermar *vi* to waste, to diminish.

mermelada *f* jam.

mero *m* pollack (fish); **~/ra** *adj* mere, pure.

merodeador *m* (*mil*) marauder.

merodear *vi* to pillage, to go marauding.

mes *m* month.

mesa *f* table; desk; plateau; **~ redonda** round table.

meseta *f* meseta, tableland.

mesón *m* inn.

mestizo/za *adj* of mixed race; crossbred; * *m/f* half-caste.

mesura *f* gravity; politeness; moderation.

mesurado/da *adj* moderate; dignified; courteous.

meta *f* goal; finish.

metabolismo *m* metabolism.

metafísica *f* metaphysics.

metafísico/ca *adj* metaphysical.

metáfora *f* metaphor.

metafórico/ca *adj* metaphorical.

metal *m* metal; (*mus*) brass; timbre (of the voice).

metálico/ca *adj* metallic.

metalurgia *f* metallurgy.

metamorfosis *f invar* metamorphosis; transformation.

meteoro *m* meteor.

meteorología *f* meteorology.

meter *vt* to place, to put; to insert, to put in; to involve; to make, to cause; **~se** *vr* to meddle, to interfere.

metódico/ca *adj* methodical.

método *m* method.

metralla *f* (*mil*) shrapnel.

metralleta *f* submachine-gun.

métrico/ca *adj* metric.

metro[1] *m* metre.

metro[2] *m* underground, tube, subway.

metrópoli *f* metropolis; mother country.

mezcla *f* mixture; medley.

mezclar *vt* to mix; **~se** *vr* to mix; to mingle.

mezquindad *f* meanness; pettiness; wretchedness.

mezquino/na *adj* mean; small-minded, petty; wretched.

mezquita *f* mosque.

mi *adj* my.

mí *pn* me; myself.

microbio *m* microbe.

microbús *m* minibus.

micrófono *m* microphone.

microondas *m inv* microwave oven.

microordenador *m* microcomputer.

microscópico/ca *adj* microscopic.

microscopio *m* microscope.

miedo *m* fear, dread.

miel *f* honey.

miembro *m* member.

mientras *adv* meanwhile; * *conj* while; as long as.

miércoles *m invar* Wednesday.

mierda *f* (*fam*) shit (*sl*).

mies *f* harvest.

miga *f* crumb; ~s *fpl* fried bread-crumbs *pl*.

migaja *f* scrap, crumb.

migración *f* migration.

mijo *m* (*bot*) millet.

mil *m* one thousand.

milagro *m* miracle, wonder.

milagroso/sa *adj* miraculous.

milano *m* kite (bird).

milésimo/ma *adj*, *m* thousandth.

mili *f*: **hacer la ~** (*fam*) to do one's military service.

milicia *f* militia; military service.

miliciano *m* militiaman.

milímetro *m* millimeter.

militante *adj* militant.

militar *adj* military; * *m* soldier; * *vi* to serve in the army; (*fig*) to be a member of a party.

milla *f* mile.

millar *m* thousand.

millón *m* million.

millonario/ria *m/f* millionaire.

mimar *vt* to spoil, pamper.

mimbre *m* wicker.

mímica *f* sign language; mimicry.

mimo *m* caress; spoiling; mime.

mimoso/sa *adj* spoilt, pampered; delicate.

mina *f* mine; underground passage.

minar *vt* to undermine; to mine.

mineral *m* mineral; * *adj* mineral.

mineralogía *f* mineralogy.

minero/ra *m/f* miner.

miniatura *f* miniature.

minicadena *f* midi system.

minifalda *f* miniskirt.

mínimo/ma *adj* minimum.

ministerio *m* ministry.

ministro/ra *m/f* minister.

minoría *f* minority.

minucioso/sa *adj* meticulous; very detailed.

minúsculo/la *adj* minute; * *f* small letter.

minusválido/da *adj* (physically) handicapped; * *m/f* (physically) handicapped person.

minuta *f* minute, first draft; menu.

minutero *m* minute hand (of a watch or clock).

minuto *m* minute.

mío/mía *adj* mine.

miope *adj* short-sighted.

mira *f* sight of a gun; (*fig*) aim.

mirada *f* glance; gaze.

mirador *m* viewpoint, vantage point.

miramiento *m* consideration; circumspection.

mirar *vt* to look at; to observe; to consider; * *vi* to look; ~se *vr* to look at oneself; to look at one another.

mirilla *f* peephole.

mirlo *m* blackbird.

mirón/ona *m/f* spectator, onlooker, bystander; voyeur.

misa *f* mass; ~ **del gallo** midnight mass.

misal *m* missal.

misantropía *f* misanthropy.

misántropo/pa *m/f* misanthropist.

miserable *adj* miserable; mean; squalid (place); (*fam*) despicable; * *m/f* rotter.

miseria *f* misery; poverty; meanness; squalor.

misericordia *f* mercy.

misil *m* missile.

misión *f* mission.

misionero/ra *m/f* missionary.

mismo/ma *adj* same; very.

misterio *m* mystery.

misterioso/sa *adj* mysterious.

mística *f* mysticism.

místico/ca *adj* mystic(al); * *m/f* mystic.

mitad *f* half; middle.

mitigación *f* mitigation.

mitigar *vt* to mitigate.

mitin *m* (political) rally.

mito *m* myth.

mitología *f* mythology.

mitológico/ca *adj* mythological.

mitones *mpl* mittens *pl*.

mixto/ta *adj* mixed.

mobiliario *m* furniture.

mochila *f* backpack.

mochuelo *m* red owl.

moción *f* motion.

moco *m* snot (*sl*), mucus.

moda *f* fashion, style.

modales *mpl* manners *pl*.

modalidad *f* kind, variety.

modelar *vt* to model, to form.

modelo *m* model, pattern.

módem *m* modem.

moderación *f* moderation.

moderado/da *adj* moderate.

moderar *vt* to moderate.

moderno/na *adj* modern.

modestia *f* modesty, decency.

modesto/ta *adj* modest.

módico/ca *adj* moderate.

modificación *f* modification.

modificar *vt* to modify.

modisto/ta *m/f* dressmaker.

modo *m* mode, method, manner.

modorra *f* drowsiness.

modulación *f* modulation.

modular *vt* to modulate.

mofa *f* mockery.

mofarse *vr*: ~ **de** to mock, to scoff at.

moflete *m* fat cheek.

moho *m* rust; mould, mildew.

mohoso/sa *adj* mouldy, musty.

mojar *vt* to wet, to moisten; ~**se** *vr* to get wet.

mojigato *adj* hypocritical.

mojón *m* landmark.

molde *m* mould; pattern; model.

moldura *f* moulding.

mole *f* bulk; pile.

molécula *f* molecule.

moler *vt* to grind, to pound; to tire out; to annoy, to bore.

molestar *vt* to annoy, to bother; to trouble; * *vi* to be a nuisance.

molestia *f* trouble; inconvenience; (*med*) discomfort.

molesto/ta *adj* annoying; inconvenient; uncomfortable; annoyed.

molinero *m* miller.

molinillo *m*: ~ **de café** coffee grinder.

molino *m* mill.

molusco *m* mollusc.

momentáneo/nea *adj* momentary.

momento *m* moment.

momia *f* mummy.

monacal *adj* monastic.

monaguillo *m* acolyte.

monarca *m/f* monarch.

monarquía *f* monarchy.

monárquico/ca *adj* monarchical; * *m/f* royalist, monarchist.

monasterio *m* monastery, convent.

monástico/ca *adj* monastic.

mondadientes *m invar* toothpick.

mondar *vt* to clean; to cleanse; to peel; ~**se** *vr*: ~ **de risa** (*fam*) to split one's sides laughing.

mondo/da *adj* clean; pure; ~ **y lirondo** bare, plain; pure and simple.

moneda *f* money; currency; coin.

monedero *m* purse.

monería *f* funny face; mimicry; prank; trifle.

monetario/ria *adj* monetary, financial.

monitor *m* monitor.

monja *f* nun.

monje *f* monk.

mono[1] *m/f* monkey; ape.

mono[2] *m* dungarees *pl*; overalls *pl*.

mono/na *adj* lovely; pretty; nice.

monólogo *m* monologue.

monopolio *m* monopoly.

monopolista *m* monopolist.

monosílabo/ba *adj* monosyllabic.

monotonía *f* monotony.

monótono/na *adj* monotonous.

monovolumen *m* people mover.

monstruo *m* monster.

monstruosidad *f* monstrosity.

monstruoso/sa *adj* monstrous.

monta *f* amount, sum total.

montaje *m* assembly; decor (of theatre); montage.

montaña *f* mountain.

montañes/esa *adj* mountain *compd*; * *m/f* highlander.

montañoso/sa *adj* mountainous.

montar *vt* to mount, to get on (a bicycle, horse, etc); to assemble, to put together; to overlap; to set up (a business); to beat, to whip (in cooking); * *vi* to mount; to ride; ~ **a** to amount to.

montaraz *adj* mountainous; wild, untamed.

monte *m* mountain; woodland; ~ **alto** forest; ~ **bajo** scrub.

montería *f* hunting, chase.

montés/esa *adj* wild, untamed.

montón *m* heap, pile; mass; **a ~ones**, abundantly, by the score.

montura *f* mount; saddle.

monumento *m* monument.

monzón *m* monsoon.

moño *m* bun.

moquillo *m* distemper (disease in dogs).

mora *f* blackberry.

morada *f* home, abode, residence.

morado/da *adj* violet, purple.

morador/ra *m/f* inhabitant.

moral[1] *m* mulberry tree.

moral[2] *f* morals *pl*, ethics *pl*; * *adj* moral.

moraleja *f* moral.

moralidad *f* morality.

moralista *m/f* moralist.

moralizar *vi* to moralize.

moralmente *adv* morally.

morar *vi* to inhabit, to dwell.

moratoria *f* moratorium.

mórbido/da *adj* morbid, diseased.

morboso/sa *adj* diseased, morbid.

morcilla *f* black pudding.

mordacidad *f* sharpness, pungency.

mordaz *adj* biting, scathing; pungent.

mordaza *f* gag; clamp.

mordedura *f* bite.

morder *vt* to bite; to nibble; to corrode, to eat away.

mordisco *m* bite.

moreno/na *adj* brown; swarthy; dark-skinned.

moribundo/da *adj* dying.

morigeración *f* temperance.

morir *vi* to die; to expire; to die down; ~**se** *vr* to die; (*fig*) to be dying.

morisco/ca *adj* Moorish.

moro/ra *adj* Moorish.

morosidad *f* slowness, sluggishness.

moroso/sa *adj* slow, sluggish; (*com*) slow to pay up.

morral *m* haversack.

morriña *f* depression; sadness.

morro *m* snout; nose (of car, plane, etc).

morsa *f* walrus.

mortaja *f* shroud; mortise; cigarette paper.

mortal *adj* mortal; fatal, deadly.

mortalidad *f* mortality.

mortandad *f* death toll.

mortero *m* mortar (cannon).

mortífero/ra *adj* deadly, fatal.

mortificación *f* mortification.

mortificar *vt* to mortify.

mortuorio *m* mortuary.

moruno/na *adj* Moorish.

mosca *f* fly.

moscardón *m* botfly, blowfly; pest (*fam*), bore.

moscatel *adj, m* muscatel.

moscón *m* pest (*fam*), bore.

mosquearse *vr* (*fam*) to get cross; (*fam*) to take offence.

mosquetero *m* musketeer.

mosquitero *m* mosquito net.

mosquito *m* gnat, mosquito.

mostaza *f* mustard.

mosto *m* must, new wine.

mostrador *m* counter.

mostrar *vt* to show, to exhibit; to explain; ~**se** *vr* to appear, to show oneself.

mota *f* speck, tiny piece; dot; defect, fault.

mote *m* nickname.

motejar *vt* to nickname.

motín *m* revolt; mutiny.

motivar *vt* to motivate; to explain, to justify.

motivo *m* motive, cause, reason.

moto (*fam*), **motocicleta** *f* motorcycle.

motor *m* engine, motor.

motriz *adj* driving, motive.

movedizo/za *adj* movable; variable, changeable; fickle.

mover *vt* to move; to shake; to drive; (*fig*) to cause; ~**se** *vr* to move; (*fig*) to get a move on.

móvil *adj* mobile, movable; moving; * *m* motive; mobile phone.

movilidad *f* mobility.

movimiento *m* movement, motion.

mozo/za *adj* young; * *m/f* youth, young man/girl; waiter/waitress.

muchacho/a *m/f* boy/girl; * *f* maid(servant).

muchedumbre *f* crowd.

mucho/cha *adj* a lot of, much; * *adv* much, a lot; long.

muda *f* change of clothes.

mudable *adj* changeable, variable; mutable.

mudanza *f* change; move.

mudar *vt* to change; to shed, to moult; ~**se** *vr* to change one's clothes; to change house; * *vi* to change;

mudo/da *adj* dumb; silent, mute.

mueble *m* piece of furniture; ~**s** *mpl* furniture.

mueca *f* grimace, funny face.

muela *f* tooth, molar.

muelle *m* spring; regulator; quay, wharf.

muérdago *m* (*bot*) mistletoe.

muerte *f* death.

muerto *m* corpse; ~/**ta** *adj* dead.

muesca *f* notch, groove.

muestra *f* pattern; indication; demonstration; proof; sample; token; model.

mugido *m* lowing.

mugir *vi* to low, to bellow.

mugre *m* dirt, filth.

mugriento/ta *adj* greasy; dirty, filthy.

mujer *f* woman.

mulato/ta *adj* mulatto.

muleta *f* crutch.

mullido/da *adj* soft; springy.

mulo/la *m/f* mule.

multa *f* fine, penalty.

multar *vt* to fine.

multimedia *adj* multimedia.

múltiple *adj* multiple; ~**s** many, numerous.

multiplicación *f* multiplication.

multiplicado *m* (*mat*) multiplicand.

multiplicar *vt* to multiply.

multiplicidad *f* multiplicity.

multitud *f* multitude.

mundano/na *adj* worldly; mundane.

mundial *adj* world-wide; world *compd*.

mundo *m* world.

munición *f* ammunition.

municipio *m* town council; municipality.

municipal *adj* municipal.

muñeca *f* wrist; child's doll.

muñeco *m* puppet; figure.

muñón *m* stump.

muralla *f* rampart, wall.

murciélago *m* bat.

murmullo *m* murmur, mutter.

murmuración *f* backbiting, gossip.

murmurador/ra *m/f* detractor, backbiter.

murmurar *vi* to murmur; to gossip, to backbite.

muro *m* wall.

muscular *adj* muscular.

músculo *m* muscle.

muselina *f* muslin.

museo *m* museum.

musgo *m* moss.

música *f* music.

musical *adj* musical.

músico/ca *m/f* musician; * *adj* musical.

muslo *m* thigh.

mustio/tia *adj* parched, withered; sad, sorrowful.

musulmán/ana *adj*, *m/f* Muslim.

mutabilidad *f* mutability.

mutación *f* mutation, change.

mutilación *f* mutilation.

mutilar *vt* to mutilate, to maim.

mutuo/tua *adj* mutual, reciprocal.

mutuamente *adv* mutually.

muy *adv* very; too; greatly; ~ **ilustre** most illustrious.

N

nabo *m* turnip.

nácar *m* mother-of-pearl, nacre.

nacarado/da *adj* mother-of-pearl *compd*; pearl-coloured.

nacer *vi* to be born; to bud, to shoot (of plants); to rise; to grow.

nacido/da *adj* born; **recién** ~ newborn.

nacimiento *m* birth; nativity.

nación *f* nation.

nacional *adj* national.

nacionalidad *f* nationality.

nacionalizar *vt* to nationalize; ~**se** to become naturalized.

nada *f* nothing; * *adv* no way, not at all, by no means.

nadador/ra *m/f* swimmer.

nadar *vi* to swim.

nadie *pn* nobody, no one.

nado *adv*: **a** ~ afloat.

nafta *f* petrol.

naipe *m* (playing) card.

nalgas *fpl* buttocks *pl*.

naranja *f* orange.

naranjada f orangeade.

naranjal m orange grove.

naranjo m orange tree.

narciso m (*bot*) daffodil; narcissus (flower); fop.

narcótico/ca adj narcotic; * m drug, narcotic.

narcotraficante m/f drug trafficker.

nardo m spikenard.

narigón/ona, narigudo/da adj big-nosed.

nariz f nose; sense of smell.

narración f narration.

narrar vt to narrate, to tell.

narrativa f narrative; story.

nata f cream.

natación f swimming.

natal adj natal, native.

natalicio m birthday.

natillas fpl custard.

natividad f nativity.

nativo/va adj, m/f native.

natural m temper; natural disposition; native; * adj natural; native; common, usual; **al** ~ unaffectedly.

naturaleza f nature.

naturalidad f naturalness.

naturalista m naturalist.

naturalizar vi to naturalize; ~**se** vr to become naturalized; to become acclimatized.

naturalmente adv in a natural way; ¡~! of course!

naturópata m/f naturopath.

naufragar vi to be shipwrecked; to suffer ruin in one's affairs.

naufragio m shipwreck.

náufrago/ga adj shipwrecked.

nauseabundo/da adj nauseating.

náuseas fpl nauseousness, nausea.

náutica f navigation.

navaja f penknife; razor.

naval adj naval.

nave f ship; nave.

navegable adj navigable.

navegación f navigation; sea journey.

navegador m browser.

navegante m navigator.

navegar vt, vi to navigate; to sail; to fly.

navidad f Christmas.

navideño/ña adj Christmas compd.

navío m ship.

nazi adj, m/f Nazi.

neblina f mist; fine rain, drizzle.

nebuloso/sa adj misty; cloudy; nebulous; foggy; hazy; drizzling; * f nebula.

necedad f gross ignorance, stupidity; imprudence.

necesario/ria adj necessary.

neceser m toilet bag; holdall.

necesidad f necessity, need, want.

necesitado/da adj necessitous, needy.

necesitar vt to need; * vi to want, to need.

necio/cia adj ignorant; stupid, foolish; imprudent.

necrología f obituary.

nectarina f nectarine.

néctar m nectar.

nefando/da adj base, nefarious, abominable.

nefasto/ta adj unlucky.

negación f negation; denial.

negado/da adj incapable, unfit.

negar vt to deny; to refuse; ~**se** vr: ~ **a hacer** to refuse to do.

negativo/va adj, m negative; * f negative; refusal.

negligencia f negligence.

negligente adj negligent; careless, heedless.

negociación f negotiation; commerce.

negociante m/f trader, dealer.

negociar vt, vi to negotiate.

negocio m business, affair; transaction; firm; place of business.

negro/gra adj black; dark; * m black; * m/f black person.

negrura f blackness.

negruzco/ca adj blackish.

nene m, **nena** f baby.

nenúfar m water lily.

neófito m neophyte.

Neptuno m Neptune (planet).

nervio m nerve.

nervioso/sa adj nervous.

neto/ta adj neat, pure; net.

neumático/ca adj pneumatic; * m tyre.

neurona f neurone.

neutral adj neutral; neuter.

neutralidad f neutrality.

neutralizar vt to neutralize; to counteract.

neutro/tra adj neutral; neuter.

neutrón m neutrone.

nevada f heavy fall of snow.

nevar vi to snow.

nevera f icebox.

nevería f ice-cream parlour.

nexo m link.

ni conj neither, nor.

nicho m niche.

nido m nest; hiding place.

niebla f fog; mist.

nieta f granddaughter.

nieto m grandson.

nieve f snow.

nigromancia f necromancy.

nimiedad f small-mindedness; triviality.

nimio/mia adj trivial.

ninfa f nymph.

ningún, **ninguno/na** adj no; * pn nobody; none; not one; neither.

niña f little girl; pupil, (of eye).

niñera f nursemaid.

niñería f childishness; childish act.

niñero/ra adj fond of children.

niñez f childhood.

niño/ña adj childish; * m/f child; infant; **desde ~** from infancy, from a child; * m boy.

níspero m medlar.

nitidez f clarity; brightness; sharpness.

nitrato m (quím) nitrate.

nitrógeno m nitrogen.

nivel m level; standard; height; **a ~** perfectly level.

niveladora f bulldozer.

nivelar vt to level; to even up; to balance.

no adv no; not; * excl no!

noble adj noble, illustrious; generous.

nobleza f nobleness, nobility.

noción f notion, idea.

nocivo/va adj harmful.

nocturno/na adj nocturnal, nightly; * m nocturne.

noche f night; evening; darkness; **¡buenas ~s!** good night!

Nochebuena f Christmas Eve.

Nochevieja f New Year's Eve.

nodriza f nurse.

nogal m walnut tree.

nómada adj nomadic; * m/f nomad.

nombramiento m nomination; appointment.

nombrar vt to name; to nominate; to appoint.

nombre m name; title; reputation.

nomenclatura f nomenclature.

nómina f list; (com) payroll.

nominador m nominator.

nominal adj nominal.

nominativo m (gr) nominative.

non *adj* odd, uneven; * *m* odd number.

nonagenario/ria *adj* ninety-year-old; * *m/f* nonagenarian.

no obstante *adv* nevertheless, notwithstanding.

nor(d)este *adj* northeast, northeastern; * *m* northeast.

nórdico/ca *adj* northern; Nordic.

noria *f* water wheel; big wheel.

normal *adj* normal; usual.

normalizar *vt* to normalize; to standardize; **~se** *vr* to return to normal.

noroeste *adj* northwest, northwestern; * *m* northwest.

norte *adj* north, northern; * *m* north; (*fig*) rule, guide.

nos *pn* us; to us; for us; from us; to ourselves.

nosotros/tras *pn* we; us.

nostalgia *f* homesickness.

nota *f* note; notice, remark; mark.

notable *adj* notable, remarkable.

notar *vt* to note; to mark; to remark; **~se** *vr* to be obvious.

notaría *f* profession of a notary; notary's office.

notario *m* notary.

noticia *f* notice; knowledge, information; note; **~s** *fpl* news.

noticiario *m* newsreel; news bulletin.

noticiero *m* news bulletin.

notificación *f* notification.

notificar *vt* to notify, to inform.

notoriedad *f* notoriety.

notorio/ria *adj* notorious.

novato/ta *adj* inexperienced; * *m/f* beginner; fresher.

novecientos/tas *adj* nine hundred.

novedad *f* novelty; modernness; newness; piece of news; change.

novela *f* novel.

novelero/ra *adj* highly imaginative.

novelesco/ca *adj* fictional; romantic; fantastic.

noveno/na *adj* ninth.

noventa *adj, m* ninety.

novia *f* bride; girlfriend; fiancée.

noviazgo *m* engagement.

novicio *m* novice.

noviembre *m* November.

novilla *f* heifer.

novillada *f* drove of young bulls; fight of young bulls.

novillo *m* young bull or ox.

novio *m* bridegroom; boyfriend; fiancé.

nubarrón *m* large cloud.

nube *f* cloud.

nublado/da *adj* cloudy; * *m* storm cloud.

nublarse *vr* to grow dark.

nuca *f* nape (of the neck); scruff of the neck.

nuclear *adj* nuclear.

núcleo *m* core; nucleus.

nudillo *m* knuckle.

nudo *m* knot.

nuera *f* daughter-in-law.

nuestro/tra *adj* our; * *pn* ours.

nuevamente *adv* again; anew.

nueve *m, adj* nine.

nuevo/va *adj* new; modern; fresh; * *f* piece of news; ¿qué hay de ~? is there any news?, what's new?

nuez *f* nut; walnut; Adam's apple; ~ **moscada** nutmeg.

nulidad *f* incompetence; nullity.

nulo/la *adj* useless; drawn; null.

numeración *f* numeration.

numerador *m* numerator.

numeral *m* numeral.

numerar *vt* to number.

numérico/ca *adj* numerical.

número *m* number; cipher.

numeroso/sa *adj* numerous.

nunca *adv* never.
nuncio *m* nuncio.
nupcial *adj* nuptial.
nupcias *fpl* nuptials *pl*, wedding.
nutria *f* otter.

nutrición *f* nutrition.
nutrir *vt* to nourish; to feed.
nutritivo/va *adj* nutritious, nourishing.
nylon *m* nylon.

Ñ

ñato/ta *adj* snubnosed.
ñoñería *f* insipidness.

ñoño/ña *adj* insipid; spineless; silly.

O

o *conj* or; either.
oasis *m invar* oasis.
obcecación *f* obduracy.
obcecar *vt* to blind; to darken.
obedecer *vt* to obey.
obediencia *f* obedience.
obediente *adj* obedient.
obelisco *m* obelisk.
obertura *f (mus)* overture.
obesidad *f* obesity.
obeso/sa *adj* obese, fat.
obispado *m* bishopric, episcopate.
obispo *m* bishop.
objeción *f* objection, opposition, exception.
objetar *vi* to object.
objetor *m* ~ **de conciencia** conscientious objector.
objetivo/va *adj, m* objective.
objeto *m* object; aim.
oblea *f* wafer.
oblicuo/cua *adj* oblique.
obligación *f* obligation; *(com)* bond.
obligar *vt* to force; ~**se** *vr* to bind oneself.
obligatorio/ria *adj* obligatory.
oblongo/ga *adj* oblong.
oboe *m* oboe.

obra *f* work; building, construction; play; **por** ~ **de** thanks to.
obrar *vt* to work, to operate; to put into practice; * *vi* to behave, to act; to have an effect.
obrero/ra *adj* working; labour *compd*; * *m/f* workman; labourer.
obscenidad *f* obscenity.
obsceno/na *adj* obscene.
obsequiar *vt* to lavish attention on; ~ **con** to present with.
obsequio *m* gift; courtesy.
obsequioso/sa *adj* obsequious, compliant; officious.
observación *f* observation; remark.
observador/ra *m/f* observer.
observancia *f* observance.
observar *vt* to observe; to notice.
observatorio *m* observatory.
obsesión *f* obsession.
obsesionar *vt* to obsess.
obstáculo *m* obstacle, impediment, hindrance.
obstar *vi*: ~ **a**, ~ **para** to oppose, to obstruct, to hinder.
obstetricia *f* obstetrics.
obstinación *f* obstinacy, stubbornness.

obstinado/da *adj* obstinate.

obstinarse *vr* to be obstinate; ~ **en** to persist in.

obstrucción *f* obstruction.

obstruir *vt* to obstruct; ~**se** *vr* to be blocked up, to be obstructed.

obtener *vt* to obtain; to gain.

obtuso/sa *adj* obtuse, blunt.

obús *m* (*mil*) shell.

obviar *vt* to obviate, to remove.

obvio/via *adj* obvious, evident.

ocasión *f* occasion, opportunity.

ocasional *adj* occasional.

ocasionar *vt* to cause, to occasion.

ocaso *m* (*fig*) decline.

occidental *adj* occidental, western.

occidente *m* occident, west.

océano *m* ocean.

ochenta *m, adj* eighty.

ocho *m, adj* eight.

ochocientos *m, adj* eight hundred.

ocio *m* leisure; pastime.

ociosidad *f* idleness, leisure.

ocioso/sa *adj* idle; useless.

ocre *m* ochre.

octavilla *f* pamphlet.

octavo/va *adj* eighth.

octogenario/ria *adj, m/f* octogenarian.

octubre *m* October.

ocular *adj* ocular; eye *compd*.

oculista *m/f* oculist.

ocultar *vt* to hide, to conceal.

oculto/ta *adj* hidden, concealed; secret.

ocupación *f* occupation; business; employment.

ocupado/da *adj* busy; occupied; engaged.

ocupar *vt* to occupy; to hold (an office); ~**se** *vr*: ~ **de**, ~ **en** to concern oneself with; to look after.

ocurrencia *f* event; bright idea.

ocurrir *vi* to occur, to happen.

oda *f* ode.

odiar *vt* to hate;~**se** *vr* to hate one another.

odio *m* hatred.

odioso/sa *adj* odious, hateful.

odontólogo/ga *m/f* dentist.

odorífero/ra *adj* odoriferous, odorous.

oeste *adj* west, western; * *m* west.

ofender *vt* to offend; to injure ~**se** *vr* to be vexed; to take offence.

ofensa *f* offence; injury.

ofensivo/va *adj* offensive, injurious.

ofensor *m* offender.

oferta *f* offer; offering.

oficial *adj* official; * *m* officer; official.

oficiar *vi* to officiate, to minister (of clergymen, etc).

oficina *f* office.

oficio *m* office; employment, occupation; ministry; function; trade, business;~**s** *mpl* divine service.

oficiosidad *f* diligence; officiousness; importunity.

oficioso/sa *adj* officious; diligent; unofficial, informal.

ofimática *f* office automation.

ofrecer *vt* to offer; to present; to exhibit; ~**se** *vr* to offer oneself; to occur, to present itself.

ofrecimiento *m* offer, promise.

ofrenda *f* offering, oblation.

ofrendar *vt* to offer, to contribute.

oftalmólogo/ga *m/f* ophthalmologist.

ofuscación *f* dimness of sight; obfuscation.

ofuscar *vt* to darken, to render obscure; to bewilder.

oídas *fpl*: **de ~** by hearsay.

oído *m* hearing; ear.

oír *vt, vi* to hear; to listen (to).

ojal *m* buttonhole.

¡ojalá! *conj* if only!, would that!

ojeada *f* glance.

ojear *vt* to eye, to view; to glance.

ojera *f* bag under the eyes.

ojeriza *f* spite, grudge, ill-will.

okupa *m/f (fam)* squatter.

ojo *m* eye; sight; eye of a needle; arch of a bridge.

ola *f* wave.

oleada *f* surge; violent emotion.

oleaje *m* succession of waves, sea swell.

óleo *m* oil.

oler *vt* to smell, to scent; * *vi* to smell; ~ **a** to smack of.

olfatear *vt* to smell; (*fig*) to sniff out.

olfato *m* sense of smell.

oligarquía *f* oligarchy.

oligárquico/ca *adj* oligarchical.

olimpíada *f*: **las O~s** the Olympics.

olímpico/ca *adj* olympic.

oliva *f* olive.

olivar *m* olive grove.

olivo *m* olive tree.

olla *f* pan; stew; ~ **podrida** dish composed of different boiled meats and vegetables; ~ **exprés**, ~ **a presión** pressure cooker.

olmo *m* elm tree.

olor *m* smell, odour; scent.

oloroso/sa *adj* fragrant; odorous.

olvidadizo/za *adj* forgetful.

olvidar *vt* to forget.

olvido *m* forgetfulness.

ombligo *m* navel.

omisión *f* omission.

omitir *vt* to omit.

omnipotencia *f* omnipotence.

omnipotente *adj* omnipotent, almighty.

once *m, adj* eleven.

onda *f* wave.

ondear *vi* to undulate; to fluctuate.

ondulado/da *adj* wavy.

oneroso/sa *adj* burdensome.

opa *f* takeover bid.

opacidad *f* opacity; gloom, darkness.

opaco/ca *adj* opaque; dark.

opción *f* option, choice.

ópera *f* opera.

operación *f* operation; ~ **de cesárea** *f* caesarean section, caesarean operation.

operador/ra *m/f* operator; projectionist; cameraman/woman.

operar *vi* to operate; to act.

opinar *vt* to think; * *vi* to give one's opinion.

opinión *f* opinion.

opio *m* opium.

oponente *m/f* opponent.

oponer *vt* to oppose; ~**se** *vr* to be opposed, ~ **a** to oppose.

oportunidad *f* opportunity.

oportunismo *m* opportunism.

oportuno/na *adj* seasonable, opportune.

oposición *f* opposition; ~**ones** *fpl* public examinations *pl*.

opositor/ra *m/f* opponent; candidate (in public examination).

opresión *f* oppression.

opresivo/va *adj* oppressive.

opresor *m* oppressor.

oprimir *vt* to oppress; to crush; to press; to squeeze.

optar *vt* to choose, to elect.

optativo/va *adj* optional.

óptica *f* optics.

óptico/ca *adj* optical; * *m/f* optician.

optimista *m/f* optimist.

óptimo/ma *adj* best.

opuesto/ta *adj* opposite; contrary; adverse.

opulencia *f* wealth, riches *pl*.

opulento/ta *adj* opulent, wealthy.

oración *f* oration, speech; prayer.

orador/ra *m/f* orator.

oral *adj* oral.

orangután *m* orang-utan.

orar *vi* to pray.

oratoria *f* oratory, rhetorical skill.

órbita *f* orbit.

orden *m/f* order; ~ **del día** order of the day; **órdenes sagradas** holy orders *pl*.

ordenación *f* arrangement; ordination; edict, ordinance.

ordenado/da *adj* methodical; orderly.

ordenador *m* computer.

ordenanza *f* order; statute, ordinance; ordination.

ordenar *vt* to arrange; to order; to ordain; ~**se** *vr* to take holy orders.

ordeñar *vt* to milk.

ordinal *adj* ordinal.

ordinario/ria *adj* ordinary, common; **de** ~ regularly, commonly, ordinarily.

orégano *m* oregano.

oreja *f* ear.

orejera *f* earflap.

orfanato *m* orphanage.

orfandad *f* orphanhood.

orgánico/ca *adj* organic; harmonious.

organigrama *m* flowchart.

organismo *m* organism; organization.

organista *m/f* organist.

organización *f* organization; arrangement.

organizar *vt* to organize.

órgano *m* organ.

orgasmo *m* orgasm.

orgía *f* orgy.

orgullo *m* pride, haughtiness.

orgulloso/sa *adj* proud, haughty.

orientación *f* position; direction.

oriental *adj* oriental, eastern.

orientar *vt* to orient; to point; to direct; to guide; ~**se** *vr* to get one's bearings; to decide on a course of action.

oriente *m* orient.

orificio *m* orifice; mouth; aperture.

origen *m* origin, source; native country; family, extraction.

original *adj* original, primitive; * *m* original, first copy.

originalidad *f* originality.

originar *vt, vi* to originate.

originario/ria *adj* original.

orilla *f* limit, border, margin; edge (of cloth); shore.

orín *m* rust.

orina *f* urine.

orinal *m* chamber pot.

orinar *vi* to pass water.

oriundo/da *adj*: ~ **de** native of.

ornamento *m* ornament, embellishment.

ornitología *f* ornithology.

oro *m* gold; ~**s** *mpl* diamonds *pl* (at cards).

orquesta *f* orchestra.

orquídea *f* orchid.

ortiga *f* (*bot*) nettle.

ortodoxia *f* orthodoxy.

ortodoxo/xa *adj* orthodox.

ortografía *f* orthography.

ortográfico/ca *adj* orthographical.

oruga *f* (*bot*) caterpillar.

orza *f* jar.

orzuelo *m* (*med*) stye.

os *pn* you; to you.

osa *f* she-bear; **O~ Mayor/Menor** Great/Little Bear.

osadamente *adv* boldly, daringly.

osadía *f* boldness, intrepidity; zeal, fervour.

osamenta *f* skeleton.

osar *vi* to dare, to venture.

óscar *m* Oscar.

oscilación *f* oscillation.

oscilar *vi* to oscillate.

oscurecer *vt* to obscure; to dark- en; * *vi* to grow dark; **~se** *vr* to disappear.

oscuridad *f* obscurity; darkness.

oscuro/ra *adj* obscure; dark.

osificarse *vr* to ossify.

oso *m* bear; **~ blanco** polar bear.

ostensible *adj* ostensible, apparent.

ostentación *f* ostentation, ambitious display, show.

ostentar *vt* to show; * *vi* to boast, to brag.

ostentoso/sa *adj* sumptuous, ostentatious.

ostra *f* oyster.

otitis *f* earache.

otoñal *adj* fall, autumnal.

otoño *m* fall, autumn.

otorgamiento *m* granting; execution.

otorgar *vt* to concede; to grant.

otorrino/na, otorrinolaringólogo/ga *m/f* ear, nose and throat specialist.

otro/tra *adj* another; other.

ovación *f* ovation.

ovalado/da *adj* oval.

óvalo *m* oval.

ovario *m* ovary.

oveja *f* sheep.

overol *m* overalls *pl*.

ovillo *m* ball of wool.

ovíparo/ra *adj* oviparous, egg-bearing.

ovulación *f* ovulation.

óvulo *m* ovum.

oxidación *f* rusting.

oxidar *vt* to rust; **~se** *vr* to go rusty.

óxido *f* (*quím*) oxide.

oxígeno *m* (*quím*) oxygen.

oyente *m/f* listener, hearer.

P

pabellón *m* pavilion; summer house; block, section.

pábilo *m* wick.

pacer *vt* to pasture, to graze.

paciencia *f* patience.

paciente *adj*, *m/f* patient.

pacificación *f* pacification.

pacificar *vt* to pacify, to appease.

pacífico/ca *adj* pacific, peaceful; * *m*: **el P~** the Pacific.

pacotilla *f*: **de ~** third-rate; cheap.

pactar *vt* to covenant; to contract; to stipulate.

pacto *m* contract, pact.

padecer *vt* to suffer; to sustain (an injury); to put up with.

padecimiento *m* suffering, sufferance.

padrastro *m* stepfather.

padrazo *m* loving, over-indulgent father.

padre *m* father; **~s** *mpl* parents *pl*.

padrino *m* godfather.

padrón *m* census; register; pattern; model.

paella *f* paella (dish of rice with shellfish, meat, etc).

paga *f* payment, fee.

pagadero/ra *adj* payable.

paganismo *m* paganism, heathenism.

pagano/na *adj*, *m/f* heathen, pagan.

pagar vt to pay; to pay for; (fig) to repay; * vi to pay.

pagaré m bond, note of hand, promissory note, IOU (I owe you).

página f page.

pago m payment; reward.

país m country; region.

paisaje m landscape.

paisano/na adj of the same country; * m/f fellow countryman/woman.

paja f straw; (fig) trash.

pajar m straw loft.

pajarita f bow tie.

pájaro m bird; sly, acute fellow.

pajarraco m large bird; cunning fellow.

paje m page.

pajita f (drinking) straw.

pajizo/za adj straw-coloured.

pala f spade, shovel.

palabra f word; **de ~** by word of mouth.

palabrota f swearword.

palaciego/ga adj pertaining or relating to the palace; * m courtier.

palacio m palace.

paladar m palate; taste, relish.

paladear vt to taste.

palanca f lever.

palangana f basin.

palco m box (in a theatre).

paleta f bat; palette; trowel.

paleto/ta m/f rustic.

paliar vt to mitigate.

paliativo/va adj, m palliative.

palidecer vi to turn pale.

palidez f paleness, wanness.

pálido/da adj pallid, pale.

palillo m small stick; toothpick; **~s** mpl chopsticks pl.

paliza f beating, thrashing.

palma f palm tree; palm of the hand; palm leaf.

palmada f slap, clap; **~s** fpl clapping of hands, applause.

palmatoria f candlestick; cane.

palmear vi to slap; to clap.

palmera f palm tree.

palmeta f cane.

palmo m palm; small amount.

palmotear vi to slap; to applaud.

palmoteo m clapping of hands.

palo m stick; cudgel; blow given with a stick; post; mast; bat; suit (at cards).

paloma f pigeon, dove; **~ torcaz** ring dove or wood pigeon; **~ mensajera** carrier pigeon, homing pigeon.

palomar m pigeon house.

palomilla f moth; wing nut; angle iron.

palomino m young pigeon.

palomitas fpl popcorn.

palpable adj palpable, evident.

palpar vt to feel, to touch.

palpitación f palpitation; panting.

palpitante adj palpitating; (fig) burning.

palta f avocado (pear).

paludismo m malaria.

palpitar vi to palpitate.

palurdo/da adj rustic, clownish, rude.

pampa f pampa(s), prairie.

pámpano m vine branch.

pamplina f trifle.

pan m bread; loaf.

pana f corduroy.

panacea f panacea, universal medicine.

panadería f baker's (shop).

panadero/ra m/f baker.

panal m honeycomb; sweet rusk.

pañal m nappy.

pancarta f placard.

panda m panda.

pandereta f tambourine.

pandilla f group; gang; clique.

panegírico/ca adj panegyrical; * m eulogy.

panel m panel.

panfleto m pamphlet.

pánico m panic.

panorama m panorama.

pantalla f screen; lampshade.

pantalón m, **pantalones** mpl trousers pl, pants pl.

pantano m fen; marsh; reservoir; obstacle, difficulty.

pantanoso/sa adj marshy, fenny, boggy.

panteísta f pantheist.

panteón m: ~ **familiar** family tomb.

pantera f panther.

pantomima f pantomime.

pantorrilla f calf (of the leg).

pantufla m slipper.

panza f belly, paunch.

panzada f bellyful of food.

panzudo/da adj big-bellied.

pañal m diaper, nappy.

paño m cloth; piece of cloth; duster, rag.

pañuelo m handkerchief.

papa f potato; * m: **el P~** the Pope.

papá m (fam) dad, pop.

papada f double chin.

papagayo m parrot.

papal adj papal.

papanatas m invar (fam) simpleton.

paparrucha f piece of nonsense.

papaya f papaya, papaw.

papel m paper; writing; part, role (acted in a play); ~ **de estraza** brown paper; ~ **sellado** stamped paper.

papeleo m red tape.

papelera f writing desk; wastepaper basket.

papelería f stationer's (shop).

papeleta f slip of paper; ballot paper; report.

paperas fpl mumps.

papilla f baby food.

papista m papist.

paquete m packet; parcel; package tour.

par adj equal; alike; even; * m pair; couple; peer; **sin** ~ matchless.

para prep for; to, in order to; toward(s).

parabién m congratulation; felicitation.

parábola f parable; parabola.

parabólico/ca adj parabolic(al).

parabrisas m invar windscreen.

paracaídas m invar parachute.

paracaidista m/f parachutist; (mil) paratrooper.

parachoques m invar bumper; shock absorber.

parada f halt; suspension; pause; stop; shutdown; stopping place; ~ **a petición** request stop; ~ **de autobús** bus stop.

paradero m halting place; term, end.

parado/da adj motionless; at a standstill; stopped; standing (up); unemployed; * m/f unemployed person.

paradoja f paradox.

parador m parador, state-owned hotel.

parafrasear vt to paraphrase.

paráfrasis f invar paraphrase.

paraguas m invar umbrella.

paraíso m paradise.

paraje m place, spot.

paralelo/la adj, m parallel.

paralítico/ca adj paralytic, palsied.

paralizar vt to paralyse; **~se** vr to become paralysed; (fig) to come to a standstill.

páramo *m* desert; wilderness.

parangón *m* paragon, model; comparison.

paranoico/ca *m/f* paranoiac.

parapente *m* paragliding.

parapeto *m* parapet.

parar *vi* to stop, to halt; * *vt* to stop, to detain; **sin ~** instantly, without delay; **~se** *vr* to stop, to halt; to stand up.

pararrayos *m invar* lightning conductor.

parásito *m* parasite; (*fig*) sponger.

parasol *m* parasol.

parcela *f* piece of ground.

parche *m* patch.

parcial *adj* partial.

parcialidad *f* prejudice; bias.

parco/ca *adj* sober, moderate.

pardo/da *adj* gray.

parear *vt* to match, to pair, to couple.

parecer *m* opinion, advice, counsel; countenance, air, mien; * *vi* to appear; to seem; **~se** *vr*: **~ a** to resemble.

parecido/da *adj* resembling, like.

pared *f* wall; **~ medianera** party-wall.

pareja *f* pair, couple; timber beam that serves as a support, brace.

parejo/ja *adj* equal; even.

parentela *f* parentage, kindred.

parentesco *m* relationship.

paréntesis *m invar* parenthesis.

parida *f* woman who has recently given birth.

paridad *f* parity, equality.

pariente/ta *m/f* relative, relation.

parir *vt* to give birth to; * *vi* to give birth.

parking *m* car park.

parlamentar *vi* to parley.

parlamentario/ria *m/f* member of parliament; * *adj* parliamentary.

parlamento *m* parliament.

parlanchín/ina *adj*, *m/f* chatterer, jabberer.

parlotear *vi* to prattle, to chatter, to gossip.

paro *m* strike; unemployment.

parodia *f* parody.

parpadear *vi* to blink; to flicker.

párpado *m* eyelid.

parque *m* park; **~ eólico** wind farm.

parque de bomberos *m*.fire station.

parquímetro *m* parking meter.

parra *f* vine raised on stakes or nailed to a wall.

párrafo *m* paragraph.

parricida *m/f* parricide (person).

parricidio *m* parricide (murder).

parrilla *f* grill; grille.

párroco *m* parish priest.

parroquia *f* parish; customers *pl*.

parroquial *adj* parochial.

parroquiano *m* parishioner; customer; **~/na** *adj* parochial.

parsimonia *f* parsimony.

parte *m* message; report; * *f* part; side; party; **de ocho días a esta ~** within these last eight days; **de ~ a ~** from side to side, through and through.

partera *f* midwife.

partición *f* partition, division.

participación *f* participation.

participante *m/f* participant.

participar *vi* to participate, to partake.

partícipe *m/f* participant.

participio *m* participle.

partícula *f* particle.

particular *adj* particular, special; * *m* private individual; particular matter or subject treated upon.

particularidad f particularity.

particularizar vt, vr to particularize; to distinguish; to specify.

partida f departure; party; item in an account; parcel; game.

partidario/ria adj partisan; * m/f supporter.

partido m party; match; team.

partidor m parter, divider.

partir vt to part; to divide, to separate; to cut; to break; * vi to depart; ~se vr to break (in two, etc.).

parto m birth.

parvulario m nursery school.

pasa f raisin.

pasada f passage, passing; **de ~** on the way, in passing.

pasadizo m narrow passage; narrow, covered way.

pasado/da adj past; bad; overdone; out of date; **~ mañana** the day after tomorrow; **la semana pasada** last week; * m past.

pasador m bolt; hair slide; grip.

pasaje m passage; fare; passengers pl.

pasajero/ra adj transient; transitory; fugitive; * m/f traveller; passenger.

pasamanos m invar (hand)rail; banister.

pasamontañas m invar balaclava helmet.

pasaporte m passport.

pasar vt to pass; to surpass; to suffer; to strain; to dissemble; * vi to pass; to happen; ~se vr to go over (to another party); to go bad or off.

pasarela f footbridge; gangway.

pasatiempo m pastime, amusement.

Pascua f Passover; Easter.

pase m pass; showing; permit.

paseante m walker.

pasear vt to walk; vi, ~se vr to walk; to walk about.

paseo m walk; shopping mall.

pasillo m passage.

pasión f passion.

pasionaria f passionflower.

pasivo/va adj passive.

pasmar vt to amaze; to numb; to chill; ~se vr to be astonished.

pasmo m astonishment, amazement.

pasmoso/sa adj marvellous, wonderful.

paso m pace, step; passage; manner of walking; flight of steps; accident; (ferro) ~ **a nivel** level crossing; **al ~** on the way, in passing.

paso de peatones m pedestrian crossing.

pasota adj, m/f (fam) dropout; **ser un ~** not to care about anything.

pasta f paste; dough; pastry; (fam) dough; ~s fpl pastries pl; pasta; ~ **de dientes** toothpaste.

pastar vt to pasture, to graze.

pastel m cake; pie; crayon (for drawing).

pastelería f cake shop.

pasteurizado/da adj pasteurized.

pastilla f bar (of soap); tablet, pill.

pasto m pasture; pasture-ground; **a ~** abundantly.

pastor m shepherd; pastor.

pastoso/sa adj mellow; doughy.

pata f leg (of animal or furniture); foot; **a la ~ coja** hopscotch (children's game); **a ~** (fam) on foot; **meter la ~** to put one's foot in it.

patada f kick.

patalear vi to kick violently.

pataleo m act of stamping one's foot.

pataleta f fit; swoon.

patán m clown; churl, countryman.

patata f potato.
patatús m swoon, fainting fit.
paté m pâté.
patear vt to kick; to stamp on.
patente adj patent, manifest, evident; * f patent; warrant.
paternal adj paternal, fatherly.
paternidad f paternity, fatherhood.
paterno/na adj paternal, fatherly.
patético/ca adj pathetic.
patíbulo m gallows.
patillas fpl sideburns pl.
patín m skate; runner.
patinaje m skating.
patinar vi to skate; to skid; (fam) to blunder.
patio m courtyard; playground (in schools).
patizambo/ba adj knock-kneed.
pato m duck.
patochada f blunder, folly; nonsense.
patología f pathology.
patológico/ca adj pathological.
patoso/sa adj (fam) clumsy.
patraña f lie.
patria f native country.
patriarca m patriarch.
patriarcado m patriarchy.
patriarcal adj patriarchal.
patrimonial adj patrimonial.
patrimonio m patrimony.
patrio/tria adj native; paternal.
patriota m/f patriot.
patriótico/ca adj patriotic.
patriotismo m patriotism.
patrocinar vt to sponsor; to back, to support.
patrocinio m sponsorship; backing, support.
patrón/ona m/f boss, master/ mistress; landlord/lady; patron saint; * m pattern.

patronal adj: **la clase ~** management.
patronato m patronage, sponsorship; trust, foundation.
patronímico m patronymic.
patrulla f patrol.
patrullar vi to patrol.
paulatino/na adj gradual, slow.
pausa f pause; repose.
pausado/da adj slow, deliberate; calm, quiet.
pausar vi to pause.
pauta f guideline.
pavesa f embers pl, hot cinders pl.
pavía f peach with hard stone.
pavimento m pavement; paving.
pavo m turkey; **~ real** peacock.
pavonearse vr to strut, to walk with affected dignity.
pavor m dread, terror.
pavoroso/sa adj awful, formidable.
payaso/sa m/f clown.
payo/ya m/f non-Gypsy (for a Gypsy).
paz f peace; tranquillity, ease.
peaje m toll.
peana f pedestal; footstool.
peatón m pedestrian.
peca f freckle; spot.
pecado m sin.
pecador/ra m/f sinner.
pecaminoso/sa adj sinful.
pecar vi to sin.
pecho m chest; breast(s) (pl); teat; bosom; (fig) courage, valour; **dar el ~ a** to breast-feed; **tomar a ~ to** take to heart.
pechuga f breast (of a fowl); (fam) bosom.
pecoso/sa adj freckled.
peculiar adj peculiar; special.
pecuniario/ria adj pecuniary.
pedagogía f pedagogy.
pedagógico/ca adj pedagogic.

pedagogo/ga *m/f* pedagogue.
pedal *m* pedal.
pedalear *vi* to pedal.
pedante *adj* pedantic; * *m/f* pedant.
pedantería *f* pedantry.
pedazo *m* piece, bit.
pedernal *m* flint.
pedestal *m* pedestal, foot.
pediatra *m/f* pediatrician.
pediatría *f.* paediatrics *pl*.
pedicuro/ra *m/f* chiropodist, podiatrist.
pedido *m* (*com*) order; request.
pedir *vt* to ask for; to petition; to beg; to order; to need; to solicit; * *vi* to ask.
pedo *m* (*fam*) fart (*sl*); **tirarse un ~** to fart (*sl*).
pedrada *f* throw (of a stone).
pedregal *m* stony place.
pedregoso/sa *adj* stony.
pedrería *f* (collection of) precious stones *pl*.
pedrisco *m* hailstone.
pedrusco *m* rough piece of stone.
pegadizo/za *adj* clammy, sticky; catchy; contagious.
pegajoso/sa *adj* sticky, viscous; contagious; attractive.
pegamento *m* glue.
pegar *vt* to cement; to join, to unite; to beat; **~ fuego a** to set fire to; * *vi* to stick; to match; **~se** *vr* to intrude; to steal in.
pegatina *f* sticker.
pegote *m* sticking plaster; intruder; hanger-on, sponger (*sl*).
peinado *m* hairstyle.
peinar *vt* to comb; to style.
peine *m* comb.
peineta *f* convex comb for women.
peladilla *f* sugared almond, burnt almond; small pebble.

pelado/da *adj* peeled; shorn; bare; broke; * *m* (*fam*) haircut.
peladura *f* peeling; plucking.
pelaje *m* fur coat; (*fig*) appearance.
pelar *vt* to cut (hair); to strip off (feathers); to peel; **~se** *vr* to peel off; to have one's hair cut.
peldaño *m* step (of a flight of stairs).
pelea *f* battle, fight; quarrel.
pelear *vt* to fight, to combat; **~se** *vr* to scuffle.
pelele *m* dummy; man of straw.
peletería *f* fur store.
peletero *m* furrier.
peliagudo/da *adj* tricky; arduous, difficult.
pelícano *m* pelican.
película *f* film; pellicle.
peligrar *vi* to be in danger; **~ de** to risk.
peligro *m* danger, peril; risk.
peligroso/sa *adj* dangerous, perilous.
pelirrojo/ja *m/f* redhead; * *adj* red-haired.
pellejo *m* skin; hide, pelt; peel; wine skin, leather bag for wine; oilskin; drunkard.
pelliza *f* fur jacket.
pellizcar *vt* to pinch.
pellizco *m* pinch; nip; small bit; (*fig*) remorse.
pelma/pelmazo/za *m/f* (*fam*) pain (in the neck).
pelo *m* hair; pile; flaw (in precious stones).
pelón/ona *adj* hairless, bald.
pelota *f* ball.
pelotazo *m* blow with a ball.
pelotera *f* quarrel.
pelotón *m* large ball; (*mil*) platoon.
peluca *f* wig.
peluche *m*: **muñeco de ~** soft toy.

peludo/da *adj* hairy.

peluquería *f* hairdresser's; barber's (shop).

peluquero/ra *m/f* hairdresser; barber.

pelusa *f* bloom (on fruit); fluff.

pena *f* punishment, pain; **a duras ~s** with great difficulty or trouble.

penacho *m* tuft on the heads of some birds; crest.

penal *adj* penal.

penalidad *f* suffering, trouble; hardship; penalty.

penalti/penalty *m* penalty (kick).

penar *vi* to suffer pain; * *vt* to chastise.

pendencia *f* quarrel, dispute.

pendenciero/ra *adj* quarrelsome.

pender *vi* to hang; to be pending; to depend.

pendiente *f* slope, declivity; * *m* earring; * *adj* pending; unsettled.

pendón *m* standard; banner.

péndulo *m* pendulum.

pene *m* penis.

penetración *f* penetration; perception.

penetrante *adj* deep; sharp; piercing; searching; biting.

penetrar *vt* to penetrate.

penicilina *f* penicillin.

península *f* peninsula.

penique *m* penny.

penitencia *f* penitence; penalty, fine.

penitenciaría *f* prison.

penitente *adj* penitent, repentant; * *m* penitent.

penoso/sa *adj* painful.

pensador/ra *m/f* thinker.

pensamiento *m* thought, thinking.

pensar *vi* to think.

pensativo/va *adj* pensive, thoughtful.

pensión *f* guest-house; pension; worry; regret.

pensionista *m/f* pensioner; lodger.

Pentecostés *m* Pentecost, Whitsuntide.

penúltimo/ma *adj* penultimate, last but one.

penumbra *f* half-light.

penuria *f* penury, poverty, neediness, extreme want.

peña *f* rock, large stone.

peñasco *m* large rock.

peñón *m* rocky mountain.

peón *m* (day)labourer; foot soldier; pawn (at chess).

peonía *f* (*bot*) peony.

peonza *f* spinning top.

peor *adj*, *adv* worse; **cada vez ~** worse and worse.

pepinillo *m* gherkin.

pepino *m* cucumber.

pepita *f* kernel; pip.

pepitoria *f* fricassée.

pequeñez *f* smallness; childhood, infancy; triviality.

pequeño/ña *adj* little, small; young.

pera *f* pear.

peral *m* pear tree.

percance *m* perquisite; bad luck, setback.

percatarse *vr*: **~ de** to notice.

percepción *f* perception; notion.

perceptible *adj* perceptible, perceivable.

percha *f* coat hook; coat hanger; perch.

percibir *vt* to receive; to perceive, to comprehend.

percusión *f* percussion.

perder *vt* to lose; to waste; to miss; **~se** *vr* to go astray; to be lost; to be spoiled.

perdición *f* loss, losing; perdition, ruin.

pérdida *f* loss, damage; lost object.

perdido/da *adj* lost; stray.
perdigón *m* young partridge; ~**ones** *mpl* buckshot, pellets.
perdiz *f* partridge.
perdón *m* pardon; mercy; **¡~!** sorry!; excuse me!
perdonable *adj* pardonable.
perdonar *vt* to pardon, to forgive; to excuse.
perdurable *adj* perpetual, everlasting.
perdurar *vi* to last; to still exist.
perecedero/ra *adj* perishable.
perecer *vi* to perish, to die; to shatter (an object).
peregrinación *f* pilgrimage.
peregrinar *vi* to go on a pilgrimage.
peregrino/na *adj* (*fig*) strange; * *m/f* pilgrim.
perejil *m* parsley.
perenne *adj* perennial; perpetual.
perentorio/ria *adj* peremptory; urgent.
pereza *f* laziness, idleness.
perezoso/sa *adj* lazy, idle.
perfección *f* perfection.
perfeccionar *vt* to perfect; to complete, to finish.
perfecto/ta *adj* perfect; complete.
perfidia *f* perfidy.
pérfido/da *adj* perfidious.
perfil *m* profile.
perfilado/da *adj* well-formed, delicate (of features).
perfilar *vt* to outline; ~**se** *vr*: ~ **en** to show up against.
perforar *vt* to perforate; to drill; to punch a hole in; * *vi* to drill.
perfumador *m* perfumer.
perfumar *vt* to perfume.
perfume *m* perfume.
perfumería *f* perfumery.
pergamino *m* parchment.

pericia *f* skill, knowledge; expertise.
periferia *f* periphery; outskirts *pl*.
periférico *m* ring-road.
perífrasis *f invar* periphrasis, circumlocution.
perímetro *m* perimeter; circumference.
periódico/ca *adj* periodical; * *m* newspaper.
periodista *m/f* journalist.
período, periodo *m* period.
peripecia *f* vicissitude; sudden change.
peripuesto/ta *adj* dressed up, very spruce.
periquito *m* budgie.
perito/ta *adj* skilful, experienced; * *m/f* expert; skilled worker; technician.
perjudicar *vt* to prejudice, to damage; to injure, to hurt.
perjudicial *adj* prejudicial, damaging.
perjuicio *m* damage, harm.
perjurar *vi* to perjure, to swear falsely; to swear.
perjurio *m* perjury; false oath.
perjuro/ra *adj* perjured; * *m/f* perjurer.
perla *f* pearl; **de ~s** fine.
permanecer *vi* to stay; to continue to be.
permanencia *f* permanence; stay.
permanente *adj* permanent.
permiso *m* permission, leave, licence.
permitir *vt* to permit, to allow.
permuta *f* permutation, exchange.
permutar *vt* to exchange, to permute.
pernera *f* trouser leg.
pernicioso/sa *adj* pernicious, destructive; wicked.

pernio *m* hinge.
perno *m* bolt.
pernoctar *vi* to spend the night.
pero *m* kind of apple; * *conj* but, yet.
perogrullada *f* truism, platitude.
perol *m* large metal pan.
perorata *f* harangue, speech.
perpendicular *adj* perpendicular.
perpetrar *vt* to perpetrate, to commit (a crime).
perpetuar *vt* to perpetuate.
perpetuidad *f* perpetuity.
perpetuo/tua *adj* perpetual.
perplejidad *f* perplexity.
perplejo/ja *adj* perplexed.
perra *f* bitch; (*fam*) money.
perrera *f* kennel.
perro *m* dog.
persecución *f* persecution; toil, trouble; fatigue.
perseguidor *m* persecutor.
perseguir *vt* to pursue; to persecute; to chase after.
perseverancia *f* perseverance, constancy.
perseverante *adj* persistent.
perseverar *vi* to persevere, to persist.
persiana *f* (Venetian) blind.
persignarse *vr* to make the sign of the cross.
persistencia *f* persistence; steadiness.
persistir *vi* to persist.
persona *f* person; **de ~ a ~** from person to person.
personaje *m* celebrity; character.
personal *adj* personal; single; * *m* personnel.
personalidad *f* personality.
personarse *vr* to appear in person.
personificar *vt* to personify.
perspectiva *f* perspective; view; outlook.

perspicacia *f* perspicacity, clear-sightedness.
perspicaz *adj* perspicacious, clear-sighted.
persuadir *vt* to persuade; **~se** *vr* to be persuaded.
persuasión *f* persuasion.
persuasivo/va *adj* persuasive.
pertenecer *vi*: **~ a** to belong to; to appertain, to concern.
pertenencia *f* ownership; **~s** *fpl* possessions *pl*.
perteneciente *adj*: **~ a** belonging to.
pértiga *f* long pole or rod.
pertinacia *f* pertinacity; obstinacy, stubbornness.
pertinaz *adj* pertinacious; obstinate.
pertinente *adj* relevant; appropriate.
pertrechar *vt* to supply with ammunition and other warlike stores; to dispose; to arrange, to prepare; **~se** *vr* to be provided with the necessary defensive stores and arms.
pertrechos *mpl* tools *pl*, instruments *pl*; ammunition.
perturbación *f* perturbation; disturbance.
perturbado/da *adj* mentally unbalanced.
perturbador *m* disturber.
perturbar *vt* to perturb, to disturb.
perversidad *f* perversity.
perversión *f* perversion; depravation, corruption.
perverso/sa *adj* perverse; extremely wicked.
pervertido/da *adj* perverted; * *m/f* pervert.
pervertir *vt* to pervert; to corrupt.
pesa *f* weight.
pesadez *f* heaviness, weight; gravity; slowness; peevishness, fretfulness; trouble; fatigue.

pesadilla *f* nightmare.

pesado/da *adj* peevish; troublesome; cumbersome; tedious; heavy, weighty.

pesadumbre *f* weightiness; gravity; quarrel, dispute; grief; trouble.

pésame *m* message of condolence.

pesar *m* sorrow, grief; repentance; **a ~ de** in spite of, notwithstanding; * *vi* to weigh; to repent; * *vt* to weigh.

pesario *m* pessary.

pesaroso/sa *adj* sorrowful, full of repentance; restless, uneasy.

pesca *f* fishing.

pescadería *f* fish market, fishmonger, fish shop.

pescado *m* fish (in general).

pescador *m* fisher, fisherman.

pescar *vt* to fish for, to catch (fish); * *vi* to fish.

pescuezo *m* neck.

pesebre *m* crib, manger.

peseta *f* peseta.

pesimista *m* pessimist.

pésimo/ma *adj* very bad.

peso *m* weight, heaviness; balance scales *pl*.

pespunte *m* back-stitching.

pesquero/ra *adj* fishing *compd*.

pesquisa *f* inquiry, examination.

pestaña *f* eyelash.

pestañear *vi* to blink.

pestañeo *m* blink.

peste *f* pest, plague, pestilence.

pesticida *m* pesticide.

pestífero/ra *adj* pestilential.

pestilencia *f* pestilence.

pestillo *m* bolt.

petaca *f* covered hamper; tobacco pouch.

pétalo *m* petal.

petardo *m* cheat, fraud; imposition.

petate *m* straw bed; sleeping mat of the Indians; (*mar*) sailors' bedding on board ship; (*mar*) passengers' baggage; poor fellow.

petición *f* petition, demand.

peto *m* breastplate; bodice.

petrificar(se) *vt* (*vr*) to petrify.

petróleo *m* oil, petroleum.

petrolero/ra *adj* petroleum *compd*; * *m* (oil) tanker; (*com*) oil man.

petulancia *f* petulance; insolence.

petulante *adj* petulant; insolent.

peyorativo/va *adj* pejorative.

pez[1] *m* fish.

pez[2] *f* pitch.

pezón *m* nipple.

pezuña *f* hoof.

piadoso/sa *adj* pious; mild; merciful; moderate.

pianista *m/f* pianist.

piano *m* piano.

piar *vi* to squeak; to chirp.

piara *f* herd (of swine); flock (of sheep).

pibe/ba *m/f* boy/girl.

pica *f* pike.

picacho *m* sharp point.

picadero *m* riding school.

picadillo *m* minced meat.

picado/da *adj* pricked; minced, chopped; bad (tooth); cross.

picador *m* riding master; picador.

picadura *f* prick; puncture.

picante *adj* hot, spicy; racy.

picapedrero *m* stonecutter.

picaporte *m* door handle; latch.

picar *vt* to prick; to sting; to mince; to nibble; * *vi* to prick; to sting; to itch; **~se** *vr* to be piqued; to take offence; to be moth-eaten; to begin to rot.

picardía *f* roguery; deceit; malice; lewdness.

picaresco/ca *adj* roguish; picaresque.

pícaro/ra *adj* roguish; mischievous, malicious; sly; * *m/f* rogue, knave.

picazón *f* itching; stinging; displeasure.

pichón *m* young pigeon.

pico *m* beak; bill, nib; peak; pick-axe.

picotazo *m* peck (of a bird).

picotear *vt* to peck (of birds).

picudo/da *adj* with a beak; sharp-pointed.

pie *m* foot; leg; basis; trunk (of trees); foundation; occasion; **a ~** on foot.

piedad *f* piety; mercy, pity.

piedra *f* stone.

piel *f* skin; hide; peel.

pienso *m* fodder.

pierna *f* leg.

pieza *f* piece; room.

pigmeo/mea *m/f*, *adj* pigmy.

pijama *m* pyjamas *pl*.

pila *f* battery; trough; font; sink; pile, heap; **nombre de ~** first name.

pilar¹ *m* basin.

pilar² *m* pillar, column; pillar box; mainstay.

píldora *f* pill.

pileta *f* basin; swimming pool.

pillaje *m* pillage, plunder.

pillar *vt* to pillage, to plunder, to foray, to seize; to catch onto; to catch.

pillo/lla *m*, *adj* rascal, scoundrel.

pilotaje *m* pilotage.

piloto *m/f* pilot.

piltrafa *f* piece of meat that is nearly all skin.

pimentón *m* paprika.

pimienta *f* pepper.

pimiento *m* pepper, pimiento.

pinacoteca *f* art gallery.

pináculo *m* pinnacle.

pinar *m* grove of pines.

pincel *m* paintbrush.

pincelada *f* dash with a paintbrush.

pinchar *vt* to prick; to puncture.

pinchazo *m* prick; puncture; (*fig*) prod.

pinchito *m* small snack.

pincho *m* thorn; snack.

pingajo *m* rag, tatter.

ping-pong *m* table tennis.

pingüe *adj* fat, greasy; fertile.

pingüino *m* penguin.

pino *m* (*bot*) pine.

pinta *f* spot, blemish; scar; mark (on playing cards); pint.

pintado/da *adj* painted, mottled; **venir ~** to fit exactly.

pintar *vt* to paint; to picture; to describe; to exaggerate; * *vi* to paint; (*fam*) to count, to be important; **~se** *vr* to put on make-up.

pintarrajear *vt* to daub.

pintarrajo *m* daub.

pintor/ra *m/f* painter.

pintoresco/ca *adj* picturesque.

pintura *f* painting.

pinza *f* claw; clothes peg; pincers *pl*; **~s** *fpl* tweezers *pl*.

piña *f* pineapple; fir cone; group.

piñón *m* pine nut; pinion.

pío/pía *adj* pious, devout; merciful.

piojo *m* louse; troublesome hanger-on.

piojoso/sa *adj* lousy; miserable, stingy.

pionero/ra *adj* pioneering; *m/f* pioneer.

pipa *f* pipe; sunflower seed.

pipí *m* (*fam*): **hacer ~** to have to go (wee-wee).

pique *m* pique, offence taken; rivalry; **echar a ~** to sink a ship; **a ~** in danger; **a ~ de** on the point of.

piquete *m* slight prick or sting; picket.

pira *f* funeral pyre.

piragua *f* canoe.

piragüismo m canoeing.

piramidal adj pyramidal.

pirámide f pyramid.

pirata m pirate.

piropo m compliment; flattery.

pirotecnia f fireworks pl.

pirueta f pirouette.

pisada f footstep; footprint.

pisar vt to tread, to trample; to stamp on (the ground); to hammer down; * vi to tread, to walk.

piscina f swimming pool; ~ **para niños** paddling pool.

Piscis m Pisces (sign of the zodiac).

piso m flat, apartment; tread, trampling; floor, pavement; floor, storey.

pisotear vt to trample, to tread under foot.

pista f trace, footprint; clue.

pisto m thick broth.

pistola f pistol.

pistolera f pistol holster.

pistolero/ra m/f gunman/woman, gangster.

pistoletazo m pistol shot.

pistón m piston; (musical) key.

pita f (bot) any plant of the family Agavaceae with tall flowers and thick, fleshy leaves.

pitar vt to blow; to whistle at; * vi to whistle; to toot one's horn; to smoke.

pitillo m cigarette.

pito m whistle; horn.

pitón m python.

pitonisa f sorceress, enchantress.

pitorreo m joke; **estar de** ~ to be joking.

pizarra f slate.

pizarral m slate quarry, slate pit.

pizca f mite; pinch.

placa f plate; badge; ~ **de matrícula** numberplate.

placentero/ra adj joyful, merry.

placer m pleasure; delight; * vt to please.

plácido/da adj placid.

plaga f plague.

plagar vt to plague, to torment.

plagio m plagiarism.

plan m plan; design; plot.

plana f trowel; page (of a book); level; ~ **mayor** (mil) staff.

plancha f plate; iron; gangway; press-up.

planchar vt to iron.

planchuela n nameplate f.

planeador m glider.

planear vt to plan; * vi to glide.

planeta m planet.

planetario/ria adj planetary.

planicie f plain.

planificación f planning; ~ **familiar** family planning.

plano/na adj plain, level, flat; * m plan; ground plot; ~ **inclinado** (ferro) dead level.

planta f plant; plantation.

plantación f plantation.

plantar vt to plant; to fix upright; to strike or hit (a blow); to found; to establish; ~**se** vr to stand upright.

plantear vt to plan; to implant.

plantilla f personnel; insole of a shoe.

plantón m long wait; (mil) sentry.

plañir vi to lament, to grieve, to bewail.

plasmar vt to mould; to represent.

plasta f paste, soft clay; mess.

plástico/ca adj plastic; * m plastic; * f (art of) sculpture.

plata f silver; plate (wrought silver); cash; **en** ~ briefly.

plataforma f platform; ~ **giratoria** (ferro) turntable.

plátano *m* banana; plane tree.

plateado/da *adj* silvered; plated.

platería *f* silversmith's shop; trade of silversmith.

plática *f* discourse, conversation.

platicar *vi* to converse.

platillo *m* saucer; ~**s** *mpl* cymbals *pl*; ~ **volador,** ~ **volante** flying saucer.

platino *m* platinum; ~**s** *mpl* contact points *pl*.

plato *m* dish; plate.

platónico/ca *adj* platonic.

plausible *adj* plausible.

playa *f* beach.

playera *f* T-shirt; ~**s** *fpl* canvas shoes *pl*.

plaza *f* square; place; office, employment; room; seat.

plazo *m* term; instalment; expiry date.

pleamar *f* (*mar*) high water.

plebe *f* common people *pl*, populace.

plebeyo/ya *adj* plebeian; * *m* commoner.

plebiscito *m* plebiscite.

plegable *adj* pliable; folding.

plegar *vt* to fold; to plait.

plegaria *f* prayer.

pleitear *vi* to plead, to litigate.

pleito *m* contract, bargain; dispute, controversy, debate; lawsuit.

plenamente *adv* fully; completely.

plenario/ria *adj* complete; full.

plenilunio *m* full moon.

plenipotenciario *m* plenipotentiary.

plenitud *f* fullness; abundance.

pleno/na *adj* full; complete; * *m* plenum.

pliego *m* sheet of paper.

pliegue *m* fold; plait.

plisado/da *adj* pleated; * *m* pleating.

plomero *m* plumber.

plomizo/za *adj* leaden.

plomo *m* lead; **a** ~ perpendicularly.

pluma *f* feather, plume.

plumaje *m* plumage; plume.

plumero *m* bunch of feathers; feather duster.

plumón *m* felt-tip pen; marker; down.

plural *adj* (*gr*) plural.

pluralidad *f* plurality.

Plutón *m* Pluto (planet).

población *f* population; town.

poblado *m* town; village; inhabited place.

poblador/ra *m/f* populator, founder.

poblar *vt* to populate, to people; to fill, to occupy.

pobre *adj* poor.

pobreza *f* poverty, poorness.

pocilga *f* pig sty.

pocillo *m* coffee cup.

pócima, poción *f* potion.

poco/ca *adj* little, scanty; (*pl*) few; * *adv* little; ~ **a** ~ gently; little by little; * *m* small part; little.

poda *f* pruning (of trees).

podadera *f* pruning knife.

podar *vt* to prune.

podenco *m* hound.

poder *m* power, authority; command; force; * *vi* to be able to; to possess the power of doing or performing.

poderío *m* power, authority; wealth, riches *pl*.

poderoso/sa *adj* powerful; eminent, excellent.

podredumbre *f* putrid matter; grief.

podrido/da *adj* rotten, bad; (*fig*) rotten.

podrir *vt* to rot, to putrefy; ~**se** *vr* to rot, to decay.

poema *m* poem.

poesía f poetry.

poeta m poet.

poético/ca adj poetical.

poetisa f poetess.

poetizar vt to poetize.

polar adj polar.

polea f pulley; (mar) tackle-block.

polémica f polemic.

polémico/ca adj polemical.

polen m pollen.

policía f police; * m/f policeman/ woman.

polideportivo m sports centre.

poligamia f polygamy.

polígamo m polygamist.

polígono m polygon.

polilla f moth.

polio f polio.

pólipo m polypus.

politécnico/ca adj polytechnic.

politeísmo m polytheism.

política f politics; policy.

político/ca adj political; * m/f politician.

póliza f written order; policy.

polizón m stowaway.

pollera f skirt.

pollería f poulterer's (shop).

pollo m chicken.

polo m pole; ice lolly; polo; polo neck.

polución f pollution.

polvareda f cloud of dust.

polvera f powder compact.

polvo m powder, dust.

pólvora f gunpowder.

polvoriento/ta adj dusty.

polvorín m powder reduced to the finest dust; powder flask.

pomada f cream, ointment.

pomelo m grapefruit.

pómez f: **piedra ~** pumice stone.

pompa f pomp; bubble.

pomposo/sa adj pompous.

pómulo m cheekbone.

ponche m punch.

poncho/cha adj soft, mild; * m poncho.

ponderación f pondering, considering; exaggeration.

ponderar vt to ponder, to weigh; to exaggerate.

ponedero/ra adj egg-laying; capable of being laid or placed; * m nest; nest egg.

poner vt to put, to place; to put on; to impose; to lay (eggs); **~se** vr to oppose; to set (of stars); to become.

poniente m west; west wind.

pontificado m pontificate.

pontífice m Pope, pontiff.

pontificio/cia adj pontifical.

pontón m pontoon.

ponzoña f poison.

ponzoñoso/sa adj poisonous.

popa f (mar) poop, stern.

populacho m populace, mob.

popular adj popular.

popularidad f popularity.

popularizarse vr to become popular.

populoso/sa adj populous.

poquedad f paucity, smallness; cowardice.

por prep for; by; about; by means of; through; on account of.

porcelana f porcelain, china.

porcentaje m percentage.

porción f part, portion; lot.

porcuno/na adj hoggish.

pordiosero/ra m/f beggar.

porfiar vt to dispute obstinately; to persist in a pursuit.

pormenor f detail.

pornografía f pornography.

poro m pore.

porosidad *f* porosity.

poroso/sa *adj* porous.

porque *conj* because; since; so that.

porqué *m* cause, reason.

porquería *f* nastiness, foulness; brutishness, rudeness; trifle; dirty action.

porqueriza *f* pig sty.

porra *f* cudgel.

porrillo: a ~ *adv* copiously, abundantly.

porrón *m* spouted wine jar.

portada *f* portal, porch; frontispiece.

portador/ra *m/f* carrier, porter.

portaequipajes *m invar* boot (in car); baggage rack.

portal *m* porch; portal.

portamonedas *m invar* purse.

portarse *vr* to behave.

portátil *adj* portable; * *m* laptop..

portaaviones *m invar* aircraft carrier.

portavoz *m/f* spokesman/woman.

portazo *m* bang of a door; banging a door in one's face.

porte *m* transportation (charges *pl*); deportment, demeanour, conduct.

portento *m* prodigy, portent.

portentoso/sa *adj* prodigious, marvellous, strange.

portería *f* porter's office; goal.

portero/ra *m/f* porter; caretaker; gatekeeper; goalkeeper.

portezuela *f* little door.

pórtico *m* portico, porch, lobby.

portilla *f*, **portillo** *m* aperture in a wall; gate; gap, breach.

portón *m* main door (of a house).

porvenir *m* future.

pos *prep*: **en ~ de** after, behind; in pursuit of.

posada *f* shelter; inn, hotel.

posaderas *fpl* buttocks *pl*.

posadero *m* innkeeper.

posar *vi* to sit, to pose; * *vt* to lay down (a burden); **~se** *vr* to settle; to perch; to land.

posdata *f* postcript.

pose *f* pose.

poseedor/ra *m/f* owner, possessor; holder.

poseer *vt* to hold, to possess.

poseído/da *adj* possessed by the devil.

posesión *f* possession.

posesivo/va *adj* possessive.

posesor/ra *m/f* possessor.

posibilidad *f* possibility.

posibilitar *vt* to make possible; to make feasible.

posible *adj* possible.

posición *f* position; posture; situation.

positivo/va *adj* positive.

poso *m* sediment, dregs *pl*.

posponer *vt* to postpone.

posta *f*: **a ~** on purpose.

postal *adj* postal; * *f* postcard.

poste *m* post, pillar.

póster *m* poster.

postergación *f* missing out, passing over; putting over.

postergar *vt* to leave behind; to postpone.

posteridad *f* posterity.

posterior *adj* posterior.

posterioridad *f*: **con ~** subsequently, later.

postigo *m* wicket; postern; pane or sash of a window.

postizo/za *adj* artificial (not natural); * *m* wig.

postor *m* bidder at a public sale; better.

postración *f* prostration.

postrar *vt* to humble, to humiliate; **~se** *vr* to prostrate oneself.

postre *m* dessert.

postrer(o)/ra *adj* last, hindmost.

postrimerías *fpl* dying moments *pl*; final stages *pl*.

póstumo/ma *adj* posthumous.

postura *f* posture, position; attitude; bet, wager; agreement, convention.

potable *adj* drinkable.

potaje *m* pottage; drink made up of several ingredients; medley of various useless things.

pote *m* pot, jar; flower pot.

potencia *f* power; mightiness.

potencial *m* potential.

potentado *m* potentate; prince.

potente *adj* potent, powerful, mighty.

potestad *f* power; dominion; jurisdiction.

potro/ra *m/f* colt; foal.

poyo *m* bench (near street door).

pozo *m* well.

práctica *f* practice.

practicable *adj* practicable, feasible.

practicante *adj* practising; * *m/f* practitioner.

practicar *vt* to practise.

práctico/ca *adj* practical; skilful, experienced.

pradera *f* meadow.

prado *m* lawn; meadow.

pragmático/ca *adj* pragmatic.

preámbulo *m* preamble; circumlocution.

prebenda *f* prebend.

precampaña *f* run-up to the election campaign.

precario/ria *adj* precarious.

precaución *f* precaution.

precaver *vt* to prevent; to guard against.

precedencia *f* precedence; preference; superiority.

precedente *adj* preceding, foregoing.

preceder *vt* to precede, to go before.

precepto *m* precept, order.

preceptor/ra *m/f* master, teacher, preceptor.

preciado/da *adj* esteemed, valued.

preciarse *vr* to boast; ~ **de** to take pride in.

precinto *m* seal.

precio *m* price; value.

preciosidad *f* excellence; preciousness.

precioso/sa *adj* precious; (*fam*) beautiful.

precipicio *m* precipice; violent, sudden fall; ruin, destruction.

precipitación *f* precipitation, rush.

precipitado/da *adj* precipitate, headlong, hasty.

precipitar *vt* to precipitate; ~**se** *vr* to act hastily; to rush.

precisamente *adv* precisely; exactly.

precisar *vt* to compel, to oblige; to need.

precisión *f* necessity, compulsion; preciseness.

preciso/sa *adj* necessary, requisite; precise, exact; abstracted.

precocidad *f* precocity.

preconizar *vt* to proclaim; to recommend.

precoz *adj* precocious.

precursor/ra *m/f* harbinger, forerunner.

predecesor/ra *m/f* predecessor.

predecir *vt* to foretell.

predestinación *f* predestination.

predestinar *vt* to predestine.

predicación *f* preaching; sermon.

predicado *m* predicate.

predicador *m* preacher.

predicar *vt* to preach.

predicción f prediction.
predilección f predilection.
predilecto/ta adj darling, favourite.
predisponer vt to predispose; to prejudice.
predisposición f inclination; prejudice.
predominar vi to predominate, to prevail.
predominio m predominant power, superiority.
preeminencia f pre-eminence; superiority.
preeminente adj pre-eminent; superior.
preescolar adj pre-school.
preexistencia f pre-existence.
preexistente adj pre-existent.
preexistir vt to pre-exist, to exist before.
prefabricado/da adj prefabricated.
prefacio m preface.
prefecto m prefect.
prefectura f prefecture.
preferencia f preference.
preferible adj preferable.
preferir vt to prefer.
prefijar vt (gr) to prefix; to fix beforehand.
prefijo m dialling code.
pregón m proclamation; hue and cry.
pregonar vt to proclaim.
pregonero m town crier.
pregunta f question; inquiry.
preguntar vt to ask; to question; to demand; to inquire.
preguntón/ona m/f inquisitive person.
prehistórico/ca adj prehistoric.
prejuicio m prejudgement; preconception; prejudice.
prelado m prelate.
preliminar adj, m preliminary.

preludio m prelude.
prematuro/ra adj premature.
premeditación f premeditation, forethought.
premeditar vt to premeditate, to think out.
premiar vt to reward, to remunerate.
premio m reward, recompense; premium.
premisa f premise.
premura f pressure, haste, hurry.
prenatal adj pre-natal.
prenda f pledge; garment; sweetheart; person or thing dearly loved; ~s fpl accomplishments pl, talents pl.
prendar vt to enchant; ~se vr: ~ de to fall in love with.
prendedor m brooch.
prender vt to seize, to catch, to lay hold of; to imprison; ~se vr to catch fire; * vi to take root.
prendimiento m seizure; capture.
prensa f press.
prensar vt to press.
preñado/da adj pregnant.
preñez f pregnancy.
preocupación f worry, preoccupation.
preocupado/da adj worried, anxious.
preocupar(se) vt (vr) to worry.
preparación f preparation.
preparador/ra m/f trainer.
preparar vt to prepare; ~se vr to be prepared.
preparativo/va adj preparatory; preliminary; qualifying; * m preparation.
preparatorio/ria adj preparatory.
preponderancia f preponderance.
preponderar vi to preponderate, to prevail.
preposición f (gr) preposition.
prepucio m foreskin.

prerrogativa *f* prerogative, privilege.

presa *f* capture, seizure; dike, dam.

presagiar *vt* to presage, to forebode.

presagio *m* omen.

presbítero *m* priest, clergyman.

presciencia *f* prescience, fore-knowledge.

prescindir *vi*: ~ **de** to do without; to dispense with.

prescribir *vt* to prescribe.

prescripción *f* prescription.

presencia *f* presence.

presenciar *vt* to attend; to be present at; to witness.

presentación *f* presentation.

presentador/ra *m/f* (*rad*, *TV*) presenter; compere.

presentar *vt* to present; to introduce; to offer; to show; ~**se** *vr* to present oneself; to appear; to run (as candidate); to apply.

presente *m* present, gift; * *adj* present.

presentemente *adv* presently, now.

presentimiento *m* presentiment.

presentir *vt* to have a premonition of.

preservación *f* preservation.

preservar *vt* to preserve; to defend.

preservativo *m* condom, sheath.

presidencia *f* presidency.

presidente/ta *m/f* president.

presidiario/ria *m/f* convict.

presidio *m* penitentiary, prison.

presidir *vt* to preside at.

presilla *f* clip; loop (in clothes).

presión *f* pressure, pressing; ~ **de los neumáticos** tyre pressure.

presionar *vt* to press; (*fig*) to put pressure on.

preso/sa *m/f* prisoner.

prestado/da *adj* on loan; **pedir** ~ to borrow.

prestamista *m* borrower, lender.

préstamo *m* loan.

prestar *vt* to lend.

presteza *f* quickness; haste, speed.

prestigio *m* prestige.

presto/ta *adj* quick; prompt; ready; * *adv* soon; quickly.

presumible *adj* presumable.

presumido/da *adj* presumptuous, arrogant.

presumir *vt* to presume, to conjecture; * *vi* to be conceited.

presunción *f* presumption, conjecture; conceit.

presunto/ta *adj* supposed; so-called.

presuntuoso/sa *adj* presumptuous.

presuponer *vt* to presuppose.

presupuesto *m* estimate; budget.

presuroso/sa *adj* hasty, quick; prompt; nimble.

pretencioso/sa *adj* pretentious.

pretender *vt* to pretend, to claim; to try, to attempt.

pretendiente *m* pretender; suitor.

pretensión *f* pretension.

pretérito/ta *adj* past.

pretextar *vt* to plead, use as an excuse.

pretexto *m* pretext, pretence; plea, excuse.

prevalecer *vi* to prevail; to triumph; to take root.

prevención *f* disposition, preparation; supply of provisions; foresight; prevention; (*mil*) police guard.

prevenido/da *adj* prepared; careful, cautious; foreseeing.

prevenir *vt* to prepare; to foresee, to know in advance; to prevent; to warn; ~**se** *vr* to be prepared; to be predisposed.

preventivo/va *adj* preventive.

prever *vt* to foresee, to forecast.

previo/via *adj* previous.

previsión *f* foresight, prevision; forecast.

previsor/ra *adj* far-sighted.

prima *f* bonus; (female) cousin.

primacía *f* priority; primacy.

primado *m* primate.

primario/ria *adj* primary.

primavera *f* spring (the season).

primeramente *adv* in the first place, mainly.

primer *adj* = **primero.**

primer(o)/ra *adj* first; prior; former; * *adv* first; rather, sooner.

primicias *fpl* first fruits *pl*.

primitivo/va *adj* primitive; original.

primo/ma *m* cousin.

primogénito/ta *adj*, *m/f* first-born.

primogenitura *f* primogeniture.

primor *m* beauty; dexterity, ability.

primordial *adj* basic, fundamental.

primoroso/sa *adj* neat, elegant; fine, excellent; handsome.

princesa *f* princess.

principal *adj*, *m* principal, chief.

príncipe *m* prince.

principiante *m* beginner, learner.

principiar *vt*, *vi* to commence, to begin.

principio *m* beginning, commencement; principle.

pringoso/sa *adj* greasy; sticky.

pringue *m/f* grease; lard; dripping.

prioridad *f* priority.

prisa *f* speed; hurry; urgency; promptness.

prisión *f* prison; imprisonment.

prisionero *m* prisoner.

prisma *m* prism.

prismáticos *mpl* binoculars *pl*.

privación *f* deprivation, want.

privado/da *adj* private; particular.

privar *vt* to deprive; to prohibit; **~se** *vr* to deprive oneself.

privativo/va *adj* private, one's own; particular, peculiar.

privilegiado/da *adj* privileged; very good.

privilegiar *vt* to privilege.

privilegio *m* privilege.

pro *m/f* profit; benefit; advantage.

proa *f* (*mar*) prow.

probabilidad *f* probability, likelihood.

probable *adj* probable, likely.

probado/da *adj* proved, tried.

probador *m* fitting room.

probar *vt* to try; to prove; to taste; * *vi* to try.

probeta *f* test tube.

problema *m* problem.

problemático/ca *adj* problematic.

procedencia *m* derivation.

procedente *adj* reasonable; proper; **~ de** coming from.

proceder *m* procedure; * *vi* to proceed, to go on; to act.

procedimiento *m* proceeding; legal procedure.

procesado/da *m/f* accused.

procesador *m*: **~ de textos** word processor.

procesar *vt* to put on trial.

procesión *f* procession.

proceso *m* process; lawsuit.

proclama *f* proclamation, publication.

proclamación *f* proclamation; acclamation.

proclamar *vt* to proclaim.

procreación *f* procreation, generation.

procrear *vt* to procreate, to generate.

procurador/ra *m/f* procurer; attorney; solicitor.

procurar *vt* to try; to obtain; to produce.

prodigalidad *f* plenty, abundance.

prodigar *vt* to waste, to lavish.

prodigio *m* prodigy; monster.

prodigioso/sa *adj* prodigious, monstrous; exquisite; excellent.

pródigo/ga *adj* prodigal.

producción *f* production.

producir *vt* to produce; (*jur*) to produce as evidence; ~se *vr* to come about; to arise; to be made; to break out.

productividad *f* productivity.

productivo/va *adj* productive.

producto *m* product.

productor/ra *adj* productive; * *m/f* producer.

proeza *f* prowess, valour, bravery.

profanación *f* desecration.

profanar *vt* to profane, to desecrate.

profano/na *adj* profane.

profecía *f* prophecy.

profesar *vt* to profess, to practise.

profesión *f* profession.

profesional *adj*, *m/f* professional.

profeso/sa *adj* professed.

profesor/ra *m/f* teacher; lecturer.

profesorado *m* teaching profession.

profeta *m* prophet.

profético/ca *adj* prophetic.

profetizar *vt* to prophesy.

prófugo/ga *m/f* fugitive.

profundidad *f* profundity, profoundness; depth; grandeur.

profundizar *vt* to go deeply into; to deepen; to penetrate.

profundo/da *adj* profound.

profusamente *adv* profusely.

profusión *f* profusion; prodigality.

progenie *f* progeny, offspring; race; generation.

progenitor *m* progenitor, ancestor, forefather.

programa *m* program(me).

programación *f* computer programming.

programador/ra *m/f* programmer.

programar *vt* to program(me).

progresar *vi* to progress.

progresión *f* progression.

progresista *adj*, *m/f* progressive.

progreso *m* progress.

progresivo/va *adj* progressive.

prohibición *f* prohibition, ban.

prohibir *vt* to prohibit, to forbid; to hinder.

prójimo *m* fellow creature; neighbour.

prole *f* offspring, progeny; race.

proletariado *m* proletariat.

proletario/ria *adj* proletarian.

proliferación *f* proliferation.

proliferar *vi* to proliferate.

prolífico/ca *adj* prolific.

prolijidad *f* prolixity; minute attention to detail.

prolijo/ja *adj* prolix; tedious.

prólogo *m* prologue.

prolongación *f* prolongation.

prolongar *vt* to prolong.

promedio *m* average; middle.

promesa *f* promise.

prometer *vt* to promise; to assure; ~se *vr* to become engaged.

prometido/da *adj* promised; engaged; * *m/f* fiancé/fiancée.

prominencia *f* protuberance.

prominente *adj* prominent, jutting out.

promiscuo/cua *adj* promiscuous; confusedly mingled; ambiguous.

promoción *f* promotion.

promontorio *m* promontory, cape.

promotor *m* promoter.

promover *vt* to promote, to advance; to stir up.

promulgación *f* promulgation.

promulgar *vt* to promulgate, to publish.

pronombre *m* (*gr*) pronoun.

pronosticar *vt* to predict, to foretell; to conjecture.

pronóstico *m* prediction; forecast.

prontitud *f* promptness.

pronto/ta *adj* prompt; ready; * *adv* promptly.

pronunciación *f* pronunciation.

pronunciamiento *m* (*jur*) publication; insurrection, sedition.

pronunciar *vt* to pronounce; to deliver; ~se *vr* to rebel.

propagación *f* propagation; extension.

propagador/ra *m/f* propagator.

propaganda *f* propaganda; advertising.

propagar *vt* to propagate.

propasar *vt* to go beyond, to exceed.

propender *vi* to incline.

propensión *f* propensity, inclination.

propenso/sa *adj* prone, inclined.

propiamente *adv* properly; really.

propiciar *vt* to favour; to cause.

propiciatorio/ria *adj* propitiatory.

propicio/cia *adj* propitious.

propiedad *f* property, possessions *pl*; right of property; propriety.

propietario/ria *adj* proprietary; * *m/f* proprietor.

propina *f* tip.

propinar *vt* to hit; to give.

propio/pia *adj* proper; own; typical; very.

proponer *vt* to propose.

proporción *f* proportion; symmetry.

proporcionado/da *adj* proportionate; fit; **bien** ~ well-proportioned.

proporcional *adj* proportional.

proporcionar *vt* to provide; to adjust, to adapt.

proposición *f* proposition.

propósito *m* aim, purpose; **a** ~ on purpose.

propuesta *f* proposal, offer; representation.

propulsar *vt* to propel; (*fig*) to promote.

prórroga *f* prolongation; extension; extra time.

prorrogable *adj* extendable.

prorrogar *vt* to extend; to postpone.

prorrumpir *vi* to break forth, to burst forth.

prosa *f* prose.

prosaico/ca *adj* prosaic.

proscribir *vt* to proscribe, to outlaw.

proscripción *f* proscription.

proscrito/ta *adj* banned.

prosecución *f* continuation.

proseguir *vt* to continue; * *vi* to continue, to go on.

prospección *f* exploration; prospecting.

prospecto *m* prospectus.

prosperar *vi* to prosper, to thrive.

prosperidad *f* prosperity.

próspero/ra *adj* prosperous.

prostíbulo *m* brothel.

prostitución *f* prostitution.

prostituir *vt* to prostitute.

prostituta *f* prostitute.

protagonista *m/f* protagonist.

protagonizar *vt* to take the chief role in.

protección *f* protection.

protector *m* to protect.

proteger *vt* to protector.

proteína *f* protein.

protesta *f* protest.

protestante *m/f* Protestant.

protestar *vt* to protest; to make public declaration (of faith); * *vi* to protest.

protocolo *m* protocol.

prototipo *m* prototype.
provecho *m* profit; advantage.
provechoso/sa *adj* profitable; advantageous.
proveedor/ra *m/f* purveyor.
proveer *vt* to provide; to provision; to decree.
provenir *vi* to arise, to originate; to issue.
proverbial *adj* proverbial.
proverbio *m* proverb; ~**s** *mpl* Book of Proverbs.
providencia *f* providence; foresight; divine providence.
providencial *adj* providential.
provincia *f* province.
provincial *adj, m* provincial.
provinciano/na *adj* provincial; country *compd*.
provisión *f* provision; store.
provisional *adj* provisional.
provisionalmente *adv* provisionally.
provocación *f* provocation.
provocador/ra *adj* provocative.
provocar *vt* to provoke; to lead to; to excite.
provocativo/va *adj* provocative.
próximamente *adv* soon.
proximidad *f* proximity, closeness.
próximo/ma *adj* next; neighbouring; close, nearby.
proyección *f* projection; showing; influence.
proyectar *vt* to throw; to cast; to screen; to plan.
proyectil *m* projectile, missile.
proyecto *m* plan; project.
proyector *m* projector.
prudencia *f* prudence, wisdom.
prudente *adj* prudent.
prueba *f* proof; reason; argument; token; experiment; essay; attempt; relish, taste.

prurito *m* itching.
psicoanálisis *m* psychoanalysis.
psicoanalista *m/f* psychoanalist.
psicología *f* psychology.
psicólogo/ga *m/f* psychologist.
psiquiatra *m/f* psychiatrist.
psiquiátrico/ca *adj* psychiatric.
psíquico/ca *adj* psychic(al).
púa *f* sharp point, prickle; shoot; pick.
pubertad *f* puberty.
publicación *f* publication.
publicar *vt* to publish; to make public.
publicidad *f* publicity.
público/ca *adj* public; * *m* public; audience; crowd.
puchero *m* pot; stew.
púdico/ca *adj* chaste, pure.
pudiente *adj* rich, opulent.
pudor *m* bashfulness.
pudrir *vt* to rot, to putrefy; ~**se** *vr* to decay, to rot.
pueblo *m* people *pl*; town, village; population; populace.
puente *m* bridge.
puenting *m* bungee-jumping.
puerco/ca *adj* nasty; filthy, dirty; rude, coarse; * *m* pig, hog; ~ **espín** porcupine.
pueril *adj* childish; peurile.
puerilidad *f* puerility.
puerro *m* leek.
puerta *f* door; doorway; gateway; ~ **trasera** back door.
puerto *m* port, harbour; haven; pass; narrow pass.
pues *adv* then; therefore; well; **¡**~**!** well, then.
puesto *m* place; particular spot; post, employment; barracks *pl*; stand.
púgil *m* boxer.
pugilato *m* boxing.

pugna *f* combat, battle.

pugnar *vi* to fight, to combat; to struggle.

pujante *adj* powerful, strong; robust; stout, strapping.

pujanza *f* power, strength.

pujar *vt* to outbid; to strain.

pulcritud *f* beauty.

pulcro/cra *adj* beautiful; affected.

pulga *f* flea; **tener malas ~s** to be easily piqued; to be ill-tempered.

pulgada *f* inch.

pulgar *m* thumb.

pulir *vt* to polish; to put the last touches to.

pulla *f* smart repartee; obscene expression.

pulmón *m* lung.

pulmonía *f* pneumonia.

pulpa *f* pulp; soft part (of fruit).

pulpería *f* small grocery store.

púlpito *m* pulpit.

pulpo *m* octopus.

pulsación *f* pulsation.

pulsador *m* push button.

pulsar *vt* to touch; to play; to press.

pulsera *f* bracelet.

pulso *m* pulse; wrist; firmness or steadiness of the hand.

pulular *vi* to swarm.

pulverización *f* pulverization.

pulverizador *m* spray gun.

pulverizar *vt* to pulverize.

puna *f* (*med*) mountain sickness.

pungir *vt* to punch, to prick.

punición *f* punishment, chastisement.

punitivo/va *adj* punitive.

punta *f* point; end; trace.

puntada *f* stitch.

puntal *m* prop, stay; buttress.

puntapié *m* kick.

puntear *vt* to tick; to pluck (the guitar); to stitch.

puntería *f* aiming.

puntero *m* pointer; **~/ra** *adj* leading.

puntiagudo/da *adj* sharp-pointed.

puntilla *f* narrow lace edging; **de ~s** on tiptoe.

punto *m* point; end; spot; stitch.

puntuación *f* punctuation.

puntual *adj* punctual; exact; reliable.

puntualidad *f* punctuality.

puntualizar *vt* to fix; to specifiy.

puntuar *vt* to punctuate; to evaluate.

punzada *f* prick; sting; pain; compunction.

punzante *adj* sharp.

punzar *vt* to punch; to prick; to sting.

punzón *m* punch.

puñado *m* handful.

puñal *m* dagger.

puñalada *f* stab.

puñetazo *m* punch.

puño *m* fist; handful; wrist-band; cuff; handle.

pupila *f* pupil (of eye).

pupitre *m* desk.

puré *m* puree; (thick) soup; **~ de patatas** mashed potatoes *pl*.

pureza *f* purity, chastity.

purga *f* purge.

purgante *m* purgative.

purgar *vt* to purge; to purify; to atone, to expiate.

purgativo/va *adj* purgative, purging.

purgatorio *m* purgatory.

purificación *f* purification.

purificador/ra *m/f* purifier; * *adj* purifying.

purificar *vt* to purify.

purismo *m* purism.

purista *m* purist.

puritano/na *adj* puritanical; * *m/f* Puritan.

puro/ra *adj* pure; mere; clear; genuine.

púrpura f purple.
purpúreo/rea adj purple.
purulento/ta adj purulent.
pus m pus.
pusilánime adj pusillanimous, faint-hearted.

pusilanimidad f pusillanimity.
pústula f pustule, pimple.
puta f whore.
putrefacción f putrefaction.
pútrido/da adj putrid, rotten.

Q

que pn that; who; which; what; * conj that; than.
qué adj what; which; * pn what; which.
quebrada f broken, uneven ground.
quebradero m breaker; ~ de cabeza worry.
quebradizo/za adj brittle; flexible.
quebrado m (mat) fraction.
quebradura f fracture; rupture, hernia.
quebrantamiento m fracture; rupture; breaking; weariness, fatigue; violation (of the law).
quebrantar vt to break; to crack; to burst; to pound, to grind; to violate; to fatigue; to weaken.
quebranto m weakness; great loss, severe damage.
quebrar vt to break; to transgress; to violate (a law); * vi to go bankrupt; ~se vr to break into pieces; to be ruptured.
queda f resting time; (mil) tattoo.
quedar vi to stay; ~se vr to remain.
quedo/da adj quiet, still; * adv softly, gently.
quehacer m task.
queja f complaint.
quejarse vr to complain of.
quejido m complaint.
quejoso/sa adj complaining, querulous.

quejumbroso/sa adj complaining, plaintive.
quema f burning, combustion; fire.
quemador m burner.
quemadura f burn.
quemar vt to burn; to kindle; ~se vr to be parched with heat; to burn oneself; * vi to be too hot.
quemarropa f: a ~ adv point-blank.
quemazón f burn; itch.
querella f charge; dispute; complaint.
querellarse vr to complain; to file a complaint.
querer vt to want; to desire; to will; to love; * m will, desire.
querido/da adj dear, beloved; * m/f darling; lover; ~ mío, ~da mía my dear, my love, my darling.
queroseno n paraffin m.
querubín m cherub.
quesería f cheesemonger, cheese shop.
queso m cheese.
quicio m hook, hinge (of a door).
quiebra f break, fracture; bankruptcy; slump.
quien pn who; whom.
quién pn who; whom.
quienquiera adj whoever.
quieto/ta adj still, peaceable.
quietud f quietness, peace, tranquillity, calmness.
quijada f jaw; jawbone.

quijotada f quixotic action.
quijote m quixotic person.
quijotesco/ca adj quixotic.
quilate m carat.
quilla f keel.
quimera f chimera.
quimérico/ca adj chimerical, fantastic.
química f chemistry.
químico/ca m/f chemist; * adj chemical.
quimioterapia f chemotheraphy.
quina f Peruvian bark, quinine.
quincalla f hardware.
quince adj, m fifteen; fifteenth.
quincena f fortnight.
quiniela f pools coupon ; ~s fpl football pools pl.
quinientos/tas adj five hundred.
quinina f quinine.
quinquenal adj quinquennial.
quinquenio m space of five years.
quinqui m delinquent.
quinta f country house; levy, drafting of soldiers.

quintaesencia f quintessence.
quintilla f (poet) metrical composition of five verses.
quinto adj fifth; * m fifth; drafted soldier.
quíntuplo/pla adj quintuple, fivefold.
quiosco m bandstand; news stand.
quirófano m operating theatre.
quiromancia f palmistry.
quirúrgico/ca adj surgical.
quisquilloso/sa adj difficult, touchy; peevish, irritable.
quiste m cyst.
quitaesmalte m nail-polish remover.
quitamanchas m invar stain remover.
quitanieves m invar snowplough.
quitar vt to take away, to remove; to take off; to relieve; to annul; ~se vr to take off (clothes, etc); to withdraw.
quitasol m parasol.
quizá, quizás adv perhaps.

R

rabadilla f coccyx; rump, croup (of a horse or other four-legged animal).
rábano m radish.
rabí m rabbi.
rabia f rage, fury.
rabiar vt to be furious, to rage.
rabieta f touchiness, petulance; fit of bad temper.
rabino m rabbi.
rabioso/sa adj rabid; furious.
rabo m tail.
racha f gust of wind; **buena/mala** ~ spell of good/bad luck.
racial adj racial, race compd.

racimo m bunch of grapes.
raciocinio m reasoning; argument.
ración f ration.
racional adj rational; reasonable.
racionalidad f rationality.
racionar vt to ration (out).
racismo m racialism.
racista adj, m/f racist.
radar m radar.
radiación f radiation.
radiactivo/va, radioactivo/va adj radioactive.
radiador m radiator.
radiante adj radiant.
radiar vt to radiate.

radicación *f* taking root; becoming rooted (of a habit).

radical *adj* radical.

radicar *vt* to take root; **~se** *vr* to establish oneself.

radio *f* radio; radio (set); * *m* radius; ray.

radiografía *f* X-ray.

radioterapia *f* radiotherapy.

raer *vt* to scrape; to grate; to erase.

ráfaga *f* gust; flash; burst.

rafting *m* rafting.

raído/da *adj* scraped; worn-out; impudent.

raíz *f* root; base, basis; origin; **bienes raíces** *mpl* landed property.

raja *f* splinter, chip (of wood); chink, fissure.

rajar *vt* to split; to chop, to cleave.

rajatabla *f*: **a ~** *adv* strictly.

ralea *f* race; breed, species.

ralladura *f* small particles *pl* taken off by grating.

rallar *vt* to grate.

ralo/la *adj* thin, rare.

rama *f* branch (of a tree, of a family); printer's chase, form.

ramadán *m* Ramadan.

ramaje *m* branches *pl*.

rambla *f* avenue.

ramera *f* whore, prostitute.

ramificación *f* ramification.

ramificarse *vr* to ramify.

ramillete *m* bunch.

ramo *m* branch (of a tree).

rampa *f* ramp.

rampante *adj* rampant.

rana *f* frog.

ranchero *m* rancher; smallholder.

rancho *m* grub; ranch; small farm.

rancio/cia *adj* rank; rancid.

rango *m* rank, standing.

ranúnculo *m* (*bot*) buttercup.

ranura *f* groove; slot.

rapacidad *f* rapacity.

rapadura *f* shaving; baldness.

rapar *vt* to shave; to plunder.

rapaz/za *adj* rapacious; * *m/f* young boy/girl.

rape *m* shaving; monkfish.

rapé *m* snuff.

rapidez *f* speed, rapidity.

rápido/da *adj* quick, rapid, swift.

rapiña *f* robbery.

rappel *m* abseiling.

raptar *vt* to kidnap.

rapto *m* kidnapping; (*fig*) ecstasy, rapture.

raqueta *f* racket.

raquítico/ca *adj* stunted; (*fig*) inadequate.

rareza *f* rarity, rareness.

raro/ra *adj* rare, scarce; extraordinary.

ras *m*: **a ~ de** level with; **a ~ de tierra** at ground level.

rasar *vt* to level.

rascacielos *m invar* skyscraper.

rascar *vt* to scratch, to scrape.

rasgar *vt* to tear, to rip.

rasgo *m* dash, stroke; grand/magnanimous action; **~s** *mpl* features *pl*.

rasguear *vi* to form bold strokes with a pen; (*mus*) to strum.

rasguñar *vt* to scratch, to scrape.

rasguño *m* scratch.

raso *m* satin; glade; **~/sa** *adj* plain; flat; **al ~** in the open air.

raspa *f* beard (of an ear of corn); backbone (of fish); stalk (of grapes); rasp.

raspadura *f* filing, scraping; filings *pl*.

raspar *vt* to scrape, to rasp.

rastra *f* rake; **a ~s** by dragging.

rastreador *m* tracker.

rastrear *vt* to trace; to inquire into;

* *vi* to skim along close to the ground (of birds).

rastrero/ra *adj* creeping; low, humble, cringing.

rastrillar *vt* to rake.

rastrillo *m* rake.

rastro *m* track; rake; trace.

rastrojera *f* stubble ground.

rastrojo *m* stubble.

rasurador *m*, **rasuradora** *f* electric shaver.

rasurarse *vr* to shave.

rata *f* rat.

ratería *f* larceny, petty theft.

ratero/ra *adj* creeping, mean, vile; * *m/f* pickpocket; burglar.

ratificación *f* ratification.

ratificar *vt* to ratify; to approve of.

rato *m* moment; **a ~s perdidos** in leisure time.

ratón *m* mouse.

ratonera *f* mousetrap.

raudal *m* torrent.

raya *f* stroke; line; part; frontier; ray (fish); roach (fish).

rayado/da *adj* ruled; crossed; striped; rifled (of firearms).

rayar *vt* to draw lines on; to cross out; to underline; to cross; to rifle.

rayo *m* ray, beam (of light).

rayón *m* rayon.

raza *f* race, lineage; quality.

razón *f* reason; right; reasonableness; account; calculation.

razonable *adj* reasonable.

razonado/da *adj* rational; prudent.

razonamiento *m* reasoning; discourse.

razonar *vi* to reason; to discourse, to talk.

reacción *f* reaction.

reaccionar *vi* to react.

reaccionario/ria *adj* reactionary.

reacio/cia *adj* stubborn.

reactor *m* reactor.

reajuste *m* readjustment.

real *adj* real, actual; royal; * *m* (*mil*) camp.

realce *m* embossment; flash; lustre, splendour.

realidad *f* reality; sincerity.

realista *m* realist; royalist.

realizador/ra *m/f* producer (in TV etc).

realizar *vt* to realize; to achieve; to undertake.

realmente *adv* really, actually.

realzar *vt* to raise, to elevate; to emboss; to heighten.

reanimar *vt* to cheer, to encourage; to reanimate.

reanudar *vt* to renew; to resume.

reaparición *f* reappearance.

reasumir *vt* to retake, to resume.

reata *f* collar, leash; string (of horses).

rebaja *f* abatement; deduction; **~s** *fpl* sale.

rebajar *vt* to abate, to lessen, to diminish; to lower.

rebanada *f* slice.

rebaño *m* flock (of sheep), herd (of cattle).

rebasar *vt* to exceed.

rebatir *vt* to resist; to parry, to ward off; to refute; to repress.

rebeca *f* cardigan.

rebelarse *vr* to revolt; to rebel; to resist.

rebelde *m/f* rebel; * *adj* rebellious.

rebeldía *f* rebelliousness, disobedience; (*jur*) contumacy; **en ~** by default.

rebelión *f* rebellion, revolt.

rebosar *vi* to run over, to overflow; to abound.

rebotar vt to bounce; to clinch; to repel; * vi to rebound.

rebote m rebound; **de ~** on the rebound.

rebozado/da adj fried in batter or breadcrumbs.

rebozar vt to wrap up; to fry in batter or breadcrumbs.

rebullir vi to stir, to begin to move.

rebuscado/da adj affected; recherché; far-fetched.

rebuznar vi to bray.

rebuzno m braying (of an ass).

recabar vt to obtain by entreaty.

recado m message; gift.

recaer vi to fall back.

recaída f relapse.

recalcar vt to stress, to emphasize.

recalcitrante adj recalcitrant.

recalentamiento m overheating.

recalentar vt to heat again; to overheat.

recámara f bedroom.

recambio m spare; refill.

recapacitar vt to reflect.

recapitulación f recapitulation.

recapitular vt to recapitulate.

recargado/da adj overloaded.

recargar vt to overload; to recharge; to charge again.

recargo m extra load; new charge or accusation.

recatado/da adj prudent; circumspect; modest.

recato m prudence; circumspection; modesty; bashfulness.

recaudación f take; recovery of debts; collector's office.

recaudador m tax collector.

recaudar vt to gather; to obtain; to recover.

recelar vt to fear; to suspect, to doubt.

recelo m dread; suspicion, mistrust.

receloso/sa adj mistrustful; shy.

recepción f reception.

recepcionista m/f receptionist.

receptáculo m receptacle.

receptor m receiver; investigating official.

recesión f (com) recession.

receta f recipe; prescription.

recetar vt to prescribe.

recetario m register of prescriptions.

rechazar vt to refuse; to repulse; to contradict.

rechazo m rebound; denial; recoil.

rechifla f booing; (fig) derision.

rechiflar vt to boo.

rechinar vi to gnash (teeth).

rechistar vi: **sin ~** without a murmur.

rechoncho/cha adj chubby.

recibidor m entrance hall.

recibimiento m reception.

recibir vt to receive, to accept; to let in; to go to meet; **~se** vr: **~ de** to qualify as.

recibo m receipt.

reciclado/da adj recycled.

reciclar vt to recycle.

recién adv recently, lately.

reciente adj recent; new, fresh; modern.

recinto m district, precinct.

recio/cia adj stout; strong, robust; coarse, thick; rude; arduous, rigid; * adv strongly, stoutly; **hablar ~** talk loud.

recipiente m container.

reciprocidad f reciprocity.

recíproco/ca adj reciprocal, mutual.

recitación f recitation.

recital m recital; reading.

recitar vt to recite.

recitativo/va adj recitative.

reclamación *f* claim; reclamation; protest.

reclamar *vt* to claim.

reclamo *m* claim; advertisement; attraction; decoy bird; catchword (in printing).

reclinar *vt* to recline; **~se** *vr* to lean back.

recluir *vt* to shut up.

reclusión *f* seclusion; prison.

recluta *f* recruitment; * *m/f* recruit.

reclutador *m* recruitment officer.

reclutar *vt* to recruit.

recobrar *vt* to recover; **~se** *vr* to recover (from sickness).

recodo *m* corner or angle jutting out.

recogedor *m* scraper (instrument).

recoger *vt* to collect; to retake, to take back; to get; to gather; to shelter; to compile; **~se** *vr* to take shelter or refuge; to retire; to withdraw from the world.

recogido/da *adj* retired, secluded; quiet.

recogimiento *m* collection; retreat; shelter; abstraction from all worldly concerns.

recolección *f* summary; recollection.

recomendación *f* recommendation.

recomendar *vt* to recommend.

recompensa *f* compensation; recompense, reward.

recompensar *vt* to recompense, to reward.

recomponer *vt* to recompose; to mend.

reconcentrar *vt* to concentrate on.

reconciliación *f* reconciliation.

reconciliar *vt* to reconcile; **~se** *vr* to make one's peace.

recóndito/ta *adj* recondite, secret, concealed.

reconfortar *vt* to comfort.

reconocer *vt* to recognize; to examine closely; to acknowledge; to consider; (*mil*) to reconnoitre.

reconocido/da *adj* recognized; grateful.

reconocimiento *m* recognition; acknowledgement; gratitude; confession; search; submission; inquiry; (*mil*) reconnaissance.

reconquista *f* reconquest.

reconquistar *vt* to reconquer.

reconstituyente *m* tonic.

reconstruir *vt* to reconstruct.

reconvenir *vt* to return the accusations of.

reconversión *f*: **~ industrial** industrial rationalization.

recopilación *f* summary, abridgement.

recopilador *m* compiler.

recopilar *vt* to compile.

récord *adj invar* record; * *m* record.

recordar *vt* to remember; to remind; * *vi* to remember.

recorrer *vt* to run over, to peruse; to cover.

recortar *vt* to cut out.

recorte *m* cutting; trimming.

recostar *vt* to lean, to recline; **~se** *vr* to lie down.

recoveco *m* cubby hole; bend.

recrear *vt* to amuse, to entertain; to delight.

recreativo/va *adj* recreational.

recreo *m* recreation; playtime (at school).

recriminación *f* recrimination.

recriminar *vt* to recriminate.

recrudecer *vt*, *vi*, **~se** *vr* to worsen.

recrudecimiento *m* upsurge.

recta *f* straight line.

rectángulo/la *adj* rectangular; * *m* rectangle.

rectificación *f* rectification.
rectificar *vt* to rectify.
rectilíneo/nea *adj* rectilinear.
rectitud *f* straightness; rectitude; justness, honesty; exactitude.
recto/ta *adj* straight; right; just, honest; * *m* rectum.
rector/ra *m/f* superior of a community or establishment; vice-chancellor (of a university); curate, rector; * *adj* governing.
rectorado *m* rectorship; vice-chancellorship.
rectoría *f* rectory; rectorship.
recua *f* drove of beasts of burden.
recuadro *m* box; inset.
recuento *m* inventory.
recuerdo *m* souvenir; memory.
recular *vi* to fall back, to recoil.
recuperable *adj* recoverable.
recuperación *f* recovery.
recuperar *vt* to recover; ~**se** *vr* to recover (from sickness).
recurrir *vi*: ~ **a** to resort to.
recurso *m* recourse.
recusación *f* refusal.
recusar *vt* to refuse; to refuse to admit.
red *f* net; network; snare.
redacción *f* editing; editor's office.
redactar *vt* to draft; to edit.
redactor/ra *m/f* editor.
redada *f*: ~ **policial** police raid.
redecilla *f* hairnet.
rededor *m* environs *pl*; **al** ~ round about.
redención *f* redemption.
redentor/ra *m/f* redeemer.
redescubrir *vt* to rediscover.
redicho/cha *adj* affected.
redil *m* sheepfold.
redimible *adj* redeemable.
redimir *vt* to redeem; to ransom.

rédito *m* revenue, rent.
redoblado/da *adj* redoubled; stout and thick; reinforced.
redoblar *vt* to redouble; to rivet.
redoble *m* doubling, repetition; (*mil*) roll of a drum.
redomado/da *adj* sly; utter.
redondear *vt* to round.
redondel *m* circle; traffic roundabout.
redondez *f* roundness, circular form.
redondo/da *adj* round; complete.
reducción *f* reduction.
reducible *adj* reducible; convertible.
reducido/da *adj* reduced; limited; small.
reducir *adj* to reduce; to limit; ~**se** *vr* to diminish.
reducto *m* (*mil*) redoubt.
redundancia *f* superfluity, redundancy, excess.
redundar *vi* to redound; to contribute.
reelegir *vt* to re-elect, to elect again.
reembolsar *vt* to refund; to reimburse.
reembolso *m* reimbursement; refund; **contra** ~ C.O.D.
reemplazar *vt* to replace; to restore.
reemplazo *m* replacement; reserve.
reenganchar *vt* (*mil*) to re-enlist; ~**se** *vr* to enlist again.
referencia *f* reference.
referéndum *m* referendum.
referir *vt* to refer, to relate, to report; ~**se** *vr* to refer or relate to.
refilón *m*: **de** ~ *adv* obliquely.
refinado/da *adj* refined; subtle, artful.
refinar *vt* to refine.
refinería *f* refinery.
reflejar *vt* to reflect.
reflejo *m* reflex; reflection.
reflexión *f* meditation, reflection.

reflexionar *vt* to reflect on; * *vi* to reflect, to meditate.

reflexivo/va *adj* reflexive; thoughtful.

reflujo *m* reflux, ebb; **flujo y ~** the tides *pl*.

reforma *f* reform; correction; repair.

reformar *vt* to reform; to correct; to restore; **~se** *vr* to mend; to have one's manners reformed or corrected.

reformatorio *m* reformatory.

reforzar *vt* to strengthen, to fortify; to encourage.

refracción *f* refraction.

refractario/ria *adj* refractory.

refrán *m* proverb.

refregar *vt* to scrub.

refrenar *vt* to refrain; to check.

refrendar *vt* to countersign; to approve.

refrescante *adj* refreshing.

refrescar *vt* to refresh; **~se** *vr* to get cooler; to go out for a breath of fresh air; * *vi* to cool down.

refresco *m* refreshment.

refriega *f* affray, skirmish, fray.

refrigerador *m*, **refrigeradora** *f* refrigerator, fridge.

refrigerar *vt* to cool; to refresh; to refrigerate; to comfort.

refrigerio *m* refrigeration; refreshment; consolation, comfort.

refuerzo *m* reinforcement.

refugiado/da *m/f* refugee.

refugiar *vt* to shelter; **~se** *vr* to take refuge.

refugio *m* refuge, asylum.

refulgir *vi* to shine.

refunfuñar *vi* to snarl; to growl; to grumble.

refutación *f* refutation.

refutar *vt* to refute.

regadera *f* watering can.

regadío *m* irrigated land.

regalar *vt* to give (as present); to give away; to pamper; to caress.

regalía *f* regalia; bonus; royalty; privilege.

regaliz *m* liquorice.

regalo *m* present, gift; pleasure; comfort.

regañadientes: a ~ *adv* reluctantly.

regañar *vt* to scold; * *vi* to growl; to grumble; to quarrel.

regañón/ona *adj* snarling, growling; grumbling; troublesome.

regar *vt* to water, to irrigate.

regata *f* irrigation ditch; regatta.

regatear *vt* (*com*) to bargain over; to be mean with; * *vi* to haggle; to dribble (in sport).

regateo *m* haggling; bartering; dribbling.

regazo *m* lap.

regencia *f* regency.

regeneración *f* regeneration.

regenerar *vt* to regenerate.

regentar *vt* to rule; to govern.

regente *m* regent; manager.

régimen *m* regime, management; diet; (*gr*) rules *pl* of verbs.

regimiento *m* regime; (*mil*) regiment.

regio/gia *adj* royal, regal.

región *f* region.

regir *vt* to rule, to govern; to direct; * *vi* to apply.

registrador/ra *m/f* registrar; controller.

registrar *vt* to survey; to inspect, to examine; to record, to enter in a register; **~se** *vr* to register; to happen.

registro *m* examining; enrolling office; register; registration.

regla f rule, ruler; period.
reglamentar vt to regulate.
reglamentario/ria adj statutory.
reglamento m regulation; by-law.
regocijar vt to gladden; ~se vr to rejoice.
regocijo m joy, pleasure; merriment, rejoicing.
regodearse vr to be delighted; to trifle, to play the fool; to joke, to jest.
regodeo m joy, merriment.
regordete adj chubby, plump.
regresar vi to return, to go back.
regreso m return, regression.
reguero m small rivulet; trickle of spilt liquid; drain, gutter.
regulación f regulation.
regulador/ra m/f regulator; knob, control.
regular vt to regulate, to adjust; * adj regular; ordinary.
regularidad f regularity.
regularizar vt to regularize.
rehabilitación f rehabilitation.
rehabilitar vt to rehabilitate.
rehacer vt to repair, to make again; to redo; ~se vr to recover; (mil) to rally.
rehén m hostage.
rehuir vt to avoid.
rehusar vt to refuse, to decline.
reimpresión f reprint.
reimprimir vt to reprint.
reina f queen.
reinado m reign.
reinante adj (fig) prevailing.
reinar vi to reign; to govern.
reincidencia f relapse.
reincidir vi: ~ en to relapse into, to fall back into.
reino m kingdom, reign.
reintegración f reintegration, restoration.

reintegrar vt to reintegrate, to restore; ~se vr to be reinstated or restored.
reintegro m reintegration.
reír(se) vi (vr) to laugh.
reiteración f repetition, reiteration.
reiterar vt to reiterate, to repeat.
reivindicación f claim; vindication.
reivindicar vt to claim.
reja f ploughshare; lattice, grating.
rejilla f grating, grille; vent; luggage rack.
rejoneador m mounted bullfighter.
rejonear vt to spear (bulls).
rejuvenecer vt, vi to rejuvenate.
relación f relation; relationship; report; account.
relacionar vt to relate.
relajación f relaxation; remission; laxity.
relajar vt to relax, to slacken; ~se vr to relax.
relamerse vr to lick one's lips; to relish.
relamido/da adj affected; overdressed.
relámpago m flash of lightning.
relampaguear vi to flash.
relatar vt to relate, to tell.
relativo/va adj relative.
relato m story; recital.
relax m relaxation.
releer vt to reread.
relegación f relegation; exile.
relegar vt to relegate; to banish, to exile.
relente m evening dew.
relevante adj excellent, great; eminent.
relevar vt to emboss, to work in relief; to exonerate; to relieve; to assist.
relevo m (mil) relief.
relicario m reliquary.

relieve *m* relief; (*fig*) prominence.
religión *f* religion.
religiosidad *f* religiousness.
religioso/sa *adj* religious.
relinchar *vi* to neigh.
relincho *m* neigh, neighing.
reliquia *f* residue, remains *pl*; (saintly) relic.
rellano *m* landing (of stairs).
rellenar *vt* to fill up; to stuff.
relleno/na *adj* satiated, full up; stuffed; * *m* stuffing.
reloj *m* clock; watch.
relojero *m* watchmaker.
relucir *vi* to shine, to glitter; to excel, to be brilliant.
relumbrar *vi* to sparkle, to shine.
remachar *vt* to rivet; (*fig*) to drive home.
remanente *m* remainder; (*com*) balance; surplus.
remangar *vt* to roll up.
remansarse *vr* to form a pool.
remanso *m* stagnant water; quiet place.
remar *vi* to row.
rematadamente *adv* entirely, totally.
rematado/da *adj* utter, complete.
rematar *vt* to terminate, to finish; to sell off cheaply; * *vi* to end.
remate *m* end, conclusion; shot; tip; last or best bid.
remedar *vt* to copy, to imitate; to mimic.
remediable *adj* remediable.
remediar *vt* to remedy; to assist, to help; to free from danger; to avoid.
remedio *m* amendment, correction; recourse; refuge.
remedo *m* imitation, copy.
remendar *vt* to patch, to mend; to correct.

remero *m* rower, oarsman.
remesa *f* shipment; remittance.
remiendo *m* patch; mend.
remilgado/da *adj* prim; affected.
remilgo *m* affected nicety or gravity.
reminiscencia *f* reminiscence, recollection.
remiso/sa *adj* remiss, careless; indolent.
remitente *m* sender.
remitir *vt* to remit, to send; to pardon (a fault); to suspend, to put off; * *vi*, **~se** *vr* to slacken.
remo *m* oar; rowing.
remojar *vt* to steep; to dunk.
remojo *m* steeping, soaking.
remolacha *f* beet.
remolcar *vt* to tow.
remolino *m* whirlwind; whirlpool; crowd.
remolón/ona *adj* stubborn; lazy.
remolque *m* tow, towing; tow rope.
remontar *vt* to mend; **~se** *vr* to tower, to soar.
remorder *vt* to disturb.
remordimiento *m* remorse.
remoto/ta *adj* remote, distant; far.
remover *vt* to stir; to move around.
remozar *vt* to rejuvenate; to renovate.
remuneración *f* remuneration, recompense.
remunerador/ra *m/f* remunerator.
remunerar *vt* to reward, to remunerate.
renacer *vi* to be born again; to revive.
renacimiento *m* regeneration; rebirth.
renacuajo *m* tadpole.
renal *adj* renal, kidney *compd*.
rencilla *f* quarrel.
rencor *m* rancour, grudge.

rencoroso/sa adj rancorous.

rendición f surrender; profit.

rendido/da adj submissive; exhausted.

rendija f crevice, crack, cleft.

rendimiento m output; efficiency.

rendir vt to subject, to subdue; **~se** vr to yield; to surrender; to be tired out.

renegado m apostate; wicked person.

renegar vt to deny; to disown; to detest, to abhor; * vi to apostatize; to blaspheme, to curse.

renglón m line; item.

renombrado/da adj renowned.

renombre m renown.

renovación f renovation; renewal.

renovar vt to renew; to renovate; to reform.

renquear vi to limp.

renta f income; rent; profit.

renuncia f renunciation; resignation.

renunciar vt to renounce; * vi to resign.

reñido/da adj at variance, at odds; hard-fought.

reñir vt, vi to wrangle, to quarrel; to scold, to chide.

reo m offender, criminal.

reojo m: **mirar de ~** to look at furtively.

reparación f repair; reparation.

reparar vt to repair; to consider, to observe; to parry * vi: **~ en** to notice; to pass (at cards).

reparo m repair, reparation; consideration; difficulty.

repartición f distribution.

repartidor m/f distributor; assessor of taxes.

repartir vt to distribute; to deliver.

reparto m distribution; delivery; cost; property development.

repasar vt to repass; to revise; to check; to mend.

repaso m revision; check-up.

repatriar vt to repatriate.

repecho m slope.

repelente adj repellent, repulsive.

repeler vt to repel; to refute, to reject.

repente: de ~ adv suddenly.

repentino/na adj sudden, unforeseen.

repercusión f reverberation.

repercutir vi to reverberate; to rebound.

repertorio m repertory; index; list.

repetición f repetition; (mus) encore.

repetidor/ra m/f repeater.

repetir vt, vi to repeat.

repicar vt to ring.

repique m chime.

repiquetear vt to ring merrily.

repisa f pedestal, stand; shelf; windowsill.

replegar vt to redouble; to fold over; **~se** vr (mil) to fall back.

repleto/ta adj replete, very full.

réplica f reply, answer; repartee.

replicar vi to reply.

repoblación f repopulation; restocking; **~ forestal** reafforestation.

repoblar vt to repopulate; to reafforest.

repollo m cabbage.

reponer vt to replace; to restore; **~se** vr to recover lost health or property.

reportaje m report, article.

reportero/ra m/f reporter.

reposado/da adj quiet, peaceful; settled (wine).

reposar *vi* to rest, to repose.
reposición *f* replacement; remake.
reposo *m* rest, repose.
repostería *f* confectioner's (shop).
repostero *m* confectioner.
reprender *vt* to reprimand.
represa *f* dam; lake.
represalia *f* reprisal.
representación *f* representation; authority.
representante *m/f* representative; understudy (stage).
representar *vt* to represent; to play on the stage; to look (age).
representativo/va *adj* representative.
represión *f* repression.
reprimenda *f* reprimand.
reprimir *vt* to repress; to check; to contain.
reprobable *adj* reprehensible.
reprobación *f* reprobation, reproof.
reprobar *vt* to reject; to condemn, to upbraid.
réprobo *m* reprobate.
reprochar *vt* to reproach.
reproche *m* reproach.
reproducción *f* reproduction.
reproducir *vt* to reproduce.
reptil *m* reptile.
república *f* republic.
republicano/na *adj*, *m/f* republican.
repudiar *vt* to repudiate.
repudio *m* repudiation.
repuesto *m* supply; spare part.
repugnancia *f* reluctance; repugnance.
repugnante *adj* repugnant.
repugnar *vt* to disgust.
repulsa *f* refusal.
repulsar *vt* to reject; to decline, to refuse.
repulsión *f* repulsion.
repulsivo/va *adj* repulsive.

reputación *f* reputation, renown.
reputar to consider.
requebrar *vt* to woo, to court.
requerimiento *m* request; requisition; intimation; summons.
requerir *vt* to intimate, to notify; to request; to require, to need; to summon.
requesón *m* cottage cheese.
requiebro *m* endearing expression.
réquiem *m* requiem.
requisa *f* inspection; (*mil*) requisition.
requisito *m* requisite.
res *f* head of cattle.
resabio *m* (unpleasant) aftertaste; vicious habit, bad custom.
resaca *f* surge, surf; (*fig*) backlash; (*fam*) hangover.
resaltar *vi* to rebound; to jut out; to be evident; to stand out.
resarcimiento *m* compensation, reparation.
resarcir *vt* to compensate, to make amends for.
resbaladizo/za *adj* slippery.
resbalar(se) *vi* (*vr*) to slip, to slide.
resbalón *m* slip, slide.
rescatar *vt* to ransom, to redeem.
rescate *m* ransom.
rescindir *vt* to rescind, to annul.
rescisión *f* rescindment, revocation.
rescoldo *m* embers *pl*, cinders *pl*.
resecarse *vr* to dry up.
reseco/ca *adj* very dry.
resentido/da *adj* resentful.
resentimiento *m* resentment.
resentirse *vr*: ~ **de** to suffer; ~ **con** to resent.
reseña *f* review; account.
reseñar *vt* to describe; to review.
reserva *f* reserve; reservation.
reservado/da *adj* reserved, cautious, circumspect.

reservar vt to keep; to reserve; **~se** vr to preserve oneself; to keep to oneself.

resfriado m cold.

resfriarse vr to catch cold.

resguardar vt to preserve, to defend; **~se** vr to be on one's guard.

resguardo m guard; security, safety; voucher; receipt.

residencia f residence.

residente adj residing, resident; * m/f resident.

residir vi to reside, to dwell.

residuo m residue, remainder.

resignación f resignation.

resignadamente adv resignedly.

resignarse vr to resign oneself.

resina f resin.

resinoso/sa adj resinous.

resistencia f resistance, opposition.

resistente adj strong; resistant.

resistir vt to resist, to oppose; to put up with; * vi to resist; to hold out.

resma f ream (of paper).

resol m glare (of the sun).

resollar vi to wheeze; to take breath.

resolución f resolution, boldness; decision.

resolver vt to resolve, to decide; to analyse; **~se** vr to resolve, to determine.

resonar vi to resound.

resoplar vi to snore; to snort.

resoplido m heavy breathing.

resorte m spring.

respaldar vt to endorse; **~se** vr to lean back.

respaldo m backing; endorsement; back of a seat.

respectivo/va adj respective.

respecto m respect; relation; **al ~** on this matter.

respetable adj respectable.

respetar vt to respect; to revere.

respeto m respect, regard, consideration; homage.

respetuoso/sa adj respectful.

respingar vi to shy.

respingo m start; jump.

respiración f respiration, breathing.

respiradero m vent, breathing hole; rest, repose.

respirar vi to breathe.

respiratorio/ria adj respiratory.

respiro m breathing; (fig) respite.

resplandecer vi to shine; to glisten.

resplandeciente adj resplendent.

resplandor m splendour, brilliance.

responder vt to answer; * vi to answer; to correspond; **~ de** to be responsible for.

respondón/ona adj ever ready to reply; cheeky.

responsable adj responsible; accountable, answerable.

responsabilidad f responsibility.

responsabilizarse vr to take charge.

responso m prayer for the dead.

respuesta f answer, reply.

resquemor m resentment.

resquicio m crack, cleft; (fig) chance.

restablecer vt to re-establish; **~se** vr to recover.

restablecimiento m re-establishment.

restallar vi to crack; to click.

restante adj remaining.

restar vt to subtract, to take away; * vi to be left.

restauración f restoration.

restaurante m restaurant.

restaurar vt to restore.

restitución f restitution.

restituir vt to restore; to return.

resto m remainder, rest.

restregar vt to scrub, to rub.

restricción f restriction, limitation.

restringir vt to restrict, to limit; to restrain.

resucitar vt to resuscitate, to revive; to renew.

resuello m breath, breathing.

resuelto/ta adj resolute, determined; prompt.

resultado m result, consequence.

resultar vi to be; to turn out; to amount to.

resumen m summary.

resumidamente adv summarily.

resumir vt to abridge; to sum up; to summarize.

resurrección f resurrection, revival.

retablo m picture drawn on a board; splendid altarpiece.

retaguardia f rearguard.

retahíla f range, series.

retal m remnant.

retar vt to challenge.

retardar vt to retard; to delay.

retardo m delay.

retazo m remnant; cutting.

retención f retention.

retener vt to retain, to keep back.

retentiva f memory.

reticencia f reticence.

retina f retina.

retintín m tinkling sound; affected tone of voice.

retirada f (mil) retreat, withdrawal; recall.

retirar vt to withdraw, to retire; to remove; ~se vr to retire, to retreat; to go to bed.

retiro m retreat, retirement; pension.

reto m challenge; threat, menace.

retocar vt to retouch; to mend; to finish off (work).

retoñar vi to sprout.

retoño m sprout; offspring.

retoque m finishing stroke; retouching.

retorcer vt to twist; to wring.

retorcimiento m twisting, contortion.

retórica f rhetoric.

retórico/ca adj rhetorical; * f rhetoric; affectedness.

retornar vt, vi to return.

retorno m return; barter, exchange.

retortero: andar al ~ to bustle about.

retortijón m twisting; ~ **de tripas** stomach cramp.

retozar vi to frisk, to skip.

retozo m romp.

retozón/ona adj wanton; romping.

retracción f retraction.

retractar vt to retract.

retraer vt to draw back; to dissuade; ~se vr to take refuge; to flee.

retraído/da adj shy.

retransmisión f broadcast.

retransmitir vt to broadcast; to relay; to retransmit.

retrasado/da adj late; (med) mentally retarded; backward.

retraso m delay; slowness; backwardness; lateness; (ferro): **el tren ha tenido ~** the train is overdue or late.

retratar vt to portray; to photograph; to describe.

retrato m portrait, effigy.

retreta f (mil) retreat.

retrete m toilet, lavatory.

retribución f retribution.

retribuir vt to repay.

retroacción f retroaction.

retroactivo/va adj retroactive.

retroceder vi to go backward(s), to fly back; to back down.

retrógrado/da adj retrograde; reactionary.

retrospectivo/va *adj* retrospective.
retrovisor *m* rear-view mirror.
retumbar *vi* to resound, to jingle.
reuma *f* rheumatism.
reumático/ca *adj* rheumatic.
reumatismo *m* rheumatism.
reunión *f* reunion, meeting.
reunir *vt* to reunite; to unite; ~**se** *vr* to gather, to meet.
revalidación *f* confirmation, ratification.
revalidar *vt* to ratify, to confirm.
revancha *f* revenge.
revelación *f* revelation.
revelado *m* developing.
revelar *vt* to reveal; to develop (photographs).
reventar *vi* to burst, to crack; to explode; to toil, to drudge.
reventón *m* (*auto*) blow-out.
reverberación *f* reverberation.
reverberar *vi* to reverberate.
reverdecer *vi* to grow green again; to revive.
reverencia *f* reverence, veneration; respect.
reverenciar *vt* to venerate, to revere.
reverendo/da *adj* reverend.
reverente *adj* respectful, reverent.
reverso *m* reverse.
revés *m* back; wrong side; disappointment, setback.
revestir *vt* to put on; to coat, to cover.
revisar *vt* to revise, to review.
revisión *f* revision.
revisor/ra *m/f* inspector; ticket collector.
revista *f* magazine; review, revision.
revivir *vi* to revive.
revocación *f* revocation.
revocar *vt* to revoke.
revolcarse *vr* to wallow.
revolotear *vi* to flutter.

revoloteo *m* fluttering.
revoltijo *m* confusion, disorder.
revoltoso/sa *adj* rebellious, unruly.
revolución *f* revolution.
revolucionario/ria *adj*, *m/f* revolutionary.
revolver *vt* to move about; to turn around; to mess up; to revolve; ~**se** *vr* to turn round; to change (of the weather).
revólver *m* revolver.
revuelo *m* fluttering; (*fig*) commotion.
revuelta *f* turn; disturbance, revolt.
rey *m* king; king (in cards or chess).
reyerta *f* quarrel, brawl.
rezagar *vt* to leave behind; to defer; ~**se** *vr* to remain behind.
rezar *vi* to pray, to say one's prayers.
rezo *m* prayer.
rezongar *vi* to grumble.
rezumar *vt* to ooze, to leak.
ría *f* estuary.
riada *f* flood.
ribera *f* shore, bank.
ribereño/ña *adj* coastal; riverside.
ribete *m* trimming; seam, border.
ribetear *vt* to hem, to border.
ricino *m*: **aceite de** ~ castor oil.
rico/ca *adj* rich; delicious; lovely; cute.
ridiculez *f* absurdity.
ridiculizar *vt* to ridicule.
ridículo/la *adj* ridiculous.
riego *m* irrigation.
riel *m* (*ferro*) rail.
rienda *f* rein of a bridle; **dar** ~ **suelta** to give free rein to.
riesgo *m* risk, danger.
rifa *f* raffle, lottery.
rifar *vt* to raffle.
rifle *m* rifle.
rigidez *f* rigidity.

rígido/da adj rigid, inflexible; severe.

rigor m rigour.

riguroso/sa adj rigorous.

rima f rhyme.

rimar vi to rhyme.

rimbombante adj pompous.

rímel, rimmel m mascara.

rincón m (inside) corner.

rinoceronte m rhinoceros.

riña f quarrel, dispute.

riñón m kidney.

río m river, stream.

rioja m rioja (wine).

riqueza f riches pl, wealth.

risa f laugh, laughter.

risco m steep rock.

risible adj risible, laughable.

risotada f loud laugh.

ristra f string.

risueño/ña adj smiling.

rítmico/ca adj rhythmic.

ritmo m rhythm.

rito m rite, ceremony.

ritual adj, m ritual.

rival adj, m/f rival.

rivalidad f rivalry.

rivalizar vi: ~ con to rival, to vie with.

rizado/da adj curly.

rizar vt to curl (hair).

rizo m curl; ripple (on water).

robar vt to rob; to steal; to break into.

roble m oak tree.

robledal m oakwood.

robo m robbery; theft.

robot m robot.

robustez f robustness.

robusto/ta adj robust, strong.

roca f rock.

rocalla f pebbles pl.

roce m rub; brush; friction.

rociada f sprinkling; spray, shower.

rociar vt to sprinkle; to spray.

rocín m nag; hack; stupid person.

rocío m dew.

rocoso/sa adj rocky.

rodada f rut, track of a wheel.

rodadura f act of rolling.

rodaja f slice.

rodaje m filming; **en ~** (auto) running in.

rodar vi to roll.

rodear vi to make a detour; * vt to surround, to enclose.

rodeo m detour; subterfuge; evasion; rodeo.

rodilla f knee; **de ~s** on one's knees.

rodillo m roller.

roedor/ra adj gnawing; * m rodent.

roedura f gnawing.

roer vt to gnaw; to corrode.

rogar vt, vi to ask for; to beg, to entreat; to pray.

rogativa f supplication, prayer.

rojez f redness.

rojizo/za adj reddish.

rojo/ja adj red; ruddy.

rol m list, roll, catalogue; role.

rollizo/za adj round; plump, chubby.

rollo m roll; coil.

romance m Romance language; romance.

romancero m collection of romances or ballads.

romanticismo m romanticism.

romántico/ca adj romantic.

rombo m rhombus.

romboide m rhomboid.

romería f pilgrimage.

romero m (bot) rosemary.

romo/ma adj blunt; snub-nosed.

rompecabezas m invar riddle; jigsaw.

romper vt to break; to tear up; to wear out; to break up (land); * vi to break (of waves); to break through.

rompimiento *m* tearing, breaking; crack.

ron *m* rum.

roncar *vi* to snore; to roar.

roncha *f* weal, bruise.

ronco/ca *adj* hoarse; husky; raucous.

ronda *f* night patrol; round (of drinks, cards, etc).

rondar *vt, vi* to patrol; to prowl around.

ronquera *f* hoarseness.

ronquido *m* snore; roar.

ronzal *m* halter.

ronronear *vi* to purr.

roña *f* scab, mange; grime; rust.

roñoso/sa *adj* filthy; mean.

ropa *f* clothes *pl*; clothing; dress.

ropaje *m* gown, robes *pl*; drapery.

ropero *m* linen cupboard; closet.

rosa *f* rose; birthmark.

rosado/da *adj* pink; rosy.

rosal *m* rosebush.

rosario *m* rosary.

rosca *f* thread (of a screw); coil, spiral.

rosetón *m* rosette; rose window.

rosquilla *f* doughnut.

rostro *m* face.

rotación *f* rotation.

roto/ta *adj* broken, destroyed; debauched.

rótula *f* kneecap; ball-and-socket joint.

rotulador *m* felt-tip pen.

rotular *vt* to inscribe, to label.

rótulo *m* inscription; label; ticket; placard, poster.

rotundo/da *adj* round; emphatic.

rotura *f* breaking; crack; tear.

roturar *vt* to plough.

rozadura *f* graze, scratch.

rozar *vt* to rub; to chafe; to nibble (the grass); to scrape; to touch lightly.

rubí *m* ruby.

rubicundo/da *adj* reddish.

rubio/bia *adj* fair-haired, blond/blonde; * *m/f* blond/blonde.

rubor *m* blush; bashfulness.

rúbrica *f* red mark; flourish at the end of a signature; title, heading, rubric.

rubricar *vt* to sign with a flourish; to sign and seal.

rudeza *f* roughness, rudeness; stupidity.

rudimento *m* principle; beginning; ~s *mpl* rudiments *pl*.

rudo/da *adj* rough, coarse; plain, simple; stupid.

rueca *f* distaff.

rueda *f* wheel; circle; slice, round.

ruedo *m* rotation; border, selvage; arena, bullring.

ruego *m* request, entreaty.

rufián *m* pimp, pander; lout.

rugby *m* rugby.

rugido *m* roar.

rugir *vi* to roar, to bellow.

rugoso/sa *adj* wrinkled.

ruibarbo *m* rhubarb.

ruido *m* noise, sound; din, row; fuss.

ruidoso/sa *adj* noisy, loud.

ruin *adj* mean, despicable; mean, stingy.

ruina *f* ruin, collapse; downfall, destruction; ~s *fpl* ruins *pl*.

ruindad *f* meanness, lowness; mean act.

ruinoso/sa *adj* ruinous, disastrous.

ruiseñor *m* nightingale.

ruleta *f* roulette.

rulo *m* curler.

rumba *f* rumba.

rumbo *m* (*mar*) course, bearing; road, route, way; course of events, pomp, ostentation.

rumboso/sa *adj* generous, lavish.
rumiante *m* ruminant.
rumiar *vt* to chew; * *vi* to ruminate.
rumor *m* rumour; murmur.
runrún *m* rumour; sound of voices, whirr.

ruptura *f* rupture.
rural *adj* rural.
rusticidad *f* rusticity; coarseness.
rústico/ca *adj* rustic; * *m/f* peasant.
ruta *f* route, itinerary.
rutina *f* routine; habit.

S

sábado *m* Saturday; (Jewish) Sabbath.
sábana *f* sheet; altar cloth.
sabandija *f* bug, insect.
sabañón *m* chilblain.
sabelotodo *m/f invar* know-all.
saber *vt* to know; to be able to; to find out, to learn; to experience; * *vi*: ~ **a** to taste of; * *m* learning, knowledge.
sabiduría *f* learning, knowledge; wisdom.
sabiendas *adv*: **a** ~ knowingly.
sabihondo/da *adj* know-all; pedantic.
sabio/bia *adj* sage, wise; * *m/f* sage, wise person.
sablazo *m* sword wound; (*fam*) sponging, scrounging.
sable *m* sabre, cutlass.
sabor *m* taste, savour, flavour.
saborear *vt* to savour, to taste; to enjoy.
sabotaje *m* sabotage.
saboteador/ora *m/f* saboteur.
sabotear *vt* to sabotage.
sabroso/sa *adj* tasty, delicious; pleasant; salted.
sabueso *m* bloodhound.
sacacorchos *m invar* corkscrew.
sacapuntas *m invar* pencil sharpener.
sacar *vt* to take out, to extract; to get

out; to bring out (a book etc); to take off (clothes); to receive, to get; (*dep*) to serve.
sacarina *f* saccharin(e).
sacerdotal *adj* priestly.
sacerdote *m* priest.
sacerdotisa *f* priestess.
saciar *vt* to satiate.
saciedad *f* satiety.
saco *m* bag, sack; jacket; ~ **de dormir** sleeping bag.
sacramental *adj* sacramental.
sacramento *m* sacrament.
sacrificar *vt* to sacrifice.
sacrificio *m* sacrifice.
sacrilegio *m* sacrilege.
sacrílego/ga *adj* sacrilegious.
sacristán *m* sacristan, sexton.
sacristía *f* sacristy, vestry.
sacro/cra *adj* holy, sacred.
sacrosanto/ta *adj* sacrosanct.
sacudida *f* shake, jerk.
sacudir *vt* to shake, to jerk; to beat, to hit.
sádico/ca *adj* sadistic; * *m/f* sadist.
sadismo *m* sadism.
saeta *f* arrow, dart.
sagacidad *f* shrewdness, cleverness sagacity.
sagaz *adj* shrewd, clever, sagacious
Sagitario *m* Sagittarius (sign of th(zodiac).
sagrado/da *adj* sacred, holy.

sagrario *m* shrine; tabernacle.

sainete *m* (*teat*) farce; flavour, relish; seasoning.

sal *f* salt.

sala *f* large room; (*teat*) house, auditorium; public hall; (*jur*) court; (*med*) ward.

salado/da *adj* salted; witty, amusing.

salamandra *f* salamander.

salar *vt* to salt.

salarial *adj* wage *compd*, salary *compd*.

salario *m* salary.

salazón *f* salting.

salchicha *f* sausage.

salchichón *m* (salami-type) sausage.

saldar *vt* to pay; to sell off; (*fig*) to settle.

saldo *m* settlement; balance; remainder; ~**s** *mpl* sale.

saledizo/za *adj* projecting, salient.

salero *m* salt cellar.

saleroso *adj* witty, amusing.

salida *f* exit, way out; leaving, departure; production, output; (*com*) sale; sales outlet.

saliente *adj* projecting; rising; (*fig*) outstanding.

salina *f* saltworks, salt mine.

salino/na *adj* saline.

salir *vi* to go out, to leave; to depart, to set out; to appear; to turn out, to prove; ~**se** *vr* to escape, to leak.

salitre *m* saltpetre.

saliva *f* saliva.

salmo *m* psalm.

salmón *m* salmon.

salmonete *m* red mullet.

salmuera *f* brine.

salobre *adj* brackish, salty.

salón *m* living room, lounge; public hall.

salpicadero *m* dashboard.

salpicar *vt* to sprinkle, to splash, to spatter.

salpicón *m* salmagundi.

salpimentar *vt* to season with pepper and salt.

salsa *f* sauce.

salsera *f* sauce boat; gravy boat.

saltamontes *m invar* grasshopper.

saltar *vt* to jump, to leap; to skip, to miss out; * *vi* to leap, to jump; to bounce; (*fig*) to explode, to blow up.

salteador *m* highwayman.

saltear *vt* to rob in a hold-up; to assault; to sauté (in cooking).

saltimbanqui *m/f* acrobat.

salto *m* leap, jump.

saltón/ona *adj* bulging; protruding.

salubre *adj* healthy.

salubridad *f* healthiness.

salud *f* health.

saludable *adj* healthy.

saludar *vt* to greet; (*mil*) to salute.

saludo *m* greeting.

salutación *f* salutation, greeting.

salva *f* (*mil*) salute, salvo.

salvación *f* salvation; rescue.

salvado *m* bran.

salvaguardar *vt* to safeguard.

salvaguardia *m* safeguard.

salvaje *adj* savage.

salvajismo *m* savagery.

salvar *vt* to save; to rescue; to overcome; to cross, to jump across; to cover, to travel; to exclude; ~**se** *vr* to escape from danger.

salvavidas *adj invar*: **bote** ~ lifeboat; **chaleco** ~ life jacket.

salvia *f* (*bot*) sage.

salvo/va *adj* safe; * *adv* save, except (for).

salvoconducto *m* safe-conduct.

san *adj* saint (as title).

sanamente *adv* healthily.

sanar *vt, vi* to heal.

sanatorio *m* sanatorium; nursing home.

sanción *f* sanction.

sancionar *vt* to sanction.

sandalia *f* sandal.

sándalo *m* sandal, sandalwood.

sandez *f* folly, stupidity.

sandía *f* watermelon.

sandwich *m* sandwich.

saneamiento *m* sanitation.

sanear *vt* to drain.

sangrar *vt, vi* to bleed.

sangre *f* blood; **a ~ fría** in cold blood; **a ~ y fuego** without mercy.

sangría *f* sangria (drink); bleeding.

sangriento/ta *adj* bloody, blood-stained, gory; cruel.

sanguijuela *f* leech.

sanguinario/ria *adj* bloodthirsty, cruel.

sanguíneo/nea *adj* blood *compd*.

sanidad *f* sanitation; health.

sanitario/ria *adj* sanitary; health; **~s** *mpl* toilets *pl*.

sano/na *adj* healthy, fit; intact, sound.

santiamén *m*: **en un ~** in no time at all.

santidad *f* sanctity.

santificar *vt* to sanctify; to make holy.

santiguarse *vr* to make the sign of the cross.

santo/ta *adj* holy; sacred; * *m/f* saint; **~ y seña** watchword.

santuario *m* sanctuary.

saña *f* anger, passion.

sañudo/da *adj* furious, enraged.

sapo *m* toad.

saque *m* (*dep*) serve, service (in tennis); throw-in (in soccer).

saqueador/ra *m/f* ransacker, looter.

saquear *vt* to ransack, to plunder.

saqueo *m* looting, sacking.

sarampión *m* measles.

sarao *m* evening party, soiree.

sarcasmo *m* sarcasm.

sarcástico/ca *adj* sarcastic.

sarcófago *m* sarcophagus.

sardina *f* sardine.

sardónico/ca *adj* sardonic; ironic(al).

sargento *m* sergeant.

sarmiento *m* vine shoot.

sarna *f* itch; mange; (*med*) scabies.

sarnoso/sa *adj* itchy, scabby, mangy.

sarpullido *m* (*med*) rash.

sarro *m* (*med*) tartar.

sarta *f* string of beads, etc; string, row.

sartén *f* frying pan.

sastre *m* tailor.

sastrería *f* tailor's shop.

Satanás *m* Satan.

satélite *m* satellite.

sátira *f* satire.

satírico/ca *adj* satirical.

satirizar *vt* to satirize.

sátiro *m* satyr.

satisfacción *f* satisfaction; apology.

satisfacer *vt* to satisfy; to pay (a debt); **~se** *vr* to satisfy oneself; to take revenge.

satisfactorio/ria *adj* satisfactory.

satisfecho/cha *adj* satisfied.

saturación *f* (*quím*) saturation.

Saturno *m* Saturn (planet).

sauce *m* (*bot*) willow.

saúco *m* (*bot*) elder.

sauna *f* sauna.

savia *f* sap.

saxofón *m* saxophone.

sazonado/da *adj* flavoured, seasoned.

sazonar *vt* to ripen; to season.

se *pn reflexivo*: himself; herself; itself; yourself; themselves; yourselves; each other; one another; oneself.

sebo *m* fat, grease.

seboso/sa *adj* fat, greasy.

secador *m*: ~ **de pelo** hairdryer.

secadora *f* tumble dryer.

secamente *adv* dryly, curtly.

secano *m* dry, arable land which is not irrigated.

secar *vt* to dry; ~**se** *vr* to dry up; to dry oneself.

sección *f* section.

seco/ca *adj* dry; dried up; skinny; cold (of character); brusque, sharp; bare.

secretaría *f* secretariat.

secretario/ria *m/f* secretary.

secreto/ta *adj* secret; hidden; * *m* secret; secrecy.

secta *f* sect.

sectario/ria *adj*, *m/f* sectarian.

sector *m* sector.

secuela *f* sequel; consequence.

secuencia *f* sequence.

secuestrador/ra *m/f* kidnapper.

secuestrar *vt* to kidnap; to confiscate.

secuestro *m* kidnapping; confiscation.

secular *adj* secular.

secularización *f* secularization.

secularizar *vt* to secularize.

secundar *vt* to second.

secundario/ria *adj* secondary.

sed *f* thirst; **tener** ~ to be thirsty.

seda *f* silk.

sedal *m* fishing line.

sedante *m* sedative.

sede *f* see; seat; headquarters.

sedentario/ria *adj* sedentary.

sedición *f* sedition.

sedicioso/sa *adj* seditious, mutinous.

sediento/ta *adj* thirsty; eager.

sedoso/sa *adj* silky.

seducción *f* seduction.

seducir *vt* to seduce; to bribe; to charm, to attract.

seductor/ra *adj* seductive; charming; attractive; * *m/f* seducer.

segador/ra *m/f* reaper, harvester.

segadora-trilladora *f* combine harvester.

segar *vt* to reap, to harvest; to mow.

seglar *adj* secular, lay.

segmento *m* segment.

segregación *f* segregation, separation.

segregar *vt* to segregate, to separate.

seguido/da *adj* continuous; successive; long-lasting; * *adv* straight (on); after; often.

seguidor/ra *m/f* follower; supporter.

seguimiento *m* pursuit; continuation.

seguir *vt* to follow, to pursue; to continue; * *vi* to follow; to carry on; ~**se** *vr* to follow, to ensue.

según *prep* according to.

segundo/da *adj* second; * *m* second (of time).

seguramente *adv* surely; for sure.

seguridad *f* security; certainty; safety; confidence; stability.

seguro/ra *adj* safe, secure; sure, certain; firm, constant; * *adv* for sure; * *m* safety device; insurance; safety, certainty.

seis *adj*, *m* six; sixth.

seiscientos/tas *adj* six hundred.

seísmo *m* earthquake.

selección *f* selection, choice.

seleccionar *vt* to select, to choose.

selecto/ta adj select, choice.
sellar vt to seal; to stamp (a document).
sello m seal; stamp.
selva f forest.
semáforo m traffic lights pl; signal.
semana f week.
semanal adj weekly.
semanario/ria m weekly (magazine).
semblante m face; (fig) look; appearance.
sembrado m sown field.
sembrar vt to sow; to sprinkle, to scatter.
semejante adj similar, like; * m fellow man.
semejanza f resemblance, likeness.
semejar vi to resemble; ~**se** vr to look alike.
semen m semen.
semental m stud.
sementera f sowing; land sown with seed.
semestral adj half-yearly.
semicircular adj semicircular.
semicírculo m semicircle.
semifinal f semi-final.
semilla f seed.
semillero m seed plot.
seminario m seedbed; seminary.
seminarista m seminarist.
sémola f semolina.
sempiterno/na adj everlasting.
senado m senate.
senador/ra m/f senator.
sencillez f plainness; simplicity; naturalness.
sencillo/lla adj simple; natural; unaffected; single.
senda f m path, footpath.
senderismo m hillwalking.
senderista m/f hillwalker.
sendero m path, footpath.

senil adj senile.
seno m bosom; lap; womb; hole, cavity; sinus; ~**s** mpl breasts pl.
sensación f sensation, feeling; sense.
sensacional adj sensational.
sensato/ta adj sensible.
sensibilidad f sensibility, sensitivity.
sensible adj sensitive; perceptible, appreciable; regrettable.
sensitivo/va adj sense compd, sensitive.
sensorial adj sensorial, sensory.
sensual adj sensuous, sensual.
sensualidad f sensuousness; sensuality; sexiness.
sentado/da adj sitting, seated; sedate; settled.
sentar vt to seat; (fig) to establish; * vi to suit; ~**se** vr to sit down.
sentencia f (jur) sentence; opinion; saying.
sentenciar vt (jur) to sentence, to pass judgement on; * vi to give one's opinion.
sentencioso/sa adj sententious.
sentido m sense; feeling; meaning; ~/**da** adj regrettable; sensitive.
sentimental adj sentimental.
sentimiento m feeling, emotion, sentiment; sympathy; regret, grief.
sentir vt to feel; to hear; to perceive; to sense; to suffer from; to regret, to be sorry for; ~**se** vr to feel; to feel pain; to crack (of walls, etc); * m opinion, judgement.
seña f sign, mark, token; signal; (mil) password; ~**s** fpl address.
señal f sign, token; symptom; signal; landmark; (com) deposit.
señalado/da adj distinct; special; distinguished, notable.
señalar vt to stamp, to mark; to signpost; to point out; to fix, to settle;

~se *vr* to distinguish oneself, to excel.

señor *m* man; gentleman; master; Mr; sir.

señora *f* lady; Mrs; madam; wife.

señorita *f* Miss; young lady.

señorito *m* young gentleman; rich kid.

señuelo *m* decoy; bait, lure.

separable *adj* separable.

separación *f* separation.

separar *vt* to separate; **~se** *vr* to separate; to come away, to come apart; to withdraw.

septentrional *adj* north, northern.

septiembre *m* September.

séptimo/ma *adj* seventh.

sepulcral *adj* sepulchral.

sepulcro *m* sepulchre, grave, tomb.

sepultar *vt* to bury, to inter.

sepultura *f* burial, interment; grave, tomb.

sepulturero *m* gravedigger, sexton.

sequedad *f* dryness; brusqueness.

sequía *f* dryness; thirst; drought.

séquito *m* retinue, suite; group of supporters; aftermath.

ser *vi* to be; to exist; **~ de** to come from; to be made of; to belong to; * *m* being.

serenarse *vr* to calm down.

serenata *f* (*mus*) serenade.

serenidad *f* serenity.

sereno *m* night watchman; **~/na** *adj* serene, calm, quiet.

serial *m* serial.

serie *f* series; sequence.

seriedad *f* seriousness, gravity; reliability; sincerity.

serio/ria *adj* serious; grave; reliable.

sermón *m* sermon.

sermonear *vt* to lecture; * *vi* to sermonize.

seronegativo/va *adj* HIV-negative.

seropositivo/va *adj* HIV-positive.

serpentear *vi* to wriggle; to wind, to snake.

serpentina *f* streamer.

serpiente *f* snake.

serranía *f* range of mountains; mountainous country.

serrano/na *m/f* highlander.

serrar *vt* to saw.

serrín *m* sawdust.

serrucho *m* handsaw.

servible *adj* serviceable.

servicial *adj* helpful, obliging.

servicio *m* service; service charge; service, set of dishes; **~s** *mpl* toilets *pl*.

servidor/ra *m/f* servant.

servidumbre *f* servitude; servants *pl*, staff.

servil *adj* servile.

servilleta *f* napkin, serviette.

servir *vt* to serve; to wait on; * *vi* to serve; to be of use; to be in service; **~se** *vr* to serve oneself, to help oneself; to deign, to please; to make use of.

sesenta *m*, *adj* sixty; sixtieth.

sesentón/ona *m/f* person of about sixty years of age.

sesgar *vt* to slope, to slant.

sesgo *m* slope.

sesión *f* session; sitting; performance; showing.

seso *m* brain.

sestear *vi* to take a nap.

sesudo/da *adj* sensible, prudent.

seta *f* mushroom.

setecientos/tas *adj* seven hundred.

setenta *adj*, *m* seventy.

setiembre *m* September.

seto *m* fence; enclosure; hedge.

seudo . . . *pref* pseudo. . . .

seudónimo *m* pseudonym.
severidad *f* severity.
severo/ra *adj* severe, strict; grave, serious.
sexagenario/ria *adj* sixty years old.
sexagésimo/ma *adj* sixtieth.
sexenio *m* space of six years.
sexo *m* sex.
sexto/ta *adj*, *m* sixth.
sexual *adj* sexual.
si *conj* whether; if.
sí *adv* yes; certainly; indeed; * *pn* oneself; himself; herself; itself; yourself; themselves; yourselves; each other; one another.
siderúrgico/ca *adj* iron and steel *compd*.
sidra *f* cider.
siega *f* harvest, mowing.
siembra *f* sowing time.
siempre *adv* always; all the time; ever; still; ~ **jamás** for ever and ever.
sien *f* temple (of the head).
sierra *f* saw; range of mountains.
siervo/va *m/f* slave.
siesta *f* siesta, afternoon nap.
siete *adj*, *m* seven.
sietemesino/na *adj* born seven months after conception; premature; (*fig*) half-witted.
sífilis *f* syphilis.
sifón *m* syphon; soda.
sigilo *m* secrecy.
sigiloso/sa *adj* reserved; silent.
sigla *f* acronym; abbreviation.
siglo *m* century.
significación *f* significance, meaning.
significado *m* significance, meaning.
significar *vt* to signify, to mean; to make known, to express.
significativo/va *adj* significant.

signo *m* sign, mark.
siguiente *adj* following, successive, next.
sílaba *f* syllable.
silbar *vt*, *vi* to hiss; to whistle.
silbato *m* whistle.
silbido, silbo *m* hiss; whistling.
silencio *m* silence; ¡~! silence! quiet!
silencioso/sa *adj* silent.
silla *f* chair; saddle; seat; ~ **de ruedas** wheelchair.
sillón *m* armchair, easy chair; rocking chair.
silo *m* silo; underground store for wheat.
silogismo *m* syllogism.
silueta *f* silhouette; outline; figure.
silvestre *adj* wild, uncultivated; rustic.
sima *f* abyss; pothole, cavern.
simbólico/ca *adj* symbolic.
simbolizar *vt* to symbolize.
símbolo *m* symbol.
simetría *f* symmetry.
simétrico/ca *adj* symmetrical.
simiente *f* seed.
similar *adj* similar.
similitud *f* similarity, similitude.
simio *m* ape.
simpatía *f* liking; kindness; solidarity; affection.
simpático/ca *adj* pleasant; kind.
simpatizante *m/f* sympathizer.
simpatizar *vi*: ~ **con** to get on well with.
simple *adj* single; simple, easy; mere; sheer; silly; * *m/f* simpleton.
simpleza *f* simpleness, gullibility; silliness.
simplicidad *f* simplicity.
simplificar *vt* to simplify.
simulación *f* simulation.
simulacro *m* simulacrum, idol.

simuladamente *adv* deceptively, hypocritically.

simular *vt* to simulate.

simultaneidad *f* simultaneity.

simultáneo/nea *adj* simultaneous.

sin *prep* without.

sinagoga *f* synagogue.

sinceridad *f* sincerity.

sincero/ra *adj* sincere.

síncope *f* (*med*) syncope, fainting fit.

sincronizar *vt* to synchronize.

sindical *adj* union *compd*.

sindicato *m* trade(s) union; syndicate.

sinfín *m*: **un ~ de** a great many.

sinfonía *f* symphony.

singular *adj* singular; exceptional; peculiar, odd.

singularidad *f* singularity.

singularizar *vt* to distinguish; to singularize; **~se** *vr* to distinguish oneself; to stand out.

siniestro/tra *adj* left; (*fig*) sinister; * *m* accident.

sinnúmero *m* = **sinfín**.

sino *conj* but; except; save; only; * *m* fate.

sinónimo/ma *adj* synonymous; * *m* synonym.

sinsabor *m* unpleasantness; disgust.

sintaxis *f* syntax.

síntesis *f* synthesis.

sintético/ca *adj* synthetic.

sintetizar *vt* synthesize.

síntoma *m* symptom.

sinuosidad *f* sinuosity; curve, wave.

sinuoso/sa *adj* sinuous; wavy.

sinvergüenza *m/f* rogue.

siquiera *conj* even if, even though; * *adv* at least.

sirena *f* siren; mermaid; car hooter/ horn.

sirviente/ta *m/f* servant.

sisa *f* petty theft; cut, percentage.

sisear *vt*, *vi* to hiss.

sistema *m* system.

sistemático/ca *adj* systematic.

sitiar *vt* to besiege.

sitio *m* place; spot; site, location; room, space; job, post; (*mil*) siege, blockade.

situación *f* situation, position; standing.

situar *vt* to place, to situate; to invest; **~se** *vr* to be established in place or business.

slip *m* pants *pl*, briefs *pl*.

smoking *m* dinner-jacket.

sobaco *m* armpit, armhole.

sobar *vt* to handle, to soften; to knead; to massage, to rub hard; to rumple (clothes); to fondle.

soberanía *f* sovereignty.

soberano/na *adj*, *m/f* sovereign.

soberbia *f* pride, haughtiness; magnificence.

soberbio/bia *adj* proud, haughty; magnificent.

sobornar *vt* to suborn, to bribe.

soborno *m* subornation, bribe.

sobra *f* surplus, excess; **de ~** spare, surplus, extra.

sobradamente *adv* too; amply.

sobrante *adj* remaining; * *m* surplus, remainder.

sobrar *vt* to exceed, to surpass; * *vi* to be more than enough; to remain, to be left.

sobrasada *f* pork sausage spread.

sobre *prep* on; on top of; above, over; more than; besides; * *m* envelope.

sobreabundancia *f* superabundance.

sobreabundar *vi* to superabound.

sobrecarga *f* extra load; (*com*) surcharge.

sobrecargar vt to overload; (com) to surcharge.

sobrecoger vt to surprise.

sobredosis f invar overdose.

sobreentender vt to deduce; ~**se** vr: **se sobreentiende que** . . . it is implied that.

sobrehumano/na adj superhuman.

sobrellevar vt to carry; to tolerate.

sobremanera adv excessively.

sobremesa f: **de** ~ immediately after dinner.

sobrenatural adj supernatural.

sobrenaturalmente adv supernaturally.

sobrenombre m nickname.

sobrepasar vt to surpass.

sobreponer vt to put (something) over or on top of; ~**se** vr to pull through.

sobresaliente adj projecting; (fig) outstanding.

sobresalir vi to project; (fig) to stand out.

sobresaltar vt to frighten.

sobresalto m start, scare; sudden shock.

sobreseer vt: ~ **una causa** (jur) to stay a case; * vi: ~ **de** to desist from.

sobreseimiento m dismissal, suspension.

sobrevenir vi to happen, to come unexpectedly; to supervene.

sobreviviente adj surviving; * m/f survivor.

sobrevivir vi to survive.

sobrevolar vt to fly over.

sobriedad f sobriety.

sobrino/na m/f nephew/niece.

sobrio/ria adj sober, frugal.

socarrón/ona adj sarcastic; ironic(al).

socarronería f sarcasm; irony.

socavar vt to undermine.

socavón m hole.

sociabilidad f sociability.

sociable adj sociable.

social adj social.

socialdemócrata adj, m/f social democrat.

socialista adj, m/f socialist.

sociedad f society.

socio/cia m/f associate, member.

sociología f sociology.

sociólogo/ga m/f sociologist.

socorrer vt to help.

socorrido/da adj well stocked or supplied.

socorrista m/f first aider; lifeguard.

socorro m help, aid, assistance, relief.

soda f soda; soda water.

sodomía f sodomy.

sodomita m sodomite.

soez adj dirty, obscene.

sofá m sofa.

sofisma m sophism.

sofista m/f sophist.

sofisticación f sophistication.

sofocar vt to suffocate.

software m software.

soga f rope.

soja f soya.

sojuzgar vt to conquer, to subdue.

sol m sun; sunshine, sunlight.

solamente adv only, solely.

solapa f lapel.

solapado/da adj cunning, crafty, artful.

solar m building site; piece of land; ancestral home of a family; * adj solar.

solariego/ga adj belonging to the ancestral home of a family.

solaz m recreation, relaxation; solace, consolation.

solazar *vt* to provide relaxation for; to comfort.

soldada *f* wages *pl*.

soldadesca *f* military profession.

soldado *m/f* soldier; ~ **raso** private.

soldador *m* welder; soldering iron.

soldadura *f* soldering; solder.

soldar *vt* to solder; to weld; to unite.

soleado/da *adj* sunny.

soledad *f* solitude; loneliness.

solemne *adj* solemn; impressive, grand.

solemnidad *f* solemnity.

solemnizar *vt* to solemnize; to praise.

soler *vi* to be accustomed to, to be in the habit of.

solfeo *m* (*mus*) solfa.

solicitar *vt* to ask for, to seek; to apply for (a job); to canvass for; to chase after, to pursue.

solícito/ta *adj* diligent; solicitous.

solicitud *f* care, solicitude; request, petition.

solidaridad *f* solidarity.

solidario/ria *adj* joint; mutually binding.

solidez *f* solidity.

sólido/da *adj* solid.

soliloquio *m* soliloquy, monologue.

solista *m/f* soloist.

solitario/ria *adj* lonely, solitary; * *m* solitaire; * *m/f* hermit.

sollozar *vi* to sob.

sollozo *m* sob.

solo *m* (*mus*) solo; ~**la** *adj* alone, single; **a solas** alone, unaided.

sólo *adv* only.

solomillo *m* sirloin.

solsticio *m* solstice.

soltar *vt* to untie, to loosen; to set free, to let out; ~**se** *vr* to get loose; to come undone.

soltero/ra *m/f* bachelor/single woman; * *adj* single, unmarried.

soltura *f* looseness, slackness; agility, activity; fluency.

soluble *adj* soluble; solvable.

solución *f* solution; denouement.

solucionar *vt* to solve; to resolve.

solvente *adj*, *m* solvent.

sombra *f* shade; shadow.

sombrear *vt* to shade.

sombrero *m* hat.

sombrilla *f* parasol.

sombrío/bría *adj* shady, gloomy; sad.

somero/ra *adj* superficial.

someter *vt* to conquer (a country); to subject to one's will; to submit; to subdue; ~**se** *vr* to give in, to submit.

sometimiento *m* submission.

somnífero *m* sleeping pill.

somnolencia *f* sleepiness, drowsiness.

son *m* sound; rumour.

sonado/da *adj* celebrated; famous; generally reported.

sonaja *f* (*mus*) timbrel.

sonajero *m* (*mus*) small timbrel.

sonámbulo/la *m/f* sleep-walker; somnambulist.

sonar *vt* to ring; * *vi* to sound; to make a noise; to be pronounced; to be talked of; to sound familiar; ~**se** *vr* to blow one's nose.

sonata *f* (*mus*) sonata.

sonda *f* sounding; (*med*) probe.

sondear *vt* (*mar*) to sound; to probe; to bore.

sondeo *m* sounding; boring; (*fig*) poll.

soneto *m* sonnet.

sónico/ca *adj* sonic.

sonido *m* sound.

sonoro/ra *adj* sonorous.
sonreír(se) *vi* (*vr*) to smile.
sonrisa *f* smile.
sonrojarse *vr* to blush.
sonrojo *m* blush.
sonsacar *vt* to wheedle, cajole; to obtain by cunning.
sonsonete *m* tapping noise; monotonous voice.
soñador/ra *m/f* dreamer.
soñar *vt*, *vi* to dream.
soñoliento/ta *adj* sleepy, drowsy.
sopa *f* soup; sop.
sopapo *m* punch, thump.
sopera *f* soup dish.
sopero *m* soup plate.
sopetón *m*: **de ~** suddenly.
soplar *vt* to blow away, to blow off; to blow up, to inflate; * *vi* to blow, to puff.
soplete *m* blowlamp.
soplo *m* blowing; puff of wind; (*fam*) tip-off.
soplón/ona *m/f* telltale.
sopor *m* drowsiness, sleepiness.
soporífero/ra *adj* soporific; * *m* sleeping pill.
soportable *adj* tolerable, bearable.
soportal *m* portico.
soportar *vt* to suffer, to tolerate; to support.
sorber *vt* to sip; to inhale; to swallow; to absorb.
sorbete *m* sherbet; iced fruit drink.
sorbo *m* sip; gulp, swallow.
sordera *f* deafness.
sordidez *f* sordidness; dirtiness; meanness.
sórdido/da *adj* sordid; dirty; mean.
sorda/da *adj* deaf; silent, quiet; * *m/ f* deaf person.
sordomudo/da *adj* deaf and dumb.
sorna *f* slyness; sarcasm; slowness.

soroche *m* mountain sickness.
sorprender *vt* to surprise.
sorpresa *f* surprise.
sortear *vt* to draw or cast (lots); to raffle; to avoid.
sorteo *m* draw; raffle.
sortija *f* ring; ringlet, curl.
sortilegio *m* sorcery.
sosegado/da *adj* quiet, peaceful.
sosegar *vt* to appease, to calm; * *vi* to rest.
sosería *f* insipidness; dullness.
sosiego *m* tranquillity, calmness.
soslayar *vt* to do or place (something) obliquely.
soslayo *adv*: **al** *o* **de ~** obliquely, sideways.
soso/sa *adj* insipid, tasteless; dull.
sospecha *f* suspicion.
sospechar *vt* to suspect.
sospechoso/sa *adj* suspicious; suspect; * *m/f* suspect.
sostén *m* support; bra; sustenance.
sostener *vt* to sustain, to maintain; **~se** *vr* to support or maintain oneself; to contrive, to remain.
sostenimiento *m* support; maintenance; sustenance.
sota *f* knave (at cards).
sotana *f* cassock.
sótano *m* basement, cellar.
sotavento *m* (*mar*) leeward, lee.
soto *m* grove, thicket.
squash *m* squash.
status *m invar* status.
su *pn* his, her, its, one's; their; your.
suave *adj* smooth, soft; delicate; gentle; mild, meek.
suavidad *f* softness, sweetness; suavity.
suavizar *vt* to soften.
subalterno/na *adj* secondary; auxiliary.

subasta *f* auction.

subastar *vt* to sell by auction.

subcampeón/ona *m/f* runner-up.

subconsciente *adj, m* subconscious.

subdesarrollado/da *adj* underdeveloped.

subdesarrollo *m* underdevelopment.

subdirector/ora *m/f* assistant director.

súbdito/ta *adj, m/f* subject.

subdividir *vt* to subdivide.

subdivisión *f* subdivision.

subestimar *vt* to underestimate.

subida *f* climb, ascent, rise in value or price.

subido/da *adj* deep-coloured; high (price).

subir *vt, vi* to raise, to lift up; to go up; to climb, to ascend; to increase, to swell; to get in, to get on, to board; to rise (in price).

súbito/ta *adj* sudden, hasty; unforeseen.

subjetivo/va *adj* subjective.

subjuntivo *m* (*gr*) subjunctive.

sublevación *f* sedition, revolt.

sublevar *vt* to excite (a rebellion); to incite (a revolt); ~**se** *vr* to revolt.

sublime *adj* sublime.

sublimidad *f* sublimity.

submarino/na *adj* underwater; * *m* submarine.

subnormal *adj* subnormal; * *m/f* subnormal person.

subordinación *f* subordination.

subrayar *vt* to underline.

subrepticio/cia *adj* surreptitious.

subsanar *vt* to excuse; to mend, to repair; to overcome.

subsidio *m* subsidy, aid; benefit, allowance.

subsistencia *f* subsistence.

subsistir *vi* to subsist.

su(b)stancia *f* substance.

su(b)stancial *adj* substantial.

su(b)stancioso/sa *adj* substantial; nutritious.

su(b)stracción *f* removal; (*mat*) subtraction.

su(b)straer *vt* to remove; (*mat*) to subtract; ~**se** *vr* to avoid; to withdraw.

subterfugio *f* subterfuge.

subterráneo/nea *adj* subterranean; underground; * *m* underground passage; (*ferro*) underground (railway).

suburbio *m* slum quarter; suburbs *pl*.

subvencionar *vt* to subsidize.

subversión *f* subversion, overthrow.

subversivo/va *adj* subversive.

subvertir *vt* to subvert, to overthrow.

subyugar *vt* to subdue, to subjugate.

sucedáneo/nea *adj* substitute; * *m* substitute (food).

suceder *vt* to succeed, to inherit; * *vi* to happen.

sucesión *f* succession; issue, offspring; inheritance.

sucesivamente *adv*: **y así** ~ and so on.

sucesivo/va *adj* successive.

suceso *m* event; incident.

sucesor/ra *m/f* successor; heir.

suciedad *f* dirtiness, filthiness; dirt.

sucinto/ta *adj* succinct, concise.

sucio/cia *adj* dirty, filthy; obscene; dishonest.

suculento/ta *adj* succulent, juicy.

sucumbir *vt* to succumb.

sucursal *f* branch (office).

sudar *vt, vi* to sweat.

sudeste *adj* southeast, southeastern; * *m* southeast.

sudoeste *adj* southwest, southwestern; * *m* southwest.

sudor *m* sweat.

sudorífico/ca *adj* sweaty.

suegra *f* mother-in-law.

suegro *m* father-in-law.

suela *f* sole (shoe).

sueldo *m* wages *pl*, salary.

suelo *m* ground; floor; soil, surface.

suelto/ta *adj* loose; free; detached; swift; * *m* loose change.

sueño *m* sleep; dream.

suero *m* (*med*) serum; whey.

suerte *f* fate, destiny, chance, lot, fortune, good luck; kind, sort.

suéter *m* sweater.

suficiencia *f* sufficiency, competence, fitness.

suficiente *adj* enough, sufficient; fit, capable.

sufragar *vt* to aid, to assist.

sufragio *m* vote, suffrage; aid, assistance.

sufrible *adj* bearable.

sufrido/da *adj* long-suffering, patient; hard-wearing.

sufrimiento *m* suffering; patience.

sufrir *vt* to suffer; to bear, to put up with; to support.

sugerencia *f* suggestion.

sugerir *vt* to suggest.

sugestión *f* suggestion.

suicida *adj* suicidal; * *m/f* suicide; suicidal person.

suicidio *m* suicide.

sujeción *f* subjection.

sujetador *m* fastener; bra.

sujetar *vt* to fasten, to hold down; to subdue; to subject; ~**se** *vr* to subject oneself.

sujeto/ta *adj* fastened, secure; subject, liable; * *m* subject; individual.

sulfúrico *adj* sulphuric.

sultán *m* sultan.

sultana *f* sultana.

suma *f* total, sum; adding up; summary.

sumamente *adv* extremely.

sumar *vt* to add, to add up; to collect, to gather; * *vi* to add up.

sumario/ria *adj* brief, concise; * *m* summary.

sumergir *vt* to submerge, to sink; to immerse.

sumidero *m* sewer, drain.

suministrador/ra *m/f* provider, supplier.

suministrar *vt* to supply, to furnish.

sumir *vt* to sink, to submerge; (*fig*) to plunge.

sumisión *f* submission.

sumiso/sa *adj* submissive, docile.

sumo/ma *adj* great, extreme; highest, greatest; **a lo ~** at most.

suntuosidad *f* sumptuousness.

suntuoso/sa *adj* sumptuous.

súper *f* four-star (petrol).

superable *adj* surmountable.

superabundancia *f* superabundance.

superabundar *vi* to superabound.

superar *vt* to surpass; to overcome; to exceed, to go beyond.

superficial *adj* superficial; shallow.

superficie *f* surface; area.

superfluo/lua *adj* superfluous.

superintendencia *f* supervision.

superintendente *m/f* superintendent, supervisor; floorwalker.

superior *adj* superior; upper; higher; better; * *m/f* superior.

superioridad *f* superiority.

superlativo/va *adj*, *m* (*gr*) superlative.

supermercado *m* supermarket.

superstición *f* superstition.

supersticioso/sa *adj* superstitious.

supervisor/ra *m/f* supervisor.
supervivencia *f* survival.
superviviente *m/f* survivor; * *adj* surviving.
suplantación *f* supplanting.
suplantar *vt* to supplant.
suplemento *m* supplement.
suplente *m/f* substitute.
supletorio/ria *adj* supplementary.
súplica *f* petition, request; supplication.
suplicante *adj*, *m/f* applicant; supplicant.
suplicar *vt* to beg (for), to plead (for); to beg; to plead with.
suplicio *m* torture.
suplir *vt* to supply; to make good, to make up for; to replace.
suponer *vt* to suppose; * *vi* to have authority.
suposición *f* supposition; authority.
supremo/ma *adj* supreme.
supresión *f* suppression; abolition; removal; deletion.
suprimir *vt* to suppress; to abolish; to remove; to delete.
supuesto *m* assumption; ~/ta *adj* supposed; ~ que *conj* since, granted that.
supuración *f* suppuration.
supurar *vt* to suppurate.
sur *adj* south, southern; * *m* south; south wind.
surcar *vt* to furrow; to cut, to score.
surco *m* furrow; groove.
surgir *vi* to emerge; to crop up.
surtido *m* assortment, supply.
surtir *vt* to supply, to furnish, to provide; * *vi* to spout, to spurt.
susceptible *adj* susceptible; impressionable.
suscitar *vt* to excite, to stir up.

suscribir *vt* to sign; to subscribe to.
suscripción *f* subscription.
suscriptor/ra *m/f* subscriber.
susodicho/cha *adj* above-mentioned.
suspender *vt* to suspend, to hang up; to stop; to fail (an exam etc).
suspensión *f* suspension; stoppage.
suspenso/sa *adj* hanging; suspended, failed.
suspicacia *f* suspicion, mistrust.
suspicaz *adj* suspicious, mistrustful.
suspirar *vi* to sigh.
suspiro *m* sigh.
sustancia *f* = **substancia**.
sustancial *adj* = **substancial**.
sustancioso *adj* = **substancioso**.
sustantivo/va *adj*, *m* (*gr*) substantive, noun.
sustentar *vt* to sustain; to support, to nourish.
sustento *m* food, sustenance; support.
sustitución *f* substitution.
sustituir *vt* to substitute.
sustituto/ta *adj*, *m/f* substitute.
susto *m* fright, scare.
sustracción *f* subtraction.
sustraer *vt* to take away; to subtract.
susurrar *vi* to whisper; to murmur; to rustle; ~se *vr* to be whispered about.
susurro *m* whisper; murmur.
sutil *adj* subtle; thin; delicate; very soft; keen, observant.
sutileza *f* subtlety; thinness; keenness.
suyo/ya *adj* his; hers; theirs; one's; his; her; its own; one's own; their own; **de** ~ per se; **los** ~s *mpl* his own, near friends, relations, family, supporters.

T

tabaco *m* tobacco; (*fam*) cigarettes *pl*.

tábano *m* horsefly.

taberna *f* bar, tavern.

tabernero/ra *m/f* barman/barmaid, bartender.

tabicar *vt* to wall up.

tabique *m* thin wall; partition wall.

tabla *f* board; shelf; plank; slab; index of a book; bed of earth in a garden.

tablado *m* scaffold; platform; stage.

tablero *m* plank, board; chessboard; draughtboard; (*auto*) dashboard; bulletin board; gambling den.

tableta *f* tablet; (chocolate) bar.

tablilla *f* small board; (*med*) splint.

tablón *m* plank; beam; ~ **de anuncios** bulletin board.

tabú *m* taboo.

taburete *m* stool.

tacañería *f* meanness; craftiness.

tacaño/ña *adj* mean, stingy; crafty.

tacha *f* fault, defect; small nail.

tachar *vt* to find fault with; to cross out, to erase.

tachuela *f* tack, nail.

tácito/ta *adj* tacit, silent; implied.

taciturno/na *adj* tacit, silent; sulky.

taco *m* stopper, plug; heel (of a shoe); wad; book of coupons; billiard cue.

tacón *m* heel.

taconear *vi* to stamp with one's heels; to walk on one's heels.

taconeo *m* stamping of the heels in dancing.

táctica *f* tactics *pl*.

tacto *m* touch, feeling; tact.

tafetán *m* taffeta.

tafilete *m* morocco leather.

tahona *f* bakery.

tahúr *m* gambler; cheat.

taimado/da *adj* sly, cunning, crafty.

tajada *f* slice; (*med*) hoarseness.

tajante *adj* sharp.

tajar *vt* to cut; to chop; to slice.

tajo *m* cut, incision; cleft, sheer drop; working area; chopping block.

tal *adj* such; **con ~ que** provided that; **no hay ~** no such thing.

tala *f* felling of trees.

taladrar *vt* to bore; to pierce.

taladro *m* drill; borer, gimlet.

talante *m* mood; appearance; aspect; will.

talar *vt* to fell (trees); to desolate.

talco *m* talc.

talega *f*, **talego** *m* bag; bagful.

talento *m* talent.

talismán *m* talisman.

talla *f* raised work; sculpture; stature, size; measure (of anything); hand, draw, turn (at cards).

tallado/da *adj* cut; carved; engraved.

tallador *m* engraver.

tallar *vt* to cut, to chop; to carve in wood; to engrave; to measure.

tallarines *mpl* noodles.

talle *m* shape; size; proportion; waist.

taller *m* workshop, laboratory.

tallo *m* shoot, sprout.

talón *m* heel; receipt; cheque.

talonario *m* cheque book; receipt book.

tamaño *m* size, shape, bulk.

tamarindo *m* tamarind tree.

tambalearse *vr* to stagger, to waver.

tambaleo *m* staggering, reeling.

también *adv* also, as well; likewise; besides.

tambor *m* drum; drummer; eardrum.

tamborilear *vi* to drum.

tamborilero *m* drummer.

tamiz *m* fine sieve.

tampoco *adv* neither, nor.

tampón *m* tampon.

tan *adv* so.

tanda *f* turn; rotation; task; gang; number of persons employed in a workforce.

tangente *f* tangent.

tangible *adj* tangible.

tanque *m* tank; tanker.

tantear *vt* to reckon (up); to measure, to proportion; to consider; to examine.

tanteo *m* computation, calculation; valuation; test; scoring.

tanto *m* certain sum or quantity; point; goal; ~/ta *adj* so much, as much; very great; * *adv* so much, as much; so long, as long.

tañido *m* tune; sound; clink.

tapa *f* lid, cover; snack; *(fam)* ~ de los sesos skull.

tapadera *f* lid (of a pot), cover.

tapar *vt* to stop up, to cover; to conceal, to hide.

taparrabo *m* loincloth.

tapete *m* table cover.

tapia *f* wall.

tapiar *vt* to brick up; to stop up (a passage).

tapicería *f* tapestry; upholstery; upholsterer's shop.

tapicero *m* tapestry-maker; upholsterer.

tapiz *m* tapestry; carpet.

tapizar *vt* to upholster.

tapón *m* cork, plug, bung.

taquigrafía *f* shorthand.

taquilla *f* booking office; takings *pl*.

taquillero/ra *m/f* ticket clerk.

tara *f* tare.

tarántula *f* tarantula.

tardanza *f* slowness, delay.

tardar *vi* to delay; to take a long time; to be late.

tarde *f* afternoon; evening; * *adv* late.

tardío/dia *adj* late; slow, tardy.

tardo/da *adj* sluggish, tardy.

tarea *f* task.

tarifa *f* tariff; price list.

tarima *f* platform; step.

tarjeta *f* card; visiting card; ~ **postal** postcard; ~ de crédito credit card.

tarro *m* pot.

tarta *f* tart; cake.

tartamudear *vi* to stutter, to stammer.

tartamudo/da *adj* stammering.

tarugo *m* wooden peg or pin.

tasa *f* rate; measure, rule; valuation; ~s de aeropuerto airport tax.

tasación *f* valuation, appraisal.

tasador *m* appraiser.

tasar *vt* to appraise, to value.

tasca *f* pub, bar.

tatarabuelo/la *m/f* great-great-grandfather/mother.

tataranieto/ta *m/f* great-great-grandson/daughter.

tatuaje *m* tattoo; tattooing.

tatuar *vt* to tattoo.

taurino/na *adj* bullfighting *compd*.

Tauro *m* Taurus (sign of the zodiac).

taxi *m* taxi.

taxista *m/f* taxi driver.

taza *f* cup; basin of a fountain.

té *m* (*bot*) tea.

te *pn* you.

tea *f* torch.

teatral *adj* theatrical.

teatro *m* theatre, playhouse.

tebeo *m* comic.

techo *m* roof; ceiling.

techumbre *f* upper roof, ceiling.

tecla *f* key (of an organ, piano, etc).

teclado *m* keyboard.

técnico/ca *adj* technical.

tecnología *f* technology.

tedio *m* boredom; dislike, abhorrence.

teja *f* tile.

tejado *m* roof covered with tiles.

tejanos *mpl* jeans *pl*.

tejar *vt* to tile.

tejedor *m* weaver.

tejemaneje *m* artfulness, cleverness; restlessness.

tejer *vt* to weave.

tejido *m* texture; web.

tejo *m* quoit (a ring of iron, plastic etc used in the game of quoits); hopscotch; (*bot*) yew tree.

tejón *m* badger.

tela *f* cloth; material.

telar *m* loom.

telaraña *f* cobweb.

tele *f* (*fam*) telly.

telebanca *f* telephone banking.

telecomedia *f* sitcom.

telediario *m* television news.

telefax *m* invar fax; fax (machine).

telefonear *vt* to telephone.

telefónico/ca *adj* telephone *compd*.

teléfono *m* (tele)phone.

teléfono público *m* payphone.

telegráfico/ca *adj* telegraphic.

telégrafo *m* telegraph.

telegrama *m* telegram.

telescopio *m* telescope.

teletienda *f* home shopping programme.

teletrabajador/ra *m/f* teleworker.

teletrabajo *m* teleworking.

televidente *m/f* viewer.

televisar *vt* to televise.

televisión *f* television; ~ **por cable** cable television.

televisor *m* television set.

télex *m* telex.

telón *m* curtain, drape.

tema *m* theme.

temblar *vi* to tremble.

temblón/ona *adj* trembling.

temblor *m* trembling; earthquake.

temer *vt* to fear, to doubt; * *vi* to be afraid.

temerario/ria *adj* rash.

temeridad *f* temerity, imprudence.

temeroso/sa *adj* timid; frightful.

temible *adj* dreadful, terrible.

temor *m* dread, fear.

témpano *m* ice-floe.

temperamento *m* temperament.

temperatura *f* temperature.

tempested *f* tempest, storm; violent commotion.

tempestuoso/sa *adj* tempestuous, stormy.

templado/da *adj* temperate, tempered.

templanza *f* temperance, moderation.

templar *vt* to temper, to moderate, to cool; to tune; ~**se** *vr* to be moderate.

temple *m* temperature; tempera; temperament; tuning; **al** ~ painted in distemper.

templo *m* temple.

temporada *f* time, season; epoch, period.

temporal *adj* temporary, temporal; * *m* tempest, storm.

temprano/na *adj* early, anticipated; * *adv* early; very early, prematurely.

tenacidad f tenacity; obstinacy.

tenacillas fpl small tongs pl.

tenaz adj tenacious; stubborn.

tenaza(s) f (pl) tongs pl, pincers pl.

tenazmente adv tenaciously; obstinately.

tendedero m clothes line.

tendencia f tendency.

tender vt to stretch out; to expand; to extend; to hang out; to lay; ~se vr to stretch oneself out.

tenderete m stall; display of goods.

tendero/ra m/f shopkeeper.

tendido/da adj lying down; hanging; * m row of seats for the spectators at a bullfight.

tendón m tendon, sinew.

tenebroso/sa adj dark, obscure.

tenedor m holder, keeper, tenant; fork.

tenencia f possession; tenancy; tenure.

tener vt to have; to take; to hold; to possess; ~se vr to stand upright; to stop, to halt; to resist; to adhere.

tenia f tapeworm.

teniente m lieutenant.

tenis m tennis.

tenista m/f tennis player.

tenor m meaning; (mus) tenor.

tensar vt to tauten; to draw.

tensión f tension.

tenso/sa adj tense.

tentación f temptation.

tentador/ra m/f tempter.

tentar vt to touch; to try; to tempt; to attempt.

tentativa f attempt.

tentempié m (fam) snack.

tenue adj thin; tenuous, slender.

tenuidad f slenderness; weakness; trifle.

teñir vt to tinge, to dye.

teología f theology, divinity.

teológico/ca adj theological.

teólogo m theologian, divine.

teorema f theorem.

teoría, teórica f theory.

teórico/ca adj theoretical.

terapéutico/ca adj therapeutic.

terapia f therapy.

tercermundista adj Third World compd.

tercer(o)/ra adj third; * m (jur) third party.

terceto m (mus) trio.

terciar vt to put on sideways; to divide into three parts; to plough the third time; * vi to mediate; to take part.

tercio/cia adj third; * m third part.

terciopelo m velvet.

terco/ca adj obstinate.

tergiversación f distortion; evasion.

tergiversar vt to distort.

termal adj thermal.

termas fpl thermal waters pl.

terminación f termination; conclusion; last syllable of a word.

terminal adj, m/f terminal.

terminante adj decisive; categorical.

terminar vt to finish; to end; to terminate; * vi to end; to stop.

término m term; end; boundary; limit; terminus.

terminología f terminology.

termodinámico/ca adj thermodynamic.

termómetro m thermometer.

termo m flask.

termostato m thermostat.

ternero/ra m/f calf; veal; heifer.

ternilla f gristle.

ternilloso/sa adj gristly.

terno m three-piece suit.

ternura f tenderness.

terquedad *f* stubbornness, obstinacy.
terrado *m* terrace.
terraplén *m* terrace; platform.
terrateniente *m/f* landowner.
terraza *f* balcony; (flat) roof; terrace (in fields).
terremoto *m* earthquake.
terrenal *adj* terrestrial, earthly.
terreno/na *adj* earthly, terrestrial; * *m* land, ground, field.
terrestre *adj* terrestrial.
terrible *adj* terrible, dreadful; ferocious.
territorial *adj* territorial.
territorio *m* territory.
terrón *m* clod of earth; lump; ~**ones** *mpl* landed property.
terror *m* terror, dread.
terrorismo *m* terrorism.
terrorista *m/f* terrorist.
terso/sa *adj* smooth, glossy.
tersura *f* smoothness; shine.
tertulia *f* club, assembly, circle.
tesis *f invar* thesis.
tesón *m* tenacity, firmness.
tesorero *m* treasurer.
tesoro *m* treasure; exchequer.
testamentaría *f* testamentary execution.
testamentario *m* executor of a will; ~/**ria** *adj* testamentary.
testamento *m* will, testament.
testar *vt, vi* to make one's will.
testarudo/da *adj* obstinate.
testículo *m* testicle.
testificación *f* attestation.
testificar *vt* to attest, to witness.
testigo *m* witness, deponent.
testimoniar *vt* to attest, to bear witness to.
testimonio *m* testimony.
teta *f* teat.
tétanos *m* tetanus.

tetera *f* teapot.
tetilla *f* nipple; teat (of a bottle).
tétrico/ca *adj* gloomy, sullen, surly.
textil *adj* textile *compd*.
texto *m* text.
textual *adj* textual.
textura *f* texture.
tez *f* complexion, hue.
ti *pn* you; yourself.
tía *f* aunt; (*fam*) bird.
tiara *f* tiara.
tibieza *f* lukewarmness.
tibio/bia *adj* lukewarm.
tiburón *m* shark.
tiempo *m* time; term; weather; (*gr*) tense; occasion, opportunity; season.
tienda *f* tent; awning; tilt; shop.
tiento *m* touch; circumspection; **a ~** or **a tientas** gropingly.
tierno/na *adj* tender.
tierra *f* earth; land, ground; native country.
tieso/sa *adj* stiff, hard, firm; robust; valiant; stubborn.
tiesto *m* large earthen pot.
tifón *m* typhoon.
tifus *m* typhus.
tigre *m* tiger.
tijeras *fpl* scissors *pl*.
tijeretada *f* cut (with scissors), clip.
tijereta *f* earwig.
tijeretear *vt* to cut (with scissors).
tildar *vt* to brand, to stigmatize.
tilde *f* tilde (ñ).
tilo *m* lime tree.
timar *vt* to steal; to swindle.
timbrar *vt* to stamp.
timbre *m* stamp; bell; timbre; stamp duty.
timidez *f* timidity.
tímido/da *adj* timid; cowardly.
timo *m* swindle.

timón m helm, rudder.

tímpano m ear-drum; small drum.

tina f tub; bath (tub).

tinaja f large earthenware jar.

tinglado m shed; trick; intrigue.

tinieblas fpl darkness; shadows pl.

tino m skill; judgement, prudence.

tinta f ink; tint, dye; colour.

tinte m tint, dye; dry cleaner's.

tintero m inkwell.

tinto/ta adj dyed; * m red wine.

tintorería f dry cleaner's.

tintura f tincture; dyeing.

tiña f scab.

tiñoso/sa adj scabby, scurvy; niggardly.

tío m uncle; (fam) guy.

tiovivo m merry-go-round.

típico/ca adj typical.

tiple m (mus) treble; * f soprano.

tipo m type; norm; pattern; guy.

tipografía f typography.

tipográfico/ca adj typographical.

tipógrafo m printer.

tiquet m ticket; cash slip.

tiquismiquis m invar fussy person.

tira f abundance; strip.

tirabuzón m curl.

tirachinas m invar catapult.

tirado/da adj dirt-cheap; (fam) very easy; * f cast; distance; series; edition.

tirador m handle.

tiranía f tyranny.

tiránico/ca adj tyrannical.

tiranizar vt to tyrannize.

tirano/na m/f tyrant.

tirante m joist; stay; strap; brace; * adj taut, extended, drawn.

tirantez f tension; tautness.

tirar vt to throw; to pull; to draw; to drop; to tend, to aim at; * vi to shoot; to pull; to go; to tend to.

Tirita® f (sticking) plaster.

tiritar vi to shiver.

tiritona f shiver; shaking with cold.

tiro m throw, shot; prank; set of coach-horses; **errar el** ~ to miss (at shooting).

tirón m pull, haul, tug.

tirotear vt to shoot at.

tiroteo m shooting; sharpshooting.

tirria f antipathy.

tísico/ca adj consumptive.

tisis f tuberculosis.

títere m puppet; ridiculous little fellow.

titiritero/ra m/f puppeteer.

titubear vi to stammer; to stagger; to hesitate.

titubeo m staggering; hesitation.

titular adj titular; * m/f occupant; * m headline; * vt to title; ~**se** vr to obtain a title.

título m title; name; **a** ~ on pretence, under pretext.

tiza f chalk.

tiznar vt to stain; to tarnish.

tizne m soot; smut.

tiznón m spot, stain.

tizón m half-burnt wood.

toalla f towel.

tobillo m ankle.

tobogán m toboggan; roller-coaster; slide.

toca f head-dress.

tocadiscos m invar record player.

tocado m head-dress, headgear.

tocador m dressing table; ladies' room.

tocante prep: ~ **a** concerning, relating to.

tocar vt to touch; to strike; (mus) to play; to ring (a bell); * vi to belong; to concern; to knock; to call; to be a duty or obligation.

tocayo/ya *m/f* namesake.

tocino *m* bacon.

todavía *adv* even; yet, still.

todo/da *adj* all, entire; every; * *pn* everything, all; * *m* whole.

todopoderoso/sa *adj* almighty.

todoterreno *m* all-terrain vehicle.

toga *f* toga; gown.

toldo *m* awning; parasol.

tolerable *adj* tolerable.

tolerancia *f* tolerance, indulgence.

tolerante *adj* tolerant.

tolerar *vt* to tolerate, to suffer.

toma *f* taking; dose; ~ (**de corriente**) socket.

tomar *vt* to take; to seize, to grasp; to understand; to interpret, to perceive; to drink; to acquire; * *vi* to drink; to take.

tomate *m* tomato.

tomavistas *m invar* cine-camera.

tomillo *m* thyme.

tomo *m* bulk; tome; volume.

ton *m*: **sin ~ ni son** without rhyme or reason.

tonada *f* tune, melody.

tonadilla *f* interlude of music; short tune.

tonalidad *f* tone.

tonel *m* cask, barrel.

tonelada *f* ton; (*mar*) tonnage duty.

tónico/ca *adj* tonic, strengthening; * *m* tonic; * *f* tonic (water); (*mus*) tonic; (*fig*) keynote.

tonificar *vt* to tone up.

tono *m* tone.

tono de marcar *m* dialling tone.

tontada *f* nonsense.

tontear *vi* to talk nonsense; to act foolishly.

tontería *f* foolery, nonsense.

tonto/ta *adj* stupid, foolish.

topacio *m* topaz.

topar *vt* to run into; to find.

tope *m* butt; scuffle; ~s *mpl* (*ferro*) buffers *pl*.

topera *f* molehill.

tópico/ca *adj* topical.

topo *m* mole; stumbler.

topografía *f* topography.

topográfico/ca *adj* topographical.

toque *m* touch; bell-ringing; crisis.

toquilla *f* head-scarf; shawl.

tórax *m* thorax.

torbellino *m* whirlwind.

torcedura *f* twisting.

torcer *vt* to twist, to curve; to turn; to sprain; ~**se** *vr* to bend; to go wrong; * *vi* to turn off.

torcido/da *adj* oblique; crooked.

torcimiento *m* bending; deflection; circumlocution.

tordo *m* thrush; ~/**da** *adj* speckled black and white.

torear *vt* to avoid; to tease; * *vi* to fight bulls.

toreo *m* bullfighting.

torero *m* bullfighter.

toril *m* bull pen (at bullfight).

tormenta *f* storm, tempest.

tormento *m* torment, pain, anguish; torture.

tornar *vt* to return; to restore; ~**se** *vr* to become; * *vi* to return; ~ **a hacer** to do again.

tornasolado *adj* iridescent; shimmering.

torneo *m* tournament.

tornillo *m* screw.

torniquete *m* turnstile; (*med*) tourniquet.

torno *m* winch; revolution.

toro *m* bull.

toronja *f* grapefruit.

torpe *adj* dull, heavy; stupid.

torpedo *m* torpedo.

torpeza f heaviness, dullness; torpor; stupidity.

torre f tower; turret; steeple of a church.

torrefacto/ta adj roasted.

torrente m torrent.

tórrido/da adj torrid, parched, hot.

torrija f French toast.

torso m torso.

torta f cake; (fam) slap.

tortícolis f invar stiff neck.

tortilla f omelette; pancake.

tórtola f turtledove.

tortuga f tortoise.

tortuoso/sa adj tortuous, circuitous.

tortura f torture.

torvo/va adj stern, grim.

tos f cough.

toscamente adv coarsely, grossly.

tosco/ca adj coarse, ill-bred, clumsy.

toser vi to cough.

tostada f slice of toast.

tostado/da adj parched; sunburnt; light-yellow; light-brown.

tostador m toaster.

tostar vt to toast, to roast.

total m whole, totality; * adj total, entire; * adv in short.

totalidad f totality.

totalitario/ria adj totalitarian.

tóxico/ca adj toxic; * m poison.

toxicómano/na m/f drug addict.

tozudo/da adj obstinate.

traba f obstacle, impediment; trammel, fetter.

trabajador/ra adj working; * m/f worker.

trabajar vt to work, to labour; to persuade; to push; * vi to strive.

trabajo m work, labour, toil; difficulty; ~s mpl troubles pl.

trabajoso/sa adj laborious; painful.

trabalenguas m invar tongue twister.

trabar vt to join, to unite; to take hold of; to fetter, to shackle.

trabucarse vr to mistake.

tracción f traction; ~ delantera/trasera front-wheel/rear-wheel drive.

tractor m tractor.

tradición f tradition.

traducción f translation.

traducir vt to translate.

traductor/ra m/f translator.

traer vt to bring, to carry; to attract; to persuade; to wear; to cause.

traficante m merchant, dealer.

traficar vi to trade, to do business, to deal.

tráfico m traffic, trade.

tragaldabas m/f invar glutton.

tragaluz m skylight.

tragaperras m/f invar slot machine.

tragar vt to swallow; to swallow up.

tragedia f tragedy.

trágico/ca adj tragic.

trago m drink; gulp; adversity, misfortune.

tragón/ona adj gluttonous.

traición f treason.

traicionar vt to betray.

traicionero/ra adj treacherous.

traidor/ra m/f traitor; * adj treacherous.

traje m suit; dress; costume.

trajín m haulage; (fam) bustle.

trajinar vt to carry; * vi to bustle about; to travel around.

trama f plot; woof.

tramar vt to weave; to plot.

tramitar vt to transact; to negotiate; to handle.

trámite m path; (jur) procedure.

tramo m section; piece of ground; flight of stairs.

tramoya f scene, theatrical decoration; trick.

tramoyista *m* scene-painter; swindler.

trampa *f* trap, snare; trapdoor; fraud.

trampear *vt* to swindle, to deceive; * *vi* to cheat.

trampolín *m* trampoline; diving board.

tramposo/sa *adj* deceitful, swindling.

tranca *f* bar, crossbeam.

trance *m* danger; last stage of life; trance.

tranco *m* long step or stride.

tranquilidad *f* tranquillity; repose, heart's ease.

tranquilizar *vt* to calm; to reassure.

tranquilo/la *adj* tranquil, calm, quiet.

transacción *f* transaction.

transbordador *m* ferry.

transbordar *vt* to transfer.

transbordo *m* transfer; **hacer ~** to change (trains).

transcribir *vt* to transcribe; to copy.

transcurrir *vi* to pass; to turn out.

transcurso *m*: **~ del tiempo** course of time.

transeúnte *adj* transitory; * *m* passer-by.

transferencia *f* transference; (*com*) transfer.

transferir *vt* to transfer; to defer.

transfiguración *f* transformation, transfiguration.

transformación *f* transformation.

transformador *m* transformer.

transformar *vt* to transform; **~se** *vr* to change one's sentiments or manners.

tránsfuga, tránsfugo *m* deserter; fugitive; defector.

transfusión *f* transfusion.

transgresión *f* transgression.

transgresor *m* transgressor.

transición *f* transition.

transido/da *adj* worn out with anguish; overcome.

transigir *vi* to compromise.

transistor *m* transistor.

transitar *vi* to travel, to pass through a place.

transitivo/va *adj* transitive.

tránsito *m* passage; transition; road, way; change; removal; death of holy or virtuous persons.

transitorio/ria *adj* transitory.

transmisión *f* transmission; transfer; broadcast.

transmitir *vt* to transmit; to broadcast.

transmutación *f* transmutation.

transmutar *vt* to transmute.

transparencia *f* transparency; clearness; slide.

transparentarse *vr* to be transparent; to shine through.

transparente *adj* transparent.

transpiración *f* perspiration; transpiration.

transpirar *vt* to perspire; to transpire.

transportar *vt* to transport, to convey.

transporte *m* transportation.

transposición *f* transposition, transposal.

transversal *adj* transverse; collateral.

tranvía *m* tram.

trapacería *f* fraud, deceit.

trapacero/ra *adj* deceitful.

trapecio *m* trapeze.

trapecista *m/f* trapeze artist.

trapero/ra *m/f* dealer in rags.

trapicheo *m* (*fam*) fiddle.

trapo *m* rag, tatter.

tráquea *f* windpipe.

traqueteo *m* rattling.

tras *prep* after, behind.

trascendencia *f* transcendency; penetration.

trascendental *adj* transcendental.

trascender *vi* to smell; to come out; ~ **de** to go beyond.

trasegar *vt* to move about; to decant.

trasero/ra *adj* back; * *m* bottom.

trasfondo *m* background.

trasgredir *vt* to contravene.

trashumante *adj* migrating.

trasiego *m* removal; decanting (of drinks).

trasladar *vt* to transport; to transfer; to postpone; to transcribe, to copy; ~**se** *vr* to move.

traslado *m* move; removal.

traslucirse *vr* to be transparent; to conjecture.

trasluz *m* reflected light.

trasnochar *vi* to watch, to sit up the whole night.

traspaperlarse *vr* to get mislaid among other papers.

traspasar *vt* to remove, to transport; to transfix, to pierce; to return; to exceed (the proper bounds); to transfer.

traspaso *m* transfer, sale.

traspié *m* trip; slip, stumble.

trasplantar *vt* to transplant.

trasplante *m* transplant.

trasquilar *vt* to shear (sheep); to clip.

trasquilón *m* cut (of the shears); badly cut hair.

traste *m* fret (of a guitar); **dar al ~ con algo** to ruin something.

trastear *vt* to move (furniture).

trastienda *f* back room behind a shop.

trasto *m* piece of junk; useless person.

trastornado/da *adj* crazy.

trastornar *vt* to overthrow, to overturn; to confuse; ~**se** *vr* to go crazy.

trastorno *m* overturning; confusion.

trastrocar *vt* to invert (the order of things).

tratable *adj* friendly.

tratado *m* treaty, convention; treatise.

tratamiento *m* treatment; style of address.

tratante *m* dealer.

tratar *vt* to traffic, to trade; to use; to treat; to handle; to address; ~**se** *vr* to treat each other.

trato *m* treatment; manner, address; trade, traffic; conversation; (*com*) agreement.

trauma *m* trauma.

través *m* (*fig*) reverse; **de** *o* **al ~** across, crossways; **a ~ de** *prep* across; over; through.

travesaño *m* cross timber; transom.

travesía *f* crossing; cross-street; trajectory; (*mar*) side wind.

travesura *f* wit; wickedness.

travieso/sa *adj* restless, uneasy, fidgety; turbulent; lively; naughty.

trayecto *m* road; journey, stretch; course.

trayectoria *f* trajectory; path.

traza *f* first sketch; trace, outline; project; manner; means; appearance.

trazar *vt* to plan out; to project; to trace.

trazo *m* sketch, plan, design.

trébedes *fpl* trivet, tripod.

trébol *m* trefoil, clover.

trece *adj*, *m* thirteen; thirteenth.

trecho *m* space, distance of time or place; **a ~s** at intervals.

tregua *f* truce, cessation of hostilities.

treinta *adj, m* thirty.

tremendo/da *adj* terrible, formidable; awful, grand.

tremolar *vt* to hoist (the colours); to wave.

trémulo/la *adj* tremulous, trembling.

tren *m* train, retinue; show, ostentation; (*ferro*) train; ~ **de alta velocidad** high-speed train; ~ **de mercancías** freight train, luggage-train.

trenza *f* plait (in hair), plaited silk.

trenzar *vt* to braid.

trepar *vi* to climb; to crawl.

tres *adj, m* three.

tresillo *m* three-piece suite; (*mus*) triplet.

treta *f* thrust (fencing); trick.

triangular *adj* triangular.

triángulo *m* triangle.

tribu *f* tribe.

tribulación *f* tribulation, affliction.

tribuna *f* tribune.

tribunal *m* tribunal, court of justice.

tributar *vt* to pay; to contribute to; to pay (homage, respect).

tributario/ria *adj* tributary.

tributo *m* tribute.

tricolor *adj* tricoloured.

tricotar *vi* to knit.

tridente *m* trident.

trienal *adj* triennial.

trienio *m* period of three years.

trigal *m* wheat field.

trigésimo/ma *adj, m* thirtieth.

trigo *m* wheat.

trigueño/ña *adj* corn-coloured; olive-skinned.

trillado/da *adj* beaten; trite, stale, hackneyed; **camino** ~ common routine.

trilladora *f* threshing machine.

trillar *vt* to thresh.

trimestral *adj* quarterly, three-monthly.

trimestre *m* period of three months.

trinar *vi* to trill, to quaver; to be angry.

trincar *vt* to tie up; to pinion.

trinchante *m* carver; carving knife.

trinchar *vt* to carve, to divide (meat).

trinchera *f* trench, entrenchment.

trineo *m* sledge.

Trinidad *f* Trinity.

trino *m* trill.

trío *m* (*mus*) trio.

tripa *f* gut, intestine; **~s** *fpl* guts; tripe.

triple *adj* triple, treble.

triplicar *vt* to treble.

trípode *m* tripod, trivet.

tripulación *f* crew.

tripulante *m/f* crewman/woman.

tripular *vt* to man; to drive.

triquiñuela *f* trick.

triquitraque *m* clack, clatter; clashing.

tris *m invar*: **estar en un** ~ **de** to be on the point of.

triste *adj* sad, mournful, melancholy.

tristeza *f* sadness, mourning.

trituración *f* pulverization.

triturar *vt* to reduce to powder; to grind, to pound.

triunfal *adj* triumphal.

triunfar *vi* to triumph; to trump (at cards).

triunfo *m* triumph; trump (at cards).

trivial *adj* trivial.

trivialidad *f* triviality.

triza *f*: **hacer ~s** to smash to bits; to tear to shreds.

trocar *vt* to exchange.

trocha *f* short cut.

troche: a ~ **y moche** *adv* helter-skelter.

trofeo *m* trophy.

tromba *f* whirlwind.

trombón *m* trombone.

trombosis *f invar* thrombosis.

trompa *f* trumpet; proboscis; spinning top.

trompazo *m* heavy blow; accident.

trompeta *f* trumpet; * *m* trumpeter.

trompetilla *f* small trumpet; speaking-trumpet.

trompicón *m* stumble.

trompo *m* spinning top.

tronar *vi* to thunder; to rage.

troncar *vt* to truncate, to mutilate.

tronchar *vt* to cut off; to shatter; to tire out.

troncho *m* sprig, stem or stalk.

tronco *m* trunk; log of wood; stock.

tronera *m* loophole; small window; pocket (of a billiard table).

trono *m* throne.

tropa *f* troop.

tropel *m* confused noise; hurry; bustle, confusion; heap of things; crowd; **en ~** in a tumultuous and confused manner.

tropelía *f* outrage.

tropezar *vi* to stumble; * *vt* to meet accidentally.

tropezón/ona *adj* stumbling; * *m* trip; **a ~ones** by fits and starts.

tropical *adj* tropical.

trópico *m* tropic.

tropiezo *m* stumble, trip; obstacle; slip, fault; quarrel; dispute.

trotamundos *m invar* globetrotter.

trotar *vi* to trot.

trote *m* trot; travelling.

trovador/ra *m/f* troubadour.

trozo *m* piece.

trucha *f* trout.

truco *m* knack; trick.

trueno *m* thunderclap.

trueque *m* exchange.

trufa *f* truffle.

truhán *adj* rogue.

truncado/da *adj* truncated.

truncamiento *m* truncation.

truncar *vt* to truncate, to maim.

tu *adj* your.

tú *pn* you.

tubérculo *m* tuber.

tuberculosis *f* tuberculosis.

tubería *f* pipe; pipeline.

tubo *m* tube.

tuerca *f* screw.

tuerto/ta *adj* one-eyed; squint-eyed; * *m/f* one-eyed person.

tuétano *m* marrow.

tufarada *f* strong scent or smell.

tufo *m* warm vapour arising from the earth; offensive smell.

tugurio *m* slum.

tul *m* tulle.

tulipán *m* tulip.

tullido/da *adj* crippled, maimed.

tumba *f* tomb.

tumbar *vt* to knock down; * *vi* to tumble (to fall down); **~se** *vr* to lie down to sleep.

tumbo *m* fall; jolt.

tumbona *f* easy chair; beach chair.

tumor *m* tumour, growth.

túmulo *m* tomb; sepulchral monument.

tumulto *m* tumult, uproar.

tumultuoso/sa *adj* tumultuous.

tuna *f* student music group.

tunda *f* beating.

túnel *m* tunnel.

túnica *f* tunic.

tuno *m* rogue.

tupé *m* toupee, wig or hairpiece.

tupido/da *adj* dense.

tupir *vt* to press close; **~se** *vr* to stuff oneself.

turbación f perturbation, confusion; trouble, disorder.
turbado/da adj disturbed.
turbante m turban.
turbar vt to disturb, to trouble; ~se vr to be disturbed.
turbina f turbine.
turbio/bia adj muddy; troubled.
turbulencia f turbulence; disturbance.
turbulento/ta adj muddy; turbulent.
turismo m tourism; ~ rural rural tourism.
turista m/f tourist, holiday-maker.

turístico/ca adj tourist compd.
turnar vi to alternate.
turno m turn; shift; opportunity.
turquesa f turquoise.
turrón m nougat (almond cake).
tutear vt to address as 'tu'.
tutela f guardianship, tutelage.
tutelar adj tutelar, tutelary.
tutor m guardian, tutor.
tutora f tutoress.
tutoría f tutelage.
tuyo/ya adj yours; ~s pl friends and relations of the party addressed.

U

u conj or (instead of o before an o or ho).
ubicar vt to place; ~se to be located.
ubre f udder.
ufanarse vr to boast.
ufano/na adj haughty, arrogant.
ujier m usher.
úlcera f ulcer.
ulcerar vi to ulcerate.
ulterior adj ulterior; farther, further.
últimamente adv lately.
ultimar vt to finalize; to finish.
ultimátum m ultimatum.
último/ma adj last; latest; bottom; top.
ultrajar vt to outrage; to despise; to abuse.
ultraje m outrage.
ultramar adj, m overseas.
ultramarinos mpl groceries.
ultrasónico/ca adj ultrasonic.
umbilical adj umbilical.
umbral m threshold.
un/una art a, an; * adj, m one (for uno).
unánime adj unanimous.

unanimidad f unanimity.
unción f unction; extreme or last unction.
ungir vt to anoint.
ungüento m ointment.
únicamente adv only, simply.
único/ca adj only; singular, unique.
unicornio m unicorn.
unidad f unity; unit; conformity; union.
unificar vt to unite.
uniformar vt to make uniform.
uniforme adj uniform; * m (mil) uniform, regimentals pl.
uniformidad f uniformity.
unilateral adj unilateral.
unión f union; ~ Europea European Union.
unir vt to join, to unite; to mingle; to bind, to tie; ~se vr to associate.
unísono/na adj unison.
universal adj universal.
universalidad f universality.
universidad f university.
universitario/ria adj university compd; * m/f student.

universo *m* universe.

uno *m* one; **~/una** *adj* one; sole, only; **~ a otro** one another; **~ a ~** one by one; **a una** jointly together.

untar *vt* to anoint; to grease; (*fam*) to bribe.

uña *f* nail; hoof; claw, talon.

¡upa! up! up!

urbanidad *f* urbanity, politeness.

uranio *m* uranium.

Urano *m* Uranus (planet).

urbanismo *m* town planning.

urbanización *f* housing estate.

urbano/na *adj* urban; urbane, polite.

urdimbre *f* warp; intrigue.

urdir *vt* to warp; to contrive.

urgencia *f* urgency; emergency; need, necessity.

urgente *adj* urgent.

urgentemente *adv* urgently.

urgir *vi* to be urgent.

urinario/ria *adj* urinary; * *m* urinal.

urna *f* urn; ballot box.

urraca *f* magpie.

usado/da *adj* used; experienced; worn.

usanza *f* usage, use, custom.

usar *vt* to use, to make use of; to wear; **~se** *vr* to be used.

uso *m* use, service; custom; mode.

usted *pn* you.

usuario *m* user.

usufructo *m* (*jur*) usufruct, use.

usura *f* usury.

usurario/ria *adj* usurious.

usurero *m* usurer.

usurpación *f* usurpation.

usurpar *vt* to usurp.

utensilio *m* utensil.

uterino/na *adj* uterine.

útero *m* uterus, womb.

util *adj* useful, profitable; * *m* utility.

utilidad *f* utility.

utilizar *vt* to use; to make useful.

utopía *f* Utopia.

utópico/ca *adj* Utopian.

uva *f* grape.

V

vaca *f* cow; beef.

vacaciones *fpl* vacation; holidays *pl*.

vacante *adj* vacant; * *f* vacancy.

vaciar *vt* to empty, to clear; to mould; * *vi* to fall, to decrease (of waters); **~se** *vr* to empty.

vacilación *f* hesitation; irresolution.

vacilar *vi* to hesitate; to falter; to fail.

vacío/cía *adj* void, empty; unoccupied; concave; vain; presumptuous; * *m* vacuum; emptiness.

vacuna *f* vaccine.

vacunar *vt* to vaccinate.

vacuno/na *adj* bovine, cow *compd*.

vadear *vt* to wade, to ford.

vagabundo/da *adj* wandering; * *m* vagrant, bum, tramp.

vagancia *f* vagrancy.

vagar *vi* to rove or loiter about; to wander.

vagido *m* cry of a child; convulsive sob.

vagina *f* vagina.

vago/ga *adj* vagrant; restless; vague.

vagón *m* (*ferro*) wagon; carriage; **~ de mercancías** goods wagon.

vaguear *vi* to rove, to loiter; to wander.

vahído *m* vertigo, giddiness.

vaho *m* steam, vapour.

vaina *f* scabbard (of a sword); pod, husk.

vainilla *f* (*bot*) vanilla.

vaivén *m* fluctuation, instability; giddiness.

vajilla *f* crockery.

vale *m* farewell; promissory note, IOU

valedero/ra *adj* valid; efficacious; binding.

valentía *f* valour, courage.

valentón *m* braggart.

valentonada *f* brag, boast.

valer *vi* to be valuable; to be deserving; to cost; to be valid; to be worth; to produce; to be current; * *vt* to protect, to favour; to be worth; to be equivalent to; ~**se** *vr* to employ, to make use of; to have recourse to.

valeroso/sa *adj* valiant, brave; strong, powerful.

valía *f* valuation; worth.

validar *vt* to validate.

validez *f* validity; stability.

válido/da *adj* valid.

valiente *adj* robust, vigorous; valiant, brave; boasting.

valija *f* suitcase.

valioso/sa *adj* valuable.

valla *f* fence; hurdle; barricade.

vallar *vt* to fence in.

valle *m* valley.

valor *m* value; price; validity; force; power; courage, valour.

valoración *f* valuation.

valorar *vt* to value; to evaluate.

valuación *f* valuation.

vals *m invar* waltz.

válvula *f* valve.

vampiro *m* vampire.

vanagloriarse *vr* to boast.

vandalismo *m* vandalism.

vándalo/la *m, adj* vandal.

vanguardia *f* vanguard.

vanidad *f* vanity; ostentation.

vanidoso/sa *adj* vain, showy; haughty; conceited.

vano/na *adj* vain; useless, frivolous; arrogant; futile; **en ~** in vain.

vapor *m* vapour, steam; breath.

vaporizador *m* atomizer.

vaporizar *vt* to vaporize.

vaporoso/sa *adj* vaporous.

vapular *vt* to whip, to flog.

vaquerizo/za *adj* cattle *compd*; * *m* cowherd.

vaquero *m* cowherd, cowman; ~/**ra** *adj* belonging to a cowherd; ~**s** *mpl* jeans *pl*.

vara *f* rod; pole, staff; stick.

variable *adj* variable, changeable.

variación *f* variation.

variado/da *adj* varied; variegated.

variar *vt* to vary; to modify; to change; * *vi* to vary.

varices *fpl* varicose veins *pl*.

variedad *f* variety; inconstancy.

varilla *f* small rod; curtain rod; spindle, pivot.

vario/ria *adj* varied, different; vague; variegated; ~**s** *pl* some; several.

varón *m* man, male.

varonil *adj* male, masculine; manful.

vasco/ca *adj*, *m/f* Basque.

vascuence *m* Basque.

Vaselina® *f* Vaseline®.

vasija *f* vessel.

vaso *m* glass; vessel; vase.

vástago *m* bud, shoot; offspring.

vasto/ta *adj* vast, huge.

vaticinar *vt* to divine, to foretell.

vaticinio *m* prophecy.

vatio *m* watt.

vecindad *f* inhabitants of a place; neighbourhood.

vecindario *m* number of inhabitants of a place; neighbourhood.

vecino/na *adj* neighbouring; near; * *m* neighbour, inhabitant.

veda *f* prohibition.

vedar *vt* to prohibit, to forbid; to impede.

vegetación *f* vegetation.

vegetal *adj* vegetable.

vegetar *vi* to vegetate.

vegetariano/na *adj, m/f* vegetarian.

vehemencia *f* vehemence, force.

vehemente *adj* vehement, violent.

vehículo *m* vehicle.

veinte *adj, m* twenty.

veintena *f* twentieth part; score.

vejación *f* vexation; embarrassment.

vejar *vt* to vex; to humiliate.

vejestorio *m* old man.

vejez *f* old age.

vejiga *f* bladder.

vela *f* wakefulness; vigil; night work; candle; sail; **hacerse a la** ~ to set sail.

velado/da *adj* veiled; blurred; * *f* soiree.

velador *m* night watchman; observer; candlestick; pedestal table.

velar *vi* to stay awake; to be attentive; * *vt* to guard, to watch.

veleidad *f* feeble will; inconstancy.

velero/ra *adj* swift-sailing.

veleta *f* weather cock.

vello *m* down; gossamer; short downy hair.

vellón *m* fleece.

velludo/da *adj* shaggy, woolly.

velo *m* veil; pretext.

velocidad *f* speed; velocity.

velocímetro *m* speedometer.

veloz(mente) *adj (adv)* swift(ly), fast.

vena *f* vein.

venado *m* deer; venison.

vencedor/ra *m/f* conqueror, victor, winner.

vencer *vt* to defeat; to conquer, to vanquish; * *vi* to win; to expire.

vencido/da *adj* defeated; due.

vencimiento *m* victory; maturity.

vendaje *m* bandage, dressing for wounds.

vendal *f* bandage.

vendar *vt* to bandage; to hoodwink.

vendaval *m* gale.

vendedor/ra *m/f* seller; ~ **de periódicos** newsagent; ~ **ambulante** pedlar.

vender *vt* to sell.

vendimia *f* grape harvest; vintage.

vendimiador/ra *m/f* vintager.

vendimiar *vt* to harvest; to gather (the vintage).

veneno *m* poison, venom.

venenoso/sa *adj* venomous, poisonous.

venerable *adj* venerable.

veneración *f* veneration, worship.

venerar *vt* to venerate, to worship.

venéreo/rea *adj* venereal.

venganza *f* revenge, vengeance.

vengar *vt* to revenge, to avenge; ~**se** *vr* to take revenge.

vengativo/va *adj* revengeful.

venia *f* pardon; leave, permission; bow.

venial *adj* venial.

venida *f* arrival; return; overflow of a river.

venidero/ra *adj* future; ~**s** *mpl* posterity.

venir *vi* to come, to arrive; to follow, to succeed; to happen; to spring from; ~**se** *vr* to ferment.

venta *f* sale.

ventaja *f* advantage.

ventajoso/sa *adj* advantageous.

ventana *f* window; window shutter; nostril.

ventanilla *f* window.

venta por correo *f* mail order.

ventarrón *m* violent wind.

ventilación *f* ventilation; draught.

ventilar *vt* to ventilate; to fan; to discuss.

ventisca *f*, **ventisco** *m* snowstorm.

ventiscar *vi* to drift, to lie in drifts (snow).

ventisquero *m* snowdrift; ~**s** *mpl* glaciers *pl*.

ventolera *f* gust; pride, loftiness.

ventosidad *f* flatulence.

ventoso/sa *adj* windy; flatulent.

ventrículo *m* ventricle.

ventrílocuo *m* ventriloquist.

ventura *f* happiness; luck, chance, fortune; **por** ~ by chance.

venturoso/sa *adj* lucky, fortunate, happy.

Venus *f* Venus (planet).

ver *vt* to see, to look at; to observe; to visit; * *vi* to understand; to see; ~**se** *vr* to be seen; to be conspicuous; to find oneself; ~**se con uno** to have a bone to pick with someone; * *m* sense of sight; appearance.

vera *f* edge; bank.

veracidad *f* truth; veracity.

veranear *vi* to spend the summer holiday, to vacation.

veraneo *m* summer holiday.

veraniego/ga *adj* summer.

verano *m* summer.

veras *fpl* truth, sincerity; **de** ~ in truth, really.

veraz *adj* truthful.

verbal *adj* verbal.

verbena *f* fair; dance.

verbo *m* word, term; (*gr*) verb.

verbosidad *f* verbosity.

verdad *f* truth, veracity; reality; reliability.

verdaderamente *adv* truly, in fact.

verdadero/ra *adj* true; real; sincere.

verde *m*, *adj* green.

verdear, verdecer *vi* to turn green.

verdín *m* bright green; verdure.

verdor *m* greenness; verdure; youth.

verdoso/sa *adj* greenish, greeny.

verdugo *m* hangman; very cruel person.

verdulero/ra *m/f* greengrocer.

verdura *f* verdure; vegetables *pl*, greens *pl*.

vereda *f* path; pavement, sidewalk.

veredicto *m* verdict.

vergel *m* orchard.

vergonzoso/sa *adj* bashful; shamefaced.

vergüenza *f* shame; bashfulness; confusion.

vericueto *m* rough road.

verídico/ca *adj* truthful.

verificación *f* verification.

verificar *vt* to check, to verify; ~**se** *vr* to happen.

verisímil *adj* probable.

verja *f* grate, lattice.

vermut *m* vermouth.

verosímil *adj* likely; credible.

verosimilitud *f* likeliness; credibility.

verraco *m* boar.

verruga *f* wart, pimple.

versado/da *adj* versed.

versátil *adj* versatile.

versículo *m* versicle; verse of a chapter.

versificar *vt* to versify.

versión *f* translation, version.

verso *m* verse.

vértebra *f* vertebra.

vertedero m sewer, drain; tip.

verter vt to pour; to spill; to empty; * vi to flow.

vertical adj vertical.

vértice m vertex, zenith; crown of the head.

vertiente f slope; waterfall, cascade.

vertiginoso/sa adj giddy.

vértigo m giddiness, vertigo.

vesícula f blister.

vespertino/na adj evening compd.

vestíbulo m vestibule, lobby; foyer.

vestido m dress; clothes pl.

vestidura f dress; clothing.

vestigio m vestige; footstep; trace.

vestimenta f clothing.

vestir vt to put on; to wear; to dress; to adorn; to cloak, to disguise; * vi to dress; **~se** to get dressed.

vestuario m clothes pl; uniform; vestry; changing room.

veta f vein (in mines, wood, etc); streak; grain.

vetado/da adj striped, veined.

vetar vt to veto.

veterano/na adj experienced, practised; * m veteran, old soldier.

veterinario/ria m/f vet; * f veterinary science.

veto m veto.

vez f time; turn; return; **cada ~** each time; **una ~** once; **a veces** sometimes, by turns.

vía f way; road, route; mode, manner, method; (ferro) railway line.

viajante m sales representative.

viajar vi to travel.

viaje m journey; voyage; travel.

viajero/ra m/f traveller.

vial adj road compd.

viático m viaticum; travel allowance.

víbora f viper.

vibración f vibration.

vibrador m vibrator.

vibrante adj vibrant.

vibrar vt, vi to vibrate.

vicaría f vicarship; vicarage.

vice- pref vice- (deputy, etc).

vicealmirante m vice-admiral.

viceconsulado m vice-consulate.

vicepresidente/ta m/f vice-president.

viciar vt to vitiate, to corrupt; to annul; to deprave.

vicio m vice.

vicioso/sa adj vicious; depraved.

vicisitud f vicissitude.

víctima f victim; sacrifice.

victoria f victory.

victorioso/sa adj victorious.

vicuña m vicuna.

vid f (bot) vine.

vida f life.

vidriado m glazed earthenware, crockery.

vídeo m video.

videocámara f video camera, camcorder.

videocasete m video cassette.

videoclip m pop video.

videojuego m video game.

vidriar vt to glaze.

vidriera f stained-glass window; shop window.

vidriero m glazier.

vidrio m glass.

vidrioso/sa adj glassy; brittle; slippery; very delicate.

vieira f scallop.

viejo/ja adj old; ancient, antiquated.

viento m wind; air.

vientre m belly.

viernes m invar Friday; **V~ Santo** Good Friday.

viga f beam; girder.

vigencia f validity.

vigente adj in force.

vigésimo/ma *adj, m* twentieth.
vigía *f* (*mar*) lookout; * *m* watchman.
vigilancia *f* vigilance, watchfulness.
vigilante *adj* watchful, vigilant.
vigilar *vt* to watch over; * *vi* to keep watch.
vigilia *f* vigil; watch.
vigor *m* vigour, strength.
vigoroso/sa *adj* vigorous.
vil *adj* mean, sordid, low; worthless; infamous; ungrateful.
vileza *f* meanness, lowness; abjectness.
vilipendiar *vt* to despise, to revile.
villa *f* villa; small town.
villancico *m* Christmas carol.
villano/na *adj* rustic, clownish; villainous; * *m* villain; rustic.
villorio *m* one horse town; (*fam*) dump; shanty town.
vilo: en ~ *adv* in the air; in suspense.
vinagre *m* vinegar.
vinagrera *f* vinegar cruet.
vinagreta *f* vinaigrette.
vinculación *f* link; linking.
vincular *vt* to link.
vínculo *m* tie, link, chain; entail.
vindicación *f* revenge.
vindicar *vt* to avenge.
vindicativo/va *adj* vindictive.
vinicultura *f* wine growing.
vino *m* wine; ~ **tinto** red wine.
viña *f* vineyard.
viñedo *m* vineyard.
viñeta *f* vignette.
viola *f* viola.
violación *f* violation; rape.
violado/da *adj* violet-coloured; violated.
violador/ra *m/f* rapist; violator; profaner.
violar *vt* to rape; to violate; to profane.

violencia *f* violence.
violentar *vt* to force.
violento/ta *adj* violent; forced; absurd; embarrassing.
violeta *f* violet.
violín *m* violin, fiddle.
violinista *m* violinist.
violón *m* double bass.
violoncelo, **violonchelo** *m* violoncello, cello.
vip *m/f* VIP.
viperino/na *adj* viperish.
viraje *m* turn; bend.
virar *vi* to swerve.
virgen *m/f* virgin.
virginidad *f* virginity.
Virgo *f* Virgo (sign of the zodiac).
viril *adj* virile, manly.
virilidad *f* virility, manhood.
virrey *m* viceroy.
virtual *adj* virtual.
virtud *f* virtue.
virtuoso/sa *adj* virtuous.
viruela *f* smallpox.
virulencia *f* virulence.
virulento/ta *adj* virulent.
virus *m invar* virus.
visa *f*, **visado** *m* visa.
viscosidad *f* viscosity.
viscoso/sa *adj* viscous, glutinous.
visera *f* visor.
visibilidad *f* visibility.
visible *adj* visible; apparent.
visillos *mpl* lace curtains *pl*.
visión *f* sight, vision; fantasy.
visionario/ria *adj* visionary.
visita *f* visit; visitor.
visitar *vt* to visit.
vislumbrar *vt* to catch a glimpse of; to perceive indistinctly.
visón *m* mink.
víspera *f* eve; evening before; ~**s** *pl* vespers.

vista *f* sight, view; vision; eyesight; appearance; looks *pl*; prospect; intention; (*jur*) trial; * *m* customs officer.

vistazo *m* glance.

visto: ~ **que** *conj* considering that.

vistoso/sa *adj* colourful, attractive, lively.

visual *adj* visual.

vital *adj* life *compd*; vital.

vitalicio/cia *adj* for life.

vitalidad *f* vitality.

vitamina *f* vitamin.

viticultor/ra *m/f* wine grower.

viticultura *f* wine growing.

vitorear *vt* to shout, to applaud.

vítreo/trea *adj* vitreous.

vitriolo *m* vitriol.

vitrina *f* showcase.

vituperación *f* condemnation, censure.

vituperar *vt* to condemn, to censure.

vituperio *m* condemnation, censure; insult.

viuda *f* widow.

viudedad *f* widowhood; widow's pension.

viudez *f* widowhood.

viudo *m* widower.

vivacidad *f* vivacity, liveliness.

vivamente *adv* in lively fashion.

vivaracho/cha *adj* lively, sprightly; bright.

vivaz *adj* lively.

víveres *mpl* provisions.

vivero *m* nursery (for plants); fish farm.

viveza *f* liveliness; sharpness.

vividor/ra *adj* (*perj*) sharp, clever; unscrupulous.

vivienda *f* housing; flat, apartment.

viviente *adj* living.

vivificar *vt* to vivify, to enliven.

vivíparo/ra *adj* viviparous.

vivir *vt* to live through; to go through; * *vi* to live; to last.

vivo/va *adj* living; lively; **al ~** to the life; very realistically.

vizconde *m* viscount.

vocablo *m* word, term.

vocabulario *m* vocabulary.

vocación *f* vocation.

vocacional *adj* vocational.

vocal *f* vowel; * *m/f* member (of a committee); * *adj* vocal, oral.

vocativo *m* (*gr*) vocative.

vocear *vt* to cry; to shout; to cheer; to shriek; * *vi* to yell.

vocería *f*, **vocerío** *m* shouting.

vociferar *vt* to shout; to proclaim in a loud voice; * *vi* to yell.

vodka *m/f* vodka.

volador/ra *adj* flying; fast.

volandas: **en ~** *adv* in the air; (*fig*) swiftly.

volante *adj* flying; * *m* (*auto*) steering wheel; note; pamphlet; shuttlecock.

volar *vi* to fly; to pass swiftly (of time); to rush, to hurry; * *vt* to blow up, to explode.

volatería *f* fowling; fowls *pl*.

volátil *adj* volatile; changeable.

volatilizar *vt* to volatilize, to vaporize.

volcán *m* volcano.

volcánico *adj* volcanic.

volcar *vt* to upset, to overturn; to make giddy; to empty out; to exasperate; **~se** *vr* to tip over.

voleibol *m* volleyball.

voleo *m* volley.

volquete *m* tipper truck; dump truck.

voltaje *m* voltage.

voltear *vt* to turn over; to overturn; * *vi* to roll over, to tumble.

voltereta f tumble; somersault.
voltio m volt.
voluble adj unpredictable; fickle.
volumen m volume; size.
voluminoso/sa adj voluminous.
voluntad f will, willpower; wish, desire.
voluntario/ria adj voluntary; * m/f volunteer.
voluptuoso/sa adj voluptuous.
volver vt to turn (over); to turn upside down; to turn inside out; * vi to return, to go back; **~se** vr to turn around.
vomitar vt, vi to vomit.
vómito m vomiting; vomit.
vomitona f violent vomiting.
voracidad f voracity.
voraz(mente) adj (adv) voracious(ly).
vórtice m whirlpool.
vos pn you.
vosotros/tras pn pl you.

votación f voting; vote.
votar vi to vote; to vote.
voto m vow; vote; opinion, advice; swearword; curse; **~s** mpl good wishes pl.
voz f voice; shout; rumour; word, term.
vuelco m overturning.
vuelo m flight; wing; projection of a building; ruffle, frill; **cazar al ~** to catch in flight; **~ chárter** charter flight.
vuelta f turn; circuit; return; row of stitches; cuff; change; bend, curve; reverse, other side; return journey.
vuestro/tra adj your; * pn yours.
vulgar adj vulgar, common.
vulgaridad f vulgar, common.
vulgaridad f vulgarity, commonness.
vulgo m common people pl.
vulnerable adj vulnerable.

W

wáter m toilet.
whisky m whisky.

windsurf m windsurfing.
windsurfista m/f windsurfer.

X

xenofobia f xenophobia.
xilófono m xylophone.
xilógrafo m xylographer (person

who prints from wooden blocks); wood engraver.

Y

y conj and.
ya adv already; now; immediately; at once; soon; * conj: **~ que** since, seeing that; **¡~!** of course!, sure!

yacer vi to lie, to lie down.
yacimiento m deposit.
yanqui m/f Yankee.
yate m yacht, sailing boat.

yedra f ivy.
yegua f mare.
yema f bud; leaf; yolk; **~ del dedo** tip of the finger.
yermo m wasteland, wilderness; **~/ma** adj waste; (fig) barren.
yerno m son-in-law.
yerro m error, mistake, fault.
yerto/ta adj stiff, inflexible; rigid.
yesca f tinder.
yeso m gypsum; plaster; **~ mate** plaster of Paris.
yo pn I; **~ mismo** I myself.
yodo m iodine.
yogur m yoghurt.
yugo m yoke.
yugular adj jugular.
yunque m anvil.
yunta f yoke; **~s** fpl couple, pair.
yute m jute.
yuxtaponer vt to juxtapose.
yuxtaposición f juxtaposition.

Z

zafar vt to loosen, to untie; to lighten (a ship); **~se** vr to escape; **~se de** to avoid; to free oneself from (trouble).
zafio/fia adj uncouth, coarse.
zafiro m sapphire.
zaga f rear; **a la ~** behind.
zagal/la m/f boy/girl.
zaguán m porch, hall.
zaherir vt to criticize; to upbraid.
zahorí m clairvoyant.
zalamería f flattery.
zalamero/ra adj flattering; * m/f wheedler.
zamarra f sheepskin; sheepskin jacket.
zambo/ba adj knock-kneed.
zambomba f rural drum.
zambullida f plunge, dive; dipping, submersion.
zambullirse vr to plunge into water, to dive.
zampar vt to gobble down; to put away hurriedly; **~se** vr to thrust oneself suddenly into any place; to crash, to hurtle.
zanahoria f carrot.
zancada f stride.

zancadilla f trip; trick.
zanco m stilt.
zancudo/da adj long-legged; * m mosquito.
zángano m drone; idler, slacker.
zanja f ditch, trench.
zanjar vt to dig (ditches); (fig) to surmount; to resolve.
zapador m (mil) sapper.
zapata f boot; **~ de freno** (auto) brake shoe.
zapatazo m (dancing) stamp.
zapatear vt to tap with the shoe; to beat time with the sole of the shoe.
zapatería f shoemaking; shoe shop; shoe factory.
zapatero/ra m/f shoemaker; **~ de viejo** cobbler.
zapatilla f slipper; pump (shoe); (dep) **~s de lona** fpl trainers pl.
zapato m shoe.
zapping m channel-hopping.
zar m czar.
zarandear vt to shake vigorously.
zarcillo m earring; tendril.
zarpa f dirt on clothes; claw.
zarpar vi to weigh anchor.
zarpazo m thud.

zarrapastroso/sa *adj* shabby, rough-looking.

zarza *f* bramble.

zarzal *m* bramble patch.

zarzamora *f* blackberry.

zarzuela *f* Spanish light opera.

zigzag *adj* zigzag.

zigzaguear *vi* to zigzag.

zinc *m* zinc.

zócalo *m* plinth, base; skirting board.

zodiaco *m* zodiac.

zona *f* zone; area, belt.

zoo *m* zoo.

zoología *f* zoology.

zoológico/ca *adj* zoological; * *m* zoo.

zoólogo/ga *m/f* zoologist.

zopenco/ca *adj* dull, very stupid.

zoquete *m* block; crust of bread; (*fam*) blockhead.

zorra *f* fox; vixen; (*fam*) whore, tart (*sl*).

zorro *m* male fox; cunning person.

zozobra *f* (*mar*) capsizing; uneasiness, anxiety.

zozobrar *vi* (*mar*) to founder; to capsize; (*fig*) to fail; to be anxious.

zueco *m* wooden shoe; clog.

zumba *f* banter, teasing; beating.

zumbar *vt* to hit; ~**se** *vr* to hit each other; * *vi* to buzz.

zumbido *m* humming, buzzing sound.

zumbón/ona *adj* waggish, funny, teasing.

zumo *m* juice.

zurcir *vt* to darn; (*fig*) to join, to unite; to hatch (lies).

zurdo/da *adj* left; left-handed.

zurra *f* flogging; drudgery.

zurrar *vt* (*fam*) to flog, to lay into; (*fig*) to criticize harshly.

zurrón *m* pouch.

zutano/na *m/f* so-and-so; ~ **y fulano** such and such a one, so and so.

English–Spanish
Dictionary

A

a *art* un, uno, una; * *prep* a, al, en.

aback *adv* detrás, atrás; **to be taken ~** quedar consternado/da.

abacus *n* ábaco *m*.

abandon *vt* abandonar, dejar.

abandonment *n* abandono *m*; desamparo *m*.

abase *vt* abatir, humillar.

abasement *n* abatimiento *m*; humillación *f*.

abash *vt* avergonzar, causar confusión.

abate *vt* disminuir, rebajar; * *vi* disminuirse.

abatement *n* rebaja, disminución *f*.

abbess *n* abadesa *f*.

abbey *n* abadía *f*.

abbot *n* abad *m*.

abbreviate *vt* abreviar, acortar.

abbreviation *n* abreviatura *f*.

abdicate *vt* abdicar; renunciar.

abdication *n* abdicación *f*; renuncia *f*.

abdomen *n* abdomen *m*.

abdominal *adj* abdominal.

abduct *vt* secuestrar.

abductor *n* músculo abductor *m*.

abed *adv* en (la) cama.

aberrant *adj* anormal.

aberration *n* error *m*; aberración *f*.

abet *vt*: **to aid and ~** ser cómplice de.

abeyance *n* desuso *m*.

abhor *vt* aborrecer, detestar.

abhorrence *n* aborrecimiento, odio *m*.

abhorrent *adj* repugnante.

abide *vt* soportar, sufrir.

ability *n* habilidad, capacidad, aptitud *f*; **abilities** *pl* talento *m*.

abject *adj* vil, despreciable, bajo/ja; **~ly** *adv* vilmente, bajamente.

abjure *vt* abjurar; renunciar.

ablative *n* (*gr*) ablativo *m*.

ablaze *adj* en llamas.

able *adj* capaz, hábil; **to be ~** poder.

able-bodied *adj* robusto/ta, vigoroso/sa.

ablution *n* ablución *f*.

ably *adv* con habilidad.

abnegation *n* abnegación, resignación *f*.

abnormal *adj* anormal.

abnormality *n* anormalidad *f*.

aboard *adv* a bordo.

abode *n* domicilio *m*.

abolish *vt* abolir, anular, revocar.

abolition *n* abolición, anulación *f*.

abominable *adj* abominable, detestable; **~bly** *adv* abominablemente.

abomination *n* abominación *f*.

aboriginal *adj* aborigen.

aborigines *npl* aborígenes *mpl*.

abort *vi* abortar.

abortion *n* aborto *m*.

abortive *adj* fracasado/da.

abound *vi* abundar; **to ~ with** abundar en.

about *prep* acerca de, acerca; **I carry no money ~ me** no traigo dinero; * *adv* aquí y allá; **to be ~ to** estar a punto de; **to go ~** andar acá y acullá; **to go ~ a thing** emprender alguna cosa; **all ~** en todo lugar.

above *prep* encima; * *adv* arriba; **~ all** sobre todo, principalmente; **~ mentioned** ya mencionado.

aboveboard *adj* legítimo/ma.

abrasion *n* abrasión *f*.

abrasive *adj* abrasivo/va.

abreast *adv* de costado.

abridge *vt* abreviar, compendiar; acortar.

abridgement *n* compendio *m*, recopilación *f*.

abroad *adv* en el extranjero; **to go ~** salir del país.

abrogate *vt* abrogar, anular.

abrogation *n* abrogación, anulación *f*.

abrupt *adj* brusco/ca; ~ly *adv* precipitadamente; bruscamente.

abscess *n* absceso *m*.

abscond *vi* esconderse; huir.

abseiling *n* rappel *m*.

absence *n* ausencia *f*.

absent *adj* ausente; * *vi* ausentarse.

absentee *n* ausente *m*.

absenteeism *n* absentismo *m*.

absent-minded *adj* distraído/da.

absolute *adj* absoluto/ta; categórico/ca; ~ly *adv* totalmente.

absolution *n* absolución *f*.

absolutism *n* absolutismo *m*.

absolve *vt* absolver.

absorb *vt* absorber.

absorbent *adj* absorbente.

absorbent cotton *n* algodón hidrófilo *m*.

absorption *n* absorción *f*.

abstain *vi* abstenerse, privarse.

abstemious *adj* abstemio/mia, sobrio/ria; ~ly *adv* moderadamente.

abstemiousness *n* sobriedad, abstinencia *f*.

abstinence *n* abstinencia *f*; templanza *f*.

abstinent *adj* abstinente, sobrio/ria.

abstract *adj* abstracto/ta; * *n* extracto *m*; sumario *m*; **in the ~** de modo abstracto.

abstraction *n* abstracción *f*.

abstractly *adv* en abstracto.

abstruse *adj* oscuro/ra; ~ly *adv* oscuramente.

absurd *adj* absurdo/da; ~ly *adv* absurdamente.

absurdity *n* absurdidad *f*.

abundance *n* abundancia *f*.

abundant *adj* abundante; ~ly *adv* abundantemente.

abuse *vt* abusar; maltratar; * *n* abuso *m*; injurias *fpl*.

abusive *adj* abusivo/va, ofensivo/va; ~ly *adv* abusivamente.

abut *vi* confinar.

abysmal *adj* abismal; insondable.

abyss *n* abismo *m*.

acacia *n* acacia *f*.

academic *adj* académico/ca.

academician *n* académico *m*.

academy *n* academia *f*.

accede *vi* acceder.

accelerate *vt* acelerar.

accelerator *n* acelerador *m*.

acceleration *n* aceleración *f*.

accent *n* acento *m*; tono *m*; * *vt* acentuar.

accentuate *vt* acentuar.

accentuation *n* acentuación *f*.

accept *vt* aceptar; admitir.

acceptable *adj* aceptable.

acceptability *n* aceptabilidad *f*.

acceptance *n* aceptación *f*.

access *n* acceso *m*; entrada *f*.

accessible *adj* accesible.

accession *n* acceso *m*.

accessory *n* accesorio *m*; (*law*) cómplice *m*.

accident *n* accidente *m*; casualidad *f*.

accidental *adj* casual; ~ly *adv* por casualidad.

acclaim *vt* aclamar, aplaudir.

acclamation *n* aclamación *f*; aplauso *m*.

acclimatize *vt* aclimatar.

accommodate *vt* alojar; complacer.

accommodating *adj* servicial.

accommodations *npl* alojamiento *m*.
accompaniment *n* (*mus*) acompañamiento *m*.
accompanist *n* (*mus*) acompañante *m*.
accompany *vt* acompañar.
accomplice *n* cómplice *m*.
accomplish *vt* efectuar, completar.
accomplished *adj* elegante, consumado/da.
accomplishment *n* cumplimiento *m*; ~s *pl* talentos, conocimientos *mpl*.
accord *n* acuerdo, convenio *m*; **with one ~** unánimemente; **of one's own ~** espontáneamente.
accordance *n*: **in ~ with** de acuerdo con.
according *prep* según, conforme; ~ **as** según que, como; ~**ly** *adv* por consiguiente.
accordion *n* (*mus*) acordeón *m*.
accost *vt* trabar conversación con.
account *n* cuenta *f*; **on no ~** de ninguna manera; bajo ningún concepto; **on ~ of** por motivo de; **to call to ~** pedir cuenta; **to turn to ~** hacer provechoso; * *vt* **to ~ for** explicar.
accountability *n* responsabilidad *f*.
accountable *adj* responsable.
accountancy *n* contabilidad *f*.
accountant *n* contable, contador *m*.
account book *n* libro de cuentas *m*.
account number *n* número *m* de cuenta.
accrue *vi* resultar, provenir.
accumulate *vt* acumular; amontonar; * *vi* crecer.
accumulation *n* acumulación *f*; amontonamiento *m*.
accuracy *n* exactitud *f*.
accurate *adj* exacto/ta; ~**ly** *adv* exactamente.

accursed *adj* maldito/ta.
accusation *n* acusación *f*.
accusative *n* (*gr*) acusativo *m*.
accusatory *adj* acusatorio/ria.
accuse *vt* acusar; culpar.
accused *n* acusado *m*.
accuser *n* acusador/a *m/f*.
accustom *vt* acostumbrar.
accustomed *adj* acostumbrado/da, habitual.
ace *n* as *m*; **within an ~ of** . . . casi; por poco no . . .
acerbic *adj* mordaz.
acetate *n* (*chem*) acetato *m*.
ache *n* dolor *m*; * *vi* doler.
achieve *vt* realizar; obtener.
achievement *n* realización *f*; hazaña *f*.
acid *adj* ácido/da; agrio/ria; * *n* ácido *m*.
acid rain *n* lluvia ácida *f*.
acidity *n* acidez *f*.
acknowledge *vt* reconocer, confesar.
acknowledgment *n* reconocimiento *m*; gratitud *f*.
acme *n* apogeo *m*.
acne *n* acne *m*.
acorn *n* bellota *f*.
acoustics *n* acústica *f*.
acquaint *vt* informar, avisar.
acquaintance *n* conocimiento *m*; conocido *m*.
acquiesce *vi* someterse, consentir, asentir.
acquiescence *n* consentimiento *m*.
acquiescent *adj* deferente.
acquire *vt* adquirir.
acquisition *n* adquisición, obtención *f*.
acquit *vt* absolver.
acquittal *n* absolución *f*.
acre *n* acre *m*.
acrid *adj* acre.
acrimonious *adj* mordaz.

acrimony n acrimonia, acritud f.
across adv de una parte a otra; * prep a través de; **to come ~** toparse con.
act vt representar; * vi hacer; * n acto, hecho m; acción f; **~s of the apostles** Hechos mpl de los Apóstoles.
acting adj interino/na.
action n acción f; batalla f.
action replay n repetición f.
activate vt activar.
active adj activo/va; **~ly** adv activamente.
activity n actividad f.
actor n actor m.
actress n actriz f.
actual adj real; efectivo/va; **~ly** adv en efecto, realmente.
actuary n actuario de seguros m.
acumen n agudeza, perspicacia f.
acupuncture n acupuntura f.
acute adj agudo/da; ingenioso/sa; **~ accent** n acento agudo m; **~ angle** n ángulo agudo m; **~ly** adv con agudeza.
acuteness n perspicacia, sagacidad f.
adage n proverbio m.
adamant adj inflexible.
adapt vt adaptar, acomodar; ajustar.
adaptability n facilidad de adaptarse f.
adaptable adj adaptable.
adaptation n adaptación f.
adaptor n adaptador m.
add vt añadir, agregar; **to ~ up** sumar.
addendum n suplemento m.
adder n culebra f; víbora f.
addict n drogadicto m.
addiction n dependencia f.
addictive adj que crea dependencia.
addition n adición f.
additional adj adicional; **~ly** adv en o por adición.

additive n aditivo m.
address vt dirigir; * n dirección f; discurso m.
adduce vt alegar, aducir.
adenoids npl vegetaciones adenoideas fpl.
adept adj hábil.
adequacy n suficiencia f.
adequate adj adecuado/da; suficiente; **~ly** adv adecuadamente.
adhere vi adherir.
adherence n adherencia f.
adherent n adherente, partidario m.
adhesion n adhesión f.
adhesive adj pegajoso/sa.
adhesiveness n adhesividad f.
adieu adv adiós; * n despedida f.
adipose adj adiposo/sa.
adjacent adj adyacente, contiguo/gua.
adjectival adj adjetivado/da; **~ly** adv como adjetivo.
adjective n adjetivo m.
adjoin vi estar contiguo/gua.
adjoining adj contiguo/gua.
adjourn vt aplazar.
adjournment n prórroga f.
adjudicate vt adjudicar.
adjunct n adjunto m.
adjust vt ajustar, acomodar.
adjustable adj ajustable.
adjustment n ajustamiento, arreglo m.
adjutant n (mil) ayudante m.
ad lib vt improvisar.
administer vt administrar; gobernar; **to ~ an oath** prestar juramento.
administration n administración f; gobierno m.
administrative adj administrativo/va.
administrator n administrador/a m/f.
admirable adj admirable; **~bly** adv admirablemente.

admiral *n* almirante *m*.
admiralship *n* almirante *f*.
admiralty *n* almirantazgo *m*.
admiration *n* admiración *f*.
admire *vt* admirar.
admirer *n* admira/a *m/f*.
admiringly *adv* con admiración.
admissible *adj* admisible.
admission *n* entrada *f*.
admit *vt* admitir; **to ~ to** confesarse culpable de.
admittance *n* entrada *f*.
admittedly *adj* de acuerdo que.
admixture *n* mixtura, mezcla *f*.
admonish *vt* amonestar, reprender.
admonition *n* amonestación *f*; consejo, aviso *m*.
admonitory *adj* exhortatorio/ria.
ad nauseam *adv* hasta el cansancio.
adolescence *n* adolescencia *f*.
adopt *vt* adoptar.
adopted *adj* adoptivo/va.
adoption *n* adopción *f*.
adoptive *adj* adoptivo/va.
adorable *adj* adorable.
adorably *adv* de modo adorable.
adoration *n* adoración *f*.
adore *vt* adorar.
adorn *vt* adornar.
adornment *n* adorno *m*.
adrift *adv* a la deriva.
adroit *adj* diestro/tra, hábil.
adroitness *n* destreza *f*.
adulation *n* adulación, zalamería *f*.
adulatory *adj* lisonjero/ra.
adult *adj* adulto/ta; * *n* adulto *m*; adulta *f*.
adulterate *vt* adulterar, corromper; * *adj* adulterado/da, falsificado/da.
adulteration *n* adulteración, corrupción *f*.
adulterer *n* adúltero *m*.
adulteress *n* adúltera *f*.

adulterous *adj* adúltero/ra.
adultery *n* adulterio *m*.
advance *vt* avanzar; promover; pagar por adelantado; * *vi* hacer progresos; **to make ~s** insinuarse; * *n* avance *m*; paga adelantada *f*.
advanced *adj* avanzado/da.
advancement *n* adelantamiento *m*; progreso *m*; promoción *f*.
advantage *n* ventaja *f*; **to take ~ of** sacar provecho de.
advantageous *adj* ventajoso/sa; **~ly** *adv* ventajosamente.
advantageousness *n* ventaja, utilidad *f*.
advent *n* venida *f*; **Advent** *n* Adviento *m*.
adventitious *adj* adventicio/cia.
adventure *n* aventura *f*.
adventurer *n* aventurero *m*.
adventurous *adj* intrépido/da; valeroso/sa; **~ly** *adv* arriesgadamente.
adverb *n* adverbio *m*.
adverbial *adj* adverbial; **~ly** *adv* como adverbio.
adversary *n* adversario, enemigo *m*.
adverse *adj* adverso/sa, contrario/ria.
adversity *n* calamidad *f*; infortunio *m*.
advertise *vt* anunciar.
advertisement *n* anuncio *m*.
advertising *n* publicidad *f*.
advice *n* consejo *m*; aviso *m*.
advisability *n* prudencia, conveniencia *f*.
advisable *adj* prudente, conveniente.
advise *vt* aconsejar; avisar.
advisedly *adv* prudentemente, avisadamente.
advisory *adj* consultivo/va.
advocacy *n* defensa *f*.

advocate n abogado m; protector m;
* vt abogar por.
advocateship n abogacía f.
aerial n antena f.
aerobics npl aerobic m.
aerometer n areómetro m.
aeroplane n avión m.
aerosol n aerosol m.
aerostat n globo aerostático m.
aesthetic adj estético/ca; ~s npl estética f.
afar adv lejos, distante; **from ~** desde lejos.
affability n afabilidad, urbanidad f.
affable adj afable, complaciente;
~**bly** adv afablemente.
affair n asunto m; negocio m.
affect vt conmover; afectar.
affectation n afectación f.
affected adj afectado/da, lleno/na de afectación; ~**ly** adv con afectación.
affectingly adv con afecto.
affection n cariño m.
affectionate adj afectuoso/sa; ~**ly** adv cariñosamente.
affidavit n declaración jurada f.
affiliate vt afiliar.
affiliation n afiliación f.
affinity n afinidad f.
affirm vt afirmar, declarar.
affirmation n afirmación f.
affirmative adj afirmativo/va; ~**ly** adv afirmativamente.
affix vt pegar; * n (gr) afijo m.
afflict vt afligir.
affliction n aflicción f; dolor m.
affluence n abundancia f.
affluent adj opulento/ta.
afflux n confluencia, afluencia f.
afford vt dar; proveer.
affray n asalto m; tumulto m.
affront n afrenta, injuria f; * vt afrentar, insultar, ultrajar.

aflame adv en llamas.
afloat adv flotante, a flote.
afraid adj espantado/da, tímido/da; **I am ~** temo.
afresh adv de nuevo, otra vez.
aft adv (mar) a popa.
after prep después; detrás; según;
* adv después; ~ **all** después de todo.
afterbirth n secundinas fpl.
after-effects npl consecuencias fpl.
afterlife n vida venidera f.
aftermath n consecuencias fpl.
afternoon n tarde f.
aftershave n aftershave m.
aftertaste n resabio m.
afterwards adv después.
again adv otra vez; ~ **and** ~ muchas veces; **as much** ~ otra vez tanto.
against prep contra; ~ **the grain** a contrapelo; de mala gana.
agate n ágata f.
age n edad f; **under** ~ menor; * vt envejecer.
aged adj viejo/ja, anciano/na.
agency n agencia f.
agenda n orden del día m.
agent n agente m.
agglomerate vt aglomerar.
agglomeration n aglomeración f.
aggrandizement n engrandecimiento m.
aggravate vt agravar, exagerar.
aggravation n agravación f.
aggregate n agregado m.
aggregation n agregación f.
aggression n agresión f.
aggressive adj ofensivo/va.
aggressor n agresor m.
aggrieved adj ofendido/da.
aghast adj horrorizado/da.
agile adj ágil; diestro/tra.
agility n agilidad f; destreza f.

agitate vt agitar.

agitation n agitación f; perturbación f.

agitator n agitador, incitador m.

ago adv pasado, largo tiempo; después; **how long ~?** ¿cuánto hace?

agog adj emocionado/da.

agonizing adj atroz.

agony n agonía f.

agree vt convenir; * vi estar de acuerdo/da.

agreeable adj agradable; amable; **~bly** adv agradablemente; **~ with** según, conforme a.

agreeableness n amabilidad, gracia f.

agreed adj establecido/da, convenido/da; **~!** adv ¡de acuerdo!

agreement n acuerdo m.

agricultural adj agrario/ria.

agriculture n agricultura f.

agriculturist n agricultor m.

agronomy n agronomía f.

aground adv (mar) encallado.

ah! excl ¡ah!, ¡ay!

ahead adv más allá, delante de otro; (mar) por la proa.

ahoy! excl (mar) ¡ohe!

aid vt ayudar, socorrer; **to ~ and abet** ser cómplice de; * n ayuda f; auxilio, socorro m.

aide-de-camp n (mil) ayudante de campo m.

AIDS n SIDA m.

ail vt afligir, molestar.

ailing adj doliente.

ailment n dolencia, indisposición f.

aim vt apuntar aspirar a; intentar; * n designio m; puntería f.

aimless adj sin designio, sin objeto; **~ly** a la deriva.

air n aire m; * vt airear; ventilar.

airbag n airbag m.

air balloon n globo aerostático m.

airborne adj aerotransportado/da.

air-conditioned adj climatizado/da.

air conditioning n aire acondicionado m.

aircraft n avión m.

air cushion n cojinete rellenado de aire m.

air force n fuerzas aéreas fpl.

air freshener n ambientador m.

air gun n escopeta de aire comprimido f.

air hole n respiradero m.

airless adj falto de ventilación, sofocado/da.

airlift n puente aéreo m.

airline n línea aérea f.

airmail n: **by ~** por avión.

airport n aeropuerto m.

airport tax n tasas de aeropuerto f.

air pump n bomba de aire f.

airsick adj mareado/da.

airstrip n pista de aterrizaje f.

air terminal n terminal f.

airtight adj herméticamente cerrado/da.

airy adj bien ventilado/da.

aisle n nave de una iglesia f.

ajar adj entreabierto/ta.

akimbo adj corvo/va.

akin adj parecido/da.

alabaster n alabastro m; * adj alabastrino/na.

alacrity n presteza f.

alarm n alarma f; * vt alarmar; inquietar.

alarm bell n timbre de alarma m.

alarmist n alarmista m.

alas adv desgraciadamente.

albeit conj aunque.

album n álbum m.

alchemist n alquimista m.

alchemy n alquimia f.

alcohol n alcohol m.
alcoholic adj alcohólico/ca; * n alcoholizado m.
alcove n nicho m.
alder n aliso m.
ale n cerveza f.
alert adj vigilante; alerto/ta; * n alerta f.
alertness n cuidado m; vigilancia f.
algae npl alga f.
algebra n álgebra f.
algebraic adj algebraico/ca.
alias adj alias.
alibi n (law) coartada f.
alien adj ajeno/na; * n forastero m.
alienate vt enajenar.
alienation n enajenación f.
alight vi apearse; * adj encendido/da.
align vt alinear.
alike adj semejante, igual; * adv igualmente.
alimentation n alimentación f.
alimony n alimentos mpl.
alive adj vivo/va, viviente; activo/va.
alkali n álcali m.
alkaline adj alcalino/na.
all adj todo/da; * adv totalmente; ~ at once, ~ of a sudden de repente; ~ the same sin embargo; ~ the better tanto mejor; not at ~! ino hay de qué!; once for ~ una vez por todas; * n todo m.
allay vt aliviar.
all clear n luz verde f.
allegation n alegación f.
allege vt alegar; declarar.
allegiance n lealtad, fidelidad f.
allegorical adj alegórico/ca; ~ly adv alegóricamente.
allegory n alegoría f.
allegro n (mus) alegro m.
allergy n alergia f.

alleviate vt aliviar, aligerar.
alleviation n alivio m; mitigación f.
alley n callejuela f.
alliance n alianza f.
allied adj aliado/da.
alligator n caimán m.
alliteration n aliteración f.
all-night adj abierto/ta toda la noche.
allocate vt repartir.
allocation n cuota f.
allot vt asignar.
allow vt conceder; permitir; dar, pagar; to ~ for tener en cuenta.
allowable adj admisible, permitido/da.
allowance n concesión f.
alloy n liga, mezcla, aleación f.
all right adv bien.
all-round adj completo/ta.
allspice n pimienta de Jamaica f.
allude vt aludir.
allure n fascinación f.
alluring adj seductor/a; ~ly adv seductoramente.
allurement n aliciente, atractivo m.
allusion n alusión f.
allusive adj alusivo/va; ~ly adv de modo alusivo.
alluvial adj aluvial.
ally n aliado m; * vt aliar.
almanac n almanaque m.
almighty adj omnipotente, todopoderoso/sa.
almond n almendra f.
almond tree n almendro m.
almost adv casi; cerca de.
alms n limosna f.
aloft prep arriba.
alone adj solo; * adv solamente, sólo; to leave ~ dejar en paz.
along adv a lo largo; ~ side al lado.
aloof adv lejos.

aloud *adj* en voz alta.
alphabet *n* alfabeto *m*.
alphabetical *adj* alfabético/ca; ~**ly** *adv* por orden alfabético.
alpine *adj* alpino/na.
already *adv* ya.
also *adv* también, además.
altar *n* altar *m*.
altarpiece *n* retablo *m*.
alter *vt* modificar.
alteration *n* alteración *f*.
altercation *n* altercado *m*.
alternate *adj* alterno/na; * *vt* alternar, variar; ~**ly** *adv* alternativamente.
alternating *adj* alterno/na.
alternation *n* alternación *f*.
alternator *n* alternador *m*.
alternative *n* alternativa *f*; * *adj* alternative; ~**ly** *adv* si no.
although *conj* aunque, no obstante.
altitude *n* altitud, altura *f*.
altogether *adv* del todo.
alum *n* alumbre *m*.
aluminium *n* aluminio *m*.
aluminous *adj* aluminoso/sa.
always *adv* siempre, constantemente.
a.m. *adv* de la mañana.
amalgam *n* amalgama *f*.
amalgamate *vt, vi* amalgamar(se).
amalgamation *n* amalgamación *f*.
amanuensis *n* amanuense, secretario *m*.
amaryllis *n* (*bot*) amarillas *f*.
amass *vt* acumular, amontonar.
amateur *n* aficionado *m*, amateur *m/f*.
amateurish *adj* torpe.
amatory *adj* amatorio/ria; erótico/ca.
amaze *vt* asombrar.
amazement *n* asombro *m*.
amazing *adj* pasmoso/sa; ~**ly** *adv* extraordinariamente.

amazon *n* amazona *f*.
ambassador *n* embajador *m*.
ambassadress *n* embajadora *f*.
amber *n* ámbar *m*; * *adj* ambarino/na.
ambidextrous *adj* ambidextro/tra, ambidiestro/tra.
ambient *adj* ambiente.
ambiguity *n* ambigüedad, duda *f*.
ambiguous *adj* ambiguo; ~**ly** *adv* ambiguamente.
ambition *n* ambición *f*.
ambitious *adj* ambicioso/sa; ~**ly** *adv* ambiciosamente.
amble *vi* andar sin prisa.
ambulance *n* ambulancia *f*.
ambush *n* emboscada *f*; **to lie in** ~ estar emboscado/da; * *vt* tender una emboscada a.
ameliorate *vt* mejorar.
amelioration *n* mejoramiento *m*.
amenable *adj* sensible.
amend *vt* enmendar.
amendable *adj* reparable, corregible.
amendment *n* enmienda *f*.
amends *npl* compensación *f*.
amenities *npl* comodidades *fpl*.
America *n* América *f*.
American *adj* americano/na.
amethyst *n* amatista *f*.
amiability *n* amabilidad *f*.
amiable *adj* amable.
amiableness *n* amabilidad *f*.
amiably *adv* amablemente.
amicable *adj* amigable, amistoso/sa; ~**bly** *adv* amistosamente.
amid(st) *prep* entre, en medio de.
amiss *adv*: **something's** ~ algo pasa.
ammonia *n* amoniaco *m*.
ammunition *n* municiones *fpl*.
amnesia *n* amnesia *f*.

amnesty n amnistía f.
among(st) prep entre, en medio de.
amoral adv amoral.
amorous adj amoroso/sa; ~ly adv amorosamente.
amorphous adj informe.
amount n importe m; cantidad f; * vi sumar.
amp(ere) n amperio m.
amphibian n anfibio m.
amphibious adj anfibio/bia.
amphitheatre n anfiteatro m.
ample adj amplio/lia.
ampleness n amplitud, abundancia f.
amplification n amplificación f; extensión f.
amplifier n amplificador m.
amplify vt ampliar, extender.
amplitude n amplitud, extensión f.
amply adv ampliamente.
amputate vt amputar.
amputation n amputación f.
amulet n amuleto m.
amuse vt entretener, divertir.
amusement n diversión f, pasatiempo, entretenimiento m.
amusing adj divertido/da; ~ly adv entretenidamente.
an art un, uno, una.
anachronism n anacronismo m.
anaemia n anemia f.
anaemic adj (med) anémico/ca.
anaesthetic n anestesia f.
analog adj (comput) analógico/ca.
analogous adj análogo.
analogy n analogía f.
analyse vt analizar.
analysis n análisis m invar.
analyst n analizador/a m/f.
analytical adj analítico/ca; ~ly adv analíticamente.
anarchic adj anárquico/ca.
anarchist adj anarquista.

anarchy n anarquía f.
anatomical adj anatómico/ca; ~ly adv anatómicamente.
anatomize vt anatomizar.
anatomy n anatomía f.
ancestor n: ~s pl antepasados mpl.
ancestral adj hereditario/ria.
ancestry n raza, alcurnia f.
anchor n ancla f; * vi anclar; to weigh ~ zarpar.
anchorage n fondeadero m.
anchovy n anchoa f.
ancient adj antiguo.
ancillary adj auxiliar.
and conj y, e.
anecdotal adj anecdótico/ca.
anecdote n anécdota f
anemone n (bot) anémona f.
anew adv de nuevo, nuevamente.
angel n ángel m.
angelic adj angélico/ca.
anger n cólera f; * vt enojar, irritar.
angle n ángulo m; * vt pescar con caña.
angled adj anguloso/sa.
angler n pescador/a de caña m/f.
anglicism n anglicismo m.
angling n pesca con caña f.
angrily adv enojado.
angry adj enojado/da.
anguish n ansia, angustia f.
angular adj angular.
angularity n forma angular f.
animal n adj animal m.
animate vt animar; * adj viviente.
animated adj vivo/va.
animation n animación f.
animosity n rencor m.
animus n odio m.
anise n anís m.
aniseed n anís m.
ankle n tobillo m; ~ bone hueso del tobillo m.

annals *n* anales *mpl*.

annex *vt* anejar; * *n* anejo *m*.

annexation *n* anexión *f*.

annihilate *vt* aniquilar.

annihilation *n* aniquilación *f*.

anniversary *n* aniversario *m*.

annotate *vi* anotar.

annotation *n* anotación *f*.

announce *vt* anunciar, publicar.

announcement *n* anuncio *m*.

announcer *n* locutor/a *m/f*.

annoy *vt* molestar.

annoyance *n* molestia *f*.

annoying *adj* molesto/ta; fastidioso/sa.

annual *adj* anual; **~ly** *adv* anualmente, cada año.

annuity *n* renta vitalicia *f*.

annul *vt* anular.

annulment *n* anulación *f*.

annunciation *n* anunciación *f*.

anodyne *adj* anodino/na.

anoint *vt* untar, ungir.

anomalous *adj* anómalo.

anomaly *n* anomalía, irregularidad *f*.

anon *adv* más tarde.

anonymity *n* anonimato *m*.

anonymous *adj* anónimo/ma; **~ly** *adj* anónimamente.

anorexia *n* anorexia *f*.

another *adj* otro/tra, diferente; **one ~** uno a otro.

answer *vt* responder, replicar; corresponder; **to ~ for** responder de *o* por; **to ~ to** corresponder a; * *n* respuesta, réplica *f*.

answerable *adj* responsable.

answering machine *n* contestador automático *m*.

ant *n* hormiga *f*.

antagonism *n* antagonismo *m*; rivalidad *f*.

antagonist *n* antagonista *m*.

antagonize *vt* provocar.

antarctic *adj* antártico/ca.

anteater *n* oso hormiguero *m*.

antecedent *n*: **~s** *pl* antecedentes *mpl*.

antechamber *n* antecámara *f*.

antedate *vt* antedatar.

antelope *n* antílope *m*.

antenna *npl* antena *f*.

anterior *adj* anterior, precedente.

anthem *n* himno *m*.

ant hill *n* hormiguero *m*.

anthology *n* antología *f*.

anthracite *n* antracita *f*.

anthropologist *n* antropólogo/ga *m/f*.

anthropology *n* antropología *f*.

anti-aircraft *adj* antiaéreo/rea.

antibiotic *n* antibiótico *m*.

antibody *n* anticuerpo *m*.

Antichrist *n* Anticristo *m*.

anticipate *vt* anticipar, prevenir.

anticipation *n* anticipación *f*.

anticlockwise *adv* en sentido contrario al de las agujas del reloj.

antidote *n* antídoto *m*.

antifreeze *n* anticongelante *m*.

antimony *n* antimonio *m*.

antipathy *n* antipatía *f*.

antipodes *npl* antípodas *fpl*.

antiquarian *n* anticuario *m*.

antiquated *adj* antiguo/gua; * *n* antigüedad *f*.

antiquity *n* antigüedad *f*.

antiseptic *adj* antiséptico/ca.

antisocial *adj* antisocial.

antithesis *n* antítesis *f*.

antler *n* cuerna *f*.

anvil *n* yunque *m*.

anxiety *n* ansiedad *f*, ansia *f*; afán *m*, zozobra *f*.

anxious *adj* ansioso/sa; **~ly** *adv* ansiosamente; **to be ~** *vi* zozobrar.

any *adj pn* cualquier, cualquiera; alguno, alguna; todo; ~**body** alguien, nadie, cualquiera; ~**how** de cualquier manera; ~**more** más; ~**place** en ninguna parte; ~**thing** algo, nada, cualquier cosa.
apace *adv* rápidamente.
apart *adv* aparte, separadamente.
apartment *n* apartamento, departamento *m*.
apartment house *n* casa de apartamentos *f*.
apathetic *adj* apático/ca.
apathy *n* apatía *f*.
ape *n* mono *m*; * *vt* remedar.
aperture *n* abertura *f*.
apex *n* ápice *m*.
aphorism *n* aforismo *m*; máxima *f*.
apiary *n* colmenar *m*.
apiece *adv* por cabeza, por persona.
aplomb *n* aplomo *m*.
Apocalypse *n* Apocalipsis *m*.
apocrypha *npl* libros apócrifos *mpl*.
apocryphal *adj* apócrifo/fa, no canónico/ca.
apologetic *adj* de disculpa.
apologist *n* apologista *m*.
apologize *vt* disculpar.
apology *n* apología, defensa *f*.
apoplexy *n* apoplejía *f*.
apostle *n* apóstol *m*.
apostolic *adj* apostólico/ca.
apostrophe *n* apóstrofe *m*.
apotheosis *n* apoteosis *f*.
appal *vt* espantar, aterrar.
appalling *adj* espantoso/sa.
apparatus *n* aparato *m*.
apparel *n* traje, vestido *m*.
apparent *adj* evidente, aparente; ~**ly** *adv* por lo visto.
apparition *n* aparición, visión *f*.
appeal *vi* apelar, recurrir a un tribunal superior; * *n* (*law*) apelación *f*.

appealing *adj* atractivo/va.
appear *vi* aparecer.
appearance *n* apariencia *f*.
appease *vt* aplacar.
appellant *n* (*law*) apelante *m*.
append *vt* anejar.
appendage *n* cosa accesoria *f*.
appendicitis *n* apendicitis *f*.
appendix *n* apéndice *m*.
appertain *vi* tocar a.
appetite *n* apetito *m*.
appetizing *adj* apetitivo/va.
applaud *vi* aplaudir.
applause *n* aplausos *mpl*.
apple *n* manzana *f*.
apple pie *n* pastelillo de manzanas *m*; **in** ~ **order** en sumo orden.
apple tree *n* manzano *m*.
appliance *n* aparato *m*.
applicability *n* aplicabilidad *f*.
applicable *adj* aplicable.
applicant *n* aspirante, candidato *m*.
application *n* aplicación *f*; solicitud *f*.
applied *adj* aplicado/da.
apply *vt* aplicar; * *vi* dirigirse a, recurrir a.
appoint *vt* nombrar.
appointee *n* persona nombrada *f*.
appointment *n* cita *f*; nombramiento *m*.
apportion *vt* repartir.
apportionment *n* repartición *f*.
apposite *adj* adaptado/da.
apposition *n* aposición *f*.
appraisal *n* estimación *f*.
appraise *vt* tasar; estimar.
appreciable *adj* sensible.
appreciably *adv* sensiblemente.
appreciate *vt* apreciar; agradecer.
appreciation *n* aprecio *m*.
appreciative *adj* agradecido/da.
apprehend *vt* arrestar.
apprehension *n* aprensión *f*.

apprehensive *adj* aprensivo/va, tímido/da.

apprentice *n* aprendiz *m*; * *vt* poner de aprendiz.

apprenticeship *n* aprendizaje *m*.

apprise *vt* informar.

approach *vt* (*vi*) aproximar(se); * *n* acceso *m*.

approachable *adj* accesible.

approbation *n* aprobación *f*.

appropriate *vt* apropiarse de; * *adj* apropiado/da.

approval *n* aprobación *f*.

approve (of) *vt* aprobar.

approximate *vi* acercarse; * *adj* aproximativo/va; ~**ly** *adv* aproximadamente.

approximation *n* aproximación *f*.

apricot *n* damasco, albaricoque *m*.

April *n* abril *m*.

apron *n* delantal *m*.

apse *n* ábside *m*.

apt *adj* apto/ta, idóneo/nea; ~**ly** *adv* oportunamente.

aptitude *n* aptitud *f*.

aqualung *n* escafandra autónoma *f*.

aquarium *n* acuario *m*.

Aquarius *n* Acuario *m*.

aquatic *adj* acuático/ca.

aqueduct *n* acueducto *m*.

aquiline *adj* aguileño/ña.

arabesque *n* arabesco *m*.

arable *adj* labrantío/tía.

arbiter *n* árbitro *m*.

arbitrariness *n* arbitrariedad *f*.

arbitrary *adj* arbitrario/ria.

arbitrate *vt* arbitrar, juzgar como árbitro.

arbitration *n* arbitrio *m*.

arbitrator *n* árbitro *m*.

arbour *n* emparrado *m*; enramada *f*.

arcade *n* galería *f*.

arch *n* arco *m*; * *adj* malicioso/sa.

archaeological *adj* arqueológico/ca.

archaeologist *n* arqueólogo/ga *m/f*.

archaeology *n* arqueología *f*.

archaic *adj* arcaico/ca.

archangel *n* arcángel *m*.

archbishop *n* arzobispo *m*.

archbishopric *n* arzobispado *m*.

archer *n* arquero *m*.

archery *n* tiro con arco *m*.

architect *n* arquitecto/ta *m/f*.

architectural *adj* arquitectónico/ca.

architecture *n* arquitectura *f*.

archives *npl* archivos *mpl*.

archivist *n* archivero/ra *m/f*.

archly *adv* maliciosamente.

archway *n* arcada, bóveda *f*.

arctic *adj* ártico/ca.

ardent *adj* apasionado/da; ~**ly** *adv* con pasión.

ardour *n* ardor *m*; vehemencia *f*; pasión *f*.

arduous *adj* arduo, difícil.

area *n* área *f*; espacio *m*, zona *f*.

arena *n* arena *f*.

arguably *adv* posiblemente.

argue *vi* discutir; * *vt* sostener.

argument *n* argumento *m*, controversia *f*.

argumentation *n* argumentación *f*.

argumentative *adj* discutidor/a.

aria *n* (*mus*) aria *f*.

arid *adj* árido/da, estéril.

aridity *n* sequedad *f*.

Aries *n* Aries *m*.

aright *adv* bien; **to set ~** rectificar.

arise *vi* levantarse; nacer.

aristocracy *n* aristocracia *f*.

aristocrat *n* aristócrata *m/f*.

aristocratic *adj* aristocrático/ca; ~**ally** *adv* aristocráticamente.

arithmetic *n* aritmética *f*.

arithmetical *adj* aritmético/ca; ~**ly** *adv* aritméticamente.

ark n arca f.
arm n brazo m; arma f; * vt, vi armar(se).
armament n armamento m.
armchair n sillón m.
armed adj armado/da.
armful n brazada f.
armhole n sobaco m.
armistice n armisticio m.
armour n armadura f.
armoured car n carro blindado m.
armoury n arsenal m.
armpit n sobaco m.
armrest n apoyabrazos m invar.
army n ejército m; tropas fpl.
aroma n aroma m.
aromatherapy n aromaterapia f.
aromatic adj aromático/ca.
around prep alrededor de; * adv alrededor.
arouse vt despertar; excitar.
arraign vt acusar.
arraignment n acusación f; proceso criminal m.
arrange vt organizar.
arrangement n colocación f; arreglo.
arrant adj consumado/da.
array n serie f.
arrears npl resto de una deuda m; atraso m.
arrest n arresto m; * vt detener, arrestar.
arrival n llegada f.
arrive vi llegar.
arrogance n arrogancia, presunción f.
arrogant adj arrogante, presuntuoso/sa; ~ly adv arrogantemente.
arrogate vt arrogarse.
arrogation n arrogación f.
arrow n flecha f.
arsenal n (mil) arsenal m; (mar) atarazana, armería f.

arsenic n arsénico m.
arson n fuego incendiario m.
art n arte m.
arterial adj arterial.
artesian well n pozo artesiano m.
artery n arteria f.
artful adj ingenioso/sa.
artfulness n astucia, habilidad f.
art gallery n pinacoteca f.
arthritis n artritis f.
artichoke n alcachofa f.
article n artículo m.
articulate vt articular, pronunciar distintamente.
articulated adj articulado/da.
articulation n articulación f.
artifice n artificio, fraude m.
artificial adj artificial; artificioso/sa; ~ly adv artificialmente; artificiosamente.
artificial insemination n inseminación artificial f.
artificiality n artificialidad f.
artillery n artillería f.
artisan n artesano/na m/f.
artist n artista m.
artistic adj artístico/ca.
artistry n habilidad f.
artless adj sencillo, simple; ~ly adv sencillamente, naturalmente.
artlessness n sencillez f.
as conj como; mientras; también; visto que, puesto que; ~ for, ~ to en cuanto a.
asbestos n asbesto, amianto m.
ascend vi ascender, subir.
ascendancy n dominio m.
ascension n ascensión f.
ascent n subida f.
ascertain vt establecer.
ascetic adj ascético/ca; * n asceta m.
ascribe vt atribuir.
ash n (bot) fresno m; ceniza f.

ashamed *adj* avergonzado/da.

ashore *adv* en tierra, a tierra; **to go ~** desembarcar.

ashtray *n* cenicero *m*.

Ash Wednesday *n* miércoles de ceniza *m*.

aside *adv* a un lado.

ask *vt* pedir, rogar; **to ~ after** preguntar por; **to ~ for** pedir; **to ~ out** invitar.

askance *adv* desconfiado/da.

askew *adv* de lado.

asleep *adj* dormido/da; **to fall ~** dormirse.

asparagus *n* espárrago *m*.

aspect *n* aspecto *m*.

aspen *n* álamo temblón *m*.

aspersion *n* calumnia *f*.

asphalt *n* asfalto *m*.

asphyxia *n* (*med*) asfixia *f*.

asphyxiate *vt* asfixiar.

asphyxiation *n* asfixia *f*.

aspirant *n* aspirante *m*.

aspirate *vt* aspirar, pronunciar con aspiración; * *n* sonido aspirado *m*.

aspiration *n* aspiración *f*.

aspire *vi* aspirar, desear.

aspirin *n* aspirina *f*.

ass *n* asno *m*; **she ~** burra *f*.

assail *vt* asaltar, atacar.

assailant *n* asaltante m/f, agresor/a m/f.

assassin *n* asesino/na m/f.

assassinate *vt* asesinar.

assassination *n* asesinato *m*.

assault *n* asalto *m*; * *vt* acometer, asaltar.

assemblage *n* multitud *f*.

assemble *vt* reunir, convocar; * *vi* juntarse.

assembly *n* asamblea, junta *f*; congreso *m*.

assembly line *n* cadena de montaje *f*.

assent *n* asentimiento *m*; * *vi* asentir.

assert *vt* sostener, mantener; afirmar.

assertion *n* aserción *f*.

assertive *adj* perentorio/ria.

assess *vt* valorar.

assessment *n* valoración *f*.

assessor *n* asesor/a m/f.

assets *npl* bienes *mpl*.

assiduous *adj* diligente, aplicado/da; **~ly** *adv* diligentemente.

assign *vt* asignar.

assignation *n* cita *f*.

assignment *n* asignación *f*; tarea *f*.

assimilate *vt* asimilar.

assimilation *n* asimilación *f*.

assist *vt* asistir, ayudar, socorrer.

assistance *n* asistencia *f*; socorro *m*.

assistant *n* asistente, ayudante *m*.

associate *vt* asociar; * *adj* asociado/da; * *n* socio *m*.

association *n* asociación, sociedad *f*.

assonance *n* asonancia *f*.

assorted *adj* surtido/da.

assortment *n* surtido *m*.

assuage *vt* mitigar, suavizar.

assume *vt* asumir; suponer.

assumption *n* supuesto *m*.

Assumption *n* Asunción *f*.

assurance *n* seguro *m*.

assure *vt* asegurar.

assuredly *adv* sin duda.

asterisk *n* asterisco *m*.

astern *adv* (*mar*) a popa.

asthma *n* asma *f*.

asthmatic *adj* asmático/ca.

astonish *vt* pasmar, sorprender.

astonishing *adj* asombroso/sa; **~ly** *adv* asombrosamente.

astonishment *n* asombro *m*.

astound *vt* pasmar.

astray *adv*: **to go ~** extraviarse; **to lead ~** llevar por mal camino.

astride *adv* a horcajadas.

astringent *adj* astringente.
astrologer *n* astrólogo/ga *m/f*.
astrological *adj* astrológico/ca.
astrology *n* astrología *f*.
astronaut *n* astronauta *m/f*.
astronomer *n* astrónomo *m*.
astronomical *adj* astronómico/ca.
astronomy *n* astronomía *f*.
astute *adj* astuto/ta.
asylum *n* asilo, refugio *m*.
at *prep* a; en; ~ **once** en seguida; ya; ~ **all** en absoluto; ~ **all events** en todo caso; ~ **first** al principio; ~ **last** por fin.
atheism *n* ateísmo *m*.
atheist *n* ateo *m*, atea *f*.
athlete *n* atleta *m/f*.
athletic *adj* atlético/ca.
atlas *n* atlas *m invar*.
atmosphere *n* atmósfera *f*.
atmospheric *adj* atmosférico/ca.
atom *n* átomo *m*.
atom bomb *n* bomba atómica *f*.
atomic *adj* atómico/ca.
atone *vt* expiar.
atonement *n* expiación *f*.
atop *adv* encima.
atrocious *adj* atroz; ~**ly** *adv* atrozmente.
atrocity *n* atrocidad, enormidad *f*.
atrophy *n* (*med*) atrofia *f*.
attach *vt* adjuntar.
attaché *n* agregado *m*.
attachment *n* afecto *m*.
attack *vt* atacar; acometer; * *n* ataque *m*.
attacker *n* asaltante *m*.
attain *vt* conseguir, obtener.
attainable *adj* asequible.
attempt *vt* intentar; probar, experimentar; * *n* intento *m*, tentativa *f*.
attend *vt* servir; asistir; **to** ~ **to** ocuparse de; * *vi* prestar atención.

attendance *n* presencia *f*.
attendant *n* sirviente *m*.
attention *n* atención *f*; cuidado *m*.
attentive *adj* atento/ta; cuidadoso/sa; ~**ly** *adv* con atención.
attenuate *vt* atenuar, disminuir.
attest *vt* atestiguar.
attic *n* desván *m*; guardilla *f*.
attire *n* atavío *m*.
attitude *n* actitud, postura *f*.
attorney *n* abogado/da *m/f*.
attract *vt* atraer.
attraction *n* atracción *f*; atractivo *m*.
attractive *adj* atractivo/va.
attribute *vt* atribuir; * *n* atributo *m*.
attrition *n* agotamiento *m*.
auburn *adj* moreno/na, castaño/ña.
auction *n* subasta *f*.
auctioneer *n* subastador/a, rematador/a *m/f*.
audacious *adj* audaz, temerario/ria; ~**ly** *adv* atrevidamente.
audacity *n* audacia, osadía *f*.
audible *adj* perceptible al oído; ~**ly** *adv* de manera audible.
audience *n* audiencia *f*; auditorio *m*.
audit *n* auditoría *f*; * *vt* auditar.
auditor *n* censor/a de cuentas *m/f*.
auditory *adj* auditivo/va.
augment *vt* aumentar, acrecentar; * *vi* crecer.
augmentation *n* aumentación *f*; aumento *m*.
August *n* agosto *m*.
august *adj* majestuoso/sa.
aunt *n* tía *f*.
au pair *n* au pair *f*.
aura *n* aura *f*.
auspices *npl* auspicios *mpl*.
auspicious *adj* propicio/cia; ~**ly** *adv* favorablemente.
austere *adj* austero/ra, severo/ra; ~**ly** *adv* austeramente.

austerity n austeridad f.
authentic adj auténtico/ca; ~**ly** adv auténticamente.
authenticate vt autenticar.
authenticity n autenticidad f.
author n autor/a m/f; escritor/a m/f.
authoress n autora; escritora f.
authoritarian adj autoritario/ria.
authoritative adj autoritativo/va; ~**ly** adv autoritativamente, con autoridad.
authority n autoridad f.
authorization n autorización f.
authorize vt autorizar.
authorship n autoría f.
automobile n coche, auto m.
autocrat n autócrata m.
autocratic adj autocrático/ca.
autograph n autógrafo m.
automated adj automatizado/da.
automatic adj automático/ca.
automaton n autómata m.
autonomy n autonomía f.
autopsy n autopsia f.
autumn n otoño m.
autumnal adj otoñal.
auxiliary adj auxiliar, asistente.
avail vt: to ~ **oneself of** aprovecharse de; * n: **to no** ~ en vano.
available adj disponible.
avalanche n alud m.
avarice n avaricia f.
avaricious adj avaro/ra.
avenge vt vengarse, castigar.
avenue n avenida f.
aver vt afirmar, declarar.
average vt tomar un término medio; * n término medio m.

aversion n aversión f, disgusto m.
avert vt desviar, apartar.
aviary n pajarera f.
avoid vt evitar, escapar, huir; * vr zafarse de.
avoidable adj evitable.
await vt aguardar.
awake vt despertar; * vi despertarse; * adj despierto/ta.
awakening n despertar.
award vt otorgar; * n premio m; sentencia, decisión f.
aware adj consciente; vigilante.
awareness n conciencia f.
away adv ausente, fuera; ~! ¡fuera!, ¡quita de ahí!, ¡marcha! **far and** ~ de mucho, con mucho.
away game n partido fuera de casa m.
awe n miedo, temor m.
awe-inspiring, awesome adj imponente.
awful adj tremendo/da; horroroso/sa; ~**ly** adv terriblemente.
awhile adv un rato, algún tiempo.
awkward adj torpe, rudo/da, poco diestro/tra; ~**ly** adv groseramente, toscamente.
awkwardness n tosquedad, grosería, poca habilidad f.
awl n lezna f.
awning n (mar) toldo m.
awry adv oblicuamente, torcidamente, al través.
axe n hacha f; * vt despedir; cortar.
axiom n axioma m.
axis n eje m.
axle n eje m.
ay(e) excl sí.

B

baa n balido m; * vi balar.

babble vi charlar, parlotear; ~, **bab-
bling** n charla, cháchara f.

babbler n charlador/a, charlatán/
ana m/f.

babe, baby n niño/a, pequeño/a,
nene/a m/f; **small ~** mamón/ona m/f.

baboon n babuino m.

babyhood n niñez f.

babyish adj niñero/ra; pueril.

baby carriage n cochecito m.

baby linen n ropita de niño f.

bachelor n soltero m; bachiller m.

bachelorship n soltería f; bachillerato m.

back n dorso m; revés de la mano m;
* adv atrás, detrás; **a few years ~**
hace algunos años; * vt sostener,
apoyar, favorecer.

backbite vt hablar mal del que está
ausente; difamar.

backbiter n detractor/a m/f.

backbone n hueso dorsal, espinazo m.

backdate vt antedatar.

backdoor n puerta trasera f.

backer n partidario/ria m/f.

backgammon n backgammon m.

background n fondo m.

backlash n reacción f.

backlog n trabajo acumulado m.

back number n número atrasado m.

backpack n mochila f.

back payment n paga atrasada f.

backside n trasero m.

back-up lights npl (auto) luces de
marcha atrás fpl.

backward adj tardo/da, lento/ta;
* adv hacia atrás.

bacon n tocino m.

bad adj mal/malo; perverso/sa; infeliz; dañoso/sa; indispuesto/ta; ~**ly**
adv malamente.

badge n señal f; símbolo m; divisa f.

badger n tejón m; * vt fatigar; cansar, atormentar.

badminton n bádminton m.

badness n maldad, mala calidad f.

baffle vt confundir, hundir; acosar.

bag n saco m; bolsa f.

baggage n bagaje, equipaje m.

bagpipe n gaita f.

bail n fianza, caución (juratoria) f;
fiador m; * vt caucionar, fiar.

bailiff n alguacil m; mayordomo m.

bait vt cebar; atraer; * n cebo m; anzuelo m.

baize n bayeta f.

bake vt cocer en horno.

bakery n panadería f.

baker n hornero/ra, panadero/ra
m/f; ~'**s dozen** trece piezas.

baking n cocción f.

baking powder n levadura f.

balance n balanza f; equilibrio m;
saldo de una cuenta m; **to lose
one's ~** caerse, dar en tierra; * vt
pesar en balanza; contrapesar; saldar; considerar, examinar.

balance sheet n balance m.

balcony n balcón m.

bald adj calvo/va.

baldness n calvicie f.

bale n bala f; * vt embalar; tirar el
agua del bote.

baleful adj triste, funesto/ta; ~**ly** adv
tristemente; míseramente.

ball n bola f; pelota f; baile m,
balón m.

ballad n balada f.
ballast n lastre, m * vt lastrar.
ballerina n bailarina f.
ballet n ballet m.
ballistic adj balístico/ca.
balloon n globo m.
ballot n voto m; escrutinio m; * vi votar.
ballpoint (pen) n bolígrafo m.
ballroom n salón de baile m.
balm, balsam n bálsamo m; * vt untar con bálsamo.
balmy adj balsámico/ca; fragante.
balustrade n balaustrada f.
bamboo n bambú m.
bamboozle vt (fam) engañar.
ban n prohibición f; * vt prohibir.
banal adj vulgar.
banana n plátano m.
band n faja f; cuadrilla f; banda (de soldados) f; orquesta f.
bandage n venda f, vendaje m; * vt vendar.
bandit n bandido/da m/f.
bandstand n quiosco m.
bandy vt pelotear; discutir.
bandy-legged adj patizambo/ba.
bang n golpe m; * vt golpear; cerrar con violencia.
bangle n brazalete m.
bangs npl flequillo m.
banish vt desterrar, echar fuera, proscribir, expatriar.
banishment n destierro m.
banister(s) n(pl) pasamanos m.
banjo n banjo m.
bank n orilla (de río) f; montón de tierra m; banco m; dique m; escollo m; * vt poner dinero en un banco; **to ~ on** contar con.
bank account n cuenta de banco f.
bank card n tarjeta bancaria f.
banker n banquero/ra m/f.

banking n banca f; **electronic ~** banca electrónica.
banknote n billete de banco m.
bankrupt adj insolvente; * n fallido/da, quebrado/da m.
bankruptcy n bancarrota, quiebra f.
bank statement n detalle de cuenta m.
banner n bandera f; estandarte m.
banquet n banquete m.
banter n zumba f.
baptism n bautismo m.
baptismal adj bautismal.
baptistery n bautisterio m.
baptize vt bautizar.
bar n bar m; barra f; tranca f; obstáculo m; (law) abogacía f; * vt impedir; prohibir; excluir.
barbarian n bárbaro/ra m/f; * adj bárbaro/ra, cruel.
barbaric adj bárbaro/ra.
barbarism n (gr) barbarismo m; crueldad f.
barbarity n barbaridad, inhumanidad f.
barbarous adj bárbaro/ra, cruel.
barbecue n barbacoa f.
barber n peluquero m.
bar code n código de barras m.
bard n bardo m; poeta m.
bare adj desnudo/da, descubierto/ta; simple; puro/ra; * vt desnudar, descubrir.
barefaced adj desvergonzado/da, impudente.
barefoot(ed) adj descalzo, sin zapatos.
bareheaded adj descubierto/ta.
barelegged adj con las piernas desnudas.
barely adv apenas, solamente.
bareness n desnudez f.
bargain n ganga f; contrato, pacto m; * vi pactar; negociar; **to ~ for** esperar.

barge n barcaza f.
baritone n (mus) barítono m.
bark n corteza f; ladrido m (del perro); * vi ladrar.
barley n cebada f.
barmaid n camarera f.
barman n barman m.
barn n granero, pajar m.
barnacles npl percebe m.
barometer n barómetro m.
baron n barón m.
baroness n baronesa f.
baronial adj de barón.
barracks npl cuartel m.
barrage n descarga f; (fig) lluvia f.
barrel n barril m; cañón de escopeta m.
barrel organ n organillo de cilindro m.
barren adj estéril, infructuoso/sa; (fig) yermo/ma.
barricade n barricada f; estacada f; barrera f; * vt cerrar con barreras, empalizar.
barrier n barrera f; obstáculo m.
barring adv excepto, fuera de.
barrow n carretilla f.
bartender n barman m.
barter vi baratar; * vt cambiar, trocar.
base n fondo m; base f; basa f; pedestal m; zócalo m; * vt apoyar; * adj bajo/ja, vil.
baseball n béisbol m.
baseless adj sin fondo o base.
basement n sótano m.
baseness n bajeza, vileza f.
bash vt golpear.
bashful adj vergonzoso/sa, modesto/ta, tímido/da; ~ly adv vergonzosamente.
basic adj básico/ca; ~ally adv básicamente.

basilisk n basilisco m.
basin n jofaina, bacía f.
basis n base f; fundamento m.
bask vi ponerse a tomar el sol.
basket n cesta, canasta f.
basketball n baloncesto m.
bass n (mus) contrabajo m.
bassoon n bajón m.
bass viol n viola f.
bass voice n bajo cantante m.
bastard n, adj bastardo/da m/f.
bastardy n bastardía f.
baste vt pringar; hilvanar.
basting n hilván m; apaleamiento m; paliza f.
bastion n (mil) bastión m.
bat n murciélago m.
batch n serie f.
bath n baño m.
bathe vt (vi) bañar(se).
bathing suit n traje de baño m.
bathos n estilo bajo en la poesía m.
bathroom n (cuarto de) baño m.
baths npl piscina f.
bathtub n baño m, bañera f.
baton n batuta f.
battalion n (mil) batallón m.
batter vt apalear; batir, cañonear; * n batido m.
battering ram n (mil) ariete m.
battery n batería f.
battle n combate m; batalla f; * vi batallar, combatir.
battle array n orden de batalla f.
battlefield n campo de batalla m.
battlement n muralla almenada f.
battleship n acorazado m.
bawdy adj indecente.
bawl vi gritar, vocear.
bay n bahía f; laurel, lauro m; * vi balar; * adj bayo.
bayonet n bayoneta f.
bay window n ventana saldiza f.

bazaar *n* bazar *m*.
be *vi* ser; estar.
beach *n* playa, orilla *f*.
beacon *n* almenara *f*.
bead *n* cuenta *f*; ~s *npl* rosario *m*.
beagle *n* sabueso *m*.
beak *n* pico *m*.
beaker *n* taza con pico *f*.
beam *n* rayo de luz *m*; travesaño *m*; pareja *f*; * *vi* brillar.
bean *n* alubia *f*, frijol *m*, judía *f*; **green ~, French ~** judía verde *f*.
beansprouts *npl* brotes de soja *mpl*.
bear *vt* llevar; sostener; soportar; producir; parir; * *vi* sufrir (algún dolor).
bear *n* oso *m*; **she ~** osa *f*.
bearable *adj* soportable.
beard *n* barba *f*.
bearded *adj* barbado/da.
bearer *n* portador/a *m/f*; árbol fructífero *m*.
bearing *n* relación *f*.
beast *n* bestia *f*; hombre brutal *m*; **~ of burden** acémila *f*.
beastliness *n* bestialidad, brutalidad *f*.
beastly *adj* bestial, brutal; * *adv* brutalmente.
beat *vt* golpear; tocar (un tambor); **to ~ time** (with the sole of the shoe) zapatear; * *vi* pulsar, palpitar; * *n* golpe *m*; pulsación *f*.
beatific *adj* beatífico/ca.
beatify *vt* beatificar, santificar.
beating *n* paliza, zurra *f*; pulsación *f*, zumba *f*.
beatitude *n* beatitud, felicidad *f*.
beautiful *adj* hermoso/sa, bello; **~ly** *adv* con belleza o perfección.
beautify *vt* hermosear; embellecer; adornar.
beauty *n* hermosura, belleza *f*; ~

salon *n* salón de belleza *m*; **~ spot** *n* lunar *m*.
beaver *n* castor *m*.
because *conj* porque, a causa de.
beckon *vi* hacer seña con la cabeza o la mano.
become *vt* convenir; estar bien; * *vi* hacerse, convertirse, venir a parar.
becoming *adj* decente, conveniente.
bed *n* cama *f*.
bedclothes *npl* cobertores *npl*, mantas o colchas *fpl*.
bedding *n* ropa de cama *f*.
bedecked *adj* adornado/da.
bedlam *n* manicomio *m*.
bedpost *n* pilar de cama *m*.
bedridden *adj* postrado/da en cama, encamado/da.
bedroom *n* dormitorio *m*.
bedspread *n* colcha *f*.
bedtime *n* hora de irse a la cama *f*.
bee *n* abeja *f*.
beech *n* haya *f*.
beef *n* carne de vaca *f*.
beefburger *n* hamburguesa *f*.
beefsteak *n* bistec *m*.
beehive *n* colmena *f*.
beeline *n* línea recta *f*.
beer *n* cerveza *f*.
beeswax *n* cera *f*.
beet *n* remolacha *f*.
beetle *n* escarabajo *m*.
befall *vi* suceder, acontecer, sobrevenir.
befit *vt* convenir, acomodarse a.
before *adv*, *prep* antes de; delante, enfrente; ante.
beforehand *adv* de antemano, anticipadamente.
befriend *vt* proteger, amparar.
beg *vt* mendigar, rogar; suplicar; suponer; * *vi* vivir de limosna.
beget *vt* engendrar.

beggar n mendigo/ga m/f.
begin vt, vi comenzar, empezar.
beginner n principiante m; novicio/ cia m/f.
beginning n principio, origen m.
begrudge vt envidiar.
behalf n on ~ of de parte de.
behave vi comportarse, portarse, conducirse.
behaviour n conducta f; modo de portarse m.
behead vt decapitar, cortar la cabeza.
behind prep detrás; atrás; a la, en zaga; * adv atrasadamente.
behold vt ver, contemplar, observar.
behove vi importar, ser útil; incumbir.
beige adj color beige.
being n existencia f; estado m; ser m.
belated adj atrasado/da.
belch vi eructar, vomitar; * n eructo m.
belfry n campanario m.
belie vt desmentir, calumniar.
belief n fe, creencia f; opinión f; credo m.
believable adj creíble.
believe vt creer; * vi pensar, imaginar.
believer n creyente, fiel, cristiano/na m/f.
belittle vt minimizar.
bell n campana f.
bellicose adj belicoso/sa.
belligerent adj beligerante.
bellow vi bramar; rugir; vociferar; * n bramido m.
bellows npl fuelle m.
belly n vientre m; panza f.
bellyful n panzada f; hartura f.
belong vi pertenecer.
belongings npl pertenencias fpl.
beloved adj querido/da, amado/da.

below adv, prep debajo, inferior; abajo.
belt n cinturón, cinto m; zona f.
bemoan vt deplorar, lamentar.
bemused adj confundido/da.
bench n banco m, banquillo m.
bend vt encorvar, inclinar, plegar; hacer una reverencia; * vi encorvarse, inclinarse; * n curva f.
beneath adv, prep debajo, abajo.
benediction n bendición f.
benefactor n bienhechor m.
benefice n beneficio m; beneficio eclesiástico m.
beneficent adj benéfico/ca.
beneficial adj beneficioso/sa, provechoso/sa, útil.
beneficiary n beneficiario/ria m.
benefit n beneficio m; utilidad f; provecho m; * vt beneficiar; * vi utilizarse; prevalerse.
benefit night n representación dramática a beneficio de un actor o de una actriz f.
benevolence n benevolencia f; donativo gratuito m.
benevolent adj benévolo/la.
benign adj benigno/na; afable; liberal.
bent n inclinación f.
benzine n (chem) bencina f.
bequeath vt legar en testamento.
bequest n legado m.
bereave vt privar.
bereavement n pérdida f.
beret n boina f.
berm n arcén m.
berry n baya f.
berserk adj loco/ca.
berth n (mar) amarradero m, camarote m.
beseech vt suplicar, implorar, conjurar, rogar.

beset *vt* acosar.

beside(s) *prep* al lado de; excepto; sobre; fuera de; * *adv* por otra parte.

besiege *vt* sitiar, bloquear.

best *adj* mejor; * *adv* (lo) mejor; * *n* lo mejor *m*.

bestial *adj* bestial, brutal; ~**ly** *adv* bestialmente.

bestiality *n* bestialidad, brutalidad *f*.

bestow *vt* dar, conferir; otorgar.

bestseller *n* bestseller *m*.

bet *n* apuesta *f*; * *vt* apostar.

betray *vt* traicionar; divulgar algún secreto.

betrayal *n* traición *f*.

betroth *vt* contraer esponsales.

betrothal *n* esponsales *mpl*.

better *adj*, *adv* mejor; **so much the** ~ tanto mejor; * *vt* mejorar, reformar.

betting *n* juego *m*.

between *prep* entre, en medio de.

bevel *n* cartabón *m*.

beverage *n* bebida *f*; trago *m*.

bevy *n* bandada (de aves) *f*.

beware *vi* guardarse.

bewilder *vt* pasmar.

bewilderment *n* perplejidad *f*.

bewitch *vt* encantar, hechizar.

beyond *prep* más allá, más adelante, fuera de.

bias *n* propensión, inclinación *f*; sesgo *m*; prejuicio *m*.

bib *n* babador *m*.

Bible *n* Biblia *f*.

biblical *adj* bíblico/ca.

bibliography *n* bibliografía *f*.

bicarbonate of soda *n* bicarbonato de soda *m*.

bicker *vi* escaramucear, reñir, disputar.

bicycle *n* bicicleta *f*.

bid *vt* mandar, ordenar; ofrecer; * *n* oferta *f*; tentativa *f*.

bidding *n* orden *f*; mandato *m*; ofrecimiento *m*.

bide *vt* sufrir, aguantar.

biennial *adj* bienal.

bifocals *npl* gafas bifocales *fpl*.

bifurcated *adj* bifurcado/da.

big *adj* grande, lleno/na; inflado/da.

bigamist *n* bígamo/ma *m/f*.

bigamy *n* bigamia *f*.

big dipper *n* montaña rusa *f*.

bigheaded *adj* engreído/da.

bigness *n* grandeza *f*.

bigot *n* fanático/ca *m/f*.

bigoted *adj* fanático/ca.

bike *n* bici *f*; bicicleta *f*; **mountain** ~ bicicleta de montaña.

bikini *n* bikini *m*.

bilberry *n* arándano *m*.

bile *n* bilis *f*.

bilingual *adj* bilingüe.

bilious *adj* bilioso/sa.

bill *n* pico de ave *m*; billete *m*; cuenta *f*.

billboard *n* cartelera *f*.

billet *n* alojamiento *m*.

billiards *npl* billar *m*.

billiard-table *n* mesa de billar *f*.

billion *n* mil millones *mpl*, millardo *m*.

billy *n* porra *f*.

bin *n* cubo de la basura *m*.

bind *vt* atar; unir; encuadernar.

binder *n* encuadernador/a *m/f*.

binding *n* venda, faja *f*.

binge *n* juerga *f*.

bingo *n* bingo *m*.

biochemistry *n* bioquímica *f*.

biodegradable *adj* biodegradable.

biodiversity *n* biodiversity *f*.

binoculars *npl* prismáticos *mpl*.

biographer *n* biógrafo/fa *m/f*.

biographical *adj* biográfico/ca.

biography *n* biografía *f*.
biological *adj* biológico/ca.
biology *n* biología *f*.
biped *n* bípedo *m*.
birch *n* abedul *m*.
bird *n* ave *f*; pájaro *m*.
bird's-eye view *n* vista de pájaro *f*.
bird-watcher *n* ornitólogo/ga *m/f*.
birth *n* nacimiento *m*; origen *m*; parto *m*.
birth certificate *n* partida de nacimiento *f*.
birth control *n* control de natalidad *m*.
birthday *n* cumpleaños *m invar*.
birthplace *n* lugar de nacimiento *m*.
birthright *n* derechos de nacimiento *mpl*; primogenitura *f*.
biscuit *n* bizcocho *m*; galleta *f*.
bisect *vt* bisecar.
bishop *n* obispo *m*.
bison *n* bisonte *m*.
bit *n* bocado *m*; pedacito *m*.
bitch *n* perra *f*; (*fig*) zorra *f*.
bite *vt* morder; picar; ~ **the dust** (*fam*) morder la tierra, morir; * *n* mordedura *f*.
bitter *adj* amargo/ga, áspero/ra; mordaz, satírico/ca; penoso/sa; ~**ly** *adv* amargamente; con pena; severamente.
bitterness *n* amargor *m*; rencor *m*; pena *f*; dolor *m*.
bitumen *n* betún *m*.
bizarre *adj* raro/ra, extravagante.
blab *vi* chismear.
black *adj* negro/gra, oscuro/ra; funesto/ta; * *n* color negro *m*.
blackberry *n* zarzamora *f*.
blackbird *n* mirlo *m*.
blackboard *n* pizarra *f*.
black box *n* caja negra *f*.
blacken *vt* teñir de negro; ennegrecer.
black ice *n* hielo invisible *m*.

blackjack *n* veintiuna *f*.
blackleg *n* esquirol *m*.
blacklist *n* lista negra *f*.
blackmail *n* chantaje *m*; * *vt* chantajear.
black market *n* mercado negro *m*.
blackness *n* negrura *f*.
black pudding *n* morcilla *f*.
black sheep *n* oveja negra *f*.
blacksmith *n* herrero *m*.
blackthorn *n* endrino *m*.
bladder *n* vejiga *f*.
blade *n* hoja *f*; filo *m*; escobilla *f*.
blame *vt* culpar; * *n* culpa *f*.
blameless *adj* inocente, irreprensible, puro/ra; ~**ly** *adv* inocentemente.
blanch *vt* blanquear.
bland *adj* blando/da, suave, dulce, apacible.
blank *adj* blanco/ca; pálido/da; * *n* blanco *m*.
blank cheque *n* cheque en blanco *m*.
blanket *n* manta *f*.
blare *vi* resonar.
blasé *adj* indiferente.
blaspheme *vt* blasfemar, jurar, decir blasfemias.
blasphemous *adj* blasfemo/ma.
blasphemy *n* blasfemia *f*.
blast *n* soplo de aire *m*; carga explosiva *f*; * *vt* volar.
blast-off *n* lanzamiento *m*.
blatant *adj* obvio.
blaze *n* llama *f*; * *vi* encenderse en llamas; brillar, resplandecer.
bleach *vt* blanquear al sol; * *vi* blanquear; * *n* lejía *f*.
bleached *adj* teñido/da de rubio; descolorado/da.
bleachers *npl* gradas al sol *fpl*.
bleak *adj* pálido/da, descolorido/da; frío, helado/da.
bleakness *n* frialdad *f*; palidez *f*.

bleary(-eyed) *adj* legañoso/sa.

bleat *n* balido *m*; * *vi* balar.

bleed *vi*, *vt* sangrar.

bleeding *n* sangría *f*.

bleeper *n* busca *m*.

blemish *vt* manchar, ensuciar; infamar; * *n* tacha *f*; deshonra, infamia *f*.

blend *vt* mezclar.

bless *vt* bendecir.

blessing *n* bendición *f*; beneficio *m*; ventaja *f*.

blight *vt* arruinar.

blind *adj* ciego/ga; ~ **alley** *n* callejón sin salida *m*; * *vt* cegar; deslumbrar; * *n* velo *m*; **(Venetian)** ~ persiana *f*.

blinders *npl* anteojeras *fpl*.

blindfold *vt* vendar los ojos; ~**ed** *adj* con los ojos vendados.

blindly *adv* ciegamente, a ciegas.

blindness *n* ceguera *f*.

blind side *n* punto ciego *m*.

blind spot *n* punto ciego *m*.

blink *vi* parpadear.

blinkers *npl* anteojeras *fpl*.

bliss *n* felicidad (eterna) *f*.

blissful *adj* feliz en sumo grado; beato/ta, bienaventurado/da; ~**ly** *adv* felizmente.

blissfulness *n* suprema felicidad *f*.

blister *n* ampolla *f*; * *vi* ampollarse.

blitz *n* bombardeo aéreo *m*.

blizzard *n* ventisca *f*.

bloated *adj* hinchado/da.

blob *n* gota *f*.

bloc *n* bloque *m*.

block *n* bloque *m*; obstáculo *m*; zoquete *m*; manzana *f*; ~ **(up)** *vt* bloquear.

blockade *n* bloqueo *m*; * *vt* bloquear.

blockage *n* obstrucción *f*.

blockbuster *n* éxito de público *m*.

blockhead *n* bruto, necio, zopenco *m*; (*fam*) zoquete *m*.

blond *adj* rubio/bia; * *n* rubio/bia *m/f*.

blood *n* sangre *f*.

blood donor *n* donante de sangre *m/f*.

blood group *n* grupo sanguíneo *m*.

bloodhound *n* sabueso *m*.

bloodily *adv* sangrientamente, inhumanamente.

bloodiness *n* (*fig*) crueldad *f*.

bloodless *adj* exangüe; sin efusión de sangre.

blood poisoning *n* septicemia *f*.

blood pressure *n* presión sanguínea *f*.

bloodshed *n* efusión de sangre *f*; matanza *f*, derramamiento de sangre *m*.

bloodshot *adj* ensangrentado/da.

bloodstream *n* corriente sanguínea *f*.

bloodsucker *n* sanguijuela *f*; (*fig*) desollador/a *m/f*.

blood test *n* análisis de sangre *m invar*.

bloodthirsty *adj* sanguinario/ria.

blood transfusion *n* transfusión sanguínea *f*.

blood vessel *n* vena *f*; vaso sanguíneo *m*.

bloody *adj* sangriento/ta, ensangrentado/da; cruel; ~ **minded** *adj* sanguinario/ria.

bloom *n* flor *f*; (*also fig*); * *vi* florecer.

blossom *n* flor *f*.

blot *vt* manchar (lo escrito); cancelar; denigrar; * *n* mancha *f*.

blotchy *adj* muy manchado/da.

blotting paper *n* papel secante *m*.

blouse *n* blusa *f*.

blow *vi* soplar; sonar; * *vt* soplar; inflar; **to** ~ **up** volar; * *n* golpe *m*.

blowout n pinchazo m.

blowpipe n soplete m.

blubber n grasa de ballena f; * vi lloriquear.

bludgeon n cachiporra f; palocorto m.

blue adj azul.

bluebell, harebell n (bot) campanilla f.

blue berets npl cascos azules mpl.

bluebottle n moscarda f.

blueness n color azul m.

blueprint n (fig) anteproyecto m.

bluff n farol m; * vt farolear.

bluish adj azulado/da.

blunder n metedura de pata f; error craso m; * vi meter la pata.

blunt adj obtuso/sa; grosero/ra; * vt embotar.

bluntly adv sin artificio; claramente; obtusamente.

bluntness n embotadura, franqueza f.

blur n contorno borroso m; * vt hacer borroso.

blurt out vt descolgarse con.

blush n rubor m; sonrojo m; * vi ponerse colorado/da, sonrojarse.

blustery adj tempestuoso/sa.

boa n boa f (serpiente).

boar n verraco m; **wild ~** jabalí m.

board n tabla f; mesa f; consejo m; * vt embarcarse en; subir a.

boarder n pensionista m/f.

boarding card n tarjeta de embarque f.

boarding house n pensión f, casa de huéspedes f.

boarding school n internado m.

boast vi jactarse; * n jactancia f; ostentación f.

boastful adj jactancioso/sa.

boat n barco m; bote m; barca f.

boating n canotaje m; paseo en barquilla m; regata f.

bobsleigh n bob m.

bode vt presagiar, pronosticar.

bodice n corsé m.

bodily adj, adv corpóreo/rea; corporalmente.

body n cuerpo m; individuo m; gremio m; **any ~** cualquier; **every ~** cada uno.

body-building n culturismo m.

bodyguard n guardaespaldas m/f invar.

bodywork n (auto) carrocería f.

bog n pantano m.

boggy adj pantanoso/sa, palustre.

bogus adj postizo.

boil vi hervir; bullir; hervirle a uno la sangre; * vt cocer; * n furúnculo m.

boiled egg n huevo duro m, huevo pasado por agua m.

boiled potatoes npl patatas hervidas fpl.

boiler n marmita f; caldero m.

boiling point n punto de ebullición m.

boisterous adj borrascoso/sa, tempestuoso/sa; violento/ta; **~ly** adv tumultuosamente, furiosamente.

bold adj ardiente, valiente; audaz; temerario/ria; impudente; **~ly** adv descaradamente.

boldness n intrepidez f; valentía f; osadía f.

bolster n travesero m; cabezal m; * vt reforzar.

bolt n cerrojo m; * vt cerrar con cerrojo.

bomb n bomba f; **~ disposal** desactivación de explosivos f.

bombard vt bombardear.

bombardier n bombardero m.

bombardment n bombardeo m.

bombshell n (fig) bomba f.

bond n ligadura f; vínculo m; vale m; obligación f.

bondage *n* esclavitud, servidumbre *f*.

bond holder *n* titular de bonos *m/f*.

bone *n* hueso *m*; * *vt* desosar.

boneless *adj* sin huesos; desosado/da.

bonfire *n* hoguera *f*.

bonnet *n* gorra *f*; bonete *m*.

bonny *adj* bonito/ta.

bonsai *n* bonsái *m*.

bonus *n* cuota, prima *f*.

bony *adj* osudo/da.

boo *vt* abuchear.

booby trap *n* trampa explosiva *f*.

book *n* libro *m*; **to bring to ~** *vt* pedir cuentas a alguien.

bookbinder *n* encuadernador/a *m/f*.

bookcase *n* estantería *f*.

bookkeeper *n* tenedor/a de libros *m/f*.

bookkeeping *n* teneduría de libros *f*.

bookmaker *n* corredor de apuestas *m*.

bookmarker *n* registro de un libro *m*.

bookseller *n* librero/ra *m/f*.

bookstore *n* librería *f*.

bookworm *n* polilla *f*; ratón de biblioteca *m*.

boom *n* trueno *m*; boom *m*; * *vi* retumbar.

boon *n* presente, regalo *m*; favor *m*.

boor *n* patán, villano/na *m/f*.

boorish *adj* rústico/ca, agreste.

boost *n* estímulo *m*; *vt* estimular.

booster *n* reinyección *f*.

boot *n(aut)* maletero *m*; bota *f*; zapata *f*; **to ~** *adv* además.

booth *n* barraca, cabaña *f*.

booty *n* botín *m*; presa *f*; saqueo *m*.

booze *vi* emborracharse; * *n* bebida *f*.

border *n* orilla *f*; borde *m*; margen *f*; frontera *f*; * *vt* lindar con.

borderline *n* frontera *f*.

bore *vt* taladrar; barrenar; fastidiar; * *n* taladro *m*; calibre *m*; pelmazo/za *m/f*.

boredom *n* aburrimiento *m*.

borehole *n* barreno *m*.

boring *adj* aburrido/da.

born *adj* nacido/da; destinado/da.

borrow *vt* pedir prestado/da.

borrower *n* prestamista *m*.

bosom *n* seno, pecho *m*.

bosom friend *n* amigo/ga íntimo/ma *m/f*.

boss *n* jefe *m*; patrón/ona *m/f*.

botanic(al) *adj* botánico/ca.

botanist *n* botánico *m*.

botany *n* botánica *f*.

botch *vt* chapuzar.

botch-up *n* mamarracho *m*.

both *adj* ambos, entrambos; ambas, entrambas; * *conj* tanto como.

bother *vt* preocupar; fastidiar; * *n* molestia *f*.

bottle *n* botella *f*; * *vt* embotellar.

bottleneck *n* embotellamiento *m*.

bottle-opener *n* abrebotellas *m invar*.

bottom *n* fondo *m*; fundamento *m*; * *adj* más bajo/ja; último/ma.

bottomless *adj* insondable; excesivo/va; impenetrable.

bough *n* brazo del árbol *m*; ramo *m*.

boulder *n* canto rodado *m*.

bounce *vi* rebotar; ser rechazado/da; * *n* rebote *m*.

bound *n* límite *m*; salto *m*; repercusión *f*; * *vi* resaltar; * *adj* destinado/da.

boundary *n* límite *m*; frontera *f*.

boundless *adj* ilimitado/da, infinito/ta.

bounteous, bountiful *adj* liberal, generoso/sa, bienhechor.

bounty *n* liberalidad, bondad *f*.

bouquet *n* ramillete de flores *m*.

bourgeois *adj* burgués/esa.

bout *n* ataque *m*; encuentro *m*.

bovine adj bovino/na.

bow¹ vt encorvar, doblar; * vi encorvarse; hacer una reverencia; * n reverencia, inclinación f.

bow² n arco m; arco de violín; corbata f; nudo m.

bowels npl intestinos mpl; entrañas fpl.

bowl n taza; bola f; * vi jugar a las bochas.

bowler hat n hongo m.

bowling n bolos mpl.

bowling alley n bolera f.

bowling-green n campo m para jugar a las bochas.

bowstring n cuerda del arco f.

bow tie n pajarita f.

box n caja, cajita f; palco de teatro m; ~ **on the ear** bofetada f; * vt encajonar; * vi boxear.

boxer n boxeador m.

boxing n boxeo m.

boxing gloves npl guantes de boxeo mpl.

boxing ring n cuadrilátero m.

box office n taquilla f.

box-seat n asiento de palco m.

boy n muchacho m; niño m; zagal m.

boycott vt boicotear; * n boicot m.

boyfriend n novio m.

boyish adj pueril; frívolo.

bra n sujetador m.

brace n abrazadera f; corrector m.

bracelet n brazalete m.

bracing adj vigorizante.

bracken n (bot) helecho m.

bracket n puntal m; paréntesis m; corchete m; * **to ~ with** vt unir, ligar.

bracing adj vigorizante.

brag n jactancia f; * vi jactarse, fanfarronear.

braid n trenza f; * vt trenzar.

brain n cerebro m; seso, juicio m; * vt descerebrar, matar a uno.

brainchild n parto del ingenio m.

brainwash vt lavar el cerebro.

brainwave n idea luminosa f.

brainy adj inteligente.

brainless adj tonto/ta, insensato/ta.

brake n freno m; * vt, vi frenar.

brake fluid n líquido de frenos m.

brake light n luz de frenado f.

brake shoe n (auto) zapata de freno f.

bramble n zarza, espina f.

bramble patch n zarzal m.

bran n salvado m.

branch n ramo m; rama f; * vt, vi ramificar(se).

branch line n (rail) empalme, ramal m.

brand n marca f; hierro m; * vt marcar (con un hierro incandescente).

brandish vt blandir, ondear.

brand-new adj flamante.

brandy n coñac m.

brash adj tosco/ca; descarado/da.

brass n bronce m.

brassiere n sujetador m.

brat n crío m.

bravado n baladronada f.

brave adj bravo/va, valiente, atrevido/da; * vt desafiar; * n bravo m; ~**ly** adv bravamente.

bravery n valor m; magnificencia f.

brawl n pelea, camorra f; * vi pelearse.

brawn n fuerza muscular f; carne de verraco f.

bray vi rebuznar; * n rebuzno (del asno) m.

braze vt soldar con latón; broncear.

brazen adj de latón; desvergonzado/da; impudente; * vi hacerse descarado/da.

brazier n brasero m.

breach n rotura f; brecha f; violación f.

bread n pan m; (fig) sustento m; **brown ~** pan moreno m.

breadbox n panera f.

breadcrumbs npl migajas fpl.

breadth n anchura f.

breadwinner n sostén de la familia m.

break vt romper; quebrantar; violar; arruinar; interrumpir; * vi romperse; **to ~ into** forzar; **to ~ out** abrirse salida; * n rotura, abertura f; interrupción f; **~ of day** despuntar del día m, aurora f.

breakage n rotura f.

breakdown n avería f; descalabro m.

breakfast n desayuno m; * vi desayunar.

breaking n rompimiento m; principio de las vacaciones en las escuelas m; fractura f.

breakthrough n avance m.

breakwater n rompeolas m invar.

breast n pecho, seno m; pechuga f; corazón m.

breastbone n esternón m.

breastplate n peto m; pectoral m; coraza f.

breaststroke n braza f.

breath n aliento m, respiración f; soplo de aire m.

breathe vt, vi respirar; exhalar.

breathing n respiración f; aliento m.

breathing space n descanso, reposo m.

breathless adj falto/ta de aliento; desalentado/da.

breathtaking adj pasmoso/sa.

breed n casta, raza f; * vt procrear; engendrar; producir; educar; * vi multiplicarse.

breeder n criador/a m/f.

breeding n crianza f; buena educación f.

breeze n brisa f.

breezy adj refrescado/da con brisas.

brethren n pl de **brother** hermanos mpl (en estilo grave).

breviary n breviario m.

brevity n brevedad, concisión f.

brew vt hacer; tramar; mezclar; * vi hacerse; tramarse; * n brebaje m.

brewer n cervecero m.

brewery n cervecería f.

briar, brier n zarza f, espino m.

bribe n cohecho, soborno m; * vt cohechar, corromper, sobornar.

bribery n cohecho, soborno m.

bric-a-brac n baratijas fpl.

brick n ladrillo m; * vt enladrillar.

bricklayer n albañil m.

bricklaying n albañilería f.

bridal adj nupcial.

bride n novia f.

bridegroom n novio m.

bridesmaid n madrina de boda f.

bridge n puente m/f; caballete de la nariz m; puente de violín m; **to build a ~ (over)** vt construir un puente (sobre).

bridle n brida f freno m; * vt embridar; reprimir, refrenar.

brief adj breve, conciso/sa, sucinto/ta; * n compendio m; breve m.

briefcase n cartera f.

briefly adv brevemente, en pocas palabras.

brier n = **briar**.

brigade n (mil) brigada f.

brigadier n (mil) general de brigada m.

brigand n bandido m.

bright adj claro/ra, luciente, brillante; **~ly** adv espléndidamente.

brighten vt pulir, dar lustre; ilustrar; * vi aclararse.

brightness n esplendor m, brillantez f; agudeza f; claridad f.

brilliance *n* brillo *m*.

brilliant *adj* brillante; **~ly** *adv* espléndidamente.

brim *n* borde extremo *m*; orilla *f*.

brimful(l) *adj* lleno/na hasta el borde.

bring *vt* llevar, traer; conducir; inducir, persuadir; **to ~ about** efectuar; **to ~ forth** producir; parir; **to ~ up** educar.

brink *n* orilla *f*; margen *m/f*; borde *m*.

brisk *adj* vivo/va, alegre, jovial; fresco/ca.

brisket *n* pecho (de un animal) *m*.

briskly *adj* vigorosamente; alegremente; vivamente.

bristle *n* cerda, seta *f*; * *vi* erizarse.

bristly *adj* cerdoso/sa, lleno/na de cerdas.

brittle *adj* quebradizo, frágil.

broach *vt* comenzar a hablar de.

broad *adj* ancho.

broad bean *n* (*bot*) haba *f*; **~s** haba gruesa *fpl*.

broadcast *n* emisión *f*; * *vt*, *vi* emitir; transmitir.

broadcasting *n* radiodifusión *f*.

broaden *vt* (*vi*) ensanchar(se).

broadly *adv* anchamente.

broad-minded *adj* tolerante.

broadness *n* ancho *m*; anchura *f*.

broadside *n* costado de navío *m*; andanada *f*.

broadways *adv* a lo ancho, por lo ancho.

brocade *n* brocado *m*.

broccoli *n* brécol *m*.

brochure *n* folleto *m*.

brogue *n* abarca *f*; acento irlandés *m*.

broil *vt* asar a la parrilla.

broken *adj* roto/ta, interrumpido/da; **~ English** inglés mal articulado *m*.

broker *n* corredor/a *m/f*.

brokerage *n* corretaje *m*.

bronchial *adj* bronquial.

bronchitis *n* bronquitis *f*.

bronze *n* bronce *m*; * *vt* broncear.

brooch *n* broche *m*.

brood *vi* empollar; meditar; * *n* raza *f*; nidada *f*.

brood-hen *n* empolladora *f*.

brook *n* arroyo *m*.

broom *n* retama *f*; escoba *f*.

broomstick *n* palo de escoba *m*.

broth *n* caldo *m*.

brothel *n* burdel *m*.

brother *n* hermano *m*.

brotherhood *n* hermandad *f*; fraternidad *f*.

brother-in-law *n* cuñado *m*.

brotherly *adj*, *adv* fraternal; fraternalmente.

brow *n* caja *f*; frente *f*; cima *f*.

browbeat *vt* intimidar.

brown *adj* moreno/na; castaño/ña; **~ paper** *n* papel de estraza *m*; **~ bread** *n* pan moreno *m*; **~ sugar** *n* azúcar terciado *m*; * *n* color moreno *m*; * *vt* volver moreno/na.

browse *vt* ramonear; * *vi* pacer la hierba.

browser *n* navegador *m*.

bruise *vt* magullar; * *n* magulladura, contusión *f*; roncha *f*.

brunch *n* desayuno-almuerzo *m*.

brunette *n* morena *f*.

brunt *n* choque *m*.

brush *n* cepillo *m*; escobilla *f*; combate *m*; * *vt* cepillar.

brushwood *n* breñal, zarzal *m*.

brusque *adj* brusco/ca.

Brussels sprout *n* col de Bruselas *f*.

brutal *adj* brutal; **~ly** *adv* brutalmente.

brutality *n* brutalidad *f*.

brutalize *vt*, *vi* embrutecer(se).

brute n bruto m; * adj feroz, bestial; irracional.

brutish adj brutal, bestial; feroz; ~ly adv brutalmente.

bubble n burbuja f; * vi burbujear, bullir.

bubblegum n chicle m.

bucket n cubo, pozal m.

buckle n hebilla f; * vt hebillar; abrochar; * vi encorvarse.

buckshot n perdigones mpl.

bucolic adj bucólico/ca.

bud n pimpollo, botón, capullo m; yema f; * vi brotar.

Buddhism n Budismo m.

budding adj en ciernes.

buddy n compañero m.

budge vi moverse, menearse.

budgerigar n periquito m.

budget n presupuesto m.

buff n entusiasta m.

buffalo n búfalo m.

buffers npl (rail) parochoques m invar, topes mpl.

buffet n buffet m; * vt abofetear.

buffoon n bufón, chocarrero m.

bug n chinche m.

bugbear n espantajo, coco m.

bugle(horn) n trompa de caza f.

build vt edificar; construir.

builder n constructor/a m/f; maestro/tra de obras m/f.

building n edificio m; construcción f.

bulb n bulbo m; cebolla f.

bulbous adj bulboso/sa.

bulge vi combarse; * n bombeo m.

bulk n masa f; volumen m; grosura f; mayor parte f; capacidad de un buque f; **in ~** a granel.

bulky adj grueso/sa, grande.

bull n toro m.

bulldog n dogo m.

bulldozer n aplanadora f.

bullet n bala f.

bulletin board n tablón de anuncios m.

bulletproof adj a prueba de balas.

bullfight n corrida de toros f.

bullfighter n torero m.

bullfighting n toreo m.

bullion n oro o plata en barras m o f.

bullock n novillo capado m.

bullring n plaza de toros f.

bull's-eye n centro del blanco m.

bully n valentón m; * vt tiranizar.

bulwark n baluarte m.

bum n vagabundo/da m/f.

bumblebee n abejorro, zángano m.

bump n hinchazón f; jiba f; bollo m; barriga f; * vt chocar contra.

bumper n parachoques m invar.

bumpkin n patán m; villano/na m/f.

bumpy adj bacheado/da.

bun n bollo m; mono m.

bunch n ramo m; grupo m.

bundle n fardo m, haz m (de leña etc); paquete m; rollo m; * vt atar, hacer un lío.

bung n tapón m; * vt atarugar.

bungalow n bungalow m.

bungee-jumping n puenting m.

bungle vt chapucear; * vi hacer algo chabacanamente.

bunion n juanete m.

bunk n litera f.

bunker n refugio m; búnker m.

buoy n (mar) boya f.

buoyancy n capacidad para flotar f.

buoyant adj boyante.

burden n carga f; * vt cargar.

bureau n armario m; escritorio m.

bureaucracy n burocracia f.

bureaucrat n burócrata m/f.

burglar n ladrón/ona m/f.

burglar alarm n alarma antirrobo f.

burglary n robo en una casa m.

burial n enterramiento m; exequias fpl; sepultura f.

burial place n cementerio m.

burlesque n, adj lengua burlesca f; burlesco/ca m/f.

burly adj fornido/da.

burn vt quemar, abrasar, incendiar; * vi arder; * n quema dura f.

burner n quemador m; mechero m.

burning adj ardiente.

burrow n madriguera f; * vi esconderse en la madriguera.

bursar n tesorero/ra m/f.

burse n bolsa, lonja f.

burst vi reventar; abrirse; **to ~ into tears** prorrumpir en lágrimas; **to ~ out laughing** estallarse de risa; * vt **to ~ into** irrumpir en; * n reventón m; rebosadura f.

bury vt enterrar, sepultar; esconder.

bus n autobús m.

bush n arbusto, espinal m; cola de zorro f.

bushy adj espeso/sa, lleno/na de arbustos.

busily adv diligentemente, apresuradamente.

business n asunto m; negocios mpl; empleo m; ocupación f.

businesslike adj serio/ria.

businessman n hombre de negocios m.

business trip n viaje de negocios m.

businesswoman n mujer de negocios f.

bus lane n carril bus m.

bust n busto m.

bus stop n parada de autobuses f.

bustle vi hacer ruido; menearse; andar al retortero; * n baraúnda f; ruido m.

bustling adj animado/da.

busy adj ocupado/da; entrometido/da.

busybody n entrometido m.

but conj pero; mas; excepto, menos; solamente.

butcher n carnicero/ra m/f; * vt matar atrozmente.

butcher's (shop) n carnicería f.

butchery n matadero m.

butler n mayordomo m.

butt n colilla f; cabo, extremo m; * vt topar.

butter n mantequilla f; * vt untar con mantequilla.

buttercup n (bot) ranúnculo m.

butterfly n mariposa f.

buttermilk n suero de manteca m.

buttocks npl posaderas fpl.

button n botón m; * vt abotonar.

buttonhole n ojal m.

buttress n estribo m; apoyo m; * vt estribar.

buxom adj frescachona, rolliza.

buy vt comprar.

buyer n comprador/a m/f.

buzz, **buzzing** n susurro, zumbido m; * vi zumbar.

buzzard n ratonero común m.

buzzer n timbre m.

by prep por; a, en; de; cerca, al lado de; **~ and ~** de aquí a poco, ahora; **~ the** ~ de paso; **~ much** con mucho; **~ all means** por supuesto.

bygone adj pasado/da.

by-law n ordenanza municipal f.

bypass n carretera de circunvalación f.

by-product n derivado m.

by-road n camino secundario m.

bystander n mirador m.

byte n (comput) byte m.

byword n proverbio, refrán m.

C

cab *n* taxi *m*.

cabbage *n* berza, col *f*.

cabin *n* cabaña, cámara de navío *f*.

cabinet *n* consejo de ministros *m*; gabinete *m*; escritorio *m*.

cabinet-maker *n* ebanista *m*.

cable *n* cable *m*.

cable car *n* teleférico *m*.

cable television *n* televisión por cable *f*.

caboose *n* (*mar*) cocina *f*.

cache *n* alijo *m*.

cackle *vi* cacarear, graznar; * *n* cacareo *m*; charla *f*.

cactus *n* cacto *m*, cactus *m invar*.

cadence *n* (*mus*) cadencia *f*.

cadet *n* cadete *m*.

cadge *vt* mangar.

caesarean section, ~ operation *n* (*med*) (operación de) cesárea *f*.

café *n* café *m*.

cafeteria *n* café *m*.

caffeine *n* cafeína *f*.

cage *n* jaula *f*; prisión *f*; * *vt* enjaular.

cagey *adj* cauteloso/sa.

cajole *vt* lisonjear, adular; sonsacar.

cake *n* bollo *m*; tortita *f*.

calamitous *adj* calamitoso/sa.

calamity *n* calamidad, miseria *f*.

calculable *adj* calculable.

calculate *vt* calcular, contar.

calculation *n* cálculo *m*.

calculator *n* calculadora *f*.

calculus *n* cálculo *m*.

calendar *n* calendario *m*.

calf *n* ternero *m*; ternera *f*; carne de ternero *f*.

calibre *n* calibre *m*.

call *vt* llamar, nombrar; llamar por teléfono; convocar, citar; apelar; **to ~ for** preguntar por, ir a buscar; **to ~ on** visitar; **to ~ attention** llamar la atención; **to ~ names** insultar; * *n* llamada *f*; instancia *f*; invitación *f*; urgencia *f*; vocación *f*; profesión *f*.

caller *n* visitador/a *m/f*.

calligraphy *n* caligrafía *f*.

calling *n* profesión, vocación *f*.

callisthenics *n* calistenia *f*.

callous *adj* calloso/sa, endurecido/da; insensible.

calm *n* calma, tranquilidad *f*; * *adj* quieto/ta, tranquilo/la; * *vt* calmar; aplacar, aquietar; **~ly** *adv* tranquilamente.

calmness *n* tranquilidad, calma *f*.

calorie *n* caloría *f*.

calumny *n* calumnia *f*.

Calvary *n* calvario *m*.

calve *vi* parir.

Calvinist *n* calvinista *m/f*.

camcorder *n* videocámara *f*.

camel *n* camello *m*.

cameo *n* camafeo *m*.

camera *n* máquina fotográfica *f*; cámara *f*.

cameraman *n* cámara *m*.

camomile *n* manzanilla *f*.

camouflage *n* camuflaje *m*.

camp *n* campo *m*; * *vi* acampar; **refugee ~** campo de refugiados.

campaign *n* campana *f*; **run-up-to-the-election ~** precampaña *f*; * *vi* hacer campana.

campaigner *n* defensor/a *m/f*.

camper *n* campista *m/f*.

camping n camping m.
camphor n alcanfor m.
campsite n camping m.
campus n ciudad universitaria f, campus m invar.
can vi poder; * n lata f.
canal n estanque m; canal m.
cancel vt cancelar; anular, invalidar.
cancellation n cancelación f.
cancer n cáncer m.
Cancer n Cáncer m (signo del zodiaco).
cancerous adj canceroso/sa.
candid adj cándido/da, sencillo/lla, sincero/ra; ~ly adv cándidamente, francamente.
candidate n candidato/ta m/f.
candied adj azucarado/da.
candle n candela f; vela f.
candlelight n luz de candela f.
candlestick n candelero m.
candour n candor m; sinceridad f.
candyfloss n algodón azucarado m.
cane n cana f; bastón m.
canine adj canino/na, perruno/na.
canister n bote m.
cannabis n cannabis m.
cannibal n caníbal m/f; antropófago/ga m/f.
cannibalism n canibalismo m.
cannon n cañón m.
cannonball n bala de artillería f.
canny adj cuerdo/da, discreto/ta.
canoe n canoa f.
canon n canon m; regla f; ~law derecho canónico m.
canonization n canonización f.
canonize vt canonizar.
can opener n abrelatas m invar.
canopy n dosel, pabellón m.
cantankerous adj áspero/ra, fastidioso/sa.
canteen n cantina f.

canter n medio galope m.
canvas n cañamazo m.
canvass vt escudriñar, examinar; controvertir; * vi solicitar votos; pretender.
canvasser n solicitador/a m/f.
canyon n cañón m.
canyoning n barranquismo m.
cap n gorra f.
capability n capacidad, aptitud, inteligencia f.
capable adj capaz.
capacitate vt hacer capaz.
capacity n capacidad f; inteligencia, habilidad f.
cape n cabo, promontorio m.
caper n cabriola f; alcaparra f; * vi hacer cabriolas.
capillary adj capilar.
capital adj capital; principal; * n capital f (la ciudad principal); capital, fondo m; mayúscula f.
capitalism n capitalismo m.
capitalist n capitalista m.
capitalize vt capitalizar; **to ~ on** aprovechar.
capital punishment n pena de muerte f.
Capitol n Capitolio m.
capitulate vi capitular.
capitulation n capitulación f.
caprice n capricho m; extravagancia f.
capricious adj caprichoso/sa; ~ly adv caprichosamente.
Capricorn n Capricornio m (signo del zodiaco).
capsize vt (mar) volcar, zozobrar.
capsizing n (mar) zozobra f.
capsule n cápsula f.
captain n capitán/ana m/f.
captaincy, captainship n capitanía f.
captivate vt cautivar.

captivation *n* atractivo *m*.

captive *n* cautivo/va, esclavo/va *m/f*.

captivity *n* cautividad, esclavitud *f*, cautiverio *m*.

capture *n* captura *f*; presa *f*; * *vt* apresar, capturar.

car *n* coche, carro *m*; vagón *m*.

carafe *n* garrafa *f*.

caramel *n* caramelo *m*.

carat *n* quilate *m*.

caravan *n* caravana *f*.

caraway *n* (*bot*) alcaravea *f*.

carbohydrates *npl* hidratos de carbono *mpl*.

car bomb *n* coche bomba *m*.

carbon *n* carbono *m*, carbón *m*.

carbon copy *n* copia al carbón *f*.

carbonize *vt* carbonizar.

carbon paper *n* papel carbón *m*.

carbuncle *n* carbúnculo, rubí *m*; carbunco, tumor maligno *m*.

carburettor *n* carburador *m*.

carcass *n* cadáver *m*.

carcinogenic *adj* cancerígeno/na.

card *n* naipe *m*; carta *f*; **pack of ~s** baraja *f*.

cardboard *n* cartón *m*.

card game *n* juego de naipes *m*.

cardiac *adj* cardíaco/ca, cardiaco/ca.

cardinal *adj* cardinal, principal; * *n* cardenal *m*.

card table *n* mesa para jugar *f*.

care *n* cuidado *m*; solicitud *f*; * *vi* cuidar, tener cuidado o pena, inquietarse; **what do I ~?** ¿a mí que me importa?; **to ~ for** *vt* cuidar a; querer.

career *n* carrera *f*; curso *m*; * *vi* correr a carrera tendida.

carefree *n* despreocupado/da.

careful *adj* cuidadoso/sa, diligente, prudente; **~ly** *adv* cuidadosamente.

careless *adj* descuidado/da, negligente; indolente; **~ly** *adv* descuidadamente.

carelessness *n* negligencia, indiferencia *f*.

caress *n* caricia *f*; * *vt* acariciar, halagar.

caretaker *n* portero *m*, conserje *m/f*.

car-ferry *n* transbordador para coches *m*.

cargo *n* cargamento *m*.

car hire *n* alquiler de coches *m*.

caricature *n* caricatura *f*; * *vt* hacer caricaturas, ridiculizar.

caries *n* caries *f*.

caring *adj* humanitario/ria.

Carmelite *n* carmelita *f*.

carnage *n* carnicería, matanza *f*.

carnal *adj* carnal; sensual; **~ly** *adv* carnalmente.

carnation *n* clavel *m*.

carnival *n* carnaval *m*.

carnivorous *adj* carnívoro/ra.

carol *n* villancico *m*, canción de alegría o piedad *f*.

car park *n* aparcamiento, estacionamiento *m*.

carpenter *n* carpintero *m*; **~'s bench** banco de carpintero *m*.

carpentry *n* carpintería *f*.

carpet *n* alfombra *f*; * *vt* cubrir con alfombras.

carpeting *n* alfombrado *m*.

car radio *n* autorradio *m*.

carriage *n* porte *m*; coche *m*; vehículo *m*.

carriage-free *adj* franco de porte.

carrier *n* portador, carretero *m*.

carrier pigeon *n* paloma correo o mensajera *f*.

carrion *n* carroña *f*.

carrot *n* zanahoria *f*.

carry *vt* llevar, conducir; **to ~ out** ejecutar; * *vi* oírse; **to ~ the day**

quedar victorioso/sa; **to ~ on** seguir.

cart n carro m; carreta f; * vt llevar (en carro).

cartel n cartel m.

carthorse n caballo de tiro m.

Carthusian n cartujo (monje) m.

cartilage n cartílago m.

cartload n carretada f.

carton n caja f.

cartoon n dibujo animado m; tira cómica f.

cartridge n cartucho m.

carve vt cincelar; trinchar; grabar.

carving n escultura f.

carving knife n cuchillo de trinchar m.

car wash n lavado de coches m.

case n caja f; maleta f; caso m; estuche m; vaina f; **in ~** por si acaso.

cash n dinero contante m; * vt cobrar.

cash card n tarjeta de cajero automático f.

cash dispenser, cash machine n cajero automático m.

cashier n cajero m.

cashmere n cachemira f.

casing n forro m; cubierta f.

casino n casino m.

cask n barril, tonel m.

casket n ataúd m.

casserole n cazuela f.

cassette n casette, cassette m.

cassette player, recorder n casette, cassette m.

cassock n sotana f.

cast vt tirar, lanzar; modelar; * n reparto m; forma f.

castanets npl castañuelas fpl.

castaway n réprobo m.

caste n casta f.

castigate vt castigar.

casting vote n voto de calidad m.

cast iron n hierro colado m.

castle n castillo m; fortaleza f.

castor oil n aceite de ricino m.

castrate vt castrar.

castration n capadura f.

cast steel n acero fundido m.

casual adj casual, fortuito/ta; **~ly** adv casualmente, fortuitamente.

casualty n víctima f; baja f.

cat n gato m; gata f.

catalogue n catálogo m.

catalyst n catalizador m.

catalytic converter n catalizador m.

catamaran n catamarán m.

catapult n catapulta, honda f.

cataract n cascada f; catarata f.

catarrh n catarro m; reuma f.

catastrophe n catástrofe f.

catcall n silbido m; reclamo m.

catch vt coger, agarrar, asir; atrapar; pillar; sorprender; **to ~ cold** resfriarse; **to ~ fire** encenderse; * n presa f; captura f; (mus) canon m; trampa f.

catching adj contagioso/sa.

catch phrase n lema m.

catchword n reclamo m.

catchy adj pegadizo/za.

catechism n catecismo m.

catechize vt catequizar, examinar.

categorical adj categórico/ca; **~ly** adv categóricamente.

categorize vt clasificar.

category n categoría f.

cater vi abastecer, proveer.

caterer n proveedor/a, abastecedor/a m/f.

catering n alimentación f.

caterpillar n oruga f.

catgut n cuerda de violín f.

cathedral n catedral f.

catholic adj, n católico/ca m/f.

Catholicism n catolicismo m.

cattle n ganado m.

cattle show n feria de ganado f.

caucus n junta electoral f.

cauliflower n coliflor f.

cause n causa f; razón f; motivo m; proceso m; * vt causar.

causeway n arrecife m.

caustic adj, n cáustico m.

cauterize vt cauterizar.

caution n prudencia, precaución f; aviso m; * vt avisar; amonestar; advertir.

cautionary adj de escarmiento.

cautious adj prudente, circunspecto/ta, cauto/ta.

cavalier adj arrogante.

cavalry n caballería f.

cave n caverna f; bodega f.

caveat n aviso m; advertencia f; (law) notificación f.

cavern n caverna f; bodega f.

cavernous adj cavernoso/sa.

caviar n caviar m.

cavity n hueco m; caries f invar.

CD-ROM n cederrón m.

cease vt parar, suspender; * vi desistir.

cease-fire n alto el fuego m.

ceaseless adj incesante, continuo/nua; ~ly adv perpetuamente.

cedar n cedro m.

cede vt ceder, transferir.

ceiling n techo m.

celebrate vt celebrar.

celebration n celebración f.

celebrity n celebridad, fama f.

celery n apio m.

celestial adj celeste, divino/na.

celibacy n celibato m, soltería f.

celibate adj soltero; soltera.

cell n celdilla f; célula f; cueva f.

cellar n sótano m; bodega f.

cello n violoncelo m.

Cellophane® n celofán m.

cellular adj celular.

cellulitis n celulitis f.

cellulose n (chem) celulosa f.

cement n cemento; (fig) vínculo m; * vt pegar con cemento.

cemetery n cementerio m.

cenotaph n cenotafio m.

censor n censor/a m/f; crítico/ca m/f.

censorious adj severo/ra, crítico/ca.

censorship n censura f.

censure n censura, reprensión f; * vt censurar, reprender; criticar.

census n censo m.

cent n centavo m.

centenarian n centenario m; centenaria f.

centenary n centena f; * adj centenario/ria.

centennial adj centenario/ria.

centigrade n centígrado m.

centilitre n centilitro m.

centimetre n centímetro m.

centipede n escolopendra f.

central adj central; ~ly adv centralmente, en el centro.

central reserve n mediana f.

centralize vt centralizar.

centre n centro m; * vt centrar; concentrar; * vi concentrarse.

centrifugal adj centrífugo/ga.

century n siglo m.

ceramic adj cerámico/ca.

cereals npl cereales fpl.

cerebral adj cerebral.

ceremonial adj, n ceremonial m; rito externo m.

ceremonious adj ceremonioso/sa; ~ly adv ceremoniosamente.

ceremony n ceremonia f.

certain adj cierto/ta, evidente; seguro/ra; ~ly adv ciertamente, sin duda.

certainty, certitude n certeza f; seguridad f.

certificate n certificado, testimonio m.
certification n certificado m.
certified mail n correo certificado m.
certify vt certificar, afirmar.
cervical adj cervical.
cessation n cesación f.
cesspool n cloaca f; sumidero m.
chafe vt frotar; enojar, irritar.
chaff n paja menuda f.
chaffinch n pinzón m.
chagrin n disgusto m.
chain n cadena f; serie, sucesión f; * vt encadenar, atar con cadena.
chain reaction n reacción en cadena f.
chain store n gran almacén m.
chair n silla f; * vt presidir.
chairman n presidente m.
chalice n cáliz m.
chalk n creta f; tiza f.
challenge n desafío m; * vt desafiar, impugnar.
challenger n desafiador/a m/f.
challenging adj desafiante.
chamber n cámara f; aposento m.
chambermaid n moza de cámara f.
chameleon n camaleón m.
chamois leather n gamuza f.
champagne n champaña m.
champion n campeón m; * vt defender.
championship n campeonato m.
chance n ventura, suerte f; oportunidad f; **by ~** por acaso; * vt arriesgar.
chancellor n canciller m.
chancery n chancillería f.
chandelier n araña de luces f; candelero m.
change vt cambiar; * vi variar, alterarse; * n mudanza, variedad f; vicisitud f; cambio m.
changeable adj variable, inconstante; mudable.

changeless adj constante, inmutable.
changing adj cambiante.
channel n canal m; estrecho m; * vt encauzar.
channel-hopping n zapping m.
chant n canto (llano) m; * vt cantar.
chaos n caos m; confusión f.
chaotic adj confuso/sa.
chapel n capilla f.
chaplain n capellán m.
chapter n capítulo m.
char vt chamuscar.
character n carácter m; personaje m.
characteristic adj característico/ca; **~ally** adv característicamente.
characterize vt caracterizar.
characterless adj sin carácter.
charade n charada f.
charcoal n carbón de leña m.
chard n (bot) acelga f.
charge vt cargar; acusar, imputar; * n cargo m; acusación f; (mil) ataque m; depósito m; carga f.
chargeable adj imputable.
charge card n tarjeta de compra f.
charitable adj caritativo/va; benigno/na, clemente; **~bly** adv caritativamente.
charity n caridad, benevolencia f; limosna f.
charlatan n charlatán/tana m/f.
charm n encanto m; atractivo m; * vt encantar, embelesar, atraer.
charming adj encantado/da.
chart n carta de navegar f.
charter n carta f; privilegio m; * vt fletar un buque; alquilar.
charter flight n vuelo chárter m, charter m.
chase vt cazar; perseguir; * n caza f.
chasm n vacío m.
chaste adj casto/ta; puro/ra; honesto/ta.

chasten vt corregir, castigar.

chastise vt castigar, reformar, corregir.

chastisement n castigo m.

chastity n castidad, pureza f.

chat vi charlar; * n charla, cháchara f.

chatter vi cotorrear; rechinar; charlar; * n chirrido m; charla f.

chatterbox n parlero/ra, hablador/a, gárrulo/la m/f.

chatty adj locuaz, parlanchín/china.

chauffeur n chófer m.

chauvinist n machista m.

cheap adj barato/ta; ~ly adv a bajo precio.

cheapen vt regatear; abaratar.

cheaper adj más barato/ta.

cheat vt engañar, defraudar; * n trampa f; fraude, engaño m; tramposo/sa m/f.

check vt comprobar; contar; reprimir, refrenar; regañar; registrar; * n restricción f; freno m.

checkmate n mate m.

checkout n caja f.

checkpoint n control m.

check-up n reconocimiento médico m.

cheek n mejilla f; (fam) desvergüenza f; atrevimiento m.

cheekbone n hueso del carrillo m.

cheeky adj descarado/da.

cheer n alegría f; aplauso m; buen humor m; * vt animar, alentar.

cheerful adj alegre, vivo/va, jovial; ~ly adv alegremente.

cheerfulness, cheeriness n alegría f; buen humor m.

cheese n queso m.

cheesemonger, cheese shop n quesería f.

chef n jefe de cocina m.

chemical adj químico/ca.

chemist n químico m.

chemistry n química f.

chemotherapy n quimioterapia f.

cheque n cheque m.

cheque account n cuenta corriente f.

chequerboard, draughtboard n tablero de damas m.

chequered adj accidentado/da.

cherish vt fomentar, proteger.

cheroot n puro m.

cherry n cereza f; * adj bermejo/ja.

cherry tree n cerezo m.

cherub n querubín m.

chess n ajedrez m.

chessboard n tablero de ajedrez m.

chessman n pieza de ajedrez f.

chest n pecho m; arca f; ~ of drawers cómoda f.

chestnut n castaña f; color de castaña m.

chestnut tree n castaño m.

chew vt mascar, masticar.

chewing gum n chicle m.

chic adj elegante.

chicanery n quisquilla f.

chick n polluelo m; (col) chica f.

chicken n pollo m.

chickenpox n varicela f.

chickpea n garbanzo m.

chicory n achicoria f.

chide vt reprobar, regañar.

chief adj principal, capital; ~ly adv principalmente; * n jefe, principal m.

chief executive n director/a general m/f.

chieftain n jefe, comandante m.

chiffon n gasa f.

chilblain n sabañón m.

child n niño m; niña f; hijo m; hija f; from a ~ desde niño/ña; with ~ preñada, embarazada.

childbirth n parto m.

childhood n infancia, niñez f; pequeñez f.

childish *adj* frívolo/la, pueril; **~ly** *adv* puerilmente.
childishness *n* puerilidad *f*.
childless *adj* sin hijos.
childlike *adj* pueril.
children *npl de* **child** niños *mpl*.
chill *adj* frío/ría, friolero/ra; * *n* frío *m*; * *vt* enfriar; helar.
chilly *adj* friolero/ra, friolento/ta.
chime *n* armonía *f*; clave *m*; * *vi* sonar con armonía; concordar.
chimney *n* chimenea *f*.
chimpanzee *n* chimpancé *m*.
chin *n* barbilla *f*.
china(ware) *n* porcelana *f*.
chink *n* grieta, hendedura *f*; * *vi* resonar.
chip *vt* astillar; * *vi* picarse; * *n* astilla *f*; chip *m*; patata o papa frita *f*.
chiropodist, podiatrist *n* pedicuro/ra *m/f*.
chirp *vi* chirriar, gorjear; * *n* gorjeo, chirrido *m*.
chirping *n* canto de las aves *m*.
chisel *n* cincel *m*; * *vt* cincelar, grabar.
chitchat *n* charla *f*.
chivalrous *adj* caballeresco/ca.
chivalry *n* caballería *f*.
chives *npl* cebollinos *f*.
chlorine *n* cloro *m*.
chloroform *n* cloroformo *m*.
chock-full *adj* de bote en bote, completamente lleno/na.
chocolate *n* chocolate *m*.
choice *n* elección, preferencia *f*; selecto *m*; * *adj* selecto/ta, exquisito/ta, excelente.
choir *n* coro *m*.
choke *vt* sofocar; oprimir; tapar.
cholera *n* cólera *m*.
choose *vt* escoger, elegir.
chop *vt* tajar, cortar; * *n* chuleta *f*; **~s** *pl* (*sl*) quijadas *fpl*.

chopper *n* helicóptero *m*.
chopping block *n* tajo de cocina *m*.
chopsticks *npl* palillos *mpl*.
chore *n* faena *f*.
choral *adj* coral.
chord *n* cuerda *f*.
chorist, chorister *n* corista *m*.
chorus *n* coro *m*.
Christ *n* Cristo *m*.
christen *vt* bautizar.
Christendom *n* cristianismo *m*; cristiandad *f*.
christening *n* bautismo *m*.
Christian *adj, n* cristiano/na *m/f*; **~ name** nombre de pila *m*.
Christianity *n* cristianismo *m*; cristiandad *f*.
Christmas *n* Navidad *f*.
Christmas card *n* tarjeta de Navidad *f*.
Christmas Eve *n* Nochebuena *f*.
chrome *n* cromo *m*.
chronic *adj* crónico/ca.
chronicle *n* crónica *f*.
chronicler *n* cronista *m*.
chronological *adj* cronológico/ca; **~ly** *adv* cronológicamente.
chronology *n* cronología *f*.
chronometer *n* cronómetro *m*.
chubby *adj* gordo/da.
chuck *vt* lanzar.
chuckle *vi* reírse a carcajadas.
chug *vi* resoplar.
chum *n* compañero/ra, compinche *m/f*.
chunk *n* trozo *m*.
church *n* iglesia *f*.
churchyard *n* cementerio *m*.
churlish *adj* hosco/ca, grosero/ra; tacaño/ña.
churn *n* mantequera *f*; * *vt* batir la leche para hacer manteca.
cider *n* sidra *f*.
cigar *n* cigarro *m*.

cigarette n cigarrillo m.
cigarette case n pitillera f.
cigarette end n colilla f.
cigarette holder n boquilla f.
cinder n carbonilla f.
cinema n cine m.
cinnamon n canela f.
cipher n cifra f.
circle n círculo m; corrillo m; asamblea f; * vt circundar; cercar; * vi circular.
circuit n circuito m; recinto m.
circuitous adj circular, tortuoso/sa.
circular adj circular, redondo/da; * n carta circular f.
circulate vi circular; moverse alrededor.
circulation n circulación f.
circumcise vt circuncidar.
circumcision n circuncisión f.
circumference n circunferencia f; circuito m.
circumflex n acento circunflejo m.
circumlocution n circunlocución f.
circumnavigate vt circunnavegar.
circumnavigation n circunnavegación f.
circumscribe vt circunscribir.
circumspect adj circunspecto/ta, prudente, reservado/da.
circumspection n circunspección, prudencia f.
circumstance n circunstancia, condición f; incidente m.
circumstantial adj accidental; accesorio/ria.
circumstantiate vt circunstanciar, detallar.
circumvent vt burlar.
circumvention n evasión f.
circus n circo m.
cistern n cisterna f.
citadel n ciudadela, fortaleza f.

citation n citación, cita f.
cite vt citar (a juicio); alegar; referirse a.
citizen n ciudadano/na m/f.
citizenship n ciudadanía f.
city n ciudad f.
civic adj cívico/ca.
civil adj civil, cortés; **~ly** adv civilmente.
civil defence n protección civil f.
civil engineer n ingeniero/ra civil m/f.
civilian n paisano m.
civility n civilidad, urbanidad, cortesía f.
civilization n civilización f.
civilize vt civilizar.
civil law n derecho civil m.
civil war n guerra civil f.
clad adj vestido/da, cubierto/ta.
claim vt pedir en juicio, reclamar; * n demanda f; derecho m.
claimant n reclamante m; demandador/a m/f.
clairvoyant n clarividente m/f; zahorí m.
clam n almeja f.
clamber vi gatear, trepar.
clammy adj viscoso/sa.
clamour n clamor, grito m; * vi vociferar, gritar.
clamp n abrazadera f; * vt afianzar; **to ~ down on** reforzar la lucha contra.
clan n familia, tribu, raza f.
clandestine adj clandestino/na, oculto/ta.
clang n rechino, sonido desapacible m; * vi rechinar.
clap vt aplaudir.
clapping n palmada f; aplauso, palmoteo m.
claret n clarete m.

clarification n clarificación f.

clarify vt clarificar, aclarar.

clarinet n clarinete m.

clarity n claridad f.

clash vi chocar; * n estruendo m; choque m.

clasp n broche m; hebilla f; abrazo m; * vt abrochar; abrazar.

class n clase f; orden f; * vt clasificar, coordinar.

classic(al) adj clásico/ca; * n autor clásico m.

classification n clasificación f.

classified advertisement n anuncio por palabras m.

classify vt clasificar.

classmate n compañero/ra de clase m/f.

classroom n aula f.

clatter vi resonar; hacer ruido; * n ruido m.

clause n cláusula f; artículo m; estipulación f.

claw n garra f; zarpa f; * vt desgarrar, arañar.

clay n arcilla f.

clean adj limpio/pia; casto/ta; * vt limpiar.

cleaning n limpieza f.

cleanliness n limpieza f.

cleanly adj limpio/pia; * adv limpiamente, aseadamente.

cleanness n limpieza f; pureza f.

cleanse vt limpiar, purificar; purgar.

clear adj claro/ra; neto/ta; diáfano/na; evidente; * adv claramente; * vt clarificar, aclarar; justificar, absolver; * vi aclararse.

clearance n despeje m; acreditación f.

clear-cut adj bien definido/da.

clearly adv claramente, evidentemente.

cleaver n cuchillo de carnicero m.

clef n clave f.

cleft n hendedura, abertura f.

clemency n clemencia f.

clement adj clemente, benigno/na.

clenched adj cerrado/da.

clergy n clero m.

clergyman n eclesiástico m.

clerical adj clerical, eclesiástico/ca.

clerk n dependiente m; oficinista m.

clever adj listo/ta; hábil, mañoso/sa; ~ly adv diestramente, hábilmente.

click vt chasquear; * vi taconear.

client n cliente m/f.

cliff n acantilado m.

climate n clima m; temperatura f.

climatic adj climático/ca.

climax n clímax m.

climb vt escalar, trepar; * vi subir.

climber n alpinista m/f.

climbing n alpinismo m.

clinch vt cerrar; remachar.

cling vi colgar, adherirse, pegarse.

clinic n clínica f.

clink vt hacer resonar; * vi resonar; * n retintín m.

clip vt cortar; * n clip m; horquilla f.

clipping n recorte m.

clique n camarilla f.

cloak n capa f; pretexto m; * vi encapotar.

cloakroom n guardarropa m.

clock n reloj m.

clockwork n mecanismo de un reloj m; * adj sumamente exacto y puntual.

clod n terrón m.

clog n zueco m; * vi atascarse.

cloister n claustro, monasterio m.

clone n clon m; * vt clonar.

cloned adj clónico/ca.

cloning n clonación f.

close vt cerrar; concluir, terminar; * vi cerrarse; * n fin m; conclusión *f;* * *adj* cercano/na; estrecho/cha; ajustado/da; denso/sa; reservado/da; * *adv* de cerca; ~ **by** muy cerca; junto.

closed *adj* cerrado/da.

closely *adv* estrechamente; de cerca.

closeness *n* proximidad *f;* estrechez; reclusión *f.*

closet *n* armario *m.*

close-up *n* primer plano *m.*

closure *n* cierre *m;* conclusión *f.*

clot *n* grumo *m;* embolia *f.*

cloth *n* paño *m;* mantel *m;* vestido *m;* lienzo *m.*

clothe *vt* vestir, cubrir.

clothes *npl* ropa *f;* ropaje *m;* ropa de cama *f;* **bed** ~ cobertores *mpl.*

clothes basket *n* cesta grande *f.*

clotheshorse *n* tendedero *m.*

clothesline *n* cuerda (de tendedero) *f.*

clothespin *n* pinza *f.*

clothing *n* vestidos *mpl.*

cloud *n* nube *f;* nublado *m;* (*fig*) adversidad *f;* * *vt* anublar; oscurecer; * *vi* anublarse; oscurecerse.

cloudiness *n* nubosidad *f;* oscuridad *f.*

cloudy *adj* nublado/da; oscuro/ra; sombrío/ría, melancólico/ca.

clout *n* tortazo *m.*

clove *n* clavo *m.*

clover *n* trébol *m.*

clown *n* payaso *m.*

club *n* cachiporra *f.*

club car *n* coche restaurante *m.*

clue *n* pista *f,* indicios *m;* idea *f.*

clump *n* grupo *m.*

clumsily *adv* torpemente.

clumsiness *n* torpeza *f.*

clumsy *adj* torpe, pesado/da; sin arte.

cluster *n* racimo *m;* manada *f;* pelotón *m;* * *vt* agrupar; * *vi* arracimarse.

clutch *n* embrague *m;* apretón *m;* * *vt* empuñar.

clutter *vt* atestar.

coach *n* autocar, autobús *m;* vagón *m;* entrenador/a *m/f;* * *vt* entrenar; enseñar.

coach trip *n* excursión en autocar *f.*

coagulate *vt* coagular, cuajar; * *vi* coagularse, cuajarse, espesarse.

coal *n* carbón *m.*

coalesce *vi* juntarse, incorporarse.

coalfield *n* yacimiento de carbón *m.*

coalition *n* coalición, confederación *f.*

coalman *n* carbonero *m.*

coalmine *n* mina de carbón, carbonería *f.*

coarse *adj* basto/ta; grosero/ra; zafio/fia; ~**ly** *adv* groseramente.

coast *n* costa *f.*

coastal *adj* costero/ra; ribereño/ña.

coastguard *n* guardacostas *m invar.*

coastline *n* litoral *m.*

coat *n* chaqueta *f;* abrigo *m;* capa *f;* * *vt* cubrir.

coat hanger *n* percha *f.*

coat hook *n* percha *f.*

coating *n* revestimiento *m.*

coax *vt* lisonjear.

cob *n* mazorca de maíz *f.*

cobbler *n* zapatero/ra *m/f.*

cobbles, cobblestones *npl* adoquines *mpl.*

cobweb *n* telaraña *f.*

cocaine *n* cocaína *f.*

coccyx *n* rabadilla *f.*

cock *n* gallo *m;* macho *m;* * *vt* armar el sombrero; amartillar, montar una escopeta.

cock-a-doodle-doo *n* quiquiriquí *m.*

cockcrow *n* canto del gallo *m.*

cockerel *n* gallito *m.*

cockfight(ing) *n* pelea de gallos *f.*

cockle *n* berberecho *m.*

cockpit n cabina f.
cockroach n cucaracha f.
cocktail n cóctel m.
cocoa n coco m; cacao m.
coconut n coco m.
cocoon n capullo (del gusano de seda) m.
cod n bacalao m.
code n código m; prefijo m.
cod-liver oil n aceite de hígado de bacalao m.
coefficient n coeficiente m.
coercion n coerción f.
coexistence n coexistencia f.
coffee n café m.
coffee break n descanso m.
coffee house n café m.
coffee-pot n cafetera f.
coffee table n mesita f.
coffer n cofre m; caja f.
coffin n ataúd m.
cog n diente (de rueda) m.
cogency n fuerza, urgencia f.
cogent adj convincente, urgente; **~ly** adv de modo convincente.
cognac n coñac m.
cognate adj cognado/da.
cognition n conocimiento m; convicción f.
cognizance n conocimiento m; competencia f.
cognizant adj informado/da; (law) competente.
cogwheel n rueda dentada f.
cohabit vi cohabitar.
cohabitation n cohabitación f.
cohere vi pegarse; unirse.
coherence n coherencia, conexión f.
coherent adj coherente; consiguiente.
cohesion n coherencia f.
cohesive adj cohesivo/va.
coil n rollo m; bobina f; * vt enrollar.
coin n moneda f; * vt acuñar.

coincide vi coincidir, concurrir, convenir.
coincidence n coincidencia f.
coincidental adj fortuito; coincidente.
coke n coque m.
Coke® n Coca-Cola® f.
colander n colador, pasador m.
cold adj frío/ría; indiferente, insensible; reservado/da; **~ly** adv fríamente; indiferentemente; * n frío m; frialdad f; resfriado m.
cold-blooded adj impasible.
coldness n frialdad f; indiferencia, insensibilidad, apatía f.
cold sore n herpes labial m.
coleslaw n ensalada de col f.
colic n cólico m.
collaborate vt cooperar.
collaboration n cooperación f.
collapse vi hundirse; * n hundimiento; (med) colapso m.
collapsible adj plegable.
collar n cuello m.
collarbone n clavícula f.
collate vt comparar, confrontar.
collateral adj colateral; * n garantía subsidiaria f.
collation n colación f.
colleague n colega, compañero/ra m/f.
collect vt recoger; coleccionar.
collection n colección f; compilación f.
collective adj colectivo/va, congregado/da; **~ly** colectivamente.
collector n coleccionista m/f.
college n colegio m.
collide vi chocar.
collision n choque m, colisión f.
colloquial adj familiar; coloquial; **~ly** adv familiarmente.
colloquialism n lengua usual f.
collusion n colusión f.

colon n dos puntos mpl; (med) colon m.

colonel n (mil) coronel m.

colonial adj colonial.

colonist n colono m.

colonize vt colonizar.

colony n colonia f.

colossal adj colosal.

colossus n coloso m.

colour n color m; ~s pl bandera f; * vt colorar; pintar; * vi ponerse colorado/da.

colour-blind adj daltónico/ca.

colourful adj lleno de color.

colouring n colorido m.

colourless adj descolorido/da, sin color.

colour television n televisión en color f.

colt n potro m.

column n columna f.

columnist n columnista m.

coma n coma f.

comatose adj comatoso/sa.

comb n peine m; * vt peinar.

combat n combate m; batalla f; **single ~** duelo m; * vt combatir.

combatant n combatiente m.

combative adj combativo/va.

combination n combinación, coordinación f.

combine vt combinar; * vi unirse.

combustion n combustión f.

come vi venir; **to ~ across/upon** vt topar con; dar con; **to ~ by** vt conseguir; **to ~ down** vi bajar; ser derribado/da; **to ~ from** vt ser de; **to ~ in for** vt merecer; **to ~ into** vt heredar; **to ~ round/to** vi volver en sí; **to ~ up with** vt sugerir.

comedian n comediante, cómico m.

comedienne n cómica f.

comedy n comedia f.

comet n cometa m.

comfort n confort m; ayuda f; consuelo m; comodidad f; * vt confortar; alentar, consolar.

comfortable adj cómodo/da.

comfortably adv agradablemente; cómodamente.

comforter n chupete m.

comic(al) adj cómico/ca, burlesco/ca; ~ly adv cómicamente.

coming n venida, llegada f; * adj venidero/ra.

comma n (gr) coma f.

command vt comandar, ordenar; * n orden f.

commander n comandante m.

commandment n mandamiento, precepto m.

commando n comando m.

commemorate vt conmemorar; celebrar.

commemoration n conmemoración f.

commence vt, vi comenzar.

commencement n principio m.

commend vt encomendar; alabar; enviar.

commendable adj recomendable.

commendably adv loablemente.

commendation n recomendación f.

commensurate adj proporcionado/da.

comment n comentario m; * vt comentar; glosar.

commentary n comentario m; interpretación f.

commentator n comentarista m/f.

commerce n comercio, tráfico, trato, negocio m.

commercial adj comercial.

commiserate vt compadecer, tener compasión.

commiseration n conmiseración, piedad f.

commissariat *n* comisaría *f.*

commission *n* comisión *f*; * *vt* comisionar; encargar.

commissioner *n* comisionado/da, delegado/da *m/f.*

commit *vt* cometer; depositar; encargar.

commitment *n* compromiso *m.*

committee *n* comité *m.*

commodity *n* comodidad *f.*

common *adj* común; bajo/ja; **in ~** comúnmente; * *n* pastos comunales *mpl.*

commoner *n* plebeyo *m.*

common law *n* derecho consuetudinario *m.*

commonly *adv* comúnmente, frecuentemente.

commonplace *n* lugar común *m*; * *adj* trivial.

common sense *n* sentido común *m.*

commonwealth *n* república *f.*

commotion *n* tumulto *m*; perturbación del ánimo *f.*

commune *vt* conversar, conferir.

communicable *adj* comunicable, impartible.

communicate *vt* comunicar, participar; * *vi* comunicarse.

communication *n* comunicación *f.*

communicative *adj* comunicativo/va.

communion *n* comunión *f.*

communiqué *n* comunicado *m.*

communism *n* comunismo *m.*

communist *n* comunista *m/f.*

community *n* comunidad *f*; colectividad *f.*

community centre *n* centro social *m.*

community chest *n* arca comunitaria *f.*

commutable *adj* conmutable, cambiable.

commutation ticket *n* billete de abono *m.*

commute *vt* conmutar.

compact *adj* compacto/ta, sólido/da, denso/sa; * *n* pacto, convenio *m*; **~ly** *adv* estrechamente; en pocas palabras.

compact disc, CD *n* compact disc *m*, disco compacto *m.*

companion *n* compañero/ra, socio/cia, compinche *m/f.*

companionship *n* sociedad, compañía *f.*

company *n* compañía, sociedad *f*; compañía de comercio *f.*

comparable *adj* comparable.

comparative *adj* comparativo/va; **~ly** *adv* comparativamente.

compare *vt* comparar.

comparison *n* comparación *f.*

compartment *n* compartimento *m.*

compass *n* brújula *f.*

compassion *n* compasión, piedad *f.*

compassionate *adj* compasivo/va.

compatibility *n* compatibilidad *f.*

compatible *adj* compatible.

compatriot *n* compatriota *m/f.*

compel *vt* compeler, obligar, constreñir.

compelling *adj* convicente.

compensate *vt* compensar.

compensation *n* compensación *f*; resarcimiento *m.*

compere *n* (*rad*, *TV*) presentador/a *m/f.*

compete *vi* concurrir, competir.

competence *n* competencia *f*; suficiencia *f.*

competent *adj* competente, adecuado/da; **~ly** *adv* competentemente.

competition *n* competencia *f*; concurrencia *f.*

competitive *adj* competitivo/va.

competitive scheduling *n* contraprogramación *f*.

competitor *n* competidor/a *m/f*, rival *m*.

compilation *n* compilación *f*.

compile *vt* compilar.

complacency *n* autocomplacencia *f*.

complacent *adj* complaciente.

complain *vi* quejarse, lamentarse, lastimarse, dolerse.

complaint *n* queja *f*; reclamación *f*.

complement *n* complemento *m*.

complementary *adj* complementario/ria.

complete *adj* completo/ta, perfecto/ta; ~**ly** *adv* completamente; * *vt* completar, acabar.

completion *n* terminación *f*.

complex *adj* complejo/ja.

complexion *n* tez *f*; aspecto *m*.

complexity *n* complejidad *f*.

compliance *n* complacencia, sumisión *f*.

compliant *adj* complaciente, oficioso/sa.

complicate *vt* complicar.

complication *n* complicación *f*.

complicity *n* complicidad *f*.

compliment *n* cumplido *m*; * *vt* cumplimentar; hacer cumplidos.

complimentary *adj* elogioso/sa, ceremonioso/sa.

comply *vi* cumplir; condescender, conformarse.

component *adj* componente.

compose *vt* componer; sosegar.

composed *adj* compuesto/ta, moderado/da.

composer *n* compositor/a *m/f*.

composite *adj* compuesto/ta.

composition *n* composición *f*.

compositor *n* cajista *m*.

compost *n* abono, estiércol *m*.

composure *n* composición *f*; tranquilidad, sangre fría *f*.

compound *vt* componer, combinar; * *adj*, *n* compuesto *m*.

comprehend *vt* comprender, contener; entender.

comprehensible *adj* comprensible; ~**ly** *adv* comprensiblemente.

comprehension *n* comprensión *f*; inteligencia *f*.

comprehensive *adj* comprensivo/va; ~**ly** *adv* comprensivamente.

compress *vt* comprimir, estrechar; * *n* cabezal *m*.

comprise *vt* comprender, incluir.

compromise *n* compromiso *m*; * *vt* comprometer.

compulsion *n* compulsión *f*; apremio *m*.

compulsive *adj* compulsivo/va; ~**ly** *adv* compulsivamente.

compulsory *adj* obligatorio/ria.

compunction *n* compunción, contrición *f*.

computable *adj* computable, calculable.

computation *n* computación *f*, cómputo *m*.

compute *vt* computar, calcular.

computer *n* ordenador *m*.

computer graphics *n* infografía *f*.

computerize *vt* computerizar, informatizar.

computer programming *n* programación *f*.

computer science *n* informática *f*.

comrade *n* camarada, compañero/ra *m/f*.

comradeship *n* compañerismo *m*.

con *vt* estafar; * *n* estafa *f*.

concave *adj* cóncavo/va.

concavity *n* concavidad *f*.

conceal vt ocultar, esconder.

concealment n ocultación f; encubrimiento m.

concede vt conceder, asentir.

conceit n concepto m; capricho m; pensamiento m; presunción f.

conceited adj afectado/da, vano/na, presumido/da.

conceivable adj concebible, inteligible.

conceive vt concebir, comprender; * vi concebir.

concentrate vt concentrar.

concentration n concentración f.

concentration camp n campo de concentración m.

concentric adj concéntrico/ca.

concept n concepto m.

conception n concepción f; sentimiento m.

concern vt concernir, importar; * n negocio m; asunto m; preocupación f.

concerning prep tocante a.

concert n concierto m.

concerto n concierto m.

concession n concesión f; privilegio m.

conciliate vt conciliar.

conciliation n conciliación f.

conciliatory adj conciliador/a.

concise adj conciso/sa, sucinto/ta; ~ly adv concisamente.

conclude vt concluir; decidir; determinar.

conclusion n conclusión, determinación f; fin m.

conclusive adj decisivo/va, conclusivo/va; ~ly adv concluyentemente.

concoct vt cocer, digerir; (fig) zurcir.

concoction n confección f; cocción f.

concomitant adj concomitante.

concord n concordia, armonía f.

concordance n concordancia f.

concordant adj concordante, conforme.

concourse n concurso m; multitud f; gentío m.

concrete n concreto m; * vt concretar.

concubine n concubina f.

concur vi concurrir; juntarse.

concurrence n concurrencia f; unión f; asistencia f.

concurrently adv al mismo tiempo.

concussion n conmoción cerebral f.

condemn vt condenar; desaprobar; vituperar.

condemnation n condena f.

condensation n condensación f.

condense vt condensar.

condescend vi condescender; consentir.

condescending adj condescendiente.

condescension n condescendencia f.

condiment n condimento m; salsa f.

condition vt condicionar; *n situación, condición, calidad f; estado m.

conditional adj condicional, hipotético/ca; ~ly adv condicionalmente.

conditioned adj condicionado/da.

conditioner n acondicionador m.

condolences npl pésame m.

condom n condón m.

condominium n condominio m.

condone vt perdonar.

conducive adj conducente, oportuno/na.

conduct n conducta f; manejo, proceder m; * vt conducir, guiar.

conductor n conductor m; guía, director m; conductor de electricidad m.

conduit n conducto m; cano m.

cone n cono m.

confection n confitura f; confección f.

confectioner n confitero/ra m/f.

confectioner's (shop) n pastelería f; confitería f.

confectionery n caramelo m.

confederacy n confederación f.

confederate vi confederarse; * adj, n confederado/da m/f.

confer vi conferenciar; * vt conferir, comparar.

conference n conferencia f.

confess vt (vi) confesar(se).

confession n confesión f.

confessional n confesionario m.

confessor n confesor m.

confetti n confeti m.

confidant n confidente, amigo/ga íntimo/ma m/f.

confide vt, vi confiar; fiarse.

confidence n confianza, seguridad f.

confidence trick n timo m.

confident adj cierto/ta, seguro/ra; confiado/da.

confidential adj confidencial.

configuration n configuración f.

confine vt limitar; aprisionar.

confinement n prisión f; confinación f.

confirm vt confirmar; ratificar.

confirmation n confirmación f; ratificación f; prueba f.

confirmed adj empedernido/da.

confiscate vt confiscar.

confiscation n confiscación f.

conflagration n conflagración f; incendio m.

conflict n conflicto m; combate m; pelea f.

conflicting adj contradictorio/ria.

confluence n confluencia f; concurso m.

conform vt (vi) conformar(se).

conformity n conformidad, conveniencia f.

confound vt turbar, confundir.

confront vt afrontar; confrontar; comparar.

confrontation n enfrentamiento m.

confuse vt confundir; desordenar.

confusing adj confuso/sa.

confusion n confusión f; perturbación f; desorden m.

congeal vt (vi) helar, congelar(se).

congenial adj congenial.

congenital adj congénito/ta.

congested adj atestado/da.

congestion n congestión f; acumulación f.

conglomerate vt conglomerar, aglomerar; * adj aglomerado/da; * n (com) conglomerado m.

conglomeration n aglomeración f.

congratulate vt congratular, felicitar.

congratulations npl felicidades fpl; * interj enhorabuena.

congratulatory adj congratulatorio/ria.

congregate vt congregar, reunir.

congregation n congregación, reunión f.

congress n congreso m; conferencia f.

congressman n miembro del Congreso m.

congruity n congruencia f.

congruous adj idóneo/nea, congruo/rua, apto/ta.

conic(al) adj cónico/ca.

conifer n conífera f.

coniferous adj (bot) conífero/ra.

conjecture n conjetura, apariencia f; * vt conjeturar; pronosticar.

conjugal adj conyugal, matrimonial.

conjugate vt (gr) conjugar.

conjugation n conjugación f.

conjunction *n* conjunción *f*; unión *f*.

conjuncture *n* coyuntura *f*; ocasión *f*; tiempo crítico *m*.

conjure *vi* conjurar, suplicar.

conjurer *n* conjurador/a, encantador/a *m/f*.

con man *n* timador *m*.

connect *vt* juntar, unir, enlazar.

connection *n* conexión *f*.

connivance *n* connivencia *f*.

connive *vi* tolerar.

connoisseur *n* conocedor/a *m/f*.

conquer *vt* conquistar; vencer.

conqueror *n* vencedor/a, conquistador/a *m/f*.

conquest *n* conquista *f*.

conscience *n* conciencia *f*; escrúpulo *m*.

conscientious *adj* concienzudo/da, escrupuloso/sa; **~ly** *adv* concienzudamente.

conscientious objector *n* objetor de conciencia *m*.

conscious *adj* sabedor, consciente; **~ly** *adv* a sabiendas.

consciousness *n* conciencia *f*.

conscript *n* conscripto *m*.

conscription *n* reclutamiento *m*.

consecrate *vt* consagrar; dedicar.

consecration *n* consagración *f*.

consecutive *adj* consecutivo/va; **~ly** *adv* consecutivamente.

consensus *n* consenso *m*.

consent *n* consentimiento *m*; aprobación *f*; * *vi* consentir; aprobar.

consequence *n* consecuencia *f*; importancia *f*.

consequent *adj* consecutivo/va, concluyente; **~ly** *adv* consiguientemente.

conservation *n* conservación *f*.

conservative *adj* conservador/a *m/f*.

conservatory *n* conservatorio *m*.

conserve *vt* conservar; * *n* conserva *f*.

consider *vt* considerar, examinar; * *vi* pensar, deliberar.

considerable *adj* considerable; importante; **~bly** *adv* considerablemente.

considerate *adj* considerado/da, prudente, discreto/ta; **~ly** *adv* juiciosamente; prudentemente.

consideration *n* consideración *f*; deliberación *f*; importancia *f*; valor, mérito *m*.

considering *conj* en vista de; **~ that** a causa de; visto que, en razón a.

consign *vt* consignar.

consignment *n* consignación *f*.

consist *vi* consistir.

consistency *n* consistencia *f*.

consistent *adj* consistente; conveniente, conforme; solido/da, estable; **~ly** *adv* conformemente.

console *n* consola *f*.

consolable *adj* consolable.

consolation *n* consolación *f*; consuelo *m*.

consolatory *adj* consolatorio/ria.

console *vt* consolar.

consolidate *vt*, *vi* consolidar(se).

consolidation *n* consolidación *f*.

consonant *adj* consonante, conforme; * *n* (*gr*) consonante *f*.

consort *n* consorte, socio *m*.

conspicuous *adj* conspicuo/cua, aparente; notable; **~ly** *adv* claramente.

conspiracy *n* conspiración *f*.

conspirator *n* conspirador/a *m/f*.

conspire *vi* conspirar, maquinar.

constancy *n* constancia, perseverancia, persistencia *f*.

constant *adj* constante; perseverante; **~ly** *adv* constantemente.

constellation *n* constelación *f*.

consternation *n* consternación *f*; terror *m*.

constipated *adj* estreñido/da.

constituency *n* circunscripción electoral *f*.

constituent *n* constitutivo *m*; * *adj* constituyente.

constitute *vt* constituir; establecer.

constitution *n* constitución *f*; estado *m*; temperamento *m*.

constitutional *adj* constitucional.

constrain *vt* constreñir, forzar; restringir.

constraint *n* constreñimiento *m*; fuerza, violencia *f*.

constrict *vt* constreñir, estrechar.

construct *vt* construir, edificar.

construction *n* construcción *f*.

construe *vt* construir; interpretar.

consul *n* cónsul *m*.

consular *adj* consular.

consulate, consulship *n* consulado *m*.

consult *vt* (*vi*) consultar(se); aconsejar(se).

consultant *n* asesor *m*.

consultation *n* consulta, deliberación *f*.

consume *vt* consumir; disipar; * *vi* consumirse.

consumer *n* consumidor/a *m/f*.

consumer goods *npl* bienes de consumo *mpl*.

consumerism *n* consumismo *m*.

consumer society *n* sociedad de consumo *f*.

consummate *vt* consumar, acabar, perfeccionar; * *adj* cumplido/da, consumado/da.

consummation *n* consumación, perfección *f*.

consumption *n* consumo *m*.

contact *n* contacto *m*.

contact lenses *npl* lentes de contacto *fpl*.

contagious *adj* contagioso/sa.

contain *vt* contener, comprender; caber, reprimir, refrenar.

container *n* recipiente *m*.

contaminate *vt* contaminar; corromper; **~d** *adj* contaminado/da, corrompido/da.

contamination *n* contaminación *f*.

contemplate *vt* contemplar.

contemplation *n* contemplación *f*.

contemplative *adj* contemplativo/va.

contemporaneous, contemporary *adj* contemporáneo/nea.

contempt *n* desprecio, desdén *m*.

contemptible *adj* despreciable, vil; **~bly** *adv* vilmente.

contemptuous *adj* desdeñoso/sa, insolente; **~ly** *adv* con desdén.

contend *vi* contender, disputar, afirmar.

content *adj* contento/ta, satisfecho/cha; * *vt* contentar, satisfacer; * *n* contenido *m*; **~s** *pl* contenido *m*; tabla de materias *f*.

contentedly *adv* de un modo satisfecho/cha; con paciencia.

contention *n* contención, altercación *f*.

contentious *adj* contencioso/sa, litigioso/sa; **~ly** *adv* contenciosamente.

contentment *n* contentamiento, placer *m*.

contest *vt* contestar, disputar, litigar; * *n* concurso *m*; contestación, altercación *f*.

contestant *n* concursante/ta *m/f*.

context *n* contexto *m*; contextura *f*.

contiguous *adj* contiguo/gua, vecino/na.

continent adj continente; * n continente m.

continental adj continental.

contingency n contingencia f; acontecimiento m; eventualidad f.

contingent n contingente m; cuota f; * adj contingente, casual; ~ly adv casualmente.

continual adj continuo/nua; ~ly adv continuamente.

continuation n continuación, serie f.

continue vt continuar; * vi durar, perseverar, persistir.

continuity n continuidad f.

continuous adj continuo/nua, unido/da; ~ly adv continuadamente.

contort vt torcer.

contortion n contorsión f.

contour n contorno m.

contraband n contrabando m; * adj prohibido/da, ilegal.

contraception n contracepción f.

contraceptive n anticonceptivo m; * adj anticonceptivo/va.

contract vt contraer; abreviar; contratar; *vi contraerse; * n contrato, pacto m.

contraction n contracción f; abreviatura f.

contractor n contratante m/f.

contradict vt contradecir.

contradiction n contradicción, oposición f.

contradictory adj contradictorio/ria.

contraption n artilugio m.

contrariness n contrariedad, oposición f.

contrary adj contrario/ria, opuesto/ta; * n contrario m; **on the ~** al contrario.

contrast n contraste m; oposición f; * vt contrastar, oponer.

contrasting adj opuesto/ta.

contravention n contravención f.

contributory adj contributario/ria.

contribute vt contribuir, ayudar.

contribution n contribución f; tributo m.

contributor n contribuidor/a m/f.

contributory adj contribuyente.

contrite adj contrito/ta, arrepentido/da.

contrition n penitencia, contrición f.

contrivance n designio m; invención f; concepto m.

contrive vt inventar, trazar, maquinar; manejar; combinar.

control n control m; inspección f; * vt controlar; manejar; restringir; gobernar.

control room n sala de mando f.

control tower n torre de control f.

controversial adj polémico/ca.

controversy n controversia f.

contusion n contusión f, magullamiento m.

conundrum n problema m.

conurbation n conurbación f.

convalesce vi convalecer.

convalescence n convalecencia f.

convalescent adj convaleciente.

convene vt convocar; juntar, unir; * vi convenir, juntarse.

convenience n conveniencia, comodidad, conformidad f.

convenient adj conveniente, apto/ta, cómodo/da, propio/pia; ~ly adv cómodamente, oportunamente.

convent n convento, claustro, monasterio m.

convention n convención f; contrato, tratado m.

conventional adj convencional, estipulado/da.

converge vi converger.

convergence *n* convergencia *f*.
convergent *adj* convergente.
conversant *adj* versado en; íntimo/ma.
conversation *n* conversación *f*.
converse *vi* conversar; platicar.
conversely *adv* mutuamente, recíprocamente.
conversion *n* conversión, transmutación *f*.
convert *vt* (*vi*) convertir(se); * *n* converso, convertido *m*.
convertible *adj* convertible, transmutable; * *n* descapotable *m*.
convex *adj* convexo/xa.
convexity *n* convexidad *f*.
convey *vt* transportar; transmitir, transferir.
conveyance *n* transporte *m*; conducción *f*; escritura de traspaso *f*.
conveyancer *n* notario *m*.
convict *vt* probar un delito; * *n* convicto/ta *m/f*.
conviction *n* convicción *f*.
convince *vt* convencer, poner en evidencia.
convincing *adj* convincente.
convincingly *adv* de modo convincente.
convivial *adj* sociable; hospitalario/ria.
conviviality *n* sociabilidad *f*.
convoke *vt* convocar, reunir.
convoy *n* convoy *m*.
convulse *vt* conmover, convulsionar.
convulsion *n* convulsión *f*; conmoción *f*; tumulto *m*.
convulsive *adj* convulsivo/va; ~**ly** *adv* convulsivamente.
coo *vi* arrullar.
cook *n* cocinero/ra *m/f*; * *vt* cocinar; * *vi* cocinar; guisar.

cookbook *n* libro de cocina *m*.
cooker *n* cocina *f*.
cookery *n* arte culinario *m*, cocina *f*.
cool *adj* fresco/ca; indiferente; * *n* frescura *f*; * *vt* enfriar, refrescar.
coolly *adv* frescamente; indiferentemente.
coolness *n* fresco *m*; frialdad, frescura *f*.
cooperate *vi* cooperar.
cooperation *n* cooperación *f*.
cooperative *adj* cooperativo/va; cooperante.
coordinate *vt* coordinar.
coordination *n* coordinación, elección *f*.
cop *n* (*fam*) poli *m*.
copartner *n* compañero/ra, socio/cia *m/f*.
cope *vi* arreglárselas.
copier *n* copiadora *f*.
copious *adj* copioso/sa, abundante; ~**ly** *adv* en abundancia.
copper *n* cobre *m*.
coppice, copse *n* bosquecillo *m*.
copulate *vi* copular.
copy *n* copia *f*; original *m*; ejemplar *m*; * *vt* copiar; imitar.
copybook *n* copiador de cartas (libro) *m*.
copying machine *n* copiadora *f*.
copyist *n* copista *m/f*.
copyright *n* propiedad de una obra literaria *f*; derechos de autor *mpl*.
coral *n* coral *m*.
coral reef *n* arrecife de coral *m*.
cord *n* cuerda *f*; cable *m*.
cordial *adj* cordial, de corazón, amistoso/sa; ~**ly** *adv* cordialmente.
corduroy *n* pana *f*.
core *n* cuesco *m*; interior, centro, corazón *m*; materia *f*.

cork *n* alcornoque *m*; corcho *m*; * *vt* encorchar.

corkscrew *n* sacacorchos *m invar*.

corn *n* maíz *m*; grano *m*; callo *m*.

corncob *n* mazorca *f*.

cornea *n* córnea *f*.

corned beef *n* carne acecinada *f*.

corner *n* rincón *m*; esquina *f*.

cornerstone *n* piedra angular *f*.

cornet *n* corneta *f*.

cornfield *n* maizal *m*.

cornflakes *npl* copos de maíz *mpl*.

cornflour *n* harina de maíz *f*.

cornice *n* cornisa *f*.

corollary *n* corolario *m*.

coronary *n* infarto *m*.

coronation *n* coronación *f*.

coroner *n* oficial que hace la inspección jurídica de los cadáveres *m*.

coronet *n* corona pequeña *f*.

corporal *n* cabo *m*.

corporate *adj* corporativo/va.

corporation *n* corporación *f*; gremio *m*.

corporeal *adj* corpóreo/rea.

corps *n* cuerpo (de ejército) *m*; regimiento *m*.

corpse *n* cadáver *m*.

corpulent *adj* corpulento/ta, gordo/da.

corpuscle *n* corpúsculo, átomo *m*.

corral *n* corral *m*.

correct *vt* corregir; enmendar; * *adj* correcto/ta, justo/ta; **~ly** *adv* correctamente.

correction *n* corrección *f*; enmienda *f*; censura *f*.

corrective *adj* correctivo/va; * *n* correctivo *m*; restricción *f*.

correctness *n* exactitud *f*.

correlation *n* correlación *f*.

correlative *adj* correlativo/va.

correspond *vi* corresponder; corresponderse.

correspondence *n* correspondencia *f*.

correspondent *adj* correspondiente, conforme; * *n* corresponsal *m*.

corridor *n* pasillo *m*.

corroborate *vt* corroborar.

corroboration *n* corroboración *f*.

corroborative *adj* corroborativo/va.

corrode *vt* corroer.

corrosion *n* corrosión *f*.

corrosive *adj*, *n* corrosivo *m*.

corrugated iron *n* chapa ondulada *f*.

corrupt *vt* corromper; sobornar; * *vi* corromperse, pudrirse; * *adj* corrompido/da; depravado/da.

corruptible *adj* corruptible.

corruption *n* corrupción *f*; depravación *f*.

corruptive *adj* corruptivo/va.

corset *n* corsé, corpiño *m*.

cortege *n* cortejo *m*.

cosily *adv* cómodamente, con facilidad.

cosmetic *adj* cosmético/ca; * *n* cosmético *m*.

cosmic *adj* cósmico/ca.

cosmonaut *n* cosmonauta *m/f*.

cosmopolitan *adj* cosmopolita.

cosset *vt* mimar.

cost *n* coste, precio *m*; * *vi* costar.

costly *adj* costoso/sa, caro/ra.

costume *n* traje *m*.

cosy *adj* cómodo/da.

cottage *n* casita, casucha *f*.

cotton *n* algodón *m*.

cotton mill *n* hilandería de algodón.

cotton wool *n* algodón hidrófilo *m*.

couch *n* sofá *m*.

couchette *n* litera *f*.

cough *n* tos *f*; * *vi* toser.

council *n* concilio, consejo *m*.

councillor *n* concejal/a *m/f*.

counsel *n* consejo, aviso *m*; abogado/da *m/f*.

counsellor n consejero/ra m/f; abogado/da m/f.

count vt contar, numerar; calcular; **to ~ on** contar con; * n cuenta f; cálculo m; conde m.

countdown n cuenta atrás f.

countenance n rostro m; aspecto m; (buena o mala) cara f.

counter n mostrador m; (games) ficha f.

counteract vt contrariar, impedir, estorbar; frustrar.

counterbalance vt contrapesar; igualar, compensar; * n contrapeso m.

counterfeit vt contrahacer, imitar, falsear; * adj falsificado/da; fingido/da.

countermand vt contramandar; revocar.

counterpart n parte correspondiente f.

counterproductive adj contraproducente.

countersign vt refrendar; firmar un decreto.

countess n condesa f.

countless adj innumerable.

countrified adj rústico/ca; tosco/ca, rudo/da.

country n país m; campo m; región f; patria f; * adj rústico/ca; campestre, rural.

country house n casa de campo, granja f.

countryman n paisano m; compatriota m.

county n condado m.

coup n golpe m.

coupé n (auto) cupé m.

couple n par m; lazo m; yuntas fpl; * vt unir, parear; casar.

couplet n copla f; par m.

coupon n cupón m.

courage n coraje, valor f.

courageous adj corajudo/da, valeroso/sa; **~ly** adv valerosamente.

courier n correo, mensajero/ra m/f, expreso m.

course n curso m; carrera f; camino m; ruta f; método m; **of ~** por supuesto, sin duda.

court n corte f; palacio m; tribunal de justicia m; * vt cortejar; solicitar, adular.

courteous adj cortés; benévolo/la; **~ly** adv cortésmente.

courtesan n cortesana f.

courtesy n cortesía f; benignidad f.

courthouse n palacio de justicia m.

courtly adj cortesano/na, elegante.

court martial n consejo de guerra m.

courtroom n sala de justicia f.

courtyard n patio m.

cousin n primo m; prima f; **first ~** primo hermano m.

cove n (mar) ensenada, caleta f.

covenant n contrato m; convención f; * vi pactar, estipular.

cover n cubierta f; abrigo m; pretexto m; * vt cubrir; tapar; ocultar; proteger.

coverage n alcance m.

coveralls npl mono m.

covering n ropa f; vestido m.

cover letter n carta de explicación f.

covert adj cubierto/ta; oculto/ta, secreto/ta; **~ly** adv secretamente.

cover-up n encubrimiento m.

covet vt codiciar, desear con ansia.

covetous adj avariento/ta, sórdido/da.

cow n vaca f.

coward n cobarde m/f.

cowardice n cobardía, timidez f.

cowardly adj, adv cobarde; pusilánime.

cowboy n vaquero m.
cower vi agacharse.
cowherd n vaquero m; vaquerizo m.
coy adj recatado/da, modesto/ta; esquivo/va; **~ly** adv con esquivez.
coyness n esquivez, modestia f.
crab n cangrejo m; manzana silvestre f.
crab apple n manzana silvestre f; **~ tree** n manzano silvestre m.
crack n crujido m; hendedura, quebraja f; * vt hender, rajar; romper; **to ~ down on** reprimandar fuertemente;* vi reventar.
cracker n buscapiés m invar; galleta f.
crackle vi crujir, chillar.
crackling n estallido, crujido m.
cradle n cuna f; * vt acunar.
craft n arte m; artificio m; barco m.
craftily adv astutamente.
craftiness n astucia, estratagema f.
craftsman n artífice, artesano m.
craftsmanship n artesanía f.
crafty adj astuto/ta, artificioso/sa.
crag n despeñadero m.
cram vt embutir; engordar; empujar; * vi empollar.
crammed adj atestado/da.
cramp n calambre m; * vt constreñir.
cramped adj apretado/da.
crampon n crampón m.
cranberry n arándano agrio m.
crane n grulla f; grúa f.
crash vi estallar; * vr zamparse; * n estallido m; choque m.
crash helmet n casco m.
crash landing n aterrizaje forzoso m.
crass adj craso/sa, grueso/sa, basto/ta, tosco/ca, grosero/ra.
crate n cesta grande f.
crater n cráter m; boca de volcán f.
cravat n pañuelo m.
crave vt rogar, suplicar.

craving adj insaciable, pedigüeño/ña; * n deseo ardiente m.
crawl vi arrastrar; **to ~ with** hormiguear.
crayfish n cangrejo de río m.
crayon n lápiz m.
craze n manía f.
craziness n locura f.
crazy adj loco/ca.
creak vi crujir, chirriar.
cream n crema f; * adj color crema.
creamy adj cremoso/sa.
crease n pliegue m; * vt plegar.
create vt crear; causar.
creation n creación f; elección f.
creative adj creativo/va.
creator n creador/a m/f.
creature n criatura f.
credence n creencia, fe f; renombre m.
credentials npl (cartas) credenciales fpl.
credibility n credibilidad f.
credible adj creíble.
credit n crédito m; reputación f; autoridad f; * vt creer, fiar, acreditar.
creditable adj estimable, honorífico/ca; **~bly** adv honorablemente.
credit card n tarjeta de crédito f.
creditor n acreedor m.
credulity n credulidad f.
credulous adj crédulo/la; **~ly** adv con credulidad.
creed n credo m.
creek n arroyo m.
creep vi arrastrar, serpear; complacer bajamente.
creeper n (bot) enredadera f.
creepy adj horripilante.
cremate vt incinerar cadáveres.
cremation n cremación f.
crematorium n crematorio m.
crescent adj creciente; * n cuarto creciente m.

cress *n* berro *m*.

crest *n* cresta *f*.

crested *adj* crestado/da.

crestfallen *adj* acobardado/da, abatido/da de espíritu.

crevasse *n* grieta (de glaciar) *f*.

crevice *n* raja, hendedura *f*.

crew *n* banda, tropa *f*; tripulación *f*.

crib *n* cuna *f*; pesebre *m*.

cricket *n* grillo *m*; críquet *m*.

crime *n* crimen *m*; culpa *f*.

criminal *adj* criminal, reo/rea; **~ly** *adv* criminalmente; * *n* criminal *m/f*.

criminality *n* criminalidad *f*.

crimson *adj*, *n* carmesí *m*.

cripple *n*, *adj* cojo/ja *m/f*; * *vt* lisiar; (*fig*) estropear.

crisis *n* crisis *f invar*.

crisp *adj* crujiente.

crispness *n* sequedad *f*.

criss-cross *adj* entrelazado/da.

criterion *n* criterio *m*.

critic *n* crítico *m*; crítica *f*.

critic(al) *adj* crítico/ca; exacto/ta; delicado/da; **~ally** *adv* exactamente, rigurosamente.

criticism *n* crítica *f*.

criticize *vt* criticar, censurar; zaherir; (*fig*) zurrar.

croak *vi* graznar.

crochet *n* ganchillo *m*; * *vt*, *vi* hacer ganchillo.

crockery *n* loza *f*; vasijas de barro *fpl*.

crocodile *n* cocodrilo *m*.

crony *n* amigote *m*; compinche *m*.

crook *n* (*fam*) ladrón *m*; cayado *m*.

crooked *adj* torcido/da; perverso/sa.

crop *n* cultivo *m*; cosecha *f*; * *vt* recortar.

cross *n* cruz *f*; carga *f*; * *adj* mal humorado/da; * *vt* atravesar, cruzar; **to ~ over** traspasar.

crossbar *n* travesaño *m*.

crossbreed *n* raza cruzada *f*.

cross-country *n* carrera a campo traviesa *f*.

cross-examine *vt* preguntar a un testigo.

crossfire *n* fuego cruzado *m*.

crossing *n* cruce *m*; paso a nivel *m*.

cross-purpose *n* disposición contraria *f*; contradicción *f*; **to be at ~s** entenderse mal.

cross-reference *n* remisión *f*.

crossroad *n* encrucijada *f*.

crotch *n* entrepierna *f*.

crouch *vi* agacharse, bajarse.

crow *n* cuervo *m*; canto del gallo *m*; * *vi* cantar el gallo.

crowd *n* público *m*; muchedumbre *f*; * *vt* amontonar; * *vi* reunirse.

crown *n* corona *f*; cumbre *f*; * *vt* coronar.

crown prince *n* príncipe real *m*.

crucial *adj* crucial.

crucible *n* crisol *m*.

crucifix *n* crucifijo *m*.

crucifixion *n* crucifixión *f*.

crucify *vt* crucificar; atormentar.

crude *adj* crudo/da, imperfecto/ta; **~ly** *adv* crudamente.

cruel *adj* cruel, inhumano/na; **~ly** *adv* cruelmente.

cruelty *n* crueldad *f*.

cruet *n* vinagrera *f*.

cruise *n* crucero *m*; * *vi* hacer un crucero.

cruiser *n* crucero *m*.

crumb *n* miga *f*.

crumble *vt* desmigajar, desmenuzar; * *vi* desmigajarse.

crumple *vt* arrugar.

crunch *vt* ronzar; * *n* (*fig*) crisis *f invar*.

crunchy *adj* crujiente.

crusade *n* cruzada *f*.

crush vt apretar, oprimir; * n choque m.

crust n costra f; corteza f; zoquete m.

crusty adj costroso/sa; bronco/ca, áspero/ra.

crutch n muleta f.

crux n lo esencial.

cry vt, vi gritar; exclamar; llorar; * n grito m; lloro m; clamor m.

crypt n cripta f.

cryptic adj enigmático/ca.

crystal n cristal m.

crystal-clear adj claro/ra como el agua.

crystalline adj cristalino/na; transparente.

crystallize vt (vi) cristalizar(se).

cub n cachorro m.

cube n cubo m.

cubic adj cúbico/ca.

cuckoo n cuco m.

cucumber n pepino m.

cud n: to chew the ~ rumiar; (fig) reflexionar.

cuddle vt abrazar; * vi abrazarse; * n abrazo m.

cudgel n garrote, palo m.

cue n taco (de billar) m.

cuff n puñada f; vuelta f.

culinary adj culinario/ria, de la cocina.

cull vt escoger, elegir.

culminate vi culminar.

culmination n colmo m.

culpability n culpabilidad f.

culpable adj culpable, criminal; ~bly adv culpablemente, criminalmente.

culprit n culpable m/f.

cult n culto f.

cultivate vi cultivar, mejorar; perfeccionar.

cultivation n cultivo m.

cultural adj cultural.

culture n cultura f.

cumbersome adj engorroso/sa, pesado/da, confuso/sa.

cumulative adj cumulativo/va.

cunning adj astuto/ta; intrigante; ~ly adv astutamente; expertamente; * n astucia, sutileza f; ~ person zorro m.

cup n taza, jícara f; (bot) cáliz m.

cupboard n armario m.

curable adj curable.

curate n teniente de cura m; párroco m.

curator n curador/a m/f; guardián/ ana m/f.

curb n freno m; bordillo m; * vt refrenar, contener, moderar.

curd n cuajada f.

curdle vt (vi) cuajar(se), coagular(se).

cure n cura f; remedio m; * vt curar, sanar.

curfew n toque de queda m.

curing n curación f.

curiosity n curiosidad f; rareza f.

curious adj curioso/sa; ~ly adv curiosamente.

curl n rizo de pelo m; * vt rizar; ondear; * vi rizarse.

curling iron n, **curling tongs** npl tenacillas de rizar fpl.

curly adj rizado/da.

currant n pasa f.

currency n moneda f; circulación f; duración f.

current adj corriente, común; * n curso, progreso m; marcha f; corriente f.

current affairs npl actualidades fpl.

currently adv actualmente.

curriculum vitae n currículum m.

curry n curry m.

curse vt maldecir; * vi imprecar; blasfemar; * n maldición f.

cursor *n* cursor *m*.

cursory *adj* precipitado/da, inconsiderado/da.

curt *adj* sucinto/ta.

curtail *vt* acortar.

curtain *n* cortina *f*; telón (en teatro) *m*.

curtain rod *n* varilla de cortinaje *f*.

curtsy *n* reverencia *f*; * *vi* hacer una reverencia.

curvature *n* curvatura *f*.

curve *vt* encorvar; * *n* curva *f*.

cushion *n* cojín *m*; almohada *f*.

custard *n* natillas *fpl*.

custodian *n* custodio *m*.

custody *n* custodia *f*; prisión *f*.

custom *n* costumbre *f*, uso *m*.

customary *adj* usual, acostumbrado/da, ordinario/ria.

customer *n* cliente *m/f*.

customs *npl* aduana *f*.

customs duty *n* derechos de aduana *mpl*.

customs officer *n* aduanero/ra *m/f*.

cut *vt* cortar; separar; herir; dividir; cortar los naipes; **to ~ short** interrumpir, cortar la palabra; **to ~ teeth** nacerle los dientes (a un niño); * *vi* traspasar; cruzarse; * *n*

corte *m*; cortadura *f*; herida *f*; **~ and dried** *adj* rutinario/ria.

cutback *n* reducción *f*.

cute *adj* lindo/da.

cutlery *n* cuchillería *f*.

cutlet *n* chuleta *f*.

cut-rate *adj* a precio reducido.

cut-throat *n* asesino *m*; * *adj* encarnizado/da.

cutting *n* cortadura *f*; * *adj* cortante; mordaz.

cyanide *n* cianuro *m*.

cyberspace *n* ciberespacio *m*.

cycle *n* ciclo *m*; bicicleta *f*; * *vi* ir en bicicleta.

cycling *n* ciclismo *m*.

cyclist *n* ciclista *m/f*.

cyclone *n* ciclón *m*.

cygnet *n* pollo del cisne *m*.

cylinder *n* cilindro *m*; rollo *m*.

cylindric(al) *adj* cilíndrico/ca.

cymbals *n* címbalo *m*.

cynic(al) *adj* cínico/ca; obsceno/na; * *n* cínico *m* (filósofo).

cynicism *n* cinismo *m*.

cypress *n* ciprés *m*.

cyst *n* quiste *m*.

czar *n* zar *m*.

D

dab *n* pedazo pequeño *m*; toque *m*.

dabble *vi* chapotear.

dad(dy) *n* papa *m*.

daddy-long-legs *n* típula *f*.

daffodil *n* narciso *m*.

dagger *n* puñal *m*.

daily *adj* diario/ria, cotidiano/na; * *adv* diariamente, cada día; * *n* diario *m*.

daintily *adv* delicadamente.

daintiness *n* elegancia *f*; delicadeza *f*.

dainty *adj* delicado/da, elegante.

dairy *n* lechería *f*.

dairy farm *n* vaquería *f*.

dairy produce *n* productos lácteos *mpl*.

daisy *n* margarita, maya *f*.

dale *n* valle *m*.

dally *vi* tardar.

dam *n* presa *f*; * *vt* represar.

damage n daño m; perjuicio m; * dañar; perjudicar.

damask n damasco m; * adj de damasco.

dame n dama f.

damn vt condenar; * adj maldito/ta.

damnable adj maldito/ta; **~bly** adv terriblemente.

damnation n perdición f.

damning adj irrecusable.

damp adj húmedo/da; * n humedad f; * vt mojar.

dampen vt mojar.

dampness n humedad f.

damson n damascena f (ciruela).

dance n danza f; baile m; * vi bailar.

dance hall n salón de baile m.

dancer n bailarín m, bailarina f.

dandelion n diente de león m.

dandruff n caspa f.

dandy adj mono/na.

danger n peligro, riesgo m.

dangerous adj peligroso/sa; **~ly** adv peligrosamente.

dangle vi estar colgado/da.

dank adj húmedo/da.

dapper adj apuesto/ta.

dappled adj rodado/da.

dare vi atreverse; * vt desafiar.

daredevil n atrevido m.

daring n osadía f; * adj atrevido/da; **~ly** adv atrevidamente, osadamente.

dark adj oscuro/ra; negro/gra; * n oscuridad f; ignorancia f.

darken vt (vi) oscurecer(se).

dark glasses npl gafas de sol fpl.

darkness n oscuridad f.

darkroom n cuarto oscuro m.

darling n, adj querido m.

darn vt zurcir.

dart n dardo m.

dartboard n diana f.

dash vi irse de prisa; * n pizca f; **at one ~** de un golpe.

dashboard n tablero de instrumentos m.

dashing adj gallardo/da.

dastardly adj cobarde.

data n datos mpl.

database n base de datos f.

data processing n proceso de datos m.

date n fecha f; cita f; (bot) dátil m; * vt fechar; salir con.

dated adj anticuado/da.

dative n dativo m.

daub vt manchar.

daughter n hija f; **~ in-law** nuera f.

daunting adj desalentador/a.

dawdle vi gastar tiempo.

dawn n alba f; * vi amanecer.

day n día m; luz f; **by ~** de día; **~ by ~** de día en día.

daybreak n alba f.

day labourer n jornalero m.

daylight n luz del día, luz natural f; **~ saving time** n hora de verano f.

daytime n día m.

daze vt aturdir.

dazed adj aturdido/da.

dazzle vt deslumbrar.

dazzling adj deslumbrante.

deacon n diácono m.

dead adj muerto/ta, marchito/ta; **~wood** n lastre m; **~ silence** n silencio profundo m; **the ~** npl los muertos.

dead-drunk adj borracho como una cuba.

deaden vt amortiguar.

dead heat n empate m.

deadline n fecha tope f.

deadlock n punto muerto m.

deadly adj mortal; * adv terriblemente.

dead march n marcha fúnebre f.
deadness n inercia f.
deaf adj sordo/da.
deafen vt ensordecer.
deaf-mute n sordomudo/da m./f.
deafness n sordera f.
deal n convenio m; transacción f; **a great ~** mucho; **a good ~** bastante; * vt distribuir; dar; * vi comerciar; **to ~ in/with** tratar en/con.
dealer n comerciante m/f; traficante m/f; mano f.
dealings npl trato m.
dean n deán m.
dear adj querido/da; caro/ra, costoso/sa; **~ly** adv caro.
dearness n carestía f.
dearth n escasez f.
death n muerte f.
deathbed n lecho de muerte m.
deathblow n golpe mortal m.
death certificate n partida de defunción f.
death penalty n pena de muerte f.
death throes npl agonía f.
death warrant n sentencia de muerte f.
debacle n desastre m.
debar vt excluir, no admitir.
debase vt degradar.
debasement n degradación f.
debatable adj discutible.
debate n debate m; polémica f; * vt discutir; examinar.
debauched adj vicioso/sa.
debauchery n libertinaje m.
debilitate vt debilitar.
debit n debe m; * vt (com) cargar en una cuenta.
debt n deuda f; obligación f; **to get into ~** contraer deudas.
debtor n deudor/a m/f.
debunk vt desacreditar.

decade n década f.
decadence n decadencia f.
decaffeinated adj descafeinado/da.
decanter n garrafa f.
decapitate vt decapitar, degollar.
decapitation n decapitación f.
decay vi decaer; pudrirse; * n decadencia f; caries f.
deceased adj muerto/ta.
deceit n engaño m.
deceitful adj engañoso/sa; **~ly** adv falsamente.
deceive vt engañar.
December n diciembre m.
decency n decencia f; modestia f.
decent adj decente, razonable; **~ly** adv decentemente.
deception n engaño m.
deceptive adj engañoso/sa.
decibel n decibelio m.
decide vt, vi decidir; resolver.
decided adj decidido/da.
decidedly adv decididamente.
deciduous adj (bot) de hoja caduca.
decimal adj decimal.
decimate vt diezmar.
decipher vt descifrar.
decision n decisión, determinación f.
decisive adj decisivo/va; **~ly** adv de modo decisivo.
deck n cubierta f; * vt adornar.
deckchair n tumbona f.
declaim vi declamar.
declamation n declamación f.
declaration n declaración f.
declare vt declarar, manifestar.
declension n declinación f.
decline vt (gr) declinar; evitar; * vi decaer; * n decadencia f.
declutch vi desembragar.
decode vt descifrar.
decoder (TV) n descodificador m.
decompose vt descomponer.

decomposition n descomposición f.
decor n decoración f.
decorate vt decorar, adornar.
decoration n decoración f.
decorative adj decorativo/va.
decorator n pintor (decorador) m.
decorous adj decoroso/sa; **~ly** adv decorosamente.
decorum n decoro, garbo m.
decoy n señuelo m.
decrease vt disminuir; * n disminución f.
decree n decreto m; * vt decretar; ordenar.
decrepit adj decrépito/ta.
decry vt desacreditar, censurar.
dedicate vt dedicar; consagrar.
dedication n dedicación f; dedicatoria f.
deduce vt deducir; concluir.
deduct vt restar.
deduction n deducción f; descuento m.
deed n acción f; hecho m; hazaña f.
deem vi juzgar.
deep adj profundo/da.
deepen vt profundizar.
deep-freeze n congeladora f.
deeply adv profundamente.
deepness n profundidad f.
deer n ciervo m.
deface vt desfigurar, afear.
defacement n desfiguración f.
defamation n difamación f.
default n defecto m; falta f; * vi faltar.
defaulter n (law) moroso/sa m/f.
defeat n derrota f; * vt derrotar; frustrar.
defect n defecto m; falta f.
defection n deserción f.
defective adj defectuoso/sa.
defend vt defender; proteger.

defendant n acusado/da m/f.
defence n defensa f; protección f.
defenceless adj indefenso/sa.
defensive adj defensivo/va; **~ly** adv de modo defensivo.
defer vt aplazar.
deference n deferencia f; respeto m.
deferential adj respetuoso/sa.
defiance n desafío m.
defiant adj insolente.
deficiency n defecto m; falta f.
deficient adj insuficiente.
deficit n déficit m.
defile vt ensuciar.
definable adj definible.
define vt definir.
definite adj definido/da, preciso/sa; **~ly** adv no cabe duda.
definition n definición f.
definitive adj definitivo/va; **~ly** adv definitivamente.
deflate vt desinflar.
deflect vt desviar.
deflower vt desvirgar.
deform vt desfigurar.
deformity n deformidad f.
defraud vt estafar.
defray vt costear.
defrost vt deshelar; descongelar.
defroster n luneta térmica f.
deft adj diestro/tra; **~ly** adv hábilmente.
defunct adj difunto/ta.
defuse vt desactivar.
degenerate vi degenerar; * adj degenerado/da.
degeneration n degeneración f.
degradation n degradación f.
degrade vt degradar.
degree n grado m; título m.
dehydrated adj deshidratado/da.
de-ice vt deshelar.
deign vi dignarse.

deity n deidad, divinidad f.

dejected adj desanimado/da.

dejection n desaliento m.

delay vt demorar; * n retraso m.

delectable adj deleitoso/sa.

delegate vt delegar; * n delegado m.

delegation n delegación f.

delete vt tachar; borrar.

deliberate vt deliberar; * adj intencionado/da; ~ly adv a propósito.

deliberation n deliberación f.

deliberative adj deliberativo/va.

delicacy n delicadeza f.

delicate adj delicado/da, exquisito/ta; ~ly adv delicadamente.

delicious adj delicioso/sa, exquisito/ta; ~ly adv deliciosamente.

delight n delicia f; gozo, encanto m; * vt (vi) deleitar(se).

delighted adj encantado/da.

delightful adj encantador/a; ~ly adv en forma encantadora.

delineate vt delinear.

delineation n delineación f.

delinquency n delincuencia f.

delinquent n delincuente m/f.

delirious adj delirante.

delirium n delirio m.

deliver vt entregar; pronunciar.

deliverance n liberación f.

delivery n entrega f; parto m.

delude vt engañar.

deluge n diluvio m.

delusion n engaño m; ilusión f.

delve vi hurgar.

demagogue n demagogo/a m/f.

demand n demanda f; reclamación f; * vt exigir; reclamar.

demanding adj exigente.

demarcation n demarcación f.

demean vi rebajarse.

demeanour n conducta f.

demented adj demente.

demise n desaparición f.

democracy n democracia f.

democrat n demócrata m/f.

democratic adj democrático/ca.

demolish vt demoler.

demolition n demolición f.

demon n demonio, diablo m.

demonstrable adj demostrable; ~bly adv manifiestamente.

demonstrate vt demostrar, probar; * vi manifestarse.

demonstration n demostración f; manifestación f.

demonstrative adj demostrativo/va.

demonstrator n manifestante m/f.

demoralization n desmoralización f.

demoralize vt desmoralizar.

demote vt degradar.

demur vi objetar.

demure adj modesto/ta; ~ly adv modestamente.

den n guarida f.

denatured alcohol n alcohol desnaturalizado m.

denial n negación f.

denims npl vaqueros mpl.

denomination n valor m.

denominator n (math) denominador m.

denote vt denotar, indicar.

denounce vt denunciar.

dense adj denso/sa, espeso/sa.

density n densidad f.

dent n abolladura f; * vt abollar.

dental adj dental.

dentifrice n dentífrico m.

dentist n dentista m/f.

dentistry n odontología f.

denture npl dentadura postiza f.

denude vt desnudar, despojar.

denunciation n denuncia f.

deny vt negar.

deodorant n desodorante m.

deodorize vt desodorizar.

depart vi partir.

department n departamento m.

department store n gran almacén m.

departure n partida f.

departure lounge n sala de embarque f.

depend vi depender; ~ **on/upon** contar con.

dependable adj seguro/ra, serio/ria.

dependant n dependiente m.

dependency n dependencia f.

dependent adj dependiente.

depict vt pintar, retratar; describir.

depleted adj reducido/da.

deplorable adj deplorable, lamentable; ~**bly** adv deplorablemente.

deplore vt deplorar, lamentar.

deploy vt (mil) desplegar.

depopulated adj despoblado/da.

depopulation n despoblación f.

deport vt deportar.

deportation n deportación f; destierro m.

deportment n conducta f.

deposit vt depositar; * n depósito m; yacimiento m.

deposition n deposición f.

depositor n depositante m.

depot n depósito m.

deprave vt depravar, corromper.

depraved adj depravado/da.

depravity n depravación f.

deprecate vt lamentar.

depreciate vi depreciarse.

depreciation n depreciación f.

depredation n pillaje m.

depress vt deprimir.

depressed adj deprimido/da.

depression n depresión f.

deprivation n privación f.

deprive vt privar.

deprived adj necesitado/da.

depth n profundidad f.

deputation n diputación f.

depute vt diputar, delegar.

deputize vi suplir a.

deputy n diputado/da m/f.

derail vt descarrilar.

deranged adj trastornado/da.

derelict adj abandonado/da.

deride vt burlar.

derision n mofa f.

derisive adj irrisorio/ria.

derivable adj deducible.

derivation n derivación f.

derivative n derivado m.

derive vt (vi) derivar(se).

dermatologist n dermatólogo/ga m/f.

dermatology n dermatología f.

derogatory adj despectivo/va.

derrick n torre de perforación f.

desalinate vt desalinizar.

desalination plant n desalinizadora f.

descant n (mus) discante m.

descend vi descender.

descendant n descendiente m.

descent n descenso m.

describe vt describir.

description n descripción f.

descriptive adj descriptivo/va.

descry vt divisar.

desecrate vt profanar.

desecration n profanación f.

desert[1] n desierto m; * adj desierto/ta.

desert[2] vt abandonar; desertar; * n mérito m.

deserter n desertor/a m/f.

desertion n deserción f.

deserve vt merecer; ser digno/na.

deservedly adv merecidamente.

deserving adj meritorio/ria.

deshabille, dishabille n deshabillé m.

desideratum n desiderátum m.

design vt diseñar; * n diseño m; dibujo m.

designate vt nombrar; designar.

designation n designación f.

designedly adv a propósito.

designer n diseñador m; modisto m.

desirability n conveniencia f.

desirable adj deseable.

desire n deseo m; * vt desear.

desirous adj deseoso/sa, ansioso/sa.

desist vi desistir.

desk n escritorio m.

desktop publishing n autoedición f.

desolate adj desierto/ta.

desolation n desolación f.

despair n desesperación f; * vi desesperarse.

despairingly adj desesperadamente.

despatch = dispatch.

desperado n bandido/da m/f.

desperate adj desesperado/da; ~ly adv desesperadamente; sumamente.

desperation n desesperación f.

despicable adj despreciable.

despise vt despreciar.

despite prep a pesar de.

despoil vt despojar.

despondency n abatimiento m.

despondent adj abatido/da.

despot n déspota m/f.

despotic adj despótico/ca, absoluto/ta; ~ally adv despóticamente.

despotism n despotismo m.

dessert n postre m.

destination n destino m.

destine vt destinar.

destiny n destino m; suerte f.

destitute adj indigente.

destitution n miseria f.

destroy vt destruir, arruinar.

destruction n destrucción, ruina f.

destructive adj destructivo/va.

desultory adj irregular; sin método.

detach vt separar.

detachable adj desmontable; de quitapón.

detachment n (mil) destacamento m.

detail n detalle m; in ~ detalladamente; * vt detallar.

detain vt retener; detener.

detect vt detectar.

detection n descubrimiento m.

detective n detective m/f.

detector n detector m.

detention n detención f.

deter vt disuadir.

detergent n detergente m.

deteriorate vt deteriorar.

deterioration n deterioro m.

determination n resolución f.

determine vt determinar, decidir.

determined adj resuelto/ta.

deterrent n fuerza de disuasión f.

detest vt detestar, aborrecer.

detestable adj detestable, abominable.

dethrone vt destronar.

dethronement n destronamiento m.

detonate vi detonar.

detonation n detonación f.

detour n desviación f.

detract vt desvirtuar.

detriment n perjuicio m.

detrimental adj perjudicial.

deuce n deuce m.

devaluation n devaluación f.

devastate vt devastar.

devastating adj devastador.

devastation n devastación, ruina f.

develop vt desarrollar.

development n desarrollo m.

deviate vi desviarse.

deviation n desviación f.

device n mecanismo m.

devil n diablo, demonio m.

devilish *adj* diabólico/ca; **~ly** *adv* diabólicamente.

devious *adj* taimado/da.

devise *vt* inventar; idear.

devoid *adj* desprovisto/ta.

devolve *vt* delegar.

devote *vt* dedicar; consagrar.

devoted *adj* fiel.

devotee *n* partidario/a *m/f*.

devotion *n* devoción *f*.

devotional *adj* devoto/ta.

devour *vt* devorar.

devout *adj* devoto/ta, piadoso/sa; **~ly** *adv* piadosamente.

dew *n* rocío *m*.

dewy *adj* rociado/da.

dexterity *n* destreza *f*.

dexterous *adj* diestro/tra, hábil.

diabetes *n* diabetes *f*.

diabetic *n* diabético/ca *m/f*.

diabolic *adj* diabólico/ca; **~ally** *adv* diabólicamente.

diadem *n* diadema *f*.

diagnosis *n* (*med*) diagnóstico *m*.

diagnostic *adj*, *n* diagnóstico *m*; **~s** *pl* diagnóstica *f*.

diagonal *adj*, *n* diagonal *f*; **~ly** *adv* diagonalmente.

diagram *n* diagrama *m*.

dial *n* cuadrante *m*; disco *m*.

dialect *n* dialecto *m*.

dialling code *n* prefijo *m*.

dialling tone *n* tono de marcar *m*.

dialogue *n* diálogo *m*.

diameter *n* diámetro *m*.

diametrical *adj* diametral; **~ly** *adv* diametralmente.

diamond *n* diamante *m*.

diamond-cutter *n* diamantista *m/f*.

diamonds *npl* (cards) diamantes *mpl*.

diaphragm *n* diafragma *m*.

diarrhoea *n* diarrea *f*.

diary *n* diario *m*.

dice *npl* dados *mpl*.

dictate *vt* dictar; * *n* dictado *m*.

dictation *n* dictado *m*.

dictatorial *adj* autoritativo/va, magistral.

dictatorship *n* dictadura *f*.

diction *n* dicción *f*

dictionary *n* diccionario *m*.

didactic *adj* didáctico/ca.

die[1] *vi* morir; **to ~ away** perderse; **to ~ down** apagarse.

die[2] *n* dado *m*.

diehard *n* reaccionario/ria *m/f*.

diesel *n* diesel *m*.

diet *n* dieta *f*; régimen *m*; * *vi* estar a dieta.

dietary *adj* dietético/ca.

differ *vi* diferenciarse.

difference *n* diferencia, disparidad *f*.

different *adj* diferente; **~ly** *adv* diferentemente.

differentiate *vt* diferenciar.

difficult *adj* difícil.

difficulty *n* dificultad *f*.

diffidence *n* timidez *f*.

diffident *adj* desconfiado/da; **~ly** *adv* desconfiadamente.

diffraction *n* difracción *f*.

diffuse *vt* difundir, esparcir; * *adj* difuso/sa.

diffusion *n* difusión *f*.

dig *vt* cavar; **to ~ ditches** zanjar; * *n* empujón *m*.

digest *vt* digerir.

digestible *adj* digerible.

digestion *n* digestión *f*.

digestive *adj* digestivo/va.

digger *n* excavadora *f*.

digit *n* dígito *m*.

digital *adj* digital.

digitize *vt* digitalizar.

dignified *adj* grave.

dignitary *n* dignatario *m*.
dignity *n* dignidad *f*.
digress *vi* divagar.
digression *n* digresión *f*.
dike *n* dique *m*.
dilapidated *adj* desmoronado/da.
dilapidation *n* ruina *f*.
dilate *vt*, *vi* dilatar(se).
dilemma *n* dilema *m*.
diligence *n* diligencia *f*.
diligent *adj* diligente, asiduo/dua; ~ly *adv* diligentemente.
dilute *vt* diluir.
dim *adj* turbio/bia; lerdo/da; oscuro/ra; * *vt* bajar.
dime *n* moneda de diez centavos *f*.
dimension *n* dimensión, extensión *f*.
diminish *vt* (*vi*) disminuir(se).
diminution *n* disminución *f*.
diminutive *n* diminutivo *m*.
dimly *adv* indistintamente.
dimmer *n* interruptor *m*.
dimple *n* hoyuelo *m*.
din *n* alboroto *m*.
dine *vi* cenar.
dinghy *n* lancha neumática *f*.
dingy *adj* sombrío/ría.
dinner *n* cena *f*.
dinner-jacket *n* smoking *m*.
dinner time *n* hora de comer *f*.
dinosaur *n* dinosaurio *m*.
dint *n*: by ~ of a fuerza de.
diocese *n* diócesis *f invar*.
dip *vt* mojar; * *n* zambullida *f*.
diphtheria *n* difteria *f*.
diphthong *n* diptongo *m*.
diploma *n* diploma *m*.
diplomacy *n* diplomacia *f*.
diplomat *n* diplomático/ca *m/f*.
diplomatic *adj* diplomático/ca.
dipsomania *n* dipsomanía *f*.
dipstick *n* (*auto*) varilla de nivel *f*.
dire *adj* calamitoso/sa.

direct *adj* directo/ta; * *vt* dirigir.
direction *n* dirección *f*; instrucción *f*.
directly *adj* directamente; inmediatamente.
director *n* director/a *m/f*.
directory *n* guía *f*.
dirt *n* suciedad *f*; ~ on clothes zarpa *f*.
dirtiness *n* suciedad *f*.
dirty *adj* sucio/cia; vil, bajo/ja.
disability *n* discapacidad *f*.
disabled *adj* discapacitado/da.
disabuse *vt* desengañar.
disadvantage *n* desventaja *f*; * *vt* perjudicar.
disadvantageous *adj* desventajoso/sa.
disaffected *adj* descontento/ta.
disagree *vi* no estar de acuerdo.
disagreeable *adj* desagradable; ~bly *adv* desagradablemente.
disagreement *n* desacuerdo *m*.
disallow *vt* rechazar.
disappear *vi* desaparecer; ausentarse.
disappearance *n* desaparición *f*.
disappoint *vt* decepcionar.
disappointed *adj* decepcionado/da.
disappointing *adj* decepcionante.
disappointment *n* decepción *f*.
disapproval *n* desaprobación, censura *f*.
disapprove *vt* desaprobar.
disarm *vt* desarmar.
disarmament *n* desarme *m*.
disarray *n* desarreglo *m*.
disaster *n* desastre *m*.
disastrous *adj* desastroso/sa, calamitoso/sa.
disband *vt* disolver.
disbelief *n* incredulidad *f*.
disbelieve *vt* desconfiar.
disburse *vt* desembolsar, pagar.
disc, disk *n* disco *m*.

discard vt descartar.

discern vt discernir, percibir.

discernible adj perceptible.

discerning adj perspicaz.

discernment n perspicacia f.

discharge vt descargar; pagar (una deuda); cumplir; * n descarga f; descargo m.

disciple n discípulo/la m/f.

discipline n disciplina f; * vt disciplinar.

disclaim vt negar.

disclaimer n negación f.

disclose vi revelar.

disclosure n revelación f.

discolour vt descolorar.

discolouration n descolorimiento m.

discomfort n incomodidad f.

disconcert vt desconcertar.

disconnect vt desconectar.

disconsolate adj inconsolable; ~ly adv desconsoladamente.

discontent n descontento/ta m/f; * adj descontento/ta.

discontented adj descontento/ta.

discontinue vi interrumpir.

discord n discordia f.

discordant adj discordante.

discotheque, disco n discoteca f.

discount n descuento m; rebaja f; * vt descontar.

discourage vt desalentar, desanimar.

discouraged adj desalentado/da.

discouragement n desaliento m.

discouraging adj desalentador/a.

discourse n discurso m.

discourteous adj descortés, grosero/ra; ~ly adv descortésmente.

discourtesy n descortesía f.

discover vt descubrir.

discovery n descubrimiento m; revelación f.

discredit vt desacreditar.

discreditable adj ignominioso/sa.

discreet adj discreto/ta; ~ly adv discretamente.

discrepancy n discrepancia, diferencia f.

discretion n discreción f.

discretionary adj discrecional.

discriminate vt distinguir.

discrimination n discriminación f.

discursive adj discursivo/va.

discuss vt discutir.

discussion n discusión f.

disdain vt desdeñar; * n desdén, desprecio m.

disdainful adj desdeñoso/sa; ~ly adv desdeñosamente.

disease n enfermedad f.

diseased adj enfermo/ma.

disembark vt, vi desembarcar.

disembarkation n desembarco m.

disenchant vt desencantar.

disenchanted adj desilusionado/da.

disenchantment n desilusión f.

disengage vt soltar.

disentangle vt desenredar.

disfigure vt desfigurar, afear.

disgrace n ignominia f; escándalo m; * vt deshonrar.

disgraceful adj ignominioso/sa; ~ly adv vergonzosamente.

disgruntled adj descontento/ta.

disguise vt disfrazar; * n disfraz m.

disgust n aversión f; * vt repugnar.

disgusting adj repugnante.

dish n fuente f; plato m; taza f; * vt servir en fuente; **to ~ up** servir.

dishcloth n paño de cocina m.

dishearten vt desalentar.

dishevelled adj desarreglado/da.

dishonest adj deshonesto/ta; ~ly adv deshonestamente.

dishonesty n falta de honradez f.

dishonour *n* deshonra, ignominia *f*;
* *vt* deshonrar.
dishonourable *adj* deshonroso/sa;
~**bly** *adv* deshonrosamente.
dishtowel *n* trapo de fregar *m*.
dishwarmer *n* escalfador *m*.
dishwasher *n* lavaplatos *m/f*; lavava-
jillas *m invar*.
disillusion *vt* desilusionar.
disillusioned *adj* desilusionado/da.
disincentive *n* freno *m*.
disinclination *n* aversión *f*.
disinclined *adj* reacio/cia.
disinfect *vt* desinfectar.
disinfectant *n* desinfectante *m*.
disinherit *vt* desheredar.
disintegrate *vi* disgregarse.
disinterested *adj* desinteresado/da;
~**ly** *adv* desinteresadamente.
disjointed *adj* inconexo/xa.
diskette *n* disco, disquete *m*.
dislike *n* aversión *f*; * *vt* tener antipatía.
dislocate *vt* dislocar.
dislocation *n* dislocación *f*.
dislodge *vt*, *vi* desalojar.
disloyal *adj* desleal; ~**ly** *adv* desleal-
mente.
disloyalty *n* deslealtad *f*.
dismal *adj* triste.
dismantle *vt* desmontar.
dismay *n* consternación *f*.
dismember *vt* despedazar.
dismiss *vt* despedir.
dismissal *n* despedida *f*.
dismount *vt* desmontar; * *vi* apearse.
disobedience *n* desobediencia *f*.
disobedient *adj* desobediente.
disobey *vt* desobedecer.
disorder *n* desorden *m*; confusión *f*.
disorderly *adj* desarreglado/da,
confuso/sa.
disorganization *n* desorganización *f*.

disorganized *adj* desorganizado/da.
disorientated *adj* desorientado/da.
disown *vt* desconocer.
disparage *vt* despreciar.
disparaging *adj* despreciativo/va.
disparity *n* disparidad *f*.
dispassionate *adj* desapasio-
nado/da.
dispatch *vt* enviar; * *n* envío *m*; informe *m*.
dispel *vt* disipar.
dispensary *n* dispensario *m*.
dispense *vt* dispensar; distribuir.
disperse *vt* dispersar.
dispirited *adj* desalentado/da.
displace *vt* desplazar.
display *vt* exponer; * *n* ostentación *f*;
despliegue *m*.
displeased *adj* disgustado/da.
displeasure *n* disgusto *m*.
disposable *adj* desechable.
disposal *n* disposición *f*.
dispose *vt* disponer; arreglar.
disposed *adj* dispuesto/ta.
disposition *n* disposición *f*.
dispossess *vt* desposeer.
disproportionate *adj* desproporcio-
nado/da.
disprove *vt* refutar.
dispute *n* disputa, controversia *f*;
* *vt* disputar.
disqualify *vt* incapacitar.
disquiet *n* inquietud *f*.
disquieting *adj* inquietante.
disquisition *n* disquisición *f*.
disregard *vt* desatender; * *n* desdén *m*.
disreputable *adj* de mala fama.
disrespect *n* irreverencia *f*.
disrespectful *adj* irreverente; ~**ly**
adv irreverentemente.
disrobe *vt* desnudar.
disrupt *vt* interrumpir.

disruption n interrupción f.

dissatisfaction n descontento/ta, disgusto m.

dissatisfied adj insatisfecho/cha.

dissect vt disecar.

dissection n disección f.

disseminate vt diseminar.

dissension n disensión f.

dissent vi disentir; * n disensión f.

dissenter n disidente m.

dissertation n disertación f.

dissident n disidente m.

dissimilar adj distinto/ta.

dissimilarity n disimilitud f.

dissimulation n disimulo m.

dissipate vt disipar.

dissipation n disipación f.

dissociate vt disociar.

dissolute adj libertino/na.

dissolution n disolución f.

dissolve vt disolver; * vi disolverse, derretirse.

dissonance n disonancia f.

dissuade vt disuadir.

distance n distancia f; **at a ~** de lejos; * vt apartar.

distant adj distante.

distaste n disgusto m.

distasteful adj desagradable.

distend vt hinchar.

distil vt destilar.

distillation n destilación f.

distillery n destilería f.

distinct adj distinto/ta, diferente; claro/ra; **~ly** adv distintamente.

distinction n distinción f.

distinctive adj distintivo/va.

distinctness n claridad f.

distinguish vt distinguir; discernir.

distort vt retorcer.

distorted adj distorsionado/da.

distortion n distorción f.

distract vt distraer.

distracted adj distraído/da; **~ly** adj distraídamente.

distraction n distracción f; confusión f.

distraught adj enloquecido/da.

distress n angustia f; * vt angustiar.

distressing adj penoso/sa.

distribute vt distribuir, repartir.

distribution n distribución f.

distributor n distribuidor m.

district n distrito m.

distrustful adj desconfiado/da; sospechoso/sa.

disturb vt molestar.

disturbance n disturbio m.

disturbed adj preocupado/da.

disturbing adj inquietante.

disuse n desuso m.

disused adj abandonado/da.

ditch n zanja f.

dither vi vacilar.

ditto adv ídem.

ditty n cancioneta f.

diuretic adj (med) diurético/ca.

dive vi sumergirse; bucear; * vr zambullirse; * n zambullida f.

diver n buzo m.

diverge vi divergir.

divergence n divergencia f.

divergent adj divergente.

diverse adj diverso/sa, diferente; **~ly** adv diversamente.

diversion n diversión f.

diversity n diversidad f.

divert vt desviar; divertir.

divest vt desnudar; despojar.

divide vt dividir; * vi dividirse.

dividend n dividendo m.

dividers npl (math) compás de puntas m.

divine adj divino/na.

divinity n divinidad f.

diving n salto m; buceo m.

diving board n trampolín m.
divisible adj divisible.
division n (math) división f; desunión f.
divisor n (math) divisor m.
divorce n divorcio m; * vi divorciarse.
divorced adj divorciado/da.
divulge vt divulgar, publicar.
dizziness n vértigo m.
dizzy adj mareado/da.
DJ n pinchadiscos m.
do vt hacer, obrar.
docile adj dócil, apacible.
dock n muelle m; * vi atracar.
docker n estibador m.
dockyard n (mar) astillero m.
doctor n médico/ca m/f.
doctrinal adj doctrinal.
doctrine n doctrina f.
document n documento m.
documentary adj documental.
dodge vt esquivar.
doe n gama f; ~ **rabbit** coneja f.
dog n perro m.
dogged adj tenaz; ~**ly** adv tenazmente.
dog kennel n perrera f.
dogmatic adj dogmático/ca; ~**ly** adv dogmáticamente.
doings npl hechos mpl; eventos mpl.
do-it-yourself n bricolaje m.
doleful adj lúgubre, triste.
doll n muñeca f.
dollar n dólar m.
dolphin n delfín m.
domain n campo m.
dome n cúpula f.
domestic adj doméstico/ca.
domesticate vt domesticar.
domestication n domesticación f.
domesticity n domesticidad f.
domicile n domicilio m.
dominant adj dominante.

dominate vi dominar.
domination n dominación f.
domineer vi dominar.
domineering adj dominante.
dominion n dominio m.
dominoes npl dominó m.
donate vt donar.
donation n donación f.
done adj hecho/cha; cocido/da.
donkey n asno, borrico m.
donor n donante m/f.
doodle vi garabatear.
doom n suerte f.
door n puerta f.
doorbell n timbre m.
door handle n tirador m.
doorman n portero m.
doormat n felpudo m.
doorstep n peldaño m.
doorway n entrada f.
dormant adj latente.
dormer window n buhardilla f.
dormitory n dormitorio m.
dormouse n lirón m.
dosage n dosis f invar.
dose n dosis f invar; * vt disponer la dosis de.
dossier n expediente m.
dot n punto m.
dote vi adorar.
dotingly adv con cariño excesivo.
double adj doble; * vt doblar; duplicar; * n doble m.
double bed n cama matrimonial f.
double-breasted adj cruzado/da.
double chin n papada f.
double-dealing n duplicidad f.
double-edged adj de doble filo.
double entry n (com) partida doble f.
double-lock vt echar la segunda vuelta a la llave a.
double room n habitación doble f.

doubly adj doblemente.
doubt n duda, sospecha f; * vt dudar; sospechar.
doubtful adj dudoso/sa.
doubtless adv sin duda.
dough n masa f.
douse vt apagar.
dove n paloma f.
dovecot(e) n palomar m.
dowdy adj mal vestido/da.
down n plumón m; flojel m; * prep abajo; **to sit ~** sentarse; **upside ~** al revés.
downcast adj cabizbajo/ja.
downfall n ruina f.
downhearted adj desanimado/da.
downhill adv cuesta abajo/ja.
down payment n entrada f.
downpour n aguacero m.
downright adj manifiesto/ta.
downstairs adv abajo/ja.
down-to-earth adj práctico/ca.
downtown adv al centro (de la ciudad).
downward(s) adv hacia abajo.
dowry n dote f.
doze vi dormitar.
dozen n docena f.
dozy adj somnoliento/ta.
drab adj gris.
draft n borrador m; quinta f; corriente de aire f.
drafty adj expuesto/ta al aire.
drag vt arrastrar; tirar con fuerza; * n lata f.
dragnet n red barredera f.
dragon n dragón m.
dragonfly n libélula f.
drain vt desaguar; secar; * n desaguadero m.
drainage n desagüe m.
draining board n escurridor m.
drainpipe n desagüe m.

drake n ánade macho m.
dram n traguito m.
drama n drama m.
dramatic adj dramático/ca; **~ally** adv dramáticamente.
dramatist n dramaturgo/ga m/f.
dramatize vt dramatizar.
drape vt cubrir.
drastic adj drástico/ca.
draughtboard n tablero de damas m.
draughts npl juego de damas m.
draw vt tirar; dibujar; **to ~ nigh** acercarse.
drawback n desventaja f.
drawer n cajón m.
drawing n dibujo m.
drawing board n tablero de dibujo m.
drawing pin n chincheta f.
drawing room n salón m.
drawl vi hablar con pesadez.
dread n terror, espanto m; * vt temer.
dreadful adj espantoso/sa; **~ly** adv terriblemente.
dream n sueño m; * vi sonar.
dreary adj triste.
dredge vt dragar.
dregs npl heces fpl.
drench vt empapar.
dress vt vestir; vendar; * vi vestirse; * n vestido m.
dresser n aparador m.
dressing n vendaje m; aliño m.
dressing gown n bata f.
dressing room n tocador m.
dressing table n tocador m.
dressmaker n modista f.
dressy adj elegante.
dribble vi caer gota a gota, babear.
dribbling n regateo m.
dried adj seco/ca.
drift n montón m; ventisquero m; significado m; * vi ir a la deriva.

driftwood n madera de deriva f.
drill n taladro m; (mil) instrucción f;
  * vt taladrar.
drink vt, vi beber; * n bebida f.
drinkable adj potable.
drinker n bebedor/a m/f.
drinking bout n borrachera f.
drinking water n agua potable f.
drip vi gotear; * n gota f; goteo m.
dripping n pringue m/f.
drive vt conducir, manejar; empujar;
  * vi conducir, manejar; * n paseo
  en coche m; entrada f.
drivel n baba f; * vi babear.
driver n conductor/a m/f; chofer m.
driver's licence n carnet m de conducir, carnet m de manejar.
driveway n entrada f.
driving n conducción f, manejo m.
driving instructor n profesor/a de
  autoescuela m/f.
driving school n autoescuela f.
driving test n examen de conducir,
  examen de manejo m.
drizzle vi lloviznar.
droll adj gracioso/sa.
drone n zumbido m; zángano m.
drool vi babear.
droop vi decaer.
drop n gota f; * vt dejar caer; * vi
  bajar; **to ~ out** retirarse.
drop-out n marginado m.
dropper n cuentagotas m invar.
dross n escoria f.
drought n sequía f.
drove n: **in ~s** en tropel.
drown vt anegar; * vi anegarse.
drowsiness n somnolencia f.
drowsy adj somnoliento/ta.
drudgery n trabajo monótono m;
  zurra f.
drug n droga f; * vt drogar.
drug addict n drogadicto/ta m/f.

drug addiction n drogadicción f.
drug trafficker n narcotraficante m/f.
drum n tambor m; **rural ~** zambomba f; * vi tocar el tambor.
drum majorette n batonista f.
drummer n batería m.
drumstick n palillo de tambor m.
drunk adj borracho/cha.
drunkard n borracho m.
drunken adj borracho/cha.
drunkenness n borrachera f.
dry adj seco/ca; * vt secar; * vi secarse.
dry-cleaning n lavado en seco m.
dryness n sequedad f.
dry rot n podredumbre f.
dual adj doble.
dual-purpose adj de doble uso.
dubbed adj doblado/da.
dubious adj dudoso/sa.
duck n pato m; * vt (vi) zambullir(se).
duckling n patito m.
dud adj estropeado/da.
due adj debido/da, apto/ta; * adv
  exactamente; * n derecho m.
duel n duelo m.
duet n (mus) dúo m.
dull adj lerdo/da; insípido/da;
  zopenco/ca; gris; * vt aliviar.
duly adv debidamente; puntualmente.
dumb adj mudo/da; **~ly** adv sin chistar.
dumbbell n pesa f.
dumbfounded adj pasmado/da.
dummy n chupete m.
dump n montón m; * vt dejar.
dumping n (com) dumping m.
dumpling n bola de masa f.
dumpy adj gordito/ta.
dunce n zopenco m.
dune n duna f.
dung n estiércol m.
dungarees npl mono m.

dungeon n calabozo m.
dupe n bobo m; * vt engañar, embaucar.
duplex n dúplex m.
duplicate n duplicado m; copia f; * vt multicopiar.
duplicity n duplicidad f.
durability n durabilidad f.
durable adj duradero/ra.
duration n duración f.
during prep mientras, durante el tiempo que.
dusk n crepúsculo m.
dust n polvo m; * vt desempolvar.
dustbin n cubo de la basura m.
dustbin man, dustman n basurero m.
duster n plumero m.
dusty adj polvoriento/ta.
Dutch courage n valor fingido m.
duteous adj fiel, leal.
dutiful adj obediente, sumiso/sa; ~ly adv obedientemente.
duty n deber m; obligación f.

duty-free adj libre de derechos de aduana.
dwarf n enano m; enana f; * vt empequeñecer.
dwell vi habitar, morar.
dwelling n habitación f; domicilio m.
dwindle vi mermar, disminuirse.
dye vt teñir; * n tinte m.
dyer n tintorero/ra m/f.
dyeing n tintorería f; tintura f.
dye-works npl taller del tintorero m.
dying adj agonizante, moribundo/da; * n muerte f; ~ **moments** postrimerías fpl.
dynamic adj dinámico/ca.
dynamics n dinámica f.
dynamite n dinamita f.
dynamiter n dinamitero/ra m/f.
dynamo n dinamo f.
dynasty n dinastía f.
dysentery n disentería f.
dyspepsia n (med) dispepsia f.
dyspeptic adj dispéptico/ca.

E

each pn cada uno, cada una; ~ **other** unos a otros, unas a otras, mutuamente.
eager adj entusiasmado/da; ~ly adv con entusiasmo.
eagerness n ansia f; anhelo m.
eagle n águila f.
eagle-eyed adj con vista de lince.
eaglet n aguilucho m.
ear n oreja f; oído m; espiga f; **by** ~ de oreja.
earache n dolor de oídos m.
eardrum n tímpano (del oído) m.
early adj temprano/na; adv temprano.
earmark vt destinar a.

earn vt ganar; conseguir.
earnest adj serio/ria; en serio; ~ly adv seriamente.
earnestness n seriedad f.
earnings npl ingresos mpl.
earphones npl auriculares mpl.
earring n zarcillo, pendiente m.
earth n tierra f; * vt conectar a tierra.
earthen adj de tierra.
earthenware n loza de barro f.
earthquake n terremoto m.
earthworm n lombriz f.
earthy adj sensual.
earwig n tijereta f.
ease n comodidad f; facilidad f; **at** ~ con desahogo; * vt aliviar; mitigar.

easel n caballete m.

easily adv fácilmente.

easiness n facilidad f.

east n este m; oriente m.

Easter n Pascua de Resurrección; Semana Santa f.

Easter egg n huevo de Pascua m.

easterly adj del este.

eastern adj del este, oriental.

eastward(s) adv hacia el este.

easy adj fácil; cómodo/da, ~ **going** acomodadizo/za.

easy chair n sillón m.

eat vt comer; * vi alimentarse.

eatable adj comestible; * ~s npl víveres mpl.

eaves npl alero m.

eau de Cologne n agua de Colonia f.

eavesdrop vt escuchar a escondidas.

ebb n reflujo m; * vi menguar; decaer, disminuir.

ebony n ébano m.

eccentric adj excéntrico/ca.

eccentricity n excentricidad f.

ecclesiastic adj eclesiástico/ca.

echo n eco m; * vi resonar, repercutir.

eclectic adj ecléctico/ca.

eclipse n eclipse m; * vt eclipsar.

ecologist, environmentalist n ecologista m/f.

ecology n ecología f.

e-commerce n comercio electrónico m.

economic(al) adj económico/ca, frugal, moderado/da.

economics npl economía f.

economist n economista m/f.

economize vt economizar.

economy n economía f; frugalidad f.

ecosystem n ecosistema m.

ecotax n ecotasa f.

ecotourism n ecoturismo m.

ecstasy n éxtasis m; rapto m.

ecstatic adj extático/ca; ~**ally** adv en éxtasis.

eczema n eczema m.

eddy n reflujo de agua m; remolino m; * vi arremolinarse.

edge n filo m; punta f; margen m/f; acrimonia f; * vt ribetear; introducir.

edgeways, edgewise adv de lado.

edging n orla, orilla f.

edgy adj nervioso/sa.

edible adj comestible.

edict n edicto, mandato m.

edification n edificación f.

edifice n edificio m; fábrica f.

edify vt edificar.

edit vt dirigir; redactar; cortar.

edition n edición f; publicación f; impresión f.

editor n director/a m/f; redactor/a m/f.

editorial adj, n editorial m.

educate vt educar; enseñar.

education n educación f.

eel n anguila f.

eerie adj espeluznante.

efface vt borrar, destruir.

effect n efecto m; realidad f; ~**s** npl efectos, bienes mpl; * vt efectuar, ejecutar.

effective adj eficaz; efectivo/va; ~**ly** adv efectivamente, en efecto.

effectiveness n eficacia f.

effectual adj eficiente, eficaz; ~**ly** adv eficazmente.

effeminacy n afeminación f.

effeminate adj afeminado/da.

effervescence n efervescencia f; hervor m.

effete adj estéril.

efficacy n eficacia f.

efficiency n eficiencia, virtud f.

efficient adj eficaz.

effigy n efigie, imagen f; retrato m.

effort n esfuerzo, empeño m.

effortless adj sin esfuerzo.

effrontery n descaro m; impudencia, desvergüenza f.

effusive adj efusivo/va.

egg n huevo m; * **to ~ on** vt animar.

eggcup n huevera f.

eggplant n berenjena f.

eggshell n cáscara de huevo f.

ego(t)ism n egoísmo m.

ego(t)ist n egoísta m/f.

ego(t)istical adj egotista.

eiderdown n edredón m.

eight adj, n ocho.

eighteen adj, n dieciocho.

eighteenth adj, n decimoctavo.

eighth adj, n octavo.

eightieth adj, n octogésimo/ma.

eighty adj, n ochenta.

either pn cualquiera; * conj o, sea, ya.

ejaculate vt exclamar; eyacular.

ejaculation n exclamación f; eyaculación f.

eject vt expeler, desechar.

ejection n expulsión f.

ejector seat n asiento eyectable m.

eke vt alargar; prolongar; hacer crecer.

elaborate vt elaborar; * adj elaborado/da; ~ly adv cuidadosamente.

elapse vi pasar, correr (el tiempo).

elastic adj elástico/ca.

elasticity n elasticidad f.

elated adj regocijado/da.

elation n regocijo m.

elbow n codo m; * vt codear.

elbow-room n anchura f; espacio suficiente m; (fig) libertad, latitud f.

elder n saúco m (árbol); * adj mayor.

elderly adj anciano/na.

elders npl ancianos, antepasados mpl.

eldest adj el mayor, la mayor.

elect vt elegir; * adj elegido/da, escogido/da.

election n elección f.

electioneering n electoralismo m.

elective adj facultativo/va.

elector n elector/a m/f.

electoral adj electoral.

electorate n electorado m.

electric(al) adj eléctrico/ca; ~ **domestic appliance** electrodoméstico m.

electric blanket n manta eléctrica f.

electric cooker n cocina eléctrica f.

electric fire n estufa eléctrica f.

electrician n electricista m/f.

electricity n electricidad f.

electrify vt electrizar.

electrocardiogram n electrocardiograma m.

electron n electrón m.

electronic adj electrónico/ca; ~s npl electrónica f.

elegance n elegancia f.

elegant adj elegante, delicado/da; ~ly adv elegantemente.

elegy n elegía f.

element n elemento m; fundamento m.

elemental, elementary adj elemental.

elephant n elefante m.

elephantine adj inmenso/sa.

elevate vt elevar, alzar, exaltar.

elevation n elevación f; altura f; alteza (de pensamientos) f.

elevator n ascensor m.

eleven adj, n once.

eleventh adj, n undécimo.

elf n duende m.

elicit vt sacar de.

eligibility *n* elegibilidad *f*.

eligible *adj* elegible.

eliminate *vt* eliminar, descartar.

elk *n* alce *m*.

elliptic(al) *adj* elíptico/ca.

elm *n* olmo *m*.

elocution *n* elocución *f*.

elocutionist *n* profesor de elocución *m*.

elongate *vt* alargar.

elope *vi* escapar, huir, evadirse.

elopement *n* fuga, huida, evasión *f*.

eloquence *n* elocuencia *f*.

eloquent *adj* elocuente; **~ly** *adv* elocuentemente.

else *pn* otro/ra.

elsewhere *adv* en otra parte.

elucidate *vt* explicar.

elucidation *n* elucidación, explicación *f*.

elude *vt* eludir, evitar.

elusive *adj* esquivo/va.

emaciated *adj* demacrado/da.

e-mail *n* correo electrónico *m*.

emanate (from) *vi* emanar.

emancipate *vt* emancipar; dar libertad.

emancipation *n* emancipación *f*.

embalm *vt* embalsamar.

embankment *n* terraplén *m*.

embargo *n* embargo *m*.

embark *vt* embarcar.

embarkation *n* embarque *m*.

embarrass *vt* avergonzar.

embarrassed *adj* avergonzado/da.

embarrassing *adj* violento/ta; embarazoso/sa.

embarrassment *n* desconcierto *m*.

embassy *n* embajada *f*.

embed *vt* empotrar; clavar.

embellish *vt* hermosear, adornar.

embellishment *n* adorno *m*.

embers *npl* rescoldo *m*.

embezzle *vt* desfalcar.

embezzlement *n* desfalco *m*.

embitter *vt* amargar.

emblem *n* emblema *m*.

emblematic(al) *adj* emblemático/ca, simbólico/ca.

embodiment *n* incorporación *f*.

embody *vt* incorporar.

embrace *vt* abrazar; contener; * *n* abrazo *m*.

embroider *vt* bordar.

embroidery *n* bordado *m*; bordadura *f*.

embroil *vt* embrollar; confundir.

embryo *n* embrión *m*.

emendation *n* enmienda, corrección *f*.

emerald *n* esmeralda *f*.

emerge *vi* salir, proceder.

emergency *n* emergencia *f*; necesidad urgente *f*.

emergency cord *n* timbre de alarma *m*.

emergency exit *n* salida de emergencia *f*.

emergency landing *n* aterrizaje forzoso *m*.

emergency meeting *n* reunión extraordinaria *f*.

emery *n* esmeril *m*.

emigrant *n* emigrante *m/f*.

emigrate *vi* emigrar.

emigration *n* emigración *f*.

eminence *n* altura *f*; eminencia, excelencia *f*.

eminent *adj* eminente, elevado/da; distinguido/da; **~ly** *adv* eminentemente.

emission *n* emisión *f*.

emit *vt* emitir; arrojar, despedir.

emolument *n* emolumento, provecho *m*.

emotion *n* emoción *f*.

emotional *adj* emocional.

emotive *adj* emotivo/va.

emperor *n* emperador *m*.

emphasis *n* énfasis *m*.

emphasize *vt* hablar con énfasis.

emphatic *adj* enfático/ca; **~ally** *adv* enfáticamente.

empire *n* imperio *m*.

employ *vt* emplear, ocupar.

employee *n* empleado/da *m/f*.

employer *n* patrón *m*; empresario/ria *m/f*.

employment *n* empleo *m*; trabajo *m*.

emporium *n* emporio *m*.

empress *n* emperatriz *f*.

emptiness *n* vaciedad *f*; futilidad *f*.

empty *adj* vacío/cía; vano/na; ignorante; * *vt* vaciar, evacuar.

empty-handed *adj* con las manos vacías.

emulate *vt* emular, competir; imitar.

emulsion *n* emulsión *f*.

enable *vt* capacitar.

enact *vt* promulgar; representar; hacer.

enamel *n* esmalte *m*; * *vt* esmaltar.

enamour *vt* enamorar.

encamp *vi* acamparse.

encampment *n* campamento *m*.

encase *vt* encajar, encajonar.

enchant *vt* encantar.

enchanting *adj* encantador/a.

enchantment *n* encanto *m*.

encircle *vt* cercar, circundar.

enclose *vt* cercar, circunvalar, circundar; incluir.

enclosure *n* cercamiento *m*; cercado *m*.

encompass *vt* abarcar.

encore *adv* otra vez, de nuevo.

encounter *n* encuentro *m*; duelo *m*; pelea *f*; * *vt* encontrar.

encourage *vt* animar, alentar.

encouragement *n* estímulo, patrocinio *m*.

encroach *vt* usurpar, avanzar gradualmente.

encroachment *n* usurpación, intrusión *f*.

encrusted *adj* incrustado/da.

encumber *vt* embarazar, cargar.

encumbrance *n* embarazo, impedimento *m*.

encyclical *adj* encíclico/ca, circular.

encyclopaedia *n* enciclopedia *f*.

end *n* fin *m*; extremidad *f*; término *m*; resolución *f*; **to the ~ that** para que; **to no ~** en vano; **on ~** en pie, de pie; * *vt* terminar, concluir, fenecer; * *vi* acabar, terminar.

endanger *vt* peligrar, arriesgar.

endear *vt* encarecer.

endearing *adj* simpático/ca.

endearment *n* ternura *f*.

endeavour *vi* esforzarse; intentar; * *n* esfuerzo *m*.

endemic *adj* endémico/ca.

ending *n* conclusión; *f*; desenlace *m*; terminación *f*.

endive *n* (*bot*) endibia *f*.

endless *adj* infinito/ta, perpetuo/tua; **~ly** *adv* sin fin, perpetuamente.

endorse *vt* endosar; aprobar.

endorsement *n* endoso *m*; aprobación *f*.

endow *vt* dotar.

endowment *n* dote, dotación *f*.

endurable *adj* sufrible, tolerable.

endurance *n* duración *f*; paciencia *f*; sufrimiento *m*.

endure *vt* sufrir, soportar; * *vi* durar.

endways, endwise *adv* de punta, derecho.

enemy *n* enemigo/ga, antagonista *m/f*.

energetic *adj* enérgico/ca, vigoroso/sa.

energy *n* energía, fuerza *f*; **renewable forms of ~** energía renovables.

enervate *vt* enervar, debilitar.

enfeeble *vt* debilitar.

enfold *vt* envolver.

enforce *vt* hacer cumplir.

enforced *adj* forzoso/sa.

enfranchise *vt* emancipar.

engage *vt* llamar; abordar; contratar.

engaged *adj* prometido/da.

engagement *n* empeño *m*; combate *m*; pelea *f*; obligación *f*.

engagement ring *n* anillo de prometida *m*.

engaging *adj* atractivo/va.

engender *vt* engendrar; producir.

engine *n* motor *m*; locomotora *f*.

engine driver *n* maquinista *m/f*.

engineer *n* ingeniero/ra *m/f*; maquinista *m/f*.

engineering *n* ingeniería *f*.

engrave *vt* grabar; esculpir; tallar.

engraving *n* grabado *m*; estampa *f*.

engrossed *adj* absorto/ta.

engulf *vt* sumergir.

enhance *vt* aumentar, realzar.

enigma *n* enigma *m*.

enjoy *vt* gozar; poseer.

enjoyable *adj* agradable; divertido/da.

enjoyment *n* disfrute *m*; placer *m*; fruición *f*.

enlarge *vt* engrandecer, dilatar, extender.

enlargement *n* aumento *m*; ampliación *f*, soltura *f*.

enlighten *vt* iluminar; instruir.

enlightened *adj* iluminado/da.

Enlightenment *n*: **the ~** el Siglo de las Luces *m*, la Ilustración *f*.

enlist *vt* alistar.

enlistment *n* alistamiento *m*.

enliven *vt* animar; avivar; alegrar.

enmity *n* enemistad *f*; odio *m*.

enormity *n* enormidad *f*; atrocidad *f*.

enormous *adj* enorme; **~ly** *adv* enormemente.

enough *adv* bastante; basta; * *n* bastante *m*.

enounce *vt* declarar.

enquire, inquire *vt*, *vi* preguntar; **to ~ about** informarse de; **to ~ after** *vt* preguntar por; **to ~ into** *vt* investigar, indagar, inquirir.

enquiry *n* pesquisa *f*.

enrage *vt* enfurecer, irritar.

enrapture *vt* arrebatar, entusiasmar; encantar.

enrich *vt* enriquecer; adornar.

enrichment *n* enriquecimiento *m*.

enrol *vt* registrar; arrollar.

enrolment *n* inscripción *f*.

en route *adv* durante el viaje.

ensign *n* (*mil*) bandera *f*; abanderado *m*; (*mar*) alférez *m*.

enslave *vt* esclavizar, cautivar.

ensue *vi* seguirse; suceder.

ensure *vt* asegurar.

entail *vt* suponer.

entangle *vt* enmarañar, embrollar.

entanglement *n* enredo *m*.

enter *vt* entrar; admitir; registrar; **to ~ for** presentarse para; **to ~ into** establecer; formar parte de/en; firmar.

enterprise *n* empresa *f*.

enterprising *adj* emprendedor/a.

entertain *vt* divertir; hospedar; mantener.

entertainer *n* artista *m/f*.

entertaining *adj* divertido/da.

entertainment *n* entretenimiento, pasatiempo *m*.

enthralled *adj* encantado/da.

enthralling *adj* cautivador/a.

enthrone *vt* entronizar.

enthusiasm *n* entusiasmo *m*.

enthusiast *n* entusiasta *m/f*.

enthusiastic *adj* entusiasta.

entice *vt* tentar; seducir.

entire *adj* entero/ra, completo/ta, perfecto/ta; **~ly** *adv* enteramente.

entitle *vt* intitular; conferir algún derecho.

entitled *adj* titulado/da.

entity *n* entidad, existencia *f*.

entourage *n* séquito *m*.

entrails *npl* entrañas *fpl*; asadura *f*.

entrance *n* entrada *f*; admisión *f*; principio *m*.

entrance examination *n* examen de ingreso *m*.

entrance fee *n* cuota *f*.

entrance hall *n* pórtico, vestíbulo *m*.

entrant *n* participante *m*; candidato *m*.

entrap *vt* enredar; engañar.

entreat *vt* rogar, suplicar.

entreaty *n* petición, suplica, instancia *f*.

entrepreneur *n* empresario/ria *m/f*.

entrust *vt* confiar.

entry *n* entrada *f*.

entry phone *n* portero automático *m*.

entwine *vt* entrelazàr, enroscar, torcer.

enumerate *vt* enumerar, numerar.

enunciate *vt* enunciar, declarar.

enunciation *n* enunciación *f*.

envelop *vt* envolver.

envelope *n* sobre *m*.

enviable *adj* envidiable.

envious *adj* envidioso/sa; **~ly** *adv* envidiosamente.

environment *n* medio ambiente *m*.

environmental *adj* ambiental, medio-ambiental.

environs *npl* vecindad *f*; contornos *mpl*.

envisage *vt* prever; concebir.

envoy *n* enviado/da *m/f*; mensajero/ra *m/f*.

envy *n* envidia, malicia *f*; * *vt* envidiar.

ephemeral *adj* efímero/ra.

epic *adj* épico/ca; * *n* épica *f*.

epidemic *adj* epidémico/ca; * *n* epidemia *f*.

epilepsy *n* epilepsia *f*.

epileptic *adj* epiléptico/ca.

epilogue *n* epílogo *m*.

Epiphany *n* Epifanía *f*.

episcopacy *n* episcopado *m*.

Episcopal *adj* episcopal.

Episcopalian *n* anglicano/na *m/f*.

episode *n* episodio *m*.

epistle *n* epístola *f*.

epistolary *adj* epistolar.

epithet *n* epíteto *m*.

epitome *n* epítome, compendio *m*.

epitomize *vt* epitomar, abreviar.

epoch *n* época *f*.

equable *adj* uniforme; **~bly** *adv* uniformemente.

equal *adj* igual; justo/ta; semejante; * *n* igual *m*; compañero *m*; * *vt* igualar; compensar.

equalize *vt* igualar.

equalizer *n* igualada *f*.

equality *n* igualdad, uniformidad *f*.

equally *adv* igualmente.

equanimity *n* ecuanimidad *f*.

equate *vt* equiparar (con).

equation *n* ecuación *f*.

equator *n* ecuador *m*.

equatorial *adj* ecuatorial, ecuatorio/ria.

equestrian *adj* ecuestre.

equilateral *adj* equilátero/ra.

equilibrium *n* equilibrio *m*.

equinox n equinoccio m.

equip vt equipar, pertrechar.

equipment n equipaje m.

equitable adj equitativo/va, imparcial; ~**bly** adv equitativamente.

equity n equidad, justicia, imparcialidad f.

equivalent adj, n equivalente m.

equivocal adj equívoco/ca, ambiguo/gua; ~**ly** adv equivocadamente, ambiguamente.

equivocate vt equivocar, usar equívocos.

equivocation n equívoco m.

era n era f.

eradicate vt desarraigar, extirpar.

eradication n extirpación f.

erase vt borrar.

eraser n goma de borrar f.

erect vt erigir; establecer; * adj derecho/ha, erguido/da, vertical.

erection n establecimiento m; estructura f; erección f.

ermine n armiño m.

erode vt erosionar; corroer.

erotic adj erótico/ca.

err vi vagar, errar; desviarse.

errand n recado, mensaje m.

errand boy n recadero m.

errata npl fe de erratas f.

erratic adj errático/ca, errante; irregular.

erroneous adj erróneo/nea; falso/sa; ~**ly** adv erróneamente.

error n error m; yerro m.

erudite adj erudito/ta.

erudition n erudición f; doctrina f.

erupt vi entrar en erupción; hacer erupción.

eruption n erupción f.

escalate vi extenderse.

escalation n intensificación f.

escalator n escalera mecánica f.

escapade n travesura f.

escape vt evitar; escapar; * vi evadirse, salvarse; * vr zafarse; * n escapada, huida, fuga f; inadvertencia f; **to make one's ~** poner los pies en polvorosa.

escapism n escapismo m.

eschew vt huir, evitar, evadir.

escort n escolta f; * vt escoltar.

esoteric adj esotérico/ca.

especial adj especial; ~**ly** adv especialmente.

espionage n espionaje m.

esplanade n (mil) esplanada f.

espouse vt desposar.

essay n ensayo m.

essence n esencia f.

essential n esencia f; * adj esencial, substancial, principal; ~**ly** adv esencialmente.

establish vt establecer, fundar, fijar; confirmar.

establishment n establecimiento m; fundación f; institución f.

estate n estado m; hacienda f; bienes mpl.

esteem vt estimar, apreciar; pensar; * n estima f; consideración f.

estimate vt estimar, apreciar, tasar; * n presupuesto m.

estimation n estimación, valuación f; opinión f.

estrange vt extrañar, apartar, enajenar.

estranged adj separado/da.

estrangement n enajenación f; extrañeza, distancia f.

estuary n estuario m, ría f.

etch vt grabar al aguafuerte.

etching n grabado al aguafuerte m.

eternal adj eterno/na, perpetuo/tua, inmortal; ~**ly** adv eternamente.

eternity n eternidad f.

ether *n* éter *m*.

ethical *adj* ético/ca; **~ly** *adv* moralmente.

ethics *npl* ética *f*.

ethnic *adj* étnico/ca.

ethos *n* genio *m*.

etiquette *n* etiqueta *f*.

etymological *adj* etimológico/ca.

etymologist *n* etimólogo/ga *m/f*, etimologista *m/f*.

etymology *n* etimología *f*.

Eucharist *n* Eucaristía *f*.

eulogy *n* elogio, encomio *m*; alabanza *f*.

eunuch *n* eunuco *m*.

euphemism *n* eufemismo *m*.

euro *n* euro *m*.

Euro MP *n* eurodiputado/da *m/f*.

Europe *n* Europa *f*.

European Community *n* Comunidad Europea *f*.

European Parliament *n* eurocámara *f*.

European Union *n* unión Europea *f*.

Eurosceptic *n* euroescéptico/ca *m/f*.

Eurotunnel, Channel Tunnel *n* eurotúnel *m*.

evacuate *vt* evacuar.

evacuation *n* evacuación *f*.

evade *vt* evadir, escapar, evitar.

evaluate *vt* evaluar; interpretar.

evangelic(al) *adj* evangélico/ca.

evangelist *n* evangelista *m*.

evaporate *vt* evaporar; * *vi* evaporarse; disiparse.

evaporated milk *n* leche evaporada *f*.

evaporation *n* evaporación *f*.

evasion *n* evasión *f*; escape *m*.

evasive *adj* evasivo/va; **~ly** *adv* con evasivas.

eve *n* víspera *f*.

even *adj* llano/na, igual; par, semejante; * *adv* aun; aun cuando, supuesto que; no obstante; * *vt* igualar, allanar; * *vi*: **to ~ out** nivelarse.

even-handed *adj* imparcial, equitativo/va.

evening *n* tarde *f*.

evening class *n* clase nocturna *f*.

evening dress *n* traje de etiqueta *m*; traje de noche *m*.

evenly *adv* igualmente, llanamente.

evenness *n* igualdad *f*; uniformidad *f*; llanura *f*; imparcialidad *f*.

event *n* acontecimiento, evento *m*; suceso *m*.

eventful *adj* lleno de acontecimientos.

eventual *adj* final; **~ly** *adv* por fin.

eventuality *n* eventualidad *f*.

ever *adv* siempre; **for ~ and ~** siempre jamás, eternamente; **~ since** después.

evergreen *adj* de hoja perenne; * *n* árbol de hoja perenne *m*.

everlasting *adj* eterno/na.

evermore *adv* eternamente, para siempre jamás.

every *adj* cada uno, cada una; **~ where** en *o* por todas partes; **~ thing** todo; **~ one, ~ body** todos, todo el mundo.

evict *vt* desahuciar.

eviction *n* desahucio *m*.

evidence *n* evidencia *f*; testimonio *m*; prueba *f*; * *vt* evidenciar.

evident *adj* evidente; patente, manifiesto/ta; **~ly** *adv* evidentemente.

evil *adj* malo/la, depravado/da, pernicioso/sa; dañoso/sa; * *n* mal *m*; maldad *f*.

evil-minded *adj* malicioso/sa, mal intencionado/da.

evocative *adj* sugestivo/va.

evoke *vt* evocar.

evolution n evolución f.

evolve vt, vi evolucionar; desenvolver; desplegarse.

ewe n oveja f.

exacerbate vt exacerbar.

exact adj exacto/ta; * vt exigir.

exacting adj exigente.

exaction n exacción, extorsión f.

exactly adj exactamente.

exactness, exactitude n exactitud f.

exaggerate vt exagerar.

exaggeration n exageración f.

exalt vt exaltar, elevar; alabar; realzar.

exaltation n exaltación, elevación f.

exalted adj exaltado/da; muy animado/da.

examination n examen m.

examine vt examinar; escudriñar.

examiner n inspector/a m/f.

example n ejemplar m; ejemplo m.

exasperate vt exasperar, irritar, enojar, provocar; agravar; amargar.

exasperation n exasperación, irritación f.

excavate vt excavar, ahondar.

excavation n excavación f.

exceed vt exceder; sobrepujar.

exceedingly adv extremamente, en sumo grado.

excel vt sobresalir, exceder; * vi descollar.

excellence n excelencia f; preeminencia f.

Excellency n Excelencia (título) f.

excellent adj excelente; ~ly adv excelentemente.

except vt exceptuar, excluir; ~(ing) prep excepto, a excepción de.

exception n excepción, exclusión f.

exceptional adj excepcional.

excerpt n extracto m.

excess n exceso m.

excessive adj excesivo/va; ~ly adv excesivamente.

exchange vt cambiar; trocar, permutar; * n cambio m; bolsa f.

exchange rate n tipo de cambio m.

excise n impuestos sobre el consumo mpl.

excitability n excitabilidad f.

excitable adj excitable.

excite vt excitar; estimular.

excited adj emocionado/da.

excitement n estímulo, excitación f.

exciting adj emocionante.

exclaim vi exclamar.

exclamation n exclamación f; clamor m.

exclamation mark n punto de admiración m.

exclamatory adj exclamatorio/ria.

exclude vt excluir; exceptuar.

exclusion n exclusión, exclusiva, excepción f.

exclusive adj exclusivo/va; ~ly adv exclusivamente.

excommunicate vt excomulgar.

excommunication n excomunión f.

excrement n excremento m.

excruciating adj atroz, enorme, grave.

exculpate vt disculpar; justificar.

excursion n excursión f; digresión f.

excusable adj excusable.

excuse vt disculpar; perdonar; * n disculpa, excusa f; pretexto m; ~ me! interj ¡perdón!.

execute vt ejecutar.

execution n ejecución f.

executioner n ejecutor/a m/f; verdugo m.

executive adj ejecutivo/va.

executor n testamentario/ria, albacea m/f.

exemplary adj ejemplar.

exemplify vt ejemplificar.
exempt adj exento/ta.
exemption n exención f.
exercise n ejercicio m; ensayo m; tarea f; practica f; * vi hacer ejercicio; * vt ejercer; valerse de.
exercise book n cuaderno m.
exert vt emplear; **to ~ oneself** esforzarse.
exertion n esfuerzo m.
exhale vt exhalar.
exhaust n escape m; * vt agotar.
exhausted adj agotado/da.
exhaustion n agotamiento m; extenuación f.
exhaustive adj comprensivo/va.
exhibit vt exhibir; mostrar; * n (law) objeto expuesto m.
exhibition n exposición, presentación f.
exhilarating adj estimulante.
exhilaration n alegría f; buen humor, regocijo m.
exhort vt exhortar, excitar.
exhortation n exhortación f.
exhume vt exhumar, desenterrar.
exile n destierro m; * vt desterrar, deportar.
exist vi existir.
existence n existencia f.
existent adj existente.
existing adj actual, presente.
exit n salida f; * vi hacer mutis.
exodus n éxodo m.
exonerate vt exonerar, descargar.
exoneration n exoneración f.
exorbitant adj exorbitante, excesivo/va.
exorcise vt exorcizar, conjurar.
exorcism n exorcismo m.
exotic adj exótico/ca, extranjero/ra.
expand vt extender, dilatar.
expanse n extensión f.

expansion n expansión f.
expansive adj expansivo/va.
expatriate vt expatriar.
expect vt esperar, aguardar.
expectance, expectancy n expectación, esperanza f.
expectant adj expectante.
expectant mother n mujer encinta f.
expectation n expectación, expectativa f.
expediency n conveniencia, oportunidad f.
expedient adj oportuno/na, conveniente; * n expediente m; **~ly** adv convenientemente.
expedite vt acelerar; expedir.
expedition n expedición f.
expeditious adj pronto/ta, expedito/ta; **~ly** adv prontamente.
expel vt expeler, desterrar.
expend vt expender; desembolsar.
expendable adj prescindible.
expenditure n gasto, desembolso m.
expense n gasto m; coste m.
expense account n cuenta de gastos f.
expensive adj caro/ra; costoso/sa; **~ly** adv costosamente.
experience n experiencia f; práctica f; * vt experimentar.
experienced adj experimentado/da.
experiment n experimento m; * vt experimentar.
experimental adj experimental; **~ly** adv experimentalmente.
expert adj experto/ta, diestro/tra.
expertise n pericia f.
expiration n expiración f; muerte f.
expire vi expirar.
explain vt explanar, explicar.
explanation n explicación f.
explanatory adj explicativo/va.
expletive adj expletivo/va.
explicable adj explicable.

explicit *adj* explícito/ta; **~ly** *adv* explícitamente.

explode *vt, vi* estallar, explotar.

exploit *vt* explotar; * *n* hazaña *f*; hecho heroico *m*.

exploitation *n* explotación *f*.

exploration *n* exploración *f*; examen *m*.

exploratory *adj* exploratorio/ria.

explore *vt* explorar, examinar; sondear.

explorer *n* explorador/a *m/f*.

explosion *n* explosión *f*.

explosive *adj, n* explosivo *m*.

exponent *n* (*math*) exponente *m*.

export *vt* exportar.

export, exportation *n* exportación *f*.

exporter *n* exportador/a *m/f*.

expose *vt* exponer; mostrar; descubrir; poner en peligro.

exposed *adj* expuesto/ta.

exposition *n* exposición *f*; interpretación *f*.

expostulate *vi* debatir, contender.

exposure *n* exposición *f*; velocidad de obturación *f*; fotografía *f*.

exposure meter *n* fotómetro *m*.

expound *vt* exponer; interpretar.

express *vt* exprimir; representar; * *adj* expreso/sa, claro/ra; a propósito; * *n* expreso, correo *m*; (*rail*) tren expreso *m*.

expression *n* expresión *f*; locución *f*.

expressionless *adj* sin expresión (cara).

expressive *adj* expresivo/va; **~ly** *adv* expresivamente.

expressly *adv* expresamente.

expressway *n* autopista *f*.

expropriate *vt* expropiar (por causa de utilidad pública).

expropriation *n* (*law*) expropiación *f*.

expulsion *n* explosión *f*.

expurgate *vt* expurgar.

exquisite *adj* exquisito/ta, perfecto/ta, excelente; **~ly** *adv* exquisitamente.

extant *adj* existente.

extempore *adv* de improviso.

extemporize *vi* improvisar.

extend *vt* extender; amplificar; * *vi* extenderse.

extension *n* extensión *f*.

extensive *adj* extenso/sa, dilatado/da; **~ly** *adv* extensivamente.

extent *n* extensión *f*.

extenuate *vt* extenuar, disminuir, atenuar.

extenuating *adj* atenuante.

exterior *adj, n* exterior *m*.

exterminate *vt* exterminar; extirpar.

extermination *n* exterminación, extirpación *f*.

external *adj* externo/na; **~ly** *adv* exteriormente; **~s** *npl* exterior *m*.

extinct *adj* extinto/ta; abolido/da.

extinction *n* extinción *f*; abolición *f*.

extinguish *vt* extinguir; suprimir.

extinguisher *n* extintor *m*.

extirpate *vt* extirpar.

extol *vt* alabar, magnificar, alzar, exaltar.

extort *vt* sacar por la fuerza.

extortion *n* extorsión *f*.

extortionate *adj* excesivo/va.

extra *adv* extra; * *n* extra *m*.

extract *vt* extraer; extractar; * *n* extracto *m*; compendio *m*.

extraction *n* extracción *f*; descendencia *f*.

extracurricular *adj* extraescolar.

extradite *vt* extraditar.

extradition *n* (*law*) extradición *f*.

extramarital *adj* extramatrimonial.

extramural *adj* extraescolar.

extraneous *adj* extraño/ña, ajeno/na.

extraordinarily adv extraordinariamente.

extraordinary adj extraordinario/ria.

extravagance n extravagancia f; gastos, excesivos mpl.

extravagant adj extravagante, exorbitante; pródigo/ga; ~ly adv extravagantemente.

extreme adj extremo/ma, supremo/ma; último/ma; * n extremo m; ~ly adv extremamente.

extremist adj, n extremista m/f.

extremity n extremidad f.

extricate vt desembarazar, desenredar.

extrinsic(al) adj extrínseco/ca, exterior.

extrovert adj, n extrovertido m.

exuberance n exuberancia, suma abundancia f.

exuberant adj exuberante, abundantísimo/ma; ~ly adv exuberantemente.

exude vi transpirar.

exult vt exultar, regocijarse, triunfar.

exultation n exultación f; regocijo m.

eye n ojo m; * vt ojear, contemplar, observar.

eyeball n globo del ojo m.

eyebrow n ceja f.

eyelash n pestaña f.

eyelid n párpado m.

eyesight n vista f.

eyesore n monstruosidad f.

eyetooth n colmillo m.

eyewitness n testigo ocular m.

eyrie n nido de águila m.

F

fable n fábula f; ficción f.

fabric n tejido m.

fabricate vt fabricar, edificar.

fabrication n fabricación f.

fabulous adj fabuloso/sa; ~ly adv fabulosamente.

facade n fachada f.

face n cara, faz f; superficie f; fachada f; aspecto m; apariencia f; * vt encararse; hacer frente; **to ~ up to** hacer frente a.

face cream n crema facial f.

face-lift n lifting m.

face powder n polvos mpl.

facet n faceta f.

facetious adj chistoso/sa, alegre, gracioso/sa; ~ly adv chistosamente.

face value n valor nominal m.

facial adj facial.

facile adj fácil, afable.

facilitate vt facilitar.

facility n facilidad, ligereza f; afabilidad f.

facing n paramento m; * prep enfrente.

facsimile n facsímil m; fax m.

fact n hecho m; realidad f; **in ~** en efecto.

faction n facción f; disensión f.

factor n factor m.

factory n fábrica f.

factual adj basado/da en hechos reales.

faculty n facultad f; personal docente m.

fad n moda f.

fade vi decaer, marchitarse, fallecer.

fail vt suspender, reprobar; fallar a; * vi suspender; fracasar; fallar; (fig) zozobrar.

failing n falta f; defecto m.

failure n falta f; culpa f; descuido m; quiebra, bancarrota f.

faint vi desmayarse, debilitarse; * n desmayo m; * adj débil; **~ly** adv débilmente.

fainthearted adj cobarde, medroso/sa, pusilánime.

faintness n flaqueza f; desmayo m.

fair adj hermoso/sa, bello/la; blanco/ca; rubio/bia; claro/ra, sereno/na; favorable; recto/ta, justo/ta; franco/ca; * adv limpio; * n feria f.

fairly adv justamente; completamente.

fairness n hermosura f; justicia f.

fair play n juego limpio m.

fair trade n comercio justo m.

fairy n hada f.

fairy tale n cuento de hadas m.

faith n fe f; dogma de fe m; fidelidad f.

faithful adj fiel, leal; **~ly** adv fielmente.

faithfulness n fidelidad, lealtad f.

fake n falsificación f; impostor/a m/f; * adj falso/sa; * vt fingir; falsificar.

falcon n halcón m.

falconry n cetrería f.

fall vi caer(se); perder el poder; disminuir, decrecer en precio; **to ~ asleep** dormirse; **to ~ back** retroceder; **to ~ back on** recurrir a; **to ~ behind** quedarse atrás; **to ~ down** caerse; **to ~ for** dejarse engañar; enamorarse de; **to ~ in** hundirse; **to ~ short** faltar; **to ~ sick** enfermar; **to ~ in love** enamorarse; **to ~ off** caerse; disminuir; **to ~ out** reñir, disputar; * n caída f; otoño m.

fallacious adj falaz, fraudulento/ta; **~ly** adv falazmente.

fallacy n falacia, sofistería f; engaño m.

fallibility n falibilidad f.

fallible adj falible.

fallow adj en barbecho; **~ deer** n gamo m.

false adj falso/sa; **~ly** adv falsamente.

false alarm n falsa alarma f.

falsehood, falseness n falsedad f.

falsify vt falsificar.

falsity n falsedad, mentira f.

falter vi tartamudear; faltar.

faltering adj vacilante.

fame n fama f; renombre m.

famed adj celebrado/da, famoso/sa.

familiar adj familiar; casero/ra; **~ly** adv familiarmente.

familiarity n familiaridad f.

familiarize vt familiarizar.

family n familia f; linaje m; clase, especie f.

family business n negocio familiar m.

family doctor n médico de familia m.

famine n hambre f; carestía f.

famished adj hambriento/ta.

famous adj famoso/sa, afamado/da; **~ly** adv famosamente.

fan n abanico m; aficionado m; fan m/f; * vt abanicar; atizar.

fanatic adj, n fanático/ca m/ca.

fanaticism n fanatismo m.

fan belt n correa del ventilador f.

fanciful adj imaginativo/va, caprichoso/sa; **~ly** adv caprichosamente.

fancy n fantasía, imaginación f; capricho m; * vt tener ganas de; imaginarse.

fancy-goods npl novedades, modas fpl.

fancy-dress ball n baile de disfraces m.

fanfare n (mus) fanfarria f.

fang n colmillo m.

fantastic adj fantástico/ca; caprichoso/sa; **~ally** adv fantásticamente.

fantasy n fantasía f.

far adv lejos, a una gran distancia; * adj lejano/na, distante, remoto/ta; **~ and away** con mucho, de mucho; **~ off** lejano/na.

faraway adj remoto/ta.

farce n farsa f.

farcical adj burlesco/ca.

fare n precio m; tarifa f; comida f; viajero m; pasaje m.

farewell n despedida f; **~!** excl ¡adiós!

farm n finca f, granja f; * vt cultivar.

farmer n agricultor/a m/f; granjero/ra m/f.

farmhand n peón m.

farmhouse n casa de hacienda f, granja f.

farming n agricultura f.

farmland n tierra de cultivo f.

farmyard n corral m.

far-reaching adj de gran alcance.

fart n (sl) pedo m; * vi tirarse un pedo.

farther adv más lejos; más adelante; * adj más lejos, ulterior.

farthest adv lo más lejos; lo más tarde; a lo más.

fascinate vt fascinar, encantar.

fascinating adj fascinante.

fascination n fascinación f; encanto m.

fascism n fascismo.

fascist n fascista m/f.

fashion n moda f; forma, figura f; uso m; manera f; estilo m; **people of ~** gente de tono f; * vt formar, amoldar.

fashionable adj a la moda; elegante; **the ~ world** el gran mundo; **~bly** adv a o segun la moda.

fashion show n desfile de modelos m.

fast vi ayunar; * n ayuno m; * adj rápido/da; firme, estable; * adv rápidamente; firmemente; estrechamente.

fasten vt abrochar; afirmar, asegurar, atar; fijar; * vi fijarse, establecerse.

fastener, fastening n cierre m; cerrojo m.

fast food n comida rápida f.

fastidious adj fastidioso/sa, desdeñoso/sa; **~ly** adv fastidiosamente.

fat adj gordo/da; * n grasa f; pringue m/f.

fatal adj fatal; funesto/ta; **~ly** adv fatalmente.

fatalism n fatalismo m.

fatalist n fatalista m/f.

fatality n fatalidad, predestinación f.

fate n hado, destino m.

fateful adj fatídico/ca.

father n padre m; **loving (over-indulgent) ~** padrazo m.

fatherhood n paternidad f.

father-in-law n suegro m.

fatherland n patria f.

fatherly adj paternal.

fathom n braza (medida) f; * vt sondar; penetrar.

fatigue n fatiga f; * vt fatigar, cansar.

fatten vt, vi engordar.

fatty adj graso/sa.

fatuous adj fatuo/tua, tonto/ta, imbécil.

fault n falta, culpa f; delito m; defecto m; yerro m.

faultfinder n censurador/a m/f.

faultless adj perfecto/ta, cumplido/da.

faulty adj defectuoso/sa.

fauna n fauna f.

faux pas n metedura de pata f.

favour n favor, beneficio m; patrocinio m; blandura f; * vt favorecer, proteger.

favourable adj favorable, propicio/cia; ~bly adv favorablemente.

favoured adj favorecido/da.

favourite n favorito/ta m/f; * adj favorecido/da.

favouritism n favoritismo m.

fawn n cervatillo m; * vi adular servilmente.

fawningly adv lisonjeramente, con adulación servil.

fax n facsímil(e) m; fax m; * vt mandar por fax.

fear vi temer; * n miedo m.

fearful adj medroso/sa, temeroso/sa; tímido/da; ~ly adv medrosamente, temerosamente.

fearless adj intrépido/da, atrevido/da; ~ly adv sin miedo.

fearlessness n intrepidez f.

feasibility n posibilidad f.

feasible adj factible, viable.

feast n banquete, festín m; fiesta f; * vi banquetear.

feat n hecho m; acción, hazaña f.

feather n pluma f;.

feather bed n plumón m.

feature n característica f; rasgo m; forma f; * vi figurar.

feature film n largometraje m.

February n febrero m.

federal adj federal.

federalist n federalista m/f.

federate vt, vi federar(se).

federation n federación f.

fed-up adj harto/ta.

fee n honorarios mpl; cuota f.

feeble adj flaco/ca, débil.

feebleness n debilidad f.

feebly adv débilmente.

feed vt nutrir; alimentar; **to ~ on** alimentarse de; * vi nutrirse; engordar; * n comida f; pasto m.

feedback n reacción f.

feel vt sentir; tocar; creer; **to ~ around** tantear; * n sensación f; tacto, sentido m.

feeler n antena f; (fig) tentativa f.

feeling n tacto m; sensibilidad f; corazonada f.

feelingly adv sensiblemente.

feign vt inventar, fingir; disimular.

feline adj felino/na.

fellow n tipo, tío m; socio/cia m/f.

fellow citizen n conciudadano/na m/f.

fellow countryman n compatriota m/f.

fellow feeling n simpatía f.

fellow men npl semejantes mpl.

fellowship n compañerismo m; beca (en un colegio) f.

fellow student n compañero/ra de curso m/f.

fellow traveller n compañero/ra de viaje m/f.

felon n criminal m/f.

felony n crimen m.

felt n fieltro m.

felt-tip pen n rotulador m.

female n hembra f; * adj femenino/na.

feminine adj femenino/na.

feminism n feminismo m.

feminist n feminista m/f.

fen n pantano m.

fence n cerca f; defensa f; * vt cercar; * vi esgrimir.

fencing n esgrima f.

fennel n (bot) hinojo m.

ferment n agitación f; * vi fermentar.

fern n (bot) helecho m.

ferocious adj feroz; fiero/ra; ~ly adv ferozmente.

ferocity n ferocidad, fiereza f.
ferret n hurón m; * vt huronear; **to ~ out** descubrir, echar fuera.
ferry n transbordador, ferry m; * vt transportar.
fertile adj fértil, fecundo/da.
fertility n fertilidad, fecundidad f.
fertilization n fertilización f.
fertilize vt fertilizar.
fertilizer n abono m.
fervent adj ferviente; fervoroso/sa; ~ly adv con fervor.
fervid adj ardiente, vehemente.
fervour n fervor, ardor m.
fester vi enconarse, inflamarse.
festival n fiesta f; festival m.
festive adj festivo/va.
festivity n festividad f.
fetch vt ir a buscar.
fetching adj atractivo/va.
fete n fiesta f.
fetid, foetid adj fétido/da, hediondo/da.
feud n riña, contienda f.
feudal adj feudal.
feudalism n feudalismo m.
fever n fiebre f.
feverish adj febril.
few adj poco/ca; **a ~** algunos; **~ and far between** pocos.
fewer adj menor; * adv menos.
fewest adj los menos.
fiancé n novio m.
fiancée n novia f.
fib n mentira f; * vi mentir.
fibre n fibra, hebra f.
fibreglass n fibra de vidrio f.
fickle adj voluble, inconstante, mudable, ligero/ra.
fiction n ficción f; invención f.
fictional adj novelesco/ca.
fictitious adj ficticio/cia; fingido/da; ~ly adv fingidamente.

fiddle n violín m; trampa f; * vi tocar el violín.
fiddler n violinista m/f.
fidelity n fidelidad, lealtad f.
fidget vi inquietarse.
fidgety adj inquieto/ta, impaciente.
field n campo m; campaña f; espacio m.
field day n (mil) día de maniobras m.
fieldmouse n ratón de campo m.
fieldwork n trabajo de campo m.
fiend n enemigo m; demonio m.
fiendish adj demoniaco/ca.
fierce adj fiero/ra, feroz; cruel, furioso/sa; ~ly adv furiosamente.
fierceness n fiereza, ferocidad f.
fiery adj ardiente; apasionado/da.
fifteen adj, n quince.
fifteenth adj, n decimoquinto/ta.
fifth adj, n quinto/ta; ~ly adv en quinto lugar.
fiftieth adj, n quincuagésimo/ma.
fifty adj, n cincuenta.
fig n higo m.
fight vt, vi reñir; batallar; combatir; * n batalla f; combate m; pelea f.
fighter n combatiente m; luchador/a m/f; caza m.
fighting n combate m.
fig-leaf n hoja de higuera f.
fig tree n higuera f.
figurative adj figurativo/va; ~ly adv figuradamente.
figure n figura, forma f; imagen f; cifra f; * vi figurar; ser lógico/ca; **to ~ out** comprender.
figurehead n testaferro m.
filament n filamento m; fibra f.
filch vi ratear.
filcher n ratero/ra, ladroncillo/lla m/f.
file n hilo m; lista f; (mil) fila, hilera f; lima f; carpeta f; fichero m; * vt

enhilar; limar; clasificar; presentar; * vi **to ~ in/out** entrar/salir en fila; **to ~ past** desfilar ante.

filing cabinet n archivador m.

fill vt llenar; hartar; **to ~ in** rellenar; **to ~ up** llenar (hasta el borde).

fillet n filete m.

fillet steak n filete de ternera m.

filling station n estación de servicio f; gasolinera f.

fillip n (fig) estímulo m.

filly n potra f.

film n película f; film m; capa f; * vt filmar; * vi rodar.

film star n estrella de cine f.

film strip n tira de película f.

filter n filtro m; * vt filtrar.

filter-tipped adj con filtro.

filth(iness) n inmundicia, porquería f; fango, lodo m.

filthy adj sucio/cia, puerco/ca.

fin n aleta f.

final adj final, último/ma; **~ly** adv finalmente; **~ stages** postrimerías fpl.

finale n final m.

finalist n finalista m/f.

finalize vt concluir.

finance n fondos mpl.

financial adj financiero/ra.

financier n financiero/ra m/f.

find vt hallar, descubrir; **to ~ out** averiguar; descubrir; **to ~ one's self** hallarse; * n hallazgo m.

findings npl fallo m; recomendaciones fpl.

fine adj fino/na; agudo/da, cortante; claro/ra, trasparente; delicado/da; astuto/ta; elegante; bello/la; * n multa f; * vt multar.

fine arts npl bellas artes fpl.

finely adv con elegancia.

finery n adorno, atavío m.

finesse n sutileza f.

finger n dedo m; * vt tocar, manosear; manejar.

fingernail n uña f.

fingerprint n huella dactilar f.

fingertip n yema del dedo f.

finicky adj delicado/da.

finish vt acabar, terminar, concluir; **to ~ off** acabar (con); **to ~ up** terminar; * vi: **to ~ up** ir a parar.

finishing line n línea de llegada, línea de meta f.

finishing school n academia para señoritas f.

finite adj finito/ta; conjugado/da.

fir n (bot) abeto m

fire n fuego m; incendio m; * vt disparar; incendiar; despertar; * vi encenderse.

fire alarm n alarma de incendios f.

firearm n arma de fuego f.

fireball n bola f de fuego.

firebreak, fire line n cortafuegos m.

fire engine n coche de bomberos m.

fire escape n escalera de incendios f.

fire extinguisher n extintor m.

firefly n luciérnaga f.

fireman n bombero m.

fireplace n hogar, fogón m.

fireproof adj a prueba de fuego.

fireside n chimenea f.

fire station n parque de bomberos m.

firewater n aguardiente m.

firewood n leña f.

fireworks npl fuegos artificiales mpl.

firing n disparos mpl.

firing squad n pelotón de ejecución m.

firm adj firme, estable, constante; * n (com) firma f; **~ly** adv firmemente.

firmament n firmamento m.

firmness n firmeza f; constancia f.

first *adj* primero/ra; * *adv* primeramente; **at ~** al principio; **~ly** *adv* en primer lugar.

first aid *n* primeros auxilios *mpl*.

first-aid kit *n* botiquín *m*.

first-class *adj* de primera (clase).

first-hand *adj* de primera mano.

first name *n* nombre de pila *m*.

first-rate *adj* de primera (clase).

fiscal *adj* fiscal.

fish *n* pez *m*; * *vi* pescar.

fishbone *n* espina *f*.

fisherman *n* pescador *m*.

fish farm *n* piscifactoría *f*.

fishing *n* pesca *f*.

fishing line *n* sedal *m*.

fishing rod *n* caña de pescar *f*.

fishing tackle *n* aparejo *m*.

fish market *n* lonja de pescado *f*.

fishseller *n* pescadero/ra *m/f*.

fishmonger, fish shop *n* pescadería *f*.

fishy *adj* (*fig*) sospechoso/sa.

fissure *n* grieta, hendedura *f*.

fist *n* puño *m*.

fit *n* paroxismo *m*; convulsión *f*; * *adj* en forma; apto/ta, idóneo/nea, justo/ta; * *vt* ajustar, acomodar, adaptar; **to ~ out** proveer; * *vi* convenir; **to ~ in** encajarse; llevarse bien (con todos).

fitness *n* salud *f*; aptitud, conveniencia *f*.

fitted carpet *n* moqueta *f*.

fitted kitchen *n* cocina amueblada *f*.

fitter *n* ajustador *m*.

fitting *adj* conveniente, idóneo/nea, justo/ta; * *n* conveniencia *f*; **~s** *pl* guarnición *f*.

five *adj*, *n* cinco.

fix *vt* fijar, establecer; **to ~ up** arreglar.

fixation *n* obsesión *f*.

fixed *adj* fijo/ja.

fixture *n* encuentro *m*.

fizz(le) *vi* silbar.

fizzy *adj* gaseoso/sa.

flabbergasted *adj* pasmado/da.

flabby *adj* blando/da, flojo/ja, lacio/cia.

flaccid *adj* flojo/ja, flaco/ca; fláccido/da.

flag *n* bandera *f*; losa *f*; * *vi* debilitarse.

flagpole *n* asta de bandera *f*.

flagrant *adj* flagrante; notorio/ria.

flagship *n* buque insignia *m*.

flair *n* aptitud especial *f*.

flak *n* fuego antiaéreo *m*; lluvia de críticas.

flake *n* copo *m*; lámina *f*; * *vi* romperse en láminas.

flaky *adj* escamoso/sa, desmenuzable.

flamboyant *adj* vistoso/sa.

flame *n* llama *f*; fuego (del amor) *m*.

flamingo *n* flamenco *m*.

flammable *adj* inflamable.

flank *n* ijada *f*; (*mil*) flanco *m*; * *vt* flanquear.

flannel *n* franela, flanela *f*.

flap *n* solapa *f*; hoja *f*; aletazo *m*; * *vt* aletear; * *vi* ondear.

flare *vi* lucir, brillar; **to ~ up** encenderse; encolerizarse; estallar; * *n* llama *f*.

flash *n* flash *m*; relámpago *m*; * *vt* **to ~ on and off** encender y apagar.

flashbulb *n* bombilla de flash *f*.

flash cube *n* cubo de flash *m*.

flashlight *n* linterna *f*.

flashy *adj* superficial.

flask *n* frasco *m*; botella *f*.

flat¹ *adj* llano/na, plano/na; insípido/da; * *n* llanura *f*; plano *m*; (*mus*) bemol *m*; **~ly** *adv* horizontalmente; llanamente; enteramente; de plano, de nivel; francamente.

flat² *n* apartamento, departamento *m*.

flatness *n* llanura *f*; insipidez *f*.

flatten *vt* allanar; abatir.

flatter *vt* adular, lisonjear.

flattering *adj* halagüeño/ña, zalamero/ra.

flattery *n* adulación, lisonja *f*; zalamería *f*.

flatulence *n* (*med*) flatulencia *f*.

flaunt *vt* ostentar.

flavour *n* sabor *m*; * *vt* sazonar.

flavoured *adj* con sabor (a).

flavourless *adj* soso/sa.

flaw *n* falta, tacha *f*; defecto *m*.

flawless *adj* sin defecto.

flax *n* lino *m*.

flea *n* pulga *f*.

flea bite *n* picadura de pulga *f*.

fleck *n* mota *f*; punto *m*.

flee *vt* huir de; * *vi* escapar; huir.

fleece *n* vellón *m*; * *vt* (*sl*) pelar.

fleet *n* flota *f*; escuadra *f*.

fleeting *adj* pasajero/ra, fugitivo/va.

flesh *n* carne *f*.

flesh wound *n* herida superficial *f*.

fleshy *adj* carnoso/sa, pulposo/sa.

flex *n* cordón *m*; * *vt* tensar.

flexibility *n* flexibilidad *f*.

flexible *adj* flexible.

flick *n* golpecito *m*; * *vt* dar un golpecito a.

flicker *vt* aletear; fluctuar.

flier *n* aviador/a *m/f*.

flight *n* vuelo *m*; huida, fuga *f*; bandada (de pájaros) *f*; (*fig*) elevación *f*.

flight attendant *n* auxiliar de vuelo *m/f*.

flight deck *n* cabina de mandos *f*.

flimsy *adj* débil; fútil.

flinch *vi* encogerse.

fling *vt* lanzar, echar.

flint *n* pedernal *m*.

flip *vt* arrojar, lanzar.

flippant *adj* petulante, locuaz.

flipper *n* aleta *f*.

flirt *vi* coquetear; * *n* coqueta *f*.

flirtation *n* coquetería *f*.

flit *vi* volar, huir; aletear.

float *vt* hacer flotar; lanzar; * *vi* flotar; * *n* flotador *m*; carroza *f*; reserva *f*.

flock *n* manada *f*; rebaño *m*; gentío *m*; * *vi* congregarse.

flog *vt* azotar; (*fam*) zurrar.

flogging *n* tunda, zurra *f*.

flood *n* diluvio *m*; inundación *f*; flujo *m*; * *vt* inundar.

flooding *n* inundación *f*.

floodlight *n* foco *m*.

floor *n* suelo, piso *m*; piso (de una casa); * *vt* dejar sin respuesta.

floorboard *n* tabla *f*.

floor lamp *n* lámpara de pie *f*.

floor show *n* cabaret *m*.

flop *n* fracaso *m*.

floppy *adj* flojo/ja.

floppy disk *n* floppy *m*, disquete *m*.

flora *n* flora *f*.

floral *adj* floral.

florescence *n* florescencia *f*.

florid *adj* florido/da.

florist *n* florista *m/f*.

florist's (shop) *n* floristería *f*.

flotilla *n* (*mar*) flotilla *f*.

flounder *n* platija (pez de mar) *f*; * *vi* tropezar.

flour *n* harina *f*.

flourish *vi* florecer; gozar de prosperidad; * *n* belleza *f*; lazo *m*; (*mus*) floreo, preludio *m*.

flourishing *adj* floreciente.

flout *vt* burlarse de.

flow *vi* fluir, manar; crecer la marea; ondear; * *n* flujo de la marea *m*; abundancia *f*; flujo *m*.

flow chart n organigrama m.

flower n flor f; * vi florear; florecer.

flowerbed n parterre m.

flowerpot n tiesto m, maceta f.

flowery adj florido/da.

flower show n exposición de flores f.

fluctuate vi fluctuar.

fluctuation n fluctuación f.

fluency n fluidez f.

fluent adj fluido/da; fácil; ~ly adv con fluidez.

fluff n pelusa f; ~y adj velloso/sa.

fluid adj, n fluido/da m.

fluidity n fluidez f.

fluke n (sl) chiripa f.

fluoride n fluoruro m.

flurry n ráfaga f; agitación f.

flush vt: to ~ out levantar; desalojar; * vi ponerse colorado/da; * n rubor m; resplandor m.

flushed adj ruborizado/da.

fluster vt confundir.

flustered adj aturdido/da.

flute n flauta f.

flutter vi revolotear; estar en agitación; * n confusión f; agitación f.

flux n flujo m.

fly vt pilotar; transportar; * vi volar; huir, escapar; to ~ away/off emprender el vuelo; * n mosca f; bragueta f.

flying n aviación f.

flying saucer n platillo volante m.

flypast n desfile aéreo m.

flysheet n doble techo m.

foal n potro m.

foam n espuma f; * vi espumar.

foam rubber n espuma de caucho f.

foamy adj espumoso/sa.

focus n foco m.

fodder n forraje m.

foe n adversario/ria m/f, enemigo/ga m/f.

foetus n feto m.

fog n niebla f.

foggy adj nebuloso/sa, brumoso/sa.

fog light n faro antiniebla m.

foible n debilidad, parte flaca f.

foil vt frustrar; * n hoja f; florete m.

fold n redil m; pliegue m; * vt plegar; * vi: to ~ up plegarse, doblarse; quebrar.

folder n carpeta f; folleto m.

folding adj plegable.

folding chair n silla de tijera f.

foliage n follaje m.

folio n folio m.

folk n gente f.

folklore n folklore m.

folk music n folk m.

folk song n canción folklórica f.

follow vt seguir; acompañar; imitar; to ~ up responder a; investigar; * vi seguir, resultar, provenir.

follower n seguidor/a m/f; imitador/a m/f; secuaz, partidario/ria m/f; adherente m; compañero/ra m/f.

following adj siguiente; * n afición f.

folly n extravagancia, bobería f.

foment vt fomentar; proteger.

fond adj cariñoso/sa; ~ly adv cariñosamente.

fondle vt acariciar.

fondness n gusto m; cariño m.

font n pila bautismal f.

food n comida f.

food mixer n batidora f.

food poisoning n intoxicación alimentaria f.

food processor n robot de cocina m.

foodstuffs npl comestibles mpl.

fool n loco/ca, tonto/ta m/f; * vt engañar.

foolhardy adj temerario/ria.

foolish adj bobo/ba, tonto/ta; ~ly adv tontamente.

foolproof *adj* infalible.

foolscap *n* papel tamaño folio *m*.

foot *n* pie *m*; pata *f*; paso *m*; **on, by ~** a pie.

footage *n* imágenes *fpl*.

football *n* balón *m*; fútbol *m*.

footballer *n* futbolista *m/f*; jugador/a de fútbol *m/f*.

football pools *npl* quinielas *fpl*.

football pools coupon *n* quiniela *f*.

footbrake *n* freno de pie *m*.

footbridge *n* puente peatonal *m*.

foothills *npl* estribaciones *fpl*.

foothold *n* pie firme *m*.

footing *n* base *f*; estado *m*; condición *f*; fundamento *m*.

footlights *npl* candilejas *fpl*.

footman *n* lacayo *m*; soldado de infantería *m*.

footnote *n* nota de pie *f*.

footpath *n* senda *f*.

footprint *n* huella, pisada *f*.

footsore *adj* con los pies doloridos.

footstep *n* paso *m*; huella *f*.

footwear *n* calzado *m*.

for *prep* por, a causa de; para; * *conj* porque, para que; por cuanto; **as ~ me** tocante a mí; **what ~?** ¿para qué?

forage *n* forraje *m*; * *vt* forrajear; saquear.

foray *n* incursión *f*.

forbid *vt* prohibir, vedar; impedir; **God ~!** ¡Dios no quiera!

forbidding *adj* inhóspito/ta; severo/ra.

force *n* fuerza *f*; poder, vigor *m*; violencia *f*; necesidad *f*; **~s** *pl* tropas *fpl*; * *vt* forzar, violentar; esforzar; constreñir.

forced *adj* forzado/da.

forced march *n* (*mil*) marcha forzada *f*.

forceful *adj* enérgico/ca.

forceps *n* fórceps *m*.

forcible *adj* fuerte, eficaz, poderoso/sa; **~bly** *adv* fuertemente, forzadamente.

ford *n* vado *m*; * *vt* vadear.

fore *n*: **to the ~** en evidencia.

forearm *n* antebrazo *m*.

foreboding *n* presentimiento *m*.

forecast *vt* pronosticar; * *n* pronóstico *m*.

forecourt *n* patio *m*.

forefather *n* abuelo, antecesor *m*.

forefinger *n* índice *m*.

forefront *n*: **in the ~ of** en la vanguardia de.

forego *vt* ceder, abandonar; preceder.

foregone *adj* pasado/da; anticipado/da.

foreground *n* delantera *f*.

forehead *n* frente *f*; insolencia *f*.

foreign *adj* extranjero/ra; extraño/ña.

foreigner *n* extranjero/ra, forastero/ra *m/f*.

foreign exchange *n* divisas *fpl*.

foreleg *n* pata delantera *f*.

foreman *n* capataz *m*; (*law*) presidente del jurado *m*.

foremost *adj* principal.

forenoon *n* mañana *f*.

forensic *adj* forense; **~ scientist** *n* forense *m/f*.

forerunner *n* precursor/a *m/f*; predecesor/a *m/f*.

foresee *vt* prever.

foreshadow *vt* pronosticar; simbolizar.

foresight *n* previsión *f*; presciencia *f*.

forest *n* bosque *m*; selva *f*.

forestall *vt* anticipar; prevenir.

forester *n* guardabosque *m/f*.

forestry *n* silvicultura *f*.

foretaste n muestra f.
foretell vt predecir, profetizar.
forethought n providencia f; premeditación f.
forever adv para siempre.
forewarn vt prevenir de antemano.
foreword n prefacio m.
forfeit n confiscación f; * vt perder derecho a.
forge n fragua f; fábrica de metales f; * vt forjar; falsificar; inventar; * vi: **to ~ ahead** avanzar constantemente.
forger n falsificador/a m/f.
forgery n falsificación f.
forget vt olvidar; * vi olvidarse.
forgetful adj olvidadizo/za; descuidado/da.
forgetfulness n olvido m; negligencia f.
forget-me-not n (bot) nomeolvides m.
forgive vt perdonar.
forgiveness n perdón m; remisión f.
fork n tenedor m; horca f; * vi bifurcarse; **to ~ out** (sl) desembolsar.
forked adj horcado/da.
fork-lift truck n carretilla elevadora f.
forlorn adj abandonado/da, perdido/da.
form n forma f; modelo m; modo m; formalidad f; método m; molde m; * vt formar.
formal adj formal, metódico/ca; ceremonioso/sa; **~ly** adv formalmente.
formality n formalidad f; ceremonia f.
format n formato m; * vt formatear.
formation n formación f.
formative adj formativo/va.
former adj precedente; anterior, pasado/da; **~ly** adv antiguamente, en tiempos pasados.
formidable adj formidable, terrible.

formula n fórmula f.
formulate vt formular, articular.
forsake vt dejar, abandonar.
fort n castillo m; fortaleza f.
forte adj fuerte.
forthcoming adj venidero/ra.
forthright adj franco/ca.
forthwith adj inmediatamente, sin tardanza.
fortieth adj, n cuadragésimo m.
fortification n fortificación f.
fortify vt fortificar; corroborar.
fortitude n fortaleza f; valor m.
fortnight n quince días mpl; dos semanas fpl; **~ly** adj, adv cada quince días.
fortress n (mil) fortaleza f.
fortuitous adj impensado/da; casual; **~ly** adv fortuitamente.
fortunate adj afortunado/da; **~ly** adv felizmente.
fortune n fortuna, suerte f.
fortune-teller n sortílego/ga, adivino/na m/f.
forty adj, n cuarenta.
forum n foro m.
forward adj avanzado/da; delantero/ra; presumido/da; **~(s)** adv adelante, más allá; * vt remitir; promover, patrocinar.
forwardness n precocidad f; audacia f.
fossil adj, n fósil m.
foster vt criar, nutrir.
foster child n hijo/ja adoptivo/va m/f.
foster father n padre adoptivo m.
foster mother n madre adoptiva f.
foul adj sucio/cia, puerco/ca; impuro/ra, detestable; **~ copy** borrador m; **~ly** adv suciamente; ilegítimamente; * vt ensuciar.
foul play n mala jugada f; muerte violenta f.

found vt fundar, establecer; edificar; fundir.

foundation n fundación f; fundamento m.

founder n fundador/a m/f; fundidor m; * vi (mar) irse a pique; zozobrar.

foundling n niño/ña expósito/ta m/f.

foundry n fundición f.

fount, fountain n fuente f.

fountainhead n origen de fuente m.

four adj, n cuatro.

fourfold adj cuádruple.

four-poster (bed) n cama de dosel f.

foursome n grupo de cuatro personas m.

fourteen adj, n catorce.

fourteenth adj, n decimocuarto/ta.

fourth adj, n cuarto/ta; * n cuarto m; ~ly adv en cuarto lugar.

fowl n ave f de corral.

fox n zorra f; (fig) zorro m.

foyer n vestíbulo m.

fracas n riña f.

fraction n fracción f.

fracture n fractura f; * vt fracturar, romper.

fragile adj frágil; débil.

fragility n fragilidad f; debilidad, flaqueza f.

fragment n fragmento m.

fragmentary adj fragmentario/ria.

fragrance n fragancia f.

fragrant adj fragante, oloroso/sa; ~ly adv con fragancia.

frail adj frágil, débil.

frailty n fragilidad f; debilidad f.

frame n armazón m; marco, cerco m; cuadro de vidriera m; estructura f; montura f; * vt encuadrar; componer, construir, formar.

frame of mind n estado de ánimo m.

framework n estructura f; esqueleto m, armazón f.

franchise n sufragio m; concesión f.

frank adj franco/ca, liberal.

frankly adv francamente.

frankness n franqueza f.

frantic adj frenético/ca, furioso/sa.

fraternal adj, ~ly adv fraternal(mente).

fraternity n fraternidad f.

fraternize vi hermanarse.

fratricide n fratricidio m; fratricida m/f.

fraud n fraude, engaño m.

fraudulence n fraudulencia f.

fraudulent adj fraudulento/ta; ~ly adv fraudulentamente.

fraught adj cargado/da, lleno/na.

fray n riña, disputa, querella f.

freak n fantasía f; fenómeno m.

freckle n peca f.

freckled adj pecoso/sa.

free adj libre; liberal; suelto/ta; exento/ta; desocupado/da; gratis; * vt soltar; librar; eximir; * vr: **to ~ oneself from trouble** zafarse de.

freedom n libertad f.

freehold n propiedad absoluta f.

free-for-all n trifulca f.

free gift n prima f.

free kick n tiro libre m.

freelance adj, adv por cuenta propia.

freely adv libremente; espontáneamente; liberalmente, gratis.

freemason n francmasón m, masón m.

freemasonry n francmasonería f, masonería f.

freepost n franqueo pagado m.

free-range adj de granja.

freethinker n librepensador/a m/f.

freethinking n librepensamiento m.

free trade n libre comercio m.

freeway n autopista f.

freewheel vi ir en punto muerto.

free will n libre albedrío m.

freeze vi helar(se); * vt congelar; helar.

freeze-dried adj liofilizado/da.

freezer n congelador m.

freezing adj helado/da.

freezing point n punto de congelación m.

freight n carga f; flete m.

freighter n fletador m.

freight train n tren de mercancías m.

French bean n judía verde f.

French fries npl patatas o papas fritas fpl.

French window n puertaventana f.

frenzied adj loco/ca, delirante.

frenzy n frenesí m; locura f.

frequency n frecuencia f.

frequent adj, ~ly adv frecuente(mente); * vt frecuentar.

fresco n fresco m.

fresh adj fresco/ca; nuevo/va, reciente; ~ **water** n agua dulce f.

freshen vt (vi) refrescar(se).

fresher n novato m.

freshly adv nuevamente; recientemente.

freshness n frescura f; fresco m.

freshwater adj de agua dulce.

fret vi agitarse, enojarse.

friar n fraile m.

friction n fricción f.

Friday n viernes m; **Good ~** Viernes Santo m.

friend n amigo/ga m/f.

friendless adj sin amigos.

friendliness n amistad, benevolencia, bondad f.

friendly adj amistoso/sa.

friendship n amistad f.

frieze n friso m.

frigate n (mar) fragata f.

fright n espanto, terror m.

frighten vt espantar.

frightened adj asustado/da.

frightening adj espantoso/sa.

frightful adj espantoso/sa, horrible; ~ly adv espantosamente, terriblemente.

frigid adj frío/ría, frígido/da; ~ly adv fríamente.

fringe n franja f.

fringe benefits npl ventajas adicionales fpl.

frisk vt cachear.

frisky adj juguetón/ona.

fritter vt: **to ~ away** desperdiciar.

frivolity n frivolidad f.

frivolous adj frívolo/la, vano/na.

frizz(le) vt frisar; rizar.

frizzy adj rizado/da.

fro adv: **to go to and ~** ir y venir.

frog n rana f.

frolic vi juguetear.

frolicsome adj juguetón/ona, travieso/sa.

from prep de; después; desde.

front n parte delantera f; fachada f; paseo marítimo m; frente m; apariencias fpl; * adj delantero/ra; primero/ra.

frontal adj de frente.

front door n puerta principal f.

frontier n frontera f.

front page n primera plana f.

front-wheel drive n (auto) tracción delantera f.

frost n helada f; hielo m; * vt escarchar.

frostbite n congelación f.

frostbitten adj helado/da, con síntomas de congelación.

frosted adj deslustrado/da.

frosty adj helado/da, frío/ría como el hielo.

froth n espuma (de algún líquido) f; * vi espumar.

frothy *adj* espumoso/sa.

frown *vt* mirar con ceño; * *n* ceño *m*.

frozen *adj* helado/da.

frugal *adj* frugal; económico/ca; sobrio/ria; ~**ly** *adv* frugalmente.

fruit *n* fruta *f*; fruto *m*; producto *m*.

fruiterer *n* frutero/ra *m/f*.

fruitful *adj* fructífero/ra, fértil; provechoso/sa, útil; ~**ly** *adv* con fertilidad.

fruitfulness *n* fertilidad *f*.

fruition *n* realización *f*.

fruit juice *n* zumo de fruta *m*.

fruitless *adj* estéril; inútil; ~**ly** *adv* vanamente, inútilmente.

fruit salad *n* ensalada de frutas *f*, macedonia *f*.

fruit seller, greengrocer *n* frutero/ra *m*.

fruit shop, greengrocer's shop *n* frutería *f*.

fruit tree *n* frutal *m*.

frustrate *vt* frustrar; anular.

frustrated *adj* frustrado/da.

frustration *n* frustración *f*.

fry *vt* freír.

frying pan *n* sartén *f*.

fuchsia *n* (*bot*) fucsia *f*.

fudge *n* caramelo blando *m*.

fuel *n* combustible *m*.

fuel tank *n* depósito *m* de combustible.

fugitive *adj*, *n* fugitivo/va *m/f*.

fugue *n* (*mus*) fuga *f*.

fulcrum *n* fulcro *m*.

fulfil *vt* cumplir; realizar.

fulfilment *n* cumplimiento *m*.

full *adj* lleno/na, repleto/ta, completo/ta; perfecto/ta; * *adv* enteramente, del todo.

full-blown *adj* hecho/cha y derecho/cha.

full-fledged *adj* hecho/cha y derecho/cha.

full-length *adj* de cuerpo entero/ra; completo/ta.

full moon *n* plenilunio *m*; luna llena *f*.

fullness *n* plenitud, abundancia *f*.

full-scale *adj* en gran escala; de tamaño natural.

full-time *adj* de tiempo completo.

fully *adv* llenamente, enteramente, ampliamente.

fulsome *adj* exagerado/da.

fumble *vi* manejar torpemente.

fume *vi* humear; encolerizarse.

fumes *npl* humo *m*.

fumigate *vt* fumigar.

fun *n* diversión *f*; alegría *f*.

function *n* función *f*.

functional *adj* funcional.

fund *n* fondo *m*; fondos públicos *mpl*; * *vt* costear.

fundamental *adj* fundamental; ~**ly** *adv* fundamentalmente.

fundamentalism *n* fundamentalismo *m*.

fundamentalist *n* fundamentalista *m/f*.

funeral service *n* misa de difuntos *f*, funeral *m*.

funeral *n* funeral *m*.

funereal *adj* funeral, fúnebre.

fungus *n* hongo *m*; seta *f*.

funnel *n* embudo *m*; cañón (de chimenea) *m*.

funny *adj* divertido/da; curioso/sa; zumbón/ona.

fur *n* piel *f*.

fur coat *n* abrigo de pieles *m*.

furious *adj* furioso/sa, frenético/ca; ~**ly** *adv* con furia.

furlong *n* estadio *m*; (octava parte de una milla).

furlough *n* (*mil*) licencia *f*; permiso *m*.

furnace *n* horno *m*; hornaza *f*.

furnish *vt* amueblar; facilitar; suministrar.

furnishings *npl* muebles *mpl*.

furniture *n* muebles *mpl*.

furrow *n* surco *m*; * *vt* surcar; estriar.

furry *adj* peludo/da.

further *adj* nuevo/va; más lejano/na; * *adv* más lejos, más allá; aún; además; * *vt* adelantar, promover, ayudar.

further education *n* educación para adultos *f*.

furthermore *adv* además.

furthest *adv* lo más lejos, lo más remoto.

furtive *adj* furtivo/va; secreto/ta; ~**ly** *adv* furtivamente.

fury *n* furor *m*; furia *f*; ira *f*.

fuse *vt, vi* fundir; derretirse; * *n* fusible *m*; *n* mecha *f*.

fuse box *n* caja de fusibles *f*.

fusion *n* fusión *f*.

fuss *n* lío *m*; alboroto *m*.

fussy *adj* jactancioso/sa.

futile *adj* fútil, frívolo/la.

futility *n* futilidad, vanidad *f*.

future *adj* futuro/ra; * *n* futuro *m*; porvenir *m*.

fuzzy *adj* borroso/sa; muy rizado/da.

G

gab *n* (*fam*) charla *f*.

gabble *vi* charlar, parlotear; * *n* algarabía *f*.

gable *n* gablete *m*.

gadget *n* dispositivo *m*.

gaffe *n* plancha *f*.

gag *n* mordaza *f*; chiste *m*; * *vt* amordazar.

gaiety *n* alegría *f*.

gaily *adv* alegremente.

gain *n* ganancia *f*; interés, provecho *m*; * *vt* ganar; conseguir.

gait *n* marcha *f*; porte *m*.

gala *n* fiesta *f*.

galaxy *n* galaxia *f*.

gale *n* vendaval *m*.

gall *n* hiel *f*.

gallant *adj* galante.

gall bladder *n* vesícula biliar *f*.

gallery *n* galería *f*.

galley *n* cocina *f*; galera *f*.

gallon *n* galón *m* (medida).

gallop *n* galope *m*; * *vi* galopar.

gallows *n* horca *f*.

gallstone *n* cálculo biliar *m*.

galore *adv* en abundancia.

galvanize *vt* galvanizar.

gambit *n* estrategia *f*.

gamble *vi* jugar; especular; * *n* riesgo *m*; apuesta *f*.

gambler *n* jugador/a *m/f*.

gambling *n* juego *m*.

game *n* juego *m*; pasatiempo *m*; partido *m*; partida *f*; caza *f*; * *vi* jugar.

gamekeeper *n* guardabosques *m invar*.

gaming *n* juego *m*.

gammon *n* jamón *m*.

gamut *n* (*mus*) gama *f*.

gander *n* ganso *m*.

gang *n* pandilla, banda *f*.

gangrene *n* gangrena *f*.

gangster *n* gángster *m*.

gangway *n* pasarela *f*.

gap *n* hueco *m*; claro *m*; intervalo *m*.

gape *vi* boquear; estar con la boca abierta.

gaping *adj* muy abierto/ta.

garage n garaje m.

garbled adj falsificado/da.

garden n jardín m.

garden-hose n regadera f.

gardener n jardinero/ra m/f.

gardening n jardinería f.

gargle vi hacer gárgaras.

gargoyle n gárgola f.

garish adj ostentoso/sa.

garland n guirnalda f.

garlic n ajo m.

garment n prenda f.

garnish vt guarnecer, adornar; * n guarnición f; adorno m.

garret n guardilla f; desván m.

garrison n (mil) guarnición f; * vt (mil) guarnecer.

garrotte, garrote vt estrangular.

garrulous adj gárrulo/la, locuaz, charlador/a.

garter n liga f.

gas n gas m; gasolina f.

gas burner n mechero de gas m.

gas cylinder n bombona de gas f.

gaseous adj gaseoso/sa.

gas fire n estufa de gas f.

gash n cuchillada f; raja f; * vt acuchillar.

gasket n junta de culata f.

gas mask n careta antigás f.

gas meter n contador de gas m.

gasp vi jadear; * n boqueada f.

gas ring n hornillo de gas m.

gassy adj gaseoso/sa.

gas tap n llave del gas f.

gastric adj gástrico/ca.

gastronomic adj gastronómico/ca.

gasworks npl fábrica de gas f.

gate n puerta f.

gateway n puerta f.

gather vt recoger, amontonar; entender; plegar; * vi juntarse.

gathering n reunión f; colecta f.

gauche adj torpe.

gaudy adj chillón/ona.

gauge n calibre m; entrevía f; indicador m; * vt medir.

gaunt adj flaco/ca, delgado/da.

gauze n gasa f.

gay adj alegre; vivo/va; gay.

gaze vi contemplar, considerar; * n mirada f.

gazelle n gacela f.

gazette n gaceta f.

gazetteer n gacetero m; diccionario geográfico m.

gear n atavío m; vestido m; aparejo m; tirantes mpl; velocidad f.

gearbox n caja de cambios f.

gear lever n palanca de cambios f.

gear wheel n rueda dentada f.

gel n gel m.

gelatin(e) n gelatina, jalea f.

gelignite n gelignita f.

gem n gema f.

Gemini n Géminis m (signo del zodiaco).

gender n género m.

gene n gen m.

genealogical adj genealógico/ca.

genealogy n genealogía f.

general adj general, común, usual; in ~ por lo general; ~ly adv generalmente; * n general m; generala f.

general election n elecciones generales fpl.

generality n generalidad, mayor parte f.

generalization n generalización f.

generalize vt generalizar.

generate vt engendrar; producir; causar.

generation n generación f.

generator n generador m.

generic adj genérico/ca.

generosity n generosidad, liberalidad f.
generous adj generoso/sa.
genetic engineering n ingeniería genética f.
genetics npl genética f.
genial adj genial, natural; alegre.
genitals npl genitales mpl.
genitive n genitivo m.
genius n genio m.
genteel adj refinado/da, elegante.
gentile n gentil, pagano/na m/f.
gentle adj suave, dócil, manso/sa, moderado/da; benigno/na.
gentleman n caballero m.
gentleness n dulzura, suavidad f.
gently adv suavemente.
gentry n alta burguesía f.
gents n aseos mpl.
genuflection n genuflexión f.
genuine adj genuino/na, puro/ra; ~ly adv puramente, naturalmente.
genus n género m.
geographer n geógrafo/fa m/f.
geographical adj geográfico/ca.
geography n geografía f.
geological adj geológico/ca.
geologist n geólogo/ga m/f.
geology n geología f.
geometric(al) adj geométrico/ca.
geometry n geometría f.
geranium n (bot) geranio m.
geriatric n, adj geriátrico/ca m/f.
germ n germen m, microbio m.
germinate vi brotar.
gesticulate vi gesticular.
gesture n gesto, movimiento expresivo m.
get vt ganar; conseguir, obtener, alcanzar; coger; agarrar; * vi hacerse, ponerse; prevalecer; introducirse; **to ~ the better** salir vencedor/a, sobrepujar.

geyser n géiser m; calentador de agua m.
ghastly adj espantoso/sa.
gherkin n pepinillo, cohombrillo m.
ghetto n gueto m.
ghost n fantasma m; espectro m.
ghostly adj fantasmal.
giant n gigante m.
gibberish n jerigonza f.
gibe vi escarnecer, burlarse, mofar; * n mofa, burla f.
giblets npl menudillos mpl.
giddiness n vértigo m.
giddy adj vertiginoso/sa.
gift n regalo m; don m; dádiva f; talento m.
gifted adj dotado/da.
gift voucher n vale de regalo m.
gigantic adj gigantesco/ca.
giggle vi reírse tontamente.
gild vt dorar.
gilding, gilt n doradura f.
gill n cuarta parte de pinta f; ~s pl agallas fpl.
gilt-edged adj de máxima garantía.
gimmick n truco m.
gin n ginebra f.
ginger n jengibre m.
gingerbread n pan de jengibre m.
ginger-haired adj pelirrojo/ja.
giraffe n jirafa f.
girder n viga f.
girdle n faja f; cinturón m.
girl n muchacha, chica f, zagala f.
girlfriend n amiga; novia f.
girlish adj de niña.
giro n giro postal m.
girth n cincha f; circunferencia f.
gist n punto principal m.
give vt, vi dar; donar; conceder; abandonar; pronunciar; aplicarse, dedicarse; **to ~ away** regalar; traicionar; revelar; **to ~ back**

devolver; **to ~ in** vi ceder; vt entregar; **to ~ off** despedir; **to ~ out** distribuir; **to ~ up** vi rendir; vt renunciar a.

gizzard n molleja f.

glacial adj glacial.

glacier n glaciar m.

glad adj alegre, contento/ta, agradable; **I am ~ to see** me alegro de ver; **~ly** adv alegremente.

gladden vt alegrar.

gladiator n gladiador m.

glamorous adj atractivo/va.

glamour n encanto, atractivo m.

glance n ojeada f; * vi mirar; echar una ojeada.

glancing adj oblicuo/cua.

gland n glándula f.

glare n deslumbramiento m; mirada feroz y penetrante f; * vi deslumbrar, brillar; echar miradas de indignación.

glaring adj deslumbrante; manifiesto/ta; notorio/ria.

glass n vidrio m, cristal m; telescopio m; vaso m; espejo m; **~es** pl gafas fpl; * adj vítreo/rea.

glassware n cristalería f.

glassy adj vítreo/rea, cristalino/na, vidrioso/sa.

glaze vt, vi driar; embarnizar.

glazier n vidriero m, cristalero m.

gleam n relámpago, rayo m; * vi relampaguear, brillar.

gleaming adj reluciente.

glean vt espigar; recoger.

glee n alegría f; gozo m; jovialidad f.

glen n valle m; llanura f.

glib adj con lab; **~ly** adv con labia.

glide vi resbalar; planear.

gliding n vuelo sin motor m.

glimmer n vislumbre f; * vi vislumbrarse.

glimpse n vislumbre f; relámpago m;

ojeada f; * vt entrever, percibir.

glint vi centellear.

glisten, glitter vi relucir, brillar.

gloat vi relamerse; saborear.

global adj mundial.

globalization n globalización f.

global warming n calentamiento global m.

globe n globo m; esfera f.

gloom, gloominess n oscuridad f; melancolía, tristeza f; **~ily** adv oscuramente; tristemente.

gloomy adj sombrío/ría, oscuro/ra; cubierto de nubes; triste, melancólico/ca.

glorification n glorificación, alabanza f.

glorify vt glorificar, celebrar.

glorious adj glorioso/sa, ilustre; **~ly** adv gloriosamente.

glory n gloria, fama, celebridad f.

gloss n glosa f; lustre m; * vt glosar, interpretar; **to ~ over** encubrir.

glossary n glosario m.

glossy adj lustroso/sa, brillante.

glove n guante m.

glove compartment n guantera f.

glow vi arder; inflamarse; relucir; * n color vivo m; viveza de color f; vehemencia de una pasión f.

glower vi mirar con ceño.

glue n cola f; cemento m; * vt pegar.

gluey adj viscoso/sa, pegajoso/sa.

glum adj abatido/da, triste.

glut n hartura, abundancia f.

glutinous adj glutinoso/sa, viscoso/sa.

glutton n glotón/ona, tragón/ona m/f.

gluttony n glotonería f.

glycerine n glicerina f.

gnarled adj nudoso/sa.

gnash vt, vi rechinar.

gnat n mosquito m.

gnaw *vt* roer.

gnome *n* gnomo *m*.

go *vi* ir, irse, andar, caminar; partir(se), marchar; huir; pasar; to ~ ahead seguir adelante; to ~ away marcharse; to ~ back volver; to ~ by pasar; to ~ for ir por; gustar; to ~ in entrar; to ~ off irse; pasarse; to ~ on seguir; pasar; to ~ out salir; apagarse; to ~ up subir.

goad *n* aguijada, aijada *f*; * *vt* aguijar; estimular, incitar.

go-ahead *adj* emprendedor/a; * *n* luz verde *f*.

goal *n* meta *f*; fin *m*.

goalkeeper *n* portero/ra *m/f*.

goalpost *n* poste (de la portería) *m*.

goatherd *n* cabrero/ra *m/f*.

gobble *vt* engullir, tragar; to ~ down zampar.

go-between *n* mediador/a *m/f*.

goblet *n* copa *f*.

goblin *n* espíritu ambulante, duende *m*.

God *n* Dios *m*.

godchild *n* ahijado, hijo de pila *m*.

goddaughter *n* ahijada, hija de pila *f*.

goddess *n* diosa *f*.

godfather *n* padrino *m*.

godforsaken *adj* dejado/da de la mano de Dios.

godhead *n* deidad, divinidad *f*.

godless *adj* infiel, impío/pía, sin Dios, ateo/tea.

godlike *adj* divino/na.

godliness *n* piedad, devoción, santidad *f*.

godly *adj* piadoso/sa, devoto/ta, religioso/sa; recto/ta, justificado/da.

godmother *n* madrina *f*.

godsend *n* don del cielo *m*.

godson *n* ahijado *m*.

goggle-eyed *adj* con ojos desorbitados.

goggles *npl* gafas *fpl*; gafas de bucear *fpl*.

going *n* ida *f*; salida *f*; partida *f*; progreso *m*.

gold *n* oro *m*.

golden *adj* áureo/rea, de oro; excelente; ~ rule *n* regla de oro *f*.

goldfish *n* pez de colores *m*.

gold-plated *adj* chapado/da en oro.

goldsmith *n* orfebre *m*.

golf *n* golf *m*.

golf ball *n* pelota de golf *f*.

golf club *n* club de golf *m*.

golf course *n* campo de golf *m*.

golfer *n* golfista *m/f*.

gondolier *n* gondolero/ra *m/f*.

gone *adj* ido/da; perdido/da; pasado/da; gastado/da; muerto/ta.

gong *n* atabal chino, gong *m*.

good *adj* bueno/na, benévolo/la, cariñoso/sa; conveniente, apto/ta; * *adv* bien; * *n* bien *m*; prosperidad, ventaja *f*; ~s *pl* bienes muebles *mpl*; mercaderías *fpl*.

goodbye ! *excl* ¡adiós!

Good Friday *n* Viernes Santo *m*.

goodies *npl* golosinas *fpl*.

good-looking *adj* guapo/pa.

good nature *n* bondad *f*.

good-natured *adj* bondadoso/sa.

goodness *n* bondad *f*.

goodwill *n* benevolencia, bondad *f*.

goose *n* ganso *m*; oca *f*.

gooseberry *n* grosella espinosa *f*.

goose bumps, goose flesh *npl* carne de gallina *f*.

goose-step *n* paso de la oca *m*.

gore *n* sangre cuajada *f*; * *vt* cornear.

gorge *n* barranco *m*; * *vt* engullir, tragar.

gorgeous *adj* maravilloso/sa.

gorilla *n* gorila *m*.

gorse *n* aulaga *f*.

gory *adj* sangriento/ta.

goshawk *n* azor *m*.

gospel *n* evangelio *m*.

gossamer *n* vello *m*; pelusa (de frutas) *f*.

gossip *n* cotilleo *m*; * *vi* cotillear.

gothic *adj* gótico/ca.

gout *n* gota *f* (enfermedad).

govern *vt* gobernar, dirigir, regir.

governess *n* gobernadora *f*.

government *n* gobierno *m*; administración publica *f*.

governor *n* gobernador/a *m/f*.

gown *n* toga *f*; vestido de mujer *m*; bata *f*.

grab *vt* agarrar.

grace *n* gracia *f*; favor *m*; merced *f*; perdón *m*; gracias *fpl*; **to say ~** bendecir la mesa; * *vt* adornar; agraciar.

graceful *adj* gracioso/sa, primoroso/sa; **~ly** *adv* elegantemente, con gracia.

gracious *adj* gracioso/sa; favorable; **~ly** *adv* graciosamente.

gradation *n* gradación *f*.

grade *n* grado *m*; curso *m*.

gradient *n* (*rail*) pendiente.

gradual *adj* gradual; **~ly** *adv* gradualmente.

graduate *vi* graduarse.

graduation *n* graduación *f*.

graffiti *n* pintadas *fpl*.

graft *n* injerto *m*; * *vt* injertar, ingerir.

grain *n* grano *m*; semilla *f*; cereales *mpl*.

gram *n* gramo *m* (peso).

grammar *n* gramática *f*.

grammatical *adj* gramatical; **~ly** *adv* gramaticalmente.

granary *n* granero *m*.

grand *adj* grande, ilustre.

grandchild *n* nieto/ta *m/f*.

grandad *n* abuelo *m*.

granddaughter *n* nieta *f*; **great ~** bisnieta *f*.

grandeur *n* grandeza *f*; pompa *f*.

grandfather *n* abuelo *m*; **great ~** bisabuelo *m*.

grandiose *adj* grandioso/sa.

grandma *n* abuelita *f*.

grandmother *n* abuela *f*; **great ~** bisabuela *f*.

grandparents *npl* abuelos *mpl*.

grand piano *n* piano de cola *m*.

grandson *n* nieto *m*; **great ~** bisnieto *m*.

grandstand *n* tribuna *f*.

granite *n* granito *m*.

granny *n* abuelita *f*.

grant *vt* conceder; **to take for ~ed** presuponer; * *n* beca *f*; concesión *f*.

granulate *vt* granular.

granule *n* gránulo *m*.

grape *n* uva *f*; **bunch of ~s** racimo de uvas *m*.

grapefruit *n* toronja *f*, pomelo *m*.

graph *n* gráfica *f*.

graphic(al) *adj* gráfico/ca; pintoresco/ca; **~ally** *adv* gráficamente.

graphics *n* artes gráficas *fpl*; gráficos *mpl*.

grapnel *n* (*mar*) arpeo *m*.

grasp *vt* empuñar, asir, agarrar; * *n* puño *m*; comprensión *f*; poder *m*.

grasping *adj* avaro/ra.

grass *n* hierba *f*.

grasshopper *n* saltamontes *m invar*.

grassland *n* pampa, pradera *f*.

grass-roots *adj* popular.

grass snake *n* culebra de agua *f*.

grassy *adj* herboso/sa.

grate n reja, verja, rejilla f; * vt rallar; rechinar (los dientes); enrejar.

grateful adj grato/ta, agradecido/da; ~ly adv agradecidamente.

gratefulness n gratitud f.

gratification n gratificación f.

gratify vt contentar; gratificar.

gratifying adj grato/ta.

grating n rejado m; * adj áspero/ra; ofensivo/va.

gratis adv gratis.

gratitude n gratitud f.

gratuitous adj gratuito/ta, voluntario/ria; ~ly adv gratuitamente.

gratuity n gratificación, recompensa f.

grave n sepultura f; * adj grave, serio/ria; ~ly adv con gravedad, seriamente.

grave digger n sepulturero m.

gravel n cascajo m.

gravestone n lápida f.

graveyard n cementerio m.

gravitate vi gravitar.

gravitation n gravitación f.

gravity n gravedad f.

gravy n jugo de la carne f; salsa f.

graze vt pastorear; tocar ligeramente; * vi pacer.

grease n grasa f; pringue m/f; * vt untar.

greaseproof adj a prueba de grasa.

greasy adj grasiento/ta.

great adj gran, grande; principal; ilustre; noble, magnánimo/ma; ~ly adv muy, mucho.

greatcoat n sobretodo m.

greatness n grandeza f; dignidad f; poder m; magnanimidad f.

greedily adv vorazmente, ansiosamente.

greediness, greed n gula f; codicia f.

greedy adj avaro/ra, codicioso/sa; goloso/sa, glotón/ona.

Greek n griego (idioma) m.

green adj verde, fresco/ca, reciente; no maduro/ra; * n verde m; llanura verde f; ~s pl verduras fpl.

green belt n zona verde f.

greenery n verdura f.

greengrocer n verdulero/ra m/f.

greenhouse n invernadero m.

greenhouse effect n efecto invernadero m.

greenish adj verdoso/sa.

green movement n ecologismo m.

greenness n verdor, vigor m; frescura, falta de experiencia f; novedad f.

greet vt saludar, congratular.

greeting n saludo m.

greeting(s) card n tarjeta de felicitación f.

grenade n (mil) granada f.

grenadier n granadero m.

grey adj gris; cano/na; * n gris m.

grey-haired adj canoso/sa.

greyhound n galgo m.

greyish adj grisáceo/a; entrecano/na.

greyness n color gris m.

grid n reja f; red f.

gridiron n parrilla f; campo de fútbol americano m.

grief n dolor m; aflicción, pena f.

grievance n pesar m; molestia f; agravio m; injusticia f; perjuicio m.

grieve vt agraviar, afligir; * vi afligirse; llorar.

grievous adj doloroso/sa; enorme, atroz; ~ly adv penosamente; cruelmente.

griffin n grifo m.

grill n parrilla f; * vt interrogar.

grille n reja f.

grim *adj* feo, fea; horrendo/da; ceñudo/da.

grimace *n* mueca *f.*

grime *n* porquería *f.*

grimy *adj* ensuciado/da.

grin *n* mueca *f*; * *vi* sonreír.

grind *vt* moler; pulverizar; afilar; picar; rechinar los dientes.

grinder *n* molinero *m*; molinillo *m*; amolador *m.*

grip *n* asimiento *m*; asidero *m*; maletín *m*; * *vt* agarrar.

gripping *adj* absorbente.

grisly *adj* horroroso/sa.

gristle *n* tendón, cartílago *m.*

gristly *adj* tendinoso/sa, cartilaginoso/sa.

grit *n* gravilla *f*; valor *m.*

groan *vi* gemir, suspirar; * *n* gemido, suspiro *m.*

grocer *n* tendero/ra, abarrotero/ra *m/f.*

groceries *npl* comestibles *mpl.*

grocer's shop *n* tienda de comestibles *f.*

groggy *adj* atontado/da.

groin *n* ingle *f.*

groom *n* establero *m*; criado *m*; novio *m*; * *vt* cuidar, almohazar.

groove *n* ranura *f.*

grope *vt, vi* tentar, buscar a oscuras; andar a tientas.

gross *adj* grueso/sa, corpulento/ta, espeso/sa; grosero/ra; estúpido/da; ~**ly** *adv* enormemente.

grotesque *adj* grotesco/ca.

grotto *n* gruta *f.*

ground *n* tierra *f*; terreno, suelo, pavimento *m*; fundamento *m*; razón fundamental *f*; campo (de batalla) *m*; fondo *m*; * *vt* mantener en tierra; conectar con tierra.

ground floor *n* planta baja *f.*

grounding *n* conocimientos básicos *mpl.*

groundless *adj* infundado/da; ~**ly** *adv* sin motivo.

ground staff *n* personal de tierra *m.*

groundwork *n* preparación *f.*

group *n* grupo *m*; * *vt* agrupar.

grouse *n* lagópodo escocés *m*; * *vi* quejarse.

grove *n* arboleda *f.*

grovel *vi* arrastrarse.

grow *vt* cultivar; * *vi* crecer, aumentarse; ~ **up** crecer.

grower *n* cultivador/a *m/f*; productor/a *m/f.*

growing *adj* creciente.

growl *vi* regañar, gruñir; * *n* gruñido *m.*

grown-up *n* adulto/ta *m/f.*

growth *n* crecimiento *m.*

grub *n* gusano *m.*

grubby *adj* sucio/cia.

grudge *n* rencor, odio *m*; envidia *f*; * *vt, vi* envidiar.

grudgingly *adv* de mala gana.

gruelling *adj* penoso/sa, duro/ra.

gruesome *adj* horrible.

gruff *adj* brusco/ca; ~**ly** *adv* bruscamente.

gruffness *n* aspereza, severidad *f.*

grumble *vi* gruñir; murmurar.

grumpy *adj* regañón/ona.

grunt *vi* gruñir; * *n* gruñido *m.*

G-string *n* taparrabo *m.*

guarantee *n* garantía *f*; * *vt* garantizar.

guard *n* guardia *f*; * *vt* guardar; defender.

guarded *adj* cauteloso/sa, mesurado/da.

guardroom *n* (*mil*) cuarto de guardia *m.*

guardian *n* tutor/ra *m/f*; curador/a *m/f*; guardián/dana *m/f.*

guardianship n tutela f.
guerrilla n guerrillero/ra m/f.
guerrilla group n guerrilla f.
guerrilla warfare n guerra de guerrillas f.
guess vt, vi conjeturar; adivinar; suponer; * n conjetura f.
guesswork n conjeturas fpl.
guest n huésped/a, convidado/da m/f.
guest room n cuarto de huéspedes m.
guffaw n carcajada f.
guidance n gobierno m; dirección f.
guide vt guiar, dirigir; * n guía m.
guide dog n perro lazarillo m.
guidelines npl directiva f.
guidebook n guía f.
guild n gremio m; corporación f.
guile n astucia f.
guillotine n guillotina f; * vt guillotinar.
guilt n culpabilidad f.
guiltless adj inocente, libre de culpa.
guilty adj reo, rea, culpable.
guinea pig n cobaya f, conejillo de Indias m.
guise n manera f.
guitar n guitarra f.
gulf n golfo m; abismo m.
gull n gaviota f.
gullet n esófago m.
gullibility n credulidad f; simpleza f.
gullible adj crédulo/la.
gully n barranco m.
gulp n trago m; * vi tragar saliva; * vr tragarse.
gum n goma f; cemento m; encía f; chicle m; * vt pegar con goma.

gum tree n árbol gomero m.
gun n pistola f; escopeta f.
gunboat n cañonera f.
gun carriage n cureña f.
gunfire n disparos mpl.
gunman n pistolero m.
gunmetal n bronce de cañones m.
gunner n artillero m.
gunnery n artillería f.
gunpoint n: at ~ a punta de pistola; a mano armada.
gunpowder n pólvora f.
gunshot n escopetazo m.
gunsmith n armero/ra m/f.
gurgle vi gorgotear.
guru n gurú m.
gush vi brotar; chorrear; * n chorro m.
gushing adj superabundante.
gusset n escudete m.
gust n ráfaga f; soplo de aire m, racha f.
gusto n entusiasmo m.
gusty adj tempestuoso/sa.
gut n intestino m; ~s npl valor m; * vt destripar.
gutter n canalón m; arroyo m.
guttural adj gutural.
guy n tío m; tipo m.
guzzle vt engullir.
gym(nasium) n gimnasio m.
gymnast n gimnasta m/f.
gymnastic adj gimnástico/ca; ~s npl gimnástica f.
gynaecologist n ginecólogo/ga m/f.
gypsy n gitano/na m/f.
gypsum n yeso m.
gyrate vi girar.

H

haberdasher n camisero/ra m/f.

haberdashery n camisería f; mercería f; prendas de caballero fpl.

habit n costumbre f.

habitable adj habitable.

habitat n hábitat m.

habitual adj habitual; ~**ly** adv por costumbre.

hack n corte m; gacetillero/ra m/f; * vt tajar, cortar.

hackneyed adj trillado/da.

haddock n especie de bacalao f.

haemorrhage n hemorragia f.

haemorrhoids npl hemorroides mpl.

hag n bruja f.

haggard adj ojeroso/sa.

haggle vi regatear.

hail n granizo m; * vt saludar; * vi granizar.

hailstone n piedra de granizo f.

hair n pelo; cabello m.

hairbrush n cepillo m.

haircut n corte de pelo m.

hairdresser n peluquero/ra m/f.

hairdryer n secador de pelo m.

hairless adj calvo/va.

hairnet n redecilla f.

hairpiece n tupé m.

hairpin n horquilla f.

hairpin curve n curva muy cerrada f.

hair remover n depilatorio m.

hairspray n laca f.

hairstyle n peinado m.

hairy adj peludo/da, cabelludo/da.

hale adj sano/na, vigoroso/sa.

half n mitad f; * adj medio/dia.

half-caste adj mestizo/za.

half-hearted adj indiferente.

half-hour n media hora f.

half-moon n media luna f.

half-price adj a mitad de precio.

half-time n descanso m.

halfway adv a medio camino.

hall n vestíbulo m; hall m.

hallmark n contraste m.

hallow vt consagrar, santificar.

hallucination n alucinación f.

halo n halo m.

halt vi parar; * n parada f; alto m.

halve vt partir por la mitad.

ham n jamón m.

hamburger n hamburguesa f.

hamlet n aldea f.

hammer n martillo m; * vt martillar.

hammock n hamaca f.

hamper n cesto f; * vt estorbar.

hamstring vt desjarretar.

hand n mano f; brazo m; aguja f; at ~ a mano; * vt alargar.

handbag n cartera f.

handbell n campanilla f.

handbook n manual m.

handbrake n freno de mano m.

handcuff n esposa f.

handful n puñado m.

handicap n desventaja f.

handicapped adj minusválido/da.

handicraft n artesanía f.

handiwork n obra f.

handkerchief n pañuelo m.

handle n mango, puño m; asa; manija f; * vt manejar; tratar.

handlebars npl manillar m.

handling n manejo m.

handrail n pasamanos m.

handshake n apretón de manos m.

handsome adj guapo/pa; ~**ly** adv primorosamente.

handwriting *n* letra *f*.
handy *adj* práctico/ca; diestro/tra.
hang *vt* colgar; ahorcar; * *vi* colgar; ser ahorcado/da.
hanger *n* percha *f*.
hanger-on *n* parásito *m*.
hangings *npl* tapicería *f*.
hangman *n* verdugo *m*.
hangover *n* resaca *f*.
hang-up *n* complejo *m*.
hanker *vi* ansiar, apetecer.
haphazard *adj* fortuito/ta.
hapless *adj* desgraciado/da.
happen *vi* pasar; acontecer, acaecer.
happening *n* suceso *m*.
happily *adv* felizmente.
happiness *n* felicidad *f*.
happy *adj* feliz.
harangue *n* arenga *f*; * *vi* arengar.
harass *vt* cansar, fatigar.
harbinger *n* precursor *m*.
harbour *n* puerto *m*; * *vt* albergar.
hard *adj* duro/ra, firme; difícil; penoso/sa; severo/ra, rígido/da; ~ **of hearing** medio sordo/da; ~ **by** muy cerca.
harden *vt* (*vi*) endurecer(se).
hard-headed *adj* realista.
hard-hearted *adj* duro de corazón, insensible.
hardiness *n* robustez *f*.
hardly *adv* apenas.
hardness *n* dureza *f*; dificultad *f*; severidad *f*.
hardship *n* penas *fpl*.
hard-up *adj* sin plata.
hardware *n* hardware *m*; quincallería *f*.
hardwearing *adj* resistente.
hardy *adj* fuerte, robusto/ta.
hare *n* liebre *f*.
hare-brained *adj* atolondrado/da.
hare-lipped *adj* labihendido/da.
haricot *n* alubia *f*.

harlequin *n* arlequín *m*.
harm *n* mal, daño *m*; perjuicio *m*; * *vt* dañar.
harmful *adj* perjudicial.
harmless *adj* inocuo/cua.
harmonic *adj* armónico/ca.
harmonious *adj* armonioso/sa; ~**ly** *adv* armoniosamente.
harmonize *vt* armonizar.
harmony *n* armonía *f*.
harness *n* arreos de un caballo *mpl*; * *vt* enjaezar.
harp *n* arpa *f*.
harpist *n* arpista *m/f*.
harpoon *n* arpón *m*.
harpsichord *n* clavicordio *m*.
harrow *n* grada *f*; rastro *m*.
harry *vt* hostigar.
harsh *adj* duro/ra; austero/ra; ~**ly** *adv* severamente.
harshness *n* aspereza, dureza *f*; austeridad *f*.
harvest *n* cosecha *f*; * *vt* cosechar.
harvester *n* cosechadora *f*.
hash *n* hachís *m*; picadillo *m*.
hassock *n* cojín de paja *m*.
haste *n* apuro *m*; **to be in** ~ estar apurado/da.
hasten *vt* acelerar, apresurar; * *vi* tener prisa.
hastily *adv* precipitadamente.
hastiness *n* precipitación *f*.
hasty *adj* apresurado/da.
hat *n* sombrero *m*.
hatbox *n* sombrerera *f*.
hatch *vt* incubar; tramar; **to** ~ **a plot or scheme** zurcir; * *n* escotilla *f*.
hatchback *n* tres puertas, cinco puertas *m invar*.
hatchet *n* hacha *f*.
hatchway *n* (*mar*) escotilla *f*.
hate *n* odio, aborrecimiento *m*; * *vt* odiar, detestar.

hateful *adj* odioso/sa.

hatred *n* odio, aborrecimiento *m*.

hatter *n* sombrerero *m*.

haughtily *adv* orgullosamente.

haughtiness *n* orgullo *m*; altivez *f*.

haughty *adj* altanero/ra, orgulloso/sa.

haul *vt* tirar; * *n* botín *m*.

hauler *n* transportista *m/f*.

haunch *n* anca *f*.

haunt *vt* frecuentar, rondar; * *n* guarida *f*; costumbre *f*.

have *vt* haber; tener, poseer.

haven *n* asilo *m*; puerto *m*.

haversack *n* mochila *f*.

havoc *n* estrago *m*.

hawk *n* halcón *m*; * *vi* cazar con halcón.

hawthorn *n* espino blanco *m*.

hay *n* heno *m*.

hay fever *n* fiebre del heno *f*.

hayloft *n* henil *m*.

hayrick, haystack *n* almiar *m*.

hazard *n* riesgo *m*; * *vt* arriesgar.

hazardous *adj* arriesgado/da, peligroso/sa.

haze *n* niebla *f*.

hazel *n* avellano *m*; * *adj* castaño/ña.

hazelnut *n* avellana *f*.

hazy *adj* oscuro/ra.

he *pn* él.

head *n* cabeza *f*; jefe *m*; juicio *m*; * *vt* encabezar; **to ~ for** dirigirse a.

headache *n* dolor de cabeza *m*.

headdress *n* cofia *f*; tocado *m*.

headland *n* promontorio *m*.

headlight *n* faro *m*.

headline *n* titular *m*.

headlong *adv* precipitadamente.

headmaster *n* director *m*.

head office *n* oficina central *f*.

headphones *npl* auriculares *mpl*.

headquarters *npl* (*mil*) cuartel general *m*; sede central *f*.

headroom *n* altura *f*.

headstrong *adj* testarudo/da, cabezudo/da.

headwaiter *n* maître *m*.

headway *n* progresos *mpl*.

heady *adj* cabezón/ona.

heal *vt, vi* curar.

health *n* salud *f*; brindis *m invar*.

healthiness *n* sanidad *f*.

healthy *adj* sano/na.

heap *n* montón *m*; * *vt* amontonar.

hear *vt* oír; escuchar; * *vi* oír; escuchar.

hearing *n* oído *m*.

hearing aid *n* audífono *m*.

hearsay *n* rumor *m*; fama *f*.

hearse *n* coche fúnebre *m*.

heart *n* corazón *m*; **by ~** de memoria; **with all my ~** con toda mi alma.

heart attack *n* infarto, infarto de miocardio *m*.

heartbreaking *adj* desgarrador.

heartburn *n* ardor de estómago *m*

heart failure *n* fallo cardíaco *m*.

heartfelt *adj* sincero/ra.

hearth *n* hogar *m*.

heartily *adv* sinceramente, cordialmente.

heartiness *n* cordialidad, sinceridad *f*.

heartless *adj* cruel; **~ly** *adv* cruelmente.

hearty *adj* cordial.

heat *n* calor *m*; * *vt* calentar.

heater *n* calentador *m*.

heather *n* (*bot*) brezo *m*.

heathen *n* pagano/na *m/f*; **~ish** *adj* salvaje.

heating *n* calefacción *f*.

heat wave *n* ola de calor *f*.

heave *vt* alzar; tirar; * *n* tirón *m*.

heaven *n* cielo *m*.

heavenly *adj* divino/na.

heavily *adv* pesadamente.

heaviness *n* pesadez *f*.

heavy *adj* pesado/da; opresivo/va.

Hebrew *n* hebreo *m*.

heckle *vt* interrumpir.

hectic *adj* agitado/da.

hedge *n* seto *m*; * *vt* cercar con seto.

hedgehog *n* erizo *m*.

heed *vt* hacer caso de; * *n* cuidado *m*; atención *f*.

heedless *adj* descuidado/da, negligente; ~ly *adv* negligentemente.

heel *n* talón *m*; **to take to one's ~s** apretar los talones, huir.

hefty *adj* grande.

heifer *n* ternera *f*.

height *n* altura *f*; altitud *f*.

heighten *vt* realzar; adelantar, mejorar; exaltar.

heinous *adj* atroz.

heir *n* heredero/ra *m/f*; ~ **apparent** heredero/ra forzoso/sa *m/f*.

heiress *n* heredera *f*.

heirloom *n* reliquia de familia *f*.

helicopter *n* helicóptero *m*.

hell *n* infierno *m*.

hellish *adj* infernal.

helm *n* (*mar*) timón *m*.

helmet *n* casco *m*.

help *vt, vi* ayudar, socorrer; **I cannot ~ it** no puedo remediarlo; no lo puedo evitar; * *n* ayuda *f*; socorro, remedio *m*.

helper *n* ayudante *m/f*.

helpful *adj* útil.

helping *n* ración *f*.

helpless *adj* indefenso/sa; ~ly *adv* irremediablemente.

helter-skelter *adv* a trochemoche, en desorden.

hem *n* ribete *m*; * *vt* ribetear.

he-man *n* macho *m*.

hemisphere *n* hemisferio *m*.

hemp *n* cáñamo *m*.

hen *n* gallina *f*.

henchman *n* secuaz *m*.

henceforth, henceforward *adv* de aquí en adelante.

henhouse *n* gallinero *m*.

hepatitis *n* hepatitis *f*.

her *pn* su; ella; de ella; a ella.

herald *n* heraldo *m*.

heraldry *n* heráldica *f*.

herb *n* hierba *f*; ~**s** *pl* hierbas *fpl*.

herbaceous *adj* herbáceo/cea.

herbalist *n* herbolario *m*.

herbivorous *adj* herbívoro/ra.

herd *n* rebaño *m*.

here *adv* aquí, acá.

hereabout(s) *adv* aquí alrededor.

hereafter *adv* en el futuro.

hereby *adv* por esto.

hereditary *adj* hereditario/ria.

heredity *n* herencia *f*.

heresy *n* herejía *f*.

heretic *n* hereje *m/f*; * *adj* herético/ca.

herewith *adv* con esto.

heritage *n* patrimonio *m*.

hermetic *adj* hermético/ca; ~ly *adv* herméticamente.

hermit *n* ermitaño/ña *m/f*.

hermitage *n* ermita *f*.

hernia *n* hernia *f*.

hero *n* héroe *m*.

heroic *adj* heroico/ca; ~**ally** *adv* heroicamente.

heroine *n* heroína *f*.

heroism *n* heroísmo *m*.

heron *n* garza *f*.

herring *n* arenque *m*.

hers *pn* suyo, de ella.

herself *pn* ella misma.

hesitant *adj* vacilante.

hesitate *vt* dudar; tardar.

hesitation *n* duda, irresolución *f*.

heterogeneous *adj* heterogéneo/nea.
heterosexual *adj*, *n* heterosexual *m*.
hew *vt* tajar; cortar; picar.
heyday *n* apogeo *m*.
hi *excl* ¡hola!
hiatus *n* (*gr*) hiato *m*.
hibernate *vi* invernar.
hiccup *n* hipo *m*; * *vi* tener hipo.
hickory *n* nogal americana *m*.
hide *vt* esconder; * *n* cuero *m*; piel *f*.
hideaway *n* escondite *m*.
hideous *adj* horrible; ~**ly** *adv* horriblemente.
hiding place *n* escondite, escondrijo *m*.
hierarchy *n* jerarquía *f*.
hieroglyphic *adj* jeroglífico/ca; * *n* jeroglífico *m*.
hi-fi *n* estéreo, hi-fi *m*.
higgledy-piggledy *adv* confusamente.
high *adj* alto/ta; elevado/da.
high altar *n* altar mayor *m*.
highchair *n* silla alta *f*.
high-handed *adj* despótico/ca.
highlands *npl* tierras montañosas, tierras altas *fpl*.
highlight *n* punto culminante *m*.
highly *adv* en sumo grado.
highness *n* altura *f*; alteza *f*.
highly strung *adj* hipertenso/sa.
high water *n* marea alta *f*.
highway *n* carretera *f*.
hike *vi* ir de excursión.
hijack *vt* secuestrar.
hijacker *n* secuestrador/a *m/f*.
hilarious *adj* alegre.
hill *n* colina *f*.
hillock *n* colina *f*.
hillside *n* ladera *f*.
hilly *adj* montañoso/sa.
hilt *n* puño de espada *m*.
him *pn* le, lo, el.

himself *pn* él mismo, se, si mismo.
hind *adj* trasero/ra, posterior; * *n* cierva *f*.
hinder *vt* impedir.
hindrance *n* impedimento, obstáculo *m*.
hindmost *adj* postrero/ra.
hindquarter *n* cuarto trasero *m*.
hindsight *n*: with ~ en retrospectiva.
hinge *n* bisagra *f*.
hint *n* indirecta *f*; * *vt* insinuar; sugerir.
hip *n* cadera *f*.
hippopotamus *n* hipopótamo *m*.
hire *vt* alquilar; * *n* alquiler *m*.
hire purchase *n* compra a plazos *f*.
his *pn* su, suyo, de él.
Hispanic *adj* hispano/na; hispánico/ca; * *n* hispanoamericano/na *m/f*.
hiss *vt*, *vi* silbar.
historian *n* historiador/a *m/f*.
historic(al) *adj* histórico/ca; ~**ally** *adv* históricamente.
history *n* historia *f*.
histrionic *adj* teatral.
hit *vt* golpear; alcanzar; zumbar; **to ~ each other** *vr* zumbarse; * *n* golpe *m*; éxito *m*.
hitch *vt* atar; * *n* problema *m*.
hitchhike *vi* hacer autostop.
hitchhiker *n* autoestopista *m/f*.
hitchhiking *n* autostop *f*.
hitherto *adv* hasta ahora, hasta aquí.
hive *n* colmena *f*.
HIV-negative *adj* seronegativo/va.
HIV-positive *adj* seropositivo/va.
hoard *n* montón *m*; tesoro escondido *m*; * *vt* acumular.
hoarfrost *n* escarcha *f*.
hoarse *adj* ronco/ca; ~**ly** *adv* roncamente.
hoarseness *n* ronquera, carraspera *f*.

hoax n trampa f; * vt engañar, burlar.

hobble vi cojear.

hobby n pasatiempo m, afición f.

hobbyhorse n caballo de batalla m.

hockey n hockey m.

hodgepodge n mezcolanza f.

hoe n azadón m; * vt azadonar.

hoist vt alzar; * n grúa f.

hold vt tener; detener; contener; celebrar; **to ~ on to** agarrarse a; * vi valer; * n presa f; poder m.

holder n poseedor/a m/f; titular m/f.

holding n tenencia, posesión f.

hold-up n atraco m; retraso m.

hole n agujero m.

holiday n día de fiesta m; **~s** pl vacaciones fpl.

holiday-maker n turista m/f.

holiness n santidad f.

hollow adj hueco/ca; * n hoyo m; * vt excavar, ahuecar.

holly n (bot) acebo m.

hollyhock n malva hortense f.

holocaust n holocausto m.

holster n pistolera f.

holy adj santo/ta, pío, pía; consagrado/da.

holy water n agua bendita f.

holy week n semana santa f.

homage n homenaje m.

home n casa f; patria f; domicilio m; **~ly** adj casero/ra.

home address n domicilio m.

homeless adj sin casa.

homeliness n simpleza f.

homely adj casero/ra.

home-made adj casero/ra.

homeopathist n homeópata m/f.

homeopathy n homeopatía f.

home shopping programme (TV) n teletienda f.

homesick adj nostálgico/ca.

homesickness n nostalgia f.

hometown n ciudad natal f.

homeward adj hacia casa; hacia su país.

homework n deberes mpl.

homicidal adj homicida.

homicide n homicidio m; homicida m/f.

homogeneous adj homogéneo/nea.

homosexual adj, n homosexual m.

honest adj honrado/da; **~ly** adv honradamente.

honesty n honradez f.

honey n miel f.

honeycomb n panal m.

honeymoon n luna de miel f.

honeysuckle n (bot) madreselva f.

honorary adj honorario/ria.

honour n honra f; honor m; * vt honrar.

honourable adj honorable; ilustre.

honourably adv honorablemente.

hood n capo m; capucha f.

hoodlum n matón m.

hoof n pezuña f.

hook n gancho m; anzuelo m; **by ~ or by crook** de un modo u otro; * vt enganchar.

hooked adj encorvado/da.

hooligan n gamberro/rra m/f.

hoop n aro m.

hooter n sirena f.

hop n (bot) lúpulo m; salto m; * vi saltar, brincar.

hope n esperanza f; * vi esperar.

hopeful adj esperanzador/a; **~ly** adv con esperanza.

hopefulness n buena esperanza f.

hopeless adj desesperado/da; **~ly** adv sin esperanza.

hopscotch n tejo m.

horde n horda f.

horizon n horizonte m.

horizontal *adj* horizontal; **~ly** *adv* horizontalmente.

hormone *n* hormona *f*.

horn *n* cuerno *m*; (*auto*) sirena *f*.

horned *adj* cornudo/da.

hornet *n* avispón *m*.

horny *adj* calloso/sa.

horoscope *n* horóscopo *m*.

horrendous *adj* horrendo/da.

horrible *adj* horrible, terrible.

horribly *adv* horriblemente; enormemente.

horrid *adj* horrible.

horrific *adj* horroroso/sa.

horrify *vt* horrorizar.

horror *n* horror, terror *m*.

horror film *n* película de horror *f*.

hors d'oeuvre *n* entremeses *mpl*.

horse *n* caballo *m*; caballete *m*.

horseback *adv*: on ~ a caballo.

horse-breaker *n* domador/a de caballos *m/f*.

horse chestnut *n* castaño de Indias *m*.

horsefly *n* moscarda *f*; moscardón *m*.

horseman *n* jinete *m*.

horsemanship *n* equitación *f*.

horsepower *n* caballo de fuerza *m*.

horse race *n* carrera de caballos *f*.

horseracing *n* hípica *f*.

horseradish *n* rábano silvestre *m*.

horseshoe *n* herradura de caballo *f*.

horsewoman *n* jineta *f*.

horticulture *n* horticultura, jardinería *f*.

horticulturist *n* jardinero/ra *m/f*.

hosepipe *n* manguera *f*.

hosiery *n* calcetería *f*.

hospitable *adj* hospitalario/ria.

hospitably *adv* con hospitalidad.

hospital *n* hospital *m*.

hospitality *n* hospitalidad *f*.

host *n* anfitrión *m*; hostia *f*.

hostage *n* rehén *m*.

hostess *n* anfitriona *f*.

hostile *adj* hostil.

hostility *n* hostilidad *f*.

hot *adj* caliente; cálido/da.

hotbed *n* semillero *m*.

hotdog *n* perro caliente *m*.

hotel *n* hotel *m*.

hotelier *n* hotelero/ra *m/f*.

hot-headed *adj* exaltado/da.

hothouse *n* invernadero *m*.

hotline *n* línea directa *f*.

hotplate *n* hornillo *m*.

hotly *adv* con calor; violentamente.

hound *n* perro de caza *m*.

hour *n* hora *f*.

hour-glass *n* reloj de arena *m*.

hourly *adv* cada hora.

house *n* casa *f*; familia *f*; * *vt* alojar.

houseboat *n* casa flotante *f*.

housebreaker *n* ladrón/ona de casa *m/f*.

housebreaking *n* allanamiento de morada *m*.

household *n* familia *f*.

householder *n* amo de casa, padre de familia *m*; dueño/ña de la casa *m/f*.

housekeeper *n* ama de llaves *f*.

housekeeping *n* trabajos domésticos *mpl*.

house-warming party *n* fiesta de estreno de una casa *f*.

housewife *n* ama de casa *f*.

housework *n* faenas de la casa *fpl*.

housing *n* vivienda *f*.

housing development *n* urbanización *f*.

hovel *n* choza, cabaña *f*.

hover *vi* flotar.

how *adv* cómo, como; **~ do you do!** ¡encantado!

however *adv* comoquiera, comoquiera que sea; aunque; no obstante.

howl *vi* aullar; * *n* aullido *m*.

hub *n* centro *m*.

hubbub *n* barullo *m*.

hubcap *n* tapacubos *m invar*.

hue *n* color *m*; matiz *m*.

huff *n*: **in a ~** picado/da.

hug *vt* abrazar; * *n* abrazo *m*.

huge *adj* vasto/ta, enorme; **~ly** *adv* inmensamente.

hulk *n* (*mar*) casco *m*; armatoste *m*.

hull *n* (*mar*) casco *m*.

hum *vi* canturrear.

human *adv* humano/na.

humane *adv* humano/na; benigno/na; **~ly** *adv* humanamente.

humanist *n* humanista *m/f*.

humanitarian *adj* humanitario/ria.

humanity *n* humanidad *f*.

humanize *vt* humanizar.

humanly *adv* humanamente.

humble *adj* humilde, modesto/ta; * *vt* humillar, postrar.

humbleness *n* humildad *f*.

humbly *adv* con humildad.

humbug *n* tonterías *fpl*.

humdrum *adj* monótono/na.

humid *adj* húmedo/da.

humidity *n* humedad *f*.

humiliate *vt* humillar.

humiliation *n* humillación *f*.

humility *n* humildad *f*.

humming *n* zumbido *m*.

humming-bird *n* colibrí *m*.

humorist *n* humorista *m/f*.

humorous *adj* gracioso/sa; **~ly** *adv* con gracia.

humour *n* sentido del humor *m*, humor *m*; jocosidad *f*; * *vt* complacer.

hump *n* giba, joroba *f*.

hunch *n* corazonada *f*; **~backed** *adj* jorobado/da, jiboso/sa.

hundred *adj* ciento; * *n* centenar *m*; un ciento.

hundredth *adj* centésimo.

hundredweight *n* quintal *m*.

hunger *n* hambre *f*; * *vi* hambrear.

hunger strike *n* huelga de hambre *f*.

hungrily *adv* con apetito.

hungry *adj* hambriento/ta.

hunt *vt* cazar; perseguir; buscar; * *vi* andar a caza; * *n* caza *f*.

hunter *n* cazador/a *m/f*.

hunting *n* caza *f*.

huntsman *n* cazador *m*.

hurdle *n* valla *f*.

hurl *vt* tirar con violencia; arrojar.

hurricane *n* huracán *m*.

hurried *adj* hecho/cha de prisa; **~ly** *adv* con prisa.

hurry *vt* acelerar, apresurar; * *vi* apresurarse; * *n* prisa *f*.

hurt *vt* hacer daño; ofender; * *n* mal, daño *m*.

hurtful *adj* dañoso/sa; **~ly** *adv* dañosamente.

hurtle *vr* zamparse.

husband *n* marido *m*.

husbandry *n* agricultura *f*.

hush! ¡chitón!, ¡silencio!; * *vt* hacer callar; * *vi* estar quieto/ta.

husk *n* cáscara *f*.

huskiness *n* ronquedad *f*.

husky *adj* ronco/ca.

hustings *n* tribuna para las elecciones *f*.

hustle *vt* empujar con fuerza.

hut *n* cabaña, barraca *f*.

hutch *n* conejera *f*.

hyacinth *n* jacinto *m*.

hydrant *n* boca de incendios *f*.

hydraulic *adj* hidráulico/ca; **~s** *npl* hidráulica *f*.

hydroelectric *adj* hidroeléctrico/ca.

hydrofoil *n* hidroala *f*.

hydrogen *n* hidrógeno *m*.
hydrophobia *n* hidrofobia *f*.
hyena *n* hiena *f*.
hygiene *n* higiene *f*.
hygienic *adj* higiénico/ca.
hymn *n* himno *m*.
hyperbole *n* hipérbole *f*; exageración *f*.
hypermarket *n* hipermercado *m*.
hyphen *n* (*gr*) guión *m*.
hypochondria *n* hipocondria *f*.

hypochondriac *adj*, *n* hipocondríaco/ca *m/f*.
hypocrisy *n* hipocresía *f*.
hypocrite *n* hipócrita *m/f*.
hypocritical *adj* hipócrita.
hypothesis *n* hipótesis *f*.
hypothetical *adj* hipotético/ca; ~ly *adv* hipotéticamente.
hysterical *adj* histérico/ca.
hysterics *npl* histeria *f*.

I

I *pn* yo; ~ **myself** yo mismo.
ice *n* hielo *m*; * *vt* helar.
ice-axe *n* piqueta *f*.
iceberg *n* iceberg *m*.
ice-bound *adj* rodeado/da de hielos.
icebox *n* nevera *f*.
ice cream *n* helado *m*.
ice rink *n* pista de hielo *f*.
ice skating *n* patinaje sobre hielo *m*.
icicle *n* carámbano *m*.
iconoclast *n* iconoclasta *m/f*.
icy *adj* helado/da; frío/ría.
idea *n* idea *f*.
ideal *adj* ideal; ~ly *adv* idealmente.
idealist *n* idealista *m/f*.
identical *adj* idéntico/ca.
identification *n* identificación *f*.
identify *vt* identificar.
identity *n* identidad *f*.
ideology *n* ideología *f*.
idiom *n* idioma *m*.
idiomatic *adj* idiomático/ca.
idiosyncrasy *n* idiosincrasia *f*.
idiot *n* idiota, necio/cia *m/f*.
idiotic *adj* tonto/ta, bobo/ba.
idle *adj* desocupado/da; holgazán/zana; inútil.
idleness *n* pereza *f*.

idler *n* holgazán/zana *m/f*; zángano *m*.
idly *adv* ociosamente; vanamente.
idol *n* ídolo *m*.
idolatry *n* idolatría *f*.
idolize *vt* idolatrar.
idyllic *adj* idílico/ca.
i.e. *adv* esto es.
if *conj* si, aunque; ~ **not** si no.
igloo *n* iglú *m*.
ignite *vt* encender.
ignition *n* (*chem*) ignición *f*; encendido *m*.
ignition key *n* llave de contacto *f*.
ignoble *adj* innoble; bajo/ja.
ignominious *adj* ignominioso/sa; ~ly *adv* ignominiosamente.
ignominy *n* ignominia, infamia *f*.
ignoramus *n* ignorante, tonto/ta *m/f*.
ignorance *n* ignorancia *f*.
ignorant *adj* ignorante; ~ly *adv* ignorantemente.
ignore *vt* no hacer caso de.
ill *adj* malo/la, enfermo/ma; * *n* mal, infortunio *m*; * *adv* mal.
ill-advised *adj* imprudente.
illegal *adj*, ~ly *adv* ilegal(mente).
illegality *n* ilegalidad *f*.
illegible *adj* ilegible.

illegibly *adv* de modo ilegible.
illegitimacy *n* ilegitimidad *f*.
illegitimate *adj* ilegítimo/ma; ~ly *adv* ilegítimamente.
ill feeling *n* rencor *m*.
illicit *adj* ilícito/ta.
illiterate *adj* analfabeto/ta.
illness *n* enfermedad *f*.
illogical *adj* ilógico/ca.
ill-timed *adj* inoportuno/na.
ill-treat *vt* maltratar.
illuminate *vt* iluminar.
illumination *n* iluminación *f*.
illusion *n* ilusión *f*.
illusory *adj* ilusorio/ria.
illustrate *vt* ilustrar; explicar.
illustration *n* ilustración *f*; elucidación *f*.
illustrative *adj* explicativo/va.
illustrious *adj* ilustre, insigne.
ill-will *n* rencor *m*.
image *n* imagen *f*.
imagery *n* imágenes *fpl*.
imaginable *adj* concebible.
imaginary *adj* imaginario/ria.
imagination *n* imaginación *f*.
imaginative *adj* imaginativo/va.
imagine *vt* imaginarse; idear, inventar.
imbalance *n* desequilibrio *m*.
imbecile *adj* imbécil, necio/cia.
imbibe *vt* beber.
imbue *vt* infundir.
imitate *vt* imitar, copiar.
imitation *n* imitación, copia *f*.
imitative *adj* imitativo/va.
immaculate *adj* inmaculado/da, puro/ra.
immaterial *adj* poco importante.
immature *adj* inmaduro/ra.
immeasurable *adj* inconmensurable.
immeasurably *adv* inmensamente.

immediate *adj* inmediato/ta; ~ly *adv* inmediatamente; ya.
immense *adj* inmenso/sa; vasto/ta; ~ly *adv* inmensamente.
immensity *n* inmensidad *f*.
immerse *vt* sumergir.
immersion *n* inmersión *f*.
immigrant *n* inmigrante *m/f*.
immigrate *vi* inmigrar.
immigration *n* inmigración *f*.
imminent *adj* inminente.
immobile *adj* inmóvil.
immobility *n* inmovilidad *f*.
immoderate *adj* inmoderado/da, excesivo/va; ~ly *adv* inmoderadamente.
immodest *adj* inmodesto/ta.
immoral *adj* inmoral.
immorality *n* inmoralidad *f*.
immortal *adj* inmortal.
immortality *n* inmortalidad *f*.
immortalize *vt* inmortalizar, eternizar.
immune *adj* inmune.
immunity *n* inmunidad *f*.
immunize *vt* inmunizar.
immutable *adj* inmutable.
imp *n* diablillo, duende *m*.
impact *n* impacto *m*.
impair *vt* disminuir.
impale *vt* empalar.
impalpable *adj* impalpable.
impart *vt* comunicar.
impartial *adj*, ~ly *adv* imparcial(mente).
impartiality *n* imparcialidad *f*.
impassable *adj* intransitable.
impasse *n* punto muerto *m*.
impassive *adj* impasible.
impatience *n* impaciencia *f*.
impatient *adj*, ~ly *adv* impaciente(mente).
impeach *vt* acusar, denunciar.

impeccable *adj* impecable.
impecunious *adj* indigente.
impede *vt* estorbar.
impediment *n* obstáculo *m*.
impel *vt* impeler, impulsar.
impending *adj* inminente.
impenetrable *adj* impenetrable.
imperative *adj* imperativo/va.
imperceptible *adj* imperceptible.
imperceptibly *adv* imperceptible-
mente.
imperfect *adj* imperfecto/ta, defec-
tuoso/sa; ~ly*adv* imperfectamente;
* *n* (*gr*) pretérito imperfecto *m*.
imperfection *n* imperfección *f*, defecto *m*.
imperial *adj* imperial.
imperialism *n* imperialismo *m*.
imperious *adj* imperioso/sa; arrogante; ~ly *adv* imperiosamente,
arrogantemente.
impermeable *adj* impermeable.
impersonal *adj*, ~ly *adv* imper-
sonal(mente).
impersonate *vt* hacerse pasar por;
imitar.
impertinence *n* impertinencia *f*; descaro *m*.
impertinent *adj* impertinente; ~ly
adv impertinentemente.
imperturbable *adj* imperturbable.
impervious *adj* impermeable.
impetuosity *n* impetuosidad *f*.
impetuous *adj* impetuoso/sa; ~ly
adv impetuosamente.
impetus *n* ímpetu *m*.
impiety *n* impiedad *f*.
impinge (on) *vt* tener influjo en.
impious *adj* impío/pía, irreligioso/
sa.
implacable *adj* implacable.
implacably *adv* implacablemente.
implant *vt* implantar; plantear.

implement *n* herramienta *f*; utensilio *m*.
implicate *vt* implicar.
implication *n* implicación *f*.
implicit *adj* implícito/ta; ~ly *adv* im-
plícitamente.
implore *vt* suplicar.
imply *vt* suponer.
impolite *adj* maleducado/da.
impoliteness *n* falta de educación *f*.
impolitic *adj* imprudente; impo-
lítico/ca.
import *vt* importar; * *n* importación *f*.
importance *n* importancia *f*.
important *adj* importante.
importation *n* importación *f*.
importer *n* importador/a *m/f*.
importunate *adj* importuno/na.
importune *vt* importunar.
importunity *n* importunidad *f*.
impose *vt* imponer.
imposing *adj* imponente.
imposition *n* imposición, carga *f*.
impossibility *n* imposibilidad *f*.
impossible *adj* imposible.
impostor *n* impostor *m*.
impotence *n* impotencia *f*.
impotent *adj* impotente; ~ly *adv* sin
poder.
impound *vt* embargar.
impoverish *vt* empobrecer.
impoverished *adj* necesitado/da.
impoverishment *n* empobrecimiento *m*.
impracticability *n* inviabilidad *f*.
impracticable *adj* impracticable, in-
viable.
impractical *adj* poco práctico/ca.
imprecation *n* imprecación, maldición *f*.
imprecise *adj* impreciso/sa.
impregnable *adj* inexpugnable.
impregnate *vt* impregnar.

impregnation n fecundación f; impregnación f.
impress vt impresionar.
impression n impresión f; edición f.
impressionable adj impresionable.
impressive adj impresionante.
imprint n sello m; * vt imprimir; estampar.
imprison vt encarcelar.
imprisonment n encarcelamiento m.
improbability n improbabilidad f.
improbable adj improbable.
impromptu adj de improviso.
improper adj impropio/pia, indecente; ~ly adv impropiamente.
impropriety n impropiedad f.
improve vt, vi mejorar.
improvement n progreso m, mejora f.
improvident adj impróvido/da, imprudente.
improvise vt improvisar.
imprudence n imprudencia f.
imprudent adj imprudente.
impudence n impudencia f.
impudent adj impudente; ~ly adv desvergonzadamente.
impugn vt impugnar.
impulse n impulso m.
impulsive adj impulsivo/va.
impunity n impunidad f.
impure adj impuro/ra; ~ly adv impuramente.
impurity n impureza f.
in prep en.
inability n incapacidad f.
inaccessible adj inaccesible.
inaccuracy n inexactitud f.
inaccurate adj inexacto/ta.
inaction n inacción f.
inactive adj inactivo/va, perezoso/sa.
inactivity n inactividad f.
inadequate adj inadecuado/da, defectuoso/sa.

inadmissible adj inadmisible.
inadvertently adv sin querer.
inalienable adj inalienable.
inane adj necio/cia.
inanimate adj inanimado/da.
inapplicable adj inaplicable.
inappropriate adj impropio/pia.
inasmuch adv visto que; en tanto en cuanto.
inattentive adj desatento/ta.
inaudible adj inaudible.
inaugural adj inaugural.
inaugurate vt inaugurar.
inauguration n inauguración f.
inauspicious adj poco propicio/cia.
in-between adj intermedio/dia.
inborn, inbred adj innato/ta.
incalculable adj incalculable.
incandescent adj incandescente.
incantation n conjuro m.
incapable adj incapaz.
incapacitate vt inhabilitar.
incapacity n incapacidad f.
incarcerate vt encarcelar.
incarnate adj encarnado/da.
incarnation n encarnación f.
incautious adj incauto/ta; ~ly adv incautamente.
incendiary n bomba incendiaria f.
incense n incienso m; * vt exasperar.
incentive n incentivo m.
inception n principio m.
incessant adj incesante, constante; ~ly adv continuamente.
incest n incesto m.
incestuous adj incestuoso/sa.
inch n pulgada f; ~ by ~ palmo a palmo.
incidence n frecuencia f.
incident n incidente m.
incidental adj casual; ~ly adv a propósito.
incinerator n incinerador m.

incipient adj incipiente.
incise vt tajar, cortar.
incision n incisión f.
incisive adj incisivo/va.
incisor n incisivo m.
incite vt incitar, estimular.
inclement adj feo, fea.
inclination n inclinación, propensión f.
incline vt (vi) inclinar(se); * n cuesta f.
include vt incluir, comprender.
including prep incluso.
inclusion n inclusión f.
inclusive adj inclusivo/va.
incognito adv de incógnito.
incoherence n incoherencia f.
incoherent adj incoherente, inconsecuente; ~ly adv de modo incoherente.
income n renta f; ingresos mpl.
income tax n impuesto sobre la renta m.
incoming adj entrante.
incomparable adj incomparable.
incomparably adv incomparablemente.
incompatibility n incompatibilidad f.
incompatible adj incompatible.
incompetence n incompetencia f.
incompetent adj, ~ly adv incompetente(mente).
incomplete adj incompleto/ta.
incomprehensibility n incomprensibilidad f.
incomprehensible adj incomprensible.
inconceivable adj inconcebible.
inconclusive adj no concluyente; * adv sin conclusión.
incongruity n incongruencia f.
incongruous adj incongruo/rua; ~ly adv incongruamente.
inconsequential adj inconsecuente.

inconsiderate adj desconsiderado/da; ~ly adv desconsideradamente.
inconsistency n inconsecuencia f.
inconsistent adj inconsecuente.
inconsolable adj inconsolable.
inconspicuous adj discreto/ta.
incontinence n incontinencia f.
incontinent adj incontinente.
incontrovertible adj incontrovertible.
inconvenience n incomodidad f; * vt incomodar.
inconvenient adj incómodo/da; ~ly adv incómodamente.
incorporate vt (vi) incorporar(se).
incorporated company (inc) n sociedad anónima f.
incorporation n incorporación f.
incorrect adj incorrecto/ta; ~ly adv incorrectamente.
incorrigible adj incorregible.
incorruptibility n incorruptibilidad f.
incorruptible adj incorruptible.
increase vt acrecentar, aumentar; * vi crecer; * n aumento m.
increasing adj creciente; ~ly adv cada vez más.
incredible adj increíble.
incredulity n incredulidad f.
incredulous adj incrédulo/la.
increment n incremento m.
incriminate vt incriminar.
incrust vt incrustar.
incubate vi incubar.
incubator n incubadora f.
inculcate vt inculcar.
incumbent adj obligatorio/ria; * n beneficiado/da m/f.
incur vt incurrir.
incurability n lo incurable.
incurable adj incurable.
incursion n incursión, invasión f.
indebted adj agradecido/da.

indecency n indecencia f.

indecent adj indecente; **~ly** adv indecentemente.

indecision n irresolución f.

indecisive adj indeciso/sa.

indecorous adj indecente.

indeed adv verdaderamente, de veras.

indefatigable adj incansable.

indefinite adj indefinido/da; **~ly** adv indefinidamente.

indelible adj indeleble.

indelicacy n falta de delicadeza, grosería f.

indelicate adj poco delicado/da.

indemnify vt indemnizar.

indemnity n indemnidad f.

indent vt mellar.

independence n independencia f.

independent adj independiente; **~ly** adv independientemente.

indescribable adj indescriptible.

indestructible adj indestructible.

indeterminate adj indeterminado/da.

index n índice m.

index card n ficha f.

indexed adj indexado/da.

index finger n dedo índice m.

indicate vt indicar.

indication n indicación f; indicio m.

indicative adj, n (gr) indicativo m.

indicator n indicador m.

indict vt acusar.

indictment n acusación f.

indifference n indiferencia f.

indifferent adj indiferente; **~ly** adv indiferentemente.

indigenous adj indígena.

indigent adj indigente.

indigestible adj indigerible.

indigestion n indigestión f.

indignant adj indignado/da.

indignation n indignación f.

indignity n indignidad f.

indigo n añil m.

indirect adj indirecto/ta; **~ly** adv indirectamente.

indiscreet adj indiscreto/ta; **~ly** adv indiscretamente.

indiscretion n indiscreción f.

indiscriminate adj indistinto/ta; **~ly** adv sin distinción.

indispensable adj indispensable.

indisposed adj indispuesto/ta.

indisposition n indisposición f.

indisputable adj indiscutible.

indisputably adv indisputablemente.

indistinct adj indistinto/ta, confuso/sa; **~ly** adv indistintamente.

indistinguishable adj indistinguible.

individual adj individual; **~ly** adv individualmente; * n individuo m.

individuality n individualidad f.

indivisible adv indivisible; **~bly** adv indivisiblemente.

indoctrinate vt adoctrinar.

indoctrination n adoctrinamiento m.

indolence n indolencia, pereza f.

indolent adj indolente; **~ly** adv con negligencia.

indomitable adj indomable.

indoors adv dentro.

indubitably adv indudablemente.

induce vt inducir, persuadir; causar.

inducement n aliciente m.

induction n inducción f.

indulge vt, vi conceder; ser indulgente.

indulgence n indulgencia f.

indulgent adj indulgente; **~ly** adv de modo indulgente.

industrial adj industrial.

industrialist n industrial m/f.

industrialization n industrialización f.

industrialize vt industrializar.

industrial park n polígono industrial m.

industrious adj trabajador/a.

industry n industria f.

inebriated adj embriagado/da.

inebriation n embriaguez f.

inedible adj incomestible.

ineffable adj inefable.

ineffective, ineffectual adj ineficaz; ~ly adv sin efecto.

inefficiency n ineficacia f.

inefficient adj ineficaz.

ineligible adj inelegible.

inept adj incompetente.

ineptitude n incompetencia f.

inequality n desigualdad f.

inert adj inerte, perezoso/sa.

inertia n inercia f.

inescapable adj ineludible.

inestimable adj inestimable, inapreciable.

inevitable adj inevitable.

inevitably adv inevitablemente.

inexcusable adj inexcusable.

inexhaustible adj inagotable.

inexorable adj inexorable.

inexpedient adj imprudente.

inexpensive adj económico/ca.

inexperience n inexperiencia f.

inexperienced adj inexperto/ta.

inexpert adj inexperto/ta.

inexplicable adj inexplicable.

inexpressible adj indecible.

inextricably adv indisolublemente.

infallibility n infalibilidad f.

infallible adj infalible; indefectible.

infamous adj vil, infame; ~ly adv infamemente.

infamy n infamia f.

infancy n infancia f; pequeñez f.

infant n niño/ña m/f.

infanticide n infanticidio m; infanticida m/f.

infantile adj infantil.

infantry n infantería f.

infatuated adj chiflado/da.

infatuation n infatuación f.

infect vt infectar.

infection n infección f.

infectious adj contagioso/sa; infeccioso/sa.

infer vt inferir.

inference n inferencia f.

inferior adj inferior; * n subordinado/da m/f.

inferiority n inferioridad f.

infernal adj infernal.

inferno n infierno m.

infest vt infestar.

infidel n infiel, pagano m.

infidelity n infidelidad f.

infiltrate vi infiltrarse.

infinite adj infinito/ta; ~ly adv infinitamente.

infinitive n infinitivo m.

infinity n infinito m; infinidad f.

infirm adj enfermo/ma, débil.

infirmary n enfermería f.

infirmity n fragilidad, enfermedad f.

inflame vt (vi) inflamar(se).

inflammation n inflamación f.

inflammatory adj inflamatorio/ria.

inflatable adj inflable.

inflate vt inflar, hinchar.

inflation n inflación f.

inflection n inflexión f; modulación de la voz f.

inflexibility n inflexibilidad f.

inflexible adj inflexible; yerto/ta.

inflexibly adv inflexiblemente.

inflict vt imponer.

influence n influencia f; * vt influir.

influential adj influyente.

influenza n gripe f.

influx n afluencia f.

inform vt informar.

informal *adj* informal.
informality *n* informalidad *f*.
informant *n* informante *m/f*.
information *n* información *f*; ~ **super highway** autopista de la información *f*.
infraction *n* infracción *f*.
infra-red *adj* infrarrojo/ja.
infrastructure *n* infraestructura *f*.
infrequent *adj* raro/ra; ~**ly** *adv* raramente.
infringe *vt* infringir; violar.
infringement *n* infracción *f*.
infuriate *vt* enfurecer.
infuse *vt* infundir.
infusion *n* infusión *f*.
ingenious *adj* ingenioso/sa; ~**ly** *adv* ingeniosamente.
ingenuity *n* ingeniosidad *f*.
ingenuous *adj* ingenuo/nua, sincero/ra; ~**ly** *adv* ingenuamente.
inglorious *adj* ignominioso/sa, vergonzoso/sa; ~**ly** *adv* ignominiosamente.
ingot *n* lingote *m*.
ingrained *adj* inveterado/da.
ingratiate *vi* congraciarse.
ingratitude *n* ingratitud *f*.
ingredient *n* ingrediente *m*.
inhabit *vt, vi* habitar.
inhabitable *adj* habitable.
inhabitant *n* habitante *m/f*.
inhale *vt* inhalar.
inherent *adj* inherente.
inherit *vt* heredar.
inheritance *n* herencia *f*.
inheritor *n* heredero/a *m/f*.
inhibit *vt* inhibir.
inhibited *adj* cohibido/da.
inhibition *n* inhibición *f*.
inhospitable *adj* inhospitalario/ria.
inhospitality *n* inhospitalidad *f*.
inhuman *adj* inhumano/na, cruel; ~**ly** *adv* inhumanamente.

inhumanity *n* inhumanidad, crueldad *f*.
inimical *adj* enemigo/ga.
inimitable *adj* inimitable.
iniquitous *adj* inicuo/cua, injusto/ta.
iniquity *n* iniquidad, injusticia *f*.
initial *adj* inicial; * *n* inicial *f*.
initially *adv* al principio.
initiate *vt* iniciar.
initiation *n* principio *m*; iniciación *f*.
initiative *n* iniciativa *f*.
inject *vt* inyectar.
injection *n* inyección *f*.
injudicious *adj* poco juicioso/sa.
injunction *n* entredicho *m*.
injure *vt* herir.
injury *n* daño *m*.
injury time *n* descuento *m*.
injustice *n* injusticia *f*.
ink *n* tinta *f*.
inkling *n* sospecha *f*.
inkstand *n* tintero *m*.
inlaid *adj* taraceado/da.
inland *adj* interior; * *adv* tierra adentro.
in-laws *npl* suegros *mpl*.
inlay *vt* taracear.
inlet *n* ensenada *f*.
inmate *n* preso *m*.
inmost *adj* más íntimo/ma.
inn *n* posada *f*; mesón *m*.
innate *adj* innato/ta.
inner *adj* interior.
innermost *adj* más íntimo/ma.
inner tube *n* cámara *f*.
innkeeper *n* posadero/ra, mesonero/ra *m/f*.
innocence *n* inocencia *f*.
innocent *adj* inocente; ~**ly** *adv* inocentemente.
innocuous *adj* inocuo/cua; ~**ly** *adv* inocentemente.

innovate *vt* innovar.
innovation *n* innovación *f*.
innuendo *n* indirecta, insinuación *f*.
innumerable *adj* innumerable.
inoculate *vt* inocular.
inoculation *n* inoculación *f*.
inoffensive *adj* inofensivo/va.
inopportune *adj* inconveniente, inoportuno/na.
inordinately *adv* desmesuradamente.
inorganic *adj* inorgánico/ca.
inpatient *n* paciente interno/na *m/f*.
input *n* entrada *f*.
inquest *n* encuesta judicial *f*.
inquire *vt*, *vi* preguntar; **to ~ about** informarse de; **to ~ after** *vt* preguntar por; **to ~ into** *vt* investigar, indagar, inquirir.
inquiry *n* pesquisa *f*.
inquisition *n* inquisición *f*.
inquisitive *adj* curioso/sa.
inroad *n* incursión, invasión *f*.
insane *adj* loco/ca, demente.
insanity *n* locura *f*.
insatiable *adj* insaciable.
inscribe *vt* inscribir; dedicar.
inscription *n* inscripción *f*; dedicatoria *f*.
inscrutable *adj* inescrutable.
insect *n* insecto *m*.
insecticide *n* insecticida *m*.
insecure *adj* inseguro/ra.
insecurity *n* inseguridad *f*.
insemination *n* inseminación *f*.
insensible *adj* inconsciente.
insensitive *adj* insensible.
inseparable *adj* inseparable.
insert *vt* introducir.
insertion *n* inserción *f*.
inshore *adj* costero/ra.
inside *n* interior *m*; * *adv* dentro.
inside out *adv* al revés; a fondo.

insidious *adj* insidioso/sa; **~ly** *adv* insidiosamente.
insight *n* perspicacia *f*.
insignia *npl* insignias *fpl*.
insignificant *adj* insignificante, frívolo/la.
insincere *adj* poco sincero/ra.
insincerity *n* falta de sinceridad *f*.
insinuate *vt* insinuar.
insinuation *n* insinuación *f*.
insipid *adj* insípido/da; insulso/sa; ñoño/ña.
insipidness *n* ñoñería *f*.
insist *vi* insistir.
insistence *n* insistencia *f*.
insistent *adj* insistente.
insole *n* plantilla *f*.
insolence *n* insolencia *f*.
insolent *adj* insolente; **~ly** *adv* insolentemente.
insoluble *adj* insoluble.
insolvency *n* insolvencia *f*.
insolvent *adj* insolvente.
insomnia *n* insomnio *m*.
insomuch *conj* puesto que.
inspect *vt* examinar, inspeccionar.
inspection *n* inspección *f*.
inspector *n* inspector, superintendente *m*.
inspiration *n* inspiración *f*.
inspire *vt* inspirar.
instability *n* inestabilidad *f*.
install, instal *vt* instalar.
installation *n* instalación *f*.
instalment *n* instalación *f*; plazo *m*.
instance *n* ejemplo *m*; **for ~** por ejemplo.
instant *adj* inmediato/ta; **~ly** *adv* en seguida; * *n* instante, momento *m*.
instantaneous *adj* instantáneo/nea; **~ly** *adv* instantáneamente.
instead (of) *prep* por, en lugar de, en vez de.

instep *n* empeine *m*.
instigate *vt* instigar.
instigation *n* instigación *f*.
instil *vt* inculcar.
instinct *n* instinto *m*.
instinctive *adj* instintivo/va; ~**ly** *adv* por instinto.
institute *vt* establecer; * *n* instituto *m*.
institution *n* institución *f*.
instruct *vt* instruir, enseñar; illustrar.
instruction *n* instrucción *f*.
instructive *adj* instructivo/va.
instructor *n* instructor/a *m/f*.
instrument *n* instrumento *m*.
instrumental *adj* instrumental.
insubordinate *adj* insubordinado/da.
insubordination *n* insubordinación *f*.
insufferable *adj* insoportable.
insufferably *adv* de modo insoportable.
insufficiency *n* insuficiencia *f*.
insufficient *adj* insuficiente; ~**ly** *adv* insuficientemente.
insular *adj* insular.
insulate *vt* aislar.
insulating tape *n* cinta aislante *f*.
insulation *n* aislamiento *m*.
insulin *n* insulina *f*.
insult *vt* insultar; * *n* insulto *m*.
insulting *adj* insultante.
insuperable *adj* insuperable.
insurance *n* (*com*) seguro *m*.
insurance policy *n* póliza de seguros *f*.
insure *vt* asegurar.
insurgent *n* insurgente, rebelde *m*.
insurmountable *adj* insuperable.
insurrection *n* insurrección *f*.
intact *adj* intacto/ta.
intake *n* admisión *f*; entrada *f*.
integral *adj* íntegro/gra; (*chem*) integrante; * *n* todo *m*.

integrate *vt* integrar.
integration *n* integración *f*.
integrity *n* integridad *f*.
intellect *n* intelecto *m*.
intellectual *adj* intelectual.
intelligence *n* inteligencia *f*.
intelligent *adj* inteligente.
intelligentsia *n* intelectualidad *f*.
intelligible *adj* inteligible.
intelligibly *adv* inteligiblemente.
intemperate *adj* inmoderado/da; ~**ly** *adv* inmoderadamente.
intend *vi* tener intención de.
intendant *n* intendente *m*.
intended *adj* deseado/da.
intense *adj* intenso/sa, hondo/da; ~**ly** *adv* intensamente.
intensify *vt* intensificar.
intensity *n* intensidad *f*.
intensive *adj* intensivo/va.
intensive care unit *n* unidad de vigilancia intensiva, unidad de cuidados intensivos *f*.
intent *adj* atento/ta, cuidadoso/sa; ~**ly** *adv* con aplicación; * *n* designio *m*.
intention *n* intención *f*; designio *m*.
intentional *adj* intencional; ~**ly** *adv* a propósito.
inter *vt* enterrar.
interaction *n* interacción *f*.
intercede *vi* interceder.
intercept *vt* interceptar.
intercession *n* intercesión, mediación *f*.
interchange *n* intercambio *m*.
intercom *n* interfono *m*.
intercourse *n* coito *m*.
interest *vt* interesar; * *n* interés *m*.
interesting *adj* interesante.
interest rate *n* tipo de interés *m*.
interface *n* interfaz, interface *f*.
interfere *vi* entrometerse.

interference *n* interferencia *f*.
interim *adj* provisional.
interior *adj* interior.
interior design *n* interiorismo *m*.
interior designer *n* interiorista *m/f*.
interjection *n* (*gr*) interjección *f*.
interlock *vi* endentarse.
interlocutor *n* interlocutor/a *m/f*.
interloper *n* intruso/sa *m/f*.
interlude *n* intermedio *m*.
intermarriage *n* matrimonio mixto *m*.
intermediary *n* intermediario/ria *m/f*.
intermediate *adj* intermedio/dia.
interment *n* entierro *m*; sepultura *f*.
interminable *adj* inacabable.
intermingle *vt, vi* entremezclar; mezclarse.
intermission *n* descanso *m*.
intermittent *adj* intermitente.
intern *n* interno *m*.
internal *adj* interno/na; **~ly** *adv* internamente.
international *adj* internacional.
Internet café *n* cibercafé *m*.
interplay *n* interacción *f*.
interpose *vt* interponer.
interpret *vt* interpretar.
interpretation *n* interpretación *f*.
interpreter *n* intérprete *m/f*.
interracial *adj* interracial.
interregnum *n* interregno *m*.
interrelated *adj* interrelacionado/da.
interrogate *vt* interrogar.
interrogation *n* interrogatorio *m*.
interrogative *adj* interrogativo/va.
interrupt *vt* interrumpir.
interruption *n* interrupción *f*.
intersect *vi* cruzarse.
intersection *n* cruce *m*.
intersperse *vt* esparcir.
intertwine *vt* entretejer.
interval *n* intervalo *m*.
intervene *vi* intervenir; ocurrir.

intervention *n* intervención *f*.
interview *n* entrevista *f*; * *vt* entrevistar.
interviewer *n* entrevistador/a *m/f*.
interweave *vt* entretejer.
intestate *adj* intestado/da.
intestinal *adj* intestinal.
intestine *n* intestino *m*.
intimacy *n* intimidad *f*.
intimate *n* amigo/ga íntimo/ma *m/f*;
* *adj* íntimo/ma; **~ly** *adv* íntimamente; * *vt* insinuar, dar a entender.
intimidate *vt* intimidar.
into *prep* en, dentro, adentro.
intolerable *adj* intolerable.
intolerably *adv* intolerablemente.
intolerance *n* intolerancia *f*.
intolerant *adj* intolerante.
intonation *n* entonación *f*.
intoxicate *vt* embriagar.
intoxication *n* embriaguez *f*.
intractable *adj* intratable.
intransitive *adj* (*gr*) intransitivo/va.
intravenous *adj* intravenoso/sa.
in-tray *n* bandeja de entrada *f*.
intrepid *adj* intrépido/da; **~ly** *adv* intrépidamente.
intrepidity *n* intrepidez *f*.
intricacy *n* complejidad *f*.
intricate *adj* intrincado/da, complicado/da; **~ly** *adv* intrincadamente.
intrigue *n* intriga *f*; * *vi* intrigar.
intriguing *adj* fascinante.
intrinsic *adj* intrínseco/ca; **~ally** *adv* intrínsecamente.
introduce *vt* introducir.
introduction *n* introducción *f*.
introductory *adj* introductorio/ria.
introspection *n* introspección *f*.
introvert *n* introvertido/da *m/f*.
intrude *vi* entrometerse.
intruder *n* intruso/sa *m/f*.
intrusion *n* invasión *f*.

intuition n intuición f.
intuitive adj intuitivo/va.
inundate vt inundar.
inundation n inundación f.
inure vt acostumbrar, habituar.
invade vt invadir.
invader n invasor/a m/f.
invalid adj inválido/da, nulo/la; * n minusválido m.
invalidate vt invalidar, anular.
invaluable adj inapreciable.
invariable adj invariable.
invariably adv invariablemente.
invasion n invasión f.
invective n invectiva f.
inveigle vt seducir, persuadir.
invent vt inventar.
invention n invento m.
inventive adj inventivo/va.
inventor n inventor m.
inventory n inventario m.
inverse adj inverso/sa.
inversion n inversión f.
invert vt invertir.
invest vt invertir.
investigate vt investigar.
investigation n investigación, pesquisa f.
investigator n investigador/a m/f.
investment n inversión f.
inveterate adj inveterado/da.
invidious adj odioso/sa.
invigilate vt vigilar.
invigorating adj vigorizante.
invincible adj invencible.
invincibly adv invenciblemente.
inviolable adj inviolable.
invisible adj invisible.
invisibly adv invisiblemente.
invitation n invitación f.
invite vt invitar.
inviting adj atractivo/va.
invoice n (com) factura f.

invoke vt invocar.
involuntarily adv involuntariamente.
involuntary adj involuntario/ria.
involve vt implicar.
involved adj complicado/da.
involvement n compromiso m.
invulnerable adj invulnerable.
inward adj interior; interno/na; ~, ~s adv hacia dentro.
iodine n (chem) yodo m.
IOU (I owe you) n pagaré m.
irascible adj irascible.
irate, ireful adj enojado/da.
iris n iris m.
irksome adj fastidioso/sa.
iron n hierro m, plancha f; * adj férreo/rea; * vt planchar.
ironic adj irónico/ca; ~ly adv con ironía.
ironing n planchado m.
ironing board n tabla de planchar f.
iron ore n mineral de hierro m.
ironwork n herraje m; ~s pl herrería f.
irony n ironía f.
irradiate vt irradiar.
irrational adj irracional.
irreconcilable adj irreconciliable.
irregular adj, ~ly adv irregular(mente).
irregularity n irregularidad f.
irrelevant adj impertinente.
irreligious adj irreligioso/sa.
irreparable adj irreparable.
irreplaceable adj irreemplazable.
irrepressible adj incontenible.
irreproachable adj irreprensible.
irresistible adj irresistible.
irresolute adj irresoluto/ta; ~ly adv irresolutamente.
irresponsible adj irresponsable.
irretrievably adv irreparablemente.
irreverence n irreverencia f.

irreverent *adj* irreverente; **~ly** *adv* irreverentemente.
irrigate *vt* regar.
irrigation *n* riego *m*.
irritability *n* irritabilidad *f*.
irritable *adj* irritable.
irritant *n* (*med*) irritante *m*.
irritate *vt* irritar.
irritating *adj* fastidioso/sa.
irritation *n* fastidio *m*; picazón *f*.
Islam *n* islam *m*.
Islamic *adj* islámico/ca.
island *n* isla *f*.
islander *n* isleño/ña *m/f*.
isle *n* isla *f*.
isolate *vt* aislar.

isolation *n* aislamiento *m*.
issue *n* asunto *m*; * *vt* expedir; publicar; repartir.
isthmus *n* istmo *m*.
it *pn* él, ella, ello, lo, la, le.
italic *n* cursiva *f*.
itch *n* picazón *f*; * *vi* picar.
item *n* artículo *m*.
itemize *vt* detallar.
itinerant *n* ambulante, errante *m*.
itinerary *n* itinerario *m*.
its *pn* su, suyo.
itself *pn* se, por sí mismo.
ivory *n* marfil *m*.
ivy *n* hiedra *f*; yedra *f*.

J

jab *vt* clavar.
jabber *vi* farfullar.
jack *n* gato *m*; sota *f*.
jackal *n* chacal *m*.
jackboots *npl* botas militares *fpl*.
jackdaw *n* grajo *m*.
jacket *n* chaqueta; funda *f*.
jack-knife *vi* colear.
jackpot *n* premio gordo *m*.
jacuzzi *n* jacuzzi *m*.
jade *n* jade *m*.
jagged *adj* dentado/da.
jaguar *n* jaguar *m*.
jail, gaol *n* cárcel *f*.
jailbird *n* preso/sa *m/f*.
jailer *n* carcelero/ra *m/f*.
jam *n* conserva *f*; mermelada de frutas *f*; (*auto*) embotellamiento *m*.
jangle *vi* sonar.
January *n* enero *m*.
jar *vi* chocar; (*mus*) discordar; reñir; * *n* jarra *f*.
jargon *n* jerigonza *f*.

jasmine *n* jazmín *m*.
jaundice *n* ictericia *f*.
jaunt *n* excursión *f*.
jaunty *adj* alegre.
javelin *n* jabalina *f*.
jaw *n* mandíbula *f*.
jay *n* arrendajo *m*.
jazz *n* jazz *m*.
jealous *adj* celoso/sa; envidioso/sa.
jealousy *n* celos *mpl*; envidia *f*.
jeans *npl* vaqueros *mpl*.
Jeep® *n* jeep *m*.
jeer *vi* befar, mofar; * *n* burla *f*.
jelly *n* jalea, gelatina *f*.
jellyfish *n* medusa *f*, aguamar *m*.
jeopardize *vt* arriesgar, poner en riesgo.
jerk *n* sacudida *f*; * *vt* tirar.
jerky *adj* espasmódico/ca.
jersey *n* jersey *m*.
jest *n* broma *f*.
jester *n* bufón/ona *m/f*.
jestingly *adv* de burlas.

Jesuit n jesuita m.
Jesus n Jesús m.
jet n avión a reacción m; azabache m.
jet engine n motor a reacción m, reactor m.
jettison vt desechar.
jetty n muelle m.
Jew n judío/día m/f.
jewel n joya f.
jeweller n joyero/ra m/f.
jeweller's shop n joyería f.
jewellery n joyería f.
Jewish adj judío/día.
jib n (mar) foque m.
jibe n mofa f.
jig n giga f.
jigsaw n rompecabezas m invar.
jilt vt dejar.
jinx n gafe m.
job n trabajo m.
jockey n jinete m/f.
jocular adj jocoso/sa, alegre.
jocularity n jocosidad f.
jog vi hacer footing.
jogging n footing m.
join vt juntar, unir; (fig) zurcir; **to ~ in** participar en; * vi unirse, juntarse.
joiner n carpintero/ra m/f.
joinery n carpintería f.
joint n articulación f; * adj común.
jointly adv conjuntamente.
joint-stock company n (com) sociedad por acciones f.
joke n broma f; * vi bromear.
joker n comodín m.
jollity n alegría f.
jolly adj alegre.
jolt vt sacudir; * n sacudida f.
jostle vt codear.
journal n revista f.
journalism n periodismo m.
journalist n periodista m/f.
journey n viaje m; * vt viajar.

jovial adj jovial, alegre; **~ly** adv con jovialidad.
joy n alegría f; júbilo m.
joyful, joyous adj alegre, gozoso/sa; **~ly** adv alegremente.
joystick n palanca de control f, joystick m.
jubilant adj jubiloso/sa.
jubilation n júbilo/la, regocijo m.
jubilee n jubileo m.
Judaism n judaísmo m.
judge n juez/a m/f; * vt juzgar.
judgement n juicio m.
judicial adj, **~ly** adv judicial(mente).
judiciary n poder judicial m, judicatura f.
judicious adj prudente.
judo n judo m.
jug n jarro m.
juggle vi hacer juegos malabares.
juggler n malabarista m/f.
jugular adj yugular.
juice n zumo, jugo m.
juicy adj jugoso/sa.
jukebox n gramola f.
July n julio m.
jumble vt mezclar; * n revoltijo m.
jump vi saltar, brincar; * n salto m.
jumper n suéter, jersey m.
jumpy adj nervioso/sa.
juncture n coyuntura f.
June n junio m.
jungle n selva f.
junior adj más joven.
juniper n (bot) enebro m.
junk n basura f; baratijas fpl.
junk food n comida basura f.
junta n junta f.
jurisdiction n jurisdicción f.
jurisprudence n jurisprudencia f.
jurist n jurista m/f.
juror, juryman n jurado/da m/f.
jury n jurado m.

just *adj* justo/ta; * *adv* justamente, exactamente; ~ **as** como; ~ **now** ahora mismo.
justice *n* justicia *f*.
justifiably *adv* con justificación.
justification *n* justificación *f*.
justify *vt* justificar.

justly *adv* justamente.
justness *n* justicia *f*.
jut *vi*; **to ~ out** sobresalir.
jute *n* yute *m*.
juvenile *adj* juvenil.
juxtapose *vt* yuxtaponer.
juxtaposition *n* yuxtaposición *f*.

K

kaleidoscope *n* caleidoscopio *m*.
kangaroo *n* canguro *m*.
karaoke *n* karaoke *m*.
karate *n* kárate *m*.
kebab *n* pincho *m* moruno.
keel *n* (*mar*) quilla *f*.
keen *adj* agudo/da; vivo/va.
keenness *n* entusiasmo *m*.
keep *vt* mantener; guardar; conservar.
keeper *n* guardián/ana *m/f*.
keepsake *n* recuerdo *m*.
keg *n* barril *m*.
kennel *n* perrera *f*.
kernel *n* fruta *f*; meollo *m*.
ketchup *n* catsup, ketchup *m*.
kettle *n* hervidor *m*.
kettle-drum *n* timbal *m*.
key *n* llave *f*; (*mus*) clave *f*; tecla *f*.
keyboard *n* teclado *m*.
keyhole *n* ojo de la cerradura *m*.
keynote *n* (*mus*) tónica *f*.
key ring *n* llavero *m*.
keystone *n* piedra clave *f*.
khaki *n* caqui *m*.
kick *vt, vi* patear; * *n* puntapié *m*; patada *f*.
kid *n* chico/ca *m/f*.
kidnap *vt* secuestrar.
kidnapper *n* secuestrador/a *m/f*.
kidnapping *n* secuestro *m*; rapto *m*.
kidney *n* riñón *m*.
killer *n* asesino/na *m/f*.

killing *n* asesinato *m*.
kiln *n* horno *m*.
kilo *n* kilo *m*.
kilobyte *n* kilobyte *m*.
kilogram *n* kilo *m*.
kilometre *n* kilómetro *m*.
kilt *n* falda escocesa *f*.
kin *n* parientes *mpl*; **next of ~** pariente próximo *m*, pariente próxima *f*.
kind *adj* cariñoso/sa; * *n* género *m*.
kindergarten *n* jardín de infancia *m*.
kind-hearted *adj* bondadoso/sa.
kindle *vt, vi* encender.
kindliness *n* benevolencia *f*.
kindly *adj* bondadoso/sa.
kindness *n* bondad *f*.
kindred *adj* emparentado/da.
kinetic *adj* cinético/ca.
king *n* rey *m*.
kingdom *n* reino *m*.
kingfisher *n* martín pescador *m*.
king prawn *n* langostino *m*.
kiosk *n* quiosco *m*.
kiss *n* beso *m*; * *vt* besar.
kissing *n* besos *mpl*.
kit *n* equipo *m*.
kitchen *n* cocina *f*.
kitchen garden *n* huerta *f*.
kitchen maid *n* fregona *f*.
kite *n* cometa *f*.
kitten *n* gatito *m*.
knack *n* don *m*.

knapsack n mochila f.
knave n bribón, pícaro m; (cards) sota f.
knead vt amasar.
knee n rodilla f.
knee-deep adj metido hasta las rodillas.
kneel vi arrodillarse.
knell n toque de difuntos m.
knife n cuchillo m.
knight n caballero m.
knit vt, vi tejer, tricotear; **to ~ the brows** fruncir el ceño.
knitter n calcetero/ra, mediero/ra m/f.
knitting needle n aguja de tejer f.
knitwear n prendas de punto fpl.
knob n bulto m; nudo en la madera m; botón de las flores m.

knock vt, vi golpear, tocar; **to ~ down** derribar; * n golpe m.
knocker n aldaba f.
knock-kneed adj patizambo/ba; zambo/ba.
knock-out n K.O. m.
knoll n cima de una colina f.
knot n nudo m; lazo m; * vt anudar.
knotty adj escabroso/sa.
know vt, vi conocer; saber.
know-all n sabelotodo m/f.
know-how n conocimientos mpl.
knowing adj entendido/da; **~ly** adv a sabiendas.
knowledge n conocimiento m.
knowledgeable adj bien informado/da.
knuckle n nudillo m.

L

laboratory n laboratorio m.
laborious adj laborioso/sa; difícil; **~ly** adv laboriosamente.
labour n trabajo m; **to be in ~** estar de parto; * vt trabajar.
labourer n peón m.
labyrinth n laberinto m.
lace n cordón; encaje m; * vt abrochar.
lacerate vt lacerar.
lack vt, vi faltar; * n falta f.
lackadaisical adj descuidado/da.
lackey n lacayo m.
laconic adj lacónico/ca.
lacquer n laca f.
lad n muchacho m.
ladder n escalera f.
ladle n cucharón m.
ladleful n cucharada f.
lady n señora f.

ladybird n mariquita f.
lady-killer n casanova m.
ladylike adj fino/na.
ladyship n señoría f.
lag vi quedarse atrás.
lager n cerveza (rubia) f.
lagoon n laguna f.
laid-back adj relajado/da.
lair n guarida f.
laity n laicado m.
lake n lago m; laguna f.
lamb n cordero m; * vi parir.
lame adj cojo/ja.
lament vt (vi) lamentar(se); * n lamento m.
lamentable adj lamentable, deplorable.
lamentation n lamentación f.
laminated adj laminado/da; plastificado/da.

lamp *n* lámpara *f*.
lampoon *n* sátira *f*.
lampshade *n* pantalla *f*.
lance *n* lanza *f*; * *vt* abrir con lanceta.
lancet *n* lanceta *f*.
land *n* país *m*; tierra *f*; * *vt*, *vi* desembarcar.
land forces *npl* tropas de tierra *fpl*.
land-holder *n* hacendado *m*.
landing *n* desembarco *m*.
landing strip *n* pista de aterrizaje *f*.
landlady *n* propietaria *f*.
landlord *n* propietario *m*.
landlubber *n* marinero de agua dulce *m*.
landmark *n* lugar conocido; hito *m*.
landowner *n* terrateniente *m/f*.
landscape *n* paisaje *m*.
landslide *n* corrimiento de tierras *m*.
lane *n* callejuela *f*.
langoustine *n* langostino *m*.
language *n* lengua *f*; lenguaje *m*.
languid *adj* lánguido/da, débil; ~**ly** *adv* lánguidamente, débilmente.
languish *vi* languidecer.
lank *adj* lacio/cia.
lanky *adj* larguirucho/cha.
lantern *n* linterna *f*; farol *m*.
lap *n* regazo *m*; * *vt* lamer.
lapdog *n* perro faldero *m*.
lapel *n* solapa *f*.
lapse *n* lapso *m*; * *vi* transcurrir.
laptop *n* portátil *m*.
larceny *n* latrocinio *m*.
larch *n* alerce *m*.
lard *n* manteca de cerdo *f*.
larder *n* despensa *f*.
large *adj* grande; **at ~** en libertad; ~**ly** *adv* en gran parte.
large-scale *adj* en gran escala.
largesse *n* liberalidad *f*.
lark *n* alondra *f*.

larva *n* larva, oruga *f*.
laryngitis *n* laringitis *f*.
larynx *n* laringe *f*.
lascivious *adj* lascivo/va; ~**ly** *adv* lascivamente.
laser *n* láser *m*.
laser printer *n* impresora láser *f*.
lash *n* latigazo *m*; * *vt* dar latigazos; atar.
lasso *n* lazo *m*.
last *adj* último/ma; pasado/da; **at ~** por fin; ~**ly** *adv* finalmente; * *n* horma de zapatero *f*; * *vi* durar.
last-ditch *adj* último/ma.
lasting *adj* duradero/ra, permanente; ~**ly** *adv* perpetuamente.
last-minute *adj* de última hora.
latch *n* picaporte *m*.
latch-key *n* llave maestra *f*.
late *adj* tarde; difunto/ta; (*rail*) **the train is ten minutes ~** el tren tiene un retraso de diez minutos; * *adv* tarde; ~**ly** *adv* recientemente.
latecomer *n* recién llegado/da *m/f*.
latent *adj* latente.
lateral *adj*, ~**ly** *adv* lateral(mente).
lathe *n* torno *m*.
lather *n* espuma *f*.
latitude *n* latitud *f*.
latrine *n* letrina *f*.
latter *adj* último/ma; ~**ly** *adv* últimamente, recientemente.
lattice *n* celosía *f*.
laudable *adj* loable.
laudably *adv* loablemente.
laugh *vi* reír; **to ~ at** *vt* reírse de; * *n* risa *f*.
laughable *adj* absurdo/da.
laughing stock *n* hazmerreír *m*.
laughter *n* risa *f*.
launch *vt* (*vi*) lanzar(se); * *n* (*mar*) lancha *f*.
launching *n* lanzamiento *m*.

launching pad n plataforma de lanzamiento f.

launder vt lavar.

Launderette™ n lavandería automática f.

laundry n lavandería f.

laurel n laurel m.

lava n lava f.

lavatory n cuarto de baño m.

lavender n (bot) espliego m, lavanda f.

lavish adj pródigo/ga; ~ly adv pródigamente; * vt disipar.

law n ley f; derecho m.

law-abiding adj respetuoso/sa con la ley.

law and order n orden público m.

law court n tribunal m.

lawful adj legal; legítimo/ma; ~ly adv legalmente.

lawless adj anárquico/ca.

lawlessness n anarquía f.

lawmaker, lawgiver n legislador/a m/f.

lawn n pasto m.

lawnmower n cortacésped m.

law school n facultad de derecho f.

lawsuit n proceso m.

lawyer n abogado/da m/f.

lax adj laxo/xa; flojo/ja.

laxative n laxante m.

laxity n laxitud f; flojedad f.

lay vt poner; **to ~ claim** reclamar; pretender; **to ~ into** (fam) zurrar; * vi poner.

layabout n vago/ga m/f.

layer n capa f.

layette n ajuar de niño m.

layman n lego, seglar m.

layout n composición f.

laze vi holgazanear.

lazily adv perezosamente; lentamente.

laziness n pereza f.

lazy adj perezoso/sa.

lead1 n plomo m.

lead2 vt conducir, guiar; * vi mandar.

leader n jefe/fa m/f.

leadership n dirección f; liderazgo m.

leading adj principal; capital; ~ **article** n artículo principal m.

leaf n hoja f, yema f.

leaflet n folleto m.

leafy adj frondoso/sa.

league n liga, alianza f; legua f.

leak n escape m; * vi (mar) hacer agua.

leaky adj agujereado/da.

lean vt (vi) apoyar(se); * adj magro/ra.

leap vi saltar; * n salto m.

leapfrog n pídola f.

leap year n año bisiesto m.

learn vt, vi aprender.

learned adj docto/ta.

learner n aprendiz m.

learning n erudición f.

lease n arriendo m; * vt arrendar.

leasehold n arriendo m.

leash n correa f.

least adj mínimo/ma; **at ~** por lo menos; **not in the ~** en absoluto.

leather n cuero m.

leathery adj correoso/sa.

leave n licencia f; permiso m; **to take ~** despedirse; * vt dejar, abandonar.

leaven n levadura f; * vt fermentar.

leavings npl sobras fpl.

lecherous adj lascivo/va.

lecture n conferencia f; * vt dar una conferencia.

lecturer n conferenciante m/f; profesor/ra m/f.

ledge n reborde m.

ledger n (com) libro mayor m.

lee n (mar) sotavento m.

leech *n* sanguijuela *f*.
leek *n* (*bot*) puerro *m*.
leer *vt* mirar de manera lasciva.
lees *npl* sedimento, poso *m*.
leeward *adj* (*mar*) sotavento.
leeway *n* libertad de acción *f*.
left *adj* izquierdo/da; zurdo/da; **on the ~** a la izquierda.
left-handed *adj* zurdo/da.
left luggage office *n* consigna *f*.
leftovers *npl* sobras *fpl*.
leg *n* pierna *f*; pie *m*.
legacy *n* herencia *f*.
legal *adj* legal, legítimo/ma; **~ly** *adv* legalmente.
legal holiday *n* fiesta oficial *f*.
legality *n* legalidad, legitimidad *f*.
legalize *vt* legalizar.
legal tender *n* moneda de curso legal *f*.
legate *n* legado *m*.
legatee *n* legado *m*.
legation *n* legación *f*.
legend *n* leyenda *f*.
legendary *adj* legendario/ria.
legible *adj* legible.
legibly *adv* legiblemente.
legion *n* legión *f*.
legislate *vt* legislar.
legislation *n* legislación *f*.
legislative *adj* legislativo/va.
legislator *n* legislador/a *m/f*.
legislature *n* cuerpo legislativo *m*.
legitimacy *n* legitimidad *f*.
legitimate *adj* legítimo/ma; **~ly** *adv* legítimamente; * *vt* legitimar.
leisure *n* ocio *m*; **~ly** *adj* sin prisa; **at ~** desocupado/da.
lemon *n* limón *m*.
lemonade *n* limonada *f*.
lemon tea *n* te con limón *m*.
lemon tree *n* limonero *m*.
lend *vt* prestar.

length *n* largo *m*; duración *f*; **at ~** finalmente.
lengthen *vt* alargar; * *vi* alargarse.
lengthways, lengthwise *adv* a lo largo.
lengthy *adj* largo/ga.
lenient *adj* indulgente.
lens *n* lente *f*.
Lent *n* Cuaresma *f*.
lentil *n* lenteja *f*.
leopard *n* leopardo *m*; mallas *fpl*.
leotard *n* leotardo *m*.
leper *n* leproso/sa *m/f*.
leprosy *n* lepra *f*.
lesbian *n* lesbiana *f*.
less *adj* menor; * *adv* menos.
lessen *vt* disminuir; * *vi* disminuirse.
lesser *adj* más pequeño/ña.
lesson *n* lección *f*.
lest *conj* para que no.
let *vt* dejar, permitir; alquilar.
lethal *adj* mortal.
lethargic *adj* letárgico/ca.
lethargy *n* letargo *m*.
letter *n* letra *f*; carta *f*.
letter bomb *n* carta bomba *f*.
letter box, postbox *n* buzón *m*.
lettering *n* letras *fpl*.
letter of credit *n* carta de crédito *f*.
lettuce *n* lechuga *f*.
leukaemia *n* leucemia *f*.
level *adj* llano/na, igual; nivelado/da; * *n* nivel *m*; * *vt* allanar; nivelar.
level crossing *n* paso a nivel *m*.
level-headed *adj* sensato/ta.
lever *n* palanca *f*.
leverage *n* influencia *f*.
levity *n* ligereza *f*.
levy *n* leva (de tropas) *f*; * *vt* recaudar.
lewd *adj* obsceno/na.
lexicon *n* lexicón *m*.

liability n responsabilidad f.
liable adj sujeto/ta; responsable.
liaise vi enlazar.
liaison n enlace m.
liar n embustero m.
libel n difamación f; * vt difamar.
libellous adj difamatorio/ria.
liberal adj liberal, generoso/sa; ~ly adv liberalmente.
liberality n liberalidad, generosidad f.
liberate vt libertar.
liberation n liberación f.
libertine n libertino m.
liberty n libertad f.
Libra n Libra f.
librarian n bibliotecario/ria m/f.
library n biblioteca f.
libretto n libreto m.
licence n licencia f; permiso m.
license vt autorizar, licenciar.
licentious adj licencioso/sa.
lichen n (bot) liquen m.
lick vt lamer.
lid n tapa f.
lie n mentira f; * vi mentir; echarse.
lie down vi yacer.
lieu n: in ~ of en vez de.
lieutenant n lugarteniente m/f; teniente m/f.
life n vida f; for ~ para toda la vida.
lifeboat n lancha de socorro f; bote salvavidas m.
lifeguard n socorrista m/ff.
life jacket n chaleco salvavidas m.
lifeless adj muerto/ta; sin vida.
lifelike adj natural.
lifeline n cordón umbilical m.
life sentence n cadena perpetua f.
life-sized adj de tamaño natural.
life span n vida f.
lifestyle n estilo de vida f.
life-support system n sistema de respiración asistida m.

lifetime n vida f.
lift vt levantar.
ligament n ligamento m.
light n luz f; * adj ligero/ra; claro/ra; * vt encender; alumbrar.
light bulb n foco m; bombilla f.
lighten vi relampaguear; * vt iluminar; aligerar; (ship) zafar.
lighter n encendedor m.
light-headed adj mareado/da.
light-hearted adj alegre.
lighthouse n (mar) faro m.
lighting n iluminación f.
lightly adv ligeramente.
lightning n relámpago m.
lightning-rod n pararrayos m invar.
light pen n lápiz óptico m.
lightweight adj ligero/ra.
light year n año luz m.
ligneous adj leñoso/sa.
like adj semejante; igual; * adv como, del mismo modo que; * vt, vi gustar.
likeable adj simpático/ca.
likelihood n probabilidad f.
likely adj probable, verosímil.
liken vt comparar.
likeness n semejanza f.
likewise adv igualmente.
liking n agrado m.
lilac n lila f.
lily n lirio m; ~ of the valley lirio de los valles.
limb n miembro m.
limber adj flexible.
lime n cal f; lima f; ~ tree tilo m.
limestone n piedra caliza f.
limit n límite, término m; * vt restringir.
limitation n limitación f; restricción f.
limitless adj inmenso/sa.
limousine n limusina f.

limp *vi* cojear; * *n* cojera *f*; * *adj* flojo/ja.

limpet *n* lapa *f*.

limpid *adj* claro/ra, transparente.

line *n* línea *f*; raya *f*; * *vt* forrar; revestir.

lineage *n* linaje *m*; filiación *f*.

linear *adj* lineal.

lined *adj* rayado/da; arrugado/da.

linen *n* lino *m*.

liner *n* transatlántico *m*.

linesman *n* juez de línea *m*.

linger *vi* persistir.

lingerie *n* ropa interior *f*.

lingering *adj* lento/ta.

linguist *n* lingüista *m/f*.

linguistic *adj* lingüístico/ca.

linguistics *n* lingüística *f*.

liniment *n* linimento *m*.

lining *n* forro *m*.

link *n* eslabón *m*; * *vt* enlazar.

linnet *n* pardillo *m*.

linoleum *n* linóleo *m*.

linseed *n* linaza *f*.

lint *n* hilas *fpl*.

lintel *n* dintel, tranquero *m*.

lion *n* león *m*.

lioness *n* leona *f*.

lip *n* labio *m*; borde *m*.

liposuction *n* liposucción *f*.

lip read *vi* leer los labios.

lipstick *n* lápiz de labios *m*.

liqueur *n* licor *m*.

liquid *adj* líquido/da; * *n* líquido *m*.

liquidate *vt* liquidar.

liquidation *n* liquidación *f*.

liquidize *vt* licuar.

liquor *n* licor *m*.

liquorice *n* regaliz *m*.

lisp *vi* cecear; * *n* ceceo *m*.

list *n* lista *f*; * *vt* hacer una lista de.

listen *vi* escuchar.

listless *adj* indiferente.

litany *n* letanía *f*.

literal *adj*, **~ly** *adv* literal(mente).

literary *adj* literario/ria.

literate *adj* culto/ta.

literature *n* literatura *f*.

lithe *adj* ágil.

lithograph *n* litografía *f*.

lithography *n* litografía *f*.

litigation *n* litigio *m*.

litigious *adj* litigioso/sa.

litre *n* litro *m*.

litter *n* litera *f*; camada *f*; * *vt* parir.

little *adj* pequeño/ña, poco/ca; **~ by ~** poco a poco; * *n* poco *m*.

liturgy *n* liturgia *f*.

live *vi* vivir; habitar; **to ~ on** alimentarse de; **to ~ up to** *vt* cumplir con; * *adj* vivo/va.

livelihood *n* vida *f*.

liveliness *n* vivacidad *f*; belleza *f*.

lively *adj* vivo/va.

liven up *vt* animar.

liver *n* hígado *m*.

livery *n* librea *f*.

livestock *n* ganado *m*.

livid *adj* lívido/da, cárdeno/na.

living *n* vida *f*; * *adj* vivo/va.

living room *n* sala de estar *f*.

lizard *n* lagarto *m*.

load *vt* cargar; * *n* carga *f*.

loaded *adj* cargado/da.

loaf *n* pan *m*.

loafer *n* holgazán, gandul *m*.

loam *n* marga *f*.

loan *n* préstamo *m*.

loathe *vt* aborrecer; tener hastío; * *vi* fastidiar.

loathing *n* aversión *f*.

loathsome *adj* asqueroso/sa.

lobby *n* vestíbulo *m*.

lobe *n* lóbulo *m*.

lobster *n* langosta *f*.

local *adj* local.

local anaesthetic n anestesia local f.
local government n gobierno municipal m.
locality n localidad f.
localize vt localizar.
locally adv en la vecindad.
locate vt localizar.
location n situación f.
loch n lago m.
lock n cerradura f; * vt cerrar con llave.
locker n vestuario m.
locket n medallón m.
lockout n cierre patronal m.
locksmith n cerrajero m.
lockup n garaje m, cochera f.
locomotive n locomotora f.
locust n langosta f.
lodge n casa del guarda f; * vi alojarse.
lodger n inquilino/na m/f.
loft n desván m.
lofty adj alto/ta.
log n leño m.
logbook n (mar) diario de a bordo m.
logic n lógica f.
logical adj lógico/ca.
logo n logotipo m.
loin n lomo m.
loiter vi merodear.
loll vi repantigarse.
lollipop n pirulí m, piruleta f.
lonely adj solitario/ria; solo/la.
loneliness n soledad f.
long adj largo/ga; * vi anhelar.
long-distance n: ~ **call** llamada interurbana f.
longevity n longevidad f.
long-haired adj de pelo largo.
longing n anhelo m.
longitude n longitud f.
longitudinal adj longitudinal.
long jump n salto de longitud m.
long-legged adj zancudo/da.

long-playing record n elepé m.
long-range adj de gran alcance.
long-term adj a largo plazo.
long wave n onda larga f.
long-winded adj prolijo/ja.
look vi mirar; parecer; **to ~ after** vt cuidar; **to ~ for** vt buscar; **to ~ forward to** vt esperar con impaciencia; **to ~ out for** vt aguardar; * n aspecto m; mirada f.
looking glass n espejo m.
lookout n (mil) centinela f; vigía f.
loom n telar m; * vi amenazar.
loop n lazo m.
loophole n escapatoria f.
loose adj suelto/ta; flojo/ja; **~ly** adv aproximadamente.
loosen vt aflojar, zafar.
loot vt saquear; * n botín m.
lop vt desmochar.
lop-sided adj desequilibrado/da.
loquacious adj locuaz.
loquacity n locuacidad f.
lord n señor m.
lore n saber popular m.
lose vt perder; * vi perder; **to ~ weight** vi adelgazar.
loss n pérdida f; **to be at a ~** no saber qué hacer.
lost and found n objetos perdidos mpl.
lot n suerte f; lote m; **a ~** mucho.
lotion n loción f.
lottery n lotería f, rifa f.
loud adj fuerte; **~ly** adv fuerte.
loudspeaker n altavoz m.
lounge n salón m.
louse n (pl **lice**) piojo m.
lousy adj vil.
lout n gamberro m.
lovable adj amable.
love n amor, cariño m; **to fall in ~** enamorarse; * vt amar; gustar.

love letter *n* carta de amor *f.*
love life *n* vida sentimental *f.*
lovely *adj* hermoso/sa.
lover *n* amante *m.*
lovesick *adj* enamorado/da.
loving *adj* amoroso/sa.
low *adj* bajo/ja; * *vi* mugir.
low-cut *adj* escotado/da.
lower *adj* más bajo/ja; * *vt* bajar.
lowest *adj* más bajo/ja, ínfimo/ma.
lowland *n* tierra baja *f.*
lowliness *n* humildad *f.*
lowly *adj* humilde.
low water, low tide *n* bajamar *f.*
loyal *adj* leal; fiel; **~ly** *adv* lealmente.
loyalty *n* lealtad *f*; fidelidad *f.*
lozenge *n* pastilla *f.*
lubricant *n* lubricante *m.*
lubricate *vt* lubricar.
lucid *adj* lúcido/da.
luck *n* suerte; fortuna *f.*
luckily *adv* afortunadamente.
luckless *adj* desdichado/da.
lucky *adj* afortunado/da.
lucrative *adj* lucrativo/va.
ludicrous *adj* absurdo/da.
lug *vt* arrastrar.
luggage *n* equipaje *m.*
lugubrious *adj* lúgubre, triste.
lukewarm *adj* tibio/bia.
lull *vt* acunar; * *n* tregua *f.*
lullaby *n* nana *f.*
lumbago *n* lumbago *m.*
lumberjack *n* maderero/ra *m/f.*
luminous *adj* luminoso/sa.
lump *n* terrón *m*; bulto *m*; chichón *m*; * *vt* juntar.

lump sum *n* suma global *f.*
lunacy *n* locura *f.*
lunar *adj* lunar.
lunatic *adj* loco/ca.
lunch, luncheon *n* almuerzo *m*, comida *f*; * *vt, vi* almorzar.
lungs *npl* pulmones *mpl.*
lurch *n* sacudida *f.*
lure *n* señuelo *m*; cebo *m*; * *vt* inducir.
lurid *adj* sensacional.
lurk *vi* esconderse.
luscious *adj* delicioso/sa.
lush *adj* exuberante.
lust *n* lujuria, sensualidad *f*; concupiscencia *f*; * *vi* lujuriar; **to ~ after** *vt* codiciar.
lustful *adj* lujurioso/sa, voluptuoso/sa; **~ly** *adv* lujuriosamente.
lustily *adv* vigorosamente.
lustre *n* lustre *m.*
lusty *adj* fuerte, vigoroso/sa.
lute *n* laúd *m.*
Lutheran *n* luterano/na *m/f.*
luxuriance *n* exuberancia, superabundancia *f.*
luxuriant *adj* exuberante, superabundante.
luxuriate *vi* crecer con exuberancia.
luxurious *adj* lujoso/sa; exuberante; **~ly** *adv* lujosamente.
luxury *n* lujo *m*, voluptuosidad *f*; exuberancia *f.*
lying *n* mentiras *fpl.*
lymph *n* linfa *f.*
lynch *vt* linchar.
lynx *n* lince *m.*
lyrical *adj* lírico/ca.
lyrics *npl* letra *f.*

M

macaroni *n* macarrones *mpl*.

macaroon *n* almendrado *m*.

mace *n* maza *f*; macis *f invar*.

macerate *vt* macerar; mortificar.

machination *n* maquinación, trama *f*.

machine *n* máquina *f*.

machine gun *n* ametralladora *f*.

machinery *n* maquinaria, mecánica *f*.

mackerel *n* caballa *f*.

mad *adj* loco/ca, furioso/sa, rabioso/sa, insensato/ta.

madam *n* madama, señora *f*.

madden *vt* enloquecer.

madder *n* (*bot*) rubia *f*.

madhouse *n* casa de locos *f*.

madly *adv* locamente.

madman *n* loco *m*.

madness *n* locura *f*.

magazine *n* revista *f*; almacén *m*.

maggot *n* gusano *m*.

magic *n* magia *f*; * *adj* mágico/ca; **~ally** *adv* mágicamente.

magician *n* mago/ga *m/f*; prestidigitador/a *m/f*.

magisterial *adj* magistral; **~ly** *adv* magistralmente.

magistracy *n* magistratura *f*.

magistrate *n* magistrado/da *m/f*.

magnanimity *n* magnanimidad *f*.

magnanimous *adj* magnánimo; **~ly** *adv* magnánimamente.

magnet *n* iman *m*.

magnetic *adj* magnetico/ca.

magnetism *n* magnetismo *m*.

magnificence *n* magnificencia *f*.

magnificent *adj* magnifico; **~ly** *adv* magníficamente.

magnify *vt* aumentar; exagerar.

magnifying glass *n* lupa *f*.

magnitude *n* magnitud *f*.

magpie *n* urraca *f*.

mahogany *n* caoba *f*.

maid *n* criada *f*.

maiden *n* doncella *f*.

maiden name *n* nombre de soltera *m*.

mail *n* correo *m*.

mailing list *n* lista de direcciones *f*.

mail order *n* venta por correo *f*.

mail train *n* (*rail*) tren correo *m*.

maim *vt* mutilar.

main *adj* principal; esencial; **in the ~** en general.

mainland *n* continente *m*.

main line *n* (*rail*) línea principal *f*.

mainly *adv* principalmente.

main street *n* calle mayor *f*.

maintain *vt* mantener; sostener.

maintenance *n* mantenimiento *m*.

maize *n* maíz *m*.

majestic *adj* majestuoso/sa; **~ally** *adv* majestuosamente.

majesty *n* majestad *f*.

major *adj* principal; * *n* (*mil*) comandante/a *m/f*.

majority *n* mayoría *f*.

make *vt* hacer, crear; **to ~ for** dirigirse hacia; **to ~ up** inventar; **to ~ up for** compensar; **to ~ off with something** alzar; * *n* marca *f*.

make-believe *n* invención *f*.

makeshift *adj* improvisado.

make-up *n* maquillaje *m*.

make-up remover *n* desmaquillador *m*.

malady *n* enfermedad *f*.

malaise *n* malestar *m*.

malaria *n* malaria *f*.

malcontent *adj*, *n* malcontento/ta *m/f*.

male *adj* masculino/na; * *n* macho *m*.

malevolence *n* malevolencia *f*.

malevolent *adj* malévolo/la; **~ly** *adv* malignamente.

malfunction *n* mal funcionamiento, fallo *m*.

malice *n* malicia *f*.

malicious *adj* malicioso/sa; **~ly** *adv* maliciosamente.

malign *adj* maligno; * *vt* calumniar.

malignant *adj* maligno/na; **~ly** *adv* malignamente.

mall (shopping) *n* centro comercial; paseo *m*.

malleable *adj* maleable.

mallet *n* mazo *m*.

mallow *n* (*bot*) malva *f*.

malnutrition *n* desnutrición *f*.

malpractice *n* negligencia *f*.

malt *n* malta *f*.

maltreat *vt* maltratar.

mammal *n* mamífero *m*.

mammoth *adj* gigantesco/ca.

man *n* hombre *m*; * *vt* (*mar*) tripular.

manacle *n* manilla *f*; **~s** *npl* esposas *fpl*.

manage *vt*, *vi* manejar, dirigir.

manageable *adj* manejable.

management *n* dirección *f*.

manager *n* director/a *m/f*.

manageress *n* directora *f*.

managerial *adj* directivo/va.

managing director *n* director/a general *m/f*.

mandarin *n* (*bot*) mandarina *f*; mandarín *m*.

mandate *n* mandato *m*.

mandatory *adj* obligatorio/ria.

mane *n* crines *fpl*, melena *f*.

manfully *adv* valerosamente.

manger *n* pesebre *m*.

mangle *n* rodillo *m*; * *vt* mutilar.

mangy *adj* sarnoso/sa.

manhandle *vt* maltratar.

manhood *n* madurez *f*; hombría *f*.

man-hour *n* hora hombre *f*.

mania *n* manía *f*.

maniac *n* maníaco/ca *m/f*.

manic *adj* frenético/ca.

manicure *n* manicura *f*.

manifest *adj* manifiesto/ta, patente; * *vt* manifestar.

manifestation *n* manifestación *f*.

manifesto *n* manifiesto *m*.

manipulate *vt* manejar; manipular.

manipulation *n* manejo; manipulación *f*.

mankind *n* género humano *m*.

manlike *adj* varonil.

manliness *n* valentía, hombría *f*.

manly *adj* varonil.

man-made *adj* artificial.

manner *n* manera *f*; modo *m*; forma *f*; **~s** *pl* modales *mpl*.

manoeuvre *n* maniobra *f*.

manpower *n* mano de obra *f*.

mansion *n* palacio *m*, mansión *f*.

manslaughter *n* homicidio (sin premeditación) *m*.

mantelpiece *n* repisa (de chimenea) *f*.

manual *adj*, *n* manual *m*.

manufacture *n* fabricación *f*; * *vt* fabricar.

manufacturer *n* fabricante *m/f*.

manure *n* abono *m*; estiércol *m*; fiemo *m*; * *vt* abonar.

manuscript *n* manuscrito *m*.

many *adj* muchos, muchas; **~ a time** muchas veces; **how ~?** ¿cuantos?; **as ~ as** tantos como.

map *n* mapa *m*; * *vt* planear, trazar el mapa de; **to ~ out** proyectar.

maple *n* arce *m*.

mar *vt* estropear.

marathon *n* maratón *m*.

marauder *n* merodeador/a *m/f*.

marble *n* mármol *m*; * *adj* marmóreo/rea.

March *n* marzo *m*.

march *n* marcha *f*; * *vi* marchar.

march past *n* desfile *m*.

mare *n* yegua *f*.

margarine *n* margarina *f*.

margin *n* margen *m*; borde *m*.

marginal *adj* marginal.

marigold *n* (*bot*) caléndula *f*.

marijuana *n* marihuana *f*.

marinate *vt* adobar.

marine *adj* marino/na; * *n* infante de marina *m*.

mariner *n* marinero/ra *m/f*.

marital *adj* marital.

maritime *adj* marítimo/ma.

marjoram *n* mejorana *f*.

mark *n* marca *f*; señal *f*; * *vt* marcar.

marker *n* registro *m*.

market *n* mercado *m*.

marketable *adj* vendible.

market garden *n* huerto de hortalizas *m*.

marketing *n* márketing *m*.

marketplace *n* mercado *m*.

market research *n* análisis de mercados *m invar*.

market value *n* valor de mercado *m*.

marksman *n* tirador *m*.

marmalade *n* mermelada de naranja *f*.

maroon *adj* marrón.

marquee *n* entoldado/da *m/f*.

marriage *n* matrimonio *m*; casamiento *m*.

marriageable *adj* casadero/ra.

marriage certificate *n* partida de casamiento *f*.

married *adj* casado/da; conyugal.

marrow *n* médula *f*.

marry *vi* casarse.

marsh *n* pantano *m*.

marshal *n* mariscal/a *m/f*.

marshy *adj* pantanoso/sa.

marten *n* marta *f*.

martial *adj* marcial; ~ **law** *n* ley marcial *f*.

martyr *n* mártir *m*.

martyrdom *n* martirio *m*.

marvel *n* maravilla *f*; * *vi* maravillar(se).

marvellous *adj* maravilloso/sa; **~ly** *adv* maravillosamente.

marzipan *n* mazapán *m*.

mascara *n* rímel *m*.

masculine *adj* masculino/na, varonil.

mash *n* mezcla *f*.

mask *n* máscara *f*; * *vt* enmascarar.

masochist *n* masoquista *m/f*.

mason *n* albañil *m*.

masonry *n* mampostería *f*.

masquerade *n* mascarada *f*.

mass *n* masa *f*; misa *f*; montón *m*.

massacre *n* carnicería, matanza *f*; * *vt* hacer una carnicería.

massage *n* masaje *m*.

masseur *n* masajista *m*.

masseuse *n* masajista *f*.

massive *adj* enorme.

mass-media *npl* medios de comunicación de masas *mpl*.

mast *n* mástil *m*.

master *n* amo/ma, dueño/ña *m/f*; maestro/tra *m/f*; * *vt* dominar.

masterly *adj* magistral.

mastermind *vt* dirigir.

masterpiece *n* obra maestra *f*.

mastery *n* maestría *f*.

masticate *vt* masticar.

mastiff *n* mastín *m*.

mat *n* estera *f*; felpudo *m*.

match *n* fósforo *m*, cerilla *f*; partido *m*; * *vt* igualar; * *vi* hacer juego.

matchbox *n* caja de fósforos *f*.

matchless *adj* incomparable, sin par.
matchmaker *n* casamentero/ra *m/f*.
mate *n* compañero/ra *m/f*; * *vt* acoplar.
material *adj,* **~ly** *adv* material(mente).
materialism *n* materialismo *m*.
maternal *adj* maternal.
maternity clothes *npl* vestido premamá *m*.
maternity hospital *n* hospital de maternidad *m*.
mathematical *adj* matemático/ca; **~ly** *adv* matemáticamente.
mathematician *n* matemático/ca *m/f*.
mathematics *npl* matemáticas *fpl*.
maths *npl* mates, matemáticas *fpl*.
matinee *n* función de la tarde *f*.
mating *n* aparejamiento *m*.
matins *npl* maitines *mpl*.
matriculate *vt* matricular.
matriculation *n* matriculación *f*.
matrimonial *adj* matrimonial.
mat, matt(e) *adj* mate.
matted *adj* enmarañado/da.
matter *n* materia, substancia *f*; asunto *m*; cuestión *f*; **what is the ~?** ¿qué pasa?; **as a ~ of fact** en realidad; * *vi* importar.
mattress *n* colchón *m*.
mature *adj* maduro/ra; * *vt* madurar.
maturity *n* madurez *f*.
maul *vt* magullar.
mausoleum *n* mausoleo *m*.
mauve *adj* malva.
maxim *n* máxima *f*.
maximum *n* máximo *m*.
may *vi* poder; **~be** acaso, quizá.
May *n* mayo *m*.
Mayday *n* primero de mayo *m*.
mayonnaise *n* mayonesa *f*.
mayor *n* alcalde *m*.
mayoress *n* alcaldesa *f*.

maze *n* laberinto *m*.
me *pn* me; mí.
meadow *n* pradera *f*; prado *m*.
meagre *adj* pobre.
meagreness *n* escasez *f*.
meal *n* comida *f*; harina *f*.
mealtime *n* hora de comer *f*.
mean *adj* tacaño/ña; **~s** *npl* medios *mpl*; * *vt, vi* significar.
meander *vi* serpentear.
meaning *n* sentido, significado *m*.
meaningful *adj* significativo/va.
meaningless *adj* sin sentido.
meanness *n* tacañería *f*.
meantime (in the), meanwhile *adv* mientras tanto.
measles *npl* sarampión *m*.
measure *n* medida *f*; (*mus*) compás *m*; * *vt* medir.
measurement *n* medida *f*.
meat *n* carne *f*.
meatball *n* albóndiga *f*.
meaty *adj* sustancioso/sa.
mechanic *n* mecánico/ca *m/f*.
mechanical *adj* mecánico; **~ly** *adv* mecánicamente.
mechanics *npl* mecánica *f*.
mechanism *n* mecanismo *m*.
medal *n* medalla *f*.
medallion *n* medallón *m*.
medallist *n* medallero/ra *m/f*.
meddle *vi* entrometerse.
meddler *n* entrometido *m*.
media *npl* medios de comunicación *mpl*.
mediate *vi* mediar.
mediation *n* mediación, interposición *f*.
mediator *n* intermediario/ria *m/f*.
medical *adj* médico/ca.
medicate *vt* medicar.
medicated *adj* medicinal.
medicinal *adj* medicinal.

medicine n medicina f; medicamento m.

medieval adj medieval.

mediocre adj mediocre.

mediocrity n mediocridad f.

meditate vi meditar.

meditation n meditación f.

meditative adj contemplativo/va.

Mediterranean adj mediterráneo/ nea; **the ~** el Mediterráneo/nea m.

medium n medio m; * adj mediano/ na.

medium wave n onda media f.

medley n mezcla m.

meek adj manso/sa; **~ly** adv mansamente.

meekness n mansedumbre f.

meet vt encontrar; **to ~ with** reunirse con; * vi encontrarse; juntarse.

meeting n reunión f; congreso m.

megaphone n megáfono m.

melancholy n melancolía f; * adj melancólico/ca.

mellow adj maduro/ra; suave; * vi madurar.

mellowness n madurez f.

melodious adj melodioso/sa; **~ly** adv melodiosamente.

melody n melodía f.

melon n melón m.

melt vt derretir; * vi derretirse.

melting point n punto de fusión m.

member n miembro m/f.

membership n número de miembros m.

membrane n membrana f.

memento n recuerdo m.

memo n memorándum m.

memoir n memoria f.

memorable adj memorable.

memorandum n memorándum m.

memorial n monumento conmemorativo m.

memorize vt memorizar, aprender de memoria.

memory n memoria f; recuerdo m.

menace n amenaza f; * vt amenazar.

menacing adj amenazador/ra.

menagerie n casa de fieras f.

mend vt reparar.

mending n reparación f.

menial adj doméstico/ca.

meningitis n meningitis f.

menopause n menopausia f.

menstruation n menstruación f.

mental adj mental, intelectual.

mentality n mentalidad f.

mentally adv mentalmente, intelectualmente.

mention n mención f; * vt mencionar.

mentor n mentor m.

menu n menú m; carta f.

mercantile adj mercantil.

mercenary adj, n mercenario/ria m/f.

merchandise n mercancía f.

merchant n comerciante m/f.

merchantman n navío mercante m.

merchant marine n marina mercante f.

merciful adj compasivo/va.

merciless adj despiadado/da; **~ly** adv despiadadamente.

mercury n mercurio m.

mercy n compasión f.

mere adj mero/ra; **~ly** adv simplemente.

merge vt fundir.

merger n fusión f.

meridian n meridiano m.

meringue n merengue m.

merit n mérito m; * vt merecer.

meritorious adj meritorio/ria.

mermaid n sirena f.

merrily adv alegremente.

merriment n diversión f; regocijo m.

merry *adj* alegre.
merry-go-round *n* tiovivo *m*.
mesh *n* malla *f*.
mesmerize *vt* hipnotizar.
mess *n* lío *m*; mamarracho *m*; (*mil*) comedor *m*; **to ~ up** *vt* desordenar.
message *n* mensaje *m*.
messenger *n* mensajero/ra *m/f*.
metabolism *n* metabolismo *n*.
metal *n* metal *m*.
metallic *adj* metálico/ca.
metallurgy *n* metalurgía *f*.
metamorphosis *n* metamorfosis *f in-var*.
metaphor *n* metáfora *f*.
metaphoric(al) *adj* metafórico/ca.
metaphysical *adj* metafísico/ca.
metaphysics *npl* metafísica *f*.
mete (out) *vt* imponer.
meteor *n* meteoro *m*.
meteorological *adj* meteorológico/ca.
meteorology *n* meteorología *f*.
meter *n* contador *m*.
method *n* método *m*.
methodical *adj* metódico/ca; **~ly** *adv* metódicamente.
Methodist *n* metodista *m/f*.
metre *n* metro *m*.
metric *adj* métrico/ca.
metropolis *n* metrópoli *f*.
metropolitan *adj* metropolitano/na.
mettle *n* valor *m*.
mettlesome *adj* brioso/sa.
mew *vi* maullar.
mezzanine *n* entresuelo *m*.
microbe *n* microbio *m*.
microchip *n* microchip *m*.
microphone *n* micrófono *m*.
microscope *n* microscopio *m*.
microscopic *adj* microscópico/ca.
microwave *n* microondas *m invar*; **~ oven** microondas *m*.
mid *adj* medio/dia.

midday *n* mediodía *m*.
middle *adj* medio/dia; * *n* medio, centro *m*.
middle name *n* segundo nombre *m*.
middleweight *n* peso medio *m*.
middling *adj* mediano/na.
midge *n* mosquito *m*.
midget *n* enano/na *m/f*.
midi system *n* minicadena *f*.
midnight *n* medianoche *f*.
midriff *n* diafragma *m*.
midst *n* medio, centro *m*.
midsummer *n* pleno verano *m*.
midway *adv* a medio camino.
midwife *n* partera *f*.
midwifery *n* obstetricia *f*.
might *n* poder *m*; fuerza *f*.
mighty *adj* fuerte.
migraine *n* jaqueca *f*.
migrate *vi* emigrar, migrar.
migration *n* emigración, migración *f*.
migratory *adj* migratorio/ria.
mike *n* micrófono *m*.
mild *adj* apacible; suave; **~ly** *adv* suavemente.
mildew *n* moho *m*.
mildness *n* dulzura *f*.
mile *n* milla *f*.
mileage *n* kilometraje *m*.
mileometer, milometer *n* cuentaki-lómetros *m invar*.
milieu *n* ambiente *m*.
militant *adj* militante.
military *adj* militar.
militate *vi* militar.
militia *n* milicia *f*.
milk *n* leche *f*; * *vt* ordenar.
milkshake *n* batido de leche *m*, mal-teada *f*.
milky *adj* lechoso/sa; **M~ Way** *n* Via Lactea *f*.
mill *n* molino *m*; * *vt* moler.
millennium *n* milenio *m*.

miller n molinero/ra m/f.
millet n (bot) mijo m.
milligram n miligramo m.
millilitre n mililitro m.
millimetre n milímetro m.
milliner n sombrerero/ra m/f.
millinery n sombrerería f.
million n millón m.
millionaire n millonario/ria m/f.
millionth adj, n millonésimo/ma m/f.
millstone n piedra de molino f.
mime n mimo m.
mimic vt imitar.
mimicry n mímica f.
mince vt picar.
mind n mente f; * vt cuidar; * vi molestar.
minded adj dispuesto/ta.
mindful adj consciente.
mindless adj sin motivo.
mine pn mío, mía, mi; * n mina; * vi minar.
minefield n campo de minas m.
miner n minero/ra m/f.
mineral adj, n mineral m.
mineralogy n mineralogía f.
mineral water n agua mineral f.
minesweeper n dragaminas m invar.
mingle vt mezclar.
miniature n miniatura f.
minimal adj mínimo/ma.
minimize vt minimizar.
minimum n mínimo m.
mining n minería f.
minion n favorito/ta m/f.
minister n ministro/tro m/f; * vt servir.
ministerial adj ministerial.
ministry n ministerio m.
mink n visón m.
minnow n vario m (pez).
minor adj menor; * n menor (de edad) m/f.

minority n minoría f.
minstrel n juglar m.
mint n (bot) menta f; casa de la moneda f; * vt acuñar.
minus adv menos.
minute¹ adj diminuto/ta; ~ly adv minuciosamente.
minute² n minuto m.
miracle n milagro m.
miraculous adj milagroso/sa.
mirage n espejismo m.
mire n fango m.
mirky adj turbio/bia.
mirror n espejo m.
mirth n alegría f.
mirthful adj alegre.
misadventure n desgracia f.
misanthrope, misanthropist n misántropo m.
misapply vt aplicar mal.
misapprehension n error m.
misbehave vi portarse mal.
misbehaviour n mala conducta f.
miscalculate vt calcular mal.
miscarriage n aborto (espontáneo) m.
miscarry vi abortar (espontáneamente); malograrse.
miscellaneous adj varios, varias.
miscellany n miscelánea f.
mischief n mal, daño m.
mischievous adj dañoso/sa; travieso/sa.
misconception n equivocación f.
misconduct n mala conducta f.
misconstrue vt interpretar mal.
miscount vt contar mal.
miscreant n malvado/da m/f.
misdeed n delito m.
misdemeanour n delito m.
misdirect vt dirigir mal.
miser n avaro/ra m/f.
miserable adj miserable, infeliz.

miserly *adj* mezquino/na, tacaño/ña.
misery *n* miseria *f*.
misfit *n* inadaptado/da *m/f*.
misfortune *n* desgracia *f*.
misgiving *n* recelo *m*; presentimiento *m*.
misgovern *vt* gobernar mal.
misguided *adj* equivocado/da.
mishandle *vt* manejar mal.
mishap *n* desgracia *f*.
misinform *vt* informar mal.
misinterpret *vt* interpretar mal.
misjudge *vi* juzgar mal.
mislay *vt* extraviar.
mislead *vt* engañar.
mismanage *vt* manejar mal.
mismanagement *n* mala administración *f*.
misnomer *n* nombre inapropriado *m*.
misogynist *n* misógino/na *m/f*.
misplace *vt* extraviar.
misprint *vt* imprimir mal; * *n* errata *f*.
misrepresent *vt* representar mal.
Miss *n* señorita *f*.
miss *vt* perder; echar de menos.
missal *n* misal *m*.
misshapen *adj* deforme.
missile *n* misil *m*.
missing *adj* perdido/da; ausente.
mission *n* misión *f*.
missionary *n* misionero/ra *m/f*.
misspent *adj* disipado/da.
mist *n* niebla *f*.
mistake *vt* entender mal; * *vi* equivocarse, engañarse; **to be mistaken** equivocarse; * *n* equivocación *f*; error *m*, yerro *f*.
Mister *n* Señor *m*.
mistletoe *n* (*bot*) muérdago *m*.
mistress *n* amante *f*.
mistrust *vt* desconfiar; * *n* desconfianza *f*.
mistrustful *adj* desconfiado/da.

misty *adj* nebuloso/sa.
misunderstand *vt* entender mal.
misunderstanding *n* malentendido *m*.
misuse *vt* maltratar; abusar de.
mitre *n* mitra *f*.
mitigate *vt* mitigar.
mitigation *n* mitigación *f*.
mittens *npl* manoplas *fpl*.
mix *vt* mezclar.
mixed *adj* surtido/da; mixto/ta.
mixed-up *adj* confuso/sa.
mixer *n* licuadora *f*.
mixture *n* mezcla *f*.
mix-up *n* confusión *f*.
moan *n* gemido *m*; * *vi* gemir; quejarse.
moat *n* foso *m*.
mob *n* multitud *f*.
mobile *adj* móvil; **~ phone** móvil *m*.
mobile home *n* caravana *f*.
mobility *n* movilidad *f*.
mobilize *vt* (*mil*) movilizar.
moccasin *n* mocasín *m*.
mock *vt* burlarse.
mockery *n* mofa *f*.
mode *n* modo *m*.
model *n* modelo *m*; * *vt* modelar.
modem *n* módem *m*.
moderate *adj* moderado/da; **~ly** *adv* medianamente; * *vt* moderar.
moderation *n* moderación *f*.
modern *adj* moderno/na.
modernize *vt* modernizar.
modest *adj* modesto/ta; **~ly** *adv* modestamente.
modesty *n* modestia *f*.
modicum *n* mínimo *m*.
modification *n* modificación *f*.
modify *vt* modificar.
modulate *vt* modular.
modulation *n* (*mus*) modulación *f*.
module *n* módulo *m*.
mogul *n* magnate *m/f*.

mohair *n* mohair *m*.
moist *adj* húmedo/da.
moisten *vt* humedecer.
moisture *n* humedad *f*.
molars *npl* muelas *fpl*.
molasses *npl* melaza *f*.
mole *n* topo *m*.
molecule *n* molécula *f*.
molehill *n* topera *f*.
molest *vt* importunar.
mollify *vt* apaciguar.
mollusc *n* molusco *m*.
mollycoddle *vt* mimar.
molten *adj* derretido/da.
moment *n* momento *m*.
momentarily *adv* momentáneamente.
momentary *adj* momentáneo/nea.
momentous *adj* importante.
momentum *n* ímpetu *m*.
monarch *n* monarca *m*.
monarchy *n* monarquía *f*.
monastery *n* monasterio *m*.
monastic *adj* monástico/ca.
Monday *n* lunes *m*.
monetary *adj* monetario/ria.
money *n* dinero *m*.
money laundering *n* blanqueo *m*.
money order *n* giro *m*.
Mongol *n* mongólico/ca *m/f*.
mongrel *adj, n* mestizo/za *m/f*.
monitor *n* monitor *m*.
monk *n* monje *m*.
monkey *n* mono *m*.
monochrome *adj* monocromo/ma.
monocle *n* monóculo *m*.
monologue *n* monólogo *m*.
monopolize *vt* monopolizar.
monopoly *n* monopolio *m*.
monosyllable *n* monosílabo *m*.
monotonous *adj* monótono/na.
monotony *n* monotonía *f*.
monsoon *n* (*mar*) monzón *m*.

monster *n* monstruo *m*.
monstrosity *n* monstruosidad *f*.
monstrous *adj* monstruoso/sa; **~ly**
  adv monstruosamente.
montage *n* montaje *m*.
month *n* mes *m*.
monthly *adj, adv* mensual(mente).
monument *n* monumento *m*.
monumental *adj* monumental.
moo *vi* mugir.
mood *n* humor *m*.
moodiness *n* mal humor *m*.
moody *adj* malhumorado/da.
moon *n* luna *f*.
moonbeams *npl* rayos lunares *mpl*.
moonlight *n* luz de la luna *f*.
moor *vt* (*mar*) atracar.
mooring rope *n* amarra *f*.
moorland, moor *n* páramo *m*.
moose *n* alce *m*.
mop *n* fregona *f*; * *vt* fregar.
mope *vi* estar triste.
moped *n* ciclomotor *m*.
moral *adj*, **~ly** *adv* moral(mente);
  ~s *npl* moralidad *f*.
morale *n* moral *f*.
moralist *n* moralista *m/f*.
morality *n* ética, moralidad *f*.
moralize *vt, vi* moralizar.
morass *n* pantano *m*.
morbid *adj* morboso/sa.
more *adj, adv* más; **never ~** nunca
  más; **once ~** otra vez; **~ and ~**
  más y más, cada vez más; **so much**
  the ~ cuanto más.
moreover *adv* además.
morgue *n* depósito de cadáveres *m*.
morning *n* mañana *f*; **good ~** buenos
  días *mpl*.
moron *n* imbécil *m/f*.
morose *adj* hosco/ca.
morphine *n* morfina *f*.
morsel *n* bocado *m*.

mortal *adj* mortal; **~ly** *adv* mortalmente; * *n* mortal *m/f*.
mortality *n* mortalidad *f*.
mortar *n* mortero *m*.
mortgage *n* hipoteca *f*; * *vt* hipotecar.
mortgage company *n* banco hipotecario *m*.
mortgager *n* deudor hipotecario *m*, deudora hipotecaria *f*.
mortification *n* mortificación *f*.
mortify *vt* mortificar.
mortuary *n* depósito de cadáveres *m*.
mosaic *n* mosaico *m*.
mosque *n* mezquita *f*.
mosquito *n* mosquito *m*; zancudo/da *m*.
moss *n* (*bot*) musgo *m*.
mossy *adj* cubierto/ta de musgo.
most *adj* la mayoría de; * *adv* sumamente; **at ~** a lo sumo; **~ly** *adv* principalmente.
motel *n* motel *m*.
moth *n* polilla *f*.
mothball *n* bola de naftalina *f*.
mother *n* madre *f*; **loving ~** madraza *f*.
motherhood *n* maternidad *f*.
mother-in-law *n* suegra *f*.
motherless *adj* sin madre.
motherly *adj* maternal.
mother-of-pearl *n* nácar *m*.
mother-to-be *n* futura madre *f*.
mother tongue *n* lengua materna *f*.
motif *n* tema *m*.
motion *n* movimiento *m*.
motionless *adj* inmóvil.
motion picture *n* película *f*.
motivated *adj* motivado/da.
motive *n* motivo *m*.
motley *adj* abigarrado/da.
motor *n* motor *m*.
motorbike *n* moto *f*.
motorboat *n* lancha motora *f*.

motorcycle *n* motocicleta *f*.
motor vehicle *n* automóvil *m*.
mottled *adj* multicolor.
motto *n* lema *m*.
mould *n* molde *m*; moho *m*; * *vt* moldear.
moulder *vi* decaer.
mouldy *adj* enmohecido/da.
moult *vt* mudar.
mound *n* montón *m*.
mount *n* monte *m*; * *vt* subir.
mountain *n* montaña *f*.
mountaineer *n* montañero/ra *m/f*.
mountaineering *n* montañismo *m*.
mountainous *adj* montañoso/sa.
mourn *vt* lamentar.
mourner *n* doliente *m/f*.
mournful *adj* triste; **~ly** *adv* tristemente.
mourning *n* luto *m*.
mouse *n* (*pl* **mice**) ratón *m*.
mouse mat *n* alfombrilla *f*.
mousse *n* mousse *f*.
moustache *n* bigote *m*.
mouth *n* boca *f*; desembocadura *f*.
mouthful *n* bocado *m*.
mouth organ *n* harmónica *f*.
mouthpiece *n* boquilla *f*.
mouthwash *n* enjuague *m*.
mouthwatering *adj* apetitoso/sa.
movable *adj* movible.
move *vt* mover; proponer; * *vi* moverse; * *n* movimiento *m*.
movement *n* movimiento *m*.
movie *n* película *f*.
movie camera *n* cámara cinematográfica *f*.
moving *adj* conmovedor/a.
mow *vt* segar.
mower *n* cortacésped *m*.
Mrs *n* señora *f*.
much *adj*, *adv* mucho/cha; con mucho.

muck n suciedad f.

mucous adj mocoso/sa.

mucus n moco m.

mud n barro m.

muddle vt confundir; * n confusión f.

muddy adj fangoso/sa.

mudguard n guardabarros m invar.

muffle vt embozar.

mug n jarra f.

muggy adj bochornoso/sa.

mulberry n mora f; ~ tree morera f.

mule n mulo m, mula f.

mull vt meditar.

multifarious adj múltiple.

multimedia adj multimedia.

multiple adj múltiplo/a; * n múltiplo m.

multiplication n multiplicación f; ~ table tabla de multiplicar f.

multiply vt multiplicar.

multitude n multitud f.

mumble vt, vi refunfuñar.

mummy[1] n mamá f.

mummy[2] n momia f.

mumps npl paperas fpl.

munch vt mascar.

mundane adj trivial.

municipal adj municipal.

municipality n municipalidad f.

munificence n munificencia f.

munitions npl municiones fpl.

mural n mural m.

murder n asesinato m; homicidio m; * vt asesinar.

murderer n asesino/na m/f.

murderess n asesina f.

murderous adj homicida.

murky adj sombrío/ría.

murmur n murmullo m;* vi murmurar.

muscle n músculo m.

muscular adj muscular.

muse vi meditar.

museum n museo m.

mushroom n (bot) seta f; champiñón m.

music n musica f.

musical adj musical; melodioso/sa.

musician n músico/ca m/f.

musk n almizcle m.

muslin n muselina f.

mussel n mejillón m.

must v aux tener que, deber; deber de.

mustard n mostaza f.

muster vt agregar.

musty adj mohoso/sa, añejo/ja.

mute adj mudo/da, silencioso/sa.

muted adj callado/da.

mutilate vt mutilar.

mutilation n mutilación f.

mutiny n motin, tumulto m; * vi amotinarse, rebelarse.

mutter vt, vi murmurar, musitar; * n murmuración f.

mutton n carnero m.

mutual adj mutuo/tua, mutual, recíproco/ca; ~ly adv mutuamente, recíprocamente.

muzzle n bozal m; hocico m; * vt embozar.

my pn mi, mis; mio, mia; mios, mias.

myriad n miríada f; gran número m.

myrrh n mirra f.

myrtle n mirto, arrayán m.

myself pn yo mismo/ma.

mysterious adj misterioso/sa; ~ly adv misteriosamente.

mystery n misterio m.

mystic(al) adj místico/ca.

mystify vt dejar perplejo/ja.

mystique n misterio m.

myth n mito m.

mythology n mitología f.

N

nab *vt* agarrar.

nag *n* jaca *f*; * *vt* regañar.

nagging *adj* persistente; * *npl* quejas *fpl*.

nail *n* uña *f*; garra *f*; clavo *m*; * *vt* clavar.

nailbrush *n* cepillo de uñas *m*.

nailfile *n* lima de uñas *f*.

nail polish *n* esmalte de uñas *m*.

nail scissors *npl* tijeras de manicura *fpl*.

naïve *adj* ingenuo/nua.

naked *adj* desnudo/da evidente; puro/ra, simple.

name *n* nombre *m*; fama, reputación *f*; * *vt* nombrar; mencionar.

nameless *adj* anónimo/ma.

nameplate *n* planchuela *f*.

namely *adv* a saber.

namesake *n* tocayo/ya *m/f*.

nanny *n* niñera *f*.

nap *n* sueño ligero *m*.

napalm *n* napalm *m*.

nape *n* nuca *f*.

napkin *n* servilleta *f*.

nappy *n* pañal *m*.

narcissus *n* (*bot*) narciso *m*.

narcotic *adj* narcótico/ca; * *n* narcótico *m*.

narrate *vt* narrar, relatar.

narrative *adj* narrativo/va; * *n* narrativa *f*.

narrow *adj* angosto/ta, estrecho/cha; ~ly *adv* estrechamente; * *vt* estrechar; limitar.

narrow-minded *adj* estrecho/cha de miras.

narrow pass *n* puerto *m*.

nasal *adj* nasal.

nasty *adj* sucio/cia, puerco/ca; obsceno/na; sórdido/da.

natal *adj* nativo/va; natal.

nation *n* nación *f*.

national *adj*, ~ly *adv* nacional(mente).

nationalism *n* nacionalismo *m*.

nationalist *adj*, *n* nacionalista *m/f*.

nationality *n* nacionalidad *f*.

nationalize *vt* nacionalizar.

nationwide *adj* a nivel nacional.

native *adj* nativo/va; * *n* natural *m/f*.

native language *n* lengua materna *f*.

Nativity *n* Navidad *f*.

natural *adj* natural; sencillo/lla; ~ly *adv* naturalmente.

natural gas *n* gas natural *m*.

naturalist *n* naturalista *m/f*.

naturalize *vt* naturalizar.

nature *n* naturaleza *f*; índole *f*.

naturopath *n* naturópata *m/f*.

naught *n* cero *m*.

naughty *adj* malo/la, malvado/da.

nausea *n* náuseas *fpl*, gana de vomitar *f*.

nauseate *vt* dar náuseas a.

nauseous *adj* fastidioso/sa.

nautical, naval *adj* náutico/ca, naval.

nave *n* nave (de la iglesia) *f*.

navel *n* ombligo *m*.

navigate *vi* navegar.

navigation *n* navegación *f*.

navy *n* marina *f*; armada *f*.

Nazi *n* nazi *m/f*.

near *prep* cerca de, junto a; * *adv* casi; cerca, cerca de; * *adj* cercano/na, proximo/ma.

nearby *adj* cercano/na.

nearly *adv* casi.

near-sighted *adj* miope.

neat *adj* hermoso/sa, pulido/da; puro/ra; neto/ta; **~ly** *adv* elegantemente.

nebulous *adj* nebuloso/sa.

necessarily *adv* necesariamente.

necessary *adj* necesario/ria.

necessitate *vt* necesitar.

necessity *n* necesidad *f*.

neck *n* cuello *m*; * *vi* besuquearse.

necklace *n* collar *m*.

nectar *n* néctar *m*.

née, nee *adj*: **~ Brown** de soltera Brown.

need *n* necesidad *f*; pobreza *f*; * *vt* necesitar.

needle *n* aguja *f*.

needless *adj* superfluo/lua, inútil.

needlework *n* costura *f*; bordado de aguja *m*; obra de punto *m*.

needy *adj* necesitado/da, pobre.

negation *n* negación *f*.

negative *adj* negativo/va; **~ly** *adv* negativamente; * *n* negativa *f*.

neglect *vt* descuidar, desatender; * *n* negligencia *f*.

negligee *n* salto de cama *m*.

negligence *n* negligencia *f*; descuido *m*.

negligent *adj* negligente, descuidado/da; **~ly** *adv* negligentemente.

negligible *adj* insignificante.

negotiate *vt, vi* negociar (con).

negotiation *n* negociación *f*; negocio *m*.

Negress *n* negra *f*.

Negro *adj* negro/gra; * *n* negro *m*.

neigh *vi* relinchar; * *n* relincho *m*.

neighbour *n* vecino/na *m/f*; * *vt* confinar.

neighbourhood *n* vecindad *f*; vecindario *m*.

neighbouring *adj* vecino/na.

neighbourly *adj* sociable.

neither *conj* ni; * *pn* ninguno/na, ni uno ni otro, ni una ni otra.

neon *n* neón *m*.

neon light *n* luz de neón *f*.

nephew *n* sobrino *m*.

nepotism *n* nepotismo *m*.

nerve *n* nervio *m*; valor *m*.

nerve-racking *adj* espantoso/sa.

nervous *adj* nervioso/sa; nervudo/da.

nervous breakdown *n* crisis nerviosa *f*.

nest *n* nido *m*; nidada *f*.

nest egg *n* (*fig*) ahorros *mpl*.

nestle *vt* anidarse.

net *n* red *f*.

netball *n* nétbol *m*.

net curtain *n* visillo *m*.

netting *n* mallado *m*.

nettle *n* ortiga *f*.

network *n* red *f*, malla *f*.

neurone *n* neurona *f*.

neurosis *n* neurosis *f* invar.

neurotic *adj*, *n* neurótico/ca *m/f*.

neuter *adj* (*gr*) neutro/tra.

neutral *adj* neutral.

neutrality *n* neutralidad *f*.

neutralize *vt* neutralizar.

neutron *n* neutrón *m*.

neutron bomb *n* bomba de neutrones *f*.

never *adv* nunca, jamás; **~ mind** no importa.

never-ending *adj* sin fin.

nevertheless *adv* no obstante.

new *adj* nuevo/va, fresco/sca, reciénte; **~ly** *adv* nuevamente.

newborn *adj* recién nacido/da.

newcomer *n* recién llegado/da *m*.

new-fangled *adj* inventado/da por novedad.

news *npl* novedad, noticias *fpl*.

news agency n agencia de noticias f.

newsagent n vendedor/a de periódicos m/f.

newscaster n presentador/a m/f.

news flash n noticia de última hora f.

newsletter n boletín m.

newspaper n periódico m.

newsreel n noticiario m.

New Year n Año Nuevo m; **~'s Day** Día de Año Nuevo m; **~'s Eve** Nochevieja f.

next adj próximo/ma; **the ~ day** el día siguiente; * adv luego, inmediatamente después.

nib n pico m; punta f.

nibble vt picar, mordiscar.

nice adj simpático/ca; agradable; lindo/da; **~ly** adv bien.

nice-looking adj guapo/pa.

niche n nicho m.

nick n mella f; * vt (sl) robar.

nickel n níquel m; moneda de cinco centavos f.

nickname n mote, apodo m; * vt poner apodos.

nicotine n nicotina f.

niece n sobrina f.

niggling adj insignificante.

night n noche f; velador m; **by ~** de noche; **good ~** buenas noches.

nightclub n cabaret m.

nightfall n anochecer m.

nightingale n ruiseñor m.

nightly adv por las noches, todas las noches; * adj nocturno/na.

nightmare n pesadilla f.

night school n clases nocturnas fpl.

night shift n turno de noche m.

night-time n noche f.

night work n vela f.

nihilist n nihilista m/f.

nimble adj ligero/ra, activo/va, listo/ta, ágil.

nine adj, n nueve.

nineteen adj, n diecinueve.

nineteenth adj, n decimonoveno/na.

ninetieth adj, n nonagésimo/ma.

ninety adj, n noventa.

ninth adj, n nono/na, noveno/na.

nip vt pellizcar; morder.

nipple n pezón m; tetilla f.

nit n liendre f.

nitrogen n nitrógeno m.

no adv no; * adj ningún, ninguno/na.

nobility n nobleza f.

noble adj noble; insigne; * n noble m/f.

nobleman n noble m.

nobody n nadie, ninguna persona f.

nocturnal adj nocturnal, nocturno/na.

nod n cabeceo m; señal f; * vi cabecear; amodorrarse.

noise n ruido, estruendo m; rumor m.

noisily adv con ruido.

noisiness n ruido, tumulto, alboroto m.

noisy adj ruidoso/sa, turbulento/ta.

nominal adj, **~ly** adv nominal(mente).

nominate vt nombrar.

nomination n nominación f.

nominative n (gr) nominativo m.

nominee n candidato/ta m/f.

nonalcoholic adj no alcóholico/ca.

nonaligned adj no alineado/da.

nonchalant adj indiferente.

noncommittal adj reservado/da.

nonconformist n inconformista m/f.

nondescript adj no descrito/ta.

none adj nadie, ninguno/na.

nonentity n nulidad f.

nonetheless adv sin embargo.

nonexistent adj inexistente.

nonfiction n no ficción f.

nonplussed adj confuso/sa.

nonsense *n* disparate, absurdo *m*.
nonsensical *adj* absurdo/da.
nonsmoker *n* no fumador/a *m/f*.
nonstick *adj* antiadherente.
nonstop *adj* directo/ta; * *adv* sin parar.
noodles *npl* fideos (chinos) *mpl*.
noon *n* mediodía *m*.
noose *n* nudo corredizo *m*.
nor *conj* ni.
normal *adj* normal.
north *n* norte *m*; * *adj* del norte.
North America *n* América del Norte, Norteamérica *f*.
northeast *n* nor(d)este *m*.
northerly, northern *adj* norteño/ña.
North Pole *n* polo norte *m*.
northward(s) *adv* hacia el norte.
northwest *n* nor(d)oeste *m*.
nose *n* nariz *f*; olfato *m*.
nosebleed *n* hemorragia nasal *f*.
nosedive *n* picado vertical *m*.
nostalgia *n* nostalgia *f*.
nostril *n* ventana de la nariz *f*.
not *adv* no.
notable *adj* notable; memorable.
notably *adv* especialmente.
notary *n* notario/ria *m/f*.
notch *n* muesca *f*; * *vt* hacer muescas.
note *n* nota, marca *f*; señal *f*; aprecio *m*; billete *m*; consecuen cia *f*; noticia *f*; indirecta *f*; * *vt* notar, marcar; observar.
notebook *n* cuaderno *m*, libreta *f*.
noted *adj* afamado/da, celebre.
notepad *n* bloc *m*.
notepaper *n* papel de cartas *m*.
nothing *n* nada *f*; **good for ~** lo que sirve para nada.
notice *n* noticia *f*; aviso *m*; * *vt* observar.
noticeable *adj* notable, reparable.
notification *n* notificación *f*.

notify *vt* notificar.
notion *n* noción *f*; opinión *f*; idea *f*.
notoriety *n* mala fama *f*.
notorious *adj* tristemente célebre; **~ly** *adv* notoriamente.
notwithstanding *conj* no obstante, aunque.
nougat *n* turrón *m*.
nought *n* cero *m*.
noun *n* (*gr*) sustantivo *m*.
nourish *vt* nutrir, alimentar.
nourishing *adj* nutritivo/va.
nourishment *n* nutrimiento, alimento *m*.
novel *n* novela *f*.
novelist *n* novelista *m/f*.
novelty *n* novedad *f*.
November *n* noviembre *m*.
novice *n* novicio/cia *m/f*.
now *adv* ya, ahora, hoy (en) día; **~ and then** de vez en cuando.
nowadays *adv* hoy (en) día.
nowhere *adv* en ninguna parte.
noxious *adj* nocivo/va, dañoso/sa.
nozzle *n* boquilla *f*.
nuance *n* matiz *m*.
nuclear *adj* nuclear; **~ power** energía nuclear *f*; **~ power station** *n* central nuclear *f*.
nucleus *n* núcleo *m*.
nude *adj* desnudo/da, en carnes, en cueros, sin vestido.
nudge *vt* dar un codazo a.
nudist *n* nudista *m/f*.
nudity *n* desnudez *f*.
nuisance *n* daño, perjuicio *m*; incomodidad *f*.
nuke *n* (*col*) bomba atómica *f*; * *vt* atacar con arma nuclear.
null *adj* nulo/la, inválido/da.
nullify *vt* anular, invalidar.
numb *adj* entorpecido/da; * *vt* entorpecer.

number n número m; cantidad f; * vt numerar.
numberplate n placa de matrícula f.
numbness n entumecimiento m.
numeral n número m.
numerical adj numérico/ca.
numerous adj numeroso/sa.
nun n monja, religiosa f.
nunnery n convento de monjas m.
nuptial adj nupcial; ~s npl nupcias fpl.
nurse n enfermera f; * vt cuidar; amamantar.

nursery n guardería infantil f; criadero m.
nursery rhyme n canción infantil f.
nursery school n parvulario m.
nursing home n clinica de reposo f.
nurture vt criar, educar.
nut n nuez f.
nutcrackers npl cascanueces m invar.
nutmeg n nuez moscada f.
nutritious adj nutritivo/va.
nutshell n cascara de nuez f.
nylon n nylon, nailon m; * adj de nylon, de nailon.

O

oak n roble m.
oar n remo m.
oasis n oasis f invar.
oath n juramento m.
oatmeal n harina de avena f.
oats npl avena f.
obedience n obediencia f.
obedient adj, ~ly adv obediente(mente).
obese adj obeso/sa, gordo/da.
obesity n obesidad f.
obey vt obedecer.
obituary n necrología f.
object n objeto m; * vt objetar.
objection n oposición, objeción, réplica f.
objectionable adj desagradable.
objective adj objetivo/va; * n objetivo m.
obligation n obligación f.
obligatory adj obligatorio/ria.
oblige vt obligar; complacer, favorecer.
obliging adj servicial.
oblique adj oblicuo/cua; indirecto/ta; ~ly adv oblicuamente.

obliterate vt borrar.
oblivion n olvido m.
oblivious adj olvidadizo/za.
oblong adj oblongo/ga.
obnoxious adj odioso/sa.
oboe n oboe m.
obscene adj obsceno/na, impudico/ca.
obscenity n obscenidad f.
obscure adj oscuro/ra; ~ly adv oscuramente; * vt oscurecer.
obscurity n oscuridad f.
observance n observancia f; reverencia f.
observant adj observante, respetuoso/sa.
observantly adv cuidadosamente, atentamente.
observation n observación f.
observatory n observatorio m.
observe vt observar, mirar.
observer n observador/a m/f.
obsess vt obsesionar.
obsessive adj obsesivo/va.
obsolete adj obsoleto/ta.
obstacle n obstáculo m.

obstinacy *n* tenacidad *f*.
obstinate *adj* obstinado/da; ~**ly** *adv* obstinadamente.
obstruct *vt* obstruir; impedir.
obstruction *n* obstrucción *f*; impedimento *m*.
obtain *vt* obtener, adquirir; ~ **by cunning** sonsacar.
obtainable *adj* asequible.
obtrusive *adj* intruso/sa, importuno/na.
obtuse *adj* obtuso/sa, sin punta; lerdo/da, torpe.
obvious *adj* obvio/via, evidente; ~**ly** *adv* naturalmente.
occasion *n* ocasión *f*; momento oportuno *m*; * *vt* ocasionar, causar.
occasional *adj* ocasional, casual; ~**ly** *adv* ocasionalmente.
occupant, occupier *n* ocupante *m/f*; poseedor/a *m/f*; inquilino/na *m/f*.
occupation *n* ocupación *f*; empleo *m*.
occupy *vt* ocupar, emplear.
occur *vi* pasar, ocurrir.
occurrence *n* incidente *m*.
ocean *n* océano *m*; alta mar *f*.
ocean-going *adj* de alta mar.
oceanic *adj* océanico/ca.
ochre *n* ocre *m*.
octave *n* octava *f*.
October *n* octubre *m*.
octopus *n* pulpo *m*.
odd *adj* impar; particular; extravagante; extraño/ña; ~**ly** *adv* extrañamente.
oddity *n* singularidad, particularidad, rareza *f*.
oddness *n* desigualdad *f*; singularidad *f*.
odds *npl* probabilidades *fpl*; apuestas *fpl*.
odious *adj* odioso/sa.

odorous *adj* odorífero/ra.
odour *n* olor *m*; fragancia *f*.
of *prep* de; tocante; segun.
of course *interj* inaturalmente!
off *adj* desconectado/da; apagado/da; cerrado/da; cancelado/da; ~! *excl* ifuera!
offence *n* ofensa *f*; injuria *f*.
offend *vt* ofender, irritar; injuriar; * *vi* pecar.
offender *n* delincuente *m*.
offensive *adj* ofensivo/va; injurioso/sa; ~**ly** *adv* ofensivamente.
offer *vt* ofrecer; * *n* oferta *f*.
offering *n* sacrificio *m*; oferta *f*.
offhand *adj* descortés; * *adv* de repente.
office *n* oficina *f*; oficio, empleo *m*; servicio *m*.
office building *n* bloque de oficinas *m*.
office hours *npl* horas de oficina *fpl*.
officer *n* oficial/a, empleado/da *m/f*.
office worker *n* oficinista *m/f*.
official *adj* oficial; ~**ly** *adv* de oficio; * *n* empleado/m.
officiate *vi* oficiar.
officious *adj* oficioso/sa; ~**ly** *adv* oficiosamente.
off-line *adj*, *adv* fuera de línea.
off-peak *adj* de temporada baja.
off-season *adj*, *adv* fuera de temporada, en tarifa reducida.
offset *vt* contrarrestar.
offshoot *n* ramificación *f*.
offshore *adj* costero/ra.
offside *adj* fuera de juego.
offspring *n* prole *f*; linaje *m*; descendencia *f*.
offstage *adv* entre bastidores.
off-the-peg *adj* confeccionado/da.
ogle *vt* comerse con los ojos.
oil *n* aceite *m*; óleo *m*; * *vt* engrasar.

oilcan *n* lata de aceite *f*.

oilfield *n* campo petrolífero *m*.

oil filter *n* filtro de aceite *m*.

oil painting *n* pintura al óleo *f*.

oil rig *n* torre de perforación *f*.

oil slick *n* marea negra *f*.

oil tanker *n* petrolero *m*.

oil well *n* pozo petrolífero *m*.

oily *adj* aceitoso/sa; grasiento/ta.

ointment *n* ungüento *m*.

OK, okay *excl* vale; * *adj* bien; * *vt* dar el visto bueno a.

old *adj* viejo/ja; antiguo/gua.

old age *n* vejez *f*.

old-fashioned *adj* pasado/da de moda.

olive *n* olivo *m*; oliva *f*.

olive oil *n* aceite de oliva *m*.

Olympic Games *n* las Olímpicos *f*.

omelette *n* tortilla (francesa) *f*.

omen *n* agüero, presagio *m*.

ominous *adj* ominoso/sa.

omission *n* omisión *f*; descuido *m*.

omit *vt* omitir.

omnipotence *n* omnipotencia *f*.

omnipotent *adj* omnipotente, todo-poderoso/sa.

on *prep* sobre, encima, en; de; a; * *adj* encendido/da; prendido/da; abierto/ta; puesto/ta.

once *adv* una vez; **at ~** en seguida; **all at ~** de una vez, en seguida; **~ more** otra vez.

oncoming *adj* que viene de frente.

one *adj* un, uno, una; **~ by ~** uno a uno, una a una, uno por uno, una por una.

one-day excursion *n* billete de ida y vuelta en un día *m*.

one-man *adj* individual.

onerous *adj* oneroso/sa, molesto/ta.

oneself *pn* sí mismo; sí misma.

one-sided *adj* parcial.

one-to-one *adj* de uno a uno; cara a cara.

ongoing *adj* continuo/nua.

onion *n* cebolla *f*.

on-line *adj, adv* en línea.

onlooker *n* espectador/a *m/f*.

only *adj* único/ca, solo/la; * *adv* solamente.

onset, onslaught *n* acometida *f*; ataque *m*.

onus *n* responsabilidad *f*.

onward(s) *adv* adelante.

ooze *vi* manar suavemente, rezumar.

opaque *adj* opaco/ca.

open *adj* abierto/ta; patente, evidente; sincero/ra, franco/ca; **~ly** *adv* con franqueza; * *vt* (*vi*) abrir(se); descubrir(se); **to ~ on to** dar a; **to ~ up** *vt* abrir; *vi* abrirse.

opening *n* abertura *f*; (*com*) salida *f*; principio *m*.

open-minded *adj* de mentalidad abierta.

openness *n* claridad *f*; franqueza, sinceridad *f*.

opera *n* ópera *f*.

opera house *n* teatro de la ópera *m*.

operate *vi* obrar, operar.

operating theatre *n* quirófano *m*.

operation *n* operación *f*; efecto *m*.

operational *adj* operacional.

operative *adj* operativo/va.

operator *n* operario/ria *m/f*; operador/a *m/f*.

ophthalmic *adj* oftálmico/ca.

opine *vi* opinar, juzgar.

opinion *n* opinión *f*; juicio *m*.

opinionated *adj* testarudo/da.

opinion poll *n* sondeo *m*.

opponent *n* antagonista *m/f*; adversario/ria *m/f*.

opportune *adj* oportuno/na.

opportunist n oportunista m/f.
opportunity n oportunidad f.
oppose vt oponerse.
opposing adj opuesto/ta.
opposite adj opuesto/ta; contrario/ria; * adv enfrente; prep frente a; * n lo contrario.
opposition n oposición f; resistencia f; impedimento m.
oppress vt oprimir.
oppression n opresión f.
oppressive adj opresivo/va, cruel.
oppressor n opresor/a m/f.
optic(al) adj óptico/ca; ~s npl óptica f.
optician n óptico/ca m/f.
optimist n optimista m/f.
optimistic adj optimista.
optimum adj óptimo/ma.
option n opción f; deseo m.
optional adj facultativo/va.
opulent adj opulento/ta.
or conj o; u.
oracle n oráculo m.
oral adj oral, vocal; ~ly adv verbalmente, de palabra.
orange n naranja f.
orator n orador/a m/f.
orbit n órbita f.
orchard n huerto m.
orchestra n orquesta f.
orchestral adj orquestal.
orchid n orquídea f.
ordain vt ordenar; establecer.
ordeal n prueba rigurosa f.
order n orden m/f; regla f; mandato m; serie, clase f; * vt ordenar, arreglar; mandar.
order form n hoja de pedido f.
orderly adj ordenado/da, regular.
ordinarily adv ordinariamente.
ordinary adj ordinario/ria.
ordination n ordenación f.

ordnance n armamento m; pertrechos mpl.
ore n mineral m.
organ n órgano m.
organic adj orgánico/ca.
organic farming n agricultura biológica f.
organism n organismo m.
organist n organista m/f.
organization n organización f.
organize vt organizar.
orgasm n orgasmo m.
orgy n orgía f.
oriental adj oriental.
orifice n orificio m.
origin n origen, principio m.
original adj original, primitivo/va; ~ly adv originalmente.
originality n originalidad f.
originate vi originar.
ornament n ornamento m; * vt ornamentar, adornar.
ornamental adj ornamental, decorativo/va.
ornate adj adornado/da, ataviado/da.
ornithology n ornitología f.
orphan adj, n huérfano/na m/f.
orphanage n orfanato m.
orthodox adj ortodoxo/xa.
orthodoxy n ortodoxia f.
orthography n ortografía f.
orthopaedic adj ortopédico/ca.
Oscar n óscar m.
oscillate vi oscilar, vibrar.
osprey n águila pescadora f.
ostensibly adv aparentemente.
ostentatious adj ostentoso/sa.
osteopath n osteópata m/f.
ostracize vt condenar al ostracismo.
ostrich n avestruz m.
other pn otro, otra.
otherwise adv de otra manera, por otra parte.

otter n nutria f.

ouch excl ¡ay!

ought v aux deber, ser menester.

ounce n onza f.

our, ours pn nuestro, nuestra, nuestros, nuestras.

ourselves pn pl nosotros mismos, nosotras mismas.

oust vt quitar; desposeer.

out adv fuera, afuera; apagado/da.

outboard adj ~ **motor** fueraborda m.

outbreak n erupción f.

outburst n explosión f.

outcast n paria m/f.

outcome n resultado m.

outcry n clamor m; griterío m.

outdated adj fuera de moda.

outdo vt exceder a otro, sobrepujar.

outdoor adj, ~**s** adv al aire libre.

outer adj exterior.

outermost adj extremo/ma; lo más exterior.

outer space n espacio exterior m.

outfit n vestidos mpl; ropa f.

outfitter n sastre m.

outgoing adj extrovertido/da.

outgrow vt sobrecrecer.

outhouse n dependencia (de una casa) f.

outing n excursión f.

outlandish adj estrafalario/ria.

outlaw n bandido m; * vt proscribir.

outlay n despensa f, gastos mpl.

outlet n salida f.

outline n contorno m; bosquejo m.

outlive vt sobrevivir.

outlook n perspectiva f.

outlying adj distante, lejos.

outmoded adj anticuado/da.

outnumber vt superar en número.

out-of-date adj caducado/da; pasado/da de moda.

outpatient n paciente externo/na m/f.

outpost n puesto avanzado m.

output n rendimiento m; salida f.

outrage n ultraje m; * vt ultrajar.

outrageous adj escandaloso/sa; atroz; ~**ly** adv escandalosamente; injuriosamente; enormemente.

outright adv absolutamente; * adj completo/ta.

outrun vt correr más que.

outset n principio m.

outshine vt exceder en brillantez, eclipsar.

outside n superficie f; exterior m; apariencia f; * adv fuera; * prep fuera de.

outsider n forástero m/f.

outsize adj de talla grande.

outskirts npl alrededores mpl.

outspoken adj muy franco/ca.

outstanding adj excepcional; pendiente.

outstretch vt extenderse, alargar.

outstrip vt dejar atrás; superar.

out-tray n bandeja de salida f.

outward adj exterior, externo/na; de ida; ~**ly** adv por fuera; exteriormente.

outweigh vt pesar más que.

outwit vt burlar.

oval n óvalo m; * adj oval.

ovary n ovario m.

oven n horno m.

ovenproof adj resistente al horno.

over prep sobre, encima; más de; durante; **all** ~ por todos lados; * adj terminado/da; de sobra; ~ **again** otra vez; ~ **and** ~ repetidas veces.

overall adj total; * adv en conjunto; ~**s** npl overol m; mono m.

overawe vt imponer respeto.

overbalance vi perder el equilibrio.

overbearing adj despótico/ca.

overboard adv (mar) por la borda, al mar.

overbook *vt* sobrereservar.

overcast *adj* encapotado/da.

overcharge *vt* sobrecargar; cobrar de más.

overcoat *n* abrigo *m*.

overcome *vt* vencer; superar.

overconfident *adj* demasiado confiado/da.

overcrowded *adj* atestado/da; superpoblado/da.

overdo *vi* hacer más de lo necesario; exagerar.

overdose *n* sobredosis *f invar*.

overdraft *n* saldo deudor, descubierto *m*.

overdrawn *adj* en descubierto.

overdress *vt* engalanar con exceso.

overdue *adj* retrasado/da.

overeat *vi* comer demasiado.

overestimate *vt* sobreestimar.

overflow *vt, vi* inundar; rebosar; * *n* inundación *f*; superabundancia *f*.

overgrown *adj* invadido/da.

overgrowth *n* vegetación exuberante *f*.

overhang *vt* colgar sobre.

overhaul *vt* revisar; * *n* revisión *f*.

overhead *adv* sobre la cabeza, en lo alto.

overhear *vt* oír por casualidad.

overjoyed *adj* muy gozoso/sa.

overkill *n* exceso de medios *m*.

overland *adj*, *adv* por tierra.

overlap *vi* traslaparse.

overleaf *adv* al dorso.

overload *vt* sobrecargar.

overlook *vt* mirar desde lo alto; examinar; repasar; pasar por alto, tolerar; descuidar.

overnight *adv* durante la noche; * *adj* de noche.

overpass *n* paso superior *m*.

overpower *vt* predominar, oprimir.

overpowering *adj* agobiante.

overrate *vt* sobrevalorar.

override *vt* no hacer caso de; anular.

overriding *adj* predominante.

overrule *vt* denegar.

overrun *vt* inundar; infestar; rebasar.

overseas *adv* fuera del país; * *adj* extranjero/ra.

oversee *vt* inspeccionar.

overseer *n* superintendente *m*.

overshadow *vt* eclipsar.

overshoot *vt* excederse.

oversight *n* yerro *m*; equivocación *f*.

oversleep *vi* dormir demasiado.

overspill *n* exceso de población *m*.

overstate *vi* exagerar.

overstep *vt* traspasar, exceder.

overt *adj* abierto/ta; publico/ca; **~ly** *adv* abiertamente.

overtake *vt* adelantar, sobrepasar.

overthrow *vt* trastornar; demoler; destruir; * *n* trastorno *m*; ruina, derrota *f*.

overtime *n* horas extra *fpl*.

overtone *n* trasfondo *m*.

overture *n* abertura *f*; (*mus*) obertura *f*.

overturn *vt* subvertir, trastornar.

overweight *adj* demasiado pesado/da.

overwhelm *vt* abrumar; oprimir; sumergir.

overwhelming *adj* arrollador/a; irresistible.

overwork *vi* trabajar demasiado.

owe *vt* deber, tener deudas; estar obligado/da.

owing *adj* que es debido/da; **~ to** por causa de.

owl *n* búho *m*.

own *adj* propio/pia; **my ~** mío, mía; * *vt* tener; poseer; **to ~ up** *vi* confesar.

owner *n* dueño/ña, propietario/ria *m/f*.
ownership *n* posesión *f*.
ox *n* buey *m*; **~en** *pl* ganado vacuno *m*.
oxidize *vt* oxidar.

oxygen *n* oxígeno *m*.
oxygen mask *n* máscara de oxígeno *f*.
oxygen tent *n* tienda de oxígeno *f*.
oyster *n* ostra *f*.
ozone *n* ozono *m*.

P

pa *n* papá *m*.
pace *n* paso *m*; * *vt* regular el ritmo de; * *vi* pasear.
pacemaker *n* marcapasos *m* invar.
pacific *adj* pacífico/ca; **P~ Ocean** el Pacífico *m*.
pacification *n* pacificación *f*.
pacify *vt* pacificar.
pack *n* lío, fardo *m*; baraja (de naipes) *f*; cuadrilla *f*; * *vt* empaquetar; hacer la maleta; llenar.
package *n* paquete *m*; acuerdo *m*.
package tour *n* viaje organizado *m*.
packet *n* paquete *m*.
packing *n* embalaje *m*.
pact *n* pacto *m*.
pad *n* bloc *m*; plataforma *f*; (*sl*) casa *f*; * *vt* rellenar.
padding *n* relleno *m*; paja *f*.
paddle *vivadear*; remar; chapotear; * *n* canalete *m*.
paddle steamer *n* vapor de ruedas *m*.
paddling pool *n* piscina para niños *f*.
paddock *n* corral *m*.
paddy field *n* arrozal *m*.
paediatrics *n* pediatría *f*.
pagan *adj*, *n* pagano/na *m/f*.
page *n* página *f*; paje *m*.
pageant *n* espectáculo público *m*.
pageantry *n* pompa *f*.
pail *n* cubo, pozal *m*.
pain *n* pena *f*; castigo *m*; dolor *m*; * *vt* afligir.

pained *adj* afligido/da.
painful *adj* dolorido/da; penoso/sa; **~ly** *adv* dolorosamente, con pena.
painkiller *n* analgésico *m*.
painless *adj* sin pena; indoloro/ra.
painstaking *adj* laborioso/sa, meticuloso/sa.
paint *vt* pintar.
paintbrush *n* pincel *m*; brocha *f*.
painter *n* pintor *m/f*.
painting *n* pintura *f*.
paintwork *n* pintura *f*.
pair *n* par *m*; yuntas *fpl*.
pal *n* compañero/ra *m/f*.
palatable *adj* sabroso/sa.
palate *n* paladar *m*; gusto *m*.
palatial *adj* palatino/na.
palaver *n* lío *m*.
pale *adj* palido/da; claro/ra.
palette *n* paleta *f*.
paling *n* estacada, palizada *f*.
pall *n* cortina de humo *f*; * *vi* perder el sabor.
palliative *adj* paliativo/va; * *n* paliativo *m*.
pallid *adj* pálido/da.
pallor *n* palidez *f*.
palm *n* (*bot*) palma *f*.
palmistry *n* quiromancia *f*.
Palm Sunday *n* Domingo de Ramos *m*.
palpable *adj* palpable; evidente.
palpitation *n* palpitación *f*.

paltry adj irrisorio/ria; mezquino/na.

pamper vt mimar.

pamphlet n folleto m.

pan n cazuela f; sartén f; olla f.

panacea n panacea f.

panache n estilo m.

pancake n crepe f.

pandemonium n jaleo m.

pane n cristal m.

panel n panel m; paño m.

panelling n paneles mpl.

pang n angustia, congoja f.

panic adj, n pánico/ca m.

panicky adj asustadizo/za.

panic-stricken adj preso/sa del pánico.

pansy n (bot) pensamiento m.

pant vi jadear.

panther n pantera f.

panties npl bragas fpl.

pantry n despensa f.

papacy n papado m.

papal adj papal.

papaw, pawpaw, papaya n papaya f.

paper n papel m; periódico m; examen m; estudio m; ~s pl escrituras fpl; (com) fondos mpl; * adj de papel; * vt empape lar; tapizar.

paperback n libro en rústica m.

paper bag n bolsa de papel f.

paperclip n clip m.

paperweight n sujetapapeles m invar.

paperwork n papeleo m.

paprika n pimentón m, paprika f.

par n equivalencia f; igualdad f; par m; **at ~** (com) a la par.

parable n parábola f.

parachute n paracaídas m invar; * vi lanzarse en paracaídas.

parade n ostentación, pompa f; (mil) parada f; * vt, vi desfilar; pasear; hacer gala.

paradise n paraiso m.

paradox n paradoja f.

paradoxical adj paradójico/ca.

paraffin n queroseno m.

paragliding n parapente m.

paragon n dechado m.

paragraph n párrafo m.

parallel adj paralelo/la; * n línea paralela f; * vt paralelizar; parangonar.

paralyse vt paralizar.

paralysis n parálisis f.

paralytic adj paralítico/ca.

paramedic n auxiliar sanitario/ria m/f.

paramount adj supremo/ma, superior.

paranoid adj paranoico/ca.

paraphernalia n parafernalia f.

parasite n parásito m.

parasol n parasol, quitasol m.

paratrooper n paracaidista m.

parcel n paquete m; porción, cantidad f; equipajes, bultos mpl; * vt empaquetar, embalar.

parch vt resecar.

parched adj reseco/ca; muerto/ta de sed.

parchment n pergamino m.

pardon n perdón m; * vt perdonar.

parent n padre m; madre f.

parentage n parentela f; extracción f.

parental adj de los padres.

parenthesis n paréntesis m invar.

parish n parroquia f; * adj parroquial.

parishioner n parroquiano/na m/f.

parity n paridad f.

park n parque m; * vt, vi aparcar, estacionar.

parking n aparcamiento, estacionamiento m.

parking meter n parquímetro m.

parking ticket n multa de estacionamiento f.

parlance n lenguaje m.

parliament n parlamento m.

parliamentary adj parlamentario/ria.

parlour n salón m.

parody n parodia f; * vt parodiar.

parole n: on ~ en libertad bajo palabra.

parricide n parricidio m; parricida m/f.

parrot n papagayo m.

parry vt parar.

parsley n (bot) perejil m.

parsnip n (bot) chirivía f.

part n parte f; partido m; oficio m; papel (de un actor) m; obligación f; raya f; ~s pl partes fpl; paraje, distrito m; * vt partir, separar, desunir; * vi partirse, separarse; to ~ with entregar; pagar; deshacerse de; ~ly adv en parte.

partial adj, ~ly adv parcial(mente).

participant n concursante m.

participate vi participar (en).

participation n participación f.

participle n (gr) participio m.

particle n partícula f.

particular adj particular, singular; ~ly adv particularmente; * n particular m; particularidad f.

parting n separación, partida f; raya (en los cabellos) f.

partisan n partidario/ria m/f.

partition n partición, separación f; * vt partir, dividir en varias partes.

partner n socio/cia, compañero/ra m/f.

partnership n compañía, sociedad de comercio f.

partridge n perdiz f.

party n partido m; fiesta f.

pass vt pasar; traspasar; transferir; adelantarse a; * vi pasar, aprobar; * n permiso m; puerto m; to ~ away vi fallecer; to ~ by vi pasar; vt pasar por alto; to ~ on vt transmitir.

passable adj pasadero/ra, transitable.

passage n pasaje m; travesía f; pasadizo m.

passbook n libreta de depósitos f.

passenger n pasajero/ra m/f.

passer-by n transeúnte m/f.

passing adj pasajero/ra.

passion n pasión f; amor m; celo, ardor m.

passionate adj apasionado/da; ~ly adv apasionadamente; ardientemente.

passive adj pasivo/va; ~ly adv pasivamente.

passkey n llava maestra f.

Passover n Pascua f.

passport n pasaporte m.

passport control n control de pasaportes m.

password n contraseña f.

past adj pasado/da; gastado/da; * n (gr) pretérito m; el pasado; * prep más allá de; después de.

pasta n pasta f.

paste n pasta f; engrudo m; * vt engrudar.

pasteurized adj pasteurizado/da.

pastime n pasatiempo m; diversión f.

pastor n pastor m.

pastoral adj pastoril; pastoral.

pastry n pastelería f.

pasture n pasto m.

pasty adj pastoso/sa; pálido/da.

pat vt dar golpecitos.

patch n remiendo m; parche m; terreno m; * vt remendar; to ~ up reparar; hacer las paces en.

patchwork n obra de retacitos f; chapuceria f.

pâté n paté m.

patent adj patente; privilegiado/da; * n patente f; * vt privilegiar.

patentee n poseedor/a de una patente m/f.

patent leather n charol m.

paternal adj paternal.

paternity n paternidad f.

path n senda f.

pathetic adj patético/ca; ~ally adv patéticamente.

pathological adj patológico/ca.

pathology n patología f.

pathos n patetismo m.

pathway n sendero m.

patience n paciencia f.

patient adj paciente, sufrido/da; ~ly adv con paciencia; * n enfermo/ma m/f.

patio n patio m.

patriarch n patriarca m.

patriot n patriota m.

patriotic adj patriotico/ca.

patriotism n patriotismo m.

patrol n patrulla f; * vi patrullar.

patrol car n coche patrulla m.

patrolman n policía m.

patron n patrón/ona, protector m/f.

patronage n patrocinio m; patronato, patronazgo m.

patronize vt patrocinar, proteger.

patter n golpeteo m; labia f; * vi tamborilear.

pattern n patrón m; dibujo m.

paunch n panza f; vientre m.

pauper n pobre m/f.

pause n pausa f; * vt pausar; deliberar.

pave vt empedrar; enlosar, embaldosar.

pavement n acera f.

pavilion n pabellón m.

paving stone n ladrillo m; losa f.

paw n pata f; garra f; * vt manosear.

pawn n peón m; * vt empeñar.

pawnbroker n prestamista m/f.

pawnshop n casa de empeños f.

pay vt pagar; sufrir por; to ~ back vt reembolsar; to ~ for pagar; to ~ off vt liquidar; vi dar resultados; * n paga f; salario m.

payable adj pagadero/ra.

payday n día de paga m.

payee n portador/a m/f.

pay envelope n sobre (de paga) m.

paymaster n pagador/a m/f.

payment n paga f; pagamento, pago m.

payphone n teléfono público m.

payroll n nómina f.

pea n guisante m.

peace n paz f.

peaceful adj tranquilo/la, pacífico/ca.

peach n melocotón, durazno m.

peacock n pavón, pavo real m.

peak n cima f.

peak hours, peak period n horas punta fpl.

peal n campaneo m; estruendo m.

peanut n cacahuete m; maní m.

pear n pera f.

pearl n perla f.

peasant n campesino/na m/f.

peat n turba f.

pebble n guija f; guijarro m.

peck n picotazo m; * vt picotear; picar.

pecking order n orden de jerarquía m.

peculiar adj peculiar, particular, singular; ~ly adv peculiarmente.

peculiarity n particularidad, singularidad f.

pedal n pedal m; * vi pedalear.

pedant n pedante m/f.

pedantic adj pedante.

pedestal n pedestal m.

pedestrian n peatón/ona m/f; * adj pedestre.

pedestrian crossing n paso de peatones m.

pedigree n genealogía f; * adj de raza.

pedlar n vendedor/a ambulante m/f.

peek vi mirar de soslayo.

peel vt pelar; * vi desconcharse; * n piel f; cáscara f.

peer n compañero/ra m/f; par m.

peerless adj incomparable.

peeved adj enojado/da.

peevish adj regañón/ona, bronco/ca; enojadizo/za.

peg n clavija f; gancho m; * vt clavar.

pelican n pelícano m.

pellet n bolita f; ~s perdigones mpl.

pelt n pellejo, cuero m; * vt arrojar; * vi llover a cántaros.

pen n bolígrafo m; pluma f; redil m.

penal adj penal.

penalty n pena f; castigo m; multa f.

penance n penitencia f.

pence n pl de **penny**.

pencil n lápiz m; lapicero m.

pencil case n estuche m.

pendant n pendiente m.

pending adj pendiente.

pendulum n péndulo m.

penetrate vt penetrar.

penguin n pingüino m.

penicillin n penicilina f.

peninsula n península f.

penis n pene m.

penitence n penitencia f.

penitent adj, n penitente m.

penknife n navaja f.

pennant n banderola f.

penniless adj sin dinero.

penny n penique m.

penpal n amigo/ga por carta m/f.

pension n pensión f; * vt dar pensión a.

pensive adj pensativo/va; ~ly adv pensativamente.

pentagon n: **the P~** el Pentágono.

Pentecost n Pentecostés m.

penthouse n ático m.

pent-up adj reprimido/da.

penultimate adj penúltimo/ma.

penury n penuria, carestía f.

people n pueblo m; nación f; gente f; * vt poblar.

people mover n monovolumen m.

pep n enérgia f; **to ~ up** vt animar.

pepper n pimienta f; * vt sazonar con pimienta.

peppermint n menta f.

per prep por.

per annum adv al año.

per capita adj, adv per cápita.

perceive vt percibir, comprender.

percentage n porcentaje m.

perception n percepción, idea, noción f.

perch n percha f.

perchance adv acaso, quizá.

percolate vt colar; filtrar.

percolator n cafetera de filtro f.

percussion n percusión f; golpe m.

perdition n pérdida, ruina f.

peremptory adj perentorio/ria; decisivo/va.

perennial adj perenne; perpetuo/tua.

perfect adj perfecto/ta, acabado/da; puro/ra; ~ly adv perfectamente; * vt perfeccionar, acabar.

perfection n perfección f.

perforate vt horadar.

perforated adj (of stamps) dentado/da.

perforation n perforación f.
perform vt ejecutar; efectuar; * vi representar, hacer papel.
performance n ejecución f; cumplimiento m; obra f; representación teatral, función f.
performer n ejecutor/a m/f; actor m, actriz f.
perfume n perfume m; fragancia f; * vt perfumar.
perhaps adv quizá, quizás.
peril n peligro, riesgo m.
perilous adj peligroso/sa; ~ly adv peligrosamente.
perimeter n perímetro m.
period n período m; época f; regla f.
periodic adj periódico/ca; ~ally adv periódicamente.
periodical n periódico m.
peripheral adj periférico/ca; * n periférico m.
perish vi perecer.
perishable adj perecedero/ra.
perjure vt perjurar.
perjury n perjurio m.
perk n extra m.
perky adj animado/da.
perm n permanente f.
permanent adj, ~ly adv permanente(mente).
permeate vt penetrar, atravesar.
permissible adj lícito/ta, permiso.
permission n permiso m.
permissive adj permisivo/va.
permit vt permitir; * n permiso m.
permutation n permutación f.
perpendicular adj, ~ly adv perpendicular(mente); * n línea perpendicular f.
perpetrate vt perpetrar, cometer.
perpetual adj perpetuo/tua; ~ly adv perpetuamente.
perpetuate vt perpetuar, eternizar.

perplex vt confundir.
persecute vt perseguir, importunar.
persecution n persecución f.
perseverance n perseverancia f.
persevere vi perseverar.
persist vi persistir.
persistence adj persistencia f.
persistent adj persistente.
person n persona f.
personable adj atractivo/va.
personage n personaje m.
personal adj, ~ly adv personal(mente).
personal assistant n secretario/ria personal m/f.
personal column n anuncios personales mpl.
personal computer n ordenador personal m, computadora personal f.
personality n personalidad f.
personification n personificación f.
personify vt personificar.
personnel n personal m.
perspective n perspectiva f.
perspiration n transpiración f.
perspire vi transpirar.
persuade vt persuadir.
persuasion n persuasión f.
persuasive adj persuasivo/va; ~ly adv de modo persuasivo.
pert adj listo/va, vivo/va; petulante.
pertaining: ~ to prep relacionado/da con.
pertinent adj pertinente; ~ly adv oportunamente.
pertness n impertinencia f; vivacidad f.
perturb vt perturbar.
perusal n lectura, lección f.
peruse vt leer; examinar atentamente.
pervade vt atravesar, penetrar.

perverse *adj* perverso/sa, depravado/da; **~ly** *adv* perversamente.
pervert *vt* pervertir, corromper.
pessimist *n* pesimista *m*.
pest *n* plaga *f*; molestia *f*.
pester *vt* molestar, cansar.
pestilence *n* pestilencia *f*.
pet *n* animal doméstico *m*; favorito/ta *m/f*; * *vt* mimar; * *vi* besuquearse.
petal *n* (*bot*) pétalo *m*.
petite *adj* chiquito/ta.
petition *n* presentación, petición *f*; * *vt* suplicar; requerir en justicia.
petrified *adj* horrorizado/da.
petrol *n* gasolina *f*; **four-star ~** súper *f*.
petroleum *n* petróleo *m*.
petticoat *n* enaguas *fpl*.
pettiness *n* mezquindad *f*; pequeñez *f*.
petty *adj* mezquino/na; insignificante.
petty cash *n* dinero para gastos menores *m*.
petty officer *n* contramaestre *m*.
petulant *adj* petulante.
pew *n* banco *m*.
pewter *n* peltre *m*.
phantom *n* fantasma *m*.
Pharisee *n* fariseo/sea *m/f*.
pharmaceutical *adj* farmacéutico/ca.
pharmacist *n* farmacéutico/ca *m/f*.
pharmacy *n* farmacia *f*.
phase *n* fase *f*.
pheasant *n* faisán *m*.
phenomenal *adj* fenomenal.
phenomenon *n* fenómeno *m*.
phial *n* vial *m*.
philanthropic *adj* filantrópico/ca.
philanthropist *n* filántropo/pa *m/f*.
philanthropy *n* filantropía *f*.

philologist *n* filólogo/ga *m/f*.
philology *n* filología *f*.
philosopher *n* filósofo/fa *m/f*.
philosophic(al) *adj* filosófico/ca; **~ally** *adv* filosóficamente.
philosophize *vi* filosofar.
philosophy *n* filosofía *f*; **natural ~** filosofía natural *f*.
phlegm *n* flema *f*.
phlegmatic(al) *adj* flemático/ca.
phobia *n* fobia *f*.
phone *n* teléfono *m*; * *vt* telefonear; **to ~ back** volver a llamar; **to ~ up** llamar por teléfono.
phone book *n* guía telefónica *f*.
phone box *n* cabina telefónica *f*.
phone call *n* llamada (telefonica) *f*.
phosphorus *n* fosforo *m*.
photocopier *n* fotocopiadora *f*.
photocopy *n* fotocopia *f*.
photograph *n* fotografía *f*; * *vt* fotografiar.
photographer *n* fotógrafo/fa *m/f*.
photographic *adj* fotográfico/ca.
photography *n* fotografía *f*.
phrase *n* frase *f*; estilo *m*; * *vt* expresar.
phrase book *n* libro de frases *m*.
physical *adj* físico/ca; **~ly** *adv* físicamente.
physical education *n* educación física *f*.
physician *n* médico/ca *m/f*.
physicist *n* físico/ca *m/f*.
physiological *adj* fisiológico/ca.
physiologist *n* fisiólogo/ga *m/f*.
physiology *n* fisiología *f*.
physiotherapy *n* fisioterapia *f*.
physique *n* físico *m*.
pianist *n* pianista *m/f*.
piano *n* piano *m*.
piccolo *n* flautín *m*.
pick *vt* escoger, elegir; recoger;

mondar, limpiar; **to ~ on** *vt* meterse con; **to ~ out** *vt* escoger; **to ~ up** *vi* ir mejor; recobrarse; * *vt* recoger; comprar; aprender; * *n* pico *m*; **the ~ of** lo más escogido de.

pickaxe *n* pico *m*.

picket *n* piquete *m*.

pickle *n* escabeche *m*; *vt* escabechar.

pickpocket *n* carterista *m/f*.

pick-up *n* (*auto*) furgoneta *f*.

picnic *n* picnic *m*.

pictorial *adj* pictórico/ca.

picture *n* pintura *f*; retrato *m*; * *vt* pintar; figurar.

picture book *n* libro de dibujos *m*.

picturesque *adj* pintoresco/ca.

pie *n* pastel *m*; tarta *f*; empanada *f*.

piece *n* pedazo *m*; pieza, obra *f*; * *vt* remendar.

piecemeal *adv* en pedazos; * *adj* dividido/da.

piecework *n* destajo *m*; * *vi* **to do ~** trabajar a destajo.

pier *n* pilar *m*; muelle *m*.

pierce *vt* penetrar, agujerear, taladrar.

piercing *adj* penetrante.

piety *n* piedad, devoción *f*.

pig *n* cerdo *m*; (*sl*) cochino *m*.

pigeon *n* paloma *f*; **carrier,homing ~** paloma mensajera *f*.

pigeonhole *n* casillero *m*.

piggy bank *n* hucha *f*.

pig-headed *adj* terco/ca.

pigsty *n* pocilga *f*.

pigtail *n* trenza *f*.

pike *n* lucio *m*; pica *f*.

pile *n* estaca *f*; pila *f*; montón *m*; pelo *m*; pelillo *m*; **~s** *pl* almorranas *fpl*; * *vt* amontonar, apilar.

pile-up *n* colisión múltiple *f*.

pilfer *vt* hurtar.

pilgrim *n* peregrino/na *m/f*.

pilgrimage *n* peregrinación *f*.

pill *n* píldora *f*.

pillage *vt* saquear.

pillar *n* pilar *m*.

pillion *n* asiento trasero *m*.

pillow *n* almohada *f*.

pillow case *n* funda de almohada *f*.

pilot *n* piloto *m/f*; * *vt* pilotar; (*fig*) guiar.

pilot light *n* piloto *m*.

pimp *n* chulo, cafiche *m*.

pimple *n* grano *m*.

pin *n* alfiler *m*; **~s and needles** *npl* hormigueo *m*; * *vt* prender con alfileres; fijar con clavija.

pinafore *n* delantal *m*.

pinball *n* flíper *m*.

pincers *n* pinzas, tenazuelas *fpl*.

pinch *vt* pellizcar; (*sl*) birlar; * *vi* apretar; * *n* pellizco *m*.

pincushion *n* acerico *m*.

pine *n* (*bot*) pino *m*; * *vi* ansiar por.

pineapple *n* piña *f*, ananás *m invar*.

ping *n* sonido agudo *m*.

pink *n* rosa *f*; * *adj* color de rosa.

pinnacle *n* cumbre *f*.

pinpoint *vt* precisar.

pint *n* pinta *f*.

pioneer *n* pionero/ra *m/f*.

pious *adj* pío, pía, devoto/ta; **~ly** *adv* piadosamente.

pip *n* pepita *f*.

pipe *n* tubo, caño *m*; pipa *f*; **~s** cañería *f*.

pipe cleaner *n* limpiapipas *m invar*.

pipe dream *n* sueño imposible *m*.

pipeline *n* tubería *f*; oleoducto *m*; gasoducto *m*.

piper *n* gaitero/ra *m/f*.

piping *adj* hirviente.

pique *n* pique *m*; desazón *f*; ojeriza *f*.

piracy *n* piratería *f*.

pirate *n* pirata *m/f*.
pirouette *n* pirueta; *vi* piruetear.
Pisces *n* Piscis *m* (signo del zodiaco).
piss *n* (*sl*) meada *f*; * *vi* mear.
pistol *n* pistola *f*.
piston *n* émbolo *m*.
pit *n* hoyo *m*; mina *f*.
pitch *n* lanzamiento *m*; tono *m*; * *vt* tirar, arrojar; * *vi* caerse; caer de cabeza.
pitch-black *adj* negro/gra como boca de lobo.
pitcher *n* cántaro *m*.
pitchfork *n* horca *f*.
pitfall *n* trampa *f*.
pithy *adj* meduloso/sa.
pitiable *adj* lastimoso/sa.
pitiful *adj* lastimoso/sa, compasivo/va; **~ly** *adv* lastimosamente.
pittance *n* pitanza, ración *f*; porioncilla *f*.
pity *n* piedad, compasión *f*; * *vt* compadecer.
pivot *n* eje *m*.
pizza *n* pizza *f*.
placard *n* pancarta *f*.
placate *vt* apaciguar.
place *n* lugar, sitio *m*; rango, empleo *m*; * *vt* colocar; poner.
placid *adj* plácido/da, quieto/ta; **~ly** *adv* plácidamente.
plagiarism *n* plagio *m*.
plague *n* peste, plaga *f*; * *vt* atormentar; infestar, apestar.
plaice *n* platija *f* (pez).
plaid *n* tartán *m*.
plain *adj* liso/so, llano/na, abierto/ta; sincero/ra; puro/ra, simple, común; claro/ra, evidente, distinto/ta; **~ly** *adv* llanamente; claramente; * *n* llano *m*.
plaintiff *n* (law) demandante *m/f*.

plait *n* pliegue *m*; trenza *f*; * *vt* plegar; trenzar.
plan *n* plano *m*; plan *m*; * *vt* proyectar.
plane *n* avión *m*; plano *m*; cepillo *m*; * *vt* allanar; acepillar.
planet *n* planeta *m*.
planetary *adj* planetario/ria.
plank *n* tabla *f*.
planner *n* planificador/a *m/f*.
planning *n* planificación *f*.
plant *n* planta *f*; fábrica *f*; maquinaria *f*; * *vt* plantar.
plantation *n* plantación *f*; colonia *f*.
plaque *n* placa *f*.
plaster *n* yeso *m*; emplasto *m*; * *vt* enyesar; emplastar.
plastered *adj* (*sl*) borracho/cha.
plasterer *n* yesero *m/f*.
plaster of Paris *n* yeso mate *m*.
plastic *adj* plástico/ca.
plastic surgery *n* cirugía plástica *f*.
plate *n* plato *m*; lámina *f*; placa *f*.
plateau *n* meseta *f*.
plate glass *n* vidrio cilindrado *m*.
platform *n* plataforma *f*.
platinum *n* platino *m*.
platitude *n* tópico *m*.
platoon *n* (*mil*) pelotón *m*.
platter *n* fuente *f*; plato grande *m*.
plaudit *n* aplauso *m*.
plausible *adj* plausible.
play *n* juego *m*; comedia *f*; * *vt*, *vi* jugar; juguetear; representar; (*mus*) tocar; **to ~ down** *vt* quitar importancia a.
playboy *n* playboy *m*.
player *n* jugador/a *m/f*; comediante/ta *m/f*, actor *m*, actriz *f*.
playful *adj* juguetón/ona, travieso/sa; **~ly** *adv* juguetonamente, retozando.
playmate *n* camarada *m/f*.

playground n patio m.

playgroup n parvulario m.

play-off n desempate m.

playpen n corral (de niños) m.

plaything n juguete m.

playwright n dramaturgo/ga m/f.

plea n defensa f; excusa f; pretexto m; * vt pretextar.

plead vt defender en juicio; alegar.

pleasant adj agradable; placentero/ra, alegre; ~ly adv alegremente, placenteramente.

please vt agradar, complacer.

pleased adj contento/ta.

pleasing adj agradable, placentero/ra.

pleasure n gusto, placer m; recreo m.

pleat n pliegue m.

pledge n prenda f; fianza f; * vt empeñar, prometer.

plentiful adj copioso/sa, abundante.

plenty n copia, abundancia f.

plethora n plétora f.

pleurisy n pleuresía f.

pliable, pliant adj flexible, dócil.

pliers npl alicates mpl.

plight n situación difícil f.

plinth n plinto m; zócalo m.

plod vi afanarse mucho, ajetrearse.

plot n terreno m; plano m; conspiración, trama f; estratagema f; * vi trazar; conspirar; tramar.

plough n arado m; * vt arar, labrar la tierra; **to ~ back** vt reinvertir; **to ~ through** abrirse paso; roer.

ploy n truco m.

pluck vt tirar con fuerza; arrancar; desplumar; * n ánimo m.

plucky adj gallardo/da.

plug n tapón m; enchufe m; bujía f; * vt tapar.

plum n ciruela f.

plumage n plumaje m.

plumb n plomada f; * adv a plomo; * vt aplomar.

plumber n fontanero/ra, plomero/ra m/f.

plume n pluma f.

plump adj gordo/da, rollizo/za.

plum tree n ciruelo m.

plunder vt saquear, pillar, robar; * n pillaje, botín m.

plunge vi sumergir(se), precipitarse; * n zambullida f.

plunger n desatascador m.

pluperfect n (gr) pluscuamperfecto m.

plural adj, n plural m.

plurality n pluralidad f.

plus n signo de más m; * prep más, y, además de.

plush adj de felpa.

plutonium n plutonio m.

ply vt trabajar con ahínco; * vi aplicarse; (mar) ir y venir.

plywood n madera contrachapada f.

pneumatic adj neumático/ca.

pneumatic drill n martillo neumático m.

pneumonia n pulmonía f.

poach vt escalfar; cazar en vedado; * vi cazar en vedado.

poached adj escalfado/da.

poacher n cazador furtivo m.

poaching n caza furtiva f.

pocket n bolsillo m; bolsa f; * vt embolsar.

pocketbook n cartera f.

pocket money n dinero para gastos m.

pod n vaina f.

podgy adj gordinflón/ona.

poem n poema m.

poet n poeta m, poetisa f.

poetic adj poético/ca.

poetry n poesía f.

poignant adj punzante.

point *n* punta *f*; punto *m*; promontorio *m*; puntillo *m*; estado *m*; ~ **of view** *n* punto de vista *m*; * *vt* apuntar; aguzar; puntuar; **to ~ a gun** encañonar.

point-blank *adv* directamente.

pointed *adj* puntiagudo/da; epigramático/ca; ~**ly** *adv* sutilmente.

pointer *n* apuntador/a *m/f*; perro de muestra *m*.

pointless *adj* sin sentido.

poise *n* peso *m*; equilibrio *m*.

poison *n* veneno *m*; * *vt* envenenar.

poisoning *n* envenenamiento *m*.

poisonous *adj* venenoso/sa.

poke *vt* hurgar; empujar.

poker *n* atizador *m*; póker *m*.

poker-faced *adj* con cara de póker.

poky *adj* estrecho/cha.

polar *adj* polar.

pole *n* polo *m*; palo *m*; pértiga *f*.

pole bean *n* judía trepadora *f*.

pole vault *n* salto con pértiga *m*.

police *n* policía *f*.

police car *n* coche patrulla *m*.

policeman *n* policía *m*.

police state *n* estado policial *m*.

police station *n* comisaría *f*.

policewoman *n* mujer policía *f*.

policy *n* política *f*.

polio *n* polio *f*.

polish *vt* pulir, alisar; limar; **to ~ off** *vt* terminar; despachar; * *n* pulimento *m*.

polished *adj* elegante, pulido/da.

polite *adj* pulido/da, cortés; ~**ly** *adv* cortésmente.

politeness *n* cortesía *f*.

politic *adj* político/ca; astuto/ta.

political *adj* político/ca.

political asylum *n* asilo político *m*.

politician *n* político/ca *m/f*.

politics *npl* política *f*.

polka *n* polca *f*; ~ **dot** *n* lunar *m*.

poll *n* voto *m*; encuesta *f*, sondeo *m*.

pollen *n* (*bot*) polen *m*.

pollute *vt* contaminar.

pollution *n* polución, contaminación *f*.

polo *n* polo *m*.

polyester *n* poliéster *m*.

polyethylene, polythene *n* polietileno *m*.

polygamy *n* poligamia *f*.

polystyrene *n* poliestireno *m*.

polytechnic *n* politécnico *m*.

pomegranate *n* granada *f*.

pomp *n* pompa *f*; esplendor *m*.

pompom *n* borla *f*.

pompous *adj* pomposo/sa.

pond *n* estanque *m*.

ponder *vt* ponderar, considerar.

ponderous *adj* ponderoso/sa, pesado/da.

pontiff *n* pontífice, papa *m*.

pontoon *n* pontón *m*.

pony *n* jaca *f*; potro *m*.

ponytail *n* cola de caballo *f*.

pool *n* charca *f*; piscina, alberca *f*; * *vt* juntar; **to form a ~** remansarse.

poor *adj* pobre; humilde; de poco valor; ~**ly** *adv* pobremente; **the ~** *n* los pobres *mpl*.

pop *n* pop *m*; papá *m*; gaseosa *f*; chasquido *m*; * **to ~ in/out** *vi* entrar *o* salir un momento.

pop concert *n* concierto pop *m*.

popcorn *n* palomitas *fpl*.

Pope *n* Papa *m*.

poplar *n* álamo *m*.

poppy *n* (*bot*) amapola *f*.

populace *n* populacho *m*.

popular *adj*, ~**ly** *adv* popular(mente).

popularity *n* popularidad *f*.

popularize *vt* popularizar.
populate *vi* poblar.
population *n* población *f*.
populous *adj* populoso/sa.
pop video *n* videoclip *m*.
porcelain *n* porcelana, china, loza fina *f*.
porch *n* pórtico, vestíbulo *m*, zaguán *m*.
porcupine *n* puerco espín *m*.
pore *n* poro *m*.
pork *n* carne de cerdo, carne de puerco *f*.
pornography *n* pornografía *f*.
porous *adj* poroso/sa.
porpoise *n* marsopa *f*.
porridge *n* gachas de avena *fpl*.
port *n* puerto *m*; (*mar*) babor *m*; vino de Oporto *m*.
portable *adj* portátil.
portal *n* portal *m*; portada *f*.
porter *n* portero *m*; mozo *m*; conserje *m/f*.
portfolio *n* cartera *f*.
porthole *n* portilla *f*.
portico *n* pórtico, portal *m*.
portion *n* porción, parte *f*.
portly *adj* rollizo/za.
portrait *n* retrato *m*.
portray *vt* retratar.
pose *n* postura *f*; pose *f*; * *vi* posar; * *vt* plantear.
posh *adj* elegante.
position *n* posición, situación *f*; * *vt* colocar.
positive *adj* positivo/va, real, verdadero/ra; ~ly *adv* positivamente; ciertamente.
posse *n* pelotón *m*.
possess *vt* poseer; gozar.
possession *n* posesión *f*.
possessive *adj* posesivo/va.
possibility *n* posibilidad *f*.

possible *adj* posible; ~ly *adv* quizá, quizás.
post *n* correo *m*; puesto *m*; empleo *m*; poste *m*; * *vt* apostar; fijar.
postage *n* franqueo *m*.
postage stamp *n* sello de correos *m*; estampilla *f*.
postal box, P O Box *n* apartado de correos *m*.
postcard *n* tarjeta *f* postal.
post code *n* código *m* postal.
postdate *vt* posfechar.
poster *n* cartel *m*.
poste restante *n* lista de correos *f*.
posterior *n* trasero *m*.
posterity *n* posteridad *f*.
postgraduate *n* posgraduado/da *m/f*.
posthumous *adj* póstumo/ma.
postman *n* cartero *m*.
postmark *n* matasellos *m*.
postmaster *n* administrador/a de correos *m/f*.
post office *n* correos *m*.
postpone *vt* diferir, suspender; posponer.
postscript *n* posdata *f*.
posture *n* postura *f*.
post-war *adj* de posguerra.
postwoman *n* cartera *f*.
posy *n* ramillete de flores *m*.
pot *n* marmita *f*; olla *f*; (*sl*) marihuana *f*; * *vt* preservar en marmitas.
potato *n* patata *f*; papa *f*.
potato peeler *n* pelapatatas *m invar*.
potbellied *adj* panzudo/da.
potent *adj* potente, poderoso/sa, eficaz.
potential *adj* potencial, poderoso/sa.
pothole *n* bache *m*.
potion *n* poción, bebida medicinal *f*.
potted *adj* en conserva; en tiesto.
potter *n* alfarero/ra *m/f*.
pottery *n* cerámica *f*.

potty adj chiflado/da.
pouch n bolsa f; petaca f; zurrón m.
poultice n cataplasma f.
poultry n aves de corral fpl.
pound n libra f; libra esterlina f; corral m; * vt machacar; * vi dar golpes.
pour vt echar; servir; * vi fluir con rapidez; llover a cántaros.
pout vi fruncir el ceño.
poverty n pobreza f.
powder n polvo m; pólvora f; * vt polvorear.
powder compact n polvera f.
powdered milk n leche en polvo f.
powder puff n borla f.
powder room n aseos mpl.
powdery adj polvoriento/ta.
power n poder m; potestad f; imperio m; potencia f; autoridad f; fuerza f; * vt impulsar.
powerful adj poderoso/sa; ~ly adv poderosamente, con mucha fuerza.
powerless adj impotente.
power station n central eléctrica f.
practicable adj factible; viable.
practical adj práctico/ca; ~ly adv prácticamente.
practicality n viabilidad f.
practical joke n broma pesada f.
practice n práctica f; uso m; costumbre f; ~s pl intrigas fpl.
practise vi practicar, ejercer.
practitioner n médico/ca m/f.
pragmatic adj pragmático/ca.
prairie n pampa f.
praise n renombre m; alabanza f; * vt celebrar, alabar.
praiseworthy adj digno/na de alabanza.
prance vi cabriolar.
prank n travesura, extravagancia f.
prattle vi charlar; * n charla f.

prawn n gamba f.
pray vi rezar; rogar; orar.
prayer n oración, súplica f.
prayer book n devocionario m.
preach vi predicar.
preacher n pastor/a; predicador/a m/f.
preamble n preámbulo m.
precarious adj precario, incierto/ta; ~ly adv precariamente.
precaution n precaución f.
precautionary adj preventivo/va.
precede vt anteceder, preceder.
precedence n precedencia f.
precedent adj, n precedente m.
precinct n límite, lindero m; barrio m; distrito electoral m.
precious adj precioso/sa.
precipice n precipicio m.
precipitate vt precipitar; * adj precipitado/da.
precise adj preciso/sa, exacto/ta; ~ly adv precisamente, exactamente.
precision n precisión, limitación exacta f.
preclude vt prevenir, impedir.
precocious adj precoz, temprano/na, prematuro/ra.
preconceive vt preconcebir.
preconception n preconcepción f.
precondition n condición previa f.
precursor n precursor/a m/f.
predator n depredador/a m/f.
predecessor n predecesor/a, antecesor/a m/f.
predestination n predestinación f.
predicament n aprieto m; dilema m.
predict vt predecir.
predictable adj previsible.
prediction n predicción f.
predilection n predilección f.
predominant adj predominante.

predominate vt predominar.
preen vt limpiarse (las plumas).
prefab n casa prefabricada f.
preface n prefacio m.
prefer vt preferir.
preferable adj preferible.
preferably adv de preferencia.
preference n preferencia f.
preferential adj preferente.
preferment n promoción f; preferencia f.
prefix vt prefijar; * n (gr) prefijo m.
pregnancy n embarazo m.
pregnant adj embarazada.
prehistoric adj prehistórico/ca.
prejudice n perjuicio, daño m; * vt perjudicar, hacer daño.
prejudiced adj predispuesto/ta; parcial.
prejudicial adj perjudicial, dañoso/sa.
preliminary adj preliminar.
prelude n preludio m.
premarital adj premarital.
premature adj prematuro/ra; ~ly adv anticipadamente.
premeditation n premeditación f.
premier n primer ministro m, primera ministra f.
première n estreno m.
premise n premisa f.
premises npl establecimiento m.
premium n premio m; remuneración f; prima f.
premonition n presentimiento m.
preoccupied adj preocupado/da; ensimismado/da.
prepaid adj con el porte pagado.
preparation n preparación f; cosa preparada f.
preparatory adj preparatorio/ria.
prepare vt (vi) preparar(se).
prepared adj abonado/da.

preponderance n preponderancia f.
preposition n preposición f.
preposterous adj absurdo/da.
prerequisite n requisito m.
prerogative n prerrogativa f.
prescribe vi prescribir; recetar.
prescription n prescripción f; receta medicinal f.
presence n presencia f; asistencia f.
present n regalo m; * adj presente; ~ly adv al presente; * vt ofrecer, presentar; regalar; acusar.
presentable adj decente, decoroso/sa.
presentation n presentación f.
present-day adj actual.
presenter n presentador/a m/f.
presentiment n presentimiento m.
preservation n preservación f.
preservative n preservativo m.
preserve vt preservar, conservar; poner en conserva; * n conserva, confitura f.
preside vi presidir; dirigir.
presidency n presidencia f.
president n presidente m/f.
presidential adj presidencial.
press vt empujar; apretar; compeler; * vi apretar; * n prensa f; armario m; apretón m; imprenta f.
press agency n agencia de prensa f.
press conference n rueda de prensa f.
pressing adj, ~ly adv urgente(mente).
press-up n plancha f.
pressure n presión f; opresión f.
pressure cooker n olla exprés, olla a presión f.
pressure group n grupo de presión m.
pressurized adj a presión.
prestige n prestigio m.
presumable adj presumible.
presumably adv es de suponer que.

presume *vt* presumir, suponer.
presumption *n* presunción *f*.
presumptuous *adj* presuntuoso/sa.
presuppose *vt* presuponer.
pretence *n* pretexto *m*; pretensión *f*.
pretend *vi* pretender; presumir.
pretender *n* pretendiente *m/f*.
pretension *n* pretensión *f*.
pretentious *adj* presumido/da; ostentoso/sa.
preterite *n* preterito *m*.
pretext *n* pretexto *m*; **to find a ~ for** pretextar.
pretty *adj* lindo/da, bien parecido/da; hermoso/sa; * *adv* algo, un poco.
prevail *vi* prevalecer, predominar.
prevailing *adj* dominante (uso, costumbre).
prevalent *adj* predominante, eficaz.
prevent *vt* prevenir; impedir.
prevention *n* prevención *f*.
preventive *adj* preventivo/va.
preview *n* preestreno *m*.
previous *adj* previo/via; antecedente; **~ly** *adv* antes.
prewar *adj* de antes de la guerra.
prey *n* presa *f*.
price *n* precio *m*.
priceless *adj* inapreciable.
price list *n* tarifa, lista de precios *f*.
pricey *adj* carero/ra.
prick *vt* punzar, picar; apuntar; excitar; * *n* puntura *f*; pica dura *f*; punzada *f*.
prickle *n* pincho *m*; espina *f*.
prickly *adj* espinoso/sa.
pride *n* orgullo *m*; vanidad *f*; jactancia *f*.
priest *n* sacerdote *m*.
priestess *n* sacerdotisa *f*.
priesthood *n* sacerdocio *m*.
priestly *adj* sacerdotal.

priggish *adj* afectado/da.
prim *adj* peripuesto/ta, afectado/da.
primacy *n* primacía *f*.
primarily *adv* primariamente, sobre todo.
primary *adj* primario/ria, principal, primero/ra.
primary school *n* escuela primaria *f*.
primate *n* primadoprimate *m*.
prime *n* (*fig*) flor, nata *f*; primavera *f*; principio *m*; * *adj* primero/ra; primoroso/sa, excelente; * *vt* cebar.
prime minister *n* primer ministro *m*, primera ministra *f*.
primeval *adj* primitivo/va.
priming *n* cebo *m*; imprimación *f*.
primitive *adj* primitivo/va; **~ly** *adv* primitivamente.
primrose *n* (*bot*) primavera *f*.
prince *n* príncipe *m*.
princess *n* princesa *f*.
principal *adj*, **~ly** *adv* principal(mente); * *n* principal, jefe *m*.
principality *n* principado/da *m*.
principle *n* principio *m*; causa primitiva *f*; fundamento, motivo *m*.
print *vt* imprimir; * *n* impresión, estampa, edición *f*; impreso *m*; **out of ~** vendido/da, agotado/da.
printed matter *n* impresos *mpl*.
printer *n* impresor/a *m/f*.
printing *n* imprenta *f*.
prior *adj* anterior, precedente; * *n* prior (prelado) *m*.
priority *n* prioridad *f*.
priory *n* priorato *m*.
prism *n* prisma *m*.
prison *n* prisión, carcel *f*.
prisoner *n* prisionero/ra *m/f*.
pristine *adj* prístino/na, antiguo/gua.
privacy *n* soledad *f*.
private *adj* secreto/ta, privado/da;

particular; ~ **soldier** n soldado raso m; **~ly** adv en secreto.
private eye n detective privado/da m/f.
privet n alheña f.
privilege n privilegio m.
prize n premio m; presa f; * vt apreciar, valuar; **to ~ open** abrir por fuerza.
prize-giving n entrega de premios f.
prizewinner n premiado/da m/f.
pro prep para.
probability n probabilidad, verosimilitud f.
probable adj probable, verosímil; **~bly** adv probablemente.
probation n prueba f.
probationary adj de prueba.
probe n sonda f; encuesta f; * vt sondar; investigar.
problem n problema m.
problematical adj problemático/ca; **~ly** adv problemáticamente.
procedure n procedimiento m; progreso, proceso m.
proceed vi proceder; provenir; originarse; **~s** npl producto m; rédito m; **gross ~s** producto íntegro; **net ~s** producto neto.
proceedings n procedimiento m; proceso m; conducta f.
process n proceso m.
procession n procesión f.
proclaim vt proclamar, promulgar; publicar.
proclamation n proclamación f; decreto m.
procrastinate vt diferir, retardar.
proctor n censor/a m/f.
procure vt procurar.
procurement n procuración f.
prod vt empujar.
prodigal adj pródigo/ga.

prodigious adj prodigioso/sa; **~ly** adv prodigiosamente.
prodigy n prodigio m.
produce vt producir, criar; causar; * n producto m.
produce dealer n verdulero/ra m/f.
producer n productor/a m/f.
product n producto m; obra f; efecto m.
production n producción f; producto m.
production line n línea de producción f.
productive adj productivo/va.
productivity n productividad f.
profane adj profano/na.
profess vt profesar; ejercer; declarar.
profession n profesión f.
professional adj profesional.
professor n profesor/a, catedratico/ca m/f.
proficiency n capacidad f.
proficient adj proficiente, adelantado/da.
profile n perfil m.
profit n ganancia f; provecho m; ventaja f; * vi aprovechar.
profitability n rentabilidad f.
profitable adj provechoso/sa, ventajoso/sa.
profiteering n explotación f.
profound adj profundo/da; **~ly** adv profundamente.
profuse adj profuso/sa, prodigo/ga; **~ly** adv profusamente.
program n programa m.
programme n programa m.
programmer n programador/a m/f.
programming n programación f.
progress n progreso m; curso m; * vi hacer progresos.
progression n progresión f; adelantamiento m.

progressive *adj* progresivo/va; ~**ly** *adv* progresivamente.
prohibit *vt* prohibir, vedar; impedir.
prohibition *n* prohibición *f*.
project *vt* proyectar, trazar; * *n* proyecto *m*.
projectile *n* proyectil *m*.
projection *n* proyección *f*; estimación *f*.
projector *n* proyector *m*.
proletarian *adj* proletario/ria.
proletariat *n* proletariado *m*.
prolific *adj* prolifico/ca, fecundo/da.
prolix *adj* prolijo/ja, difuso/sa.
prologue *n* prólogo *m*.
prolong *vt* prolongar; diferir.
prom *n* baile de gala; concierto *m*.
promenade *n* paseo *m*.
prominence *n* prominencia *f*.
prominent *adj* prominente, saledizo/za.
promiscuous *adj* promiscuo/cua.
promise *n* promesa *f*; * *vt* prometer.
promising *adj* prometedor/a.
promontory *n* promontorio *m*.
promote *vt* promover.
promoter *n* promotor/a, promovedor/a *m/f*.
promotion *n* promoción *f*.
prompt *adj* pronto/ta; ~**ly** *adv* prontamente; * *vt* sugerir, insinuar; apuntar (en el teatro).
prompter *n* apuntador/a *m/f*.
prone *adj* inclinado/da.
prong *n* diente *m*.
pronoun *n* pronombre *m*.
pronounce *vt* pronunciar; recitar.
pronounced *adj* marcado/da.
pronouncement *n* declaración *f*.
pronunciation *n* pronunciación *f*.
proof *n* prueba *f*; * *adj* impenetrable; de prueba.
prop *vt* sostener; * *n* apoyo, puntal *m*; sostén *m*.

propaganda *n* propaganda *f*.
propel *vt* impeler.
propeller *n* hélice *f*.
propensity *n* propensión, tendencia *f*.
proper *adj* propio/pia; conveniente; exacto/ta; bien parecido/da; ~**ly** *adv* propiamente, justamente.
property *n* propiedad *f*.
prophecy *n* profecía *f*.
prophesy *vt* profetizar.
prophet *n* profeta *m*.
prophetic *adj* profético/ca.
proportion *n* proporción *f*; simetría *f*.
proportional *adj* proporcional.
proportionate *adj* proporcionado/da.
proposal *n* propuesta, proposición *f*; oferta *f*.
propose *vt* proponer.
proposition *n* proposición, propuesta *f*.
proprietor *n* propietario/ria *m/f*.
propriety *n* propiedad *f*.
pro rata *adv* de forma prorrateada.
prosaic *adj* prosaico/ca, en prosa.
prose *n* prosa *f*.
prosecute *vt* proseguir.
prosecution *n* prosecución *f*; acusación *f*.
prosecutor *n* fiscal *m/f*.
prospect *n* perspectiva *f*; esperanza *f*; * *vt* explorar; * *vi* buscar.
prospecting *n* prospección *f*.
prospective *adj* probable; futuro/ra.
prospector *n* explorador/a *m/f*.
prospectus *n* prospecto *m*.
prosper *vi* prosperar.
prosperity *n* prosperidad *f*.
prosperous *adj* próspero/ra, feliz.
prostitute *n* prostituta *f*.
prostitution *n* prostitución *f*.
prostrate *adj* postrado/da.
protagonist *n* protagonista *m*.

protect *vt* proteger; amparar.

protection *n* protección *f*.

protective *adj* protectorio/ria.

protector *n* protector/a, patrono/na *m/f*.

protégé(e) *n* protegido/da *m/f*.

protein *n* proteína *f*.

protest *vi* protestar; * *n* protesta *f*.

Protestant *n* protestante *m/f*.

protester *n* manifestante *m/f*.

protocol *n* protocolo *m*.

prototype *n* prototipo *m*.

protracted *adj* prolongado/da.

protrude *vi* sobresalir.

proud *adj* soberbio/bia, orgulloso/sa; ~ly *adv* soberbiamente.

prove *vt* probar, justificar; * *vi* resultar; salir (bien o mal).

proverb *n* proverbio *m*.

proverbial *adj*, ~ly *adv* proverbial(mente).

provide *vt* proveer; **to ~ for** mantener a; tener en cuenta.

provided *conj*: ~ **that** con tal que.

providence *n* providencia *f*.

province *n* provincia *f*; campo de acción *m*.

provincial *adj* provincial; * *n* provincial/a *m/f*.

provision *n* provisión *f*; precaución *f*.

provisional *adj*, ~ly *adv* provisional(mente).

proviso *n* estipulación *f*.

provocation *n* provocación *f*; apelación *f*.

provocative *adj* provocativo/va.

provoke *vt* provocar; apelar.

prow *n* (*mar*) proa *f*.

prowess *n* proeza, valentía *f*.

prowl *vi* rondar, vagar.

prowler *n* merodeador/a *m/f*.

proximity *n* proximidad *f*.

proxy *n* poder *m*; apoderado/da *m/f*.

prudence *n* prudencia *f*.

prudent *adj* prudente, circunspecto/ta; ~ly *adv* con juicio.

prudish *adj* gazmoño/ña, mojigato/ta.

prune *vt* podar; * *n* ciruela pasa *f*.

prussic acid *n* ácido prúsico *m*.

pry *vi* espiar, acechar; **to ~ open** *vt* abrir por fuerza.

psalm *n* salmo *m*.

pseudonym *n* seudónimo *m*.

psyche *n* psique *f*.

psychiatric *adj* psiquiátrico/ca.

psychiatrist *n* psiquiatra *m/f*.

psychiatry *n* psiquiatría *f*.

psychic *adj* psíquico/ca.

psychoanalysis *n* psicoanálisis *m*.

psychoanalyst *n* psicoanalista *m/f*.

psychological *adj* psicológico/ca.

psychologist *n* psicólogo/ga *m/f*.

psychology *n* psicología *f*.

puberty *n* pubertad *f*.

public *adj* público/ca; común; notorio/ria; ~ly *adv* publicamente; * *n* público *m*.

public address system *n* megafonía *f*.

publican *n* publicano *m*; tabernero/ra *m/f*.

publication *n* publicación *f*; edición *f*.

publicity *n* publicidad *f*.

publicize *vt* publicitar; hacer propaganda para.

public opinion *n* opinión pública *f*.

public school *n* instituto; colegio privado *m*.

publish *vt* publicar.

publisher *n* editorial *f*; editor/a *m/f*.

publishing *n* industria del libro *f*.

pucker *vt* arrugar, hacer pliegues.

pudding *n* pudín *m*; morcilla *f*.

puddle *n* charco *m*.

puerile *adj* pueril.

puff n soplo m; bocanada f; resoplido m; * vt chupar; * vi bufar; resoplar.

puff pastry n hojaldre m.

puffy adj hinchado/da, entumecido/da.

pull vt tirar; coger; rasgar, desgarrar; **to ~ down** derribar; **to ~ in** parar; llegar a la estación; **to ~ off** cerrar; **to ~ out** vi irse; salir; * vt arrancar; **to ~ through** salir adelante; **to ~ up** vi parar; * vt arrancar; parar; * n tirón m; sacudida f.

pulley n polea, garrucha f.

pullover n jersey m.

pulp n pulpa f; pasta f.

pulpit n púlpito m.

pulsate vi pulsar, latir.

pulse n pulso m; legumbres fpl.

pulverize vt pulverizar.

pumice n piedra pómez f.

pummel vt aporrear.

pump n bomba f; (shoe) zapatilla f; * vt bombear; sondear; sonsacar.

pumpkin n calabaza f.

pun n juego de palabras m; * vi hacer juegos de palabras.

punch n puñetazo m; punzón m; taladro m; ponche m; * vt golpear; perforar.

punctual adj puntual, exacto/ta; **~ly** adv puntualmente.

punctuate vi puntuar.

punctuation n puntuación f.

pundit n experto/ta m/f.

pungent adj picante, acre, mordaz.

punish vt castigar.

punishment n castigo m; pena f.

punk n punk m/f; música punk f; rufián/fiana m/f.

punt n barco llano m.

puny adj joven, pequeño/ña; inferior.

pup n cachorro m; * vi parir (la perra).

pupil n alumno/na m/f; pupila f.

puppet n títere, muñeco m.

puppy n perrito m.

purchase vt comprar; * n compra f; adquisición f.

purchaser n comprador/a m/f.

pure adj puro/ra; **~ly** adv puramente.

purée n puré m.

purge vt purgar.

purification n purificación f.

purifier n depuradora f.

purify vt purificar.

purist n purista m/f.

puritan n puritano/na m/f.

purity n pureza f.

purl n punto del revés m.

purple adj purpureo/rea; * n púrpura f.

purport vi: **to ~ to** dar a entender que.

purpose n intención f; designio, proyecto m; **to the ~** al propósito; **to no ~** inútilmente; **on ~** a propósito.

purposeful adj resuelto/ta.

purr vi ronronear.

purse n bolsa f; cartera f.

purser n comisario m/f.

pursue vt perseguir; seguir, acosar.

pursuit n perseguimiento m; ocupación f.

purveyor n abastecedor m.

push vt empujar; estrechar, apretar; **to ~ aside** apartar; **to ~ off** (sl) largarse; **to ~ on** seguir adelante; * n impulso m; empujón m; esfuerzo m; asalto m.

pusher n traficante de drogas m/f.

put vt poner, colocar; proponer; imponer, obligar; **to ~ away** guardar; **to ~ away hurriedly** zampar; **to ~ down** poner en el suelo; sacrificar; apuntar; sofocar; **to ~ forward**

adelantar; **to ~ off** aplazar; desanimar; **to ~ on** ponerse; encender; presentar; ganar; echar; **to ~ out** apagar; extender; molestar; **to ~ up** alzar; aumentar; alojar.
putrid *adj* podrido/da.
putt *n* putt *m*; *vt* hacer un putt.
putty *n* masilla *f*.

puzzle *n* acertijo *m*; rompecabezas *m* inv ar.
puzzling *adj* extraño/ña.
pyjamas *npl* pijama *m*.
pylon *n* torre de alta tensión *f*.
pyramid *n* pirámide *f*.
python *n* pitón *m*.

Q

quack *vi* graznar; * *n* graznido *m*; (*sl*) curandero/ra *m/f*.
quadrangle *n* cuadrángulo *m*.
quadrant *n* cuadrante *m*.
quadrilateral *adj* cuadrilátero/ra.
quadruped *n* cuadrúpedo *m*.
quadruple *adj* cuádruplo.
quadruplet *n* cuatrillizo/za *m/f*.
quagmire *n* barrizal *m*, cenagal *m*.
quail *n* codorniz *f*.
quaint *adj* pulido/da; exquisito/ta.
quake *vi* temblar; tiritar.
Quaker *n* cuáquero/ra *m/f*.
qualification *n* calificación *f*; título *m*.
qualified *adj* capacitado/da; titulado/da.
qualify *vt* calificar; modificar; * *vi* clasificarse.
quality *n* calidad *f*.
qualm *n* escrúpulo *m*.
quandary *n* incertidumbre, duda *f*.
quantitative *adj* cuantitativo/va.
quantity *n* cantidad *f*.
quarantine *n* cuarentena *f*.
quarrel *n* riña, contienda *f*; * *vi* reñir, disputar.
quarrelsome *adj* pendenciero/ra.
quarry *n* cantera *f*.
quarter *n* cuarto *m*; cuarta parte *f*; **~ of an hour** cuarto de hora; * *vt* cuartear.

quarterly *adj* trimestral; * *adv* trimestralmente.
quartermaster *n* (*mil*) comisario/ria *m/f*.
quartet *n* (*mus*) cuarteto *m*.
quartz *n* (*min*) cuarzo *m*.
quash *vt* fracasar; anular, abrogar.
quay *n* muelle *m*.
queasy *adj* nauseabundo/da.
queen *n* reina *f*; dama *f*.
queer *adj* extraño/ña; ridículo/la; * *n* (*sl*) maricón *m*.
quell *vt* calmar; sosegar.
quench *vt* apagar; extinguir.
query *n* cuestión, pregunta *f*; * *vt* preguntar.
quest *n* pesquisa, inquisición, busca *f*.
question *n* pregunta *f*; cuestión *f*; asunto *m*; duda *f*; * *vt* dudar de; interrogar.
questionable *adj* cuestionable, dudoso/sa.
questioner *n* interrogador/a *m/f*.
question mark *n* signo de interrogación *m*.
questionnaire *n* cuestionario *m*.
quibble *vi* buscar evasivas.
quick *adj* rapido/da; vivo/va; pronto/ta; ágil; **~ly** *adv* rápidamente.
quicken *vt* apresurar; * *vi* darse prisa.
quicksand *n* arenas movedizas *f/pl*.

quicksilver n azogue, mercurio m.
quick-witted adj agudo/da, perspicaz.
quiet adj callado/da; **~ly** adv tranquilamente.
quietness n tranquilidad f.
quinine n quinina f.
quintet n (mus) quinteto m.
quintuple adj quíntuplo.
quintuplet n quintillizo/za m/f.
quip n indirecta f; * vt echar pullas.
quirk n peculiaridad f.
quit vt dejar; desocupar; * vi renunciar; irse; * adj libre, descargado/da.

quite adv bastante; totalmente, enteramente, absolutamente.
quits adv ¡en paz!
quiver vi temblar.
quixotic adj quijotesco/ca.
quiz n concurso m; programa concurso m; * vt interrogar.
quizzical adj burlón/ona.
quota n cuota f.
quotation n citación, cita f.
quotation marks npl comillas fpl.
quote vt citar.
quotient n cociente m.

R

rabbi n rabino/na m/f.
rabbit n conejo m.
rabbit hutch n conejera f.
rabble n gentuza f.
rabid adj rabioso/sa; furioso/sa.
rabies n rabia f.
race n raza, casta f; carrera f; * vt
hacer correr a; competir contra;
acelerar; * vi correr; competir; latir rápidamente.
racehorse n caballo de carreras m.
racial adj racial.
raciness n vivacidad f.
racing n carreras fpl.
racist adj, n racista m/f.
rack n rejilla f; estante m; * vt atormentar; trasegar.
racket n ruido m; raqueta f.
rack-rent n alquiler abusivo m.
racy adj picante, vivo/va.
radiance n brillantez f, resplandor m.
radiant adj radiante, brillante.
radiate vt, vi radiar, irradiar.
radiation n radiación f.
radiator n radiador m.

radical adj radical; **~ly** adv radical-
mente.
radicalism n radicalismo m.
radio n radio f.
radioactive adj radioactivo/va; **~
fallout** lluvia radioactiva f.
radish n rábano m.
radius n radio f.
raffle n rifa f (juego); * vt rifar.
raft n balsa, almadía f.
rafter n par m; viga f.
rafting n rafting m.
rag n trapo, andrajo m.
ragamuffin n granuja, galopín/ina
m/f.
rage n rabia f; furor m; * vi rabiar;
encolerizarse.
ragged adj andrajoso/sa.
raging adj furioso/sa, rabioso/sa.
ragman, ~ picker n trapero m.
raid n incursión f; * vt invadir.
raider n invasor/a m/f.
rail n baranda, barandilla f; (rail)
raíl, carril m; * vt cercar con baran-
dillas.

raillery n burlas fpl.
railway n ferrocarril m.
raiment n vestido m.
rain n lluvia f; * vi llover.
rainbow n arco iris m.
rainwater n agua de lluvia f.
rainy adj lluvioso/sa.
raise vt levantar, alzar; fabricar, edificar; elevar.
raisin n pasa f.
rake n rastro, rastrillo m; libertino/na m/f; * vt rastrillar.
rakish adj libertino/na, disoluto/ta.
rally vt (mil) reunir; * vi reunirse.
ram n carnero, morueco m; ariete m; * vt chocar con.
ramble vi divagar; salir de excursión a pie; * n excursión a pie, caminata f.
rambler n excursionista m/f.
ramification n ramificación f.
ramify vi ramificarse.
ramp n rampa f.
rampant adj exuberante.
rampart n terraplén m; (mil) muralla f.
ramrod n baqueta f; atacador m.
ramshackle adj en ruina.
ranch n hacienda, estancia f.
rancid adj rancio/cia.
rancour n rencor m.
random adj fortuito/ta, sin orden; at ~ al azar.
range vt colocar, ordenar; *vi vagar; * n clase f; orden m; hilera f; cordillera f; campo de tiro m; reja de cocina f.
ranger n guardabosques m invar.
rank adj exuberante; rancio/cia; fétido/da; * n fila, hilera, clase f.
rankle vi doler.
rankness n exuberancia f; olor o gusto rancio m.

ransack vt saquear, pillar.
ransom n rescate m.
rant vi vociferar.
rap vi dar un golpecito; * n golpecito m.
rapacious adj rapaz; ~ly adv con rapacidad.
rapacity n rapacidad f.
rape n violación f; estupro m; (bot) colza f; * vt violar.
rapid adj rápido/da; ~ly adv rápidamente.
rapidity n rapidez f.
rapier n espadín m.
rapist n violador m.
rapt adj arrebatado/da; absorto/ta.
rapture n rapto m; éxtasis m invar.
rapturous adj arrebatado/da.
rare adj raro/ra, extraordinario/ria; ~ly adv raramente.
rarity n raridad, rareza f.
rascal n pícaro/ra m/f.
rash adj precipitado/da, temerario/ria; ~ly adv temerariamente; * n salpullido m; erupción (cutánea) f.
rashness n temeridad f.
rasp n raspador m; * vt raspar, escofinar.
raspberry n frambuesa f; ~ bush frambueso m.
rat n rata f.
rate n tasa f, precio, valor m; grado m; * vt tasar, apreciar.
rather adv más bien; antes.
ratification n ratificación f.
ratify vt ratificar.
rating n tasación f; clasificación f; índice m.
ratio n razón f.
ration n ración f; (mil) víveres mpl.
rational adj racional; razonable; ~ly adv racionalmente.
rationality n racionalidad f.

rattan n (bot) rota f.

rattle vi golpear; traquetear; * vt sacudir; * n traqueteo m; sonajero m.

rattlesnake n serpiente de cascabel f.

ravage vt saquear, pillar; estragar; * n saqueo m.

rave vi delirar.

rave music n (fam) bakalao m.

raven n cuervo m.

ravenous adj, ~ly adv voraz(mente).

ravine n barranco m.

ravish vt encantar; raptar.

ravishing adj encantador/a.

raw adj crudo/da; puro/ra; novato/ta.

rawboned adj huesudo/da; magro/gra.

rawness n crudeza f; falta de experiencia f.

ray n rayo de luz m; raya f (pez).

raze vt arrasar.

razor n navaja f; máquina de afeitar f.

reach vt alcanzar; llegar hasta; * vi extenderse, llegar; alcanzar, penetrar; * n alcance m.

react vi reaccionar.

reaction n reacción f.

read vt leer; * vi estudiar.

readable adj legible.

reader n lector/a m/f.

readily adv pronto; de buena gana.

readiness n voluntad, gana f; prontitud f.

reading n lectura f.

reading room n sala de lectura f.

readjust vt reajustar.

ready adj listo/ta, pronto/ta; inclinado/da; abonado/da; fácil.

real adj real, verdadero/ra; ~ly adv realmente.

reality n realidad f.

realization n realización f.

realize adv darse cuenta de; realizar.

realm n reino m.

ream n resma f.

reap vt segar.

reaper n segador/a m/f.

reappear vi reaparecer.

rear n parte trasera f; retaguardia f; zaga f; * vt levantar, alzar.

rearmament n rearme m.

reason n razon f; causa f; * vt, vi razonar.

reasonable adj razonable.

reasonableness n lo razonable.

reasonably adv razonablemente.

reasoning n razonamiento m.

reassure vt tranquilizar, alentar; (com) asegurar.

rebel n rebelde m/f; * vi rebelarse.

rebellion n rebelión f.

rebellious adj rebelde.

rebound vi rebotar.

rebuff n desaire m; * vt rechazar.

rebuild vt reedificar.

rebuke vt reprender; * n reprensión f.

rebut vi repercutir.

recalcitrant adj recalcitrante.

recall vt recordar; retirar; * n retirada f.

recant vt retractar, desdecirse.

recantation n retractación f.

recapitulate vt, vi recapitular.

recapitulation n recapitulación f.

recapture n recobra f.

recede vi retroceder.

receipt n recibo m; recepción f; ~s npl ingresos mpl.

receivable adj por cobrar.

receive vt recibir; aceptar, admitir.

recent adj reciente, nuevo/va; ~ly adv recientemente.

receptacle n receptáculo m.

reception n recepción f.

recess n descanso m; recreo m; hueco m.

recession n retirada f; (com) recesión f.

recipe n receta f.
recipient n recipiente m.
reciprocal adj recíproco/ca; ~**ly** adv recíprocamente.
reciprocate vi reciprocar.
reciprocity n reciprocidad f.
recital n recital m.
recite vt recitar; referir, relatar.
reckless adj temerario/ria; ~**ly** adv temerariamente.
reckon vt contar, computar; * vi calcular.
reckoning n cuenta f; cálculo m.
reclaim vt reformar; reclamar.
reclaimable adj reclamable.
recline vt (vi) reclinar(se); recostar(se).
recluse n recluso/sa m/f.
recognition n reconocimiento; recuerdo m.
recognize vt reconocer.
recoil vi recular.
recollect vt acordarse de; recordar.
recollection n recuerdo m.
recommence vt empezar de nuevo.
recommend vt recomendar.
recommendation n recomendación f.
recompense n recompensa f; * vt recompensar.
reconcilable adj reconciliable.
reconcile vt reconciliar.
reconciliation n reconciliación f.
recondite adj recóndito/ta, reservado/da.
reconnaissance n (mil) reconocimiento m.
reconnoitre vt (mil) reconocer.
reconsider vt reconsiderar.
reconstruct vt reedificar.
record vt registrar; grabar; * n registro, archivo m; disco; récord m; ~**s** pl anales mpl.

recorder n registrador/a, archivero/ra m/f; (mus) flauta de pico f.
recount vt contar de nuevo; relatar.
recourse n recurso m; remedio m.
recover vt recobrar; recuperar; restablecer; * vi convalecer, restablecerse.
recoverable adj recuperable.
recovery n convalecencia f; recuperación f.
recreation n recreación f; recreo m.
recriminate vi recriminar.
recrimination n recriminación f.
recruit vt reclutar; * n (mil) recluta m/f.
recruiting n recluta f.
rectangle n rectángulo m.
rectangular adj rectangular.
rectification n rectificación f.
rectify vt rectificar.
rectilinear adj rectilíneo/nea.
rectitude n rectitud f.
rector n rector/a m/f.
recumbent adj recostado/da, reclinado/da.
recur vi repetirse.
recurrence n repetición f.
recurrent adj repetido/da.
recycle vt reciclar.
recycled adj reciclado/da.
red adj rojo/ja; tinto/ta; * n rojo m.
redden vt enrojecer; * vi ponerse colorado/da.
reddish adj rojizo/za.
redeem vt redimir, rescatar.
redeemable adj redimible.
redeemer n redentor/a m/f.
redemption n redención f.
redeploy vt reorganizar.
red-handed adj to catch somebody ~ pillar a alguien con las manos en la masa.
red-hot adj candente, ardiente.

red-letter day *n* dia señalado *m*.

redness *n* rojez, bermejura *f*.

redolent *adj* fragante, oloroso/sa.

redouble *vt* (*vi*) redoblar(se).

redress *vt* corregir; reformar; rectificar; * *n* reparación, compensación *f*.

red tape *n* (*fig*) trámites *mpl*.

reduce *vt* reducir; disminuir; rebajer.

reducible *adj* reducible.

reduction *n* reducción *f*; rebaja *f*.

redundancy *n* despido *m*.

redundant *adj* superfluo/lua.

reed *n* caña *f*.

reedy *adj* lleno de canas.

reef *n* (*mar*) rizo *m*; arrecife *m*.

reek *n* mal olor *m*; * *vi* humear; vahear.

reel *n* carrete *m*; bobina *f*; rollo *m*; * *vi* tambalear(se).

re-election *n* reelección *f*.

re-engage *vt* empeñar de nuevo.

re-enter *vt* volver a entrar.

re-establish *vt* restablecer, volver a establecer.

re-establishment *n* restablecimiento *m*; restauración *f*.

refectory *n* refectorio; comedor *m*.

refer *vt*, *vi* referir, remitir; referirse.

referee *n* arbitro/ra *m/f*.

reference *n* referencia, relación *f*.

refine *vt* refinar, purificar.

refinement *n* refinación *f*; refinadura *f*; cultura *f*.

refinery *n* refinería *f*.

refit *vt* reparar; (*mar*) reparar.

reflect *vt*, *vi* reflejar; reflexionar.

reflection *n* reflexión, meditación *f*.

reflector *n* reflector *m*; captafaros *m* invar.

reflex *adj* reflejo.

reform *vt* (*vi*) reformar(se).

reform, reformation *n* reformación *f*.

reformer *n* reformador/a *m/f*.

reformist *n* reformista *m/f*.

refract *vt* refractar.

refraction *n* refracción *f*.

refrain *vi*: **to ~ from something** abstenerse de algo.

refresh *vt* refrescar.

refreshment *n* refresco, refrigerio *m*.

refrigerator *n* nevera *f*; refrigerador *m*.

refuel *vi* repostar (combustible).

refuge *n* refugio, asilo *m*.

refugee *n* refugiado/da *m/f*.

refund *vt* devolver; * *n* reembolso *m*.

refurbish *vt* restaurar, renovar.

refusal *n* negativa *f*.

refuse *vt* rehusar; * *n* basura *f*.

refuse collector *n* basurero *m*.

refute *vt* refutar.

regain *vt* recobrar, recuperar.

regal *adj* real.

regale *vt* regalar.

regalia *n* insignias *fpl*.

regard *vt* estimar; considerar; * *n* consideración *f*; respeto *m*.

regarding *pr* en cuanto a.

regardless *adv* a pesar de todo.

regatta *n* regata *f*.

regency *n* regencia *f*.

regenerate *vt* regenerar; * *adj* regenerado/da.

regeneration *n* regeneración *f*.

regent *n* regente *m/f*.

regime *n* régimen *m*.

regiment *n* regimiento *m*.

region *n* región *f*.

register *n* registro *m*; * *vt* registrar; **~ed letter** *n* carta certificada *f*.

registrar *n* registrador/a *m/f*.

registration *n* registro *m*.

registry *n* registro *m*.

regressive *adj* regresivo/va.

regret *n* sentimiento *m*; remordimiento *m*; pensión *f*; * *vt* sentir.

regretful *adj* pesaroso/sa.

regular *adj* regular; ordinario/ria; ~ly *adv* regularmente; * *n* regular *m*.

regularity *n* regularidad *f*.

regulate *vt* regular, ordenar.

regulation *n* regulación *f*; arreglo *m*.

regulator *n* regulador *m*.

rehabilitate *vt* rehabilitar.

rehabilitation *n* rehabilitación *f*.

rehearsal *n* repetición *f*; ensayo *m*.

rehearse *vt* repetir; ensayar.

reign *n* reinado, reino *m*; * *vi* reinar; prevalecer.

reimburse *vt* reembolsar.

reimbursement *n* reembolso *m*.

rein *n* rienda *f*; * *vt* refrenar.

reindeer *n* reno *m*.

reinforce *vt* reforzar.

reinstate *vt* reintegrar.

reinsure *vt* (*com*) reasegurar.

reissue *n* reedición *f*.

reiterate *vt* reiterar.

reiteration *n* reiteración, repetición *f*.

reject *vt* rechazar.

rejection *n* rechazo *m*.

rejoice *vt* (*vi*) regocijar(se).

rejoicing *n* regocijo *m*.

relapse *vi* recaer; * *n* reincidencia *f*; recaída *f*.

relate *vt, vi* relatar, referirse.

related *adj* emparentado/da.

relation *n* relación *f*; pariente *m*.

relationship *n* parentesco *m*; relación *f*.

relative *adj* relativo/va; ~ly *adv* relativamente; * *n* pariente *m/f*.

relax *vt, vi* relajar; descansar.

relaxation *n* relajación *f*; descanso *m*; relax *m*.

relay *n* relevo *m*; * *vt* retransmitir.

release *vt* soltar, libertar; * *n* liberación *f*; descargo *m*.

relegate *vt* relegar.

relegation *n* relegación *f*, descenso *m*.

relent *vi* ablandarse.

relentless *adj* implacable.

relevant *adj* pertinente.

reliable *adj* fiable, de confianza.

reliance *n* confianza *f*.

relic *n* reliquia *f*.

relief *n* relieve *m*; alivio *m*.

relieve *vt* aliviar, consolar; socorrer.

religion *n* religión *f*.

religious *adj* religioso/sa; ~ly *adv* religiosamente.

relinquish *vt* abandonar, dejar.

relish *n* sabor *m*; gusto *m*; salsa *f*; * *vt* gustar de, agradar.

reluctance *n* repugnancia *f*.

reluctant *adj* reticente.

rely *vi* confiar en; contar con.

remain *vi* quedar, restar, permanecer, durar.

remainder *n* resto, residuo *m*.

remains *npl* restos, residuos *mpl*; sobras *fpl*.

remand *vt*: to ~ in custody mantener bajo prisión preventiva.

remark *n* observación, nota *f*; * *vt* notar, observar.

remarkable *adj* notable, interesante.

remarkably *adv* notablemente.

remarry *vi* volver a casarse.

remedial *adj* curativo/va.

remedy *n* remedio, recurso *m*; * *vt* remediar.

remember *vt* acordarse de; recordar.

remembrance *n* memoria *f*; recuerdo *m*.

remind *vt* recordar.

reminiscence *n* reminiscencia *f*.

remiss *adj* negligente.

remission *n* remisión *f*.

remit *vt*, *vi* remitir, perdonar; disminuir.

remittance *n* remesa *f*.

remnant *n* resto, residuo *m*.

remodel *vt* remodelar.

remonstrate *vi* protestar.

remorse *n* remordimiento *m*; compunción *f*.

remorseless *adj* implacable.

remote *adj* remoto/ta, lejano/na; ~ly *adv* remotamente, lejos.

remote control *n* mando a distancia *m*.

remoteness *n* alejamiento *m*; distancia *f*.

removable *adj* de quita y pon, de quitapón.

removal *n* remoción *f*; mudanza *f*.

remove *vt* quitar; * *vi* mudarse.

remunerate *vt* remunerar.

remuneration *n* remuneración *f*.

render *vt* devolver, restituir; traducir; rendir.

rendezvous *n* cita *f*; lugar de encuentro *m*.

renegade *n* renegado/da *m/f*.

renew *vt* renovar, restablecer.

renewal *n* renovación *f*.

rennet *n* cuajo *m*.

renounce *vt* renunciar.

renovate *vt* renovar.

renovation *n* renovación *f*.

renown *n* renombre *m*; celebridad *f*.

renowned *adj* célebre.

rent *n* renta *f*; arrendamiento *m*; alquiler *m*; * *vt* alquilar.

rental *n* alquiler *m*.

renunciation *n* renuncia *f*.

reopen *vt* reabrir.

reorganization *n* reorganización *f*.

reorganize *vt* reorganizar.

repair *vt* reparar; resarcir; * *n* reparación *f*.

reparable *adj* reparable.

reparation *n* reparación *f*.

repartee *n* réplica aguda o picante *f*.

repatriate *vt* repatriar.

repay *vt* devolver; pagar, restituir.

repayment *n* pago *m*.

repeal *vt* abrogar, revocar; * *n* revocación, anulación *f*.

repeat *vt* repetir.

repeatedly *adv* repetidamente.

repeater *n* reloj de repetición *m*.

repel *vt* repeler, rechazar.

repent *vi* arrepentirse.

repentance *n* arrepentimiento *m*.

repentant *adj* arrepentido/da.

repertory *n* repertorio *m*.

repetition *n* repetición, reiteración *f*.

replace *vt* reemplazar; reponer.

replant *vt* replantar.

replenish *vt* llenar, surtir.

replete *adj* repleto/ta, lleno/na.

reply *n* respuesta *f*; * *vi* responder.

report *vt* referir, contar; dar cuenta de; * *n* informe *m*; repor taje *m*; relación *f*.

reporter *n* reportero/ra *m/f*.

repose *vt*, *vi* reposar; * *n* reposo *m*.

repository *n* depósito *m*.

repossess *vt* reobrar.

reprehend *vt* reprender.

reprehensible *adj* reprensible.

represent *vt* representar.

representation *n* representación *f*.

representative *adj* representativo/va; * *n* representante *m/f*.

repress *vt* reprimir, domar.

repression *n* represión *f*.

repressive *adj* represivo/va.

reprieve *vt* suspender una ejecución; indultar; * *n* indulto *m*.

reprimand *vt* reprender, corregir; * *n* reprensión *f*; repri menda *f*.

reprint *vt* reimprimir.

reprisal n represalia f.

reproach n improperio, oprobio m; * vt hacer reproches a.

reproachful adj ignominioso/sa; ~ly adv ignominiosamente.

reproduce vt reproducir.

reproduction n reproducción f.

reptile n reptil m.

republic n república f.

republican adj, n republicano/a m/f.

republicanism n republicanismo m.

repudiate vt repudiar.

repugnance n repugnancia f.

repugnant adj repugnante; ~ly adv con repugnancia.

repulse vt repulsar, desechar; * n repulsa f; rechazo m.

repulsion n repúlsion, repulsa f.

repulsive adj repulsivo/va.

reputable adj honroso/sa.

reputation n reputación f.

repute vt reputar.

request n petición, súplica f; * vt rogar, suplicar.

request stop n parada a petición f.

require vt requerir, demandar.

requirement n requisito m; exigencia f.

requisite adj necesario/ria, indispensable; * n requisito m.

requisition n petición, demanda f.

requite vt recompensar.

rescind vt rescindir, abrogar.

rescue vt librar, rescatar; * n libramiento, recobro m.

research vt investigar; * n investigación f.

resemblance n semejanza f.

resemble vt asemejarse.

resent vt resentirse.

resentful adj resentido/da; vengativo/va; ~ly adv con resentimi ento.

resentment n resentimiento m.

reservation n reserva f.

reserve vt reservar; * n reserva f.

reservedly adv con reserva.

reservoir n depósito m; pantano m.

reside vi residir, morar.

residence n residencia, morada f.

resident adj residente.

residuary adj sobrado/da; ~ **legatee** n (law) legatario/ria universal m/f.

residue n residuo, resto m.

residuum n (chem) residuo m.

resign vt, vi resignar, renunciar, ceder; resignarse, rendirse.

resignation n resignación f; dimisión f.

resin n resina f.

resinous adj resinoso/sa.

resist vt resistir, oponerse.

resistance n resistencia f.

resolute adj resuelto/ta; ~ly adv resueltamente.

resolution n resolución f.

resolve vt, vr resolver(se); (fig) zanjar.

resonance n resonancia f.

resonant adj resonante.

resort vi recurrir, frecuentar; * n recurso m; resorte m.

resound vi resonar.

resource n recurso m; expediente m.

respect n respecto m; respeto m; motivo m; ~s pl recuerdos mpl; * vt apreciar; respetar; venerar.

respectability n respetabilidad f.

respectable adj respetable; considerable; ~bly adv notablemente.

respectful adj respetuoso/sa; ~ly adv respetuosamente.

respecting prep con respecto a.

respective adj respectivo/va, relativo/va; ~ly adv respectivamente.

respirator n respirador m.

respiratory adj respiratorio/ria.

respite *n* suspensión *f*; respiro *m*; * *vt* suspender, diferir.
resplendence *n* resplandor, brillo *m*.
resplendent *adj* resplandeciente.
respond *vt* responder; corresponder.
respondent *n* (*law*) defensor/a *m*.
response *n* respuesta, réplica *f*.
responsibility *n* responsabilidad *f*.
responsible *adj* responsable.
responsive *adj* sensible.
rest *n* reposo *m*; sueño *m*; quietud *f*; (*mus*) pausa *f*; resto, residuo *m*; * *vt* descansar; apoyar; * *vi* dormir, reposar; descansarse.
restaurant *n* restaurante (económico) *m*.
resting place *n* última morada *f*.
restitution *n* restitución *f*.
restive *adj* inquieto/ta; obstinado/da.
restless *adj* insomne; inquieto/ta.
restoration *n* restauración *f*.
restorative *adj* restaurativo/va.
restore *vt* restaurar, restituir.
restrain *vt* restringir, restriñir.
restraint *n* refrenamiento, constreñimiento *m*.
restrict *vt* restringir, limitar.
restriction *n* restricción *f*.
restrictive *adj* restrictivo/va.
result *vi* resultar; * *n* resultado *m*.
resume *vt* resumir; empezar de nuevo.
resurrection *n* resurrección *f*.
resuscitate *vt* resucitar.
retail *vt* vender al por menor; * *n* venta por menor *f*.
retain *vt* retener, guardar.
retainer *n* adherente, partidario/ria *m/f*; **~s** *pl* comitiva *f*; séquito *m*.
retake *vt* volver a tomar.
retaliate *vt* tomar represalias.
retaliation *n* represalias *fpl*.

retardation *n* retraso *m*.
retarded *adj* retrasado/da.
retch *vi* tener arcadas.
retention *n* retención *f*.
retentive *adj* retentivo/va.
reticence *n* reticencia *f*.
reticule *n* retículo *m*.
retina *n* retina *f*.
retire *vt* (*vi*) retirar(se); jubilar(se).
retired *adj* apartado/da, retirado/da; jubilado/da.
retirement *n* retiro *m*, jubilación *f*.
retort *vt* replicar; * *n* réplica *f*.
retouch *vt* retocar.
retrace *vt* volver a trazar.
retract *vt* retraer; retractar.
retrain *vt* reciclar.
retraining *n* reciclaje profesional *m*.
retreat *n* retirada *f*; * *vi* retirarse.
retribution *n* retribución, recompensa *f*.
retrievable *adj* recuperable; reparable.
retrieve *vt* recuperar, recobrar.
retriever *n* sabueso *m*.
retrograde *adj* retrógrado/da.
retrospect, retrospection *n* reflexión *f*.
retrospective *adj* retrospectivo/va.
return *vt* retribuir; restituir; devolver; * *n* retorno *m*; vuelta *f*; recompensa, rendimiento *m*; recaída *f*.
reunion *n* reunión *f*.
reunite *vt* (*vi*) reunir(se).
rev counter *n* cuentarrevoluciones *m invar*.
reveal *vt* revelar.
revel *vi* andar de juerga.
revelation *n* revelación *f*.
reveller *n* juerguista *m/f*.
revelry *n* juerga *f*.
revenge *vt* vengar; * *n* venganza *f*.
revengeful *adj* vengativo/va.

revenue n renta f; rédito m.

reverberate vt, vi reverberar; resonar, retumbar.

reverberation n rechazo m; reverberación f.

revere vt reverenciar, venerar.

reverence n reverencia f; * vt reverenciar.

reverend adj reverendo/da; venerable; * n padre m.

reverent, reverential adj reverencial, respetuoso/sa.

reversal n revocación f; cambio total m.

reverse vt trastrocar; abolir; poner en marcha atrás; * n vicisi tud f; contrario m; reverso m (de una moneda).

reversible adj revocable; reversible.

reversion n reversión f.

revert vt, vi trastrocar; volverse atrás.

review vt rever; (mil) revistar; * n revista f; reseña f.

reviewer n revisor/a m/f; crítico/ca m/f.

revile vt ultrajar; difamar.

revise vt rever; repasar.

reviser n revisor/a m/f.

revision n revisión f.

revisit vt volver a visitar.

revival n restauración f; restablecimiento m.

revive vt avivar; restablecer; * vi revivir.

revocation n revocación f.

revoke vt revocar, anular.

revolt vi rebelarse; * n rebelión f.

revolting adj asqueroso/sa.

revolution n revolución f.

revolutionary adj, n revolucionario/ria m/f.

revolve vt revolver; meditar; * vi girar.

revolver n revólver m.

revolving adj giratorio/ria.

revue n revista f.

revulsion n revulsión f.

reward n recompensa f; * vt recompensar.

rhapsody n rapsodia f.

rhetoric n retórica f.

rhetorical adj retórico/ca.

rheumatic adj reumático/ca.

rheumatism n reumatismo m.

rhinoceros n rinoceronte m.

rhomboid n romboide m.

rhombus n rombo m.

rhubarb n ruibarbo m.

rhyme n rima f; poema m; * vi rimar.

rhythm n ritmo m.

rhythmical adj rítmico/ca.

rib n costilla f.

ribald adj escabroso/sa.

ribbon n listón m; cinta f.

rice n arroz m.

rich adj rico/ca; opulento/ta; abundante; ~ly adv ricamente.

riches npl riqueza f.

richness n riqueza f; abundancia f.

rickets n raquitismo m.

rickety adj raquítico/ca.

rid vt librar, desembarazar.

riddance n: good ~! ¡enhoramala!

riddle n enigma m; criba f; * vt cribar.

ride vi cabalgar; andar en coche; * n paseo a caballo o en coche m.

rider n caballero/ra, jinete m, amazona f.

ridge n espinazo, lomo m; cumbre f; * vt formar lomos o surcos.

ridicule n ridiculez f; ridiculo m; * vt ridiculizar.

ridiculous adj ridículo/la; ~ly adv ridiculamente.

riding n equitación f.

riding habit n traje de amazona m.

riding school *n* picadero *m*.

rife *adj* común, frecuente.

riffraff *n* desecho, desperdicio *m*.

rifle *vt* robar, pillar; estriar, rayar;
* *n* rifle *m*.

rifleman *n* fusilero *m*.

rig *vt* ataviar; (*mar*) aparejar; * *n*
torre de perforación *f*; plataforma
petrolera *f*.

rigging *n* (*mar*) aparejo *m*.

right *adj* derecho/cha, recto/ta;
justo/ta; honesto/ta; ~! ¡bien!,
¡bueno!; ~ly *adv* rectamente, justamente; * *n* justicia *f*; razón *f*; derecho *m*; mano derecha *f*; * *vt* hacer
justicia.

righteous *adj* justo/ta, honrado/da;
~ly *adv* justamente.

righteousness *n* equidad *f*; honradez *f*.

rigid *adj* rígido/da; austero/ra, seve-
ro/ra; yerto/ta; ~ly *adv* con rigidez.

rigidity *n* rigidez, austeridad *f*.

rigmarole *n* galimatías *m*.

rigorous *adj* riguroso/sa; ~ly *adv* ri-
gorosamente.

rigour *n* rigor *m*; severidad *f*.

rim *n* margen *m/f*; orilla *f*.

rind *n* corteza *f*.

ring *n* círculo, cerco *m*; anillo *m*;
campaneo *m*; * *vt* sonar; * *vi* reti-
ñir, retumbar; **to ~ the bell** pulsar
el timbre.

ringer *n* campanero/ra *m/f*.

ringleader *n* cabecilla *m/f*.

ringlet *n* anillejo *m*.

ring road *n* periférico *m*; carretera
de circunvalación *f*.

ringworm *n* (*med*) tina favosa *f*.

rink *n* (*also* **ice ~**) pista de hielo *f*.

rinse *vt* lavar, limpiar.

riot *n* tumulto, bullicio *m*; * *vi* amotinarse.

rioter *n* amotinado/da *m/f*.

riotous *adj* bullicioso/sa, sedicioso/
sa; disoluto/ta; ~ly *adv* disoluta-
mente.

rip *vt* rasgar, lacerar; descoser.

ripe *adj* maduro/ra, sazonado/da.

ripen *vt*, *vi* madurar.

ripeness *n* madurez *f*.

rip-off *n* (*sl*): **it's a ~!** ¡es una estafa!

ripple *vi* rizarse; * *vt* rizar; * *n* onda
f, rizo *m*.

rise *vi* levantarse; nacer, salir; rebelarse; ascender; hincharse; elevarse; resucitar; * *n* levantamiento *m*;
elevación *f*; subida *f*; salida (del
sol) *f*; causa *f*.

rising *n* salida (del sol) *f*; fin (de una
junta *o* sesión) *m*.

risk *n* riesgo, peligro *m*; * *vt* arriesgar.

risky *adj* peligroso/sa.

rissole *n* croqueta *f*.

rite *n* rito *m*.

ritual *adj*, *n* ritual *m*.

rival *adj*, *n* rival *m/f*; * *vt* competir,
emular.

rivalry *n* rivalidad *f*.

river *n* río *m*.

riverside *adj* ribereño/ña.

rivet *n* remache *m*; * *vt* remachar,
roblar.

rivulet *n* riachuelo *m*.

roach *n* rubio *m*.

road *n* camino *m*.

road sign *n* señal de trafico *f*.

roadstead *n* (*mar*) rada *f*.

roadworks *npl* obras *fpl*.

roam *vt*, *vi* corretear; vagar.

roan *adj* ruano/na.

roar *vi* rugir, aullar; bramar; * *n* rugido *m*; bramido, trueno *m*; mugido *m*.

roast *vt* asar; tostar.

roast beef n rosbif m.

rob vt robar, hurtar.

robber n ladrón/ona m/f.

robbery n robo m.

robe n manto m; toga f; * vt vestir de
gala.

robin (redbreast) n petirrojo m.

robust adj robusto/ta.

robustness n robustez f.

rock n roca f; escollo m; rueca f; * vt
mecer; arrullar; ape drear; * vi
bambolear.

rock and roll n rocanrol m.

rock crystal n cuarzo m.

rocket n cohete m.

rocking chair n mecedora f.

rock salt n sal gema f.

rocky adj peñascoso/sa.

rod n varilla, verga, cana f.

rodent n roedor/a m/f.

roe n corzo m; hueva f.

roebuck n corzo m.

rogation n rogaciones fpl.

rogue n bribón/ona, pícaro/ra,
villano/na m/f.

roguish adj pícaro/ra.

roll vt rodar; volver; arrollar; * vi rodar; girar; * n rodadura f; rollo m;
lista f; catalogo m; bollo m; paneci-
llo m.

roller n rodillo, cilindro m.

roller skates npl patines de rueda
mpl.

rolling pin n rodillo de cocina m.

Roman Catholic adj, n católico/ca
m/f (romano/na).

romance n romance m; ficción f;
cuento m; fábula f.

romantic adj romántico/ca.

romp vi retozar.

roof n tejado m; paladar m; * vt techar.

roofing n techado, tejado m.

rook n grajo m; torre f (en el juego
de ajedrez).

room n habitación, sala f; lugar, espacio m; aposento m.

roominess n espaciosidad, capacidad f.

roomy adj espacioso/sa.

roost n pértiga del gallinero f; * vi
dormir en una pértiga.

root n raíz f; origen m; * vt, vi **to ~
out** desarraigar; arraigar.

rooted adj inveterado/da.

rope n cuerda f; cordel m; * vi hacer
hebras.

rope maker n cordelero/ra m/f.

rosary n rosario m.

rose n rosa f.

rose bed n campo de rosales m.

rosebud n capullo de rosa m.

rosemary n (bot) romero m.

rose tree n rosal m.

rosette n roseta f.

rosé wine n vino rosado m.

rosewood n palo de rosa m.

rosiness n color rosado m.

rosy adj rosado/da.

rot vi pudrirse; * n putrefacción f.

rotate vt, vi girar.

rotation n rotación f.

rote n uso m; práctica f.

rotten adj podrido/da, corrompido/
da.

rottenness n podredumbre, putrefacción f.

rotund adj rotundo/da, redondo/da,
circular, esférico/ca.

rouble n rublo m.

rouge n arrebol, colorete m.

rough adj áspero/ra, tosco/ca;
bronco/ca, bruto/ta, brusco/ca;
tempestuoso/sa; **~-looking** zarra-
pastroso/sa; **~ly** adv rudamente.

roughcast n mezcla gruesa f.

roughen *vt* poner áspero/ra.

roughness *n* aspereza *f*; rudeza, tosquedad *f*; tempestad *f*.

roulette *n* ruleta *f*.

round *adj* redondo/da; cabal; franco/ca, sincero/ra; * *n* círculo *m*; redondez *f*; vuelta *f*; giro *m*; escalón *m*; ronda *f*; andanada de cañones *f*; descarga *f*; * *adv* alrededor; por todos lados; ~**ly** *adv* redondamente; francamente; * *vt* cercar, rodear; redondear.

roundabout *adj* amplio/lia; indirecto/ta, vago/ga; * *n* jubón *m*; glorieta *f*.

roundness *n* redondez *f*.

rouse *vt* despertar; excitar.

rout *n* derrota *f*; * *vt* derrotar.

route *n* ruta *f*; camino *m*.

routine *adj* rutinario/ria; * *n* rutina *f*; número *m*.

rove *vi* vagar, vaguear.

rover *n* vagabundo/da *m/f*; pirata *m/f*.

row *n* camorra *f*; rina *f*.

row *n* (*line*) hilera, fila *f*; * *vt* (*mar*) remar, bogar.

rowdy *n* alborotador/a, bullanguero/ra *m/f*.

rower *n* remero/ra *m/f*.

royal *adj* real; regio/gia; ~**ly** *adv* regiamente.

royalist *n* realista *m/f*.

royalty *n* realeza, dignidad real *f*; honorarios que paga el editor al autor por cada ejemplar vendido de su obra *mpl*; ~ **ties** *npl* regalías *fpl*.

rub *vt* estregar, fregar, frotar; raspar; * *n* frotamiento *m*; (*fig*) embarazo *m*; dificultad *f*.

rubber *n* caucho *m*, goma *f*; condón *m*.

rubber-band *n* goma, gomita *f*.

rubbish *n* basura *f*; tonterías *fpl*; escombro *m*; ruinas *fpl*.

rubric *n* rúbrica *f*.

ruby *n* rubí *m*.

rucksack *n* mochila *f*.

rudder *n* timón *m*.

ruddiness *n* tez encendida; rubicundez *f*.

ruddy *adj* colorado/da, rubio/bia.

rude *adj* rudo/da, brutal, rústico/ca, grosero/ra; tosco/ca; ~**ly** *adv* rudamente, groseramente.

rudeness *n* descortesía *f*; rudeza, insolencia *f*.

rudiment *n* rudimentos *mpl*.

rue *vi* compadecerse; * *n* (*bot*) ruda *f*.

rueful *adj* lamentable, triste.

ruffian *n* malhechor/a, bandolero/ra *m/f*; * *adj* brutal.

ruffle *vt* desordenar, desazonar; rizar.

rug *n* alfombra *f*.

rugby *n* rugby *m*.

rugged *adj* áspero/ra, tosco/ca; brutal; peludo/da.

ruin *n* ruina *f*; perdición *f*; escombros *mpl*; * *vt* arruinar; destruir.

ruinous *adj* ruinoso/sa.

rule *n* mando *m*; regla *f*; regularidad *f*; dominio *m*; * *vt* gobernar; reglar, arreglar, dirigir.

ruler *n* gobernador/a *m/f*; regla *f*.

rum *n* ron *m*.

rumble *vi* crujir, rugir.

ruminate *vt* rumiar.

rummage *vt* rebuscar.

rumour *n* rumor *m*; * *vt* rumorearse.

rump *n* ancas *fpl*.

run *vt* dirigir; organizar; llevar; pasar; **to ~ the risk** aventurar, arriesgar; * *vi* correr; fluir, manar; pasar rápidamente; proceder; ir; desteñirse; ser candidato/ta; * *n* corrida, carrera *f*; paseo *m*; curso *m*; serie *f*; moda *f*; ataque *m*.

runaway *n* fugitivo/va, desertor/a *m/f*.

rung *n* escalón, peldaño *m* (de escalera de mano).

runner *n* corredor/a *m/f*; correo, mensajero/ra *m/f*.

running *n* carrera, corrida *f*; curso *m*.

runway *n* pista de aterrizaje *f*.

rupture *n* rotura *f*; hernia, quebradura *f*; * *vt* reventar, romper.

rural *adj* rural, campestre, rústico/ca.

ruse *n* astucia, maña *f*.

rush *n* junco *m*; ráfaga *f*; ímpetu *m*; * *vt* apresurar; * *vi* abalanzarse, tirarse.

rusk *n* galleta *f*.

russet *adj* bermejo/ja.

rust *n* herrumbre *f*; * *vi* oxidarse.

rustic *adj* rústico/ca; * *n* patán/ana, rústico/ca *m/f*.

rustiness *n* herrumbre *f*.

rustle *vi* crujir, rechinar; * *vt* hacer crujir.

rustling *n* estruendo *m*; crujido *m*.

rusty *adj* oriniento/ta, mohoso/sa; oxidado/da.

rut *n* celo *m*; carril *m*.

ruthless *adj* cruel, insensible; ~**ly** *adv* inhumanamente.

rye *n* (*bot*) centeno *m*.

S

Sabbath *n* sábado *m*.

sable *n* cebellina *f*.

sabotage *n* sabotaje *m*.

sabre *n* sable *m*.

saccharin *n* sacarina *f*.

sachet *n* sobrecito *m*.

sack *n* saco *m*; * *vt* despedir; saquear.

sacrament *n* sacramento *m*; Eucaristía *f*.

sacramental *adj* sacramental.

sacred *adj* sagrado/da, sacro/cra; inviolable.

sacredness *n* santidad *f*.

sacrifice *n* sacrificio *m*; * *vt*, *vi* sacrificar.

sacrificial *adj* de sacrificio.

sacrilege *n* sacrilegio *m*.

sacrilegious *adj* sacrílego/ga.

sad *adj* triste, melanólico/ca; infausto/ta; obscuro/ra; ~**ly** *adv* tristemente.

sadden *vt* entristecer.

saddle *n* silla *f*; sillín *m*; * *vt* ensillar.

saddlebag *n* alforja *f*.

saddler *n* sillero *m/f*.

sadness *n* tristeza *f*.

safari *n* safari *m*.

safe *adj* seguro/ra; ileso/sa; fuera de peligro; de fiar; ~**ly** *adv* seguramente; ~ **and sound** sano y salvo; * *n* caja fuerte *f*.

safe-conduct *n* salvoconducto *m*.

safeguard *n* salvaguardia *f*; * *vt* proteger, defender.

safety *n* seguridad *f*; salvamento *m*.

safety belt *n* cinturón (de seguridad) *m*.

safety match *n* cerilla *f*.

safety pin *n* imperdible, seguro *m*.

saffron *n* azafrán *m*.

sage *n* (*bot*) salvia *f*; sabio/bia *m/f*; * *adj* sabio/bia; ~**ly** *adv* sabiamente.

Sagittarius n Sagitario m (signo del zodíaco).
sago n (*bot*) sagú m.
sail n vela f; * vt gobernar; * vi dar a la vela, navegar.
sailing n navegación f.
sailing boat n yate m.
sailor n marinero/ra m/f.
saint n santo/ta m/f.
sainted, saintly adj santo/ta.
sake n causa, razón f; **for God's ~** por amor de Dios.
salad n ensalada f.
salad bowl n ensaladera f.
salad dressing n aliño m.
salad oil n aceite para ensaladas m.
salamander n salamandra f.
salary n sueldo m.
sale n venta f; liquidación f.
saleable adj vendible.
salesman n vendedor m.
saleswoman n vendedora f.
salient adj saliente, saledizo/za.
saline adj salino/na.
saliva n saliva f.
sallow adj cetrino/na, pálido/da.
sally n (*mil*) salida, surtida f; * vi salir.
salmon n salmón m.
salmon trout n trucha salmonada f.
saloon n bar m.
salt n sal f; * vt salar.
salt cellar n salero m.
salting n saladura f.
saltpetre n salitre m.
saltworks npl salinas fpl.
salubrious adj salubre, saludable.
salubrity n salubridad f.
salutary adj salubre, salutífero/ra.
salutation n salutación f.
salute vt saludar; * n saludo m.
salvage n (*mar*) salvamento, rescate m.

salvation n salvación f.
salve n emplasto, ungüento m.
salver n salvilla, bandeja f.
salvo n salva, excusa f.
same adj mismo/ma, idéntico/ca.
sameness n identidad f.
sample n muestra f; ejemplo m; * vt probar.
sampler n muestra f; dechado, modelo m.
sanatorium n sanatorio m.
sanctify vt santificar.
sanctimonious adj santurrón/ona.
sanction n sanción f; * vt sancionar.
sanctity n santidad f.
sanctuary n santuario m; asilo m.
sand n arena f; * vt lijar.
sandal n sandalia f.
sandbag n (*mil*) saco de tierra m.
sandpit n arenal m.
sandstone n arenisca f.
sandwich n bocadillo, sandwich m.
sandy adj arenoso/sa.
sane adj sano/na.
sanguinary adj sanguinario/ria.
sanguine adj sanguíneo/nea.
sanitary towel n compresa f.
sanity n juicio sano, sentido común m.
sap n savia f; * vt minar.
sapient adj sabio/bia, cuerdo/da.
sapling n arbolito m.
sapper n (*mil*) zapador m.
sapphire n zafiro m.
sarcasm n sarcasmo m.
sarcastic adj sarcástico/ca; **~ally** adv sarcásticamente.
sarcophagus n sarcófago, sepulcro m.
sardine n sardina f.
sash n cíngulo m, cinta f.
sash window n ventana o vidriera corrediza f.
Satan n Satanás m.
satanic(al) adj diabólico/ca.

satchel *n* mochila *f*.
satellite *n* satélite *m*.
satellite dish *n* antena parabólica *f*.
satiate, sate *vt* saciar, hartar.
satin *n* raso *m*; * *adj* de raso.
satire *n* satira *f*.
satiric(al) *adj* satírico/ca; ~ly *adv* satíricamente.
satirist *n* autor satírico *m*, autora satírica *f*.
satirize *vt* satirizar.
satisfaction *n* satisfacción *f*.
satisfactorily *adv* satisfactoriamente.
satisfactory *adj* satisfactorio/ria.
satisfy *vt* satisfacer; convencer.
saturate *vt* saturar.
Saturday *n* sábado *m*.
saturnine *adj* saturnino/na, melancólico/ca.
satyr *n* sátiro *m*.
sauce *n* salsa *f*; crema *f*; * *vt* condimentar.
saucepan *n* cazo *m*.
saucer *n* platillo *m*.
saucily *adv* desvergonzadamente.
sauciness *n* insolencia, impudencia *f*.
saucy *adj* insolente.
saunter *vi* callejear, corretear.
sausage *n* salchicha *f*.
savage *adj* salvaje, bárbaro/ra; ~ly *adv* bárbaramente; * *n* salvaje *m/f*.
savageness *n* salvajería, *f*; crueldad *f*.
savagery *n* crueldad *f*.
savanna(h) *n* sabana *f*.
save *vt* salvar; economizar; ahorrar; evitar; conservar; * *adv* salvo, excepto; * *n* parada *f*.
saveloy (sausage) *n* chorizo *m*.
saver *n* libertador/a *m/f*; ahorrador/a *m/f*.
saving *adj* frugal, económico/ca; * *prep* fuera de, excepto; * *n* salva-

miento *m*; ~s *pl* ahorro *m*, economía *f*.
savings account *n* cuenta de ahorros *f*.
savings bank *n* caja de ahorros *f*.
Saviour *n* Salvador *m*.
savour *n* olor *m*; sabor *m*; * *vt* gustar, saborear.
savouriness *n* paladar; sabor *m*.
savoury *adj* sabroso/sa.
saw *n* sierra *f*; * *vt* serrar.
sawdust *n* serrín *m*.
sawfish *n* priste *m*.
sawmill *n* aserradero *m*.
sawyer *n* aserrador/a *m/f*.
saxophone *n* saxofóno *m*.
say *vt* decir, hablar.
saying *n* dicho, proverbio *m*.
scab *n* roña *f*; roñoso *m*.
scabbard *n* vaina (de espada) *f*; cobertura *f*.
scabby *adj* sarnoso/sa.
scaffold *n* tablado *m*; cadalso *m*.
scaffolding *n* andamio *m*.
scald *vt* escaldar; * *n* escaldadura *f*.
scale *n* balanza *f*; escama *f*; escala *f*; gama *f*; * *vt, vi* escalar; descostrarse.
scallop *n* vieira *f*; festón *m*; * *vt* festonear.
scalp *n* cuero cabelludo *m*; * *vt* escalpar.
scamp *n* bribón/ona, ladrón/ona *m/f*.
scamper *vi* escapar, huir.
scampi *npl* gambas *fpl*.
scan *vt* escudriñar; registrar; escandir; escanear.
scandal *n* escándalo *m*; infamia *f*.
scandalize *vt* escandalizar.
scandalous *adj* escandaloso/sa; ~ly *adv* escandalosamente.
scanner *n* escáner *m*.
scant, scanty *adj* escaso/sa, parco/ca.

scantily *adv* escasamente, estrechamente.

scantiness *n* estrechez, escasez *f*.

scapegoat *n* chivo expiatorio *m*.

scar *n* cicatriz *f*; * *vt* dejar cicatriz en.

scarce *adj* raro/ra; ~**ly** *adv* apenas.

scarcity *n* escasez *f*; raridad *f*.

scare *vt* espantar; * *n* susto *m*.

scarecrow *n* espantapájaros *m invar*.

scarf *n* bufanda *f*.

scarlet *n* escarlata *f*; * *adj* escarlata.

scarlet fever *n* escarlatina *f*.

scarp *n* escarpa *f*.

scat *interj* (*sl*) izape!

scatter *vt* esparcir; disipar.

scavenger *n* basurero/ra *m/f*; carroñero/ra *m/f*.

scenario *n* argumento *m*; guión *m*; (*fig*) escenario *m*.

scene *n* escena *f*; panorama *m*; escándalo *m*; paisaje *m*.

scenery *n* vista *f*; decoración (de teatro) *f*.

scenic *adj* escénico/ca.

scent *n* olfato *m*; olor *m*; rastro *m*; * *vt* oler.

scent bottle *n* frasco de perfume *m*.

scentless *adj* sin olfato; inodoro/ra.

sceptic *n* escéptico/ca *m/f*.

sceptic(al) *adj* escéptico/ca.

scepticism *n* escepticismo *m*.

sceptre *n* cetro *m*.

schedule *n* horario *m*; programa *m*; lista *f*.

scheme *n* proyecto, plan *m*; esquema *m*; sistema *m*; modelo *m*; * *vt* proyectar; * *vi* intrigar.

schemer *n* proyectista, intrigante *m/f*.

schism *n* cisma *m*.

schismatic *adj* cismático/ca.

scholar *n* estudiante *m/f*; erudito/ta *m/f*, escolástico/ca *m/f*.

scholarship *n* ciencia *f*; erudición *f*.

scholastic *adj* escolástico/ca.

school *n* escuela *f*, colegio *m*; * *vt* enseñar.

schoolboy *n* alumno *m*.

schoolgirl *n* alumna *f*.

schooling *n* instrucción *f*.

schoolmaster *n* maestro de escuela *m*.

schoolmistress *n* maestra de niños o niñas *f*.

schoolteacher *n* maestro/tra *m/f*; profesor/a *m/f*.

schooner *n* (*mar*) goleta *f*.

sciatica *n* ciática *f*.

science *n* ciencia *f*.

scientific *adj* científico/ca; ~**ally** *adv* científicamente.

scientist *n* científico/ca *m/f*.

scimitar *n* cimitarra *f*.

scintillate *vi* chispear, centellar.

scintillating *adj* brillante, ingenioso/sa.

scission *n* separación, partición *f*.

scissors *npl* tijeras *fpl*.

scoff *vi* mofarse, burlarse.

scold *vt, vi* regañar, reñir, refunfuñar.

scoop *n* cucharón *m*; pala *f*; exclusiva *f*; * *vt* cavar, socavar.

scooter *n* moto *f*; patinete *m*.

scope *n* objeto, intento, designio, blanco, espacio *m*; alcance *m*; libertad *f*.

scorch *vt* quemar; tostar; * *vi* quemarse, secarse.

score *n* muesca, canalita *f*; consideración *f*; cuenta *f*; puntuación *f*; razón *f*; motivo *m*; veintena *f*; * *vt* ganar; señalar con una línea; * *vi* marcar.

scoreboard *n* marcador *m*.

scorn *vt, vi* despreciar; mofar; * *n* desdén, menosprecio *m*.

scornful *adj* desdeñoso/sa; **~ly** *adv* con desdén.

Scorpio *n* Escorpión *m* (signo del zodíaco).

scorpion *n* escorpión *m*.

scotch *vt* descartar.

Scotch *n* whisky escocés *m*.

scoundrel *n* pícaro/ra *m/f*.

scour *vt* fregar, estregar; limpiar; * *vi* corretear.

scourge *n* azote *m*; castigo *m*; * *vt* azotar, castigar.

scout *n* (*mil*) explorador/a *m/f*; espía *m/f*; * *vi* ir de reconocimiento.

scowl *vi* fruncir el ceño; * *n* ceño, semblante ceñudo *m*.

scragginess *n* flaqueza, aspereza *f*.

scraggy *adj* áspero/ra; macilento/ta.

scramble *vi* arrapar; trepar; disputar; * *n* disputa *f*; subida *f*.

scrap *n* migaja *f*; sobras *fpl*; pedacito *m*; riña *f*; chatarra *f*.

scrape *vt, vi* raer, raspar; arañar; tocar mal un instrumento; * *n* embarazo *m*; dificultad *f*.

scraper *n* rascador *m*.

scratch *vt* rascar, raspar; raer, garrapatear; * *n* rasguño *m*.

scrawl *vt, vi* garrapatear; * *n* garabatos *mpl*.

scream, screech *vi* chillar, dar alaridos; * *n* chillido, grito, alarido *m*.

screen *n* pantalla *f*; biombo *m*; mampara *f*; abanico de chimenea *m*; * *vt* abrigar, esconder; proyectar; cribar, cerner.

screenplay *n* guión *m*.

screw *n* tornillo *m*; * *vt* atornillar; forzar, apretar, estrechar.

screwdriver *n* destornillador *m*.

scribble *vt* escarabajear; * *n* escrito de poco mérito *m*.

scribe *n* escritor/a *m/f*; escriba *m/f*.

scrimmage *n* tumulto *m*.

script *n* guión *m*; letra *f*.

scriptural *adj* bíblico/ca.

Scripture *n* Sagrada Escritura *f*.

scroll *n* rollo (de papel o pergamino) *m*.

scrounger *n* mamón/ona *m/f*.

scrub *vt* restregar; anular; * *n* maleza *f*.

scruffy *adj* desaliñado/da.

scruple *n* escrúpulo *m*.

scrupulous *adj* escrupuloso/sa; **~ly** *adv* escrupulosamente.

scrutinize *vt* escudriñar, examinar.

scrutiny *n* escrutinio, examen *m*.

scuffle *n* quimera, riña *f*; * *vi* reñir, pelear.

scull *n* barquillo *m*.

scullery *n* fregadero *m*.

sculptor *n* escultor/a *m/f*.

sculpture *n* escultura *f*; * *vt* esculpir.

scum *n* espuma *f*; escoria *f*; canalla *m/f*.

scurrilous *adj* vil, bajo/ja; injurioso/sa; **~ly** *adv* injuriosamente.

scurvy *n* escorbuto *m*; * *adj* escorbútico/ca; vil, despreciable.

scuttle *n* carbonera *f*; * *vt* barrenar.

scythe *n* guadaña *f*.

sea *n* mar *m/f*; * *adj* de mar; **heavy ~** oleada *f*.

sea breeze *n* viento de mar *m*.

seacoast *n* costa marítima *f*.

sea fight *n* combate naval *m*.

seafood *n* mariscos *mpl*.

sea front *n* paseo marítimo *m*.

sea-green *adj* verdemar.

seagull *n* gaviota *f*.

sea horse *n* caballito de mar *m*.

seal *n* sello *m*; foca *f*; * *vt* sellar.

sealing wax *n* lacre *m*.

seam *n* costura *f*; * *vt* coser.

seaman *n* marinero *m*.

seamanship n pericia en la navegación m.

seamstress n costurera f.

seamy adj sórdido/da.

seaplane n hidroavión m.

seaport n puerto de mar m.

sear vt cauterizar.

search vt examinar; escudriñar; inquirir, tentar; investigar, buscar; * n pesquisa f; busca f; buscada f.

searchlight n reflector m.

seashore n ribera f, litoral m.

seasick adj mareado/da.

seasickness n mareo m.

seaside n orilla o ribera del mar f.

season n estación f; tiempo oportuno m; sazón f; * vt sazonar; imbuir.

seasonable adj oportuno/na, a propósito.

seasonably adv oportunamente.

seasoning n condimento m.

season ticket n abono m.

season ticket holder n abonado/da m/f.

seat n asiento m; silla f; escaño m; situación f; * vt situar; colocar; asentar.

seat belt n cinturón de seguridad m.

seaward adj del litoral; ~s adv hacia el mar.

seaweed n alga marina f.

seaworthy adj en condiciones de navegar.

secede vi apartarse, separarse.

secession n secesión f; separación f.

seclude vt apartar, excluir.

seclusion n separación f; exclusión f.

second adj segundo/da; ~(ly) adv en segundo lugar; * n defensor/a m/f; segundo m; (mus) segunda f; * vt ayudar; segundar.

secondary adj secundario/ria.

secondary school n centro de enseñanza secundaria m; escuela secundaria f.

secondhand adj de segunda mano.

secrecy n secreto m, confidencialidad f.

secret adj secreto/ta; * n secreto m; ~ly adv secretamente.

secretary n secretario/ria m/f.

secrete vt esconder; (med) secretar.

secretion n secreción f.

secretive adj misterioso/sa.

sect n secta f.

sectarian n sectario/ria m/f.

section n sección f.

sector n sector m.

secular adj secular, seglar.

secularize vt secularizar.

secure adj seguro/ra; salvo/va; ~ly adv seguramente; * vt asegurar; salvar.

security n seguridad f; defensa f; confianza f; fianza f.

sedan, saloon n sedán m.

sedate adj sosegado/da, tranquilo/la; ~ly adv tranquilamente.

sedateness n tranquilidad f.

sedative n sedativo m.

sedentary adj sedentario/ria.

sedge n (bot) juncia f.

sediment n sedimento m; hez f; poso m.

sedition n sedición f; tumulto, alboroto, motín m; revuelta f.

seditious adj sedicioso/sa.

seduce vt seducir; engañar.

seducer n seductor/a m/f.

seduction n seducción f.

seductive adj seductor/a.

sedulous adj asiduo/dua; ~ly adv asiduamente.

see vt, vi ver, observar, descubrir; advertir; conocer, juzgar; comprender; ~! ¡mira!

seed *n* semilla, simiente *f*; * *vi* granar.
seedling *n* plantón *m*.
seedsman *n* tratante en semillas *m*.
seed time *n* sementera, siembra *f*.
seedy *adj* desaseado/da.
seeing *conj*: ~ **that** visto que, ya que.
seek *vt, vi* buscar; pretender.
seem *vi* parecer, semejarse.
seeming *n* apariencia *f*; **~ly** *adv* al parecer.
seemliness *n* decensia *f*.
seemly *adj* decente, propio/pia.
seer *n* profeta *m*, profetisa *f*.
seesaw *n* vaivén *m*; * *vi* balancear.
seethe *vi* hervir, bullir.
segment *n* segmento *m*.
seize *vt* asir, agarrar; secuestrar (bienes o efectos).
seizure *n* captura *f*; secuestro *m*.
seldom *adv* raramente, rara vez.
select *vt* elegir, escoger; * *adj* selecto/ta, escogido/da.
selection *n* selección *f*.
self *n* uno/na mismo/ma; **the** ~ el yo; * *pref* auto- .
self-command *n* autocontrol *m*.
self-conceit *n* presunción *f*.
self-confident *adj* que tiene confianza en sí mismo/ma.
self-defence *n* defensa propia *f*.
self-denial *n* abnegación de sí mismo/ma *f*.
self-employed *adj* autónomo/ma.
self-evident *adj* obvio/via.
self-governing *adj* autónomo/ma.
self-interest *n* interés propio *m*.
selfish *adj* egoísta; **~ly** *adv* interesadamente.
selfishness *n* egoísmo *m*.
self-medication *n* automedicación *f*.
self-pity *n* lástima de sí mismo/ma *f*.
self-portrait *n* autorretrato *m*.

self-possession *n* sangre fría, tranquilidad de ánimo *f*.
self-reliant *adj* independiente.
self-respect *n* amor propio *m*.
selfsame *adj* mismísimo/ma.
self-satisfied *adj* pagado/da de sí mismo/ma.
self-seeking *adj* egoísta.
self-service *adj* de autoservicio.
self-styled *adj* autoproclamado/da.
self-sufficient *adj* autosuficiente.
self-taught *adj* autodidacta.
self-willed *adj* obstinado/da.
sell *vt, vi* vender; traficar.
seller *n* vendedor/a *m/f*.
selling-off *n* privatización *f*.
Sellotape® *n* celo *m*.
semblance *n* semejanza, apariencia *f*.
semen *n* semen *m*.
semester *n* semestre *m*.
semicircle *n* semicirculo *m*.
semicircular *adj* semicircular.
semicolon *n* punto y coma *m*.
semiconductor *n* semiconductor *m*.
semi-final *n* semifinal *f*.
seminarist *n* seminarista *m*.
seminary *n* seminario *m*.
semitone *n* (*mus*) semitono *m*.
senate *n* senado *m*.
senator *n* senador/a *m/f*.
senatorial *adj* senatorio/ria.
send *vt* enviar, despachar, mandar; enviar; producir.
sender *n* remitente *m/f*.
senile *adj* senil.
senility *n* senectud *f*; vejez *f*.
senior *n* mayor *m*; * *adj* mayor; superior.
seniority *n* antigüedad, ancianidad *f*.
senna *n* (*bot*) sena *f*.
sensation *n* sensación *f*.
sense *n* sentido *m*; entendimiento *m*; razón *f*; juicio *m*; sentimiento *m*.

senseless *adj* insensible; insensato/ta; ~**ly** *adv* insensatamente.

senselessness *n* tontería, insensatez *f*.

sensibility *n* sensibilidad *f*.

sensible *adj* sensato/ta; juicioso/sa.

sensibly *adv* sensatamente.

sensitive *adj* sensible.

sensual, sensuous *adj*, ~**ly** *adv* sensual(mente).

sensuality *n* sensualidad *f*.

sentence *n* oración *f*; sentencia *f*; * *vt* sentenciar, condenar.

sententious *adj* sentencioso/sa; ~**ly** *adv* sentenciosamente.

sentient *adj* sensitivo/va.

sentiment *n* sentimiento *m*; opinión *f*.

sentimental *adj* sentimental.

sentinel, sentry *n* centinela *m*.

sentry box *n* garita *f*.

separable *adj* separable.

separate *vt* (*vi*) separar(se); * *adj* separado/da; distinto/ta; ~**ly** *adv* separadamente.

separation *n* separación *f*.

September *n* septiembre *m*.

septennial *adj* sieteñal.

septuagenarian *n* septuagenario/ria *m/f*.

sepulchre *n* sepulcro *m*.

sequel *n* continuación *f*; consecuencia *f*.

sequence *n* serie, continuación *f*.

sequester, sequestrate *vt* secuestrar.

sequestration *n* secuestro *m*.

seraglio *n* serallo *m*.

seraph *n* serafín *m*.

serenade *n* serenata *f*; * *vt* dar serenatas.

serene *adj* sereno/na; ~**ly** *adv* serenamente.

serenity *n* serenidad *f*.

serf *n* siervo/va, esclavo/va *m/f*.

serge *n* sarga *f*.

sergeant *n* sargento/ta *m/f*; alguacil *m/f*.

serial *adj* consecutivo/va, en serie; * *n* serial *m*; telenovela *f*.

series *n* serie *f*.

serious *adj* serio/ria, grave; ~**ly** *adv* seriamente.

sermon *n* sermón *f*; oración evangélica *f*.

serous *adj* seroso/sa.

serpent *n* serpiente, sierpe *f*.

serpentine *adj* serpentino/na; * *n* (*chem*) serpentina *f*.

serrated *adj* serrado/da.

serum *n* suero *m*.

servant *n* criado *m*; criada *f*.

servant girl *n* criada *f*.

serve *vt, vi* servir; asistir (a la mesa); hacer; cumplir; sacar; ser a propósito; **to ~ a warrant** ejecutar un auto de prisión.

service *n* servicio *m*; servidumbre, utilidad *f*; culto divino *m*; acomodo *m*; * *vt* mantener; reparar.

serviceable *adj* servible; oficioso/sa.

servile *adj* servil.

servitude *n* servidumbre, esclavitud *f*.

session *n* junta *f*; sesión *f*.

set *vt* poner, colocar, fijar; establecer, determinar; * *vi* ponerse (el sol o los astros); cuajarse; aplicarse; * *n* juego, conjunto *m*; servicio (de plata) *m*; conjunto *o* agregado de muchas cosas *m*; decorado *m*; set *m*; cuadrilla, bandada *f*; * *adj* puesto/ta, fijo/ja; listo/ta; decidido/da.

settee *n* sofá *m*.

setter *n* setter *m*.

setting *n* establecimiento *m*; marco *m*; montadura *f*; **~ of the sun** puesta del sol *f*.

settle *vt* colocar, fijar, afirmar; arreglar; calmar; * *vi* repo sarse; establecerse; sosegarse.

settlement *n* establecimiento *m*; domicilio *m*; contrato *m*; empleo *m*; poso *m*; colonia *f*.

settler *n* colono/na *m/f*.

set-to *n* riña *f*; combate *m*.

seven *adj, n* siete.

seventeen *adj, n* diecisiete.

seventeenth *adj, n* decimoséptimo/ma.

seventh *adj, n* séptimo/ma.

seventieth *adj, n* septuagésimo/ma.

seventy *adj, n* setenta.

sever *vt, vi* separar.

several *adj, pn* varios/as, algunos/nas.

severance *n* separación *f*.

severe *adj* severo/ra, riguroso/sa, áspero/ra, duro/ra; **~ly** *adv* severamente.

severity *n* severidad *f*.

sew *vt, vi* coser.

sewer *n* alcantarilla *f*.

sewerage *n* alcantarillado *m*.

sewing machine *n* máquina de coser *f*.

sex *n* sexo *m*.

sexist *adj, n* sexista *m/f*.

sextant *n* sextante *m*.

sexton *n* sepulturero/ra *m/f*.

sexual *adj* sexual.

sexy *adj* sexy.

shabbily *adv* vilmente, mezquinamente.

shabbiness *n* miseria *f*.

shabby *adj* desharrapado/da, zarrapastroso/sa.

shackle *vt* poner grilletes; **~s** *npl* grilletes *mpl*.

shade *n* sombra, oscuridad *f*; matiz *m*; sombrilla *f*; * *vt* dar sombra a; abrigar; proteger.

shadiness *n* sombraje *m*; umbría *f*.

shadow *n* sombra *f*; protección *f*.

shadowy *adj* umbroso/sa; oscuro/ra; quimerico/ca.

shady *adj* opaco/ca, oscuro/ra, sombrío/ría.

shaft *n* flecha, saeta *f*; fuste de columna *m*; pozo *m*; hueco *m*; rayo *m*.

shag *n* tabaco picado *m*; cormorán moñudo *m*.

shaggy *adj* lanoso/sa.

shake *vt* sacudir; agitar; **to ~ vigorously** zarandear; **to ~ hands** darse las manos; * *vi* vacilar; temblar; * *n* sacudida *f*; vibración *f*.

shaking *n* temblor *m*.

shaky *adj* titubeante.

shallow *adj* somero/ra, superficial; trivial.

shallowness *n* poca profundidad *f*; necedad *f*.

sham *vt* engañar; * *n* fingimiento *m*; impostura *f*; * *adj* fingido/da, disimulado/da.

shambles *npl* confusión *f*.

shame *n* vergüenza *f*; deshonra *f*; * *vt* avergonzar, deshonrar.

shamefaced *adj* vergonzoso/sa, pudoroso/sa.

shameful *adj* vergonzoso/sa; deshonroso/sa; **~ly** *adv* ignominiosamente.

shameless *adj* desvergonzado/da; **~ly** *adv* desvergonzadamente.

shamelessness *n* desvergüenza, impudencia *f*.

shammy, chamois *n* gamuza *f*.

shampoo *vt* lavar con champú; * *n* champú *m*.

shamrock *n* trébol *m*.

shank *n* caña *f*; asta (de ancla) *f*; cañón (de pipa) *m*.

shanty *n* chabola *f*.

shanty town n barrio de chabolas m.

shape vt, vi formar; proporcionar; concebir; * n forma, figura f; modelo m.

shapeless adj informe.

shapely adj bien hecho/cha.

share n parte, porción f; (com) acción f; reja del arado f; * vt, vi repartir; compartir.

sharer n partícipe m/f.

shark n tiburón m.

sharp adj agudo/da, aguzado/da; astuto/ta; perspicaz; penetrante; acre, mordaz, severo/ra, rígido/da; vivo/va, violento/ta; * n (mus) sostenido m; * adv en punto.

sharpen vt afilar, aguzar.

sharply adv con filo; severamente, agudamente; ingenios amente.

sharpness n agudeza f; sutileza, perspicacia f; acrimonia f.

shatter vt destrozar, estrellar; * vi hacerse pedazos.

shave vt afeitar, rasurar; * vi afeitarse, rasurarse; * n afeite m.

shaver n máquina de afeitar f.

shaving n rasurado m.

shaving brush n brocha de afeitar f.

shaving cream n crema de afeitar f.

shawl n chal m.

she pn ella.

sheaf n gavilla f; haz m.

shear vt atusar; tundir; ~s npl tijeras de podar fpl.

sheath n vaina f.

shed vt verter, derramar; esparcir; * n tejadillo m; cabaña f.

sheen n resplandor m.

sheep n oveja f.

sheepfold n redil m.

sheepish adj vergonzoso/sa; tímido/da.

sheepishness n timidez, cortedad de genio f.

sheep-run n dehesa f; carneril, pasto de ovejas m.

sheepskin n piel de carnero m; zamarra f; ~ **jacket** zamarra f.

sheer adj puro/ra, claro/ra, sin mezcla; escarpado/da; * adv verticalmente.

sheet n sábana f; lámina f; pliego de papel f; (mar) escota f.

sheet anchor n áncora mayor de un navio f.

sheeting n tela para sábanas f.

sheet iron n chapa de hierro batido f.

sheet lightning n relampagueamiento m.

shelf n anaquel m; (mar) arrecife m; escollera f; **on the** ~ desecho/cha.

shell n cáscara f; proyectil m; concha f; corteza f; * vt descas carar, descortezar; bombardear; * vi descascararse.

shellfish npl invar crustáceo m; marisco m.

shelter n guardia f; amparo, abrigo m; asilo, refugio m; * vt guarecer, abrigar; acoger; * vi abrigarse.

shelve vt echar a un lado, arrinconar.

shelving n estantería f.

shepherd n pastor m.

shepherdess n pastora f.

sherbet n sorbete m.

sheriff n sheriff m/f.

sherry n jerez m.

shield n escudo m; patrocinio m; * vt defender.

shift vi cambiarse; moverse; * vt mudar, cambiar; transpor tar; * n cambio m; turno m.

shinbone n espinilla f.

shine vi lucir, brillar, resplandecer; * vt lustrar; * n brillo m.

shingle n guijarros mpl; ~s pl (med) herpes m invar.

shining *adj* resplandeciente; * *n* esplendor *m*.

shiny *adj* brillante, luciente.

ship *n* nave *f*; barco *m*; navío, buque *m*; * *vt* embarcar; transportar.

shipbuilding *n* construcción naval *f*.

shipmate *n* (*mar*) ayudante *m/f*.

shipment *n* cargamento *mf*.

shipowner *n* naviero/ra *m/f*.

shipwreck *n* naufragio *m*.

shirt *n* camisa *f*.

shit *excl* (*sl*) ¡mierda!

shiver *vi* tiritar de frío.

shoal *n* banco *m*.

shock *n* choque *m*; descarga *f*; susto *m*; * *vt* asustar; ofender.

shock absorber *n* amortiguador *m*.

shoddy *adj* de pacotilla.

shoe *n* zapato *m*; herradura *f*; * *vt* calzar; herrar.

shoeblack *n* limpiabotas *m invar*.

shoe factory *n* zapatería *f*.

shoehorn *n* calzador *m*.

shoelace *n* cordón de zapato *m*.

shoemaker *n* zapatero/ra *m/f*.

shoemaking *n* zapatería *f*.

shoe shop *n* zapatería *f*.

shoestring *n* lazo de zapato *m*.

shoot *vt* tirar, arrojar, lanzar, disparar; * *vi* brotar, germinar; sobresalir; lanzarse; * *n* vástago *m*.

shooter *n* tirador *m*.

shooting *n* caza con escopeta *f*; tiroteo *m*.

shop *n* tienda *f*; taller *m*.

shopfront *n* escaparate *m*.

shopkeeper *n* tendero/ra *m/f*.

shoplifter *n* ladrón/ona de tiendas *m/f*.

shopper *n* comprador/a *m/f*.

shopping *n* compras *fpl*.

shopping centre *n* centro comercial *m*.

shopping mall *n* paseo *m*.

shore *n* costa, ribera, playa *f*.

short *adj* corto/ta, breve, sucinto/ta, conciso/sa; ~ly *adv* brevemente; pronto; en pocas palabras.

shortcoming *n* insuficiencia *f*; déficit *m*.

shorten *vt* acortar; abreviar.

shortness *n* cortedad *f*; brevedad *f*.

short-sighted *adj* miope, corto de vista.

short-sightedness *n* miopía *f*.

shortwave *n* onda corta *f*.

shot *n* tiro *m*; alcance *m*; perdigones *mpl*; tentativa *f*; toma *f*.

shotgun *n* escopeta *f*.

shoulder *n* hombro *m*; brazuelo *m*; * *vt* cargar al hombro.

shout *vi* gritar, aclamar; * *vt* gritar; * *n* aclamación *f*, grito *m*.

shouting *n* gritos *mpl*.

shove *vt, vi* empujar; impeler; * *n* empujon *m*.

shovel *n* pala *f*; * *vt* traspalar.

show *vt* mostrar; descubrir, manifestar; probar; ensenar, explicar; * *vi* parecer; * *n* espectaculo *m*; muestra *f*; exposición, parada *f*.

show business *n* el mundo del espectaculo *m*.

shower *n* nubada *f*; llovizna *f*; ducha *f*; (*fig*) abundancia *f*; * *vi* llover.

showery *adj* lluvioso/sa.

showjumping *n* hípica *f*.

showroom *n* sala de muestras *f*.

showy *adj* ostentoso/sa, suntuoso/sa.

shred *n* cacho, pedazo pequeño *m*; * *vt* hacer trizas.

shrew *n* mujer de mal genio *f*; musaraña *f*.

shrewd *adj* astuto/ta; maligno/gna; ~ly *adv* astutamente.

shrewdness *n* astucia *f*.

shriek *vt, vi* chillar; * *n* chillido *m*.

shrill *adj* agudo/da, penetrante.

shrillness *n* aspereza (del sonido *o* de la voz) *f*.

shrimp *n* camarón *m*; enano/na *m/f*, hombrecillo *m*.

shrine *n* relicario *m*.

shrink *vi* encogerse; angostarse; acortarse.

shrivel *vi* arrugarse, encogerse; * *vt* encoger.

shroud *n* cubierta *f*; mortaja *f*; * *vt* cubrir, defender; amortajar; proteger.

Shrove Tuesday *n* martes de carnaval *m*.

shrub *n* arbusto *m*.

shrubbery *n* plantío de arbustos *m*.

shrug *vt* encogerse de hombros; * *n* encogimiento de hombros *m*.

shudder *vi* estremecerse; * *n* temblor *m*.

shuffle *vt* desordenar; barajar.

shun *vt* huir, evitar.

shunt *vt* (*rail*) maniobrar.

shut *vt* cerrar, encerrar; *vi* cerrarse.

shutter *n* contraventana *f*.

shuttle *n* lanzadera *f*.

shuttlecock *n* volante, rehilete *m*.

shy *adj* tímido/da; reservado/da; vergonzoso/sa, contenido/da; ~**ly** *adv* tímidamente.

shyness *n* timidez *f*.

sibling *n* hermano/na *m/f*.

sibyl *n* sibila, profetisa *f*.

sick *adj* malo/la, enfermo/ma; disgustado/da.

sicken *vt* enfermar; * *vi* caer enfermo/ma.

sickle *n* hoz *f*.

sick leave *n* baja por enfermedad *f*.

sickliness *n* indisposición habitual *f*.

sickly *adj* enfermizo/za.

sickness *n* enfermedad *f*.

sick pay *n* subsidio por enfermedad *m*.

side *n* lado *m*; costado *m*; facción *f*; partido *m*; * *adj* lateral; oblicuo/cua; * *vi* unirse.

sideboard *n* aparador *m*; alacena *f*.

sidelight *n* luz lateral *f*.

sidelong *adj* lateral.

sideways *adv* de lado, al través.

siding *n* toma de partido *f*; (*rail*) aguja *f*.

sidle *vi* ir de lado.

siege *n* (*mil*) sitio *m*.

sieve *n* tamiz *m*; criba *f*; colador *m*; * *vt* cribar.

sift *vt* cerner; cribar; examinar; investigar.

sigh *vi* suspirar, gemir; * *n* suspiro *m*.

sight *n* vista *f*; mira *f*; espectáculo *m*.

sightless *adj* ciego/ga.

sightly *adj* vistoso/sa, hermoso/sa.

sightseeing *n* excursionismo, turismo *m*.

sign *n* señal *f*, indicio *m*; letrero *m*; signo *m*; firma *f*; seña *f*; * *vt* firmar.

signal *n* señal *f*, aviso *m*; * *adj* insigne, señalado/da.

signalize *vt* señalar.

signal lamp *n* (*rail*) reflector de señales *m*.

signalman *n* (*rail*) guardavía *m*.

signature *n* firma *f*.

signet *n* sello *m*.

significance *n* importancia *f*.

significant *adj* significante.

signify *vt* significar.

signpost *n* indicador *m*.

silence *n* silencio *m*; * *vt* imponer silencio.

silent *adj* silencioso/sa; ~**ly** *adv* silenciosamente.

silex *n* sílex *m*.
silicon chip *n* chip de silicio *m*.
silk *n* seda *f*.
silken *adj* hecho/cha de seda; sedeño/ña.
silkiness *n* blandura, molicie *f*.
silkworm *n* gusano de seda *m*.
silky *adj* hecho/cha de seda; sedoso/sa.
sill *n* repisa *f*; umbral de puerta *m*.
silliness *n* simpleza, bobería, tontería, necedad *f*.
silly *adj* tonto/ta, imbécil; ñoño/ña.
silver *n* plata *f*; * *adj* de plata.
silversmith *n* platero/ra *m/f*.
silvery *adj* plateado/da.
similar *adj* similar; semejante; ~ly *adv* del mismo modo.
similarity *n* semejanza *f*.
simile *n* símil *m*.
simmer *vi* hervir a fuego lento.
simony *n* simonía *f*.
simper *vi* sonreír; * *n* sonrisa *f*.
simple *adj* simple, puro/ra, sencillo/lla.
simpleton *n* simplón/ona, simplonazo/za *m/f*.
simplicity *n* sencillez *f*; simpleza *f*.
simplification *n* simplificación *f*.
simplify *vt* simplificar.
simply *adv* sencillamente; solo.
simulate *vt* simular, fingir.
simulation *n* simulación *f*.
simultaneous *adj* simultáneo/nea.
sin *n* pecado *m*; * *vi* pecar, faltar.
since *adv* desde, entonces, después; * *prep* desde; * *conj* desde que; ya que.
sincere *adj* sencillo/lla; sincero/ra; ~ly *adv* sinceramente; **yours ~ly** le saluda atentamente.
sincerity *n* sinceridad *f*.
sinecure *n* sinecura *f*.
sinew *n* tendón *m*; nervio *m*.

sinewy *adj* nervioso/sa, robusto/ta.
sinful *adj* pecaminoso/sa, malvado/da; ~ly *adv* malvadamente.
sinfulness *n* corrupción *f*.
sing *vi*, *vt* cantar; gorjear; (*poet*) celebrar.
singe *vt* chamuscar.
singer *n* cantante *m/f*.
singing *n* canto *m*.
single *adj* sencillo/lla, simple, solo/la; soltero/ra; * *n* billete sencillo *m*; sencillo *m*; * *vt* singularizar; separar.
singly *adv* separadamente.
singular *adj* singular, peculiar; * *n* singular *m*; ~ly *adv* singularmente.
singularity *n* singularidad *f*.
sinister *adj* siniestro/tra, izquierdo/da; infeliz, funesto/ta.
sink *vi* hundirse; sumergirse; bajarse; arruinarse, decaer; * *vt* hundir, echar a lo hondo; destruir; * *n* fregadero *m*.
sinking fund *n* fondo de amortización *m*.
sinner *n* pecador/a *m/f*.
sinuosity *n* sinuosidad *f*.
sinuous *adj* sinuoso/sa.
sinus *n* seno *m*.
sip *vt* sorber; * *n* sorbo *m*.
siphon *n* sifón *m*.
sir *n* señor *m*.
sire *n* caballo padre *m*.
siren *n* sirena *f*.
sirloin *n* solomillo *m*.
sister *n* hermana *f*.
sisterhood *n* hermandad *f*.
sister-in-law *n* cuñada *f*.
sisterly *adj* de hermana.
sit *vi* sentarse; estar situado/da; * *vt* presentarse a.
sitcom *n* telecomedia *f*.
site *n* sitio *m*; situación *f*.

sit-in n ocupación f.

sitting n sesión, junta f; sentada f.

sitting room n sala de estar f.

situated adj situado/da.

situation n situación f.

six adj, n seis.

sixteen adj, n dieciséis.

sixteenth adj, n decimosexto/ta.

sixth adj, n sexto/ta.

sixtieth adj, n sexagésimo/ma.

sixty adj, n sesenta.

size n tamaño, talle m; calibre m; dimensión f; estatura f; condición f.

sizeable adj considerable.

skate n patín m; * vi patinar.

skateboard n monopatín m.

skating n patinaje m.

skating rink n pista de patinaje f.

skein n madeja f.

skeleton n esqueleto m.

skeleton key n llave maestra f.

sketch n esbozo m; esquicio m; * vt esquiciar, bosquejar.

skewer n aguja de lardear f; espetón m; * vt espetar.

ski n esquí m; * vi esquiar.

ski boot n bota de esquí f.

skid n patinazo m; * vi patinar.

skier n esquiador/a m/f.

skiing n esquí m.

skilful adj práctico/ca, diestro/tra; ~ly adv diestramente.

skilfulness n destreza f.

skill n destreza, arte, pericia f.

skilled adj práctico/ca, instruido/da.

skim vt espumar; tratar superficialmente.

skimmed milk n leche desnatada f.

skimmer n espumadera f.

skin n piel f; cutis m; * vt desollar.

skin diving n buceo m.

skinned adj desollado/da.

skinny adj flaco/ca, macilento/ta.

skip vi saltar, brincar; * vt pasar, omitir; * n salto, brinco m; cuba f.

ski pants npl pantalones de esquí mpl.

skipper n capitán/ana m/f.

skirmish n escaramuza f; * vi escaramuzar.

skirt n falda, orla f; * vt orillar.

skirting board n zócalo m.

skit n burla, zumba f.

skittish adj espantadizo/za, retozón/ona; terco/ca; inconstante; ~ly adv caprichosamente.

skittle n bolo m.

skulk vi escuchar, acechar.

skull n cráneo m.

skullcap n casquete m.

sky n cielo, firmamento m.

skylight n claraboya f.

skyrocket n cohete m.

skyscraper n rascacielos m invar.

slab n losa f.

slack adj flojo/ja, perezoso/sa, negligente, lento/ta.

slack(en) vt, vi aflojar; ablandar; entibiarse; decaer; relajar; aliviar.

slacker n zángano m.

slackness n flojedad, remisión f; descuido m.

slag n escoria f.

slam vt cerrar de golpe; * vi cerrarse de golpe.

slander vt calumniar, infamar; * n calumnia f.

slanderer n calumniador/a, maldiciente m/f.

slanderous adj calumnioso/sa; ~ly adv calumniosamente.

slang n argot m; jerigonza f.

slant vi pender oblicuamente; * n sesgo m; interpretación f.

slanting adj sesgado/da, oblicuo/cua.

slap n manotazo m; (on the face) bofetada f; * adv directamente; * vt golpear, dar una bofetada.
slash vt acuchillar; * n cuchillada f.
slate n pizarra f.
slater n pizarrero/ra m/f.
slating n techo de pizarras m.
slaughter n carnicería, matanza f; * vt matar atrozmente; hacer una matanza de.
slaughterer n matador/a, asesino/na m/f.
slaughterhouse n matadero m.
slave n esclavo/va m/f; * vi trabajar como esclavo/va.
slaver n baba f; * vi babosear.
slavery n esclavitud f.
slavish adj servil, humilde; ~ly adv servilmente.
slavishness n bajeza, servidumbre f.
slay vt matar, quitar la vida.
slayer n matador/a m/f.
sleazy adj de mala fama.
sledge, sleigh n trineo m.
sledgehammer n mazo m.
sleek adj liso/sa, brunido/da.
sleep vi dormir; * n sueño m.
sleeper n durmiente m.
sleepily adv con somnolencia o torpeza.
sleepiness n sueño m.
sleeping bag n saco m de dormir.
sleeping pill n somnífero m.
sleepless adj desvelado/da.
sleepwalking n sonambulismo m.
sleepy adj soñoliento/ta.
sleet n aguanieve f.
sleeve n manga f.
sleight n: ~ of hand escamoteo m.
slender adj delgado/da, débil, pequeño/ña, escaso/sa; ~ly adv delgadamente.
slenderness n delgadez f; tenuidad f; pequeñez f.

slice n rebanada f; espátula f; * vt rebanar.
slide vi resbalar, deslizarse; correr por encima del hielo; * n resbalón m; corredera f; diapositiva f; tobogán m.
sliding adj corredizo/za.
slight adj ligero/ra, leve, pequeño/ña; * n descuido m; * vt despreciar.
slightly adv ligeramente.
slightness n debilidad f; negligencia f.
slim adj delgado/da; * vi adelgazar.
slime n lodo m; substancia viscosa f.
sliminess n viscosidad f.
slimming n adelgazamiento m.
slimy adj viscoso/sa, pegajoso/sa.
sling n honda f; cabestrillo m; * vt tirar.
slink vi escaparse; esconderse.
slip vi resbalar; escapar, huirse; * vt deslizar; * n resbalón m; tropiezo m; escapada f; papelito m.
slipper n zapatilla f.
slippery adj resbaladizo/za.
slip road n vía de acceso f; rampa de acceso f.
slipshod adj descuidado/da.
slipway n grada f, gradas fpl.
slit vt rajar, hender; * n raja, hendedura f.
slobber n baba f.
sloe n endrina f.
slogan n eslogan, lema m.
sloop n (mar) balandro m.
slop n aguachirle f; lodazal m; ~s pl gachas fpl.
slope n cuesta f; sesgo m; declivio m; escarpa f; * vt sesgar.
sloping adj oblicuo/cua; en declive.
sloppy adj descuidado/da; desaliñado/da.
sloth n pereza f.

slouch *vt, vi* estar cabizbajo/ja; bambolearse pesadamente.

slovenliness *n* desaliño *m*; porquería *f*.

slovenly *adj* desaliñado/da, puerco/ca, sucio/cia.

slow *adj* tardío/día, lento/ta, torpe, perezoso/sa; ~ly *adv* lentamente, despacio.

slowness *n* lentitud, tardanza, pesadez *f*.

slow worm *n* lución *m*.

slug *n* holgazán/ana *m/f*, zángano *m*; babosa *f*; ficha *f*; trago *m*.

sluggish *adj* perezoso/sa; lento/ta; ~ly *adv* perezosamente.

sluggishness *n* pereza *f*.

sluice *n* compuerta *f*; * *vt* soltar la compuerta de.

slum *n* tugurio *m*; barrio bajo *m*.

slumber *vi* dormitar; * *n* sueño ligero *m*.

slump *n* depresión *f*.

slur *vt* ensuciar; calumniar; pronunciar mal; * *n* calumnia *f*.

slush *n* lodo, barro, cieno *m*.

slut *n* marrana *f*.

sly *adj* astuto/ta; ~ly *adv* astutamente.

slyness *n* astucia, maña *f*.

smack *n* sabor, gusto *m*; beso fuerte (que se oye) *m*; chasquido de latigo *m*; * *vi* saber; besar con ruido; * *vt* golpear.

small *adj* pequeño/ña, menudo/da.

smallish *adj* algo pequeño/ña.

smallness *n* pequeñez *f*.

smallpox *n* viruelas *fpl*.

small talk *n* charla, prosa *f*.

smart *adj* elegante; listo/ta, ingenioso/sa; vivo/va; * *vi* escocer.

smartly *adv* agudamente, vivamente; elegantemente; inteligentemente.

smartness *n* agudeza, viveza, sutileza *f*.

smash *vt* romper, quebrantar; estrellar; batir; * *vi* hacerse pedazos; estrellarse; * *n* fracaso *m*; choque *m*.

smattering *n* conocimiento superficial *m*.

smear *n* (*med*) frotis *m invar*; * *vt* untar; difamar.

smell *vt, vi* oler; * *n* olfato *m*; olor *m*; hediondez *f*.

smelly *adj* maloliente.

smelt *n* espirenque de *mar m*; * *vt* fundir (el metal).

smelter *n* fundidor/a *m/f*.

smile *vi* sonreír; * *n* sonrisa *f*.

smirk *vi* sonreír.

smite *vt* herir; afligir.

smith *n* herrero/rra *m/f*.

smithy *n* herrería *f*.

smock *n* camisa de mujer *f*.

smoke *n* humo *m*; vapor *m*; * *vt, vi* ahumar; humear; fumar.

smoked herring, kipper *n* arenque ahumado *m*.

smokeless *adj* sin humo.

smoker *n* fumador/a *m/f*.

smoking: 'no ~' 'prohibido fumar'.

smoky *adj* humeante; humoso/sa.

smooth *adj* liso/sa, pulido/da, llano/na; suave; afable; * *vt* allanar; alisar; lisonjear.

smoothly *adv* llanamente; con blandura.

smoothness *n* lisura *f*; llanura *f*; suavidad *f*.

smother *vt* sofocar; suprimir.

smoulder *vi* arder debajo la ceniza.

smudge *vt* manchar; * *n* mancha *f*.

smug *adj* presumido/da.

smuggle *vt* pasar de contrabando.

smuggler *n* contrabandista *m/f*.

smuggling *n* contrabando *m*.

smut n tiznón m; suciedad f.
smuttiness n obscenidad f.
smutty adj tiznado/da; obsceno/na.
snack n bocado, bocadillo m, pinchito m.
snack bar n cafetería f.
snag n problema m.
snail n caracol m.
snake n serpiente, culebra f.
snaky adj serpentino/na.
snap vt, vi romper; agarrar; morder; insultar; **to ~ one's fingers** castañetear; * n estallido m; foto f.
snapdragon n (bot) boca de dragón f.
snap fastener n automático m.
snare n lazo m; trampa f.
snarl vi regañar, gruñir.
snatch vt arrebatar; agarrar; * n arrebatamiento m; robo m; bocado m.
sneak vi arrastrar; * n soplón/ona m/f.
sneer vi hablar con desprecio.
sneeringly adv con desprecio.
sneeze vi estornudar.
sniff vt oler; * vi resollar con fuerza.
snigger vi reír disimuladamente.
snip vt tijeretear; * n tijeretada f, pedazo pequeño m; porción f.
snipe n agachadiza f; zopenco m.
sniper n francotirador/a m/f.
snivel n moquita f; * vi moquear.
sniveller n lloraduelos m invar.
snob n (e)snob m/f.
snobbish adj esnob.
snooze n sueño ligero m; * vi echar una siesta.
snore vi roncar.
snorkel n (tubo)respirador m.
snort vi resoplar.
snout n hocico m; morro m.
snow n nieve f; * vi nevar.
snowball n bola de nieve f.

snowdrop n (bot) campanilla blanca f.
snowman n muñeco de nieve m.
snowplough n quitanieves m invar.
snowy adj nevoso/sa; nevado/da.
snub vt reprender, regañar.
snub-nosed adj chato/ta; ñato/ta.
snuff n rapé m.
snuffbox n tabaquera f.
snuffle vi ganguear, hablar gangoso.
snug adj abrigado/da; conveniente, cómodo/da, agradable, grato/ta.
so adv así; de este modo; tan.
soak vi, vt remojarse; calarse; empapar, remojar.
so-and-so n zutano/na m/f.
soap n jabón m; * vt jabonar.
soap bubble n burbuja de jabón f.
soap opera n telenovela f.
soap powder n jabón en polvo m.
soapsuds fpl jabonaduras fpl.
soapy adj jabonoso/sa.
soar vi remontarse, sublimarse.
sob n sollozo m; * vi sollozar.
sober adj sobrio/ria; serio/ria; **~ly** adv sobriamente; juiciosamente.
sobriety n sobriedad f; seriedad, sangre fria f.
soccer n fútbol m.
sociability n sociabilidad f.
sociable adj sociable, comunicativo/va.
sociably adv sociablemente.
social adj social, sociable; **~ly** adv sociablemente.
socialism n socialismo m.
socialist n socialista m/f.
social work n asistencia social f.
social worker n asistente/ta social m/f.
society n sociedad f; compañia f.
sociologist n sociólogo/ga m/f.
sociology n sociología f.
sock n calcetín m; media f.

socket *n* enchufe *m*.

sod *n* césped *m*.

soda *n* sosa *f*; gaseosa *f*.

sofa *n* sofá *m*.

soft *adj* blando/da, suave; benigno/na, tierno/na; afeminado/da; mullido/da; ~ly *adv* suavemente; paso a paso.

soften *vt* ablandar, mitigar; enternecer.

soft-hearted *adj* compasivo/va.

softness *n* blandura, dulzura *f*.

soft-spoken *adj* de voz suave.

software *n* (*comput*) software *m*.

soil *vt* ensuciar, emporcar; * *n* mancha, porquería *f*; terreno *m*; tierra *f*.

sojourn *vi* residir, morar; * *n* morada *f*; residencia *f*.

solace *vt* solazar, consolar; * *n* consuelo *m*.

solar *adj* solar; ~ energy energía solar *f*.

solder *vt* soldar; * *n* soldadura *f*.

soldier *n* soldado/da *m/f*; militar *m*.

soldierly *adj* soldadesco/ca.

sole *n* planta (del pie) *f*; suela (del zapato) *f*; lenguado *m*; * *adj* único/ca, solo/la.

solecism *n* (*gr*) solecismo *m*.

solemn *adj*, ~ly *adv* solemne(mente).

solemnity *n* solemnidad *f*.

solemnize *vt* solemnizar.

solicit *vt* solicitar; implorar.

solicitation *n* solicitación *f*.

solicitor *n* representante, agente *m/f*.

solicitous *adj* solícito/ta, diligente; ~ly *adv* solícitamente.

solicitude *n* solicitud *f*.

solid *adj* sólido/da, compacto/ta; * *n* sólido *m*; ~ly *adv* sólidamente.

solidify *vt* solidificar.

solidity *n* solidez *f*.

soliloquy *n* soliloquio *m*.

solitaire *n* solitario *m*.

solitary *adj* solitario/ria, retirado/da; * *n* ermitaño/ña *m/f*.

solitude *n* soledad *f*; vida solitaria *f*.

solo *n* (*mus*) solo/la *m*.

solstice *n* solsticio *m*.

soluble *adj* soluble.

solution *n* solución *f*.

solve *vt* resolver.

solvency *n* solvencia *f*.

solvent *adj* solvente; *n* (*chem*) solvente *m*.

some *adj* algo de, un poco, algún, alguno, alguna, unos, pocos, ciertos.

somebody *n* alguien *m*.

somehow *adv* de algún modo.

someplace *adv* en alguna parte; a alguna parte.

something *n* alguna cosa, algo.

sometime *adv* algún día.

sometimes *adv* a veces.

somewhat *adv* algo; algún tanto, un poco.

somewhere *adv* en alguna parte; a alguna parte.

somnambulism *n* sonambulismo *m*.

somnambulist *n* sonámbulo/la *m/f*.

somnolence *n* somnolencia *f*.

somnolent *adj* somnoliento/ta.

son *n* hijo *m*.

sonata *n* (*mus*) sonata *f*.

song *n* canción *f*.

son-in-law *n* yerno *m*.

sonnet *n* soneto *m*.

sonorous *adj* sonoro/ra.

soon *adv* ya, pronto; as ~ as luego que.

sooner *adv* antes, más pronto.

soot *n* hollín *m*.

soothe *vt* adular; calmar.

soothsayer *n* adivino/na *m/f*.

sop *n* sopa *f*.

sophism *n* sofisma *m*.

sophist *n* sofista *m/f*.

sophistical *adj* sofístico/ca.

sophisticate *vt* sofisticar; falsificar.

sophisticated *adj* sofisticado/da.

sophistry *n* sofistería *f*.

soporific *adj* soporífero/ra.

sorcerer *n* hechicero *m*.

sorceress *n* hechicera *f*.

sorcery *n* hechizo, encanto *m*.

sordid *adj* sórdido/da, sucio/cia; asqueroso/sa.

sordidness *n* sordidez, suciedad *f*.

sore *n* llaga, úlcera *f*; * *adj* doloroso/sa, penoso/sa; resentido/da; ~**ly** *adv* penosamente.

sorrel *n* (*bot*) acedera *f*; * *adj* alazán rojo/ja.

sorrow *n* pesar *m*; tristeza *f*; * *vi* entristecerse.

sorrowful *adj* pesaroso/sa, afligido/da; ~**ly** *adv* con aflicción.

sorry *adj* triste, afligido/da; arrepentido/da; **I am** ~ lo siento.

sort *n* suerte *f*; género *m*; especie *f*; calidad *f*; manera *f*; * *vt* separar en distintas clases; escoger, elegir.

soul *n* alma *f*; esencia *f*; persona *f*.

sound *adj* sano/na; entero/ra; puro/ra; firme; ~**ly** *adv* sanamente, vigorosamente; * *n* sonido, ruido *m*; estrecho *m*; * *vt* sonar; tocar; celebrar; sondar; * *vi* sonar, resonar; parecer.

sounding board *n* diapasón *m*; sombrero de púlpito *m*.

sound effects *npl* efectos sonoros *mpl*.

soundings *npl* (*mar*) sondeo *m*; (*mar*) surgidero *m*.

soundness *n* sanidad *f*; fuerza, solidez *f*.

soundtrack *n* banda sonora *f*.

soup *n* sopa *f*.

sour *adj* agrio/ria, ácido/da; cortado/da; áspero/ra; ~**ly** *adv* agriamente; * *vt*, *vi* agriar, acedar; agriarse.

source *n* manantial *m*; principio *m*.

sourness *n* acedía, agrura *f*; acrimonia *f*.

souse *n* (*sl*) borracho/cha *m/f*; * *vt* escabechar; chapuzar.

souvenir *n* recuerdo *m*.

south *n* sur *m*; * *adj* del sur; * *adv* al sur.

southerly, southern *adj* del sur, meridional.

southward(s) *adv* hacia el sur.

southwester *n* (*mar*) viento de sudoeste *m*; sombrero grande de los marineros *m*.

sovereign *adj*, *n* soberano/na *m/f*.

sovereignty *n* soberanía *f*.

sow *n* puerca, marrana *f*.

sow *vt* sembrar; esparcir.

sowing-time *n* sementera, siembra *f*.

soy *n* soja *f*.

space *n* espacio *m*; intersticio *m*; * *vt* espaciar.

spacecraft *n* nave espacial *f*.

spaceman *n* astronauta *m*.

spacewoman *n* astronauta *f*.

spacious *adj* espacioso/sa, amplio/lia; ~**ly** *adv* con bastante espacio.

spaciousness *n* espaciosidad *f*.

spade *n* laya, azada *f*; pica *f* (en los naipes).

spaghetti *n* espaguetis *mpl*.

span *n* palmo *m*; envergadura *f*; * *vt* cruzar; abarcar.

spangle *n* lentejuela *f*; * *vt* adornar con lentejuelas.

spaniel *n* perro de aguas *m*.

Spanish *adj*, *n* español/a *m/f*.

Spanish America *n* Hispanoamérica *f*.

Spanish American *adj* hispano-americano/na; * *n* hispano-americano/na *m/f*.

Spanish light opera *n* zarzuela *f*.

spar *n* palo *m*; * *vi* entrenarse.

spare *vt, vi* ahorrar, economizar; perdonar; pasarse sin; vivir con economía; * *adj* de más; de reserva.

sparing *adj* escaso/sa, raro/ra, económico/ca; ~ly *adv* parcamente, frugalmente.

spark *n* chispa *f*.

sparkle *n* centella, chispa *f*; * *vi* chispear; espumar.

spark plug *n* bujía *f*.

sparrow *n* gorrión *m*.

sparrowhawk *n* gavilán *m*.

sparse *adj* delgado/da; tenue; ~ly *adv* tenuemente.

spasm *n* espasmo *m*.

spasmodic *adj* espasmódico/ca.

spatter *vt* salpicar, manchar.

spatula *n* espátula *f*.

spawn *n* freza *f*; * *vt, vi* desovar; engendrar.

spawning *n* freza *f*.

speak *vt, vi* hablar; decir; conversar; pronunciar.

speaker *n* altavoz; bafle *m*; orador/a *m/f*.

spear *n* lanza *f*; arpón *m*; * *vt* herir con lanza.

special *adj* especial, particular; ~ly *adv* especialmente.

speciality *n* especialidad *f*.

species *n* especie *f*.

specific *adj* específico/ca; * *n* específico *m*.

specifically *adv* específicamente.

specification *n* especificación *f*.

specify *vt* especificar.

specimen *n* muestra *f*; prueba *f*.

specious *adj* especioso/sa.

speck(le) *n* mácula, tacha *f*; * *vt* abigarrar, manchar.

spectacle *n* espectáculo *m*.

spectacles *npl* gafas *fpl*.

spectator *n* espectador/a *m/f*.

spectral *adj* espectral; ~ analysis *n* análisis espectral *m invar*.

spectre *n* espectro *m*.

speculate *vi* especular; reflexionar.

speculation *n* especulación *f*; especulativa *f*; meditación *f*.

speculative *adj* especulativo/va, teórico/ca.

speculum *n* espéculo *m*.

speech *n* habla *m*; discurso *m*; lenguaje *m*; conversación *f*.

speechify *vi* arengar.

speechless *adj* sin habla.

speed *n* prisa *f*; velocidad *f*; * *vt* apresurar; despachar; * *vi* darse prisa.

speedboat *n* lancha motora *f*.

speedily *adv* aceleradamente, de-prisa.

speediness *n* celeridad, prontitud, precipitación *f*.

speed limit *n* límite de velocidad *m*, velocidad maxima *f*.

speedometer *n* velocímetro *m*.

speedway *n* pista de carreras *f*.

speedy *adj* veloz, pronto/ta, diligente.

spell *n* hechizo, encanto *m*; período *m*; * *vt, vi* escribir correc tamente; deletrear; hechizar, encantar.

spelling *n* ortografía *f*.

spend *vt* gastar; pasar; disipar; consumir.

spendthrift *n* despilfarrador/a *m/f*.

spent *adj* agotado/da.

sperm *n* esperma *f*.

spermaceti *n* espermaceti *m*.

spew *vi* (*sl*) vomitar.

sphere *n* esfera *f*.

spherical *adj* esférico/ca; **~ly** *adv* en forma esférica.

spice *n* especia *f*; * *vt* especiar.

spick-and-span *adj* aseado/da, (bien) arreglado/da.

spicy *adj* aromático/ca.

spider *n* araña *f*.

spigot *n* grifo *m*.

spike *n* espiga de grano *f*; espigón *m*; * *vi* clavar con espi gones.

spill *vt* derramar, verter; * *vi* derramarse.

spin *vt* hilar; alargar, prolongar; girar; * *vi* dar vueltas; * *n* vuelta *f*; paseo (en coche) *m*.

spinach *n* espinaca *f*.

spinal *adj* espinal.

spindle *n* huso *m*; quicio *m*.

spine *n* espinazo *m*, espina *f*.

spineless *adj* ñoño/ña.

spinet *n* (*mus*) espineta *f*.

spinner *n* hilador/a *m/f*; hilandero/ra *m/f*.

spinning top *n* trompa *f*.

spinning wheel *n* rueca *f*.

spin-off *n* derivado, producto secundario *m*.

spinster *n* soltera *f*.

spiral *adj* espiral; **~ly** *adv* en figura de espiral.

spire *n* espira *f*; pirámide *m*; aguja *f* (de una torre).

spirit *n* aliento *m*; espíritu *m*; ánimo, valor *m*; brío *m*; humor *m*; fantasma *m*; * *vt* incitar, animar; **to ~ away** quitar secretamente.

spirited *adj* vivo/va, brioso/sa; **~ly** *adv* con espíritu.

spirit lamp *n* velón *o* quinque de alcohol *m*.

spiritless *adj* abatido/da, sin espíritu.

spiritual *adj*, **~ly** *adv* espiritual(mente).

spiritualist *n* espiritista *m/f*.

spirituality *n* espiritualidad *f*.

spit *n* asador *m*; saliva *f*; * *vt, vi* espetar; escupir.

spite *n* rencor *m*, malevolencia *f*; **in ~ of** a pesar de, a despe cho; * *vt* dar pesar.

spiteful *adj* rencoroso/sa, malicioso/sa; **~ly** *adv* malignamente, con tirria.

spitefulness *n* malicia *f*; rencor *m*.

spittle *n* saliva *f*; baba *f*, esputo *m*.

splash *vt* salpicar, enlodar; * *vi* chapotear; * *n* chapoteo *m*; mancha *f*.

spleen *n* bazo *m*; esplín *m*.

splendid *adj* espléndido/da, magnífico/ca; **~ly** *adv* espléndidamente.

splendour *n* esplendor *m*; pompa *f*.

splice *vt* (*mar*) empalmar, empleitar.

splint *n* tablilla *f*.

splinter *n* cacho *m*; astilla *f*; brisna *f*; * *vt* (*vi*) hender(se).

split *n* hendedura *f*; división *f*; * *vt* hender, rajar; * *vi* hen derse.

splutter, sputter *vi* escupir con frecuencia; babosear; barbotar.

spoil *vt* despojar; arruinar; mimar.

spoiled *adj* pasado/da; cortado/da.

spoke *n* radio (de la rueda) *m*.

spokesman *n* portavoz *m*.

spokeswoman *n* portavoz *f*.

sponge *n* esponja *f*; * *vt* limpiar con esponja; * *vi* meterse de mogollón.

sponger *n* mogollón *m*.

sponginess *n* esponjosidad *f*.

spongy *adj* esponjoso/sa.

sponsor *n* patrocinador/a *m/f*; padrino *m*; madrina *f*.

sponsorship *n* patrocinio *m*.

spontaneity *n* espontaneidad, voluntariedad *f*.

spontaneous *adj* espontáneo/nea; ~**ly** *adv* espontaneamente.

spool *n* carrete *m*; canilla, broca *f*.

spoon *n* cuchara *f*.

spoonful *n* cucharada *f*.

sporadic(al) *adj* esporádico/ca.

sport *n* deporte *m*; juego, retozo *m*; juguete, divertimiento, recreo, pasatiempo *m*.

sports car *n* coche deportivo *m*.

sports jacket *n* chaqueta deportiva *f*.

sportsman *n* deportista *m*.

sportswear *n* ropa de deporte *o* sport *f*.

sportswoman *n* deportista *f*.

spot *n* mancha *f*; borrón *m*; sitio, lugar *m*; grano *m*; * *vt* notar; manchar.

spotless *adj* limpio/pia, inmaculado/da.

spotlight *n* foco, reflector *m*.

spotted, spotty *adj* lleno/na de manchas; con granos.

spouse *n* esposo/a *m/f*.

spout *vi* borbotar; chorrear; * *vt* arrojar; vomitar; (*fig*) declamar; * *n* piton *m*, pico *m*.

sprain *adj* descoyuntar; * *n* dislocación *f*.

sprat *n* meleta, nuesa *f* (pez).

sprawl *vi* revolcarse.

spray *n* rociada *f*; espray *m*; ramita *f*; espuma de la mar *f*.

spread *vt* extender, desplegar; esparcir, divulgar; * *vi* extenderse, desplegarse; * *n* extensión, dilatación *f*.

spree *n* fiesta *f*; juerga *f*.

sprig *n* ramito *m*.

sprightliness *n* alegría, vivacidad *f*.

sprightly *adj* alegre, despierto/ta, vivaracho/cha.

spring *vi* brotar, arrojar; nacer, provenir; dimanar, originarse; saltar, brincar; * *n* primavera *f*; elasticidad *f*; muelle, resorte *m*; salto *m*; manantial *m*.

springiness *n* elasticidad *f*.

spring onion *n* cebolleta *f*.

springtime *n* primavera *f*.

spring water *n* agua de fuente *f*.

springy *adj* elástico/ca; mullido/da.

sprinkle *vt* rociar.

sprinkling *n* rociadura *f*.

sprout *n* vástago, renuevo *m*; ~**s** *npl* coles de Bruselas *fpl*; * *vi* brotar.

spruce *adj* pulido/da, gentil; ~**ly** *adv* bellamente, lindamente; * *vr* vestirse con afectación.

spruceness *n* lindeza, hermosura *f*.

spur *n* espuela *f*; espolón (del gallo) *m*; estímulo *m*; * *vt* espolear; estimular.

spurious *adj* espurio/ria, falso/sa; contrahecho/cha; supuesto/ta; bastardo/da.

spurn *vt* despreciar.

spy *n* espía *m/f*; * *vt*, *vi* espiar.

squabble *vi* reñir, disputar; * *n* riña, disputa *f*.

squad *n* escuadra *f*; brigada *f*; equipo *m*.

squadron *n* (*mil*) escuadrón *m*.

squalid *adj* sucio/cia, puerco/ca.

squall *n* ráfaga *f*; chubasco *m*; * *vi* chillar.

squally *adj* borrascoso/sa.

squalor *n* porquería, suciedad *f*.

squander *vt* malgastar, disipar.

square *adj* cuadrado/da, cuadrángulo/la; exacto/ta; cabal; * *n* cuadro *m*; plaza *f*; escuadra *f*; * *vt* cuadrar; ajustar, arreglar; * *vi* ajustarse.

squareness *n* cuadratura *f*.

squash *vt* aplastar; * *n* squash *m*.

squat *vi* agacharse; * *adj* agachado/da; rechoncho/cha.

squatter n ocupante ilegal m/f; (fam) okupa m/f.

squeak vi plañir, chillar; * n grito, plañido m.

squeal vi plañir, gritar.

squeamish adj fastidioso/sa; demasiado delicado/da.

squeeze vt apretar, comprimir; estrechar; * n presión f; apre ton m; restricción f.

squid n calamar m.

squint adj bizco/ca; * vi bizquear; * n estrabismo.

squirrel n ardilla f.

squirt vt jeringar; * n jeringa f; chorro m; pisaverde m.

stab vt apuñalar; * n puñalada f.

stability n estabilidad, solidez f.

stable n establo m; * vt poner en el establo; * adj estable.

stack n pila f; * vt hacinar.

staff n personal m, plantilla f; palo m; apoyo m.

stag n ciervo m.

stage n etapa f; escena f; tablado m; teatro m; parada f; escalón m.

stagger vi vacilar, titubear; estar incierto/ta; * vt asustar; esca lonar.

stagnant adj estancado/da.

stagnate vi estancarse.

stagnation n estancamiento m.

staid adj grave, serio/ria.

stain vt manchar; empañar la reputación de; * n mancha f; deshonra f.

stainless adj limpio/pia; inmaculado/da.

stair n escalón m; ~s pl escalera f.

staircase n escalera f.

stake n estaca f; apuesta f (en el juego); * vt estacar; apostar.

stale adj añejo/ja, viejo/ja, rancio/cia.

staleness n vejez f; rancidez f.

stalk vi andar con paso majestuoso; * n tallo, pie, tronco m; troncho m (de ciertas hortalizas).

stall n pesebre m; puesto m; tabanco m; emplazamiento m; * vt parar; * vi pararse; buscar evasivas.

stallion n semental m; caballo entero m.

stalwart n partidario/ria leal m/f.

stamen n estambre m; fundamento m.

stamina n resistencia f.

stammer vi tartamudear; * n tartamudeo m.

stamp vt patear; estampar, imprimir; acuñar; andar con mucha pesadez; * vi patear; * n cuño m; sello m; impresión f; huella f; estampilla f; (dancing) zapatazo m.

stampede n estampida f.

stand vi estar de pie; ponerse de pie; sostenerse; permanecer; pararse, hacer alto, estar situado/da; hallarse; erizarse (el pelo); * vt poner; aguantar; sostener, defender; * n puesto, sitio m; posición, situación f; parada f; estado m (fijo); tribuna f; stand m.

standard n estandarte m; modelo m; precio ordinario m; norma f; * adj normal.

standing adj permanente, fijado/da, establecido/da; de pie; estancado/da; * n duración f; posición f; puesto m.

standstill n pausa f; alto m.

staple n grapa f; * adj básico/ca, establecido/da; * vt grapar.

star n estrella f; asterisco m.

starboard n estribor m.

starch n almidón m; * vt almidonar.

stare vi: **to ~ at** clavar la vista en; * n mirada fija f.

stark adj fuerte, áspero/ra; puro/ra; * adv del todo.

starling *n* estornino *m*.

starry *adj* estrellado/da.

start *vi* empezar; sobrecogerse, sobresaltarse; levantarse de repente; salir; * *vt* empezar; causar; fundar; poner en marcha; * *n* principio *m*; salida *f*; sobresalto *m*; ímpetu *m*; paso primero *m*.

starter *n* estárter *m*; juez de salida *m*.

starting point *n* punto de partida *m*.

startle *vt* sobresaltar.

startling *adj* alarmante.

starvation *n* hambre, inanición *f*.

starve *vi* pasar hambre.

state *n* estado *m*; condición *f*; estado (político); pompa, gran deza *f*; **the S~s** los Estados Unidos *mpl*; * *vt* afirmar; exponer.

stateliness *n* grandeza, pompa *f*.

stately *adj* augusto/ta, majestuoso/sa.

statement *n* afirmación, cuenta *f*.

statesman *n* estadista, político *m*.

statesmanship *n* política *f*.

static *adj* estático/ca; * *n* parásitos *mpl*.

station *n* estación *f*; emisora *f*; empleo, puesto *m*; situación *f*; condición *f*; (*rail*) estación *f*; * *vt* apostar.

stationary *adj* estacionario/ria, fijo/ja.

stationer *n* papelero/ra *m/f*.

stationery *n* papelería *f*.

station wagon *n* ranchera *f*.

statistical *adj* estadístico/ca.

statistics *npl* estadística *f*.

statuary *n* estatuario/ria, escultor/a *m/f*.

statue *n* estatua *f*.

stature *n* estatura, talla *f*.

statute *n* estatuto *m*; reglamento *m*.

stay *n* estancia *f*; ~s *npl* corsé, justillo *m*; * *vi* quedarse, estarse; detenerse; esperarse; **to ~ in** quedarse en casa; **to ~ on** quedarse; **to ~ up** velar.

stead *n* lugar, sitio, paraje *m*.

steadfast *adj* firme, estable, sólido/da; ~**ly** *adv* firmemente, con constancia.

steadily *adv* firmemente; invariablemente.

steadiness *n* firmeza, estabilidad *f*.

steady *adj* firme, fijo/ja; * *vt* hacer firme.

steak *n* filete *m*; bistec *m*.

steal *vt*, *vi* robar.

stealth *n* hurto *m*; **by ~** a hurtadillas.

stealthily *adv* furtivamente.

stealthy *adj* furtivo/va.

steam *n* vapor *m*; humo *m*; * *vt* cocer al vapor; * *vi* echar humo.

steam-engine *n* máquina de vapor *f*.

steamer, steamboat *n* vapor, buque de vapor *m*.

steel *n* acero *m*; * *adj* de acero.

steelyard *n* romana *f*.

steep *adj* escarpado/da; excesivo/va; * *vt* empapar.

steeple *n* torre *f*; campanario *m*.

steeplechase *n* carrera de obstáculos *f*.

steepness *n* lo escarpado; lo abrupto.

steer *n* novillo *m*; * *vt* manejar, conducir; dirigir; gobernar; * *vi* conducir.

steering *n* dirección *f*.

steering wheel *n* volante *m*.

stellar *adj* estrellado/da.

stem *n* vástago, tallo *m*; estirpe *f*; pie *m*; cañón *m*; * *vt* cortar la corriente.

stench *n* hedor *m*.

stencil *n* cliché *m*.

stenographer *n* taquígrafo/fa *m/f*.

stenography *n* taquigrafía *f*.

step n paso, escalón m; huella f; * vi
dar un paso; andar.

stepbrother n hermanastro m.

stepdaughter n hijastra f.

stepfather n padrastro m.

stepmother n madrastra f.

stepping stone n pasadera f.

stepsister n hermanastra f.

stepson n hijastro m.

stereo n estérreo m.

stereotype n estereotipo m; * vt estereotipar.

sterile adj estéril.

sterility n esterilidad f.

sterling adj esterlín/ina, genuino/na,
verdadero/ra; * n libras esterlinas
fpl.

stern adj austero/ra, rígido/da,
severo/ra; * n (mar) popa f; ~ly
adv austeramente.

stethoscope n (med) estetoscopio m.

stevedore n (mar) estibador/a m/f.

stew vt estofar; * n estufa, olla f.

steward n mayordomo m; (mar)
despensero m.

stewardess n azafata f.

stewardship n mayordomía f.

stick n palo, palillo, bastón m; vara f;
* vt pegar, hincar; aguantar; picar;
* vi pegarse; detenerse; perseverar;
dudar.

stickiness n viscosidad, gomosidad f.

sticking plaster n esparadrapo m.

stick-up n asalto, atraco m.

sticky adj viscoso/sa, tenaz.

stiff adj tieso/sa; duro/ra, torpe;
rígido/da; yerto/ta; obstinado/da;
~ly adv obstinadamente.

stiffen vt atiesar, endurecer; * vi en-
durecerse.

stiff neck n tortícolis m.

stiffness n tesura, rigidez f; obstinación f.

stifle vt suofocar.

stifling adj bochornoso/sa.

stigma n estigma m.

stigmatize vt estigmatizar.

stile n portillo con escalones m
(para pasar de un cercado a otro).

stiletto n estilete m; tacón de aguja m.

still vt aquietar, aplacar; destilar;
* adj silencioso/sa, tranquilo/la;
* n alambique m; * adv todavía;
hasta ahora; no obstante; aún así.

stillborn adj nacido/da muerto/ta.

stillness n calma, quietud f.

stilts npl zancos mpl.

stimulant n estimulante m.

stimulate vt estimular, aguijonear.

stimulation n estímulo m; estimula-
ción f.

stimulus n estímulo m.

sting vt picar o morder (un insecto);
* vi escocer; * n aguijón m; punzada, picadura, picada f; timo m.

stingily adv avaramente.

stinginess n tacañería, avaricia f.

stingy adj mezquino/na, tacaño/ña,
avaro/ra.

stink vi heder; * n hedor m.

stint n tarea f.

stipulate vt estipular.

stipulation n estipulación f; condición f.

stir vt remover; agitar; incitar; * vi moverse; * n tumulto m; turbulencia f.

stirrup n estribo m.

stitch vt coser; * n punzada f; punto m.

stoat n armiño m.

stock n existencias fpl; ganado m;
caldo m; estirpe f, linaje m; capital,
principal m; fondo m; ~s pl acciones en los fondos públicos fpl; * vt
proveer, abastecer.

stockade n prisión militar f.

stockbroker n agente de bolsa m/f.

stock exchange n bolsa f.
stockholder n accionista m/f.
stocking n media f.
stock market n bolsa f.
stoic n estoico/ca m/f.
stoical adj estoico/ca; ~ly adv estoicamente.
stoicism n estoicismo m.
stole n estola f.
stomach n estómago m; apetito m; * vt aguantar.
stone n piedra f; pepita f; hueso de fruta m; * adj de piedra; * vt apedrear; deshuesar; empedrar; trabajar de albañil.
stone deaf adj sordo/da como una tapia.
stoning n apedreamiento m.
stony adj de piedra, pétreo/rea; duro/ra.
stool n banquillo, taburete m.
stoop vi encorvarse, inclinarse; bajarse; * n inclinación hacia abajo f.
stop vt detener, parar; tapar; * vi pararse, hacer alto; * n parada f; punto m; pausa f; obstáculo m.
stopover n parada; rescala f.
stoppage, stopping n obstrucción f; impedimento m; (rail) alto m.
stopwatch n cronómetro m.
storage n almacenamiento m; almacenaje m.
store n abundancia f; provisión f; almacén m, tienda f; * vt surtir, proveer, abastecer.
storey n piso m (de una casa).
stork n cigüeña f.
storm n tempestad, borrasca f; asalto m; * vt tomar por asalto; * vi rabiar.
stormily adv violentamente.
stormy adj tempestuoso/sa; violento/ta.

story n historia f; chiste m.
stout adj robusto/ta, corpulento/ta, vigoroso/sa; terco/ca; ~ly adv valientemente; obstinadamente.
stoutness n valor m; fuerza f; corpulencia f.
stove n cocina f; estufa f.
stow vt ordenar, colocar; (mar) estibar.
straggle vi rezagarse.
straggler n rezagado/da m/f.
straight adj derecho/cha; estrecho/cha; franco/ca; * adv directamente.
straightaway adv inmediatamente.
straighten vt enderezar.
straightforward adj derecho/cha; franco/ca; leal.
straightforwardness n derechura f, franqueza f.
strain vt colar, filtrar; apretar (a uno contra sí); forzar, violen tar; * vi esforzarse; * n tensión f; retorcimiento m; raza f; linaje m; estilo m; sonido m; armonía f.
strainer n colador m; coladera f.
strait n estrecho m; aprieto, peligro m; penuria f.
strait-jacket n camisa de fuerza f.
strand n hebra f; costa, playa f.
strange adj raro/ra; extraño/ña; ~ly adv extrañamente, extraordinariamente.
strangeness n rareza f; extrañeza f.
stranger n desconocido/da m/f; extranjero/ra m/f.
strangle vt estrangular.
strangulation n estrangulamiento m.
strap n correa, tira de cuero f; tirante de bota m; * vt atar con correa.
strapping adj abultado/da, corpulento/ta.
stratagem n estratagema f; astucia f.

strategic *adj* estratégico/ca.

strategy *n* estrategia *f*.

stratum *n* estrato *m*.

straw *n* paja *m*; pajita *f*.

strawberry *n* fresa *f*.

stray *vi* extraviarse; perder el camino; * *adj* extraviado/da; perdido/da.

streak *n* raya, lista *f*; vena *f*; * *vt* rayar.

stream *n* arroyo, río, torrente *m*; * *vi* correr.

streamer *n* serpentina *f*.

street *n* calle *f*.

strength *n* fuerza, robustez *f*; vigor *m*; fortaleza *f*.

strengthen *vt* fortificar; corroborar.

strenuous *adj* arduo/dua; ágil.

stress *n* presión *f*; estrés *m*; fuerza *f*; peso *m*; importancia *f*; acento *m*; * *vt* subrayar; acentuar.

stretch *vt, vi* extender, alargar; estirar; extenderse; esforzarse; * *n* extensión *f*; trecho *m*; estirón *m*.

stretcher *n* camilla *f*.

strew *vt* esparcir; sembrar.

strict *adj* estricto/ta, estrecho/cha; exacto/ta, riguroso/sa, severo/ra; ~**ly** *adv* exactamente, con severidad.

strictness *n* exactitud *f*; severidad *f*, estrechez *f*.

stride *n* tranco *m*; zancada *f*; * *vi* atrancar.

strife *n* contienda, disputa *f*.

strike *vt, vi* golpear; herir; castigar; tocar; chocar; sonar; cesar de trabajar; * *n* ataque *m*; descubrimiento *m*; huelga *f*.

striker *n* huelguista *m/f*.

striking *adj* llamativo/va; notorio/ria; ~**ly** *adv* sorprendentemente.

string *n* cordón *m*; hilo *m*; cuerda *f*; hilera *f*; fibra *f*; * *vt* encordar; enhilar; estirar.

stringent *adj* astringente.

stringy *adj* fibroso/sa.

strip *vt* desnudar, despojar; * *vi* desnudarse; * *n* tira *f*; franja *f*; cinta *f*.

stripe *n* raya, lista *f*; azote *m*; * *vt* rayar.

strive *vi* esforzarse; empeñarse; disputar, contender; oponerse.

stroke *n* golpe *m*; toque (en la pintura) *m*; sonido (del reloj) *m*; pluma da *f*; acaricia *f*; apoplejía *f*; * *vt* acariciar.

stroll *n* paseo *m*; * *vi* dar un paseo.

strong *adj* fuerte, vigoroso/sa, robusto/ta; poderoso/sa; violento/ta; ~**ly** *adv* fuertemente, con violencia.

strongbox *n* caja fuerte *f*.

stronghold *n* plaza fuerte *f*.

strophe *n* estrofa *f*.

structure *n* estructura *f*; edificio *m*.

struggle *vi* esforzarse; luchar; agitarse; * *n* lucha *f*.

strum *vt* (*mus*) rasguear.

strut *vi* pavonearse; * *n* contoneo *m*.

stub *n* talón *m*; colilla *f*; tronco *m*.

stubble *n* rastrojo *m*; cerda *f*.

stubborn *adj* obstinado/da, testarudo/da; ~**ly** *adv* obstinadamente.

stubbornness *n* obstinación, pertinacia *f*.

stucco *n* estuco *m*.

stud *n* corchete *m*; taco *m*; cabelleriza *f*.

student *n* estudiante *m/f*; * *adj* estudiantil.

studio *n* estudio *m*.

studio flat *n* estudio *m*.

studious *adj* estudioso/sa; diligente; ~**ly** *adv* estudiosamente, diligentemente.

study n estudio m; aplicación f; meditación profunda f; * vt estudiar; observar; * vi estudiar; aplicarse.

stuff n materia f; material m; estofa f; * vt henchir, llenar; disecar.

stuffing n relleno m.

stuffy adj cargado/da; de miras estrechas.

stumble vi tropezar; * n traspié, tropiezo m.

stumbling block n tropiezo m; escollo m.

stump n tronco m; tocón m; muñón m.

stun vt aturdir, ensordecer.

stunner n cosa estupenda f.

stunt n vuelo acrobático m; truco publicitario m; * vt no dejar crecer.

stuntman n especialista m.

stuntwoman n especialista f.

stupefy vt atontar, atolondrar.

stupendous adj estupendo/da, maravilloso/sa.

stupid adj estúpido/da; **very ~** zopenco/ca; **~ly** adv estúpidamente.

stupidity n estupidez f.

stupor n estupor m.

sturdily adv fuertemente.

sturdiness n fuerza, fortaleza f; obstinación f.

sturdy adj fuerte, tieso/sa, robusto/ta; bronco/ca, insolente.

sturgeon n esturión m.

stutter vi tartamudear.

sty n zahurda f; pocilga f.

sty(e) n orzuelo m.

style n estilo m; moda f; * vt titular; nombrar; estilizar.

stylish adj elegante, en buen estilo.

suave adj afable.

subdivide vt subdividir.

subdivision n subdivisión f.

subdue vt sojuzgar, sujetar; conquistar; mortificar.

subject adj sujeto/ta; sometido/da; * n sujeto m; súbdito/ta m/f; tema m; * vt sujetar; exponer.

subjection n sujeción f.

subjugate vt sojuzgar, subyugar.

subjugation n subyugación f.

subjunctive n subjuntivo m.

sublet vt subarrendar.

sublimate vt sublimar.

sublime adj sublime, excelso/sa; **~ly** adv de modo sublime; * n sublime m.

sublimity n sublimidad f.

submachine gun n metralleta f.

submarine adj submarino/na; * n submarino m.

submerge vt sumergir.

submersion n inmersión f; zambullida f.

submission n sumisión f.

submissive adj sumiso/sa, obsequioso/sa; **~ly** adv con sumisión.

submissiveness n obsequio m; sumisión f.

submit vt (vi) someter(se).

subordinate adj subordinado/da, inferior; * vt subordinar.

subordination n subordinación f.

subpoena n citación f; * vt citar.

subscribe vt, vi suscribir, certificar con su firma; consentir.

subscriber n suscriptor/a m/f.

subscription n suscripción f.

subsequent adj, **~ly** adv subsiguiente(mente).

subservient adj subordinado/da; servil.

subside vi sumergirse, irse a fondo.

subsidence n derrumbamiento m.

subsidiary adj subsidiario/ria.

subsidize vt subvencionar, dar subsidios.

subsidy *n* subvención *f*; subsidio, socorro *m*.

subsist *vi* subsistir; existir.

subsistence *n* existencia *f*; subsistencia *f*.

substance *n* substancia *f*; entidad *f*; esencia *f*.

substantial *adj* substancial; real, material; substancioso/sa; fuerte; ~**ly** *adv* substancialmente.

substantiate *vt* probar.

substantive *n* sustantivo *m*.

substitute *vt* sustituir; * *n* suplente *m/f*.

substitution *n* sustitución *f*.

substratum *n* sustrato *m*.

subterfuge *n* subterfugio *m*; evasión *f*.

subterranean *adj* subterráneo/nea.

subtitle *n* subtítulo *m*.

subtle *adj* sutil, astuto/ta.

subtlety *n* sutileza, astucia *f*.

subtly *adv* sutilmente.

subtract *vt* (*math*) sustraer.

suburb *n* zona residencial *f*.

suburban *adj* suburbano/na.

subversion *n* subversión *f*.

subversive *adj* subversivo/va.

subvert *vt* subvertir, destruir.

succeed *vt*, *vi* seguir; conseguir, lograr, tener éxito.

success *n* éxito *m*.

successful *adj* exitoso/sa; próspero/ra, dichoso/sa; ~**ly** *adv* con éxito; prósperamente.

succession *n* sucesión *f*; descendencia *f*; herencia *f*.

successive *adj* sucesivo/va; ~**ly** *adv* sucesivamente.

successor *n* sucesor/a *m/f*.

succinct *adj* sucinto/ta, compendioso/sa; ~**ly** *adv* con brevedad.

succulent *adj* suculento/ta, jugoso/sa.

succumb *vi* sucumbir.

such *adj* tal, semejante; ~ **as** tal como.

such and such a one *n* zutano/na y fulano *m/f*.

suck *vt*, *vi* chupar; mamar.

suckle *vt* amamantar.

suckling *n* mamantón/ona *m/f*.

suction *n* (*med*) succión *f*.

sudden *adj* repentino/na, no previsto/ta; ~**ly** *adv* de repente, súbitamente.

suddenness *n* precipitación *f*.

suds *npl* jabonaduras *fpl*.

sue *vt* demandar.

suede *n* ante *m*, gamuza *f*.

suet *n* sebo *m*.

suffer *vt*, *vi* sufrir, padecer; tolerar, permitir.

suffering *n* pena *f*; dolor *m*.

suffice *vi* bastar, ser suficiente.

sufficiency *n* suficiencia *f*; capacidad *f*.

sufficient *adj* suficiente; ~**ly** *adv* bastante.

suffocate *vt* asfixiar; sofocar; * *vi* asfixiarse.

suffocation *n* asfixia *f*.

suffrage *n* sufragio, voto *m*.

suffuse *vt* difundir, derramar.

sugar *n* azúcar *m*; * *vt* azucarar.

sugar beet *n* remolacha *f*.

sugar cane *n* caña de azúcar *f*.

sugar loaf *n* pan de azúcar *m*.

sugary *adj* azucarado/da.

suggest *vt* sugerir.

suggestion *n* sugestión *f*.

suicidal *adj* suicida.

suicide *n* suicidio *m*; suicida *m/f*.

suit *n* conjunto *m*; petición *f*; traje *m*; pleito *m*; surtido *m*; * *vt* convenir; sentar a; adaptar.

suitable *adj* conforme, conveniente.

suitably *adv* convenientemente.

suitcase *n* maleta, valija *f*.

suite *n* suite *f*; serie *f*; tren *m*, comitiva *f*.

suitor *n* suplicante *m*; amante, cortejo *m*; pleiteante *m/f*; galanteador *m*.

sulkiness *n* mal humor *m*.

sulky *adj* regañon, terco/ca.

sullen *adj* hosco/ca; intratable; ~ly *adv* de mal humor; tercamente.

sullenness *n* hosquedad *f*; obstinación, pertinacia, terquedad *f*.

sulphur *n* azufre *m*.

sulphurous *adj* sulfureo, azufroso/sa.

sultan *n* sultán *m*.

sultana *n* sultana *f*; pasa *f*.

sultry *adj* caluroso/sa; sofocante.

sum *n* suma *f*; total *m*.

summarily *adv* sumariamente.

summary *adj* sumario/ria; * *n* sumario *m*; resumen *m*.

summer *n* verano, estío *m*.

summerhouse *n* glorieta de jardín *f*.

summit *n* ápice *m*; cima *f*.

summon *vt* citar, requerir por auto de juez; convocar, convidar; (*mil*) intimar la rendición.

summons *n* citación *f*; requerimiento *m*.

sumptuous *adj* suntuoso/sa; ~ly *adv* suntuosamente.

sum up *vt* resumir; sumar; recopilar.

sun *n* sol *m*.

sunbathe *vi* tomar el sol.

sunburnt *adj* quemado/da por el sol.

Sunday *n* domingo *m*; * *adj* dominical; **done or worn on ~** dominguero/ra.

Sunday driver *n* dominguero/ra *m/f*.

sundial *n* reloj de sol, cuadrante *m*.

sundry *adj* diversos/sas.

sunflower *n* girasol *m*.

sunglasses *npl* gafas de sol *fpl*.

sunless *adj* sin sol; sin luz.

sunlight *n* luz del sol *f*.

sunny *adj* soleado/da; brillante.

sunrise *n* salida del sol *f*; amanecer *m*.

sun roof *n* techo corredizo *m*.

sunset *n* puesta del sol *f*.

sunshade *n* quitasol *m*.

sunshine *n* solana *f*; claridad del sol *f*.

sunstroke *n* insolación *f*.

suntan *n* bronceado *m*.

suntan oil *n* aceite bronceador *m*.

super *adj* (*fam*) bárbaro/ra.

superannuated *adj* añejado/da; pensionado/da.

superannuation *n* pensión, jubilación *f*; retiro *m*.

superb *adj* magnífico/ca; ~ly *adv* magníficamente.

supercargo *n* (*mar*) sobrecargo *m*.

supercilious *adj* arrogante, altanero/ra; ~ly *adv* con altivez.

superficial *adj*, ~ly *adv* superficial(mente).

superfluity *n* superfluidad *f*.

superfluous *adj* superfluo/lua.

superhuman *adj* sobrehumano/na.

superintendent *n* superintendente *m/f*.

superior *adj* superior; * *n* superior/a *m/f*.

superiority *n* superioridad *f*.

superlative *adj* superlativo/va; * *n* superlativo *m*; ~ly *adv* superlativamente, en sumo grado.

supermarket *n* supermercado *m*.

supernatural *adj* sobrenatural.

supernumerary *adj* supernumerario/ria.

superpower *n* superpotencia *f*.

supersede *vt* sobreseer; sustituir; invalidar.

supersonic *adj* supersónico/ca.

superstition *n* superstición *f*.

superstitious *adj* supersticioso/sa; **~ly** *adv* supersticiosamente.

superstructure *n* superestructura *f*.

supertanker *n* superpetrolero *m*.

supervene *vi* sobrevenir.

supervise *vt* supervisar, revistar.

supervision *n* supervisión *f*.

supervisor *n* supervisor/a *m/f*.

supine *adj* supino/na; negligente.

supper *n* cena *f*.

supplant *vt* suplantar.

supple *adj* flexible, manejable; blando/da.

supplement *n* suplemento *m*.

supplementary *adj* adicional.

suppleness *n* flexibilidad *f*.

suppli(c)ant *n* suplicante *m/f*.

supplicate *vt* suplicar.

supplication *n* súplica, suplicación *f*.

supplier *n* proveedor/a *m/f*.

supply *vt* suministrar; suplir, completar; surtir; * *n* provisión *f*; suministro *m*.

support *vt* sostener; soportar, asistir; * *n* apoyo *m*.

supportable *adj* soportable.

supporter *n* partidario/ria *m/f*; aficionado/da *m/f*.

suppose *vt*, *vi* suponer.

supposition *n* suposición *f*.

suppress *vt* suprimir.

suppression *n* supresión *f*.

supremacy *n* supremacía *f*.

supreme *adj* supremo/ma; **~ly** *adv* supremamente.

surcharge *vt* sobrecargar; * *n* sobretasa *f*.

sure[1] *adj* seguro/ra, cierto/ta; firme; estable; **to be ~** estar seguro/ra; **~ly** *adv* ciertamente, seguramente, sin duda.

sure![2] *interj* ¡ya!

sureness *n* certeza, seguridad *f*.

surety *n* seguridad *f*; fiador *m/f*.

surf *n* (*mar*) resaca *f*.

surface *n* superficie *f*; * *vt* revestir; * *vi* salir a la superficie.

surfboard *n* plancha de surf *f*.

surfeit *n* exceso *m*.

surge *n* ola, onda *f*; * *vi* avanzar en tropel.

surgeon *n* cirujano/na *m/f*.

surgery *n* cirugía *f*.

surgical *adj* quirúrgico/ca.

surliness *n* mal humor *m*.

surly *adj* hosco/ca.

surmise *vt* sospechar; * *n* sospecha *f*.

surmount *vt* sobrepujar; (*fig*) zanjar.

surmountable *adj* superable.

surname *n* apellido, sobrenombre *m*.

surpass *vt* sobresalir, sobrepujar, exceder, aventajar.

surpassing *adj* sobresaliente.

surplice *n* sobrepelliz *f*.

surplus *n* excedente *m*; sobrante *m*; * *adj* sobrante.

surprise *vt* sorprender; * *n* sorpresa *f*.

surprising *adj* sorprendente.

surrender *vt*, *vi* rendir; ceder; rendirse; * *n* rendición *f*.

surreptitious *adj* subrepticio/cia; **~ly** *adv* subrepticiamente.

surrogate *vt* subrogar; * *n* subrogado/da *m/f*.

surrogate mother *n* madre de alquiler *f*.

surround *vt* circundar, cercar, rodear.

surrounding area *n* inmediaciones *fpl*.

survey *vt* inspeccionar, examinar; apear; * *n* inspección *f*; apeo (de tierras) *m*.

survive *vi* sobrevivir; * *vt* sobrevivir a.

survivor n superviviente m/f.
susceptibility n susceptibilidad f.
susceptible adj susceptible.
suspect vt, vi sospechar; * n sospechoso/sa m/f.
suspend vt suspender.
suspense n suspense m; detención f; incertidumbre f.
suspension n suspensión f.
suspension bridge n puente colgante m.
suspicion n sospecha f.
suspicious adj suspicaz; ~ly adv sospechosamente.
suspiciousness n suspicacia f.
sustain vt sostener, sustentar, mantener; apoyar; sufrir.
sustenance n sostenimiento, sustento m.
suture n sutura, costura f.
swab n algodón m; frotis m invar.
swaddle vt fajar.
swaddling-clothes npl pañales mpl.
swagger vi baladronear.
swallow n golondrina f; * vt tragar, engullir.
swamp n pantano m.
swampy adj pantanoso/sa.
swan n cisne m.
swap vt canjear; * n intercambio m.
swarm n enjambre m; gentío m; hormiguero m; * vi enjambrar; hormiguear de gente; abundar.
swarthy adj atezado/da.
swarthiness n tez morena f.
swashbuckling adj fanfarrón/ona.
swath n tranco m.
swathe vt fajar; * n faja f.
sway vt mover; * vi ladearse, inclinarse; * n balanceo m; poder, imperio, influjo m.
swear vt, vi jurar; hacer jurar; juramentar.

sweat n sudor m; * vi sudar; trabajar con fatiga.
sweater, sweatshirt n suéter m.
sweep vt, vi barrer; arrebatar; deshollinar; pasar o tocar ligeramente; oscilar; * n barredura f; vuelta f; giro m.
sweeping adj rápido/da; ~s pl barreduras fpl.
sweepstake n lotería f.
sweet adj dulce, grato/ta, gustoso/sa; suave; oloroso/sa; melodioso/sa; hermoso/sa; amable; * adv dulcemente, suavemente; * n dulce, caramelo m.
sweetbread n mellejas de ternera fpl.
sweeten vt endulzar; suavizar; aplacar; perfumar.
sweetener n edulcorante m.
sweetheart n novio/via m/f; querida f.
sweetmeats npl dulces secos mpl.
sweetness n dulzura, suavidad f.
swell vi hincharse; ensoberbecerse; embravecerse; * vt hinchar, inflar, agravar; * n marejada f; * adj (fam) estupendo/da, fenomenal.
swelling n hinchazón f; tumor m.
swelter vi ahogarse de calor.
swerve vi vagar; desviarse.
swift adj veloz, ligero/ra, rápido/da; * n vencejo m.
swiftly adv velozmente.
swiftness n velocidad, rapidez f.
swill vt beber en exceso; * n bazofia f.
swim vi nadar; abundar en; * vt pasar a nado; * n nadada f.
swimming n natación f.
swimming pool n piscina f.
swimsuit n traje de baño m.
swindle vt estafar.
swindler n estafador/a m/f.
swine n puerco, cochino m.
swing vi balancear, columpiarse;

vibrar; agitarse; * *vt* colum piar; balancear; girar; * *n* vibración *f*; balanceo *m*.

swinging *adj* (*fam*) alegre.

swinging door *n* puerta giratoria *f*.

swirl *n* remolino.

switch *n* varilla *f*; interruptor *m*; (*rail*) aguja *f*; * *vt* cambiar de; **to ~ off** apagar; parar; **to ~ on** encender, prender.

switchboard *n* centralita *f*.

swivel *vt* girar.

swoon *vi* desmayarse; * *n* desmayo, deliquio, pasmo *m*.

swoop *vi* calarse; * *n* calada; redada *f*; **in one ~** de un golpe.

sword *n* espada *f*.

swordfish *n* pez espada *f*.

swordsman *n* guerrero, espadachín *m*.

sycamore *n* sicomoro *m* (árbol).

sycophant *n* sicofante *m*.

syllabic *adj* silábico/ca.

syllable *n* sílaba *f*.

syllabus *n* programa de estudios *m*.

syllogism *n* silogismo *m*.

sylph *n* silfio *m*; sílfide *f*.

symbol *n* simbolo *m*.

symbolic(al) *adj* simbólico/ca.

symbolize *vt* simbolizar.

symmetrical *adj* simétrico/ca; **~ly** *adv* con simetría.

symmetry *n* simetría *f*.

sympathetic *adj* simpático/ca; **~ally** *adv* simpáticamente.

sympathize *vi* compadecerse.

sympathy *n* simpatía *f*.

symphony *n* sinfonía *f*.

symposium *n* simposio *m*.

symptom *n* síntoma *m*.

synagogue *n* sinagoga *f*.

synchronism *n* sincronismo *m*.

syndicate *n* sindicato *m*.

syndrome *n* síndrome *m*.

synod *n* sínodo *m*.

synonym *n* sinónimo *m*.

synonymous *adj* sinónimo/ma; **~ly** *adv* con sinonimia.

synopsis *n* sinopsis *f invar*; sumario *m*.

synoptic *adj* sinóptico/ca.

syntax *n* sintaxis *f*.

synthesis *n* síntesis *f invar*.

syringe *n* jeringa, lavativa *f*; * *vt* jeringar.

system *n* sistema *m*.

systematic *adj* sistemático/ca; **~ally** *adv* sistemáticamente.

systems analyst *n* analista de sistemas *m/f*.

T

tab *n* lengüeta *f*; etiqueta *f*.

tabernacle *n* tabernáculo *m*.

table *n* mesa *f*; tabla *f*; * *vt* someter a discusión; poner sobre la mesa; **~ d'hôte** menu *m*.

tablecloth *n* mantel *m*.

tablespoon *n* cuchara para comer *f*.

tablet *n* tableta *f*; pastilla *f*; comprimido *m*.

table tennis *n* ping-pong, tenis de mesa *m*.

taboo *adj* tabú; * *n* tabú *m*; * *vt* interdecir.

tabular *adj* tabular.

tacit *adj* tácito/ta; **~ly** *adv* tácitamente.

taciturn *adj* taciturno/na, callado/da.

tack *n* tachuela *f*; bordo *m*; * *vt* atar; pegar; * *vi* virar.

tackle n equipo m, aparejos mpl; placaje m; (mar) cordaje m, jarcia f.
tact n tacto m.
tactician n táctico/ca m/f.
tactics npl táctica f.
tadpole n renacuajo m.
taffeta n tafetán m.
tag n herrete m; * vt herretear.
tail n cola f; rabo m; * vt vigilar a.
tailgate n puerta trasera f.
tailor n sastre m.
tailoring n corte m.
tailor-made adj hecho/cha a la medida.
tailwind n viento de cola m.
taint vt tachar, manchar; viciar; * n mancha f.
tainted adj contaminado/da; manchado/da.
take vt tomar, coger, asir; recibir, aceptar; pillar; prender; admitir; entender; * vi prender el fuego; **to ~ apart** vt descoser; **to ~ away** quitar; llevar; **to ~ back** devolver; retractar; **to ~ down** derribar; apuntar; **to ~ in** entender, abarcar; acoger; **to ~ off** vi despegar; vt quitar; imitar; **to ~ on** aceptar; contratar; desafiar; **to ~ out** sacar; quitar; **to ~ to** encariñarse con; **to ~ up** acortar; ocupar; dedicarse a; * n toma f.
takeoff n despegue m.
takeover n absorción f; ~ **bid** opa f.
takings npl ingresos mpl.
talc n talco m.
talent n talento m; capacidad f.
talented adj con talento.
talisman n talismán m.
talk vi hablar, conversar; charlar; * n habla f; charla f; fama f.
talkative adj locuaz.
talk show n programa de entrevistas m.

tall adj alto/ta, elevado/da; robusto/ta.
tally vi corresponder.
talon n garra f.
tambourine n pandereta f.
tame adj amansado/da, domado/da, domesticado/da; ~**ly** adv mansamente; bajamente; * vt domar, domesticar.
tameness n domesticidad f; sumisión f.
tamper vi tocar.
tampon n tampón m.
tan vt broncear; * vi broncearse, ponerse moreno/na; * n bronceado m.
tang n sabor fuerte m.
tangent n tangente f.
tangerine n mandarina f.
tangible adj tangible.
tangle vt enredar, embrollar.
tank n cisterna f; aljibe m.
tanker n petrolero m; camión cisterna m.
tanned adj bronceado/da.
tantalizing adj tentador/a.
tantamount adj equivalente.
tantrum n rabieta f.
tap vt tocar ligeramente; utilizar; intervenir; zapatear; * n grifo m; palmada suave f; toque ligero m; llave f; espita f.
tape n cinta f; * vt grabar.
tape measure n metro m.
taper n cirio m.
tape recorder n grabadora f.
tapestry n tapiz m; tapicería f.
tar n brea f, alquitrán m.
target n blanco m (para tirar).
tariff n tarifa f.
Tarmac®, tarmac n asfalto m, alquitranado m.
tarnish vt deslustrar.
tarpaulin n lona f alquitranada.
tarragon n (bot) estragón m.

tart *adj* acedo/da, acre; * *n* tarta, torta *f*; (*sl*) zorra *f*.

tartan *n* tela escocesa *f*.

tartar *n* tártaro *m*.

task *n* tarea *f*.

tassel *n* borlita *f*.

taste *n* gusto *m*; sabor *m*; saboreo *m*; ensayo *m*; * *vt*, *vi* gustar; probar; experimentar; agradar; tener sabor.

tasteful *adj* sabroso/sa; ~**ly** *adv* sabrosamente.

tasteless *adj* insípido/da, sin sabor.

tasty *adj* sabroso/sa.

tattoo *n* tatuaje *m*; * *vt* tatuar.

taunt *vt* mofar; ridiculizar; * *n* mofa, burla *f*.

Taurus *n* Tauro *m* (signo del zodíaco).

taut *adj* tieso/sa.

tautological *adj* tautológico/ca.

tautology *n* tautología *f*.

tawdry *adj* jarifo/fa, vistoso/sa, chabacano/na.

tax *n* impuesto *m*; contribución *f*; * *vt* gravar; poner a prueba.

taxable *adj* sujeto/ta a impuestos.

taxation *n* imposición de impuestos *f*.

tax collector *n* recaudador/a *m/f* de impuestos.

tax-free *adj* libre de impuestos.

taxi *n* taxi *m*; * *vi* rodar por la pista.

taxi driver *n* taxista *m/f*.

taxi rank *n* parada de taxis *f*.

tax payer *n* contribuyente *m/f*.

tax relief *n* desgravación fiscal *f*.

tax return *n* declaración de la renta *f*.

tea *n* té *m*.

teach *vt* enseñar, instruir; * *vi* enseñar.

teacher *n* profesor/a *m/f*; maestro/tra *m/f*.

teaching *n* enseñanza *f*.

teacup *n* taza de té *f*.

teak *n* teca *f* (árbol).

team *n* equipo *m*.

teamster *n* camionero/ra *m/f*.

teamwork *n* trabajo de equipo *m*.

teapot *n* tetera *f*.

tear *vt* despedazar, rasgar; **to ~ up** hacer trizas.

tear *n* lágrima *f*; gota *f*.

tearful *adj* lloroso/sa; ~**ly** *adv* con lloro.

tear gas *n* gas lacrimógeno *m*.

tease *vt* tomar el pelo.

tea service, tea set *n* servicio para té *m*.

teasing *adj* zumbón/ona; * *n* zumba *f*.

teaspoon *n* cucharita *f*.

teat *n* ubre, teta *f*.

technical *adj* técnico/ca.

technicality *n* detalle técnico *m*.

technician *n* técnico/ca *m*

technique *n* técnica *f*.

technological *adj* tecnológico/ca.

technology *n* tecnología *f*.

teddy (bear) *n* osito de felpa *m*.

tedious *adj* tedioso/sa, fastidioso/sa; ~**ly** *adv* fastidiosamente.

tedium *n* tedio, fastidio *m*.

tee *n* tee *m*.

teem *vi* rebosar de.

teenage *adj* juvenil; ~**r** *n* adolescente *m/f*.

teens *npl* adolescencia *f*.

tee-shirt, T-shirt *n* camiseta *f*.

teeth *n pl* de **tooth**.

teethe *vi* echar los dientes.

teetotal *adj* abstemio/mia, sobrio/ria.

teetotaller *n* abstemio/mia *m/f*.

telegram *n* telegrama *m*.

telegraph *n* telégrafo *m*.

telegraphic *adj* telegráfico/ca.

telegraphy *n* telegrafía *f*.

telepathy *n* telepatía *f*.

telephone *n* teléfono *m*.

telephone banking *n* telebanca *f*.

telephone booth *n* cabina telefónica *f*.

telephone call *n* llamada telefónica *f*.
telephone directory *n* guía *f* telefónica.
telephone number *n* número de teléfono *m*.
telescope *n* telescopio *m*.
telescopic *adj* telescópico/ca.
televise *vt* televisar.
television *n* televisión *f*.
television news *n* telediario *m*.
television set *n* televisor *m*.
teleworker *n* teletrabajador/ra *m/f*.
teleworking *n* teletrabajo *m*.
telex *n* télex *m*; *vt*, *vi* enviar un télex.
tell *vi* decir; informar, contar.
teller *n* cajero/ra *m/f*.
telling *adj* contundente; revelador/a.
telltale *adj* indicador/a.
telly *n* (*fam*) tele *f*.
temper *vt* templar, moderar; * *n* mal genio *m*.
temperament *n* temperamento *m*.
temperance *n* templanza, moderación *f*.
temperate *adj* templado/da, moderado/da, sobrio/ria.
temperature *n* temperatura *f*.
tempest *n* tempestad *f*.
tempestuous *adj* tempestuoso/sa.
template *n* plantilla *f*.
temple *n* templo *m*; sien *f*.
temporarily *adv* temporalmente.
temporary *adj* temporal.
tempt *vt* tentar; provocar.
temptation *n* tentación *f*.
tempting *adj* tentador/a.
ten *adj*, *n* diez.
tenable *adj* defendible.
tenacious *adj*, **~ly** *adv* tenaz(mente).
tenacity *n* tenacidad *f*; porfía *f*.
tenancy *n* tenencia *f*.
tenant *n* arrendatario/ria, inquilino/na *m/f*.

tend *vt* guardar, velar; * *vi* tener tendencia a.
tendency *n* tendencia *f*.
tender *adj* tierno/na, delicado/da; sensible; **~ly** *adv* tiernamente; * *n* oferta *f*; * *vt* ofrecer; estimar.
tenderness *n* ternura *f*.
tendon *n* tendón *m*.
tendril *n* zarcillo *m*.
tenement *n* casa de pisos *f*.
tenet *n* dogma *m*; aserción *f*.
tennis *n* tenis *m*.
tennis court *n* cancha de tenis *f*.
tennis player *n* tenista *m/f*.
tennis racket *n* raqueta de tenis *f*.
tennis shoes *npl* zapatillas de tenis *fpl*.
tenor *n* (*mus*) tenor *m*; contenido *m*; substancia *f*.
tense *adj* tieso/sa, tenso/sa; * *n* (*gr*) tiempo *m*.
tension *n* tensión, tirantez *f*.
tent *n* tienda de campaña *f*.
tentacle *n* tentáculo *m*.
tentative *adj* de ensayo, de prueba; **~ly** *adv* como prueba.
tenth *adj*, *n* décimo/ma.
tenuous *adj* tenue.
tenure *n* tenencia *f*.
tepid *adj* tibio/bia.
term *n* término *m*; dicción *f*; vocablo *m*; condición, estipulación *f*; * *vt* nombrar, llamar.
terminal *adj* mortal; * *n* terminal *m*; terminal *f*.
terminate *vt* terminar.
termination *n* terminación, conclusión *f*.
terminus *n* terminal *f*.
terrace *n* terraza *f*.
terrain *n* terreno *m*.
terrestrial *adj* terrestre, terreno/na.
terrible *adj* terrible.

terribly *adv* terriblemente.
terrier *n* terrier *m*.
terrific *adj* fantástico/ca; maravilloso/sa.
terrify *vt* aterrar, espantar.
territorial *adj* territorial.
territory *n* territorio, distrito *m*.
terror *n* terror *m*.
terrorism *n* terrorismo *m*.
terrorist *n* terrorista *m/f*.
terrorist attack *n* atentado *m*.
terrorize *vt* aterrorizar.
terse *adj* tajante.
test *n* examen *m*; prueba *f*; * *vt* probar; examinar.
testament *n* testamento *m*.
tester *n* ensayador/a *m/f*.
testicles *npl* testículos *mpl*.
testify *vt* testificar, atestiguar.
testimonial *n* atestación *f*.
testimony *n* testimonio *m*.
test pilot *n* piloto de pruebas *m/f*.
test tube *n* probeta *f*.
testy *adj* tétrico/ca.
tetanus *n* tétanos *m invar*.
tether *vt* atar.
text *n* texto *m*.
textbook *n* libro de texto *m*.
textiles *npl* textiles *mpl*.
textual *adj* textual.
texture *n* textura *f*; tejido *m*.
than *adv* que, de.
thank *vt* agradecer, dar las gracias a.
thankful *adj* grato/ta, agradecido/da; ~ly *adv* con gratitud.
thankfulness *n* gratitud *f*.
thankless *adj* ingrato/ta.
thanks *npl* gracias *fpl*.
Thanksgiving *n* día de acción de gracias *m*.
that *pn* aquel, aquello, aquella; que; este; * *conj* porque; para que; **so ~** de modo que.

thatch *n* techo de paja *m*; * *vt* techar con paja.
thaw *n* deshielo *m*; * *vi* deshelarse.
the *art* el, la, lo; los, las.
theatre *n* teatro *m*.
theatregoer *n* aficionado/da al teatro *m/f*.
theatrical *adj* teatral.
theft *n* robo *m*.
their *pn* su, suyo, suya; de ellos, de ellas; ~s el suyo, la suya, los suyos, las suyas; de ellos, de ellas.
them *pn* los, las, les; ellos, ellas.
theme *n* tema *m*.
themselves *pn pl* ellos mismos, ellas mismas; sí mismos; se.
then *adv* entonces, después; en tal caso; * *conj* en ese caso; * *adj* entonces; **now and ~** de vez en cuando.
theologian *n* teólogo/ga *m/f*.
theological *adj* teológico/ca.
theology *n* teología *f*.
theorem *n* teorema *m*.
theoretic(al) *adj* teórico/ca; ~ly *adv* teóricamente.
theorist *n* teórico/ca *m/f*.
theorize *vt* teorizar.
theory *n* teoría *f*.
therapeutics *n* terapéutica *f*.
therapist *n* terapeuta *m/f*.
therapy *n* terapia *f*.
there *adv* allí, allá.
thereabout(s) *adv* por ahí, acerca de.
thereafter *adv* después; según.
thereby *adv* así; de ese modo.
therefore *adv* por eso, por lo tanto.
thermal *adj* termal.
thermal printer *n* impresora térmica *f*.
thermometer *n* termómetro *m*.
thermostat *n* termostato *m*.
thesaurus *n* diccionario de sinónimos *m*.

these *pn pl* éstos, éstas; *adj* estos, estas.

thesis *n* tesis *f invar*.

they *pn pl* ellos, ellas.

thick *adj* espeso/sa, denso/sa; grueso/sa; torpe.

thicken *vi* espesar, condensar; condensarse.

thicket *n* espesura *f*.

thickness *n* espesor *m*.

thickset *adj* grueso/sa; rechoncho/cha.

thick-skinned *adj* duro/ra de pellejo.

thief *n* ladrón/ona *m/f*.

thigh *n* muslo *m*.

thimble *n* dedal *m*.

thin *adj* delgado/da, delicado/da, flaco/ca; claro/ra; * *vt* atenuar; adelga zar; aclarar.

thing *n* cosa *f*; objeto *m*; chisme *m*.

think *vi* pensar, imaginar, meditar, considerar; creer, juzgar; **to ~ over** reflexionar; **to ~ up** imaginar.

thinker *n* pensador/a *m/f*.

thinking *n* pensamiento *m*; juicio *m*; opinión *f*.

third *adj* tercero/ra; * *n* tercio *m*; **~ly** *adv* en tercer lugar.

third rate *adj* mediocre.

thirst *n* sed *f*.

thirsty *adj* sediento/ta.

thirteen *adj, n* trece.

thirteenth *adj, n* decimotercero/ra.

thirtieth *adj, n* trigésimo/ma.

thirty *adj, n* treinta.

this *adj* este, esta; * *pn* éste, ésta, esto.

thistle *n* cardo *m*.

thorn *n* espino *m*; espina *f*.

thorny *adj* espinoso/sa; arduo/dua.

thorough *adj* entero/ra, perfecto/ta; **~ly** *adv* enteramente, profundamente.

thoroughbred *adj* de sangre, de casta.

thoroughfare *n* paso, tránsito *m*.

those *pn pl* ésos, ésas; aquéllos, aquéllas; * *adj* esos, esas; aquellos, aquellas.

though *conj* aunque, no obstante; * *adv* sin embargo.

thought *n* pensamiento, juicio *m*; opinión *f*; cuidado *m*.

thoughtful *adj* pensativo/va.

thoughtless *adj* descuidado/da; insensato/ta; **~ly** *adv* descuidadamente, sin reflexión.

thousand *adj, n* mil.

thousandth *adj, n* milésimo/ma.

thrash *vt* golpear; derrotar.

thread *n* hilo *m*; rosca *f*; * *vt* enhebrar.

threadbare *adj* raído/da, muy usado/da.

threat *n* amenaza *f*.

threaten *vt* amenazar.

three *adj, n* tres.

three-dimensional *adj* tridimensional.

three-monthly *adj* trimestral.

three-ply *adj* triple.

threshold *n* umbral *m*.

thrifty *adj* económico/ca.

thrill *vt* emocionar; * *n* emoción *f*.

thriller *n* película *o* novela de suspense *f*.

thrive *vi* prosperar; crecer.

throat *n* garganta *f*.

throb *vi* palpitar; vibrar; dar punzadas.

throne *n* trono *m*.

throng *n* tropel de gente *m*; * *vt* venir en tropel.

throttle *n* acelerador *m*; * *vt* estrangular.

through *prep* por; durante; mediante; * *adj* directo/ta; * *adv* completamente.

throughout *prep* por todo; * *adv* en todas partes.

throw *vt* echar, arrojar, tirar, lanzar; * *n* tiro *m*; golpe *m*; **to ~ away** tirar; **to ~ off** desechar; **to ~ out** tirar; **to ~ up** vomitar, devolver.

throwaway *adj* desechable.

thrush *n* tordo *m* (ave).

thrust *vt* empujar, introducir; * *vr* zamparse; * *n* empuje *m*.

thud *n* ruido sordo *m*; zarpazo *m*.

thug *n* gamberro/rra *m/f*.

thumb *n* pulgar *m*.

thump *n* golpe *m*; * *vt*, *vi* golpear.

thunder *n* trueno *m*; * *vi* tronar.

thunderbolt *n* rayo *m*.

thunderclap *n* trueno *m*.

thunderstorm *n* tormenta *f*.

thundery *adj* tormentoso/sa.

Thursday *n* jueves *m invar*.

thus *adv* así, de este modo.

thwart *vt* frustrar.

thyme *n* (*bot*) tomillo *m*.

thyroid *n* tiroides *m invar*.

tiara *n* tiara *f*.

tic *n* tic *m*.

tick *n* tictac *m*; palomita *f*; * *vt* marcar; **to ~ over** girar en marcha; ir tirando.

ticket *n* billete, boleto *m*; etiqueta *f*; tarjeta *f*.

ticket collector *n* (*rail*) revisor/a *m/f*.

ticket office *n* taquilla *f*, boletería *f*; despacho de boletos *m*.

tickle *vt* hacer cosquillas.

ticklish *adj* con cosquillas.

tidal *adj* (*mar*) de marea.

tidal wave *n* maremoto *m*.

tide *n* curso *m*; marea *f*.

tidy *adj* ordenado/da; arreglado/da; aseado/da.

tie *vt* anudar, atar; * *vi* empatar; **to ~ up** envolver; atar; amarrar; con-

cluir; * *n* atadura *f*; lazo *m*; corbata *f*; empate *m*.

tier *n* grada *f*; piso *m*.

tiger *n* tigre *m*.

tight *adj* tirante, tieso/sa, tenso/sa; cerrado/da; apretado/da; * *adv* con fuerza.

tighten *vt* tirar, estirar.

tightfisted *adj* tacaño/ña.

tightly *adv* muy fuerte.

tightrope *n* cuerda floja *f*.

tights *npl* medias *fpl*.

tigress *n* tigresa *f*.

tile *n* teja *f*; baldosa *f*; azulejo *m*; * *vt* tejar.

tiled *adj* embaldosado/da.

till *n* caja *f*; * *vt* cultivar, labrar.

tiller *n* cana del timón *f*.

tilt *vt* inclinar; * *vi* inclinarse.

timber *n* madera de construcción *f*; árboles *mpl*.

time *n* tiempo *m*; época *f*; hora *f*; momento *m*; (*mus*) compás *m*; **in ~** a tiempo; **from ~ to ~** de vez en cuando; * *vt* medir el tiempo; cronometrar.

time bomb *n* bomba de relojería *f*.

time lag *n* desfase *m*.

timeless *adj* eterno/na.

timely *adj* oportuno/na.

time off *n* tiempo libre *m*.

timer *n* interruptor *m*; programador horario *m*.

time scale *n* escala de tiempo *f*.

time trial *n* contrarreloj *f*.

time zone *n* huso horario *m*.

timid *adj* tímido/da, temeroso/sa; **~ly** *adv* con timidez.

timidity *n* timidez *f*.

timing *n* cronometraje *m*; oportunidad *f*.

tin *n* estaño *m*; hojalata *f*.

tinder *n* yesca *f*.

tinfoil n papel de estaño m.

tinge n matiz m.

tingle vi zumbar; latir, punzar.

tingling n zumbido m; latido m.

tinker n calderero remendón m; gitano/na m/f.

tinkle vi tintinear.

tinplate n hojalata f.

tinsel n oropel m.

tint n tinte m; * vt teñir.

tinted adj teñido/da; ahumado/da.

tiny adj pequeño/ña, chico/ca.

tip[1] n punta, extremidad f.

tip[2] n propina f; consejo m; * vt dar una propina a.

tip[3] vt inclinar; vaciar.

tip-off n advertencia f.

tipsy adj alegre.

tiptop adj excelente, perfecto/ta.

tirade n invectiva f.

tire vt cansar, fatigar; * vi cansarse; fastidiarse.

tireless adj incansable.

tiresome adj tedioso/sa, molesto/ta.

tiring adj cansado/da.

tissue n tejido m; pañuelo de papel m.

tissue paper n papel de seda m.

titbit n golosina f; pedazo m.

titillate vt estimular.

title n título m.

title deed n derecho de propiedad m.

title page n portada f.

titter vi reírse disimuladamente; * n risa disimulada f.

titular adj titular.

to prep a; para; por; de; hasta; en; con; que.

toad n sapo m.

toadstool n (bot) seta venenosa f.

toast vt tostar; brindar; * n tostada f; brindis m.

toaster n tostadora f.

tobacco n tabaco m.

tobacconist n tabaquero/ra, estanquero/ra m/f.

tobacconist's (shop) n estanco m, tabaquería f.

tobacco pouch n petaca f.

toboggan n tobogán m.

today adv hoy.

toddler n niño/ña (que empieza a andar) m/f.

toddy n ponche m.

toe n dedo del pie m; punta f.

together adv juntamente, juntos; al mismo tiempo.

toil vi fatigarse, trabajar mucho; afanarse; * n trabajo m; fatiga f; afán m.

toilet n servicios mpl; sanitario m; * adj de aseo.

toilet bag n bolsa de aseo f.

toilet bowl n taza del retrete f.

toilet paper n papel higiénico m.

toiletries npl artículos de aseo mpl.

token n señal f; muestra f; recuerdo m; vale m; (games) ficha f.

tolerable adj soportable; pasable.

tolerance n tolerancia f.

tolerant adj tolerante.

tolerate vt tolerar.

toll n peaje m; número de victimas m; * vi doblar.

tomato n tomate m.

tomb n tumba f; sepulcro m, sepultura f.

tomboy n muchachota f.

tombstone n piedra sepulcral f.

tomcat n gato m.

tomorrow adv mañana; * n mañana f.

ton n tonelada f.

tone n tono m; acento m; * vi armonizar; **to ~ down** suavizar.

tone-deaf adj sin oído musical.

tongs npl tenacillas fpl.

tongue n lengua f.

tongue-tied *adj* mudo/da.
tongue-twister *n* trabalenguas *m invar*.
tonic *n* (*med*) tónico *m*.
tonight *adv*, *n* esta tarde (*f*).
tonnage *n* tonelaje *m*.
tonsil *n* amígdala *f*; ~s *npl* agallas *fpl*.
tonsillitis *n* agalla *f*.
tonsure *n* tonsura *f*.
too *adv* demasiado; también.
tool *n* herramienta *f*; utensilio *m*.
tool box *n* caja de herramientas *f*.
toot *vi* tocar la bocina.
tooth *n* diente *m*.
toothache *n* dolor de muelas *m*.
toothbrush *n* cepillo de dientes *m*.
toothless *adj* desdentado/da.
toothpaste *n* pasta de dientes *f*.
toothpick *n* palillo *m*.
top *n* cima, cumbre *f*; último grado *m*; lo alto; superficie *f*; tapa *f*; cabeza *f*; * *adj* de arriba; primero/ra; * *vt* elevarse por encima; sobrepujar, exceder; **to ~ off** llenar.
topaz *n* topacio *m*.
top floor *n* último piso *m*.
top-heavy *adj* inestable.
topic *n* tema *m*; ~al *adj* actual.
topless *adj* topless.
top-level *adj* al más alto nivel.
topmost *adj* lo más alto.
topographic(al) *adj* topográfico/ca.
topography *n* topografía *f*.
topple *vt* derribar; * *vi* volcarse.
top-secret *adj* de alto secreto.
topsy-turvy *adv* al revés.
torch *n* antorcha *f*.
torment *vt* atormentar; * *n* tormento *m*.
tornado *n* tornado *m*.
torrent *n* torrente *m*.
torrid *adj* apasionado/da.

tortoise *n* tortuga *f*.
tortoiseshell *adj* de carey.
tortuous *adj* tortuoso/sa, sinuoso/sa.
torture *n* tortura *f*; * *vt* torturar.
toss *vt* tirar, lanzar, arrojar; agitar, sacudir.
total *adj* total, entero/ra; ~ly *adv* totalmente.
totalitarian *adj* totalitario/ria.
totality *n* totalidad *f*.
totter *vi* vacilar.
touch *vt* tocar, palpar; **to ~ on** aludir a; **to ~ up** retocar; * *n* contacto *m*; tacto *m*; toque *m*; prueba *f*.
touch-and-go *adj* arriesgado/da.
touchdown *n* aterrizaje *m*; ensayo *m*.
touched *adj* conmovido/da; chiflado/da.
touching *adj* patético/ca, conmovedor/a.
touchstone *n* piedra de toque *f*.
touchwood *n* yesca *f*.
touchy *adj* quisquilloso/sa.
tough *adj* duro/ra; difícil; resistente; fuerte; * *n* gorila *m*.
toughen *vt* endurecer.
toupee *n* tupé *m*.
tour *n* viaje *m*; visita *f*; * *vt* visitar.
touring *n* viajes turísticos *mpl*.
tourism *n* turismo *m*; **bicycle ~** cicloturismo; **rural ~** turismo rural.
tourist *n* turista *m/f*.
tourist office *n* oficina de turismo *f*.
tournament *n* torneo *m*.
tow *n* remolque *m*; * *vt* remolcar.
toward(s) *prep*, *adv* hacia, con dirección a; cerca de, respecto a.
towel *n* toalla *f*.
towelling *n* toalla *f*.
towel rack *n* toallero *m*.
tower *n* torre *m*.
towering *adj* imponente.
town *n* ciudad *f*.

town clerk n secretario/ria del ayuntamiento m/f.

town hall n ayuntamiento m.

towrope n cable de remolque m.

toy n juguete m.

toyshop n juguetería f.

trace n huella, pisada f; * vt trazar, delinear; encontrar.

track n vestigio m; huella f; camino m; vía f; pista f; canción f; * vt rastrear.

tracksuit n chándal m.

tract n región, comarca f; serie f; tratado m.

traction n tracción f.

trade n comercio, tráfico m; negocio, trato m; ocupación f; * vi comerciar, traficar.

trade fair n feria de muestras f.

trademark n marca comercial f.

trade name n nombre comercial m.

trader n comerciante, traficante m.

tradesman n tendero m.

trade(s) union n sindicato m.

trade unionist n sindicalista m/f.

trading n comercio m; * adj comercial.

tradition n tradición f

traditional adj tradicional.

traffic n tráfico m; tránsito m; * vi traficar, comerciar.

traffic jam n embotellamiento m.

trafficker n traficante, comerciante m/f.

traffic lights npl semáforo m.

tragedy n tragedia f.

tragic adj trágico/ca; ~ally adv trágicamente.

tragicomedy n tragicomedia f.

trail vt, vi rastrear; arrastrar; * n rastro m; pista f; cola f.

trailer n remolque m; avance m.

trailer n tráiler m.

train vt entrenar; amaestrar, enseñar, criar, adiestrar; disciplinar; vr ejercitarse; * n tren m; cola f; serie f; **high-speed** ~ tren de alta velocidad m.

trained adj cualificado/da; amaestrado/da.

trainee n aprendiz/a m/f.

trainer n entrenador/a m/f.

trainers npl zapatillas de lona fpl.

training n entrenamiento m; formación f.

trait n rasgo m.

traitor n traidor/a m/f.

tram n tranvía f.

tramp n vagabundo/da m/f; (sl) puta f; * vi andar pesadamente; * vt pisotear.

trample vt pisotear.

trampoline n cama elástica f.

trance n rapto m; éxtasis m.

tranquil adj tranquilo/la.

tranquillize vt tranquilizar.

tranquillizer n tranquilizante m.

transact vt negociar.

transaction n transacción f; negociación f.

transatlantic adj transatlántico/ca.

transcend vt trascender, pasar; exceder.

transcription n transcripción f.

transfer vt transferir, trasladar; * n transferencia f; traspaso m; calcomanía f.

transform vt transformar.

transformation n transformación f.

transfusion n transfusión f.

transient adj pasajero/ra, transitorio/ria.

transit n tránsito m.

transition n tránsito m; transición f.

transitional adj de transición.

transitive adj transitivo/va.

translate *vt* traducir.
translation *n* traducción *f*.
translator *n* traductor/ra *m/f*.
transmission *n* transmisión *f*.
transmit *vt* transmitir.
transmitter *n* transmisor *m*; emisora *f*.
transparency *n* transparencia *f*.
transparent *adj* transparente, diáfano/na.
transpire *vi* resultar; ocurrir.
transplant *vt* trasplantar; * *n* trasplante *m*.
transport *vt* transportar; * *n* transporte *m*.
transportation *n* transporte *m*.
trap *n* trampa *f*; * *vt* atrapar, bloquear.
trap door *n* trampilla *f*; escotillón *m*.
trapeze *n* trapecio *m*.
trappings *npl* adornos *mpl*.
trash *n* basura *f*; tonterías *fpl*.
trash can *n* cubo de la basura *m*.
trashy *adj* vil, despreciable, de ningún valor.
travel *vi* viajar; * *vt* recorrer; * *n* viaje *m*.
travel agency *n* agencia de viajes *f*.
travel agent *n* agente de viajes *m*.
traveller *n* viajante, viajero/ra *m/f*.
traveller's cheque *n* cheque de viaje *m*.
travelling *n* viajes *mpl*.
travel-sickness *n* mareo *m*.
travesty *n* parodia *f*.
trawler *n* arrastrero *m*.
tray *n* bandeja *f*; cajón *m*.
treacherous *adj* traidor/a, perfido/da.
treachery *n* traición *f*.
tread *vi* pisar; pistoear; * *n* pisada *f*; ruido de pasos *m*; banda de rodadura *f*.

treason *n* traición *f*; **high ~** alta traición *f*.
treasure *n* tesoro *m*; * *vt* atesorar.
treasurer *n* tesorero/ra *m/f*.
treat *vt* tratar; regalar; * *n* regalo *m*; placer *m*.
treatise *n* tratado *m*.
treatment *n* trato *m*.
treaty *n* tratado *m*.
treble *adj* triple; * *vt* (*vi*) triplicar(se); * *n* (*mus*) tiple *m*.
treble clef *n* clave de sol *f*.
tree *n* árbol *m*.
trek *n* caminata *f*; expedición *f*.
trellis *n* enrejado *m*.
tremble *vi* temblar.
trembling *n* temor *m*; trino *m*.
tremendous *adj* tremendo/da; enorme; estupendo/da.
tremor *n* temblor *m*.
trench *n* foso *m*; (*mil*) trinchera *f*; zanja *f*.
trend *n* tendencia *f*; curso *m*; moda *f*.
trendy *adj* de moda.
trepidation *n* inquietud *f*.
trespass *vt* transpasar, violar.
tress *n* trenza *f*; rizo de pelo *m*.
trestle *n* caballete de serrador *m*.
trial *n* proceso *m*; prueba *f*; ensayo *m*; desgracia *f*.
triangle *n* triángulo *m*.
triangular *adj* triangular.
tribal *adj* tribal.
tribe *n* tribu *f*; raza, casta *f*.
tribulation *n* tribulación *f*.
tribunal *n* tribunal *m*.
tributary *adj*, *n* tributario/ria *m/f*.
tribute *n* tributo *m*.
trice *n* momento, tris *m*.
trick *n* engaño, fraude *m*; burla *f*; baza *f*; zancadilla *f*; * *vt* engañar.
trickery *n* engaño *m*.
trickle *vi* gotear; * *n* reguero *m*.

tricky *adj* difícil; delicado/da.

tricycle *n* triciclo *m*.

trifle *n* bagatela, nineria *f*; * *vi* bobear; juguetear.

trifling *adj* frívolo/la, inútil.

trigger *n* gatillo *m*.

trigger off *vt* desencadenar.

trigonometry *n* trigonometría *f*.

trill *n* trino *m*; * *vi* trinar.

trillion *n* billón *m*.

trim *adj* aseado/da; en buen estado; arreglado/da; * *vt* arreglar; recortar; adornar.

trimester *n* trimestre *m*.

trimmings *npl* accesorios *mpl*.

Trinity *n* Trinidad *f*.

trinket *n* joya, alhaja *f*; adorno *m*.

trio *n* (*mus*) trío *m*.

trip *vt* hacer caer; * *vi* tropezar; resbalar; **to ~ up** *vi* caerse; *vt* hacer caer; * *n* resbalón *m*; viaje corto *m*; zancadilla *f*.

tripe *n* callos *mpl*; bobadas *fpl*.

triple *adj* triple; * *vt* triplicar.

triplets *npl* trillizos/zas *m/fpl*.

triplicate *n* triplicado *m*.

tripod *n* trípode *m*.

trite *adj* trivial; usado/da.

triumph *n* triunfo *m*; * *vi* triunfar.

triumphal *adj* triunfal.

triumphant *adj* triunfante; victorioso/sa; **~ly** *adv* en triunfo.

trivia *npl* trivialidades *fpl*.

trivial *adj* trivial, vulgar; **~ly** *adv* trivialmente.

triviality *n* trivialidad *f*.

trolley *n* carrito *m*.

trombone *n* trombón *m*.

troop *n* grupo *m*; **~s** *npl* tropas *fpl*.

trooper *n* soldado a caballo *m*.

trophy *n* trofeo *m*.

tropical *adj* trópico/ca.

trot *n* trote *m*; * *vi* trotar.

trouble *vt* afligir; molestar; * *n* problema *m*; disturbio *m*; inquietud *f*; aflicción, pena *f*.

troubled *adj* preocupado/da; agitado/da.

troublemaker *n* agitador/a *m/f*.

troubleshooter *n* conciliador/a *m/f*.

troublesome *adj* molesto/ta.

trough *n* abrevadero *m*; comedero *m*.

troupe *n* grupo *m*.

trousers *npl* bragas *fpl*; pantalones *mpl*.

trout *n* trucha *f*.

trowel *n* paleta *f*.

truce *n* tregua *f*.

truck *n* camión *m*; vagón *m*.

truck driver *n* camionero/ra *m/f*.

truculent *adj* truculento/ta, cruel.

trudge *vi* andar fatigosamente, andar con dificultad.

true *adj* verdadero/ra, cierto/ta; sincero/ra; exacto/ta.

truelove *n* amor verdadero *m*.

truffle *n* trufa *f*.

truly *adv* en verdad; sinceramente.

trump *n* triunfo (en el juego de naipes) *m*.

trumpet *n* trompeta *f*.

trunk *n* baúl, cofre *m*; trompa *f*.

truss *n* braguero *m*; * *vt* atar; espetar.

trust *n* confianza *f*; trust *m*; fideicomiso *m*; * *vt* tener confianza en; confiar algo a.

trusted *adj* de confianza.

trustee *n* fideicomisario/ria, curador/a *m/f*.

trustful *adj* fiel; confiado/da.

trustily *adv* fielmente.

trusting *adj* confiado/da.

trustworthy *adj* digno/na de confianza.

trusty *adj* fiel, leal; seguro/ra.

truth *n* verdad *f*; fidelidad *f*; realidad *f*; **in ~** en verdad.

truthful *adj* verídico/ca; veraz.

truthfulness *n* veracidad *f*.

try *vt* examinar, ensayar, probar; experimentar; tentar; inte ntar; juzgar; * *vi* probar; **to ~ on** probarse; **to ~ out** probar; * *n* tentativa *f*; ensayo *m*.

trying *adj* pesado/da; cansado/da.

tub *n* balde *m*, barreño *m*, cubo *m*; tina *f*.

tuba *n* tuba *f*.

tube *n* tubo, cañon, canuto *m*.

tuberculosis *n* tuberculosis *f invar*.

tubing *n* caería *f*.

tuck *n* pliegue *m*; * *vt* poner.

Tuesday *n* martes *m invar*.

tuft *n* mechón *m*; manojo *m*.

tug *vt* remolcar; * *n* remolcador *m*.

tuition *n* matrícula *f*; enseñanza *f*.

tulip *n* tulipán *m*.

tumble *vi* caer, hundirse; revolcarse; * *vt* revolver; volcar; * *n* caída *f*; vuelco *m*.

tumbledown *adj* destartalado/da.

tumbler *n* vaso *m*.

tummy *n* barriga *f*.

tumour *n* tumor *m*.

tumultuous *adj* tumultuoso/sa.

tuna *n* atún *m*.

tune *n* tono *m*; armonia *f*; aria *f*; * *vt* afinar; sintonizar.

tuneful *adj* armonioso/sa, acorde, melodioso/sa.

tuner *n* sintonizador/a *m*.

tunic *n* túnica *f*.

tuning fork *n* (*mus*) diapasón *m*.

tunnel *n* túnel *m*; * *vt* construir un tunel por.

turban *n* turbante *m*.

turbine *n* turbina *f*.

turbulence *n* turbulencia, confusión *f*.

turbulent *adj* turbulento/ta, tumultuoso/sa.

tureen *n* sopera *f*.

turf *n* césped *m*; * *vt* cubrir con césped.

turgid *adj* pesado/da.

turkey *n* pavo *m*.

turmoil *n* disturbio *m*; baraúnda *f*.

turn *vi* volver; cambiar; girar; dar vueltas; volverse a, mudarse, transformarse; **to ~ around** volverse; girar; **to ~ back** volverse; **to ~ down** rechazar; doblar; **to ~ in** acostarse; **to ~ off** *vi* desviarse; *vt* apagar; parar; **to ~ on** encender, prender; poner en marcha; **to ~ out** apagar; **to ~ over** *vi* volverse; *vt* volver; **to ~ up** *vi* llegar; aparecer; *vt* subir; * *n* vuelta *f*; giro *m*; rodeo *m*; turno *m*; vez *f*; inclinación *f*.

turncoat *n* desertor/a, renegado/da *m/f*.

turning *n* vuelta *f*.

turnip *n* nabo *m*.

turn-off *n* salida *f*.

turnout *n* concurrencia *f*.

turnover *n* facturación *f*.

turnpike *n* autopista de peaje *f*.

turnstile *n* torniquete *m*.

turntable *n* plato *m*.

turpentine *n* trementina *f*.

turquoise *n* turquesa *f*.

turret *n* torrecilla, torreta *f*.

turtle *n* tortuga marina *f*.

turtledove *n* tórtola *f*.

tusk *n* colmillo *m*.

tussle *n* pelea *f*.

tutor *n* tutor/a *m/f*; profesor/a *m/f*; * *vt* enseñar, instruir.

tuxedo *n* smoking *m*.

twang *n* gangueo *m*; sonido agudo *m*.

tweezers *npl* tenacillas *fpl*.

twelfth *adj*, *n* duodécimo/ma.

twelve *adj, n* doce.

twentieth *adj, n* vigésimo/ma.

twenty *adj, n* veinte.

twice *adv* dos veces.

twig *n* ramita *f*; * *vi* caer en la cuenta.

twilight *n* crepúsculo *m*.

twin *n* gemelo/la *m/f*.

twine *vi* entrelazarse; caracolear; * *n* bramante *m*.

twinge *vt* punzar, pellizcar; * *n* dolor agudo o punzante *m*; punzada *f*.

twinkle *vi* centellear; parpadear.

twirl *vt* dar vueltas a; * *vi* piruetear; * *n* rotación *f*.

twist *vt* torcer, retorcer; entretejer; * *vi* serpentear; * *n* torsión *f*; vuelta *f*; doblez *f*.

twit *n* (*sl*) tonto/ta *m/f*.

twitch *vi* moverse nerviosamente; * *n* tirón; tic *m*.

twitter *vi* gorjear; * *n* gorjeo *m*.

two *adj, n* dos.

two-door *adj* de dos puertas.

two-faced *adj* falso/sa.

twofold *adj* doble, duplicado/da; * *adv* al doble.

two-seater *n* avión *o* coche de dos plazas *m*.

twosome *n* pareja *f*.

tycoon *n* magnate *m*.

type *n* tipo *m*; letra *f*; modelo *m*; * *vt* escribir a máquina.

typecast *adj* encasillado/da.

typeface *n* tipo *m*.

typescript *n* texto mecanografiado *m*.

typewriter *n* máquina de escribir *f*.

typewritten *adj* mecanografiado/da.

typical *adj* típico/ca.

tyrannical *adj* tiránico/ca.

tyranny *n* tiranía *f*; crueldad *f*.

tyrant *n* tirano/na *m/f*.

tyre *n* neumático *m*; llanta *f*.

tyre pressure *n* presión de los neumáticos *f*.

U

ubiquitous *adj* ubicuo/cua.

udder *n* ubre *f*.

ugh *excl* ¡puaj!

ugliness *n* fealdad *f*.

ugly *adj* feo, fea; peligroso/sa.

ulcer *n* úlcera *f*.

ulterior *adj* ulterior.

ultimate *adj* último/ma; ~**ly** *adv* al final; a fin de cuentas.

ultimatum *n* ultimátum *m*.

ultramarine *n* ultramar *m*; * *adj* ultramarino/na.

ultrasound *n* ultrasonido *m*.

ultrasound scan *n* ecografía *f*.

umbilical cord *n* cordón umbilical *m*.

umbrella *n* paraguas *m invar*.

umpire *n* árbitro/tra *m/f*.

umpteen *adj* enésimos/mas.

unable *adj* incapaz.

unaccompanied *adj* solo/la, sin acompañamiento.

unaccomplished *adj* incompleto/ta, no acabado/da.

unaccountable *adj* inexplicable, extraño/ña.

unaccountably *adv* extrañamente.

unaccustomed *adj* desacostumbrado/da, desusado/da.

unacknowledged *adj* desconocido/da; negado/da.

unacquainted *adj* desconocido/da; ignorado/da.

unadorned *adj* sin adorno.

unadulterated *adj* genuino/na, puro/ra; sin mezcla.

unaffected *adj* sincero/ra, sin afectación.

unaided *adj* sin ayuda.

unaltered *adj* invariado/da.

unambitious *adj* poco/ca ambicioso/sa.

unanimity *n* unanimidad *f*.

unanimous *adj* unánime; **~ly** *adv* unánimemente.

unanswerable *adj* incontrovertible, incontestable.

unanswered *adj* no contestado/da.

unapproachable *adj* inaccesible.

unarmed *adj* inerme, desarmado/da.

unassuming *adj* nada presuntuoso/sa, modesto/ta.

unattached *adj* independiente; disponible.

unattainable *adj* inasequible.

unattended *adj* sin atender.

unauthorized *adj* no autorizado/da.

unavoidable *adj* inevitable.

unavoidably *adv* inevitablemente.

unaware *adj* ignorante.

unawares *adv* inadvertidamente; de improviso.

unbalanced *adj* desequilibrado/da; trastornado/da.

unbearable *adj* insoportable.

unbecoming *adj* indecente, indecoroso/sa.

unbelievable *adj* increíble.

unbend *vi* relajarse; * *vt* enderezar.

unbiased *adj* imparcial.

unblemished *adj* sin mancha, sin tacha, irreprensible.

unborn *adj* no nacido/da.

unbreakable *adj* irrompible.

unbroken *adj* intacto/ta; indómito/ta; entero/ra; no batido/da.

unbutton *vt* desabotonar.

uncalled-for *adj* fuera de lugar.

uncanny *adj* extraordinario/ria.

unceasing *adj* sin cesar, continuo/nua.

unceremonious *adj* brusco/ca.

uncertain *adj* incierto/ta, dudoso/sa.

uncertainty *n* incertidumbre *f*.

unchangeable *adj* inmutable.

unchanged *adj* no alterado/da.

unchanging *adj* inalterable, immutable.

uncharitable *adj* nada caritativo/va, duro/ra.

unchecked *adj* desenfrenado/da, incontrolado/da.

unchristian *adj* poco cristiano/na.

uncivil *adj* grosero/ra, descortés.

uncivilized *adj* tosco/ca, salvaje, incivilizado/da.

uncle *n* tío.

uncomfortable *adj* incómodo/da; molesto/ta.

uncomfortably *adv* incómodamente; inquietantemente.

uncommon *adj* raro/ra, extraordinario/ria.

uncompromising *adj* irreconciliable.

unconcerned *adj* indiferente.

unconditional *adj* sin condiciones, incondicional.

unconfined *adj* libre, ilimitado/da.

unconfirmed *adj* no confirmado/da.

unconnected *adj* inconexo/xa.

unconquerable *adj* invencible, insuperable.

unconscious *adj* inconsciente; **~ly** *adv* inconscientemente.

unconstrained *adj* libre, voluntario/ria.

uncontrollable *adj* incontrolable; desenfrenado/da.

unconventional *adj* poco convencional.

unconvincing *adj* no convincente.

uncork *vt* destapar.

uncorrected *adj* sin corregir, no corregido/da.

uncouth *adj* grosero/ra, zafio/fia.

uncover *vt* descubrir.

uncultivated *adj* inculto/ta.

uncut *adj* no cortado/da, entero/ra.

undamaged *adj* ileso/sa, libre de daño.

undaunted *adj* intrépido/da.

undecided *adj* indeciso/sa.

undefiled *adj* impoluto/ta, puro/ra.

undeniable *adj* innegable, incontestable; **~bly** *adv* indubitablemente.

under *prep* debajo de; menos de; según; * *adv* debajo.

under-age *adj* menor de edad.

undercharge *vt* cobrar de menos.

underclothing *n* ropa íntima *f*.

undercoat *n* primera mano *f*.

undercover *adj* clandestino/na.

undercurrent *n* corriente subyacente *f*.

undercut *vt* vender más barato que.

underdeveloped *adj* subdesarrollado/da.

underdog *n* desvalido/da *m/f*.

underdone *adj* poco cocido/da.

underestimate *vt* subestimar.

undergo *vt* sufrir; sostener.

undergraduate *n* estudiante universitario/ria *m/f*.

underground *n* metro *m*; movimiento clandestino *m*.

undergrowth *n* soto *m*, maleza *f*.

underhand *adv* clandestinamente; * *adj* secreto/ta, clandestino/na.

underlie *vi* estar debajo.

underline *vt* subrayar.

undermine *vt* minar.

underneath *adv* debajo; * *prep* debajo de.

underpaid *adj* mal pagado/da.

underpants *npl* calzoncillos *mpl*.

underprivileged *adj* desvalido/da.

underrate *vt* menospreciar.

undersecretary *n* subsecretario/ria *m/f*.

underside *n* revés *m*.

understand *vt* entender, comprender.

understandable *adj* comprensible.

understanding *n* entendimiento *m*; inteligencia *f*; conocimiento *m*; correspondencia *f*; * *adj* comprensivo/va.

understatement *n* subestimación *f*; modestia *f*.

undertake *vt, vi* emprender.

undertaker *n* director de pompas fúnebres.

undertaking *n* empresa *f*; empeño *m*.

undervalue *vt* menospreciar.

underwater *adj* submarino/na; * *adv* bajo el agua.

underwear *n* ropa íntima *f*.

underworld *n* hampa *f*.

underwrite *vt* suscribir; asegurar contra riesgos.

underwriter *n* asegurador/a *m/f*.

undeserved *adj* inmerecido/da; **~ly** *adv* sin haberlo merecido.

undeserving *adj* indigno/na.

undesirable *adj* indeseable.

undetermined *adj* indeterminado/da, indeciso/sa.

undigested *adj* no digerido/da.

undiminished *adj* entero/ra, no disminuido/da.

undisciplined *adj* indisciplinado/da.

undisguised *adj* sin disfraz, cándido/da, sincero/ra.

undismayed *adj* intrépido/da.

undisputed *adj* incontestable.

undisturbed *adj* quieto/ta, tranquilo/la.

undivided *adj* indiviso/sa, entero/ra.

undo *vt* deshacer, destar, descoser.

undoing *n* ruina *f*.

undoubted *adj* indudable; **~ly** *adv* indudablemente.

undress *vi* desnudarse.

undue *adj* indebido/da; injusto/ta.

undulating *adj* ondulante.

unduly *adv* indebidamente.

undying *adj* inmortal.

unearth *vt* desenterrar.

unearthly *adj* inverosímil.

uneasiness *n* inquietud *f*; zozobra *f*.

uneasy *adj* inquieto/ta, desasosegado/da; incomodo/da.

uneducated *adj* ignorante.

unemployed *adj* desmpleado/da, parado/da; **~ person** parado/da *m/f*.

unemployment *n* desempleo, paro *m*.

unending *adj* interminable.

unenlightened *adj* no iluminado/da.

unenviable *adj* poco envidiable.

unequal *adj*, **~ly** *adv* desigual(mente).

unequalled *adj* incomparable.

unerring *adj*, **~ly** *adv* infalible(mente).

uneven *adj* desigual; impar; **~ly** *adv* desigualmente.

unexpected *adj* inesperado/da; inopinado/da; **~ly** *adv* de repente; inopinadamente.

unexplored *adj* inexplorado/da, no descubierto/ta.

unfailing *adj* infalible, seguro/ra.

unfair *adj* falso/sa; injusto/ta; **~ly** *adv* injustamente.

unfaithful *adj* infiel, pérfido/da.

unfaithfulness *n* infidelidad, perfidia *f*.

unfaltering *adj* firme, asegurado/da.

unfamiliar *adj* desacostumbrado/da, poco común.

unfashionable *adj* pasado/da de moda; **~bly** *adv* contra la moda.

unfasten *vt* desatar, soltar, aflojar.

unfathomable *adj* insondable, impenetrable.

unfavourable *adj* desfavorable.

unfeeling *adj* insensible, duro/ra de corazón.

unfinished *adj* imperfecto/ta, no acabado/da.

unfit *adj* indispuesto/ta; incapaz.

unfold *vt* desplegar; revelar; * *vi* abrirse.

unforeseen *adj* imprevisto/ta.

unforgettable *adj* inolvidable.

unforgivable *adj* imperdonable.

unforgiving *adj* implacable.

unfortunate *adj* desafortunado/da, infeliz; **~ly** *adv* por desgracia, infelizmente.

unfounded *adj* sin fundamento.

unfriendly *adj* antipático/ca.

unfruitful *adj* estéril; infructuoso/sa.

unfurnished *adj* sin muebles; desprovisto/ta.

ungainly *adj* desmañado/da.

ungentlemanly *adj* indigno/na de un hombre bien criado.

ungovernable *adj* indomable, ingobernable.

ungrateful *adj* ingrato/ta; desagradable; **~ly** *adv* ingratamente.

ungrounded *adj* infundado/da.

unhappily *adv* infelizmente.

unhappiness *n* infelicidad *f*.

unhappy *adj* infeliz.

unharmed *adj* ileso/sa, sano/na y salvo/va.

unhealthy *adj* malsano/na; enfermizo/za.

unheard-of *adj* inaudito/ta, extraño/ña, sin ejemplo.

unheeding *adj* negligente; distraído/da.

unhitch *vt* (beasts) desaparejar.

unhook *vt* desenganchar; descolgar; desabrochar.

unhoped (for) *adj* inesperado/da.

unhurt *adj* ileso/sa.

unicorn *n* unicornio *m*.

uniform *adj*, **~ly** *adv* uniforme(mente); * *n* uniforme *m*.

uniformity *n* uniformidad *f*.

unify *vt* unificar.

unimaginable *adj* inimaginable.

unimpaired *adj* no disminuido/da, no alterado/da.

unimportant *adj* poco importante.

uninformed *adj* desinformado/da.

uninhabitable *adj* inhabitable.

uninhabited *adj* inhabitado/da, desierto/ta.

uninjured *adj* ileso/sa, no dañado/da.

unintelligible *adj* ininteligible.

unintelligibly *adv* de modo ininteligible.

unintentional *adj* involuntario/ria, no intencionado/da.

uninterested *adj* desinteresado/da.

uninteresting *adj* poco interesante.

uninterrupted *adj* sin interrupción, continuo/nua.

uninvited *adj* no convivado/da.

union *n* unión *f*; sindicato *m*.

unionist *n* sindicalista *m/f*.

unique *adj* único/ca, uno/na, singular.

unison *n* unísono *m*.

unit *n* unidad *f*.

unitarian *n* unitario/ria *m/f*.

unite *vt* (*vi*) unir(se), juntarse; (*fig*) zurcir.

unitedly *adv* unidamente, de acuerdo.

United States (of America) *npl* Estados Unidos (de América) *mpl*.

unity *n* unidad, concordia, conformidad *f*.

universal *adj*, **~ly** *adv* universal(mente).

universe *n* universo *m*.

university *n* universidad *f*.

unjust *adj* injusto/ta; **~ly** *adv* injustamente.

unkempt *adj* despeinado/da; descuidado/da.

unkind *adj* poco amable; severo/ra.

unknowingly *adv* sin saberlo.

unknown *adj* incógnito/ta.

unlawful *adj* ilegal; **~ly** *adv* ilegalmente.

unlawfulness *n* ilegalidad *f*.

unleash *vt* desencadenar.

unless *conj* a menos que, si no.

unlicensed *adj* sin licencia.

unlike, unlikely *adj* diferente; improbable; inverosímil.

unlikelihood *n* inverisimilitud *f*.

unlimited *adj* ilimitado/da.

unlisted *adj* que no viene en la guía.

unload *vt* descargar.

unlock *vt* abrir.

unluckily *adv* desafortunadamente.

unlucky *adj* desafortunado/da.

unmanageable *adj* inmanejable, intratable.

unmannered *adj* rudo/da, brutal, grosero/ra.

unmannerly *adj* malcriado/da, descortés.

unmarried *adj* soltero/ra.

unmask *vt* desenmascarar.

unmentionable *adj* que no se puede mencionar.

unmerited *adj* desmerecido/da.

unmindful *adj* olvidadizo/za, negligente.

unmistakable *adj* inconfundible; **~ly** *adv* indudablemente.

unmitigated *adj* absoluto/ta.

unmoved *adj* inmoto, firme.

unnatural *adj* antinatural; perverso/sa; afectado/da.

unnecessary *adj* inútil, innecesario/ria.

unneighbourly *adj* poco atento/ta con sus vecinos; descortés.

unnoticed *adj* inadvertido/da.

unnumbered *adj* innumerable.

unobserved *adj* no observado/da.

unobtainable *adj* inconseguible; inexistente.

unobtrusive *adj* modesto/ta.

unoccupied *adj* desocupado/da.

unoffending *adj* sencillo/lla, inocente.

unofficial *adj* no oficial.

unorthodox *adj* heterodoxo/xa.

unpack *vt* desempacar; desenvolver.

unpaid *adj* no pagado/da.

unpalatable *adj* desabrido/da, desgradable.

unparalleled *adj* sin paralelo; sin par.

unpleasant *adj*, **~ly** *adv* desagradable(mente).

unpleasantness *n* desagrado *m*.

unplug *vt* desconectar.

unpolished *adj* que no está pulido/da; rudo/da, grosero/ra.

unpopular *adj* impopular.

unpractised *adj* inexperto/ta, no versado/da.

unprecedented *adj* sin precedentes.

unpredictable *adj* imprevisible.

unprejudiced *adj* imparcial.

unprepared *adj* no preparado/da.

unprofitable *adj* inútil, vano/na; poco lucrativo/va.

unprotected *adj* desvalido/da, sin protección.

unpublished *adj* no publicado/da; inédito/ta.

unpunished *adj* impune.

unqualified *adj* sin títulos; total.

unquestionable *adj* indubitable, indisputable; **~ly** *adv* sin duda, sin disputa.

unquestioned *adj* incontestable, no preguntado/da.

unravel *vt* desenredar.

unread *adj* no leído/da; ignorante.

unreal *adj* irreal.

unrealistic *adj* poco realista.

unreasonable *adj* poco razonable; disparatado/da.

unreasonably *adv* poco razonablemente; disparatadamente.

unrelated *adj* sin relación; inconexo/xa.

unrelenting *adj* implacable.

unreliable *adj* poco fiable.

unremitting *adj* constante, incansable.

unrepentant *adj* impenitente.

unreserved *adj* sin restricción; franco/ca; **~ly** *adv* abiertamente.

unrest *n* malestar *m*; disturbios *mpl*.

unrestrained *adj* desenfrenado/da; ilimitado/da.

unripe *adj* inmaduro/ra.

unrivalled *adj* sin rival, sin igual.

unroll *vt* desenrollar.

unruliness *n* turbulencia *f*; desenfreno *m*.

unruly *adj* desenfrenado/da.

unsafe *adj* inseguro/ra, peligroso/sa.

unsatisfactory *adj* insatisfactorio/ria.

unsavoury *adj* desabrido/da, insípido/da.

unscathed *adj* ileso/sa.

unscrew *vt* destornillar.

unscrupulous *adj* sin escrúpulos.

unseasonable *adj* intempestivo/va, fuera de propósito.

unseemly *adj* indecente.

unseen *adj* invisible.

unselfish *adj* desinteresado/da.

unsettle *vt* perturbar.

unsettled *adj* inquieto/ta; inestable; variable.

unshaken *adj* firme, estable.

unshaven *adj* sin afeitar.

unsightly *adj* desagradable a la vista, feo/a.

unskilful *adj* inhábil, poco mañoso/sa.

unskilled *adj* no cualificado/da.

unsociable *adj* insociable, intratable.

unspeakable *adj* inefable, indecible.

unstable *adj* instable, inconstante.

unsteadily *adv* ligeramente, inconstantemente.

unsteady *adj* inestable.

unstudied *adj* no estudiado/da; no premeditado/da.

unsuccessful *adj* infeliz, desafortunado/da; **~ly** *adv* sin éxito.

unsuitable *adj* inapropiado/da; inoportuno/na.

unsure *adj* ineguro/ra.

unsympathetic *adj* poco comprensivo/va.

untamed *adj* indomado/da.

untapped *adj* sin explotar.

untenable *adj* insostenible.

unthinkable *adj* inconcebible.

unthinking *adj* desatento/ta, irreflexivo/va.

untidiness *n* desaliño *m*.

untidy *adj* desordenado/da; sucio/cia.

untie *vt* desatar, deshacer, soltar, zafar.

until *prep* hasta; * *conj* hasta que.

untimely *adj* intempestivo/va.

untiring *adj* incansable.

untold *adj* nunca dicho/cha; indecible; incalculable.

untouched *adj* intacto/ta.

untoward *adj* impropio/pia; adverso/sa.

untried *adj* no ensayado/da *o* probado/da.

untroubled *adj* no perturbado/da, tranquilo/la.

untrue *adj* falso/sa.

untrustworthy *adj* indigno/na de confianza.

untruth *n* falsedad, mentira *f*.

unused *adj* sin usar, no usado/da.

unusual *adj* inusual, inusitado/da, raro/ra; **~ly** *adv* inusitadamente, raramente.

unveil *vt* quitar el velo, descubrir.

unwavering *adj* inquebrantable.

unwelcome *adj* desagradable, inoportuno/na.

unwell *adj* enfermizo/za, malo/la.

unwieldy *adj* pesado/da.

unwilling *adj* desinclinado/da; **~ly** *adv* de mala gana.

unwillingness *n* mala gana, repugnancia *f*.

unwind *vt* desenredar, desenmarañar; * *vi* relajarse.

unwise *adj* imprudente.

unwitting *adj* inconsciente.

unworkable *adj* poco práctico/ca.

unworthy *adj* indigno/na.

unwrap *vt* desenvolver.

unwritten *adj* no escrito/ta.

up *adv* arriba, en lo alto; levantado/da; * *prep* hacia; hasta.

upbraid *vt* zaherir.

upbringing *n* educación *f*.

update *vt* poner al día.

upheaval *n* agitación *f*.

uphill *adj* difícil, penoso/sa; * *adv* cuesta arriba.

uphold *vt* sostener, apoyar.

upholstery *n* tapicería *f*.

upkeep *n* mantenimiento *m*.

uplift *vt* levantar.

upon *prep* sobre, encima.

upper adj superior; más elevado/da.
upper-class adj de la clase alta.
upper-hand n (fig) superioridad f.
uppermost adj más alto/ta, supremo/ma; **to be ~** predominar.
upright adj derecho/cha, perpendicular, recto/ta; puesto/ta en pie; honrado/da.
uprising n sublevación f.
uproar n tumulto, alboroto m.
uproot vt desarraigar.
upset vt trastornar; derramar, volcar; * n revés m; trastorno m; * adj molesto/ta; revuelto/ta.
upshot n remate m; fin m; conclusión f.
upside-down adv al revés.
upstairs adv arriba.
upstart n advenedizo/za m/f.
uptight adj nervioso/sa.
up-to-date adj al día.
upturn n mejora f.
upward adj ascendente; **~s** adv hacia arriba.
urban adj urbano/na.
urbane adj cortés.
urchin n golfillo/lla m/f.
urge vt animar; * n impulso m; deseo m.
urgency n urgencia f.
urgent adj urgente.
urinal n orinal m.

urinate vi orinar.
urine n orina f.
urn n urna f.
us pn nos; nosotros, nosotras.
usage n tratamiento m; uso m.
use n uso m; utilidad, práctica f; * vt usar, emplear.
used adj usado/da.
useful adj, **~ly** adv útil(mente).
usefulness n utilidad f.
useless adj inútil; **~ly** adv inútilmente.
uselessness n inutilidad f.
user-friendly adj fácil de utilizar.
usher n ujier m/f; acomodador/a m/f.
usherette n acomodadora f.
usual adj usual, común, normal; **~ly** adv normalmente.
usurer n usurero/ra m/f.
usurp vt usurpar.
usury n usura f.
utensil n utensilio m.
uterus n útero m.
utility n utilidad f.
utilize vt utilizar.
utmost adj extremo/ma, sumo/ma; último/ma.
utter adj total; todo; entero/ra; * vt proferir; expresar; publicar.
utterance n expresion f.
utterly adv enteramente, del todo.

V

vacancy n cuarto libre m, vacante f.
vacant adj vacío/cía; desocupado/da; vacante.
vacant lot n solar m.
vacate vt desocupar; dejar.
vacation n vacaciones fpl.
vaccinate vt vacunar.

vaccination n vacunación f.
vaccine n vacuna f.
vacuous adj vacío/cía, vacuo/cua.
vacuum n vacío m.
vacuum flask n termo m.
vagina n vagina f.
vagrant n vagabundo/da m/f.

vague *adj* vago/ga; **~ly** *adv* vagamente.

vain *adj* vano/na, inútil; vanidoso/sa.

valet *n* criado *m*.

valiant *adj* valiente, valeroso/sa.

valid *adj* válido/da.

valley *n* valle *m*.

valour *n* valor, aliento, brío, esfuerzo *m*.

valuable *adj* valioso/sa; **~s** *npl* objetos de valor *mpl*.

valuation *n* tasa, valuación *f*.

value *n* valor, precio *m*; * *vt* valuar; estimar, apreciar.

valued *adj* apreciado/da.

valve *n* válvula *f*.

vampire *n* vampiro *m*.

van *n* camioneta *f*.

vandal *n* gamberro/rra *m/f*.

vandalism *n* vandalismo *m*.

vandalize *vt* dañar.

vanguard *n* vanguardia *f*.

vanilla *n* vainilla *f*.

vanish *vi* desvanecerse, desaparecer.

vanity *n* vanidad *f*.

vanity case *n* neceser *m*.

vanquish *vt* vencer, conquistar.

vantage point *n* punto panorámico *m*.

vapour *n* vapor *m*; exhalación *f*.

variable *adj* variable; voluble.

variance *n* discordia, desavenencia *f*.

variation *n* variación *f*.

varicose vein *n* variz *f*.

varied *adj* variado/da.

variety *n* variedad *f*.

variety show *n* espectáculo de variedades *m*.

various *adj* vario/ria, diverso/sa, diferente.

varnish *n* barniz *m*; * *vt* barnizar.

vary *vt, vi* variar; cambiar.

vase *n* florero, jarrón *m*.

vast *adj* vasto/ta; inmenso/sa.

vat *n* tina *f*.

vault *n* bóveda *f*; cueva *f*; caverna *f*; * *vt* saltar.

veal *n* ternera *f*.

veer *vi* (*mar*) virar.

vegetable *adj* vegetal; * *n* vegetal *m*; **~s** *pl* verduras *fpl*.

vegetable garden *n* huerta *f*.

vegetarian *n* vegetariano/na *m/f*.

vegetate *vi* vegetar.

vegetation *n* vegetación *f*.

vehemence *n* vehemencia, violencia *f*.

vehement *adj* vehemente, violento/ta; **~ly** *adv* vehementemente.

vehicle *n* vehículo *m*; **all-terrain ~** todoterreno *m*.

veil *n* velo *m*; * *vt* encubrir, ocultar.

vein *n* vena *f*; cavidad *f*; inclinación del ingenio *f*.

velocity *n* velocidad *f*.

velvet *n* terciopelo *m*.

vending machine *n* máquina expendedora *f*.

vendor *n* vendedor/a *m/f*.

veneer *n* chapa *f*; barniz *m*.

venerable *adj* venerable.

venerate *vt* venerar, honrar.

veneration *n* veneración *f*.

venereal *adj* venéreo.

vengeance *n* venganza *f*.

venial *adj* venial.

venison *n* (carne de) venado *f*.

venom *n* veneno *m*.

venomous *adj* venenoso/sa; **~ly** *adv* venenosamente.

vent *n* respiradero *m*; salida *f*; * *vt* desahogar.

ventilate *vt* ventilar.

ventilation *n* ventilación *f*.

ventilator *n* ventilador *m*.

ventriloquist *n* ventrílocuo/cua *m/f*.

venture *n* empresa *f*; * *vi* aventurarse; * *vt* aventurar, arriesgar.

venue *n* lugar de reunión, local *m*.

veranda(h) *n* terraza *f*, porche *m*.

verb *n* (*gr*) verbo *m*.

verbal *adj* verbal, literal; **~ly** *adv* verbalmente.

verbatim *adv* literalmente.

verbose *adj* verboso/sa.

verdant *adj* verde.

verdict *n* (*law*) veredicto *m*; opinión *f*.

verification *n* verificación *f*.

verify *vt* verificar.

veritable *adj* verdadero/ra.

vermicelli *npl* fideos *mpl*.

vermin *n* bichos *mpl*.

vermouth *n* vermut *m*.

versatile *adj* versátil; polifacético/ca.

verse *n* verso *m*; versículo *m*.

versed *adj* versado/da.

version *n* versión *f*.

versus *prep* contra.

vertebra *n* vértebra *f*.

vertebral, vertebrate *adj* vertebral.

vertex *n* cenit, vértice *m*.

vertical *adj*, **~ly** *adv* vertical(mente).

vertigo *n* vértigo *m*.

verve *n* brío *m*.

very *adj* idéntico/ca, mismo/ma; * *adv* muy, mucho, sumamente.

vessel *n* vasija *f*; vaso *m*; barco *m*.

vest *n* camiseta *f*.

vestibule *n* vestíbulo *m*.

vestige *n* vestigio *m*.

vestment *n* vestido *m*; vestidura *f*.

vestry *n* sacristía *f*.

vet *n* veterinario/ria *m/f*.

veteran *adj*, *n* veterano/na *m/f*.

veterinary *adj* veterinario/ria.

veterinary surgeon *n* veterinario/ria *m/f*.

veto *n* veto *m*; * *vt* vetar.

vex *vt* molestar.

vexed *adj* molesto/ta; controvertido/da.

via *prep* por.

viaduct *n* viaducto *m*.

vial *n* ampolla *f*, vial *m*.

vibrate *vi* vibrar.

vibration *n* vibración *f*.

vicarious *adj* sustituto/ta.

vice *n* vicio *m*; culpa *f*; tornillo *m*.

vice-chairman *n* vice-presidente *m*.

vice-chancellor (of a university) *n* rector/ra *m/f*.

vice-chancellorship *n* rectorado *m*.

vice versa *adv* viceversa.

vicinity *n* vecindad, proximidad *f*; **immediate ~** inmediaciones *fpl*.

vicious *adj* vicioso/sa; **~ly** *adv* de manera viciosa.

victim *n* víctima *f*.

victimize *vt* victimizar.

victor *n* vencedor/a *m/f*.

victorious *adj* victorioso/sa.

victory *n* victoria *f*.

video *n* vídeo *m*.

video camera *n* videocámara *f*.

video cassette *n* videocasete *m*.

video game *n* videojuego *m*.

video tape *n* cinta de vídeo *f*.

vie *vi* competir.

view *n* vista *f*; perspectiva *f*; aspecto *m*; opinión *f*; paisaje *m*; * *vt* mirar; ver; examinar.

viewer *n* televidente *m/f*.

viewfinder *n* visor *m*.

viewpoint *n* punto de vista *m*.

vigil *n* vela *f*; vigilia *f*.

vigilance *n* vigilancia *f*.

vigilant *adj* vigilante, atento/ta.

vigorous *adj* vigoroso/sa; **~ly** *adv* vigorosamente.

vigour *n* vigor *m*; energía *f*.

vile *adj* vil, bajo/ja; asqueroso/sa.

vilify *vt* envilecer.

villa *n* chalet *m*; casa de campo *f*.

village *n* aldea *f*.

villager n aldeano/na m/f.
villain n malvado/da m/f.
vindicate vt vindicar, defender.
vindication n vindicación f; justificación f.
vindictive adj vengativo/va.
vine n vid f.
vinegar n vinagre m.
vineyard n viña f.
vintage n vendimia f.
vinyl n vinilo m.
viola n (mus) viola f.
violate vt violar.
violation n violación f.
violence n violencia f.
violent adj violento/ta; ~ly adv violentamente.
violet n (bot) violeta f.
violin n (mus) violín m.
violinist n violinista m/f.
violoncello, cello n (mus) violoncelo, violonchelo m.
VIP n vip m/f.
viper n víbora f.
virgin n virgen f; * adj virgen.
virginity n virginidad f.
Virgo n Virgo f (signo del zodiaco).
virile adj viril.
virility n virilidad f.
virtual adj, ~ly adv virtual(mente).
virtue n virtud f.
virtuous adj virtuoso/sa.
virulent adj virulento/ta.
virus n virus m invar.
visa n visado m, visa f.
vis-à-vis prep con respecto a.
viscous adj viscoso/sa, glutinoso/sa.
visibility n visibilidad f.
visible adj visible.
visibly adv visiblemente.
vision n vista f; visión f.
visit vt visitar; * n visita f.
visitation n visitación, visita f.

visiting hours npl horas de visita fpl.
visitor n visitante m/f; turista m/f.
visor n visera f.
vista n vista, perspectiva f.
visual adj visual.
visual aid n medio visual m.
visualize vt imaginarse.
vital adj vital; esencial; imprescindible; ~ly adv vitalmente; ~s npl partes vitales fpl.
vitality n vitalidad f.
vital statistics npl medidas vitales fpl.
vitamin n vitamina f.
vitiate vt viciar, corromper.
vivacious adj vivaz.
vivid adj vivo/va; gráfico/ca; intenso/sa; ~ly adv vivamente; gráficamente.
vivisection n vivisección f.
vixen n zorra f.
vocabulary n vocabulario m.
vocal adj vocal.
vocation n vocación f; oficio m; carrera, profesión f; ~al adj profesional.
vocative n vocativo m.
vociferous adj vocinglero/ra, clamoroso/sa.
vodka n vodka m.
vogue n moda f; boga f.
voice n voz f; * vt expresar.
void adj nulo * n vacío m.
volatile adj volátil; voluble.
volcanic adj volcánico/ca.
volcano n volcán m.
volition n voluntad f.
volley n descarga f; salva f; rociada f; volea f.
volleyball n voleibol m.
volt n voltio m.
voltage n voltaje m.
voluble adj locuaz.
volume n volumen m; libro m.

voluntarily adv voluntariamente.

voluntary adj voluntario/ria.

volunteer n voluntario/ria m/f; * vi ofrecerse voluntariamente.

voluptuous adj voluptuoso/sa.

vomit vt, vi vomitar; * n vómito m.

voracious adj, ~ly adv voraz(mente).

vortex n remolino, torbellino m.

vote n voto, sufragio m; votación f; * vt votar.

voter n votante m/f.

voting n votación f.

voucher n vale m.

vow n voto m; * vi jurar.

vowel n vocal f.

voyage n viaje m; travesía f.

vulgar adj vulgar, ordinario/ria; de mal gusto.

vulgarity n vulgaridad f, grosería f; mal gusto m.

vulnerable adj vulnerable.

vulture n buitre m.

W

wad n fajo m; bolita f.

waddle vi anadear.

wade vi vadear.

wafer n galleta f; oblea f.

waffle n gofre m.

waft vt hacer flotar; * vi flotar.

wag vt menear; * vi menearse.

wage n salario m.

wage earner n asalariado/da m/f.

wager n apuesta f; * vt apostar.

wages npl salario m.

waggish adj zumbón/ona.

waggle vt menear.

wagon n carro m; (rail) vagón m.

wail n lamento, gemido m; * vi gemir.

waist n cintura f.

waistline n talle m.

wait vi esperar; * n espera f; pausa f.

waiter n camarero m.

waiting list n lista de espera f.

waiting room n sala de espera f.

waive vt suspender.

wake vi despertarse; * vt despertar; * n vela f; (mar) estela f.

wakefulness n vela f.

waken vt (vi) despertar(se).

walk vt, vi pasear, ir; andar, caminar; * n paseo m; caminata f.

walker n paseante m/f.

walkie-talkie n walkie-talkie m.

walking n paseos mpl.

walking stick n bastón m.

walkout n huelga f.

walkover n (sl) pan comido m.

walkway n paseo m.

wall n pared f; muralla f; muro m.

walled adj amurallado/da.

wallet n cartera, billetera f.

wallflower n (bot) alhelí m.

wallow vi revolcarse.

wallpaper n papel pintado m.

walnut n nogal m; nuez f.

walrus n morsa f.

waltz n vals m invar.

wan adj pálido/da.

wand n varita mágica f.

wander vt, vi errar; vagar.

wane vi menguar.

want vt querer; necesitar; faltar; * n necesidad f; falta f.

wanting adj falto/ta, defectuoso/sa.

wanton adj lascivo/va; juguetón/ona.

war n guerra f.

ward n sala f; pupilo/la m/f.

wardrobe n guardarropa f, ropero m.

warehouse n almacén m.

warfare n guerra f.
warhead n ojiva f.
warily adv prudentemente.
wariness n cautela, prudencia f.
warm adj cálido/da; caliente; efusivo/va; * vt calentar; **to ~ up** vi calentarse; entrar en calor; acalorarse; vt calentar.
warm-hearted adj afectuoso/sa.
warmly adv con calor, ardientemente.
warmth n calor m.
warn vt avisar; advertir.
warning n aviso m.
warning light n luz de advertencia f.
warp vi torcerse; * vt torcer; pervertir.
warrant n orden judicial f; mandamiento judicial m.
warranty n garantía f.
warren n conejero m.
warrior n guerrero/ra, soldado/da m/f.
warship n barco de guerra m.
wart n verruga f.
wary adj cauto/ta, prudente.
wash vt lavar; bañar; * vi lavarse; * n lavado m; baño m.
washable adj lavable.
washbowl n lavabo m.
washcloth n manopla f.
washer n arandela f.
washing n ropa sucia f; colada f.
washing machine n lavadora f.
washing-up n fregado m.
wash out n (sl) fracaso m.
washroom n aseos mpl.
wasp n avispa f.
wastage n desgaste m; pérdida f.
waste vt malgastar; destruir, arruinar; perder; * vi gastarse; * n desperdicio m; destrucción f; despilfarro m; basura f; yermo m.

wasteful adj destructivo/va; pródigo/ga; **~ly** adv pródigamente.
wasteland n yermo m.
waste paper n papel usado m.
waste pipe n tubo de desagüe m.
watch n reloj m; centinela f; guardia f; * vt mirar; ver; vigilar; tener cuidado; * vi ver; montar guardia.
watchdog n perro guardián m.
watchful adj vigilante; **~ly** adv vigilantemente.
watchmaker n relojero/ra m/f.
watchman n sereno m; vigilante m.
watchtower n atalaya, garita f.
watchword n santo y seña m.
water n agua f; * vt regar, humedecer, mojar; * vi hacerse agua.
water closet n váter m.
watercolour n acuarela f.
waterfall n cascada f.
water heater n calentador de agua m.
watering-can n regadera f.
water level n nivel del agua m.
water lily n ninfea f.
water line n línea de flotación f.
waterlogged adj anegado/da.
water main n cañería del agua f.
watermark n filigrana f.
water melon n sandía f.
watershed n momento crítico m.
watertight adj impermeable.
waterworks npl depuradora de agua f.
watery adj aguado/da; desvaído/da; lloroso/sa.
watt n vatio m.
wave n ola, onda f; oleada f; senal f; * vi agitar la mano; ondear; * vt agitar.
wavelength n longitud de onda f.
waver vi vacilar, balancear.
wavering adj inconstante.
wavy adj ondulado/da.
wax n cera f; * vt encerar; * vi crecer.

wax paper n papel de cera m.

waxworks n museo de cera m.

way n camino m; vía f; ruta f; modo m; recorrido m; **to give** ~ ceder.

waylay vt salir al paso.

wayward adj caprichoso/sa.

we pn nosotros, nosotras.

weak adj, **~ly** adv débil(mente).

weaken vt debilitar.

weakling n enclenque m/f.

weakness n debilidad f; punto débil m.

weal, wheal n roncha f.

wealth n riqueza f; bienes mpl.

wealthy adj rico/ca.

wean vt destetar.

weapon n arma f.

wear vt gastar, consumir; usar, llevar; * vi consumirse; **to ~ away** vt gastar; vi desgastarse; **to ~ down** gastar; agotar; **to ~ off** pasar; **to ~ out** desgastar; agotar; * n uso m; desgaste m.

weariness n cansancio m; fatiga f; enfado m.

wearisome adj tedioso/sa.

weary adj cansado/da, fatigado/da; tedioso/sa.

weasel n comadreja f.

weather n tiempo m; **to ~ out** vt aguantar, sufrir, superar.

weather-beaten adj curtido/da.

weather cock n gallo de campanario m; veleta f.

weather forecast n boletín meteorológico m.

weave vt tejer; trenzar; (fig) zurcir.

weaving n tejido m.

web n telaraña f; membrana f; red f.

wed vt (vi) casar(se).

wedding n boda f; nupcias fpl; casamiento m.

wedding day n día de la boda m.

wedding dress n traje de novia m.

wedding present n regalo de boda m.

wedding ring n alianza f.

wedge n cuña f; * vt acuñar; apretar.

wedlock n matrimonio m.

Wednesday n miércoles m invar.

wee adj pequeñito/ta.

weed n mala hierba f; * vt escardar.

weedkiller n herbicida m.

weedy adj lleno/na de malas hierbas.

week n semana f; **tomorrow ~** mañana en una semana; **yesterday ~** ayer hace ocho días.

weekday n día laborable m.

weekend n fin de semana m.

weekly adj semanal; * adv semanalmente, por semana.

weep vt, vi llorar; lamentar.

weeping willow n sauce llorón m.

weigh vt, vi pesar.

weight n peso m.

weightily adv pesadamente.

weightlifter n levantador/a de pesas m/f.

weighty adj ponderoso/sa; importante.

welcome adj bienvenido/da; ~! ¡bienvenido!; * n bienvenida f; * vt dar la bienvenida a.

weld vt soldar; * n soldadura f.

welfare n prosperidad f; bienestar m; subsidio de paro m.

welfare state n estado del bienestar m.

well n fuente f; manantial m; pozo m; * adj bueno/na, sano/na; * adv bien, felizmente; favorablemente; suficientemente; convenientemente; **as ~ as** así como, además de, lo mismo que.

well-behaved adj bien educado/da.

wellbeing n felicidad, prosperidad f.

well-bred *adj* bien criado/da, bien educado/da.

well-built *adj* fornido/da.

well-deserved *adj* merecido/da.

well-dressed *adj* bien vestido/da.

well-known *adj* conocido/da.

well-mannered *adj* educado/da.

well-meaning *adj* bien intencionado/da.

well-off *adj* acomodado/da.

well-to-do *adj* acomodado/da.

well-wisher *n* partidario/ria *m/f*.

wench *n* mozuela, cantonera *f*.

west *n* oeste, occidente *m*; * *adj* occidental; * *adv* hacia el oeste.

westerly, western *adj* occidental.

westward *adv* hacia el oeste.

wet *adj* húmedo/da, mojado/da; * *n* humedad *f*; * *vt* mojar, hume decer.

wet-nurse *n* ama de leche *f*.

wet suit *n* traje de buzo *m*.

whack *vt* aporrear; * *n* golpe *m*.

whale *n* ballena *f*.

wharf *n* muelle *m*.

what *pn* que, ¿qué?, el que, la que, lo que; * *adj* ¿qué?; * *excl* ¡cómo!

whatever *pn* cualquier, cualquiera cosa que, lo que sea.

wheat *n* trigo *m*.

wheedle *vt* halagar, engañar con lisonjas, sonsacar.

wheedler *n* zalamero/ra *m/f*.

wheel *n* rueda *f*; volante *m*; timón *m*; * *vt* (hacer) rodar; volver, girar; * *vi* rodar.

wheelbarrow *n* carretilla *f*.

wheelchair *n* silla de ruedas *f*.

wheel clamp *n* cepo *m*.

wheeze *vi* jadear.

when *adv* ¿cuándo?; mientras que; * *conj* cuando.

whenever *adv* cuando; cada vez que.

where *adv* ¿dónde?; * *conj* donde;

any~ en cualquier parte; **every~** en todas partes.

whereabout(s) *adv* ¿dónde?

whereas *conj* mientras que; pues que, ya que.

whereby *pn* por lo cual, con lo cual.

whereupon *conj* con lo cual.

wherever *adv* dondequiera que.

wherewithal *npl* recursos *mpl*.

whet *vt* excitar.

whether *conj* si.

which *pn* qué; lo que; el que, el cual; cuál; * *adj* ¿qué?; cuyo.

whiff *n* bocanada de humo *f*.

while *n* rato *m*; vez *f*; * *conj* durante; mientras; aunque.

whim *n* antojo, capricho *m*.

whimper *vi* sollozar, gemir.

whimsical *adj* caprichoso/sa, fantástico/ca.

whine *vi* llorar, lamentar; * *n* quejido, lamento *m*.

whinny *vi* relinchar.

whip *n* azote *m*; látigo *m*; * *vt* azotar; batir.

whipped cream *n* nata montada *f*.

whirl *vt*, *vi* girar; hacer girar; mover(se) rápidamente.

whirlpool *n* remolino *m*.

whirlpool bath *n* hidromasaje *m*.

whirlwind *n* torbellino *m*.

whisky *n* whisky *m*.

whisper *vi* cuchichear; susurrar.

whispering *n* cuchicheo *m*; susurro *m*.

whistle *vi* silbar; * *n* silbido *m*.

white *adj* blanco/ca, pálido/da; cano/na; puro/ra; * *n* color blanco *m*; clara del huevo *f*.

white elephant *n* maula *f*.

white-hot *adj* incandescente.

white lie *n* mentirijilla *f*.

whiten *vt*, *vi* blanquear; emblanquecerse.

whiteness n blancura f; palidez f.
whitewash n enlucimiento m; * vt encalar; jalbegar.
whiting n pescadilla f.
whitish adj blanquecino/na.
who pn ¿quién?, que.
whoever pn quienquiera, cualquiera.
whole adj todo/da, total; sano/na, entero/ra; * n total m; conjunto m.
wholehearted adj sincero/ra.
wholemeal adj integral.
wholesale n venta al por mayor f.
wholesome adj sano/na, saludable.
wholly adv enteramente.
whom pn ¿quién?; que.
whooping cough n tos ferina f.
whore n puta f; (fam) zorra f.
why n ¿por qué?; * conj por qué; * excl ¡hombre!
wick n mecha f.
wicked adj malvado/da, perverso/sa; ~ly adv malamente.
wickedness n perversidad, malignidad f.
wicker n mimbre m; * adj tejido/da de mimbre.
wide adj ancho/cha, vasto/ta; grande; ~ly adv muy; **far and** ~ por todos lados.
wide-awake adj despierto/ta.
widen vt ensanchar, extender.
wide open adj de par en par.
widespread adj extendido/da.
widow n viuda f.
widower n viudo m.
width n anchura f.
wield vt manejar, empuñar.
wife n esposa f; mujer f.
wig n peluca f; tupé m.
wiggle vt menear; * vi menearse.
wild adj silvestre, feroz; desierto/ta; descabellado/da; salvaje.
wilderness n desierto m; yermo m.

wild life n fauna f.
wildly adv violentamente; locamente; desatinadamente.
wilful adj deliberado/da; testarudo/da.
wilfulness n obstinación f.
wiliness n fraude, engaño m.
will n voluntad f; testamento m; * vt querer, desear.
willing adj inclinado/da, dispuesto/ta; ~ly adv de buena gana.
willingness n buena voluntad, buena gana f.
willow n sauce m (árbol).
willpower n fuerza de voluntad f.
wilt vi marchitarse.
wily adj astuto/ta.
win vt ganar, conquistar; alcanzar; lograr.
wince vi encogerse, estremecerse.
winch n torno m.
wind n viento m; aliento m; flatulencia f.
wind vt enrollar; envolver; dar cuerda a; * vi serpentear.
windfall n golpe de suerte m.
wind farm n parque eólico m.
winding adj tortuoso/sa.
windmill n molino de viento m.
window n ventana f.
window box n jardinera de ventana f.
window cleaner n limpiacristales m invar.
window ledge n repisa f.
windowpane n cristal m.
windowsill n repisa f.
windpipe n tráquea f.
windscreen n parabrisas m invar.
windscreen washer n lavaparabrisas m invar.
windscreen wiper n limpiaparabrisas m invar.
windsurfer n windsurfista m/f.
windsurfing n windsurf m.

wind turbine n aerogenerador m.

windy adj de mucho viento.

wine n vino m.

wine cellar n bodega f.

wine glass n copa de vino f.

wine list n carta de vinos f.

wine merchant n vinatero/ra m/f.

wine-tasting n degustación de vinos f.

wing n ala f.

winged adj alado/da.

winger n extremo m.

wink vi guiñar; * n pestañeo m; guino m.

winner n ganador/a m/f; vencedor/a m/f.

winning post n meta f.

winter n invierno m; * vi invernar.

winter sports npl deportes de invierno mpl.

wintry adj invernal.

wipe vt limpiar; borrar.

wire n alambre m; telegrama m; * vt instalar el alambrado en; conectar.

wiring n alambrado m.

wiry adj delgado/da y fuerte.

wisdom n sabiduría, prudencia f.

wisdom teeth npl muelas del juicio fpl.

wise adj sabio/bia, docto/ta, juicioso/sa, prudente.

wisecrack n broma f.

wish vt querer, desear, anhelar; * n anhelo, deseo m.

wishful adj deseoso/sa.

wisp n mechón m; voluta f.

wistful adj pensativo/va, atento/ta.

wit n entendimiento, ingenio m.

witch n bruja, hechicera f.

witchcraft n brujería f; sortilegio m.

with prep con; por, de, a.

withdraw vt quitar; privar; retirar; * vi retirarse, apartarse.

withdrawal n retirada f.

withdrawn adj reservado/da.

wither vi marchitarse, secarse.

withhold vt detener, impedir, retener.

within prep dentro de, adentro; * adv interiormente; en casa.

without prep sin.

withstand vt resistir.

witless adj necio/cia, tonto/ta, falto/ta de ingenio.

witness n testimonio m; testgo m/f; * vt atestiguar, testificar.

witness stand n estrado de los testigos m.

witticism n ocurrencia f.

wittily adv ingeniosamente.

wittingly adv adrede, de propósito.

witty adj ingenioso/sa, agudo/da, chistoso/sa.

wizard n brujo, hechicero m.

wobble vi tambalearse.

woe n dolor m; miseria f.

woeful adj triste, funesto/ta; ~ly adv tristemente.

wolf n lobo m; **she** ~ loba f.

woman n mujer f.

womanish adj mujeril.

womanly adj mujeril, mujeriego/ga.

womb n útero m.

women's lib n la liberación de la mujer f.

wonder n milagro m; maravilla f; asombro m; * vi maravil larse de; preguntarse si.

wonderful adj maravilloso/sa; ~ly adv maravillosamente.

wondrous adj maravilloso/sa.

won't abrev de **will not**.

wont n uso m; costumbre f.

woo vt cortejar.

wood n bosque m; selva f; madera f; leña f.

wood alcohol n alcohol metílico m.

wood carving n tallado en madera m.

woodcut n estampa de madera f.

woodcutter n leñador/a m/f; grabador en láminas de madera, xilógrafo m/f.

wooded adj arbolado/da.

wooden adj de madera.

wood engraver n xilógrafo m.

wooden shoe n zueco m.

woodland n arbolado m.

woodlouse n cochinilla f.

woodman n cazador m; guardabosque m.

woodpecker n pájaro carpintero m.

woodwind n intrumento de viento de madera m.

woodwork n carpintería f.

woodworm n carcoma f.

wool n lana f.

woollen adj de lana.

woollens npl géneros de lana mpl.

woolly adj lanudo/da, lanoso/sa.

word n palabra f; noticia f; * vt expresar; componer en escri tura.

wordiness n verbosidad f.

wording n redacción f.

word processing n tratamiento de textos m.

word processor n procesador de textos m.

wordy adj verboso/sa.

work vi trabajar; obrar; estar en movimiento o en acción; fermentar; * vt trabajar; labrar; fabricar, manufacturar; **to ~ out** vi salir bien; * vt resolver; * n trabajo m; fábrica f; obra f; empleo m.

workable adj práctico/ca.

workaholic n trabajador obsesivo m, trabajadora obsesiva f.

worker n trabajador/a m/f; obrero/ra m/f.

workforce n mano de obra f.

working-class adj obrero/ra, de clase trabajadora.

workman n labrador m.

workmanship n manufactura f; destreza del artífice f.

workmate n compañero/ra de trabajo m/f.

workshop n taller, obrador m.

world n mundo m; * adj del mundo; mundial.

worldliness n mundanería f.

worldly adj mundano/na, terreno/na.

worldwide adj mundial.

worm n gusano m; (of a screw) rosca de tornillo f.

worn-out adj gastado/da; rendido/da.

worried adj preocupado/da.

worry vt preocupar; * n preocupación f; pensión f.

worrying adj inquietante.

worse adj, adv peor; **~ and ~** cada vez peor; * n lo peor.

worship n culto m; adoración f; **your ~** su señoría; * vt adorar, venerar.

worst adj el/la peor; * adv peor; * n lo peor m.

worth n valor, precio m; mérito m.

worthily adv dignamente, convenientemente.

worthless adj sin valor; inútil.

worthwhile adj que vale la pena; valioso/sa.

worthy adj digno/na; respetable; honesto/ta.

would-be adj aspirante.

wound n herida, llaga f; * vt herir, llagar.

wrangle vi reñir; * n riña f.

wrap vt envolver.

wrath n ira, rabia, cólera f.

wreath n corona, guirnalda f.

wreck n naufragio m; ruina f; destrucción f; navío naufragado m; * vt naufragar; arruinar.

wreckage *n* restos *mpl*; escombros *mpl*.

wren *n* chochín *m*.

wrench *vt* arrancar; dislocar; torcer; * *n* llave inglesa *f*; tirón *m*.

wrest *vt* arrancar, arrebatar.

wrestle *vi* luchar; disputar.

wrestling *n* lucha *f*.

wretched *adj* infeliz, miserable.

wriggle *vi* menearse, agitarse.

wring *vt* torcer; arrancar; estrujar.

wrinkle *n* arruga *f*; * *vt* arrugar; * *vi* arrugarse.

wrist *n* muñeca *f*.

wristband *n* puno de camisa *m*.

wristwatch *n* reloj de pulsera *m*.

writ *n* escrito *m*; escritura *f*; orden *f*.

write *vt* escribir; componer; **to ~ down** apuntar; **to ~ off** borrar; desechar; **to ~ up** redactar.

write-off *n* pérdida total *f*.

writer *n* escritor/a, *m/f*; autor/a *m/f*.

writhe *vi* retorcerse.

writing *n* escritura *f*; letra *f*; obras *fpl*; escrito *m*.

writing desk *n* escritorio *m*.

writing paper *n* papel para escribir *m*.

wrong *n* injuria *f*; injusticia *f*; perjuicio *m*; error *m*; * *adj* malo/la; injusto/ta; equivocado/da, inoportuno/na; falso/sa; * *adv* mal, equivocadamente; * *vt* agraviar, injuriar.

wrongful *adj* injusto/ta.

wrongly *adv* injustamente.

wry *adj* irónico/ca.

X

xenophobia *n* xenofobia *f*.

Xmas *n* Navidad *f*.

X-ray *n* radiografía *f*.

xylographer *n* xilógrafo *m*.

xylophone *n* xilófano *m*.

Y

yacht *n* yate *m*.

yachting *n* vela *f*.

Yankee *n* yanqui *m/f*.

yard *n* corral *m*; yarda *f*.

yardstick *n* criterio *m*.

yarn *n* estambre *m*; hilo de lino *m*.

yawn *vi* bostezar; * *n* bostezo *m*.

yawning *adj* muy abierto/ta.

yeah *adv* sí.

year *n* año *m*.

yearbook *n* anuario *m*.

yearling *n* añal *m*.

yearly *adj* anual; * *adv* anualmente, todos los años.

yearn *vi* añorar.

yearning *n* añoranza *f*.

yeast *n* levadura *f*.

yell *vi* aullar; * *n* aullido *m*.

yellow *adj* amarillo/lla; * *n* amarillo *m*.

yellowish *adj* amarillento/ta.

yelp *vi* latir, gañir; * *n* aullido *m*.

yes *adv* sí; * *n* sí *m*.

yesterday *adv* ayer; * *n* ayer *m*.

yet *conj* sin embargo; pero; * *adv* todavía.

yew *n* tejo *m*.

yield *vt* dar, producir; rendir; * *vi* rendirse; ceder el paso; * *n* producción f; cosecha f; rendimiento m.

yoga n yoga m.

yoghurt n yogur m.

yoke n yugo m; (of oxen) yunta f.

yolk n yema (de huevo) f.

yonder adv allá.

you pn vosotros/tras, tú, usted, ustedes.

young adj joven, mozo/za; **~er** adj menor.

youngster n jovencito/ta m/f; joven m/f.

your(s) pn tuyo, tuya, vuestro, vuestra, suyo, suya.

yourself pn tú mismo, tú misma, usted mismo, usted misma.

yourselves pn pl vosotros mismos, vosotras mismas, ustedes mismos, ustedes mismas.

youth n juventud, adolescencia f; joven m/f.

youthful adj juvenil.

youthfulness n juventud f.

yuppie adj, n yupi m/f.

Z

zany adj estrafalario/ria.

zap vt borrar.

zeal n celo m; ardor m.

zealous adj celoso/sa.

zebra n cebra f.

zenith n cénit m.

zero n zero, cero m.

zest n ánimo m.

zigzag n zigzag m; * adj zigzag; * vi zigzaguear.

zinc n zinc m.

zip n cremallera f; cierre m.

zodiac n zodíaco m.

zone n banda, faja f; zona f.

zoo n zoo, zoológico m.

zoological adj zoológico/ca.

zoologist n zoólogo/ga m/f.

zoology n zoología f.

zoom vi zumbar.

zoom lens n zoom m.

Verbos Irregulares en Ingles

Infinitivo	*Pretérito*	*Participio de pasado*
arise	arose	arisen
awake	awoke	awaked, awoken
be [I am, you/we/they are, he/she/it is, gerundio being]		
	was, were	been
bear	bore	borne
beat	beat	beaten
become	became	become
begin	began	begun
behold	beheld	beheld
bend	bent	bent
beseech	besought, beseeched	besought, beseeched
beset	beset	beset
bet	bet, betted	bet, betted
bid	bade, bid	bade, bid, bidden
bite	bit	bitten
bleed	bled	bled
bless	blessed	blessed, blest
blow	blew	blown
break	broke	broken
breed	bred	bred
bring	brought	brought
build	built	built
burn	burnt, burned	burnt, burned
burst	burst	burst
buy	bought	bought
can	could	(been able)
cast	cast	cast
catch	caught	caught
choose	chose	chosen
cling	cling	clung
come	came	come
cost	cost	cost
creep	crept	crept
cut	cut	cut
deal	dealt	dealt
dig	dug	dug
do [he/she/it does]	did	done

Infinitivo	Pretérito	Participio de pasado
draw	drew	drawn
dream	dreamed, dreamt	dreamed, dreamt
drink	drank	drunk
drive	drove	driven
dwell	dwelt, dwelled	dwelt, dwelled
eat	ate	eaten
fall	fell	fallen
feed	fed	fed
feel	felt	felt
fight	fought	fought
find	found	found
flee	fled	fled
fling	flung	flung
fly [he/she/it flies]	flew	flown
forbid	forbade	forbidden
forecast	forecast	forecast
forget	forgot	forgotten
forgive	forgave	forgiven
forsake	forsook	forsaken
foresee	foresaw	foreseen
freeze	froze	frozen
get	got	got, gotten
give	gave	given
go [he/she/it goes]	went	gone
grind	ground	ground
grow	grew	grown
hang	hung, hanged	hung, hanged
have [I/you/we/they have, he/she/it has, *gerundio* having]		
	had	had
hear	heard	heard
hide	hid	hidden
hit	hit	hit
hold	held	held
hurt	hurt	hurt
keep	kept	kept
kneel	knelt, kneeled	knelt, kneeled
know	knew	known
lay	laid	laid
lead	led	led
lean	leant, leaned	leant, leaned

Infinitivo	*Pretérito*	*Participio de pasado*
leap	leapt, leaped	leapt, leaped
learn	learnt, learned	learnt, learned
leave	left	left
lend	lent	lent
let	let	let
lie [*gerundio* lying]	lay	lain
light	lighted, lit	lighted, lit
lose	lost	lost
make	made	made
may	might	–
mean	meant	meant
meet	met	met
mistake	mistook	mistaken
mow	mowed	mowed, mown
must	(had to)	(had to)
overcome	overcame	overcome
pay	paid	paid
put	put	put
quit	quit, quitted	quit, quitted
read	read	read
rid	rid	rid
ride	rode	ridden
ring	rang	rung
rise	rose	risen
run	ran	run
saw	sawed	sawn
say	said	said
see	saw	seen
seek	sought	sought
sell	sold	sold
send	sent	sent
set	set	set
sew	sewed	sewn
shake	shook	shaken
shall	should	–
shear	sheared	sheared, shorn
shed	shed	shed
shine	shone	shone
shoot	shot	shot
show	showed	shown, showed

Infinitivo	*Pretérito*	*Participio de pasado*
shrink	shrank	shrunk
shut	shut	shut
sing	sang	sung
sink	sank	sunk
sit	sat	sat
slay	slew	slain
sleep	slept	slept
slide	slid	slid
sling	slung	slung
smell	smelt, smelled	smelt, smelled
sow	sowed	sown, sowed
speak	spoke	spoken
speed	sped, speeded	sped, speeded
spell	spelt, spelled	spelt, spelled
spend	spent	spent
spill	spilt, spilled	spilt, spilled
spin	spun	spun
spit	spat	spat
split	split	split
spoil	spoilt, spoiled	spoilt, spoiled
spread	spread	spread
spring	sprang	sprung
stand	stood	stood
steal	stole	stolen
stick	stuck	stuck
sting	stung	stung
stink	stank	stunk
stride	strode	stridden
strike	struck	struck
strive	strove	striven
swear	swore	sworn
sweep	swept	swept
swell	swelled	swelled, swollen
swim	swam	swum
swing	swung	swung
take	took	taken
teach	taught	taught
tear	tore	torn
tell	told	told
think	thought	thought

Infinitivo	*Pretérito*	*Participio de pasado*
throw	threw	thrown
thrust	thrust	thrust
tread	trod	trodden
understand	understood	understood
upset	upset	upset
wake	woke	woken
wear	wore	worn
weave	wove, weaved	woven, weaved
wed	wed, wedded	wed, wedded
weep	wept	wept
win	won	won
wind	wound	wound
withdraw	withdrew	withdrawn
withhold	withheld	withheld
withstand	withstood	withstood
wring	wrung	wrung
write	wrote	written

Spanish Verbs

Regular

	comprar	temer	partir
	to buy	*to fear*	*to divide*
Gerund	comprando	temiendo	partiendo
Part participle	comprado	temido	partido
Present indicative	compro	temo	parto
	compras	temes	partes
	compra	teme	parte
	compramos	tememos	partimos
	compráis	teméis	partís
	compran	temen	parten
Imperfect indicative	compraba	temía	partía
	comprabas	temías	partías
	compraba	temía	partía
	comprábamos	temíamos	partíamos
	comprabais	temíais	partíais
	compraban	temían	partían
Past absolute	compré	temí	partí
(or preterit)	compraste	temiste	partiste
	compró	temió	partió
	compramos	temimos	partimos
	comprasteis	temisteis	partisteis
	compraron	temieron	partieron
Future	compraré	temeré	partiré
	comprarás	temerás	partirás
	comprará	temerá	partirá
	compraremos	temeremos	partiremos
	compraréis	temeréis	partiréis
	comprarán	temerán	partirán

Conditional	compraría	temería	partiría
	comprarías	temerías	partirías
	compraría	temería	partiría
	compraríamos	temeríamos	partiríamos
	compraríais	temeríais	partiríais
	comprarían	temerían	partirían

Imperative	compra	teme	parte
	compre	tema	parta
	compremos	temamos	partamos
	comprad	temed	partid
	compren	teman	partan

Present subjunctive	compre	tema	parta
	compres	temas	partas
	compre	tema	parta
	compreemos	temamos	partamos
	compreéis	temáis	partáis
	compren	teman	partan

Imperfect subjunctive	comprara	temiera	partiera
	ase	iese	iese
	compraras	temieras	partieras
	ases	ieses	ieses
	comprara	temiera	partiera
	ase	iese	iese
	compráramos	temiéramos	partiéramos
	ásemos	iésemos	iésemos
	comprarais	temierais	partierais
	aseis	ieseis	ieseis
	compraran	temieran	partieran
	asen	iesen	iesen

Auxiliary Verbs

Infinitive	haber	ser	tener	estar
	to have	*to be*	*to have*	*to be*
Gerund	habiendo	siendo	teniendo	estando
Part participle	habido	sido	tenido	estado
Present indicative	he	soy	tengo	estoy
	has	eres	tienes	estás
	ha	es	tiene	está
	hemos	somos	tenemos	estamos
	habéis	sois	tenéis	estáis
	han	son	tienen	están
Imperfect indicative	había	era	tenía	estaba
	habías	eras	tenías	estabas
	había	era	tenía	estaba
	habíamos	éramos	teníamos	estábamos
	habíais	erais	teníais	estabais
	habían	eran	tenían	estaban
Past absolute	hube	fui	tuve	estuve
(or preterit)	hubiste	fuiste	tuviste	estuviste
	hubo	fue	tuvo	estuvo
	hubimos	fuimos	tuvimos	estuvimos
	hubisteis	fuisteis	tuvisteis	estuvisteis
	hubieron	fueron	tuvieron	estuvieron
Future	habré	seré	tendré	estaré
	habrás	serás	tendrás	estarás
	habrá	será	tendrá	estará
	habremos	seremos	tendremos	estaremos
	habréis	seréis	tendréis	estaréis
	habrán	serán	tendrán	estarán

Conditional	habría	sería	tendría	estaría
	habrías	serías	tendrías	estarías
	habría	sería	tendría	estaría
	habríamos	seríamos	tendríamos	estaríamos
	habríais	seríais	tendríais	estaríais
	habrían	serían	tendrían	estarían

Imperative	–	sé(tu)	ten(tu)	está(tu)

Present subjunctive	haya	sea	tenga	esté
	hayas	seas	tengas	estés
	haya	sea	tenga	esté
	hayamos	seamos	tengamos	estémos
	hayáis	seáis	tengáis	estéis
	hayan	sean	tengan	estén

Imperfect subjunctive	hubiera	fuera	tuviera	estuviera
	iese	ese	iese	iese
	hubieras	fueras	tuvieras	estuvieras
	ieses	eses	ieses	ieses
	hubiera	fuera	tuviera	estuviera
	iese	ese	iese	iese
	hubiéramos	fuéramos	tuviéramos	estuviéramos
	iésemos	ésemos	iésemos	iésemos
	hubierais	fuerais	tuvierais	estuvierais
	ieseis	eseis	ieseis	ieseis
	hubieran	fueran	tuvieran	estuvieran
	iesen	esen	iesen	iesen